Nelson's
Illustrated
Encyclopedia
of the Bible

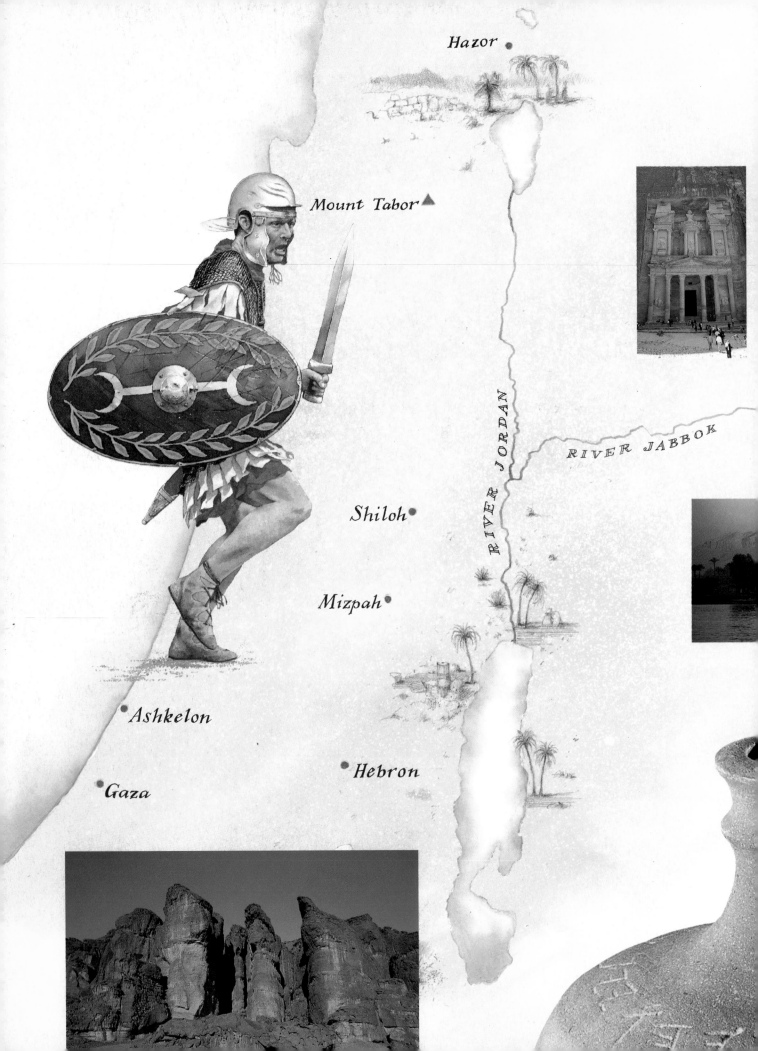

Hazor

Mount Tabor ▲

RIVER JORDAN

RIVER JABBOK

Shiloh

Mizpah

Ashkelon

Hebron

Gaza

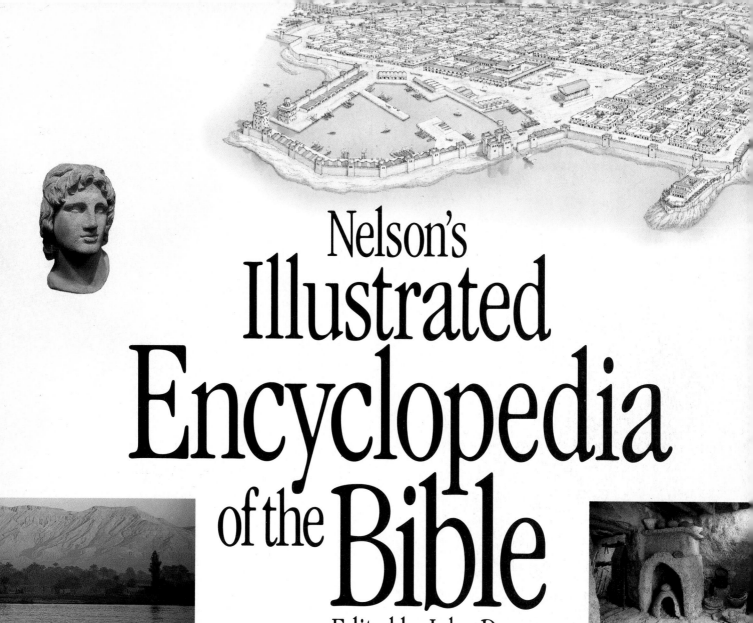

Nelson's
Illustrated
Encyclopedia
of the Bible

Edited by John Drane

NELSON

First North American paperback edition published 2001 by
Thomas Nelson, Inc., Nashville, Tennessee

Library of Congress Cataloging-in-Publication Data
Nelson's illustrated encyclopedia of the Bible / John W. Drane. editor
Updated ed. of: The Lion encyclopedia of the Bible.
Includes index.
ISBN 0-7852-4614-2. - ISBN 0-7862-4615-0
1. Bible-Criticism, interpretation. etc. I. Drane, John William. II. Lion
encyclopedia of the Bible (1986)
BS510.2.L56 1998
220.3-DC21
98-13164 CIP

Copyright © 1998 Lion Publishing
Published by
Lion Publishing plc
Sandy Lane West, Oxford, England
www.lion-publishing.co.uk
ISBN 0 7459 3922 8

First paperback edition 2000
10 9 8 7 6 5 4 3 2 1 0

Printed and bound in Spain

A catalogue record for this book is available from the British Library

Acknowledgments

We are grateful to the following contributors to the original
Lion Encyclopedia of the Bible, whose material has been
included in this book:

David Clines MA

John Drane MA, PhD

Margaret Embry BA, BD

David Gillett BA, MPhil

Ralph Gower MEd, BD

Colin Hemer MA, PhD

Kenneth Kitchen BA, PhD

Robin Keeley BA

Alan Millard, MA, MPhil, FSA

Margaret Moore BA, BD

Stephen Parish Dip Th

John Paterson MA

Project editor: Sarah Medina

Designer: Nicholas Rous

PICTURE ACKNOWLEDGMENTS

Front Cover

Pyramids: Jon Arnold
Philistine ship: Lion Publishing/David Alexander
Dagger from the Royal Graves at Ur: © The British Museum,
  by courtesy of the Trustees
Drawing showing trees being transported (based on a mural
  from Hatshepsut's temple): Roger Kent
Phoenician perfume jar: Zev Radovan

Back Cover
Exodus timeline: David Atkinson

Prelims and Introduction

Title page (anticlockwise)
Background map: David Atkinson
Roman soldier: Martin Sanders
Solomon's pillars, Timna Park, Negev: Jon Arnold
Wine jar from Judea: Zev Radovan
Persepolis: PowerStock Photo Library
Rural house reconstruction: Zev Radovan
Caesarea: Stephen Conlin
Alexander the Great: Zev Radovan
Treasury at Petra: Jon Arnold
View across the Nile: Jon Arnold

Page 5
Dagger, Royal Treasure at Ur: © The British Museum,
  by courtesy of the Trustees
Gold jewellery, mid-second millennium BC: Zev Radovan
Israelite seal inscribed 'belonging to Shallum',
  seventh century BC: Zev Radovan
Seal with four-winged creature, eighth century BC: Zev Radovan

Page 6
Sacred tree plaque from Ahab's ivory palace: Zev Radovan
Seal inscribed 'Amos the scribe', 8000–7000 BC: Zev Radovan
Roman glass cosmetics container: Zev Radovan

Page 7
Gold Astarte, Gezer, 14th century BC: Zev Radovan
Phoenician seal, Dor: Zev Radovan
Israelite seal inscribed 'To Pedajah son of the King',
  sixth century BC: Zev Radovan
Spearhead, about 2000 BC: Zev Radovan

Page 8
Tools of a Roman doctor: Zev Radovan
Egyptian pen case: Ashmolean Museum, Oxford
Israelite seal inscribed 'belonging to Abdi, servant of Hoshea':
  Zev Radovan

Part-openers

All part-opener illustrations: Simon Bull

CONTENTS

PART 1. Outline of Biblical History

PART 2. Peoples and Empires

PART 3. The World of the Bible

PART 7. Rapid Factfinder

INTRODUCTION

What is the Bible?

The Bible is one of the great classics of world literature. Its stories may well have happened long ago in a handful of small countries at the eastern end of the Mediterranean Sea, but today they are still read enthusiastically by millions of people all over the world. Its most recent parts are nearly 2,000 years old, while the origins of its earliest works are lost forever in the mists of antiquity. But its unique combination of epic stories, history, reflective philosophy, poetry, political commentary – and much more – is held together with all the elements of adventure, excitement and suspense that we might expect from a modern television drama. In fact, the Bible has provided the story line for many Hollywood movies. It has been translated into more languages than any other book in history, and the best-known parts of it are available today in more than 2,000 languages.

The Bible has also been the inspiration behind many great social movements. In 19th-century Britain, for example, William Wilberforce was inspired by what he read in its pages, and launched himself into a campaign to abolish slavery. During the same period, the British politician Earl Shaftesbury read the Bible and committed himself to stop the exploitation of women and children by their employers. In the mid-20th century the African-American church leader Martin Luther King challenged and changed the whole course of race relations in the United States on the basis of what he knew of the Bible and its message. And at the end of the 20th century, much of the pressure that brought about the collapse of the system of apartheid that segregated the races in South Africa came from church groups who were fired by the vision of a better way of living which they read about in the Bible.

A library of books

Surprisingly, perhaps, the Bible is not just one book, but a whole library. Like any library, it contains many different kinds of literature, written by different people at different times, and for different purposes. There are stories, songs, poetry and history, as well as religious teachings – and even the teachings are presented in many forms, including ancient stories along with everyday letters, visions and other types of literature.

The Bible today is divided into two main sections, referred to by Christians as the Old Testament and the New Testament – as they see these as two halves of the same story. The Old Testament is, in fact, the original Hebrew Bible, which had a life of its own long before Christianity came on the scene, and which consists of the sacred writings of the Jewish faith, Judaism. The Hebrew Bible is also respected and referred to by Muslims. The New Testament is a collection of writings written by Christians in the first century AD.

The Hebrew Bible

There are 39 books in the original Hebrew Bible. These books are the literary archives of the nation of Israel. In different ways, their stories cover about 1,500 years of the nation's early history, beginning with Abraham, who was regarded as the founder of the nation, and ending in the time of the Greek empire of Alexander the Great and his successors. There is great diversity in the books of the Hebrew Bible. From the stories of heroes such as Moses, Deborah, Joshua, David and Esther, to the more reflective books such as Job and Ecclesiastes, there is something that will appeal to everyone. Enchanting stories of human intrigue and passion stand side by side with philosophical enquiries into the meaning of human life.

The books of the Hebrew Bible were traditionally arranged in three groups: the Law, the Prophets and the Writings.

The Law

This consists of the first five books of the Hebrew Bible (Genesis, Exodus, Leviticus, Numbers and Deuteronomy). These were believed to be of special importance as they were supposedly written by one of the earliest leaders of Israel, a man called Moses, whose story is told in some of them. They are not all 'law' in the modern sense of the word. Indeed, the book of Genesis consists entirely of stories, and contains nothing at all that could be understood as rules and regulations. Even the other four books, which do have community laws in them, also contain many narratives. The Hebrew term for 'law' (*torah*) really means 'guidance' or 'instruction'; this can include theoretical rules, but it also needed to incorporate stories which could serve as everyday illustrations of how the people were meant to live.

These five books became known later as the 'Pentateuch', and they were always grouped together because of the tradition that Moses wrote them all. Some parts of the Pentateuch might easily go back to ancient times, but as time passed, life changed – and old laws needed to be updated and new ones produced, and these would have been added by later editors.

The Prophets

This is the largest section of the Hebrew Bible. It takes its name from a number of religious and political activists who sought to influence the life of the nation of Israel over a long period of several centuries. This collection of books itself falls into two distinct sections, the former prophets and the latter prophets. It will be most useful here to look at the latter prophets first.

THE LATTER PROPHETS

Prophets are mentioned throughout the history of the Israelite people. They were not primarily writers, but speakers and political activists. The faith of Israel was based on the belief that religion is not just concerned with the kind of rituals that go on in shrines and temples, but was to be a way of life. As the people looked back to the stories of how their ancestors had lived, they came to the conclusion that God's values were essentially concerned with justice and freedom. One group of their own forebears had been enslaved in Egypt, and God had stood by them in their distress, finally orchestrating their freedom. From that time onwards, they were convinced that God was on the side of the poor and the oppressed – and this belief was enshrined in all their laws.

It is easy to hold such beliefs – but more difficult to put them into practice. The prophets were the conscience of the nation, always reminding the people of how much they themselves owed to God's generosity and love – and encouraging them to demonstrate these same values in their dealings with one another and with other nations. It was an uphill struggle, and many of the prophets were persecuted, imprisoned – even killed. But this message was at the heart of authentic Hebrew faith, which is why it plays such a large part in the books of the Old Testament.

Not all the prophets had books named after them. Of those who did, Isaiah, Jeremiah and Ezekiel have the longest, while 12 others are credited with much shorter books: Hosea, Joel, Amos, Obadiah, Jonah,

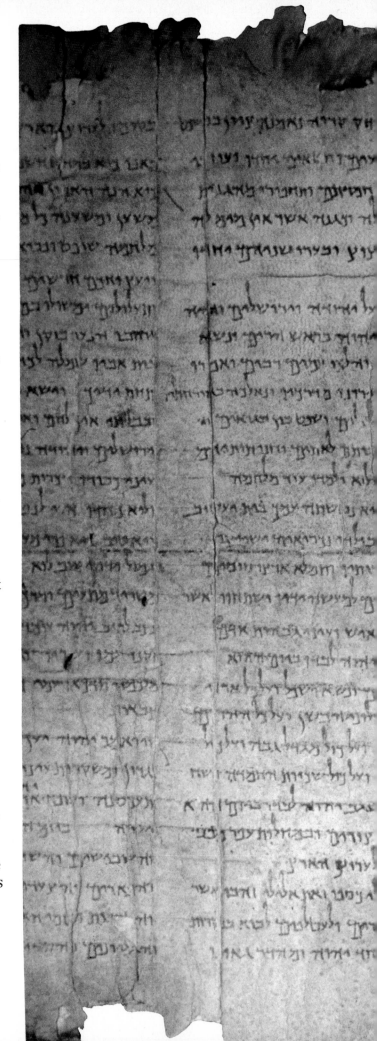

Part of the Isaiah scroll, one of the Dead Sea Scrolls found at Qumran. Dating from about 100 BC. (Credit: Zev Radovan)

Micah, Nahum, Habakkuk, Zephaniah, Haggai, Zechariah and Malachi. The prophets themselves rarely made long speeches. They usually delivered short messages that could be easily remembered – many of them in poetry. They were also mime artists and dramatists, acting out their messages.

THE FORMER PROPHETS

These are the books of Joshua, Judges, 1–2 Samuel and 1–2 Kings. They appear in the Hebrew Bible before the latter prophets, and at first sight they look to be so different that it is not obvious why they too should be included as part of the Prophets. They read more like history books, telling the story of the nation of Israel from the time when their ancestors escaped from slavery, through to the time in the sixth century BC when their national capital was destroyed by the Babylonian empire and its people were deported. In between, we read of how, under kings David and Solomon, Israel briefly enjoyed a period of political stability and influence. But most of the rest of the story describes how this grand kingdom split into two parts (Israel and Judah), both of which struggled to maintain their independence in the face of increasing pressure from the great superpowers of the day, especially Egypt, Assyria, Babylon and Syria.

The thing that makes these history books also 'prophets' is that they do not merely relate the stories but – like all good history books – they interpret them, and tell their readers what the stories mean and how they are to be understood in relation to the grand sweep of wider world history of the time. And in doing that, their writers looked at things the way the prophets had taught them. As they looked at the nation, they could see that whenever the people committed themselves to God's values and ways of doing things, they prospered – but when God's demands for justice and love were forgotten, then the nation suffered. Israelite faith was not focused on philosophical theories, but began with the way God had dealt with people in the experiences of everyday life. History was therefore very important: it was one of the key places where God's activity could be seen, and by a proper appreciation of its meaning, as explained by the prophets, the people could discover how they were meant to live.

The Writings

This section includes all the remaining books of the Hebrew Bible. They are not all the same kind of works. Psalms, Proverbs and Job are very different from one another in content, for example, but they are all poetry. Then there are those books known as the 'Megilloth', or 'five scrolls': Ruth, Song of Solomon,

Ecclesiastes, Lamentations and Esther. Again, these are all different styles, but they were grouped together because each of them had a particular association with significant religious festivals: Ruth was used at Pentecost, Song of Solomon at Passover, Ecclesiastes at Tabernacles, Lamentations to commemorate the destruction of Jerusalem, and Esther at Purim. There are also the books of Ezra, Nehemiah and 1–2 Chronicles, all of which relate to the situation in which the remnants of the people of Judah found themselves after they were allowed to return to their homeland in 538 BC by the Persian emperor Cyrus the Great, following his destruction of the Babylonian empire. And last of all, there is the book of Daniel, containing visions and some stories, and relating to a later period still.

Compiling the Hebrew Bible

Just as the books were written over a long period of time, so it took a long time for them to be gathered together in the form they now have. There seem to have been several stages in this. Nations tend to reflect on their history at times of great prosperity, and in times of great crisis. The compilation of the Hebrew Bible probably began in the days of success enjoyed by the people under King Solomon (970–930 BC), and there is evidence that at this time the earliest stories of the nation's life now contained in the books of Genesis to 1 Samuel were gathered together. They were not written then, of course, but collated from material that had been handed on by memory over many generations. People wanted to understand where they had come from and the experiences they had shared, so that they could celebrate their achievements. Slightly later, after the great kingdom of Israel had split in two, the people of the north (Israel) enjoyed great prosperity under King Jeroboam II, and collected together their own national story.

But it was mostly during times of great trouble that the Hebrew Bible was compiled, as the people tried to work out what had gone wrong, and how to put it all right again. In 722 BC, the kingdom of Israel, with its capital in Samaria, was devastated by an Assyrian invasion. Its economy was wrecked, its land given to others and its people were scattered throughout the Middle East. The smaller kingdom of Judah, based on Jerusalem, still survived, but it was obvious that it too would be overcome if it failed to learn the lessons of the disaster that had overtaken its larger neighbour. The prophets Micah and Isaiah spoke into this situation, and reminded the people of the need to uphold God's standards, especially justice and fairness for everyone in the whole community. At this time, the earlier histories of the Israelite people were brought together and the laws were revised so that the people could see clearly how they needed to live if they were to do God's will. By 622 BC, a new law book was in circulation in Jerusalem, spelling it all out in great detail. Sadly, things were already too corrupt, and less than 40 years later Jerusalem was destroyed by the Babylonians. Taken to live far away in exile, the people reflected again on the stories from their past, and gradually they were written in the form we now have them, to help the nation avoid making the same mistakes ever again.

Not long after, the Persians allowed the Jewish people to return to their homeland, and during the next two centuries there was much reading and re-reading of the ancient stories, along with the collection of the words of the prophets, and the writing and editing of further works such as those contained in the Writings. Jewish tradition identifies Ezra (whose story is told in the book of that name) as a key person in the arrangement and collection of the books of the Hebrew Bible at this time. But what happened during this period was the end of a long process of development, and it is important not to forget that much of the material already existed long before it was gathered together and edited in this way.

Translating the Hebrew Bible

The world changed very rapidly after the time of the Persian empire. Soon, the ancient language of Hebrew was forgotten by all but a few, and Jewish people were living in many different countries. By the time of the Roman empire, there were more Jewish people in Alexandria in Egypt than there were in Jerusalem! And the language most of them spoke was Greek. According to legend it was the Jews of Alexandria who decided to translate their scriptures from Hebrew into Greek, with the support of Pharaoh Ptolemy II Philadelphus (284–247 BC). By the time of the New Testament the Hebrew scriptures were widely read in Greek, in a translation known as the 'Septuagint'. It was this translation that put the books into the order

they have today, and it also included some other writings which had not originally been among the 39 books of the Hebrew Bible. There has been great debate ever since about the value of these books. Most Bibles today print them separately, as 'the Deuterocanonical books'. Like the Hebrew Bible, they include history, poetry, stories and religious philosophy.

The New Testament

By the start of the Christian era, Palestine was firmly under the control of the Roman empire. But the Christian faith began very much in a Jewish context. Jesus himself was a Jew, along with all his first followers. Naturally, therefore, the first Bible of the Christians was the Greek translation of the Hebrew scriptures, the Septuagint. They read it carefully because they believed that what Jesus had said and done was in some way the fulfilment of the ancient message given by God to the people of Israel centuries before. But within a short time, Christians felt moved by God to begin producing their own literature, which then came to form what is known today as the New Testament. Like the Hebrew Bible, the New Testament is not all one book, but a collection of different books. In this case, there are 27 of them. But whereas the books of the Hebrew Bible were written and gathered together over a period of hundreds of years, all the New Testament books were written in little more than 50 years, between the middle of the first century AD and its end.

The letters

As with the Old Testament, so with the New, the actual order in which the books appear is not an accurate guide to when they were written. The earliest parts of the New Testament to be written were the various letters written by Paul and others to Christian communities and individuals in different parts of the Roman empire. This reflects the rapid spread of the Christian church, which had established itself in all the major cities of the Mediterranean area within less than a generation following the crucifixion of Jesus.

Stories about the life and teaching of Jesus must have circulated from the very beginning, but these seem to have been handed on almost exclusively by word of mouth for some considerable time. The church grew so quickly that the nurture of new converts was of much greater importance than the production of literary works, and that is the context in which the various letters were written. They were for the most part not carefully worked out presentations of Christian belief, but ad hoc responses to particular situations that arose as people in different cultural contexts struggled to work out how to express their new faith using the language and ideas available to them. Questions had to be answered, quarrels needed to be resolved, personal advice was sought on a variety of issues, and Christians suffering persecution needed encouragement. All these factors contributed to the writing of the letters that are now found in the New Testament. Each of them was addressed to Christians in particular localities, but since they often gave general guidance on Christian life and beliefs, their usefulness for the whole church was soon recognized, and collections of letters seem to have been brought together by at least the later years of the first century AD.

The gospels

The first four books in the New Testament are the gospels, and these contain stories of the life of Jesus and accounts of his teachings. They are not all identical, though between the first three (Matthew, Mark and Luke) there are significant overlaps, while the fourth gospel (John) is quite different in style and, for the most part, in content as well. They were put together from the stories of Jesus that were circulating by word of mouth in the early Christian communities and, as such, their origins must have been with those who had known Jesus during his lifetime. But almost from the beginning, such reminiscences were preserved not just out of historical interest, but so they could, like the letters, give guidance and direction to the Christian believers. Just as the history writers of the Hebrew Bible interpreted the meaning of the events they reported, so the gospel writers explained and applied the stories of Jesus to their readers. This is why there was more than one version: there was no disagreement over the fundamental shape of the story, but since each of the writers was addressing the needs of quite different groups of people, in different places around the Roman empire, they needed freedom to apply Jesus' teaching directly to their readers.

It was out of this process that the four written gospels of the New Testament emerged: as the churches grew in numbers, and as the first generation of Jesus' disciples began to die, the only satisfactory way to preserve these stories was to write them all down. That also gave them a wider circulation, of course. One of the gospels – Luke – had a companion volume, the Acts of the Apostles. This continued the story from the time of Jesus, through a selective account of the activities of some of his followers, up to the point where the missionary Paul arrived in the city of Rome itself.

Collecting the New Testament books

The actual collecting of all these different books together, to form what we now know as the New Testament, must have started in the context of Christian worship. The first gatherings of Christians probably followed the practice of Jewish worship, and had regular readings from the Old Testament. It would be natural to read the new Christian books at the same time, and by the beginning of the second century almost all the New Testament books were widely used and valued. A few of them were less popular than others, particularly Hebrews, Revelation, 2 Peter and 2–3 John. But Christians eventually came to recognize that the 27 books in the New Testament spoke with a particular authority and were especially useful for solving the problems of the growing churches. It was not until the Council of Carthage in AD 397 that the churches actually published a list of New Testament books, but there had been an informal acceptance of these 27 books long before that, and the list merely confirmed what Christians were already agreed upon.

Texts and manuscripts

With the exception of some small sections that were written in Aramaic, the books of the Hebrew Bible were, as its name suggests, originally compiled in Hebrew. They were handed on from one generation to another as scribes made new copies of them from time to time. But documents did not last long in the climate of the Bible lands, and so relatively few truly ancient copies have survived. Prior to 1947 the oldest known Hebrew manuscripts dated back only as far as the ninth and tenth centuries AD – and these only contained the first five books of the Hebrew Bible, not the entire collection. Then in 1947 there was the remarkable discovery of the Dead Sea Scrolls. These documents originally formed the library of a religious community living at Qumran, near the Dead Sea in Palestine, in the years just before and after the start of the Christian era. These archives contained Hebrew manuscripts that were almost 1,000 years older than any previously known. Surprisingly, perhaps, the text they contained was very little different from the one that had always been known. Naturally, there are a few places where different words and expressions are used, and sometimes it is no longer possible to discern what the Hebrew words mean. But the copyists over many centuries clearly did a good job and made very few errors or alterations – which means we can be

confident that the Old Testament as we have it today is substantially the same as its authors wrote many centuries ago.

Prayer book, Jerusalem. (Credit: Jon Arnold)

The text of the Old Testament books has also come down to us in other early translations, the most important one being the Greek version known as the Septuagint. As Christianity spread to people who spoke other languages, the Old Testament was also translated into Latin (the Vulgate), Syriac (the Peshitta) and Egyptian (Coptic). All these early versions confirm what we already knew: that the text of the Hebrew scriptures had been accurately preserved over many generations, not only in its original language but also in the process of translation.

The New Testament books were originally written in Greek, and many thousands of ancient manuscripts of these books survive, either in part or in whole. In addition, experts also have available a number of early translations of the New Testament into Latin, Syriac, Coptic and other languages – as well as quotations contained in the writings of early Christian leaders.

At the very beginning, the New Testament books would have been written on scrolls made of papyrus, leather or parchment. But by the second century, Christians had invented a new form of document. This was the 'codex', which had sheets stitched down one edge just like a modern book. Two of the most important groups of New Testament manuscripts are the Bodmer Papyri (one of which dates from the late second century AD) and the Chester Beatty Papyri (from the early third century AD). These contain only parts of the New Testament, but the Codex Sinaiticus, which dates from the fourth century AD, contains the complete New Testament, while the Codex Vaticanus has everything up to the first part of the book of Hebrews. These two codex manuscripts were made by professional copyists in Alexandria, Egypt, and when 19th-century scholars first began looking in detail at the history of the New Testament text, these were the main sources available to them. Since then, many more papyrus documents have been discovered. Over the last two centuries, experts in ancient texts and languages have worked hard to compare them all, weighing up their evidence to make sure that what is in today's New Testament is as close as possible to what its authors originally wrote. The few small areas of debate which remain are over very minor matters of wording – and none of these questions raises any doubt at all about the central message of the New Testament.

Different types of literature

There are many different forms of writing contained in the Bible. Here are the main ones:

History

Much of the Bible is history. In the Old Testament, this includes books such as Joshua, Judges, 1–2 Samuel, 1–2 Kings, 1–2 Chronicles, Ezra and Nehemiah, all of which tell the story of the nation of Israel (continued in the Deuterocanonical books of Maccabees). In the New Testament, the Acts of the Apostles reports some events in the life of the earliest Christian communities. But none of these books merely records past events. They all report some things and not others, and they always interpret what they include, explaining its significance in the light of the religious faith of their writers. The nearest we get to historical archives would be some sections of the Old Testament books of Chronicles.

Poetry

The Bible contains a lot of poetry. The Old Testament prophets seem to have put many of their messages into poetic form, and Jesus often did the same (the Lord's Prayer, for example, is poetry). This would make it easier to remember and repeat. But many other books also contain poetry: the Old Testament books of Job, Psalms and Proverbs, for example, and the Wisdom of Solomon and Wisdom of Ben Sira in the Deuterocanonical books. The Old Testament Song of Songs is one long poem, celebrating the love between a royal bridegroom and his bride.

Stories

People have always loved good stories, and the Hebrews were no exception. This was one of Jesus' favourite ways of putting across his message, and almost all his teaching in the New Testament gospels is in story form. Other Bible books that fall into this category would be the Old Testament stories of Job, Jonah and Esther, and maybe parts of Daniel and the Joseph stories in the book of Genesis. All these are certainly carefully crafted narratives that have been designed, like a good novel, to engage the reader's attention and to get a message across at the same time. Some experts believe that the stories of Job and Jonah may originally have been meant to be performed as drama. In the Deuterocanonical books, Tobit, Judith and various additions to the stories of Daniel and Esther all fall into this category.

Visions

Visions are to be found scattered throughout the Bible stories, but three books in particular are full of them: Daniel in the Old Testament and Revelation in the New Testament, with 2 Esdras in the Deuterocanonical collection. These books share one thing in common: they were all written in what is called the apocalyptic style, and at a time when their writers and readers were being persecuted. By looking at what is going on from God's angle in some other world, they put present suffering in perspective and show that it is only a temporary situation: God and the forces of good will always win through over the powers of evil.

Letters

These are all found in the New Testament, written by Paul and other church leaders to keep in touch with their friends. Greek and Latin literature has many examples of writings that look like letters, but which are actually just ordinary books written in that style. The New Testament letters are all real letters, written by real people to other real people, and sent in the care of a messenger or through the normal Roman postal system.

Gospels

The four gospels of the New Testament are difficult to categorize. They contain elements of history and biography, along with Jesus' teaching, but none of these labels by itself can adequately describe them. The gospels seem to have been a unique form of literature, used by their writers to inspire and encourage faith in Jesus, but doing so by telling stories of Jesus and then explaining and applying their meaning to their readers, and inviting them to follow Jesus for themselves.

Worship materials

Some New Testament books contain instructions relating to worship in the early church, including a few hymns that would be sung in praise of God. But the book of Psalms in the Old Testament is the largest collection of worship materials. This book is a specialized form of poetry, and includes songs – together with instructions for the musicians – and detailed directions for dancers and other worship leaders.

Philosophy and ethics

Many Bible books contain advice about how to live. Much of it, like the teaching of Proverbs in the Old Testament and James in the New Testament, is simple and straightforward, and is quite similar to other ethical teaching of the day. But other books wrestle with the great issues of life and death, and the meaning of things. These include the Old Testament books of Job and Ecclesiastes; the Wisdom of Solomon and Wisdom of Ben Sira in the Deuterocanonical books; and the New Testament book of Hebrews.

Faith stories

Books of philosophy tend to address big questions in abstract ways. But people of all cultures have usually preferred to tell stories to explain ideas that just could not be put any other way. These stories are sometimes called 'myths', which can suggest they are somehow untrue or unreliable. We prefer to use the term 'faith stories' here because, far from being untrue, these stories express profound truths about some of life's most complex questions – questions such as, 'Where did the world come from?', 'What is the point of being alive?' and 'Why are there so many catastrophes in the world?' The Bible begins with stories of this kind in the book of Genesis and, in doing so, sets the scene for all that then follows.

There are obviously many different kinds of literature in the Bible. This is one of the secrets of its continuing popularity so many centuries after it was written. There is something here for everybody, and it is not shrouded in religious jargon. Instead, the Bible's story of God is closely related to the kind of things that ordinary people do and think every day. The authors saw their different books as related parts of one common story, through which they could get across what they believed to be the most important thing of all: the knowledge that this world and all its affairs are not just a haphazard sequence of coincidences, but are looked over by a God who is not a remote, unknowable, divine force, but a personal being with whom women and men can have personal dealings.

OUTLINE
OF BIBLICAL
HISTORY

P a r t   1

The patriarchs and their world

The world of Israel's early ancestors was one of rich and powerful kingdoms in the river valleys of Egypt and Mesopotamia. In the lands between there were many walled cities and tiny kingdoms. These strongholds protected the settlers who farmed the surrounding country. But there were also nomadic tribes who moved from place to place in search of good grazing for their flocks and herds.

Ancestor of a great nation

Israel's earliest ancestor was Abraham. He was originally from the south Mesopotamian city of Ur on the River Euphrates. Some of his family settled at Harran, several hundred miles to the north of Ur. But when his father Terah died, Abraham moved on to Canaan. There, he and his family lived a nomadic existence, moving from place to place in search of pasture and water.

A new land

When Abraham arrived in Canaan, he first set up camp in the hills at Shechem. The coastal plain and the Jordan valley, where there was good farm land, were already settled. However, the Jordan valley looked attractive to Abraham's nephew Lot, who decided to move down from the hills to settle near Sodom. But life there had its dangers, and when Sodom was later threatened with destruction by raiding kings, Abraham was called upon to rescue his nephew.

Promises fulfilled

Apart from a brief visit to Egypt at a time of famine, Abraham spent most of his life in Canaan, based near Hebron. The Bible says that this was the land God had promised to give to Abraham and his descendants.

God also promised a son to Abraham and his wife Sarah. They had been childless for many years and Sarah had given Abraham an Egyptian concubine, Hagar. When Abraham was 86 years old, Hagar gave birth to a son, Ishmael. Years later, Sarah was to bear the promised son, Isaac.

A group of Semitic visitors to Egypt is portrayed on this painting from the tomb of Khnom-hotpe at Beni-Hasan. The artist has carefully depicted details of their appearance and clothing, and the painting gives a good idea of what the patriarchs may have looked like.

Abraham's son, Isaac

The Bible recounts that when Isaac was a boy, God tested his father Abraham's faith to the limit by asking him to sacrifice Isaac. Just as Abraham was about to obey, an angel intervened and Isaac's life was spared. At the age of 40, Isaac married Rebekah, who was one of Abraham's relations from Harran. After many years, Isaac and Rebekah had twin sons: Esau and Jacob.

GOSHEN

CANAAN

EDOM

EGYPT

RIVER NILE

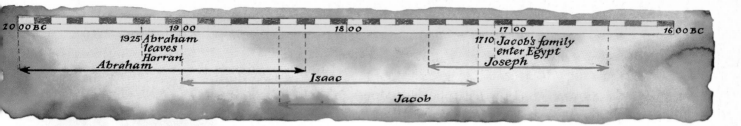

20 00 BC 19 00 18 00 17 00 16 00 BC

1925 Abraham leaves Harran

Abraham

Isaac

Jacob

1710 Jacob's family enter Egypt
Joseph

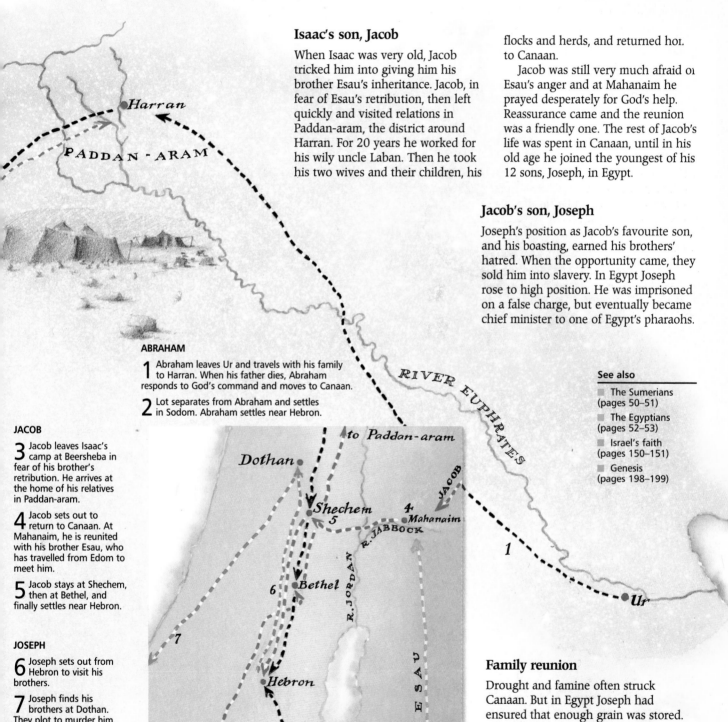

Isaac's son, Jacob

When Isaac was very old, Jacob tricked him into giving him his brother Esau's inheritance. Jacob, in fear of Esau's retribution, then left quickly and visited relations in Paddan-aram, the district around Harran. For 20 years he worked for his wily uncle Laban. Then he took his two wives and their children, his flocks and herds, and returned hoɪ. to Canaan.

Jacob was still very much afraid oɪ Esau's anger and at Mahanaim he prayed desperately for God's help. Reassurance came and the reunion was a friendly one. The rest of Jacob's life was spent in Canaan, until in his old age he joined the youngest of his 12 sons, Joseph, in Egypt.

Jacob's son, Joseph

Joseph's position as Jacob's favourite son, and his boasting, earned his brothers' hatred. When the opportunity came, they sold him into slavery. In Egypt Joseph rose to high position. He was imprisoned on a false charge, but eventually became chief minister to one of Egypt's pharaohs.

ABRAHAM

1 Abraham leaves Ur and travels with his family to Harran. When his father dies, Abraham responds to God's command and moves to Canaan.

2 Lot separates from Abraham and settles in Sodom. Abraham settles near Hebron.

JACOB

3 Jacob leaves Isaac's camp at Beersheba in fear of his brother's retribution. He arrives at the home of his relatives in Paddan-aram.

4 Jacob sets out to return to Canaan. At Mahanaim, he is reunited with his brother Esau, who has travelled from Edom to meet him.

5 Jacob stays at Shechem, then at Bethel, and finally settles near Hebron.

JOSEPH

6 Joseph sets out from Hebron to visit his brothers.

7 Joseph finds his brothers at Dothan. They plot to murder him, but instead sell him to traders, who take him to Egypt as a slave.

8 Joseph overcomes many obstacles in Egypt and becomes chief minister to the pharaoh. His entire family is invited to settle in Goshen.

See also

- The Sumerians (pages 50–51)
- The Egyptians (pages 52–53)
- Israel's faith (pages 150–151)
- Genesis (pages 198–199)

Family reunion

Drought and famine often struck Canaan. But in Egypt Joseph had ensured that enough grain was stored. When his brothers came from Canaan to buy corn, Joseph first tested them and then told them who he was. He invited his father Jacob and his brothers' families to live in Egypt. They eventually settled in Goshen, in the eastern Nile Delta, near to the court.

The exodus from Egypt

Jacob's descendants lived in Egypt for more than 450 years, during which time they grew into a nation – the nation of Israel. The Egyptians, under the rule of a more hostile dynasty of kings, or pharaohs, began to see them as a threat. They tightened their control, forcing the Israelites to work as slaves in the brick-fields. To reduce their growing numbers, newborn Israelite babies were drowned in the River Nile.

The Israelite slaves were forced to make bricks for the pharaohs' building programme. Scenes painted on the walls of tombs in ancient Egypt show how the mixture of clay and straw was placed in wooden moulds, to be baked in the sun.

Exodus to freedom

The Israelites' journey from slavery in Egypt is known as the 'exodus'. The word 'exodus' means simply a going out or departure. But this 'going out' of Egypt, *the* exodus, was the key event in the history of Old Testament Israel. All future generations were to look back to it and commemorate it.

A new leader

The Bible records that the Israelites cried out for help to God, who sent them a leader: Moses. The date was probably early in the 13th century BC. Moses was to lead the Israelites out of slavery into the land of Canaan: the so-called 'promised land'.

A series of plagues

Moses and his brother Aaron repeatedly asked the pharaoh to allow the Israelites to leave Egypt, but it took a series of terrible plagues sent by God before he would agree. The 10th plague was the deciding factor. 'All through Egypt,' Moses announced, 'on a certain night, the first-born sons in every household will die.' The first-born sons of the Israelites would be safe if the people carefully followed the instructions Moses gave to them. They must mark their door posts with the blood of a lamb killed in sacrifice. They must cook the lamb and eat it that night, with bitter herbs and bread made without yeast. They must pack their belongings and get dressed, ready for a journey.

Pharaoh Ramesses II ruled ancient Egypt during 1279–1212 BC. He was responsible for many great building projects, including the temple at Luxor. It is widely believed that Ramesses II was the pharaoh that Moses and Aaron had to confront in order to secure Israel's freedom.

Out of Egypt

After death 'passed over' the families of Israel, the pharaoh let them go. Even so, at the last minute he changed his mind and sent his army in pursuit – but the Israelites escaped across the 'sea of reeds' to Sinai. Every year afterwards, the people of Israel kept the anniversary of this event during a festival known as the Passover.

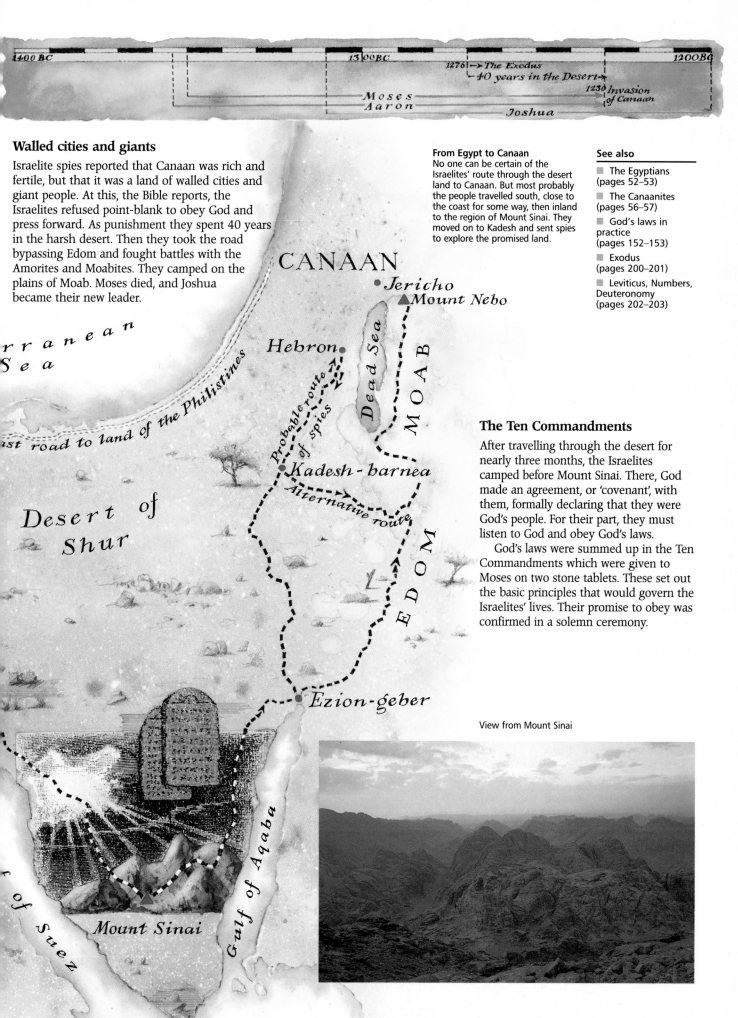

1400 BC   1300 BC   1276 → The Exodus
   40 years in the Desert →
   1230 Invasion of Canaan   1200 BC

Moses
Aaron

Joshua

Walled cities and giants

Israelite spies reported that Canaan was rich and fertile, but that it was a land of walled cities and giant people. At this, the Bible reports, the Israelites refused point-blank to obey God and press forward. As punishment they spent 40 years in the harsh desert. Then they took the road bypassing Edom and fought battles with the Amorites and Moabites. They camped on the plains of Moab. Moses died, and Joshua became their new leader.

From Egypt to Canaan

No one can be certain of the Israelites' route through the desert land to Canaan. But most probably the people travelled south, close to the coast for some way, then inland to the region of Mount Sinai. They moved on to Kadesh and sent spies to explore the promised land.

See also

- The Egyptians (pages 52–53)
- The Canaanites (pages 56–57)
- God's laws in practice (pages 152–153)
- Exodus (pages 200–201)
- Leviticus, Numbers, Deuteronomy (pages 202–203)

The Ten Commandments

After travelling through the desert for nearly three months, the Israelites camped before Mount Sinai. There, God made an agreement, or 'covenant', with them, formally declaring that they were God's people. For their part, they must listen to God and obey God's laws.

God's laws were summed up in the Ten Commandments which were given to Moses on two stone tablets. These set out the basic principles that would govern the Israelites' lives. Their promise to obey was confirmed in a solemn ceremony.

View from Mount Sinai

The Israelites enter Canaan

Joshua took over leadership of the Israelites from Moses, and at last, in about 1230 BC, they crossed the River Jordan to enter the 'promised land', Canaan, from the west. Canaan at this time was divided into a large number of small independent states, each centred on a fortified town with its own ruler. In front of the Israelites was the walled town of Jericho. The whole land God had promised them was waiting to be possessed.

The remains of a tower nearly 8 m/26 ft high built at Jericho in the eighth millennium BC attest to the great age of the town. The tower had a door and an internal staircase, and possibly served as a watchtower.

The fall of Jericho

Joshua's first aim was to take Jericho, a strategic walled town in the land of Canaan. Jericho fell after a remarkable siege. The Bible describes how each day for six days the Israelite forces marched round the town without a sound except for their tramping feet and the blast of trumpets. On the seventh day they marched round seven times and then gave a tremendous shout. The walls collapsed. The Israelites moved in and completely destroyed the town.

Jericho was established around an oasis on the edge of the Jordan valley. It had been occupied for more than 6,000 years before the Israelites came against it.

Mt Ebal
Shechem
Libnah
Beth-horon
Gibeon
Makkedah
Ai
Eglon
Lachish
Jerusalem
Debir
Hebron
Gilgal
Jericho
RIVER

Victory in the south

After an initial setback Joshua took Ai and then marched on to establish himself at Shechem, a key hill town on the road through the centre of Canaan. This gave him a good foothold in the region. However, enemies remained to the south and north.

The Gibeonites, fearful of defeat by Joshua, tricked the Israelites into making a peace treaty with them. When the kings of Jerusalem, Hebron and three neighbouring cities, alarmed by this treaty, then made war on Gibeon, Joshua was obliged to help his allies, and the enemies were defeated at the battle of Beth-horon. Joshua executed the five kings and destroyed their cities. When he returned to Gilgal, the south of Canaan was in his hands.

INTO CANAAN

1 Joshua's forces cross the River Jordan and take Jericho and then Ai.

2 Joshua takes the Israelites north to Mount Ebal, where he builds an altar to God.

3 The kings of Jerusalem, Hebron, Jarmuth, Lachish and Eglon form a coalition to besiege Gibeon. They are in turn attacked by the Israelites and chased down the mountain pass of Beth-horon.

4 Joshua swiftly moves south and destroys the cities of Makkedah, Libnah, Lachish, Eglon, Hebron and Debir.

5 With the south of Canaan subdued, the Israelites march north to confront and defeat King Jabin of Hazor and his allies at the Waters of Merom.

The northern alliance

News of the Israelite victories in the south travelled fast. In the north, the king of Hazor gathered his allies and they marched out to deal with the invaders. Joshua took them by surprise in their camp by the spring waters of Merom and won another victory. He captured the important city of Hazor and burned it down. He killed the kings who opposed him but left the other cities standing.

The Canaanite stronghold of Hazor lay on important trade routes. Archaeological findings indicate that Hazor was destroyed at the end of the 13th century BC. To the left of the picture are the Solomonic gate and pillared building, and in the centre is the ninth-century BC water system.

See also

■ The Canaanites (pages 56–57)

■ Regional geography (pages 84–85)

■ Joshua, Judges (pages 206–207)

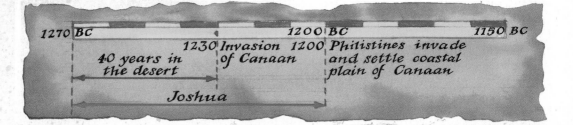

1270 BC — 1200 BC — 1150 BC

40 years in the desert — 1230 Invasion of Canaan 1200 — Philistines invade and settle coastal plain of Canaan

Joshua

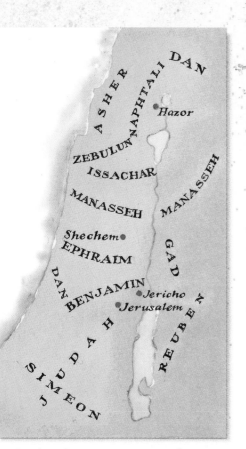

Twelve tribes

The Israelites were traditionally divided into 12 tribes, descended from the 12 sons of Jacob, and bound together by their special relationship with God. Different parts of Canaan were allocated to the various tribes.

The tribes of Reuben and Gad settled in the east of Canaan, together with half the tribe of Manasseh. The tribes of Asher, Naphtali, Zebulun, Issachar and Ephraim, the half-tribe of Dan and the other half-tribe of Manasseh, settled in the north-west. The tribes of Benjamin, Judah and Simeon, and the other half-tribe of Dan, settled in the south-west.

Settling the land

Joshua defeated the kings of Canaan and destroyed many key cities – and with them many Canaanite religious centres. The conquest was not complete, but Joshua had done enough for his people to begin settling in the land.

The Israelites never fully succeeded in possessing the whole of Canaan. Enemies remained to harass them, and the Israelites often simply adopted the Canaanite way of life and worshipped Canaanite gods. But there were some outstanding victories and the Israelites established themselves as the dominant power in the land.

The time of the judges

Having moved into the promised land of Canaan, the Israelite tribes settled into the areas allotted to them. But the tribes found themselves scattered, surrounded by hostile neighbours, and it began to seem impossible for the Israelites to gain full control of the land. Gradually they began to compromise with surrounding nations, and with their gods, for the sake of peace.

Freedom fighters

As at so many times in their history, the Israelites cried out to God for help in their time of need. The Bible recounts that, at this, God 'raised up judges, who saved them'. These 'judges' were not simply judges of the law; they were, in a very real sense, 'deliverers' or freedom-fighters. They won at least a temporary respite from the onslaught of the Israelites' enemies. The most famous of these judges were Deborah and Barak, Gideon, Jephthah, Samson and Samuel.

Samson

The Philistines, who had invaded and settled on the coastal plain of Canaan in about 1200 BC, grew into a strong and powerful nation. They began to infiltrate the same territory as Israel was fighting for, bringing with them the promise of economic benefit. Achieved without warfare, this insidious domination was a threat to the Israelites' continued independence.

Dedicated to God at birth, Samson was bound by a vow never to cut his hair; in return, God endowed Samson with enormous strength. Samson was a judge in Israel for about 20 years. During this time, he single-handedly struggled against the Philistines in numerous conflicts, bringing into the open the danger of the Philistine infiltration. Samson died in his final confrontation with the Philistines. Though high hopes had been attached to Samson, in the event it took many more years before the Israelites finally overcame their enemies.

SAMSON'S EXPLOITS

1 Samson marries a Philistine woman at Timnah. At the wedding feast, he sets a riddle to 30 guests, who trick him by extracting the answer from his bride. Samson kills 30 Philistines in Ashkelon and gives his bride to a close friend.

2 The Philistines come to capture Samson at Lehi, but he kills 1,000 of them using the jawbone of an ass.

3 Samson visits a prostitute in Gaza. As he leaves he takes with him the doors of the city gate and carries them to Hebron.

4 Samson falls in love with Delilah in Sorek; she collaborates with the Philistines to obtain the secret of his strength. Samson's hair is cut and he is overcome by the Philistines, who blind him and take him in chains to Gaza. After a time he is put on show in the temple, where he brings down the roof in a final display of strength.

Under siege

The Israelites' enemies took advantage of their evident weakness. The surrounding nations returned to the attack: the Canaanites at Hazor from the north; the Midianites from the east; the Ammonites from across the River Jordan. And from the coastlands the Philistines pushed the Israelites further and further into the hills.

Mount Tabor, the scene of Barak's defeat of Sisera.

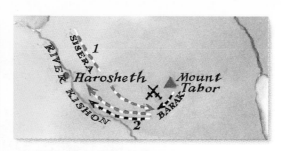

BARAK ATTACKS

1 Barak's forces assemble on Mount Tabor. Sisera's Canaanite forces, armed with 900 iron chariots, are deployed in the Plain of Jezreel below.

2 Barak's forces attack and rout the Caananites, whose chariots are rendered useless by the wet ground surrounding the River Kishon. Barak pursues the Canaanites towards Harosheth.

Deborah and Barak

For 20 years the Israelites had been ruled by Jabin, the king of Hazor. Deborah, a prophet, was one of the Israelite judges in about 1125 BC. She summoned Barak, an Israelite from Naphtali, to recruit an army to fight Sisera, the commander of the Canaanite forces. Barak agreed, on condition that Deborah accompanied him. The Canaanites were defeated in battle on the plain of Jezreel. The victory is graphically described in the 'Song of Deborah' in the Old Testament book of Judges.

2 30 BC — Start of conquest of the Promised Land — 12 00 — Approximate period of the Judges — 11 00 — Saul 1050 - 1010 — 10 00 BC

Jephthah

Israel was under threat of invasion again, this time by the Ammonites. When the elders of Gilead invited Jephthah to be their commander, he first attempted a diplomatic resolution to the conflict. This having failed, Jephthah raised troops to fight the Ammonite enemies.

Before going into battle, Jephthah made a vow to God: if he was successful, he would sacrifice whoever first came out of his house to meet him on his return. He went on to defeat the Ammonites decisively. Imagine his distress when the first person he saw on his triumphant return was his only child, a daughter. Despite his grief, and despite the fact that child sacrifice was forbidden under Israelite law, Jephthah kept his vow and offered his daughter as a burnt-offering. Jephthah was a judge of Israel for six years.

Gideon

After the victory gained by Deborah and Barak over Jabin, Israel again fell into difficulties. For seven consecutive years, their land was invaded by the Midianites, a nomadic group. Gideon was called by God to rescue Israel from the invaders. From an army of thousands, Gideon selected 300 men to attack the Midianites at night. In fear and confusion, the Midianites killed one another in large numbers, and the rest fled. After this decisive victory, the Israelites lived in peace for 40 years, until Gideon died.

GIDEON'S SUCCESS

1 Midianite invaders camp in the Plain of Jezreel.

2 Gideon attacks the Midianites in a surprise three-pronged attack at night.

3 The Midianites flee towards the Jordan valley, but are overtaken and destroyed by Gideon's forces.

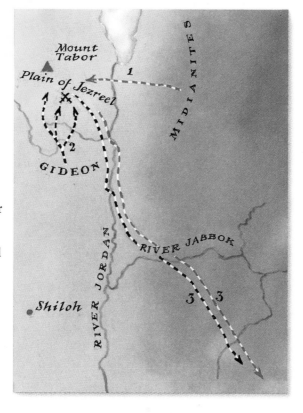

Samuel

The last and greatest of the judges was Samuel. Under his leadership, the Philistines were finally defeated in battle at Mizpeh, probably in about 1095 BC. Following this victory, the Israelites lived in peace for many years. Samuel brought the Israelites back to God's laws, and he ruled Israel for his whole life.

See also:

■ The Canaanites (pages 56–57)

■ The Philistines (pages 58–59)

■ Nations to the east and west (pages 78–79)

■ Judges (pages 206–207)

The first kings

When Samuel, the last of the Israelite judges, grew old, the people asked for a king to rule them, like the other nations. Samuel resisted at first, and warned them that a king would result in conscription to the army, forced labour and oppression. But the Israelites insisted and, at last, Samuel did as they asked.

The spring of Engedi, by the shore of the Dead Sea, was one place where David sought refuge from King Saul.

The sling was a common weapon in Bible times, and David used one to kill the Philistine, Goliath. This carving dates from the ninth century BC.

Saul

The first king of the Israelites, Saul, was from the tribe of Benjamin. He was appointed king in 1050 BC. Soon afterwards, he was faced with a challenge from the Ammonites, who moved from the east to besiege Jabesh-gilead. Saul gathered an army and launched a three-pronged attack which drove them off. Following this, and all through his life, Israel was engaged in war against the Philistines.

Power soon went to Saul's head and the Bible states that he began to disregard God's clear instructions. Because of Saul's disobedience, his son Jonathan did not inherit the throne. Instead, during Saul's lifetime, God sent Samuel to anoint David as Israel's next king.

David

David was a shepherd in Bethlehem, a member of the tribe of Judah and a gifted harpist. He was taken to the king's court to play his music to soothe Saul, who was by now suffering from spells of madness. At first, David was popular with the king. But after David killed the Philistine champion, Goliath, Saul became very jealous. Saul's son, Jonathan, warned David that he was in danger of his life. For a number of years, David was forced to live as an outlaw. Then Saul and Jonathan were killed in a battle against the Philistines on Mount Gilboa.

David was made king at Hebron in 1002 BC, when he was 30 years old. For the first two years, however, he was king only of his own tribal region in the south. This was a period of civil war between David's army and supporters of the former king, Saul. David united the kingdom, and was appointed king over all 12 of the Israelite tribes. He captured Jerusalem and made it his capital. During his lifetime he expanded the kingdom and drove off old enemies. He was a very popular king, and his legacy to his son Solomon was peace and security.

David reigned at Hebron as king of Judah. A thousand years earlier, Abraham had used Hebron as a base, and was buried there.

PHILISTIA

Aphek

Ramah

Gath

7

Adullam

Keilah

2

2

Hereth

3

Gibeah

Jerusalem

Nob

4

9

Bethlehem

JUDAH

BESOR RAVINE

7

Ziklag

8

Hebron

6

Horesh

Maon

5

4

Engedi

MOAB

DAVID'S PATH TO KINGSHIP

1 Saul is jealous of David's military successes, and becomes aware that David would eventually succeed him as king. David fears for his life and finds sanctuary among the priests at Nob, where he collects the sword of Goliath. Saul orders the murder of the priests for assisting David.

2 David finds refuge in the Philistine city of Gath, but becomes afraid of the Philistines, and flees to Adullam. He is joined by a band of about 600 men discontented with Saul's rulership and they move to Moab.

3 He returns to Judah in response to a prophecy, and fights against the Philistines who are besieging Keilah.

4 Saul pursues David with a force of 3000 men to Horesh and Maon, but withdraws when he learns the Philistines are invading Judah. David moves on to Engedi. Saul returns to the pursuit of David, who spares his life.

5 David moves to Maon. Saul follows him and again David spares Saul's life.

6 David seeks refuge again at Gath. King Achish of Gath believes David is an enemy of Israel and gives him Ziklag as a base.

7 The Philistines assemble to attack Israel. Saul summons his troops and meets them on Mount Gilboa. David reaches Aphek but is prevented from joining the battle. He returns to Ziklag to discover that the Amalekites have raided the city. He sets off in pursuit across the Besor Ravine and destroys them. Meanwhile, the Israelites have been defeated on Mount Gilboa. Saul and his sons are killed, and their bodies fixed to the walls of Beth-shan. The men of Jabesh-gilead take down the bodies and bury them.

8 David moves to Hebron, where he is made king over Judah. There is civil war between the supporters of David and those of Saul's family. Gradually, David's position becomes stronger until all Israel recognises him as king.

9 He reigns for seven and a half years in Hebron, then captures Jerusalem from the Jebusites and makes it his capital.

See also:

■ The Philistines (pages 58–59)

■ Three temples (pages 160–161)

■ 1 and 2 Samuel (pages 208–209)

■ 1 and 2 Kings (pages 210–211)

This aerial photograph shows the mound of Beth-shan, with the Roman amphitheatre in the foreground. The bodies of King Saul and his son Jonathan were fixed to the walls of Beth-shan after they were defeated by the Philistines.

Philistine army

▲ *Mount Gilboa*

Israelite army

Beth-shan

Jabesh-gilead

AMMON

The Jebusites were confident that Jerusalem was impregnable, but David's forces found a way into the city using a tunnel which had been dug to give access to the water supply of the Gihon spring.

Solomon

Solomon's wisdom as king was legendary. He became king in 970 BC, and he protected Israel by building fortresses and maintaining a powerful army. A strong, secure kingdom made it possible for Israel to prosper through trade alliances.

Solomon's kingdom included all the nations from the River Euphrates to Philistia and the Egyptian border. These nations paid him taxes and were subject to him all his life.

Peace and security freed the king to attend to other affairs, among them government and administration. At Solomon's court there was time for culture and the enjoyment of beauty. He built a magnificent temple in Jerusalem, and many other fine buildings. His reign was Israel's golden age. But there was another side to the picture. The introduction of heavy taxes, forced labour and foreign gods angered his subjects, and sowed the seeds that were to divide the kingdom after his death.

1070 BC   1000 BC   900 BC

Reign of David in Israel and Judah 1002–970

966 *Work on temple started*
959 *Work on temple finished*

Reign of Saul 1050–1010

Reign of David in Judah 1010–1002

Reign of Solomon 970–930

Two kingdoms

Under King Solomon Israel became a rich and powerful kingdom, but the people were oppressed and burdened with heavy taxes and forced labour. When Solomon's son Rehoboam came to the throne the Israelites appealed to him to lighten their burdens. He refused. The people rebelled, and the nation was divided.

The kingdom of Judah

In the south, the new kingdom of Judah comprised the tribes of Judah and Benjamin. It was a small kingdom, about 5,630 square km/3,500 square miles in area, one-third of the size of the kingdom of Israel. Rehoboam continued to rule the kingdom from its capital, Jerusalem.

The kingdom of Israel

Ten of the Israelite tribes set up a new kingdom, which they called the kingdom of Israel. Jeroboam I was appointed as king, and ruled from his capital at Shechem. He established new centres of worship at the cities of Dan and Bethel for this northern kingdom, which was now cut off from Jerusalem.

Shechem was chosen by Jeroboam I to be the capital of the new kingdom of Israel.

Good kings or bad?

The historians who wrote the Old Testament books of Kings and Chronicles classified the kings of Israel and Judah as 'good' or 'bad', depending on whether they reformed religion or allowed the non-Israelite practices adopted by the people to continue.

Uzziah and Hezekiah were two of the reforming kings of Judah. King Ahab of Israel had one of the worst records. He and his foreign wife Jezebel supported the worship of Baal, opposed the prophet Elijah and persecuted those who worshipped Israel's own God. The remains of Ahab's 'ivory house' at Samaria can still be seen today.

War and reconciliation

Rehoboam and later kings of Judah attempted to re-establish their authority over the remaining 10 tribes, and the kingdoms of Israel and Judah were in a state of civil war for 60 years. It was King Jehoshaphat who eventually formed an alliance with King Ahab of Israel. After this, the two kingdoms cooperated against the onslaught of their surrounding enemies.

King Ahab of Israel married Jezebel, daughter of Ethbaal, the king of Tyre. Jezebel enforced the worship of the weather god, Baal. Ahab built a temple for Baal at his capital, Samaria.

An era of prophecy

Against the backdrop of the division and later cooperation of the tribes of Israel, the Bible tells of the prophets who were active during this period. A prophet was considered to be a spokesperson for God, actively concerned with the conduct of God's people. Many prophets lived together in communities. The prophet Elisha was a leader of such a community, as also was the later prophet Isaiah.

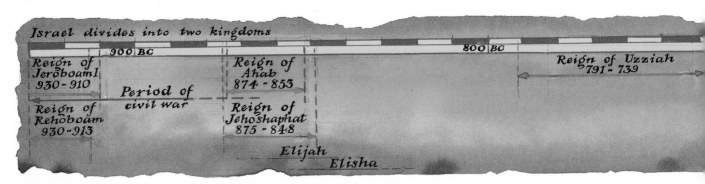

Israel divides into two kingdoms

| 900 BC | | 800 BC |

Reign of Jeroboam I 930 - 910

Period of civil war

Reign of Ahab 874 - 853

Reign of Uzziah 791 - 739

Reign of Rehoboam 930 - 913

Reign of Jehoshaphat 875 - 848

Elijah

Elisha

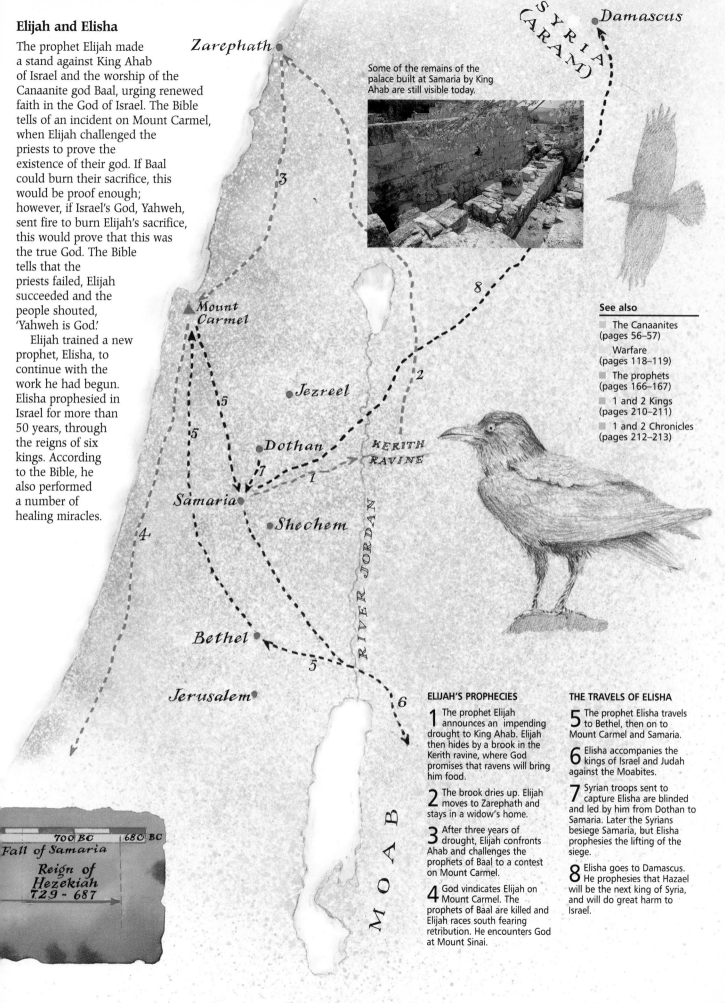

Elijah and Elisha

The prophet Elijah made a stand against King Ahab of Israel and the worship of the Canaanite god Baal, urging renewed faith in the God of Israel. The Bible tells of an incident on Mount Carmel, when Elijah challenged the priests to prove the existence of their god. If Baal could burn their sacrifice, this would be proof enough; however, if Israel's God, Yahweh, sent fire to burn Elijah's sacrifice, this would prove that this was the true God. The Bible tells that the priests failed, Elijah succeeded and the people shouted, 'Yahweh is God.'

Elijah trained a new prophet, Elisha, to continue with the work he had begun. Elisha prophesied in Israel for more than 50 years, through the reigns of six kings. According to the Bible, he also performed a number of healing miracles.

Some of the remains of the palace built at Samaria by King Ahab are still visible today.

See also
- The Canaanites (pages 56–57)
- Warfare (pages 118–119)
- The prophets (pages 166–167)
- 1 and 2 Kings (pages 210–211)
- 1 and 2 Chronicles (pages 212–213)

Zarephath

Damascus

SYRIA (ARAM)

Mount Carmel

Jezreel

Dothan

KERITH RAVINE

Samaria

Shechem

RIVER JORDAN

Bethel

Jerusalem

MOAB

Fall of Samaria
Reign of Hezekiah 729 – 687
700 BC   680 BC

ELIJAH'S PROPHECIES

1 The prophet Elijah announces an impending drought to King Ahab. Elijah then hides by a brook in the Kerith ravine, where God promises that ravens will bring him food.

2 The brook dries up. Elijah moves to Zarephath and stays in a widow's home.

3 After three years of drought, Elijah confronts Ahab and challenges the prophets of Baal to a contest on Mount Carmel.

4 God vindicates Elijah on Mount Carmel. The prophets of Baal are killed and Elijah races south fearing retribution. He encounters God at Mount Sinai.

THE TRAVELS OF ELISHA

5 The prophet Elisha travels to Bethel, then on to Mount Carmel and Samaria.

6 Elisha accompanies the kings of Israel and Judah against the Moabites.

7 Syrian troops sent to capture Elisha are blinded and led by him from Dothan to Samaria. Later the Syrians besiege Samaria, but Elisha prophesies the lifting of the siege.

8 Elisha goes to Damascus. He prophesies that Hazael will be the next king of Syria, and will do great harm to Israel.

The rise of Assyria

Because of their strategic position between Egypt and the Mesopotamian powers, Israel and Judah were very vulnerable to military aggression. Kings David and Solomon had been successful partly because none of the larger nations were powerful enough to attack during their reigns. But after the division of the Israelites into two kingdoms, surrounding nations – Syria, Ammon and Moab – gave the subsequent kings of Israel and Judah increasing trouble. However, it was the growth of the major powers further north-east that proved decisive.

Judah and Israel subdued

From the mid-ninth century BC, the time of King Ahab in Israel, the kings of Assyria repeatedly attacked Israel. Soon King Jehu of Israel (841–814 BC) was paying an annual tribute to Shalmaneser III of Assyria.

Ahaz, king of Judah in about 735–715 BC, asked Tiglath-pileser III of Assyria to help him to fight Syria and Israel. The Assyrian king agreed, and defeated them both. But Judah had to become a subject kingdom of the Assyrians in return for their help.

ASSYRIAN INVASIONS

1 In 853 BC Shalmaneser III's army is confronted at Qarqar by 12 kings who have come together to oppose him: one is King Ahab of Israel.

2 In 841 BC Shalmaneser III again marches on the area, laying siege to Damascus. King Jehu of Israel pays him tribute. Shalmaneser then has to secure his northern borders against attack, and Damascus seizes the opportunity to attack Israel and Judah.

3 King Tiglath-pileser III campaigns as far as 'the brook of Egypt' in 734 BC. Then in 733 BC he attacks Israel, destroying Megiddo and Hazor, and turning the coastal plain, Galilee and the area beyond the River Jordan into Assyrian provinces. In 732 BC Samaria is spared only because their rebellious King Pekah is assassinated.

4 Shalmaneser V captures King Hoshea of Israel in 724 BC and lays siege to Samaria. In 722 BC, he takes Samaria and sends the Israelites into exile, thus bringing the northern kingdom to an end.

The growth of the Assyrian empire

The Assyrian empire had an earlier period of power under King Tiglath-pileser I in about 1100 BC. But the ruthless aggression for which Assyria was so much feared reached its peak in the period between 880 BC and 612 BC. The Assyrian empire was based on three great cities: Asshur, Calah and Nineveh.

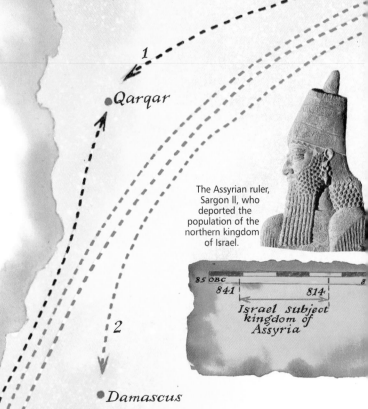

The Assyrian ruler, Sargon II, who deported the population of the northern kingdom of Israel.

85 OBC   841   814   8

Israel subject kingdom of Assyria

The decline of the Assyrian empire

The Assyrians dominated the affairs of the kingdoms of Israel and Judah, as well as conquering several other nations, including Egypt, Syria and Babylonia. However, the Assyrians had to fight many battles to protect their empire which, in effect, grew too large to defend adequately. Over time, several provinces regained their freedom. The empire lasted until Asshur fell to the Medes in 614 BC, and the capital, Nineveh, was destroyed by the Medes and Babylonians in 612 BC.

Qarqar

Damascus

Hazor

Megiddo

Samaria

A detail from the Black Obelisk of the Assyrian King Shalmaneser (858–824 BC) from Calah. King Jehu of Israel is shown on his knees before the Assyrian ruler.

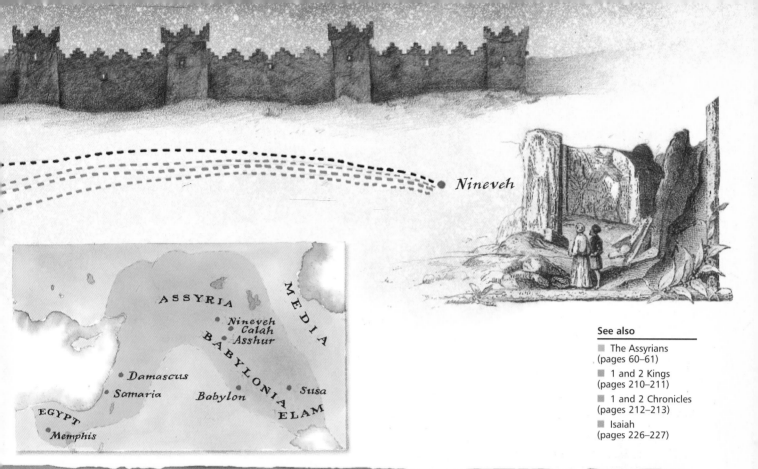

Nineveh

See also

- The Assyrians
(pages 60–61)
- 1 and 2 Kings
(pages 210–211)
- 1 and 2 Chronicles
(pages 212–213)
- Isaiah
(pages 226–227)

700 BC — 600 BC

733 Judah subject
kingdom of Assyria
722 Assyria besieges Samaria;
end of northern kingdom
701 Assyria unsuccessfully
besieges Jerusalem

614 Medes take
Asshur
612 Babylonians
destroy Nineveh

Isaiah

Jeremiah

The northern kingdom destroyed

When King Hoshea of Israel rebelled
and refused to pay the yearly tribute,
the Assyrian king Shalmaneser V began
a three-year siege of Samaria, then the
capital of Israel. The Israelites were
exiled to Assyria and the northern
kingdom of Israel was destroyed
(722–721 BC). The 10 tribes of Israel
were never heard of again.

Jerusalem besieged

Soon after the destruction of Israel, the
Assyrians defeated Egypt. Then, in
701 BC, the powerful King Sennacherib
besieged Jerusalem, because King
Hezekiah of Judah had stopped paying
tribute to the Assyrians and had joined
a rebellion. The Bible records that
Hezekiah trusted God and Jerusalem
was saved. King Sennacherib returned
to Nineveh, where he was murdered by
two of his sons.

This relief from
the palace of the
Assyrian king
Sennacherib in
Nineveh depicts
the siege of
Lachish in 701 BC.
Infantry and
archers use a siege
ramp to scale the
walls.

The Babylonian invasion

If Assyria in the Bible represented oppression, Babylon represented power. Nabopolassar, governor of the area around the Persian Gulf, freed Babylon from the Assyrians and was made king in 626 BC. He continued to gain victories over the Assyrians, and in 612 BC the Babylonians and Medes captured the Assyrian capital, Nineveh. They were not content with taking over Assyria itself, but set out to conquer the entire Assyrian empire.

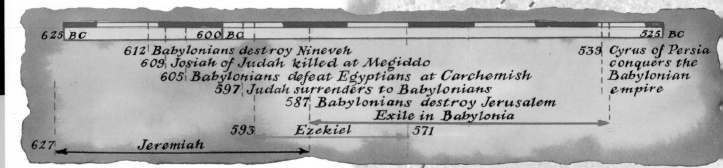

Carchemish
2

625 BC   600 BC   525 BC
612 Babylonians destroy Nineveh   539 Cyrus of Persia
609 Josiah of Judah killed at Megiddo   conquers the
605 Babylonians defeat Egyptians at Carchemish   Babylonian
597 Judah surrenders to Babylonians   empire
587 Babylonians destroy Jerusalem
Exile in Babylonia
593   Ezekiel   571
627   Jeremiah

JUDAH UNDER PRESSURE

1 In 609 BC King Josiah of Judah is killed in battle against Egyptian troops at Megiddo. Judah becomes a subject state of Egypt.

2 Four years later, in 605 BC, King Nebuchadnezzar of Babylon, having defeated the Egyptians at Carchemish, invades Judah and occupies the coastal plain.

3 In 597 BC Jerusalem is forced to surrender to King Nebuchadnezzar. Ten years later Nebuchadnezzar again marches on Jerusalem, following a rebellion. In 587 BC the city is taken and destroyed, and its citizens are taken into exile.

The fall of Jerusalem

Shortly after Jehoiachin became king of Judah in 597 BC, the Babylonians conquered Jerusalem. The king and many of Judah's leaders were taken into exile in Babylon. The policy of the invaders was not just to plunder and destroy, but also to weaken the subject nations and prevent further rebellions by deporting their leading citizens.

Despite this, 10 years later, Zedekiah, a puppet king placed on the throne of Judah by Nebuchadnezzar of Babylon, appealed to the Egyptians for help. To crush this rebellion, the Babylonians laid siege to Jerusalem for 18 months, before taking the city in 587 BC. King Zedekiah was captured and blinded. Jerusalem and its temple were destroyed. Valuable objects, including the temple treasure, were plundered; and the people were deported to Babylon. Only the very poor were left to cultivate the land. This was the beginning of the period of Jewish history known as the 'exile'.

Megiddo

3

1

Jerusalem

This clay tablet, part of the Babylonian Chronicle, records a number of key events in the history of Babylon and Judah. These include the accession to the throne of Babylon of Nebuchadnezzar II, the battle of Carchemish, the fall of Jerusalem in 597 BC, and the appointment of Zedekiah as king of Judah.

1

The rise of the Babylonian empire

After the Babylonians captured Nineveh, the Assyrians retreated to Harran. The Egyptians, realizing that their own nation might be in danger, marched north to support the Assyrians.

King Josiah of Judah intercepted the Egyptian army at Megiddo. In the resulting battle he was killed and Judah became subject to Egypt. Four years later, in 605 BC, the Babylonian army, led by the new king of Babylon, Nebuchadnezzar, defeated the Egyptians at Carchemish. The Babylonian empire was spreading. It was to remain all-powerful until it was conquered by Cyrus of Persia in 539 BC.

See also
■ The Egyptians (pages 52–53)
■ The Babylonians (pages 62–63)
■ The prophets (pages 166–167)
■ 1 and 2 Kings (pages 210–211)
■ Jeremiah (pages 230–231)

The site of ancient Babylon. The River Euphrates divided the city into two parts, connected by a bridge resting on stone piers. The walls of Babylon extended for 8 km/5 miles around the city, and were wide enough for a four-horse chariot to turn around on top. In the foreground are the remains of the Etemenanki ziggurat, the so-called 'Tower of Babel'.

Babylon

From exile to return

For more than 200 years, the prophets warned the people of Israel and Judah that judgment would befall them if they refused to listen to God and to keep God's laws. They ignored the warning. The northern kingdom of Israel was destroyed by the Assyrians in 721 BC, and the Israelite tribes disappeared. Judah was conquered in 587 BC, and many of its people were exiled to Babylonia.

The Persian king, Darius I, began the construction of a huge complex of palaces at Persepolis. It was completed by King Artaxerxes I. The remains of the buildings still indicate something of their orginal scale and grandeur.

The exiles

In Babylonia the exiles lived in their own settlements in the capital, Babylon, and other towns. They were free to build houses, earn a living, and keep their own customs and religion. They could not return to Judah, but they were not ill-treated. Some Jews even rose to high positions in government service. Many became so much at home in Babylon that when the opportunity came to rebuild Jerusalem they did not want to go. But some Jews longed to return to Judah.

590 BC		500 BC		420 BC
587 Exile in Babylonia		519 Prophecies of Haggai and Zechariah		Ezra arrives in Jerusalem
	538 Jews return to Jerusalem			Nehemiah arrives in Jerusalem and rebuilds walls
	Jews rebuild the temple			
	539 Cyrus conquers Babylon			
	Reign of Cyrus 559 - 530	Reign of Darius I 522 - 486		Reign of Artaxerxes I 464 - 423

Faith in practice

Solomon's temple in Jerusalem had been the centre of Jewish faith and worship. After its destruction, there was nowhere to offer temple sacrifices. The people living in exile began to lay new stress on those parts of their religion that they were able to observe anywhere in the world, including keeping the sabbath day of rest, circumcision, and the laws about what was clean and unclean. And the Jews began to value the written records of God's message as never before.

34

The Persian empire

In the first half of the sixth century BC Babylonia appeared all-powerful. But when King Cyrus of Persia united the two kingdoms of Persia and Media, the end of the Babylonian empire was in sight. In 539 BC, Cyrus conquered Babylon, and took over and expanded the entire Babylonian empire, taking Egypt and all of what is now Turkey.

See also

■ The Persians (pages 66–67)
■ The prophets (pages 166–167)
■ Three temples (pages 160–161)
■ Ezra, Nehemiah (pages 212–213)
■ Ezekiel (pages 232–233)

The first Jewish coins struck in Israel date from about 333 BC. This one bears the Hebrew inscription 'Yehud', the Aramaic name for the Persian satrapy of Judea.

Return to Jerusalem

When Babylon fell, King Cyrus divided the Persian empire into provinces, each with its own ruler, called a 'satrap'. These were mainly Persians, but under them were local rulers who retained some power. The different peoples were encouraged to keep their own customs and religions.

As part of this policy, in 538 BC Cyrus issued a decree saying that the Jews could return to Jerusalem and rebuild the temple. They were to be given money and all the supplies they needed. Cyrus returned to them the gold and silver bowls and other items that King Nebuchadnezzar of Babylon had taken from the temple. The first party of exiles made the long journey back home.

King Cyrus of Persia united Persia and Media in 550 BC, and founded the city of Pasargadae as his new capital. Little remains of the city today apart from King Cyrus' tomb, shown in this photograph.

Rebuilding the temple

In Jerusalem Zerubbabel, a descendant of the last king of Judah, and the priest Joshua took charge of the work to rebuild the temple. Conditions were difficult. The people had first to build homes and make a living for themselves. Their enemies harassed them. They soon grew discouraged and work on the temple came to a standstill – for 15 years.

Then the prophets Haggai and Zechariah spoke out, stirring the people to action. Word came from the new Persian king, Darius, confirming Cyrus' decree and ordering the governor of the province to give the Jews whatever help they needed. Four years later, in 515 BC, the temple was finished and dedicated to God.

Rebuilding the city walls

When the Jews returned from exile to Judah, they remained a small and struggling community, and the city of Jerusalem had no walls to protect it. During the reign of King Artaxerxes I of Persia (464–423 BC), two new leaders came to Jerusalem: Ezra and Nehemiah.

Ezra was a priest. Many of the Jews in Jerusalem had married foreign wives and were worshipping other gods. Ezra called on the people to return to their own faith.

Nehemiah, who was King Artaxerxes' wine steward in Susa, returned to Jerusalem to rebuild the city walls. He organized the work, making certain families responsible for building particular sections. After 52 days, the wall was completed and dedicated to God.

The reformers

For 12 years Nehemiah was governor of Judah, appointed by the Persians. Together, he and Ezra guided the community and made a number of reforms in line with the Torah's teaching. Nehemiah prevented wealthy Jews from over-charging their poorer neighbours for food. Ezra read and explained God's law to the people. And in a written document signed in their name by their leaders, the Jews made a solemn promise that in future they would obey all God's commands and laws.

The 'dispersion'

After the exile, many Jews did not return to Jerusalem, but remained settled in other parts of the Persian empire. This 'dispersion' became significant in New Testament times. Because of their distance from the temple at Jerusalem, these Jews developed the practice of having a local synagogue, which was a centre of teaching and worship. This laid the basis for the rapid spread of Jewish communities throughout the Mediterranean world.

The Greek and Roman empires

The Old Testament story ends with the rebuilding of the temple and the city walls of Jerusalem. There is a gap of several hundred years before the New Testament story begins. This period was one of enormous changes of fortune for the Persians, the Greeks and the Romans – and for the Jews who lived in their midst.

Alexander and the Greek empire

The Persian empire was set to expand into the whole of Greece. Numerous battles between the Persians and the Greeks led to deadlock – until finally, in 334 BC, the Greek soldier Alexander of Macedon began his meteoric career.

Alexander was only 22 when he set out on a campaign which swept across the ancient world. Having taken Egypt, he marched east, to the heart of the Persian empire. He pressed on as far as India, conquering all who stood in his way and founding Greek city-states wherever he went. His title 'Alexander the Great' was well earned. He died of a fever in Babylon, when only 33, in 323 BC.

The empire divided

Following the death of Alexander, the Greek empire was divided up by his four generals. Ptolemy took control of Egypt, ruling from Alexandria. Seleucus initially controlled the eastern areas of the Greek empire. Over the following decades, the Ptolemaic and Seleucid rulers each fought to expand their separate empires. Culturally, however, the Greek or 'Hellenistic' world continued as a unity.

Ptolemy I

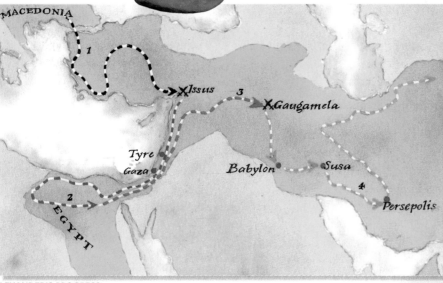

ALEXANDER'S PROGRESS

1 In 334 BC Alexander of Macedon crosses the Hellespont into Asia Minor to challenge the Persian king Darius III.

2 Alexander defeats the Persians at Issus, then proceeds to take Phoenicia, Palestine and Egypt, destroying the cities of Tyre and Gaza on the way.

3 At the battle of Gaugamela in 331 BC, Alexander finally defeats Darius III and conclusively breaks Persian power.

4 Alexander takes the Persian capitals of Babylon, Susa and Persepolis, and continues his conquests towards India.

The Greek ideal

Alexander's ambition was not simply one of conquest. He believed in Greek ideals, and wanted to spread Greek culture and thought. He encouraged army veterans to settle in distant places and to build up societies based on the Greek way of life. City-states were built and organized on the Greek pattern. Each city had a market-place, public buildings, temples and theatres built in Greek architectural style.

Greek thought was as powerful an influence for change as Greek building. Greek plays performed in the theatres were linked with Greek religious festivals. And Greek became the international language. It was not long before the Hebrew scriptures were translated into Greek, so they could be read more widely.

350 BC   300

333 Battle of Issus
331 Battle of Gaugamela
Alexander 323
the Great

The Maccabean revolt

After the death of Alexander the Great, Palestine – the area encompassing the former kingdoms of Judah and Israel – was initially ruled by the Ptolemaic rulers. In 198 BC, however, Palestine fell under Seleucid control. This marked the beginning of a period of persecution against the Jews.

Finally, the Seleucid king, Antiochus IV Epiphanes, desecrated the temple at Jerusalem and decreed that the Jewish religion be outlawed. Many Jews succumbed to the king's decree. Others, refusing to abandon their faith, were killed or went into hiding. Judas, the son of a priest called Mattathias, led a revolt against King Antiochus, who was soundly defeated by 164 BC. Thanks to the endeavours of Judas and his brothers, the 'Maccabeans', there followed a century of Jewish independence.

Antioch

SYRIA

The Roman empire

The Greek empire gradually fell to the Romans. Corinth was taken in 146 BC and Athens in 86 BC. In the first century BC Julius Caesar conquered Gaul, and Pompey brought Syria and Palestine under Roman control. He occupied Jerusalem in 63 BC.

The Romans absorbed Greek ideas, language and culture. Their legacy to the world was essentially practical: fine straight roads, aqueducts, plumbing and central heating, and the baths. To the Greek games were added Roman spectator sports and contests. In 31 BC Octavian became in effect the first ruler of the Roman empire, adopting the title Augustus in AD 27. It was during his reign that Jesus Christ was born.

Pompey

Augustus

Jerusalem

The Romans in Palestine

The Romans brought law, order and stability to the nations they ruled. Peace was maintained by garrisons of soldiers, whose presence was not generally appreciated. Four legions were stationed in Palestine, and there were heavy taxes to pay. The atmosphere was highly charged and revolt – especially where the Jewish religion was concerned – was a constant danger.

When the time was ripe

In many ways, the time was ripe for Jesus and his teaching. After the philosophy of the Greeks and the materialism of the Romans, people were searching for more 'spiritual' answers to life's questions. But all too often they simply lapsed into superstition. In an age of degenerate religion, many non-Jews were attracted to the Jewish faith. And because of Roman roads and the Roman peace, the news of Jesus' message and activities could travel quickly throughout the Roman empire.

200		100		20 BC
198	142	Jewish independence	63 Romans occupy Jerusalem	31 Octavian first ruler of the Roman empire
Ptolemies control Palestine	164 Temple rededicated			27 Octavian adopts the title 'Augustus'
	Seleucids control Palestine			
	168	165 Maccabean revolt		

A brief history of Jerusalem

Jerusalem has been a political and religious focal point of the Jewish people since it was captured by King David in the 10th century BC. Referred to even today as the 'holy city', it was the scene of the biblical account of the arrest, trial, crucifixion and resurrection of Jesus. Today Jerusalem has a special significance in the three great faiths, Judaism, Christianity and Islam.

City in the hills

The city of Jerusalem was built high in the Judean hills, about 800 m/2,640 ft above sea level, and about 50 km/31 miles from the Mediterranean Sea. Surrounded by steep hills to the west and the Judean desert to the east, it was a natural fortress. However, enemies could approach the city along the high plateau from the north or south.

An aerial view of Jerusalem looking towards the north-west with part of the City of David in the left foreground. Crossing the picture is the Kidron valley. The platform now occupied by the Dome of the Rock was built on Mount Moriah. It was the site of the intended sacrifice of Isaac by Abraham, and the place where both Solomon's and Herod's temples stood.

The Jerusalem captured by King David from the Jebusites was located on the Eastern Hill. King Solomon extended the city northwards, building the temple, a royal palace and a millo, which appears to have been a fortified watchtower. The extent of the city from Solomon's time through to the first century BC is the subject of much dispute. However, the small map (left) shows the likely minimum and maximum extent of the city walls during this period. The fine line indicates the position of a later wall, and provides a point of reference with the main map (opposite).

Temple
Royal Palace
Millo
City of David

A chequered history

From the time of King David in about 1002 BC, Jerusalem had a chequered history. During the reign of King Solomon in 970–930 BC, the city – with its magnificent temple and fine buildings – was the centre of all the civil and religious affairs of the Israelites. After the division of the tribes of Israel into two separate kingdoms, Jerusalem became the capital of Judah. The city was subsequently besieged by the Egyptians, the Assyrians and the kings of the northern kingdom of Israel, and then destroyed by the Babylonians in 587 BC.

Rebuilt by the Jews in the years following their return from exile in Babylon, Jerusalem was absorbed by the Persian empire and the later Greek empire. After only one century of independence, the city fell under the control of the Romans. In AD 66, the Jews rebelled against the Romans, and AD 70 saw the destruction of Jerusalem yet again. Modern Jerusalem is built on the site of the ancient city.

100 BC | 0
63 Romans occupy Jerusalem | 19 Work on Herod's temple started
Reign of Herod 37 – 4

New Testament Jerusalem

In Jesus' day, there may have been as many as a quarter of a million people living in Jerusalem. Its streets were crowded with people buying and selling. The shops and stalls sold everything, from necessities such as sandals and cloth, meat, and fruit and vegetables, to the luxury goods offered by goldsmiths and jewellers, and the silk, linen and perfume merchants. There were seven different markets, and two market days each week.

Jerusalem had restaurants and wine shops for ordinary people, as well as grander buildings such as the palaces, Roman amphitheatre and the fortress of Antonia.

See also
- Regional geography (pages 84–85)
- Cities, towns and villages (pages 120–121)
- Trade and commerce (pages 124–125)
- Three temples (pages 160–161)

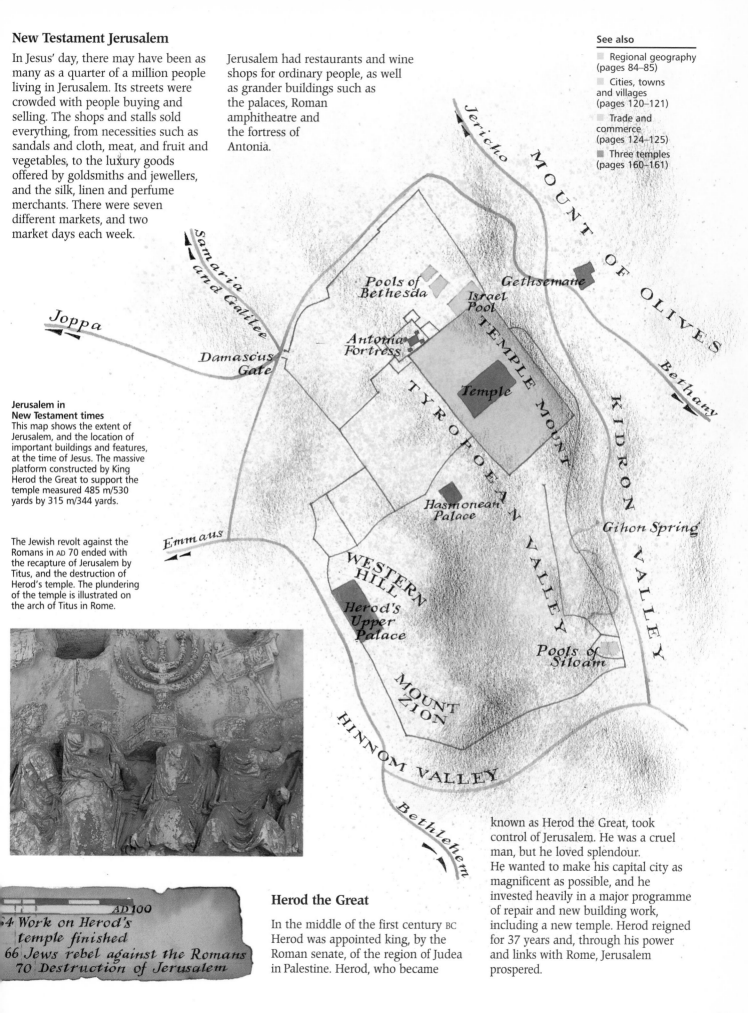

Jerusalem in New Testament times
This map shows the extent of Jerusalem, and the location of important buildings and features, at the time of Jesus. The massive platform constructed by King Herod the Great to support the temple measured 485 m/530 yards by 315 m/344 yards.

The Jewish revolt against the Romans in AD 70 ended with the recapture of Jerusalem by Titus, and the destruction of Herod's temple. The plundering of the temple is illustrated on the arch of Titus in Rome.

Map labels: Jericho · MOUNT OF OLIVES · Pools of Bethesda · Gethsemane · Israel Pool · Samaria and Galilee · Antonia Fortress · TEMPLE MOUNT · Temple · Bethany · KIDRON VALLEY · Joppa · Damascus Gate · TYROPOEAN VALLEY · Gihon Spring · Hasmonean Palace · Emmaus · WESTERN HILL · Herod's Upper Palace · Pools of Siloam · MOUNT ZION · HINNOM VALLEY · Bethlehem

Timeline: AD 100 · 64 Work on Herod's temple finished · 66 Jews rebel against the Romans · 70 Destruction of Jerusalem

Herod the Great

In the middle of the first century BC Herod was appointed king, by the Roman senate, of the region of Judea in Palestine. Herod, who became known as Herod the Great, took control of Jerusalem. He was a cruel man, but he loved splendour. He wanted to make his capital city as magnificent as possible, and he invested heavily in a major programme of repair and new building work, including a new temple. Herod reigned for 37 years and, through his power and links with Rome, Jerusalem prospered.

In the steps of Jesus

Jesus was born, the Bible records, at the time when the Roman emperor Augustus had ordered a census throughout his empire. This was towards the end of the reign of King Herod the Great. Although his parents, Mary and Joseph, came from Nazareth, Jesus was born in Bethlehem, the birthplace of his illustrious ancestor, King David.

45 BC | 0 | AD 45

Reign of Augustus
31 BC – AD 14

Reign of Tiberius
AD 14 – 37

Reign of Herod the Great
37 – 4 BC

Pontius Pilate governor of Judea
AD 26 – 36

Probable lifetime of Jesus 4 BC – AD 30

The promised one

The Bible clearly identifies Jesus, who was born into an ordinary family, as the Messiah, or 'Christ' – the one that God had long promised would save his people. Many Jews were ready and waiting for him – though he was not to be the kind of king they imagined.

Jesus' childhood

Jesus' early years were spent in Nazareth, where his father Joseph ran a building business. An annual highlight was the visit to Jerusalem to celebrate the Passover festival. When Jesus was 12 years old, Mary and Joseph took him with them for the first time.

A public figure

It was in about AD 27, in the 13th year of the rule of the Roman emperor Tiberius, that Jesus' public work began. The Bible records that Jesus joined the crowds that flocked to John the Baptist beside the River Jordan and was baptized by John, identifying himself with the struggle of his people. Forty days of fasting and testing in the desert prepared Jesus for his return to the region of Galilee and the start of a new life as a travelling teacher. Quickly gathering a following of his own, Jesus soon chose 12 companions to go with him on his travels. From this time until his death (probably about three years later) Jesus was a public figure.

The Bible records an incident in which Jewish teachers of God's law questioned Jesus about the legality of paying tax to the Roman emperor. The denarius was the coin used for paying this tax. This denarius bears the image of Tiberius, who was emperor during the time of Jesus' ministry.

Caesarea

SAMARIA

Samaria/
Sebaste

Sychar

Jerusalem

JUDEA

Jerusalem

Bethany

Bethlehem

RIVER JORDAN

Bethlehem

DEAD SEA

PEREA

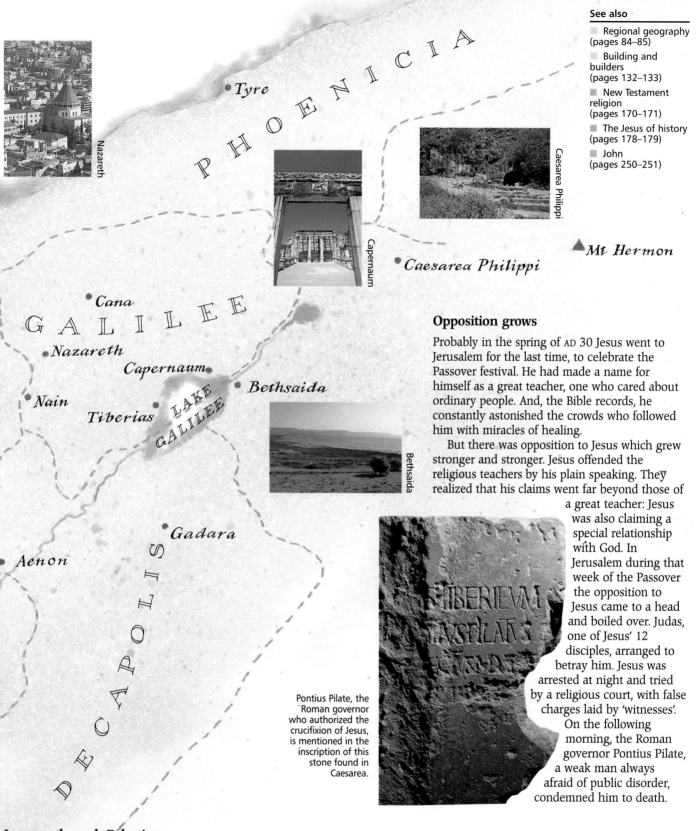

See also
■ Regional geography (pages 84–85)
■ Building and builders (pages 132–133)
■ New Testament religion (pages 170–171)
■ The Jesus of history (pages 178–179)
■ John (pages 250–251)

PHOENICIA

Tyre

Nazareth

Caesarea Philippi

Capernaum

▲ Mt Hermon

• Caesarea Philippi

Cana

GALILEE

Nazareth

Capernaum

• Bethsaida

Nain

Tiberias

LAKE GALILEE

Bethsaida

Gadara

Aenon

DECAPOLIS

Opposition grows

Probably in the spring of AD 30 Jesus went to Jerusalem for the last time, to celebrate the Passover festival. He had made a name for himself as a great teacher, one who cared about ordinary people. And, the Bible records, he constantly astonished the crowds who followed him with miracles of healing.

But there was opposition to Jesus which grew stronger and stronger. Jesus offended the religious teachers by his plain speaking. They realized that his claims went far beyond those of a great teacher: Jesus was also claiming a special relationship with God. In Jerusalem during that week of the Passover the opposition to Jesus came to a head and boiled over. Judas, one of Jesus' 12 disciples, arranged to betray him. Jesus was arrested at night and tried by a religious court, with false charges laid by 'witnesses'. On the following morning, the Roman governor Pontius Pilate, a weak man always afraid of public disorder, condemned him to death.

Pontius Pilate, the Roman governor who authorized the crucifixion of Jesus, is mentioned in the inscription of this stone found in Caesarea.

Journey through Palestine

The Bible names many of the places Jesus visited, although it is not possible to work out a precise sequence of his travels. Much of his time was spent in Palestine in the area around Lake Galilee. But it is evident that there were frequent visits to Jerusalem, especially for major festivals. On at least one occasion, he chose to go through Samaria. And he travelled to the far north, to the district of Caesarea Philippi, close to Mount Hermon.

Death, burial and beyond

Jesus was condemned to death by crucifixion, and he died on a cross on a hill outside Jerusalem's city wall. A hasty burial followed. But the Bible recounts that when some women friends came to observe the last rites, they found that Jesus' tomb was empty. Later, many of Jesus' followers saw him alive.

The birth of Christianity

The Bible records that six weeks after his resurrection, Jesus left his disciples with instructions to make him known throughout the world. They were to wait in Jerusalem to receive the power of God's Holy Spirit. On the day of Pentecost that power came – and the disciples' lives were transformed.

The spread of Christianity was aided by the superb network of roads and shipping routes built by the Romans. The inset map shows the greatest extent of the Roman empire, under the emperor Trajan. The main map indicates the location of many of the Roman provinces mentioned in the New Testament.

New followers

Under the disciples' leadership, many people in Jerusalem became followers of Jesus. And in towns and villages all over Palestine, new groups of believers were established. The Bible records that at this time (about AD 34) two important events occurred. A Pharisee named Saul (later known as Paul), who was a fierce opponent of the new sect, was converted as he went to arrest believers in Damascus. And in Caesarea a Roman centurion, Cornelius, became a notable convert to Christianity.

The first missionaries

In Antioch, the capital of the province of Syria, many people became believers; they were nicknamed 'Christians'. It was from Antioch that the missionaries Paul and Barnabas set out in about AD 45 or 46. They preached in Cyprus and what is now Turkey, and many non-Jews (known as 'Gentiles') as well as Jews became Christians. This led to a major problem. Could Gentiles become Christians without first becoming Jews? A conference held at Jerusalem in AD 49 decided that they could. This was a crucial step forward for the church.

Paul continued to undertake missionary journeys into Europe. And many others were also preaching the message about Jesus, the 'gospel', and helping the Christian churches. By AD 64, there were churches in all the main centres of the Roman empire. From these, the gospel spread out to surrounding areas.

0   AD 100

34 Conversion of Saul (later Paul)
45-46 Paul and Barnabas sent out as missionaries
49 Conference about the Gentiles held in Jerusalem
64 Churches in all main centres of the Roman empire

BITHYNIA AND PONTUS

GALATIA

CILICIA

LYCIA PAMPHYLIA

SYRIA

JUDEA

EGYPT

Antioch

Damascus

Caesarea

Jerusalem

See also

■ Roman religion and beliefs (pages 74–75)

■ The earliest Christians (pages 172–173)

■ Jesus the saviour (pages 190–191)

■ Acts of the Apostles (pages 248–249)

Antioch
Antioch was a major centre of the new Christian church, where followers of Jesus were first called 'Christians'. Paul left from here on his missionary journeys.

Damascus
It was en route to Damascus that the Pharisee Saul, later known as Paul, became a follower of Jesus. Paul was on his way from Jerusalem to persecute the Christians.

Caesarea
Caesarea was built by King Herod the Great in honour of the Roman emperor Augustus. It was here that the missionary Peter preached to non-Jews for the first time, in the home of a Roman centurion.

Jerusalem
Jerusalem was the centre of the early Christian church. A conference to decide how far non-Jews should keep the Jewish law was held here in about AD 49.

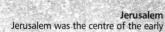

43

The journeys of Paul

Paul, who was converted to Christianity on the road to Damascus, became a key figure in the spread of Christianity to the western world. In the letters to Christian groups which form a large part of the New Testament, Paul refers to his frequent journeys and to the constant dangers he faced. Three of those missionary journeys are fully recorded by his companion, Luke, in the New Testament – and Paul made a fourth journey as a prisoner sent for trial in Rome.

Corinth was an important trade centre, and attracted people of many nationalities. The remains of the temple of Apollo in Corinth date from about 540 BC.

The first journey

Paul's first missionary journey took Paul and Barnabas from their base at Antioch in Syria by ship to Cyprus, and from there to present-day Turkey. They visited Attalia, Perga, Pisidian Antioch, Iconium, Derbe and Lystra. They returned by the same route and took a ship back to Antioch. John Mark, who had set out with them, returned home from Perga. The date was about AD 45 or 46.

The second journey

Paul's second missionary journey took place in AD 48–51, and included an 18-month stay at Corinth. This time Paul took Silas with him, after a disagreement with Barnabas about John Mark.

They went overland from Antioch, revisiting the churches established on the first journey, They were joined by Timothy at Lystra. From this region they went to Troas on the coast and crossed to northern Greece, travelling from Philippi to Thessalonica, Berea, Athens and Corinth, and returning by ship from Corinth via Ephesus and Caesarea to Antioch.

The third journey

Paul's third missionary journey began in AD 53. Paul and his companions again went overland through Galatia and Phrygia in Turkey. They stayed for more than two years at Ephesus where the response to the news about Jesus was so great that the silversmiths lost their trade in statuettes of the goddess Diana and started a riot. From Ephesus Paul went to Philippi, Corinth and back, taking a ship around the coast from Troas to Assos, Mitylene, Miletus, Rhodes, Patara, then from Tyre to Ptolemais and Caesarea en route for Jerusalem.

Paul preached to the Greek philosophers at Athens, beginning by affirming their creation-centred beliefs before speaking of Jesus.

Voyage to Rome

In Jerusalem Paul was arrested. He spent the next two years, AD 58–60, in prison, before appealing to be heard by the emperor and setting sail for Rome. This fourth journey, in the autumn, was very different from Paul's previous travels. Although Paul had Luke with him, he was under guard. After his ship set out from Crete, it was caught in a fierce gale and wrecked off Malta. The travellers, having escaped with their lives, stayed in Malta during the winter months, before completing their journey to Rome. As Paul entered the capital, Christians came out to meet him. For the next two years Paul continued to preach the message of Jesus, though under house arrest and awaiting trial.

Rome

Rhegium

Athens

Corinth

Syracuse

Malta

CRETE

Lasea

See also
- Hellenistic civilization (pages 70–71)
- Roman religion and beliefs (pages 74–75)
- The earliest Christians (pages 172–173)
- Acts of the Apostles (pages 248–249)
- Writings of the apostles: overview (pages 252–253)

The first Christian church in Europe was established at Philippi in northern Greece. This photograph shows the site of the market-place in this ancient city.

Philippi

Berea Thessalonica

Troas

Ephesus Pisidian Antioch GALATIA

Miletus Colossae

PHYRGIA Iconium

Rhodes Lystra

Attalia Perga Derbe

Patara

Tarsus

CYPRUS Syrian Antioch

SYRIA

Sidon

Tyre Damascus

Ptolemais

Caesarea

Jerusalem

------- First journey
------- Second journey
------- Third journey
------- Voyage to Rome

45

The earliest churches

By the end of the first century AD Christianity had spread throughout much of the Roman empire. Jesus' followers travelled far and wide to tell others about their new-found faith and to establish new communities of believers. Despite sometimes strong opposition and even persecution, the new Christians held firmly to their beliefs and the church took root so deeply that it could never be eradicated.

Rome
Paul is thought to have ended his life here, at the heart of the Roman empire. Paul wrote to the Romans before visiting them to set out the main facts about the Christian faith.

Good news travels fast

The early apostles were crucial to the establishment of new churches. Paul visited Asia Minor, Peter worked in Rome, and other ancient traditions mention John in Asia, Mark in Alexandria, Thomas in India and Thaddeus in Mesopotamia. Some – like Paul – were quite rich, while others were supported by the generosity of other Christians who paid for their travels throughout the Roman empire. And undoubtedly the 'good news' about Jesus spread still further as many unknown believers simply talked about their own experiences with others. The map indicates the location of known centres of Christianity in AD 100.

Athens
The cultural and religious heart of the ancient world. Paul visited Athens on his second missionary journey, and addressed the court convened to settle matters of religion.

Corinth
A cosmopolitan port. Paul's letters to the Corinthians show how the church was affected by problems in society, such as immorality, idol worship and mystery religions.

Early Christianity in practice

The earliest Christian church was effectively one among several Jewish groups in Palestine, including the Pharisees and Sadducees. And yet – in contrast to such groups – the early Christians welcomed non-Jews, too, which made them highly distinctive. Indeed, by AD 100, when the focal point of Christianity had moved to Rome, the church was made up mainly of non-Jews.

The early Christians were united by their acceptance of the Old Testament scriptures, as well as by their acknowledgment that Jesus was God's son and their 'Lord and saviour'. They shared a regular meal in remembrance of Jesus and the 'last supper', confessing their sins and offering thanks before they ate. They also practised baptism, recited the Lord's Prayer and fasted regularly.

In the latter half of the first century AD, the early Christian church came under attack in various parts of the Roman empire. Large numbers of Christians died for their faith. The scene of many such martyrdoms was the Colosseum in Rome. Opened in AD 80, it could accommodate up to 70,000 spectators.

Philippi
This city was a Roman colony, home to people who had made a special contribution to the empire. Paul was illegally imprisoned here. The letter to the Philippians was written to the church in Philippi.

Thessalonica
Paul wrote two letters to the Thessalonians addressing the issue of the return of Jesus.

Ephesus
This great city and port was the site of the temple of Diana, the theatre where crowds cried for Paul's blood, and the hall of Tyrannus where Paul taught for two years. The letter to the Ephesians was written to the Christians in this area.

See also

■ New Testament religion
(pages 170–171)

■ The earliest Christians
(pages 172–173)

■ The practice of prayer
(pages 174–175)

■ Writings of the apostles: overview
(pages 252–253)

Patmos
While an exile on Patmos, John wrote the book of Revelation to the Christians on the mainland who were suffering persecution. He included letters to seven churches.

Colossae
Paul wrote his letter to the Colossians to Christians in this Hellenistic city.

Philippi
Apollonia
Thessalonica

Troas

Pergamum
Thyatira

Sardis
Smyrna
Tralles
Philadelphia
Hierapolis
Laodicea

Pisidian Antioch

Ephesus
Magnesia
Miletus

Colossae

Iconium

Lystra

Edessa

Athens
Aegina
Corinth
Cenchreae

Derbe

Tarsus

Perge

Syrian Antioch

Salamis

Paphos

Sidon
Tyre
Ptolemais

Damascus

Caesarea
Joppa
Lydda

Pella
Sebaste

Jerusalem

Alexandria

Part 1: Picture acknowledgments

Abbreviations:

t = top, tl = top left, tc = top centre, tr = top right,
c = centre, cl = centre left, cr = centre right
b = bottom, bl = bottom left, bc = bottom centre, br = bottom right

Illustrations

Maps and timelines by David Atkinson
RN = Rex Nicholls

Photographs:

JA = Jon Arnold, ZR = Zev Radovan

Part 2

PEOPLES
AND
EMPIRES

The Sumerians

The Sumerians lived in the southern part of ancient Mesopotamia for about 3,000 years. Their history can be divided into three main periods: Early Sumerian, Classic Sumerian and Neo-Sumerian. The Sumerians were responsible for many of the hallmarks of later civilization, including writing, art and architecture.

The invention of writing

The Sumerians are believed to have invented writing. The earliest known examples of writing, dating from about 3300 BC, were discovered on clay tablets from the city of Uruk. They used a form of writing known as cuneiform in which, at first, picture symbols were used to represent words. This early Sumerian cuneiform script was made up of more than 700 different picture symbols, and was used to record economic transactions. Scribes quickly saw how to use the word signs for their sound values in order to write words which were hard to draw (as in 'thin' + 'king' = 'thinking'), making the system flexible so that other languages, such as Babylonian and Hittite, could adopt it. The script could then be used to record literature and religious ideas, as well as legal deeds.

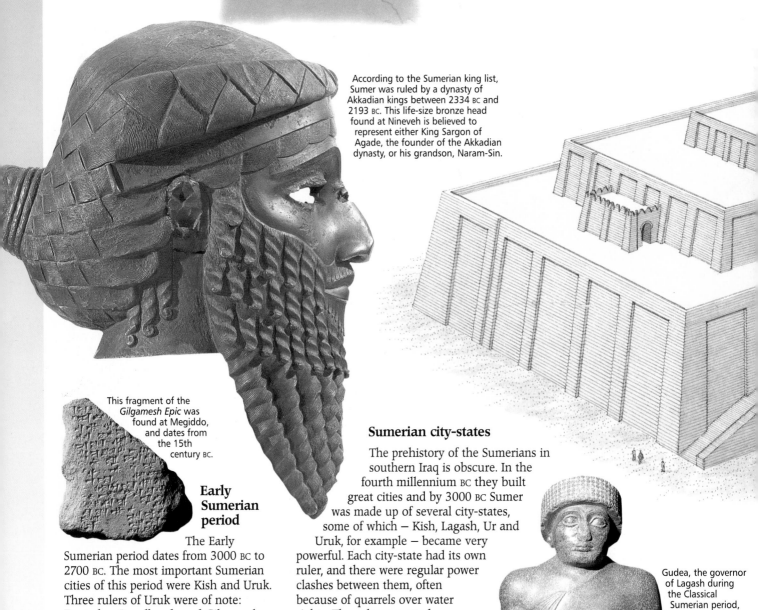

According to the Sumerian king list, Sumer was ruled by a dynasty of Akkadian kings between 2334 BC and 2193 BC. This life-size bronze head found at Nineveh is believed to represent either King Sargon of Agade, the founder of the Akkadian dynasty, or his grandson, Naram-Sin.

This fragment of the *Gilgamesh Epic* was found at Megiddo, and dates from the 15th century BC.

Early Sumerian period

The Early Sumerian period dates from 3000 BC to 2700 BC. The most important Sumerian cities of this period were Kish and Uruk. Three rulers of Uruk were of note: Enmerkar, Lugalbanda and Gilgamesh. Gilgamesh was the most famous hero of all Sumerian history. Poems telling of his exploits were later combined in the Babylonian *Gilgamesh Epic*.

Sumerian city-states

The prehistory of the Sumerians in southern Iraq is obscure. In the fourth millennium BC they built great cities and by 3000 BC Sumer was made up of several city-states, some of which – Kish, Lagash, Ur and Uruk, for example – became very powerful. Each city-state had its own ruler, and there were regular power clashes between them, often because of quarrels over water rights. They also mounted expeditions into Iran to obtain minerals, and traded widely, exporting surplus grain, dates and woollen cloth.

Gudea, the governor of Lagash during the Classical Sumerian period, is portrayed in this statue from a Sumerian temple. The statue dates from about 2130 BC.

Sumerian gods

Sumerian scribes recorded the names of hundreds of gods and goddesses. Each city had a guardian god. Sud was the god of Shuruppak, for example, and Nanna was the city god of Ur. The main city temple was dedicated to the city god. Nationally important gods included An, the god of the sky and the heavens, and Inanna, the goddess of love and of war. Sumerian mythology indicates that Sumerian gods took human form and behaved very much like people – often interfering in human affairs.

See also

■ The world of the patriarchs (pages 18–19)

■ The Babylonians (pages 62–63)

■ Ancient beliefs (pages 146–147)

The ziggurat at Ur, constructed by King Ur-Nammu, is one of the earliest examples of a design which became standard throughout Mesopotamia. It is likely that the Tower of Babel recorded in the Bible followed a similar form of construction.

Treasures discovered in the royal graves at Ur date from perhaps 500 years before the time of Abraham. They include this statue of a goat (above), made from gold, silver, lapis lazuli and shell, and a gold dagger (right).

Neo-Sumerian period

The capital of the Neo-Sumerian period (2100–2000 BC) was the city of Ur. The oldest known code of law was issued here, requiring payments in money rather than physical retribution for crimes. The first of Ur's kings during this period, Ur-namma, built a magnificent ziggurat in the city, the remains of which can still be seen today. Over time, the Sumerians began to intermarry with the many immigrants, especially Amorites, into their nation. After that, Sumerian identity disappeared and the spoken language gradually died out. Nonetheless, Sumerian remained the language of religion, science, business and law for many centuries.

Classic Sumerian period

The second period in Sumer's history dates from 2700–2250 BC. During this time, the most powerful Sumerian cities were Ur, Kish, Umma and Lagash. The tensions between Umma and Lagash are recorded in a series of historical documents inscribed in about 2400 BC, which also include economic and social data of the time. Later documents, from the time of the governor Gudea of Lagash, also detail economic data, as well as describing religious life.

Sumerian art and architecture

Sumerian art and architecture had a major influence on the culture of the ancient Near East. Sculpture – clay, wood and metal – was highly advanced. Examples of fine Sumerian art include an alabaster vase from Erech dating from about 3500 BC and an intricate wooden harp from Ur (about 2650 BC). The Sumerians constructed massive ziggurat temples which could extend over 46,500 square metres (more than half a million square feet).

The Egyptians

The Egyptian civilization is one of the world's oldest. It developed in the narrow valley of the River Nile more than 5,000 years ago, and was pivotal for thousands of years, enjoying three periods of greatness during this time.

Egyptian writing systems

The idea of writing was carried to Egypt soon after it was invented. Egyptian clerks made up their own writing system of picture word-signs, which we call hieroglyphs, and this system was used for inscriptions on buildings and other monuments until the fifth century AD. For ordinary records, letters, accounts and books, however, a simpler handwriting script – hieratic – was developed. A form of shorthand, now called demotic, grew out of that after 1000 BC.

Ancient Egypt

Initially there were two kingdoms in Egypt: the Nile Valley (Upper Egypt) and the Nile Delta (Lower Egypt). But before 3000 BC the king of the Nile Valley, Menes, defeated the king of the Nile Delta and became the first king of all Egypt. Menes was first in a line of kings, or pharaohs, who ruled Egypt for the next 3,000 years.

This hieroglyph represents the name of the pharaoh Menes. The bird symbolizes the god Horus, of which Menes was believed to be a manifestation.

The Middle Kingdom

The second great age in Egypt was the 'Middle Kingdom'. Its new pharaohs took over Nubia in the south of Egypt to obtain gold and other African products. By improving the use of the Nile waters for farming, these kings also increased the crops grown and, consequently, the wealth of the people. The Old Testament story of Abraham visiting Egypt at a time of famine in Canaan is set in this period.

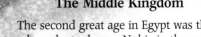

THE MIDDLE KINGDOM
Second intermediate
THE NEW
1550 BC
1640 BC
First intermediate
THE OLD KINGDOM
2040 BC
2134 BC
2575 BC
Early dynastic
Pre-dynastic
2920 BC
3050 BC. Founding of Egyptian state

The Old Kingdom

The first great age in Egypt was the 'Old Kingdom', also known as the 'Pyramid Age' because of the huge, pointed stone tombs built by the pharaohs during this period. The Pyramid Age came to an end under the rule of less able kings. Egypt became poor and, once more, rival kings came to power in the south and north of the land, until a prince from Thebes again reunited Egypt.

The highly decorated columns and walls of the mortuary temple of Pharaoh Ramesses III at Thebes. Amongst other events, the reliefs record the pharaoh's campaigns against Libyans, Asiatics and Philistines, and show the king presenting captives to the god Amun.

Foreign kings

When the Middle Kingdom came to an end under the rule of weaker pharaohs, Egypt came under the control of kings, known as the Hyksos, who rose from amongst the foreigners living in the eastern part of the Nile Delta. But it was not long before Egyptian princes from Thebes again came north to expel the Hyksos rulers and reunite Egypt once more.

Part of the victory document of Pharoah Shoshenq I in the temple of Amun at Karnak. The relief lists 138 towns in Palestine which were conquered in his campaign to restore Egyptian supremacy in the region.

See also

■ The exodus from Egypt (pages 20–21)

■ Genesis (pages 198–199)

Egypt under threat

The New Kingdom was threatened when the Hittites in the far north conquered part of Egypt's empire in Syria. A new line of pharaohs tried to win back the lost provinces, especially Sethos I and Ramesses II in the 13th century BC. These pharaohs built a new royal city, Pi-Ramesse, in the eastern Nile Delta. This was the climax of the 'oppression' of the Israelites who, as recorded in the Old Testament, were used as slave-labour by the pharaohs.

The New Kingdom

The last great age of the Egyptians was the 'New Kingdom', also known as the 'empire'. The pharaohs of the New Kingdom fought and won control of the lands of Canaan and Syria. In Egypt, they built many huge temples, the most important at the capital city, Memphis, and their sacred city, Thebes.

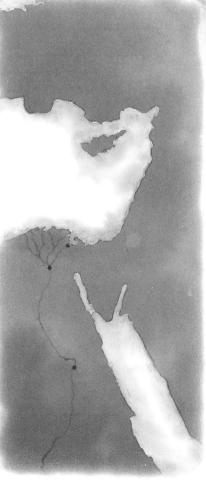

The Late Period and Greek rule

The so-called 'Late Period' saw a decline in Egypt's power and influence. It never regained the glory of earlier times, and by 525 BC, Egypt was part of the Persian empire along with surrounding nations it had formerly ruled. Sometimes rebelling and regaining its freedom, Egypt was finally conquered by Alexander the Great (332–323 BC) and remained under Greek rule until the time of the Roman empire.

GDOM

Third intermediate

1070BC

712BC

THE LATE PERIOD

332BC

GRECO-ROMAN PERIOD

AD395

Egyptian religion and beliefs

The pharaoh was the supreme ruler of ancient Egypt, and was the go-between for the Egyptian gods and people. Through his priests, the pharaoh made offerings to the gods on behalf of the people in order that, in return, the gods might shower their gifts on Egypt. He also appeared as the representative of the gods to the people, and directed the building and upkeep of the temples, which were always built in his name.

The religion of the people

Ordinary Egyptians could not enter the temples. They only saw the great gods on festival days, when their veiled images were carried in procession in small sacred boats by the priests. Instead, ordinary people worshipped at small, local shrines, or the chapels at the gateways of the great temples. Their worship was mostly the presentation of offerings, following certain set rituals. When troubles such as illness struck them, the Egyptians sometimes thought this was punishment from the gods for wrong-doing. They then confessed their sins, and prayed for healing and help.

A group of mourners depicted on a wall of the funerary temple of Amenophis II at Thebes.

The gods of Egypt

The Egyptians had many gods. Some came from nature: Re', the sun god; Thoth and Khons, the moon gods; Nut, the sky goddess; Geb, the earth god; Hapi, the god of the Nile flood; and Amun, the god of hidden life-powers in nature. Some gods stood for ideas: Maat was goddess of truth, justice and right order; Thoth was also the god of learning and wisdom; and Ptah was the god of craftsmanship.

The process of mummification involved removing the brain and other large organs from the dead body, packing the body in salt to dry it out, and then filling the cavities with linen soaked with fragrant resins. The surface of the body was then treated with resin, bandaged and placed in an elaborately decorated wooden coffin.

Part of the papyrus of Hunefer known as the *Book of the Dead*. On the left, Anubis weighs the deceased's heart, while Thoth records the result. Horus then presents Hunefer before the enthroned Osiris.

Life after death

The early Egyptians buried their dead along the edges of the dry deserts that bordered the Nile Valley. The dry sand and hot sun often dried, and so preserved, the bodies of those early people in their shallow graves. The Egyptians later came to believe that the body was a home for the soul, and that the soul needed its personal belongings in a life after death. So, when tombs became too big and deep for the sun's heat to dry the body, the Egyptians did this artificially through a process called 'mummification'. The Old Testament book of Genesis records that Joseph was embalmed in this way, and placed in a coffin in Egypt.

Anubis, the god of embalming, was represented by a jackal resting on a funerary chest.

This image of the pharaoh Tutankhamun and his queen was found on the back of Tutankhamun's throne. The throne is made of wood overlaid with gold and silver, and decorated with blue faience, calcite and glass.

See also

■ Ancient beliefs (pages 146–147)

■ The creator-God of Israel (pages 148–149)

■ Death and the afterlife (pages 164–165)

Magic

Magic was used by the Egyptians to grasp at supernatural power. Good, or 'white', magic was designed to ward off life's troubles. Harmful, or 'black', magic was a crime, and was punished as such. People often wore lucky charms, or amulets. The scarab-beetle, the symbol for renewal, was popular.

This Egyptian scarab seal dates from about 1200–1000 BC.

Live images

Certain animals which were considered sacred could act as 'live images' for the Egyptian gods. For example, the Apis-bull was sacred to Ptah, the ibis-birds to Thoth, falcons were sacred to Horus and cats to the goddess Bastet. A god was sometimes shown wearing the head of its sacred animal, to make it easier to recognize.

On this wall painting from a burial chamber at Thebes, a dead person is depicted kneeling before the god Osiris as he enters the after-life.

The realm of Osiris

Most Egyptians turned to the god Osiris for hope of a life after death. The Egyptians had papyrus-roll books of magical spells to help them pass the judgment of the dead. The most famous collection of spells is the *Book of the Dead*. It was believed that the souls of dead kings spent their after-life with the sun-god, crossing the sky in his heavenly boat by day. Then, at night, they passed through the realm of Osiris, providing for their dead subjects.

Worship in the temples

The Egyptians believed that the great state temples were home to the gods. Only the pharaoh, priests and higher officials could go into the sacred inner room of the temple. The temple priests were the god's servants. Each morning, noon and evening, they carried out regular rituals to honour the god, and gave offerings of food and drink.

The Canaanites

Canaan's great legacy to the world is almost certainly the alphabet, invented here between 2000 and 1600 BC. However, because the common writing material papyrus (which was made from reeds) has not survived the centuries, examples of this infant alphabet are very rare. They are limited to those found on more durable items – names scratched on cups, for instance.

This statuette of the god Baal, which comes from Ras Shamra, dates from the 13th century BC.

The goddess Hathor is portrayed on this gold pendant discovered at Tell el-Ajjul. It dates from the second millennium BC.

The peoples of Canaan

About 1300 BC, 'Canaan' was an Egyptian province covering Lebanon, southern Syria and what later became the land of Palestine. The name may have belonged at first to the coastal plain, then have been extended to include the people of the forested hills – the Amorites. Besides the Canaanites and Amorites, there were other groups living in the land, and the term 'Canaanites' came to include a mixture of peoples.

Metal ores

Cedar wood, oil, wine

Luxury goods

Ras Shamra/ Ugarit

Byblos
Beirut
Sidon
Tyre

CANAAN

EGYPT

Canaanite gods

Canaanite gods and goddesses were the powers of nature personified. Baal, which means 'lord', was the title of Hadad, the weather god. He controlled the rains, mist and dew, and so held the key to the good harvests which were essential if the Canaanites were to survive.

Baal's female companion was Astarte, also known as Anat, goddess of love and war. His father was El, the chief of the gods, but at the time of the Israelite settlement in Canaan he had become a shadowy figure. El's wife was Asherah, mother goddess and goddess of the sea. Both Asherah and Astarte were often simply called 'Mistress' (Baalat).

Other leading deities were Shamash, the sun; Reshef, lord of war and of the underworld; Dagon, the corn god; and many lesser ones who made up the families and courts of each senior god. This general picture varied from place to place, as each town had its own patron or favourite deity, often called 'Lord' or 'Mistress' of a given place.

Canaanite trade

Trade was so much a part of Canaanite life that the word 'Canaanite' came to mean 'merchant' in the Hebrew language. The major ports were Tyre, Sidon, Beirut and Byblos. From them, cedar wood, jars of oil and wine and other goods were exported to Egypt, Crete and Greece. In return came Egyptian luxuries and writing paper, Greek pottery, and metal ores.

Temples and priests

The important Canaanite gods had richly endowed temples in the leading cities, with priests, choirs and temple servants. On holy days the kings would go in procession to offer animal or plant sacrifices. Some of these were burnt entirely; some were shared between the god and the worshippers. On occasions of great celebration, the ordinary people probably joined the processions and watched the ceremonies from a distance. But the temple buildings were not large, and only the privileged could go into them.

It was a matter of pride for a Canaanite king to make the temple as grand as he could, covering the statues of the gods and the walls of the shrine with precious metal, and supplying golden

A Canaanite incense burner decorated with snakes. It dates from 1000–900 BC, and was found at Beth-shan.

dishes for the god's food. As well as a statue of the god, or of an animal that was its emblem (Baal was represented by a bull, Asherah by a lion), there was also an altar for the sacrifices, an altar for incense and perhaps a number of stone pillars inside the temple which were thought to be the homes of gods or spirits.

See also

■ The Israelites enter Canaan
(pages 22–23)

■ Ancient beliefs
(pages 146–147)

■ Joshua, Judges
(pages 206–207)

The Canaanite high place at Megiddo.

Sacrifices

The sacrifices offered to the Canaanite gods were normally animals and foodstuffs. When a sacrifice was offered, the priest often examined the entrails of the animal to forecast the fortune of the worshipper. Human sacrifice was also practised, but was probably a rite used in extreme circumstances, when only the greatest sacrifice was thought adequate to persuade the god to act favourably. The god Molech, who is named in connection with this sacrifice, seems to have been a god of the underworld.

A 'horned' altar found at Megiddo. Similar altars have been found at many sites in Israel.

Canaanite cities and rulers

Canaanite cities were surrounded by defensive walls of earth and stone to keep out raiders and wild animals. Inside the walls, the houses were crowded together. The ordinary people worked on the land or at various crafts, or were employed by the king, landowners and merchants. The rulers of the cities were constantly quarrelling and fighting with each other, as recorded in the Amarna Letters found in Egypt and the Old Testament books of Joshua and Judges.

One of the Amarna letters, a series of 380 clay tablets found at Amarna in Egypt. The letters are written in the Akkadian language.

The alphabet

The alphabet appears to have been invented in Canaan when a scribe realized that it was possible to write a language without the many signs used in cuneiform and hieroglyphic scripts. The scribe studied the Canaanite language, and drew one sign for each consonant. There were no separate signs for vowels, a fact which creates problems in reading Hebrew and Arabic even now.

Examples of the early alphabet have been found in Canaan. These are very

short, probably people's names, and are written on pottery, stone and metal. Canaanites working in Egyptian mines in south-western Sinai scratched prayers on rocks and stones, using the alphabet. Their work preserves some of the best surviving examples of the alphabet at an early stage of its development (about 1500 BC).

This gold necklace with carnelian beads dates from about the 14th century BC. It was discovered amongst a hoard of jewellery at Deir-el Balach, near Gaza.

The Philistines

The Philistines settled the south-west area of Canaan in the 12th century BC. They extended their rule northwards along the coast, and inland, whenever they could. Although they were never in control of much of the land for long, it was the Philistines who eventually gave their name to the whole of the region, which came to be known as Palestine.

Invasion of Canaan

After the Philistines were defeated by the Egyptians, they established five main city-states in Canaan – Ashdod, Ashkelon, Ekron, Gath and Gaza – each ruled by a 'seren'. They controlled the coast road from Egypt. It may have been to avoid the Philistines that the Israelites, as recorded in the Old Testament book of Exodus, did not enter Canaan 'by the road that goes up the coast to Philistia, although it was the shortest way'.

Origins of the Philistines

Evidence from archaeological discoveries, and Egyptian and Old Testament writings, suggests that the Philistines were intruders into the Near East from Crete and the Aegean. Philistine pottery dating from 1200–1100 BC found in Palestine, for example, belongs to a type known to have been made in Greece, Crete and Cyprus. And the Old Testament books of Amos and Jeremiah state that the Philistines came from Caphtor, a place commonly linked with Crete.

Geometric designs in red and black, as seen on this Philistine beer jug, were popular in the 12th century BC.

The 'peoples of the sea'

Egyptian pharaohs from the 13th and 12th centuries BC recorded how they beat off invasions by the so-called 'peoples of the sea'. One of these peoples was the Philistines. The Philistine warriors reached Egypt by ship and fought the Egyptians on water. However, according to an Egyptian text, their families and household goods travelled down the coast of Syria and Canaan. Ancient Egyptian reliefs depict Philistine soldiers with spears, long swords, round shields, triangular daggers and what look like head-dresses with vertical feathers.

The Philistine 'peoples of the sea' are thought to have travelled from the Aegean, settling on the coast of Canaan possibly at the same time that the Israelites were arriving there from Egypt.

The demise of the Philistines

The Philistines continued to live in the south of Canaan until at least the late eighth century BC, when they were defeated by Sargon, the king of Assyria. However, it was the Babylonians who finally brought the Philistines to an end in the early sixth century BC.

Philistine language and culture

Very little is known about Philistine language and culture. The Philistines left no recognizable writings, and excavation of their cities has revealed too little information to build up a picture of their culture. It is apparent that, while bringing some traditions of their own, the Philistines largely adopted the Canaanite culture and language around them.

Enmity with Israel

The Philistines were a constant threat to the Israelites in Canaan. Both peoples wanted control of the same land. The Old Testament books of Judges and 1 Samuel record the conflict between the two peoples. It was probably because of this constant pressure from the Philistines that the Israelites petitioned the last judge, Samuel, for a king. By this time, the Philistines had clearly gained the upper hand over at least some of the Israelite tribes. The Old Testament records that the Philistines prevented the Israelites from owning iron weapons; they also charged exorbitant prices for sharpening even agricultural tools.

A Philistine soldier wearing the typical feathered head-dress.

See also

- The time of the judges (pages 24–25)
- The first kings (pages 26–27)
- Ancient beliefs (pages 146–147)
- Judges (pages 206–207)

The first Israelite king, Saul, never succeeded in defeating the Philistines. King David, however, managed to end the Philistine attacks, but only after fierce struggles. The Old Testament book of 2 Samuel states that David drove the Philistines 'back from Geba all the way to Gezer'. Nonetheless, the Philistines remained independent and continued to cause occasional disturbances in later times.

Philistine religion

The main Philistine gods were Dagon, Ashtoreth and Baalzebub. These gods are all of Near Eastern origin, suggesting that the Philistines adapted their own religion to that of the Canaanites. The Philistines built temples at Gaza, Ashdod and Ekron, and offered sacrifices to the gods.

A relief from the temple of Ramesses III at Medinet Habu portrays Philistine soldiers being led into captivity by their Egyptian conquerors.

This anthropoid Philistine sarcophagus found at Beth-shan dates from 1200–1100 BC.

The Assyrians

The story of the Assyrians is one of constant warfare. Assyria was a prosperous nation. A favourable climate and ample water supplies from the River Tigris resulted in an abundance of crops: barley and wheat on the plains; grapes, olives, apricots, cherries and other fruit on the hills. Neighbouring peoples, who lived in harsh desert and mountain terrains, were attracted to this abundance, and posed a constant threat to the Assyrians.

Ashur

Ancient records show that the Assyrians, a Semitic people, were settled in their land in about 2300 BC. They called their country, their capital city and their national god by one name: Ashur. The city of Ashur was in the south of the country, on the west bank of the River Tigris. The second city, Nineveh, lay east of the river, opposite modern Mosul, 109 km/68 miles north of Ashur.

The city of Calah in Assyria, as portrayed by a 19th-century artist.

The Assyrian empire

Between 1500 and 1100 BC, Assyria became a leading state in the Near East, ruling as far west as the River Euphrates. The kings of Assyria wrote letters, as equals, to the kings of Egypt. Then Aramaean invaders from the desert completely overran the Assyrian homeland. This began a period of weakness that lasted until about 900 BC.

Over time, a line of vigorous Assyrian kings began to regain their lost lands. The warrior kings Ashurnasirpal II (883–859 BC) and Shalmaneser III (858–824 BC) captured many cities and made their kings vassals. But often, as soon as the Assyrian army had gone home, the subject kings rebelled. Tiglath-pileser III (745–727 BC) was the first Assyrian king to establish an effective system of provincial governors with firm control over their regions.

Eventually, under kings Esarhaddon (681–669 BC) and Ashurbanipal (669–627 BC), the Assyrian empire grew too large, covering Egypt, Syria, Israel, north Arabia, and parts of Turkey and Persia. It was impossible to defend all the frontiers and defeat all the rebels. In 625 BC, Babylon won independence and, with help from the Medes, destroyed Nineveh – and the Assyrian empire – in 612 BC.

Works of art

Assyria's great empire generated enormous wealth through taxes and trade. The Assyrian kings were able to build great palaces and temples, each aiming to do better than ever before. Walls were lined with stone slabs carved in low relief to depict the king in religious, military and sporting life. Furniture was decorated with ivory panels, carved or engraved, often plated with gold. The king lay on a couch and drank from golden goblets shaped like animals' heads. His queen sat beside him. In the palace stores there were vast collections of iron weapons for the army.

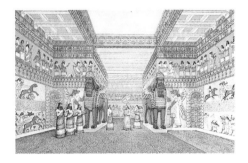

A reconstruction of the throne room of King Ashurnasirpal II at Calah (below) by A.H. Layard, who began excavating the site in 1845. The carved reliefs, which are now just plain stone, were originally painted in bright colours as the drawing suggests.

In 701 BC King Sennacherib of Assyria invaded Judah in response to a rebellion by King Hezekiah. Assyrian forces swept through the land, taking all the major fortified cities in Judah, with the exception of Jerusalem. The siege of the city of Lachish is well documented. In this relief from Sennacherib's palace at Nineveh (above), the king is pictured receiving his generals after the surrender of Lachish.

Cruel imperialists?

The Assyrians are commonly thought of as cruel imperialists. This picture comes partly from their wars with Israel, which are reported in the Old Testament. However, this needs to be balanced against the situation for Assyria. Even when the Assyrian frontiers seemed secure, threats existed — or could be imagined — from foreign rulers a little further away. These threats could only be dealt with by new campaigns. No doubt, success encouraged further military adventures. But the Assyrians, like most people, prized peace and prosperity.

See also

■ The rise of Assyria (pages 30–31)

■ 1 and 2 Kings (pages 210–211)

■ Isaiah (pages 226–227)

This relief (above) from the north-west palace at Calah depicts King Ashurnasirpal II hunting lions.

King Ashurbanipal feasting with his queen Ashur-sharrat (left). Hanging from a pine tree is the severed head of the Elamite King Teumman, who was defeated by the Assyrians in 653 BC. The relief was originally on a wall of the north palace at Nineveh.

Babylonian influence

The basic culture of Assyria was drawn very much from that of Babylonia. Not only did the Assyrians use a language which was very closely related to Babylonian, but they also adopted the Babylonian cuneiform writing system. Thousands of clay tablets have been found in the Assyrian ruins. Some deal with the administration of the empire. Some are diplomatic documents. Some are private legal deeds. Some are the records of the deeds of kings. Most outstanding of all is the library collected by King Ashurbanipal. This library held copies of every piece of literature and knowledge that had been handed down from the past.

The Babylonians

Babylonian contributions to the world at large stem from about 3000–1600 BC, when the Babylonian writing system spread throughout the Near East. It brought with it the knowledge of astronomy and mathematics, which the Greeks borrowed. Other influences are harder to trace, but were undoubtedly strong.

Babylonian peoples

Ancient Babylonian documents have identified the Sumerians as early inhabitants of Babylonia. Alongside the Sumerians in the north lived the Akkadian tribes. Their Semitic language was an early form of Babylonian, related to Arabic and Hebrew. The scholars of ancient Babylonia made translations from Sumerian into Akkadian, and these have enabled modern students to translate the Sumerian language.

In about 2300 BC, the Semites under King Sargon gained control of Babylonia. His capital was at Akkad, and his rule extended into north Syria. From this time on, the Sumerian language was less important than Akkadian. Sargon's family maintained his empire for about a century, until attackers from the east broke their power. From about 2100–2000 BC a line of kings based at Ur had a kingdom which was almost as large.

The Babylonian kings of the 15th to the 12th centuries BC recorded royal land transfers on *kudurrus*. These were stone tablets carved with symbols of the gods who had witnessed the transaction. This one dates from about 1000 BC.

The Babylonian empire

It was the Babylonian Nabopolassar who freed Babylon from the grip of the Assyrians before being made king in 626 BC. Nabopolassar went on to win further decisive battles against the Assyrians, before capturing Nineveh in 612 BC. The Babylonian empire now contained most of the Assyrian provinces, although Nabopolassar's son, Nebuchadnezzar (605–562 BC), had to crush some rebels in the west, including Judah. The wealth of the new empire enabled these two kings to rebuild Babylon on an immense scale, with lavish decoration.

Nebuchadnezzar's son was killed by the Babylonian general Neriglissar, but Nabonidus in turn displaced Neriglissar's son. This king held strong religious convictions. He left Babylon in the care of his son, Belshazzar, and lived for 10 years in Arabia. After his return, the army of Cyrus the Persian took Babylon. The centre of world history moved away from the city of Babylon for the last time.

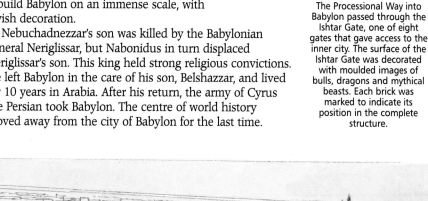

King Hammurabi
The most outstanding of the Babylonian kings was Hammurabi, who ruled in about 1792–1750 BC. Hammurabi gained power by war and by diplomacy. During his reign he revised the laws of the land and had them engraved on stone. However, despite royal authority, these laws soon fell into disuse, although they were copied in schools for another 1,000 years.

See also

■ The rise of Assyria (pages 30–31)

■ The Babylonian invasion (pages 32–33)

□ Education (pages 100–101)

■ 1 and 2 Kings (pages 210–211)

The Processional Way into Babylon passed through the Ishtar Gate, one of eight gates that gave access to the inner city. The surface of the Ishtar Gate was decorated with moulded images of bulls, dragons and mythical beasts. Each brick was marked to indicate its position in the complete structure.

Art and crafts

Craftspeople in the third millennium BC made fine jewellery in gold, silver and semi-precious stones imported from the east and south. Smiths cast copper and bronze for weapons and statues. Stone carvers produced some of the finest pieces of Babylonian art – from great monuments to tiny cylinder seals which were rolled across clay to leave impressions of the pictures engraved on them.

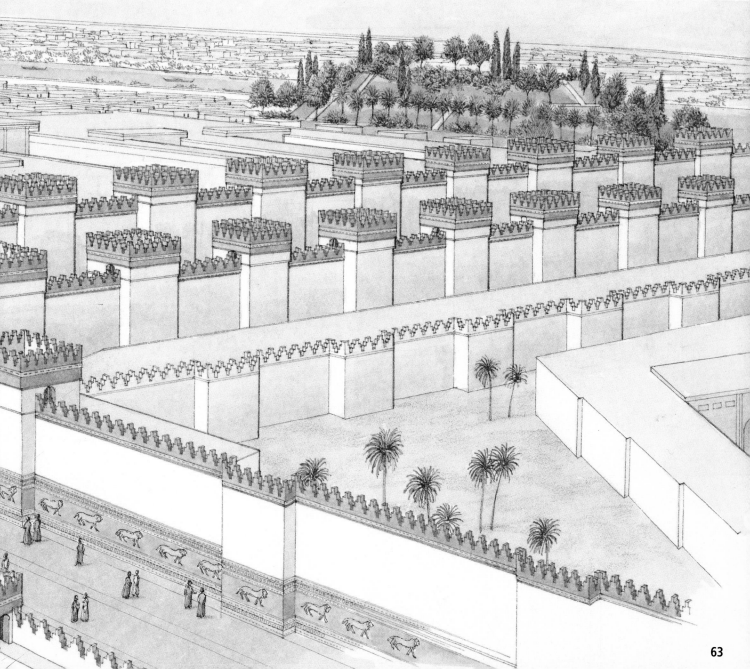

Babylonian religion and beliefs

Like most peoples in the ancient world, the Babylonians honoured the great powers of the universe, and had favourite gods or goddesses of their own. They told stories about their gods, gave offerings to them in great temples and small shrines, asked for their help and hoped for their good will. The gods were in control of everything, though their behaviour was generally unpredictable.

The Babylonian Chronicle names Nabonidus as the last king of Babylon. Here he is portrayed with carvings of the moon, the sun and the planet Venus, representing the deities Sin, Shamash and Ishtar.

Worship

Each city had a main temple where the patron god of the city was worshipped. Here the people would gather for major festivals at the New Year and on the god's own special day. Ordinary citizens normally worshipped at small shrines set amongst the houses of a town. There they could ask the gods or goddesses for a son, pray for success in business, give them 'thank-you presents', or make offerings to win attention or persuade the deities to rid them of some misfortune. A priest would perform rites, speak the correct prayers, and accept the animal or goods offered in sacrifice.

This stone, which may have been used to mark a boundary, is inscribed with the symbols of some of the Babylonian gods. The star-shaped symbol at the top identifies Ishtar, the goddess of love and fertility. The moon represents the moon-god Sin, and the star within the circle stands for the sun-god Shamash. The scorpion is the symbol of the goddess Ishara.

Babylonian gods

Anu, king of heaven, was the chief of the Babylonian gods. His son, Enlil, ruled over the earth's surface, and was treated as the king of the gods. Enki, or Ea, had charge of the fresh waters that gave life. Each had a wife and family. Ishtar was the wife of Anu; she was in charge of war and of love. Enki was given a son – Marduk – who became the patron god of Babylon. His worship began to grow as Babylon's power increased during the period 2000–1000 BC. As time passed, he was elevated to be king of all the gods.

The Ishtar Gate in Babylon (below) was decorated with moulded and glazed bricks portraying images of animals, either real or mythical, which represented different gods. The bull was associated with the weather god Adad.

Myths

Stories about the gods occur in the Sumerian and Akkadian languages. One of these is the well-known Babylonian creation story, *Enuma elish*, which was composed not long before 1000 BC, although it was based on much older stories. It was recited during the New Year feast in Babylon, and on other occasions, to celebrate the elevation of Marduk, because he conquered the ocean of chaos and created the world.

This clay tablet (left) is inscribed with a map of the world, a copy from an original drawn in about 700 BC. The circle represents the ocean, outside of which are various lands which are described in the text. In the centre is the known world, and Babylon, Assyria, Urartu and Susa are all marked. The two vertical lines in the centre are thought to indicate the River Euphrates as it flows through Babylon.

See also

■ The Babylonian invasion
(pages 32–33)

■ Ancient beliefs
(pages 146–147)

■ Death and the afterlife
(pages 164–165)

■ 1 and 2 Kings
(pages 210–211)

Death and the afterlife

The Babylonians believed that all the dead inhabited the underworld. There they lived in a land of dust, fed by offerings of food and drink made by their descendants. If no offerings were made, the ghosts of the dead would come back to haunt their families. So, too, would the ghosts of those who were not properly buried. Ideas about death were very vague and, unlike the ancient Egyptians, Babylonians had little expectation of a future life.

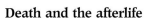

A clay model of a sheep's liver (below right), used for divination. It is marked off into 50 sections, each inscribed with omens and magical formulae.

Divination

The gods controlled everything, according to Babylonian thought, but they did not reveal the future. So the Babylonians consulted omens. The livers and other parts of sacrificed animals were inspected for unusual symptoms, to see if the gods had 'written a message' in them. They also used other unpredictable things, such as the flight of birds or patterns of oil on water.

Astrologers worked out 'omens' from the movements of the stars. The clear night skies made observation easy. And because each star was linked to a god or goddess, it was possible to make all sorts of deductions about the will of the gods. Some of these arts passed to the Greeks, and so to modern astrology. The zodiac is one legacy of the Babylonian astrologers. The 360° circle and the 60-minute hour were also first worked out by Babylonian star-gazers.

This bronze figure (right) is Pazuzu, a demon associated with the Assyrian and Babylonian cultures. The figure bears the inscription: 'I am Pazuzu, son of Hanbi, king of the evil wind-demons.' Amulets engraved with images of Pazuzu were sometimes worn to protect the wearer against attacks from other demons.

Demons

The Babylonians believed that evil spirits and demons lurked ready to catch anyone they could. They would slide under the door to attack people as they slept or to snatch children from their parents' safekeeping, or they would bring diseases with the wind. Special priests recited prayers and spells over the sick or injured person, calling on the gods for help. Sometimes the affliction would be transferred, by a ritual, to a goat or some other substitute, which would then be killed or destroyed. People wore charms and amulets to ward off these evils. They also hung them in doorways and buried them under their doorsteps.

The Persians

The Persians first appear as a nation about 650 BC, under King Cyrus I. Although no one knows where they came from, their language shows they were one of the Indo-European peoples. It is related to Greek, Latin, French, German and English, but even more closely to Sanskrit and other Indian languages.

Cyrus the Great

It was Cyrus' grandson, King Cyrus II (the Great), who changed the course of Persian history. In 550 BC, he took control of Ecbatana, the capital of the Medes. He conquered what is now Turkey, and moved east into north-west India. By 540 BC he was ready to challenge the power of the Babylonian empire.

The 'Cyrus cylinder', buried in the foundations of a building in Babylon, contains the king's own account of how he captured the city of Babylon. It fell without a battle in 539 BC. The course of the River Euphrates had been diverted, allowing the invaders to make their way into the city along the dried-up river-bed.

The baked clay cylinder (left) records an account by the Persian king Cyrus of his conquest of Babylon, and his release of statues of gods held by the Babylonians.

The hollow spaces in this Persian gold armlet would originally have been inlaid with pieces of coloured glass or semi-precious stones. This example was discovered near the River Oxus in modern Kazakhstan.

The Persian empire

The Persian kings extended their borders even further than the earlier empires. The Persian empire stretched east to India, and Turkey and Egypt were also under their control. King Darius I (522–486 BC), who built a magnificent palace at Persepolis, took Macedonia in northern Greece in 513 BC. After a setback at Marathon, his son, Xerxes I (486–464 BC), pushed south as far as Athens before losing the sea battle of Salamis (480 BC).

Despite attacks from Greeks and revolts in Egypt, the Persians held their empire for 200 years. Then, in 333 BC, the Greek conqueror Alexander crossed the Hellespont and brought the Persian empire to a rapid end.

Persian government

Wise government and administration, and a policy of peaceful relations throughout the empire, made it possible for Persia to control distant nations. Cyrus the Great divided the empire into provinces, each with its own ruler or 'satrap'. These were Persian or Median nobles, but there were nationals under them who retained power locally. The different peoples were encouraged to keep their own customs and religions. King Darius I made further improvements to the system of government. He also introduced coinage, and a legal system. His new postal system was a vital aid to communication. A further unifying factor was the use of Aramaic as the administrative language of the empire.

A reconstruction of part of the palace at Persepolis built by Darius I and his son Xerxes.

Persian religion

Ancient Persian beliefs were based upon the life of the herdsman: the gods were partly nature-gods, partly ideas such as 'contract' (Mitra) and 'true speech' (Varuna). There was animal sacrifice, and the drinking of *haoma* or *soma*, which produced a state of intoxication. At an unknown date, the prophet Zoroaster arose in eastern Persia, preaching the worship of Ahura-mazda as the supreme deity worshipped through fire – yet a god to whom people can talk – and the battle between Good and Evil, in which humanity has a part. Zoroaster's ideas influenced the Persian kings, and spread widely, even affecting Jewish thought.

See also

■ From exile to return (pages 34–35)

■ Ancient beliefs (pages 146–147)

■ Esther (pages 214–215)

This winged figure probably represents the supreme god Ahura-mazda. The colours used here are based on an example at the Hall of 100 Columns in Persepolis, on which traces of paint are still visible.

Persian art and crafts

The Persian empire created great wealth, and crafts of all descriptions flourished. They were brought from every part of the empire to decorate the new palaces at Persepolis, Pasargadae and Susa, whose ruins still show their former magnificence. Quantities of gold plate and jewellery reveal the highly developed skills in the making of luxury goods. The Old Testament book of Esther is set in the splendour of palace life in Persia.

Persian and Median officials are depicted in conversation in this detail from the relief on the eastern staircase of the Apadana at Persepolis.

This glazed brick relief of a Persian archer comes from the palace of King Darius at Susa.

The king shown hunting a lion on this cylinder seal is probably King Darius.

The Greeks

Until relatively recent times, the beginnings of Greece were a puzzle. Two works written in about 800 BC by the Greek poet, Homer – *The Iliad* and *The Odyssey* – gave a picture of an early Greek civilization. It is now known that Homer's poems were based on fact, and that Greeks were settled in Mycenae on the mainland of southern Greece as long ago as the second millennium BC.

Early history

Greek-speaking people had entered Greece from the north. They lived in small towns separated by the mountains. After the great days of Mycenae, the land was never united. Town fought against town. It was often easier to travel by sea than by land.

Greece was a poor and rocky land, with too little fertile land to support the people. And so the Greeks became adventurous sailors. The regular summer winds and the shelter of the many islands helped them to voyage across the Aegean Sea to Asia. They imported food, and founded new cities on many parts of the Mediterranean coast, especially in Asia Minor.

Greek gods

The Greeks were very religious, and their supreme god was Zeus. He ruled over the other gods who lived on Olympus, the highest mountain in Greece. The Greeks were a logical people, and they attempted to build complete family histories of the gods. The gods were pictured vividly. They behaved like human beings – often jealous, vengeful or immoral – but, of course, they were far more powerful.

Among the other Greek gods were Ares, the god of war; Hermes, the messenger of the gods; Hades or Pluto, the god of the dead; Hephaestus, the lame craftsman; and Apollo, the god of wisdom. The best-known goddesses were Artemis, the huntress and twin sister of Apollo; Athena, the patroness of art and war; Aphrodite, the goddess of love; and Demeter, the goddess of the harvest. These names were remembered long after people ceased to believe in these gods. Some of them are still in use today as the names of planets.

Alexander the Great

Greece was a divided and weakened nation – the result of frequent and bitter local wars. After 336 BC, Alexander, the king of Macedon (to the north of Greece), conquered and united the whole country. Alexander proved to be a brilliant soldier. He overthrew the great empire of Persia, and made conquests as far east as India. But he was also more than a conqueror. He aimed to spread Greek culture and language – Hellenistic civilization – throughout this whole area. However, Alexander's hopes were thwarted by his early death in 323 BC.

This mosaic from Pompeii portrays Alexander the Great in battle with the Persian army at Gaugamela.

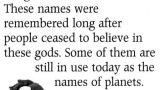

Zeus

The 'golden age' of Greece

In the fifth century BC the most famous of the Greek cities was Athens. The Athenians took a leading part in defeating two great attacks on Greece by the Persians in 490 BC and 480 BC. They became rich and powerful, and built many beautiful temples, including the Parthenon, which can still be seen today. Athens also became the home of some remarkable leaders, thinkers, writers and poets, including Pericles, Socrates, Plato, Sophocles and Euripides.

Sophocles

Democracy

The city of Athens was the perfect example of the Greek way of life. It was a 'democracy'. That is a Greek word for a very Greek idea. To an Athenian it meant that every male citizen ought to play his part in the affairs of his city. 'Politics' was the business of the 'city' (Greek *polis*). The Greeks were a very gifted people, clever and active, quick to argue, with a great love of freedom, and a feeling for beauty in art and writing. Although they were so divided, they were all very proud of being Greek. They thought of themselves as different from other races, whom they called 'barbarians'. Every four years, all the cities met at Olympia in southern Greece for the Olympic Games, and wars between them stopped for that time.

See also

■ Greek and Roman empires (pages 36–37)

■ Ancient beliefs (pages 146–147)

■ Between the Testaments: overview (pages 238–239)

The theatre of Dionysus in Athens, viewed from the Acropolis.

Greek religion

Greek religion was based on the city. There were great festivals in which everybody took part together, and social events were based on religion. The Olympic games were first held as a religious event to honour Zeus. The plays in the theatre at Athens, tragedies and comedies, were performed at the festival of the god Dionysus. And the greatest works of Greek art all had a religious meaning.

Socrates

Early Greek philosophers

As belief in the gods waned, many Greeks turned to philosophy to answer the fundamental questions of good and evil, and life and death. Plato (429–347 BC) wrote down the discussions of his master, Socrates (469–399 BC), about subjects such as justice and life after death, and built up a noble system of thought. Later, the Stoics advised people to live in harmony with reason. The Epicureans believed the world had come about by the chance meeting of atoms. They thought that people should live quietly without fear. Others made new moral lessons from the old stories of the gods. But many had no idea what was worth believing. They worshipped Tyche ('Chance'), and hoped that the chances of life might favour them. Or they turned to astrology or magic.

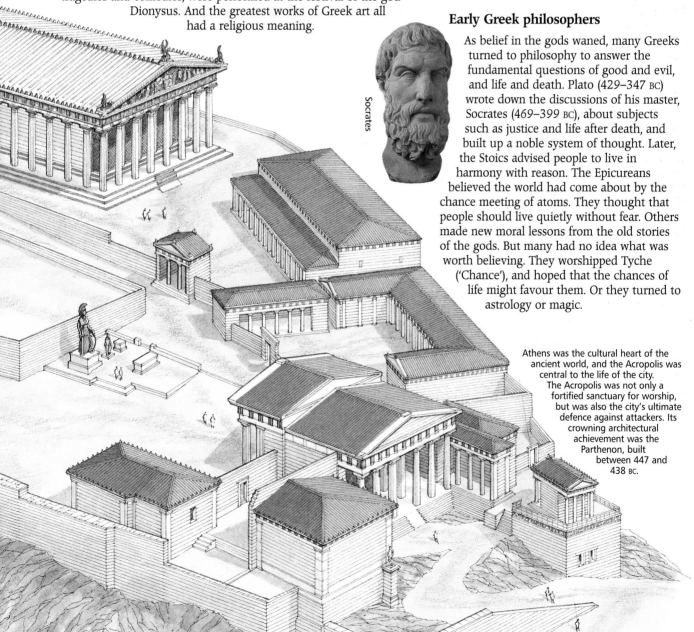

Athens was the cultural heart of the ancient world, and the Acropolis was central to the life of the city. The Acropolis was not only a fortified sanctuary for worship, but was also the city's ultimate defence against attackers. Its crowning architectural achievement was the Parthenon, built between 447 and 438 BC.

Hellenistic civilization

Following the death of Alexander the Great in 323 BC, control of the Greek empire was disputed by his generals. It was divided from the start. Nonetheless, the impact of Greek civilization remained strong, and the period from 330 BC to 30 BC is known as the Hellenistic age (from *Hellen*, meaning 'Greek').

The empire divided

The Greek empire was eventually divided into three distinct dynasties, descended from Alexander's generals. The Ptolemies won control of Egypt; the Seleucids held the East, and made their capital at Antioch in Syria; and the Antigonids ruled Macedonia. There was a struggle for Palestine between the Seleucids and the Ptolemies. One of the Seleucid kings, Antiochus IV Epiphanes (175–164 BC), became the bitter enemy of the stricter Jews.

In 275 BC the empire of the Greek king Pyrrhus of Epirus fell to the Romans. Pyrrhus was regarded as the ruler who most closely resembled Alexander the Great, both in appearance and ability, and his defeat sent shock waves throughout the Greek world.

Fall of an empire

By the end of the third century BC Rome was increasing its influence in the eastern Mediterranean region. As the power of Rome increased, the Romans became involved in the affairs of Greece. In 146 BC they destroyed Corinth, which had resisted them, and Athens fell in 86 BC. This marked the end of Greek political freedom.

The Seleucid rulers used elephants in their efforts to suppress the Maccabbean revolt. This plate shows a war elephant being followed by its calf.

The influence of the Greek language

During the Hellenistic age, Greek became an international language for the eastern Mediterranean and beyond. It was the language of trade, and of education and writing, even for people who still usually spoke their own languages. Even the Jews were influenced by it. In the second century BC the Old Testament was translated into Greek at Alexandria in Egypt, for the Greek-speaking Jews there. This translation, called the *Septuagint*, was the version of the Old Testament used by the first Christians.

Hellenistic philosophy

Hellenistic philosophy can be traced back to the Greek Sophists of the fifth century BC and particularly to Socrates (469–399 BC). And yet it was distinct from earlier Greek philosophy, as well as from later philosophical endeavours. Philosophy in the Hellenistic age was popular throughout society. For many people it was, in effect, a religion, and offered a clear spiritual and moral direction. Each school of philosophy had its own beliefs, practices and way of life, but the focus was on ethics and how to live. Self-sufficiency, freedom and happiness were the goals, and the philosophers encouraged people to turn from the self-indulgence and superstition which they saw in traditional Greek religion.

Aspects of Hellenistic life, such as sport, were often portrayed on Greek vases. Physical exercise had religious significance in Greek culture, and was dedicated to the gods. This, together with the fact that athletes often ran naked, triggered the opposition of orthodox Jews.

Greeks in the New Testament

The New Testament often mentions 'Greeks'. This sometimes means simply non-Jews, also called Gentiles, or Greek-speaking people of the Roman world. Very little of the New Testament story takes place in the land of Greece. Yet the missionary Paul, though a strict Jew, wrote in Greek and understood Greek ways of thinking. Most of his work was in Greek-style cities, especially in Asia Minor, which at that time contained some of the largest and richest Greek towns, such as Ephesus. These cities still had some power, but by then the real power belonged to the Roman governor.

The city of Ephesus was a bridge between east and west, with a population of about a third of a million people in New Testament times. The remains of the library of Celsus (above) indicate something of the splendour of this ancient city.

See also

■ Greek and Roman empires (pages 36–37)

■ The journeys of Paul (pages 44–45)

■ Between the Testaments: overview (pages 238–239)

■ Acts of the Apostles (pages 248–249)

Philosophy played an important part in Greek life. This mosaic of the school of Plato depicts philosophers in debate.

The Romans

The beginnings of the city of Rome are lost in legend. According to Roman mythology, the city was named after its founder, Romulus, in 753 BC. And it was from this year that the later Romans dated the beginning of their history.

Roman engineering achievements were impressive, and often conceived on a grand scale. This example is the aqueduct constructed over the River Gard during the time of the emperor Augustus. The accuracy of the surveyors and engineers was such that the aqueduct carried water for a distance of 50 km and yet the water dropped by only 17 m from beginning to end.

Early Roman history

For centuries Rome was a small and struggling city-state. But it was well placed at a crossing of the River Tiber in the centre of Italy. At first Rome had kings, some of whom probably came from the nation of the Etruscans. When these kings were driven out, Rome became a 'republic', headed by two 'consuls' elected for a year and a council called the 'Senate'. After times of strife, poverty and war, Rome slowly won ground, and by 275 BC controlled all Italy.

Rome increased its power partly through war, but also by a policy of alliances in which Roman citizenship and other rights were freely granted to its allies. The Romans were good organizers. They built fine roads and unified the whole of Italy. They were very different in character from the Greeks. They were not very original. But they were practical, loyal to the state, hard-working and disciplined.

Struggle for power

In 63 BC the Roman general, Pompey, occupied Jerusalem. From that time on, Rome had a controlling influence on Palestine. Later, the ambitious Julius Caesar defeated Pompey and took the title 'dictator', a position which gave him special emergency powers. Caesar was a brilliantly able and vigorous ruler. He defeated the Celts and conquered Gaul (modern France and Germany), as well as invading Britain. But he was murdered in 44 BC by the republicans, Brutus and Cassius. Caesar's friend, Antony, and his heir, Octavian, defeated the republicans in 42 BC, at Philippi in Macedonia. Then the two victors quarrelled. Octavian defeated Antony and his ally, Cleopatra, queen of Egypt.

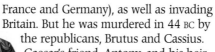

Julius Caesar

Roman empire and emperors

People were weary of so many years of war. Octavian gave them peace. In 27 BC he received the title 'Augustus'. Augustus became the first ruler of the Roman empire, uniting the whole Mediterranean world under one peaceful government until his death in AD 14. It became possible to travel safely by land or sea to every part of the empire.

Life in Rome

Rome, the centre of the Roman empire and the world, was a city of well over a million people. There are vivid pictures of life in Rome: the tall buildings and narrow, congested streets, where people lived in fear of fire, and the constant noise of carts which kept them awake all night. The emperors and nobles lived in great luxury. There were free men and slaves of many races thronging the streets. The emperors tried to keep the peace by bringing corn from Egypt and organizing bloodthirsty public shows where men or beasts fought to the death.

Rome, a world power

After the Romans won control of Italy, they began to extend their power base into new territories. Carthage, on the coast of modern Tunisia, was destroyed by Rome in 146 BC. Rome now controlled the sea-routes and trade of the western Mediterranean Sea. In the Near East, the Romans defeated King Antiochus III of Syria. And they destroyed Corinth in 146 BC and Athens in 86 BC.

By winning control of Greece, Rome became a world power. However, the Greeks had a remarkable influence on their conquerors. The Romans studied Greek language and thought, and copied Greek styles of art and writing. But Roman officials also became corrupt, enriching themselves by robbing their subjects. The Senate in Rome was unable to control them. It was not possible to govern a world empire in the same way as a small city. Large armies and regular organization were needed. Ambitious men began to struggle for power. As a result, there were several civil wars in the first century BC.

Roman warship

The emperor Trajan conducted successful campaigns against Dacia in AD 102 and AD 106. His victories were recorded on the Column of Trajan (left) in the Roman forum.

See also

- Greek and Roman empires (pages 36–37)

- Kings and rulers (pages 116–117)

- Travel and transport (pages 122–123)

Roman religion and beliefs

The Roman empire covered a very large area, and included peoples with many different beliefs. Those living in the eastern empire were the ones whom the early Christians first met. They were often influenced by Eastern ideas which had been handed down from long before Greek civilization came to them.

Roman gods

When the Romans conquered the Greeks they took over all their gods and gave them Roman names. Zeus, for example, became the Roman god Jupiter. His wife, Hera, became the Roman Juno, and his brother, Poseidon, god of the sea, was given the name Neptune. Other famous Roman gods and goddesses were Mars, Mercury, Vulcan, Apollo, Diana, Minerva and Venus.

The Pantheon, or 'shrine of all the gods' in Rome. The dome was the largest ever built by pre-industrial methods, and is 45 m/146 ft in diameter, and the same distance from the top to the floor, so that it forms an exact hemisphere. Niches in the walls were occupied by statues of the gods, and as the sun shone through the hole in the ceiling, it illuminated each one in turn.

Roman religion

Little is really known about the earliest Roman religion, but it was clearly at that time very different from that of the Greeks. The early Romans felt that a divine power (*numen*) existed in nature, and they wanted to harness it to their needs. So there were 'gods' for every area of life: gods of the house and of its doorway, of the fields, and so on. Most of these seem to have had a vague kind of existence. Only a few of the official gods of the state, such as Jupiter, were clearly pictured as persons. But when Greek ideas began to influence Roman thought, the old Roman gods were fitted into the Greek system. Roman beliefs merged with Greek ideas in such a way that it is hard to separate out what is purely Roman.

Religion and the emperor

Augustus (27 BC– AD 14) tried to revive Roman religion. His chosen title, 'Augustus', had a sense of religious awe.

An inscription from Ephesus (above) refers to the 'divine' Caesar Augustus.

He wanted to use religion to bind people in loyalty to his own government. He was worshipped as a god in his lifetime, for he had brought peace and good government to a world torn by war. A great temple was built to Rome and Augustus at Pergamum, and Herod the Great built others at Caesarea and Samaria.

Greek and Roman gods

Greek	Roman	Description
Zeus	Jupiter (Jove)	Chief god, father of other gods
Hera	Juno	Sister and consort of Zeus
Athena	Minerva	Goddess of wisdom and the arts
Apollo	Apollo	God of sun, prophecy, music, medicine, poetry
Artemis	Diana	Virgin goddess of the hunt and the moon; twin sister of Apollo
Poseidon	Neptune	God of sea, earthquakes, horses; brother of Zeus
Aphrodite	Venus	Goddess of love and beauty; Cytherea
Hermes	Mercury	God of commerce, invention, cunning, theft; messenger for other gods; patron of travellers and rogues; conductor of the dead to Hades
Hephaestus	Vulcan	Disabled god of fire and metalworking
Ares	Mars	God of war
Demeter	Ceres	Goddess of agriculture, fertility, marriage
Dionysus	Bacchus	God of wine and ecstasy, orgasm

See also

■ The journeys of Paul (pages 44–45)

■ Kings and rulers (pages 116–117)

■ Ancient beliefs (pages 146–147)

■ The gospels and Acts: overview (pages 242–243)

Religion and ordinary people

The Romans worshipped many gods, but their religion had little effect on the way the worshipper lived. Neither belief nor behaviour was really important. People might believe what they wished, as long as they did what was expected of good citizens, and remained loyal to the state. There was no great stress on a search for truth, nor was there any powerful body of priests. The gods were distant. They were to be paid due honour. But they were not deeply interested in human affairs.

Educated Romans in the time of Julius Caesar in the first century BC often had little regard for these gods. They would use the forms of religion for their own ends when there was some personal advantage, or a political point to gain. But if they thought seriously about life, they turned, like the Greeks, to philosophy or new religions.

The mysteries

People who wanted a more personal faith often turned to the 'mystery' religions. Here the worshipper was admitted step by step into the secret inner spiritual knowledge of the faith. The mysteries at Eleusis in Greece had been known since early times. But many new foreign cults became popular in the Roman world of the first century AD.

This marble sculpture from Rome portrays Mithras slaying the bull.

The Egyptian goddess Isis had many priests and an impressive ritual, and was thought to answer prayer. The Persian Mithras was the soldier's god. Men advanced from rank to rank in his service in the fight against evil. For a time, Mithraism was one of the most serious rivals to Christianity.

Rome and the Christians

Rome normally allowed different beliefs to flourish throughout the empire, although groups which might not be loyal to the state were always banned. Judaism was allowed and, at first, Christianity also, because it seemed to be a kind of Judaism. However, as time went on, the Romans began to use emperor-worship as a test of loyalty. The emperor Domitian (AD 81–96) required people to worship him as 'lord and god'. This meant that the Christians, who would not agree to this, now had to be ready to suffer for their faith.

Nations to the north and south

The great powers to the north of Israel in Bible times were Assyria and Babylon. But the closest of Israel's northern neighbours was a Canaanite people: the Phoenicians. Other related tribes had settled inland from Phoenicia during the time when the Israelites were moving into Canaan.

Hittites

Before the time of the Israelites and Aramaeans, Syria was controlled by the Hittites from Turkey. They were an Indo-European race who built up an empire which was very powerful from about 1600–1200 BC. Their capital city was Hattusha; and royal archives have been found in its ruins. They are written in the Babylonian cuneiform script on clay tablets, but in the Hittite languages. Amongst the important documents are many treaties made with subject states. The Hittites also developed their own hieroglyphic writing system.

This Hittite bronze axe-head dates from the 13th century BC.

Small states

After the fall of the Hittites, a number of smaller states appeared in Turkey. In the south-west was Caria. The Carians served as mercenary soldiers in Egypt, where their inscribed grave stones have been discovered, and in Judah.

The Lydians (Lud in the Bible) lived on the west coast. Inscriptions and objects unearthed in their capital, Sardis, are beginning to reveal their culture and history. Lydia had rich deposits of gold; and it was here that coinage began. From 133 BC Lydia was part of the Roman province of Asia.

East of Lydia was Phrygia. In Assyrian records and the Old Testament it is called Meshech. Phrygia traded in copper and slaves. After the middle of the seventh century BC, Phrygia came under Lydian rule. In 116 BC it became part of the Roman empire.

Still further to the east lay the kingdom of the Urartians. In about 800–650 BC, strong Urartian kings tried to dominate northern Syria and check the Assyrians. Their temples and palaces show distinctive designs and decoration. But they used the cuneiform script to write their language.

The horse-riding Scythians came from central Asia. They destroyed Urartu in the seventh century BC and joined with the Medes, in alliance with Babylon, to overthrow Assyria.

Phoenician craftworkers produced glass utensils such as this brightly decorated perfume jar.

Phoenicians

After the Israelites settled in Canaan in 1230 BC, other Canaanite peoples remained in parts of the land. The Phoenicians lived on the coast to the north-west. They spoke a language which was a form of Canaanite, similar to Hebrew, and their religion, too, contained Canaanite ideas. One of their towns was the ancient city of Byblos, which may have been where the alphabet was invented. After 1000 BC the cities of Tyre and Sidon overtook Byblos in importance. King Hiram of Tyre supplied goods and craftworkers to the Israelite kings David and Solomon at about this time.

Cush

To the south of Egypt lies the Sudan, which was known as Cush in the Old Testament. Usually dominated by Egypt, the Cushite soldiers served in the Egyptian armies. An independent kingdom existed in Cush in Hellenistic and Roman times, with its capital at Meröe. Queens, referred to as 'the Candace', often ruled this state.

Mercenaries from Cush and Nubia (modern Sudan) served in the armies of Egypt. This painted wooden model of a Nubian bowman is one of 40 found in a grave at Asyut in Upper Egypt, and is thought to be nearly 4,000 years old.

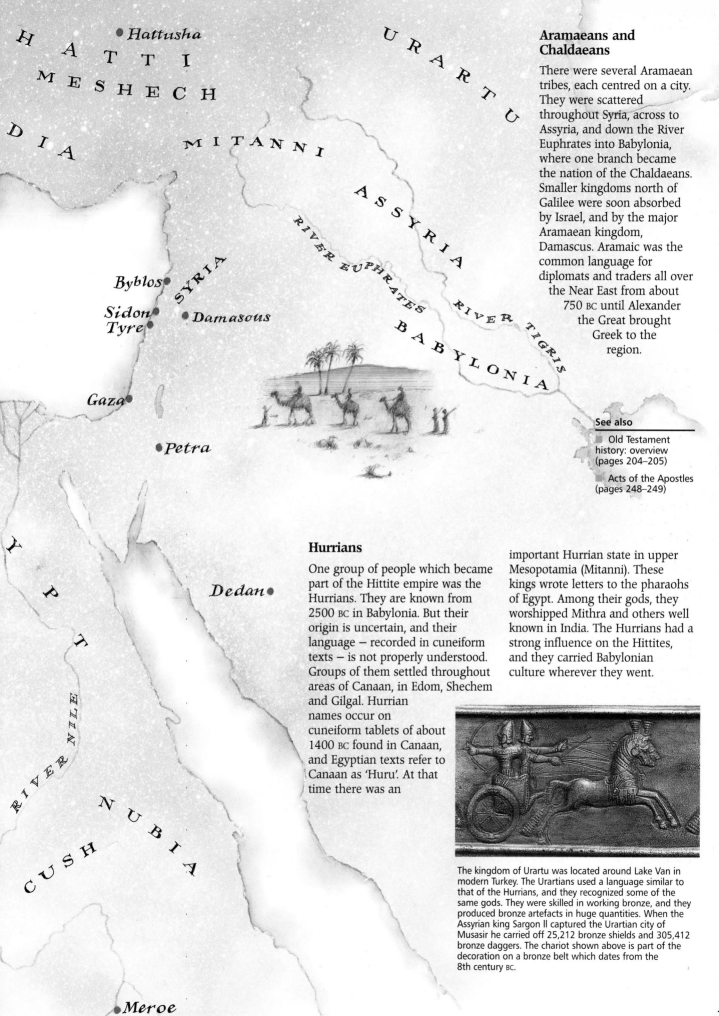

Map labels

HATTI

Hattusha

URARTU

MESHECH

DIA

MITANNI

ASSYRIA

Byblos

SYRIA

RIVER EUPHRATES

RIVER TIGRIS

Sidon

Damascus

Tyre

BABYLONIA

Gaza

Petra

Dedan

Y
P
P
T

RIVER NILE

NUBIA

CUSH

Meroe

Aramaeans and Chaldaeans

There were several Aramaean tribes, each centred on a city. They were scattered throughout Syria, across to Assyria, and down the River Euphrates into Babylonia, where one branch became the nation of the Chaldaeans. Smaller kingdoms north of Galilee were soon absorbed by Israel, and by the major Aramaean kingdom, Damascus. Aramaic was the common language for diplomats and traders all over the Near East from about 750 BC until Alexander the Great brought Greek to the region.

See also

■ Old Testament history: overview (pages 204–205)

■ Acts of the Apostles (pages 248–249)

Hurrians

One group of people which became part of the Hittite empire was the Hurrians. They are known from 2500 BC in Babylonia. But their origin is uncertain, and their language – recorded in cuneiform texts – is not properly understood. Groups of them settled throughout areas of Canaan, in Edom, Shechem and Gilgal. Hurrian names occur on cuneiform tablets of about 1400 BC found in Canaan, and Egyptian texts refer to Canaan as 'Huru'. At that time there was an important Hurrian state in upper Mesopotamia (Mitanni). These kings wrote letters to the pharaohs of Egypt. Among their gods, they worshipped Mithra and others well known in India. The Hurrians had a strong influence on the Hittites, and they carried Babylonian culture wherever they went.

The kingdom of Urartu was located around Lake Van in modern Turkey. The Urartians used a language similar to that of the Hurrians, and they recognized some of the same gods. They were skilled in working bronze, and they produced bronze artefacts in huge quantities. When the Assyrian king Sargon II captured the Urartian city of Musasir he carried off 25,212 bronze shields and 305,412 bronze daggers. The chariot shown above is part of the decoration on a bronze belt which dates from the 8th century BC.

Nations to the east and west

Israel's closest eastern neighbours were the Moabites, Edomites and Ammonites, who settled alongside the River Jordan at about the same time as the Israelites occupied Canaan. Further east lived the Midianites, and a number of tribes mentioned in the Bible who settled in Arabia. To the west, the Israelites were only vaguely aware of the existence of the island peoples of Cyprus and Crete.

Ammonites

North of the Dead Sea, between the rivers Arnon and Jabbok, lived the Ammonites. The Ammonite kingdom was protected from raiders by a series of stone watch-towers. Excavation work in Ammon has revealed ruined houses and tombs with pottery similar to that of the Israelites, stone statues, seals engraved with their owners' names, and a few brief inscriptions, which show that their language was similar to Hebrew. The main road east of the River Jordan – the King's Highway – brought traders through the Ammonite kingdom on their way from Damascus to the Gulf of Aqaba. These were a source of wealth, and a strong cultural and religious influence.

Edomites

The land of Edom lay south of Moab, stretching down to the Gulf of Aqaba. The Edomites lived here, ruled by kings, from an early date. Some Edomites travelled as traders; others worked at copper mining and farming. Like their neighbours, they were hostile to Israel. They were conquered more than once, but often broke free again.

Moabites

South of the River Arnon was Moabite country. These people constantly harassed the Israelites throughout much of the Old Testament period. Moab is listed among the countries attacked by Ramesses II of Egypt (about 1283 BC). The city of Dibon was taken. Here, much later, King Mesha recorded his triumph over Israel's king Omri on the famous Moabite Stone. The inscription shows that his language was similar to Hebrew.

The Moabite stone (left) dates from about 840–820 BC. It records the success of the Moabite king Mesha in overthrowing his Israelite overlords and releasing himself from the requirement to pay annual tribute to Israel. Moab had previously been required to supply Israel with 100,000 lambs and the wool of 100,000 rams.

Island nations

Two major island nations lay to the west of Israel in the Mediterranean Sea. In early times, Cyprus was known as Elisha or Alashiya, and was a major source of copper. Cyprus came under the rule of Rome in 58 BC, and was governed by a proconsul from 27 BC. It was a natural stopping-place for ships passing from the eastern Mediterranean coast to Turkey or Rome.

Crete is known in the Old Testament and other ancient texts as Caphtor. The Minoan civilization flourished there from 2000 BC, merging with the Mycenaean. It fell in the 12th century BC. The Cretan scripts Linear A and Linear B represent a local form of writing. Linear B script was adapted for writing an early form of Greek.

Painted terracotta horse from Cyprus.

Medes

The Medes joined with the Scythians, in alliance with Babylon, to bring about the downfall of Assyria in 612 BC. Astyages, the next king of the Medes, was overthrown by his son-in-law, Cyrus the Persian, in 549 BC. Media then became a province of the new Persian empire. They played their part in the fall of Babylon. Media's capital, Ecbatana, then became a Persian capital.

PRUS

Byblos

Sidon
Tyre *Damascus*

Gaza

Petra

A R A B I A

RED SEA

Dedan

RIVER EUPHRATES

RIVER TIGRIS

M E D I A

Ecbatana

E L A M

Susa

See also

- The time of the judges (pages 24–25)
- Ancient beliefs (pages 146–147)
- Old Testament history: overview (pages 204–205)

This Elamite stone relief was found in Susa. It shows a woman spinning, and dates from 800–700 BC.

Midianites

The Midianites lived south of Edom, along the Red Sea coast, engaging in trade and riding in on camels to raid the settled lands. The Bible records that Moses met them in the Sinai Desert and married a Midianite woman.

Late Bronze Age Midianite pottery found at Timnah in the southern Negev.

Dedan

Within the general area of Midian, the city of Dedan (now Al-'Ula) later grew up. This major trading centre was known even to the Babylonians.

The Nabatean city of Petra lay on important trade routes and was protected by huge rock masses. The 'treasury' is a tomb carved out of the cliff face and given a Hellenistic pillared facade.

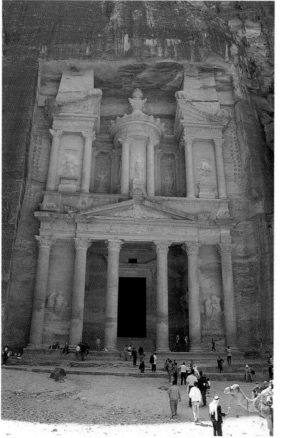

Elamites

Far to the east of Israel were the Elamites, an isolated nation whose chief city was Susa. The Elamites were often under the thumb of their western neighbours. When the Assyrians destroyed the northern kingdom of Israel in 721 BC, they sent some of the citizens of Samaria to Elam, and Elamites were sent to Israel to replace them. Elam became part of the Persian kingdom.

Nabataeans

After the time of Alexander the Great, an Arab tribe, the Nabataeans, made their home in Edomite and Midianite territory, building up a strong kingdom by controlling the trade which brought incense from southern Arabia to Damascus, and across to Gaza. For a few years they ruled Damascus, but were conquered by Trajan of Rome in AD 106. Their chief city was Petra.

THE
WORLD
OF THE
BIBLE

P a r t   3

The lands of the Bible

The land in which the Israelites made their home has changed its name and boundaries several times. The Israelites settled in Canaan, then separated into the kingdoms of Israel and Judah. Under the Romans, their homeland was divided into several regions, including Judea and Galilee. The name 'Palestine' derives from the Philistines who invaded the land in about 1200 BC.

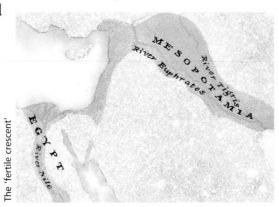

The 'fertile crescent'

The 'fertile crescent'

Most of the Bible story takes place in a very small area at the eastern end of the Mediterranean Sea, in the narrow coastlands that lie between the sea and the vast Arabian deserts. The two worlds of the sea and the desert are separated by the 'fertile crescent'. This is the name given to a belt of well-watered lands extending from Egypt in the south, through an area of natural rainfall on the east Mediterranean coast, to the fertile irrigated lands of Mesopotamia with their great rivers, the Tigris and the Euphrates.

The fertile crescent forms an attractive feature of the Middle East. It has always appealed to desert peoples from the south and mountain peoples from the north. This is why it has been invaded, or overrun, or changed hands, so many times during its history. The Israelites themselves never took to the sea – they left that to the Phoenicians. But certainly the desert is never far away in the Bible story. And in the south of Palestine it reaches westwards almost to the coast.

This scene at Nahal Bezet illustrates the undulating landscape of much of Palestine, where limestone forms a series of hills and valleys. Springs occur in valleys where water permeating through the limestone reaches an impermeable rock beneath and then finds an outlet to the surface. Early settlements in Palestine were normally established close to such springs, or in places where a well could be sunk to reach the water.

Dunes and alluvium

Chalk, chalky limestone and marls

Marble limestone and limestone

Sandstone, sand and marls

Basalt and volcanic tufa

• Acco

Jericho •
Jerusalem •

• Gaza

• Beersheba

Geology

Geologically, most of the materials making up the land of Palestine are young, with limestone occupying a large part of the surface. There are certain characteristic landscape features wherever limestone occurs. Limestone is permeable and there is little surface drainage. But underground streams normally develop and this water can be tapped by sinking wells. Limestone also contains many caves. On the surface it often develops a kind of stony pavement, which makes cultivation difficult and yields only a patchy soil. All of these features are found in the hills of Palestine.

The desert climate of the land also has its effects on the landscape and its structures. In the desert, regardless of rock type, there is usually a surface covering of sand, flint or salt.

Much of the southern part of Palestine is covered by these infertile deposits. Wind and water are the forces which shape the desert rock. The wind scours the desert rocks into fantastic shapes. The force of water, made all the more powerful and dramatic because it is so rare, gouges out steep-sided valleys and overhanging crags. Occasional 'flash' floods can fill a dry valley several metres deep with water in a few minutes.

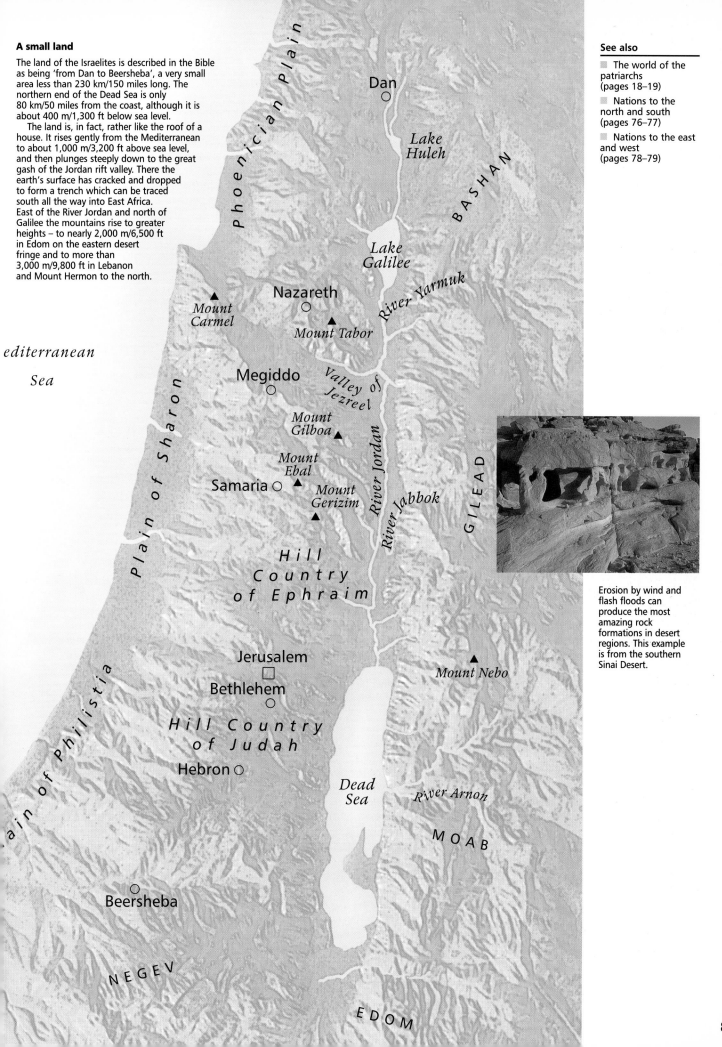

A small land

The land of the Israelites is described in the Bible as being 'from Dan to Beersheba', a very small area less than 230 km/150 miles long. The northern end of the Dead Sea is only 80 km/50 miles from the coast, although it is about 400 m/1,300 ft below sea level.

The land is, in fact, rather like the roof of a house. It rises gently from the Mediterranean to about 1,000 m/3,200 ft above sea level, and then plunges steeply down to the great gash of the Jordan rift valley. There the earth's surface has cracked and dropped to form a trench which can be traced south all the way into East Africa. East of the River Jordan and north of Galilee the mountains rise to greater heights – to nearly 2,000 m/6,500 ft in Edom on the eastern desert fringe and to more than 3,000 m/9,800 ft in Lebanon and Mount Hermon to the north.

See also

■ The world of the patriarchs (pages 18–19)

■ Nations to the north and south (pages 76–77)

■ Nations to the east and west (pages 78–79)

Phoenician Plain

Dan

Lake Huleh

BASHAN

Lake Galilee

River Yarmuk

Mediterranean Sea

Mount Carmel

Nazareth

Mount Tabor

Megiddo

Valley of Jezreel

Mount Gilboa

River Jordan

Mount Ebal

Samaria

Mount Gerizim

River Jabbok

GILEAD

Plain of Sharon

Hill Country of Ephraim

Erosion by wind and flash floods can produce the most amazing rock formations in desert regions. This example is from the southern Sinai Desert.

Jerusalem

Mount Nebo

Bethlehem

Hill Country of Judah

Hebron

Plain of Philistia

Dead Sea

River Arnon

MOAB

Beersheba

NEGEV

EDOM

Regional geography

The regional geography of Palestine encompasses seven major natural divisions in the land: the coastal plain, the region of Galilee, the Jordan valley, the central highlands, the Transjordan, the 'Shephelah' and the plain of Megiddo.

The coastal plain

When the Israelites occupied the land of Canaan, they settled the central highlands and then made sporadic attempts to spread their control down to the Mediterranean coast. But this region was occupied by the Philistines, and it was they who in fact exerted more pressure from their five cities on the coastlands up into the hills.

The coastal plain was not, at this time, a particularly attractive area, comprising a belt of sand dunes backed by forest, lagoons and swamp. There were no large natural harbours south of Mount Carmel, and the first major port on this coast was the artificial harbour at Caesarea, built by King Herod the Great not long before Jesus was born.

South of Mount Carmel, the plain was known as the plain of Philistia and the plain of Sharon. North of Mount Carmel, it became the plain of Asher. Going north, it narrows, but is much better provided with natural harbours. It was from here that the sea-going Phoenicians traded.

Galilee

North of the plain of Megiddo, the highland ranges begin again in the region of Galilee. They rise towards the high mountains of Lebanon in a series of steps, with scarp edges facing generally south or south-east. The lower steps in the 'staircase' were, and still are, fertile basin lands, separated from each other by barren limestone. In the time of Jesus, these basins were known for their grain, fruit and olives. They formed a prosperous, well-populated area. But the higher steps rise to a bleak and windswept upland. This area is isolated and infertile, and lacks the forests of the higher mountain slopes further north.

Galilee is sometimes divided into Lower and Upper Galilee. The southern and eastern edges of the region are clearly drawn, but to the north, it merges into the mountains. In the past this northern boundary area was always the area where foreign influences were strongest, and the Israelites seldom really had it under control.

Galilee was the region where Jesus spent his childhood years. It was a busy area, full of coming and going, with a very mixed community. Its trade routes linked it with the outside world, bringing an awareness of non-Jewish ideas. The people of the region lived off its fertile farmlands and lake fisheries. They were far more alert to the realities of life in the Roman Empire than the aloof inhabitants of Jerusalem – who despised their northern cousins as country bumpkins, and because they were racially mixed.

The Jordan valley

The River Jordan rises near Mount Hermon and flows south through Lake Huleh (now largely drained) and into Lake Galilee. At the southern end of Lake Galilee it enters a deep valley known as the Ghor. Not only is the valley itself steep-sided but the river has cut into the floor and has created a winding, cliff-lined 'valley within a valley', filled with dense, jungle-like vegetation. This made crossing the River Jordan very difficult before the first modern bridges were built.

The Jordan valley is a geological rift. The sides follow parallel faults in the earth's crust. These faults carry on the line of the valley down to the Dead Sea and beyond it, producing the deepest natural depression in the world. The deepest point of the Dead Sea is more than 800 m/2,600 ft below sea level, despite the deposits brought down by the River Jordan for thousands of years.

The distance from the mountain rim on one side of the valley to that on the other is 15–20 km/9–12 miles. But no major road follows the valley, partly due to the broken and difficult ground created by the Jordan and its tributaries.

The central highlands

The core area occupied by the Israelites lay in the 'hill country', the central highlands, along the watershed. Here the land slopes away to the coast on one side and to the Jordan Valley on the other. The western slope is gentle, the eastern slope abrupt. The fortified towns of the central highlands made good defence points.

At the northern end of this region a number of isolated hills look down on the neighbouring region, the plain of Megiddo. But the hill country continues north-westwards to the coast in the

jutting promontory of Mount Carmel. The 600 m/1,970 ft ridge cuts the coastal plain in two, breaking the general north-south pattern of the region.

Even today the central highlands have few roads apart from the main Hebron-Jerusalem-Nablus road. The main roads of both the ancient and modern worlds pass north of the hills or run parallel with them along the coast. So, although this region contains Jerusalem, it has always stood a little apart from the everyday comings and goings through the land.

The 'Shephelah'

Between the coastal plain and the central highlands is an area of low foothills, known as the 'Shephelah', formerly covered by forests of sycamores. When the Philistines fought the Israelites the hills formed a kind of no-man's-land, where there were constant skirmishes, and most of the routes through it were therefore fortified or guarded.

The Transjordan

The Transjordan is an area of mountains similar to, but higher than, the central highlands. They are well-watered and provided good pasture for the huge flocks of sheep and herds of cattle formerly raised in Moab.

The mountains here rise from 600–700 m/1,900–2,300 ft east of Galilee to almost 2,000 m/6,560 ft south and east of the Dead Sea. They attract a rainfall which increases with their height and makes them a fertile belt between the dry Jordan valley on one side and the Arabian Desert on the other.

The plain of Megiddo

Some distance back from the Mediterranean coast, mountain ranges run along the length of Palestine. But there is one important break where a fault in the underlying rock has caused a section of mountain to drop to a height of 100 m/300 ft or less. This break divides the central highlands from Galilee and the northern mountains. It is known as the plain of Megiddo or the plain of Esdraelon.

The plain of Megiddo forms a rough triangle, with each side about 24 km/15 miles long. Although originally the floor of the valley was marshy, it has always had great strategic importance. The principal north-south route of the ancient world (which the Romans called Via Maris, 'the way of the sea') cut through the plain on the way from Egypt to Damascus and Mesopotamia. It was an obvious route for trade – or for invasion. This may account for the long list of battles which have been fought in the plain, right up to modern times.

See also

▪ The world of the patriarchs
(pages 18–19)

▪ A brief history of Jerusalem
(pages 38–39)

▪ In the steps of Jesus (pages 40–41)

Climate and natural resources

The lands on the Mediterranean coast have a climate which is midway between temperate and tropical. The winters are wet, like those of northern countries. The summers are hot and dry, influenced by the tropical deserts that lie beyond the sea's southern rim. Thanks to this seasonal contrast, snow will lie on the coastal mountains but tropical fruits will ripen in the plain.

Sandy soil grassland or shrubs with remnants of Tabor oak and carob forest

Sand dunes

Cultivated land

Forest and 'maquis'

Semi-arid dwarf shrubs

Desert and semi-desert

Oases

Temperature

The temperature range in Palestine is very large. Temperatures by the Dead Sea, for example, reach 40°C as a matter of course, yet at the same time 100 miles away in Upper Galilee freezing rain may be falling. There are daily changes, too, especially in low-lying areas. Jericho has a January average temperature of 15°C, but this is made up of high daytime temperatures and freezing nights.

Temperatures are affected generally by the height of the land above sea level and, from time to time, by the winds. In the daytime, cooling breezes blow in from the Mediterranean Sea to make the summer heat less intense. But the effect of the 'hamsin' is much less pleasant. This fiercely hot and dry wind blows from the south, out of Arabia, and is well-known to the people of Palestine.

The arid land of the rift valley is broken by scattered oases. This one is at Engedi by the shore of the Dead Sea.

Vegetation

The vegetation of Palestine is as varied as its climate: desert scrub, steppeland with shrubs and grasses, grassland, transitional woodland and forests all feature in and around this relatively small region. There are forests in Lebanon to the north, and desert scrub is found to the south. The steppeland and grassland form a narrow band around the highlands of Judea and east of the River Jordan. In the coastal areas, most of the original grassland has long since been ploughed and sown. And some of the desert was cultivated by irrigation agriculture in Roman times just as it is in modern Palestine.

The vegetation of Palestine during Bible times was clearly influenced by geology, rainfall and temperature (see charts below and right). The most densely forested areas are the limestone hills where rainfall is high.

Acco

Jericho
Jerusalem

Guzu

Beersheba

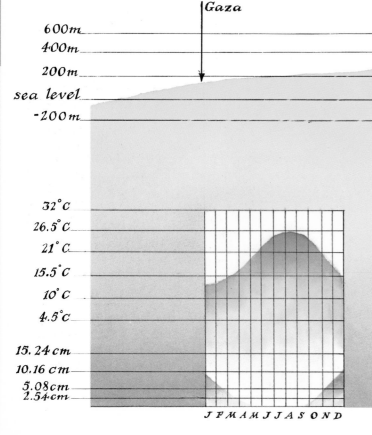

Gaza

600m
400m
200m
sea level
-200m

32°C
26.5°C
21°C
15.5°C
10°C
4.5°C

15.24cm
10.16cm
5.08cm
2.54cm

J F M A M J J A S O N D

Water resources

Palestine is a land where it has always been important to save and store water. The River Jordan is the only river of any size in the region – but it empties into the Dead Sea, where water evaporates from the surface at a rate of 1,500 mm/60 in a year. The River Jordan flows all the year round, fed by snow from Mount Hermon. Most streams, however, flow in sudden spates followed by months when their beds are dry.

From the earliest times, the towns and villages of Palestine have relied on wells and springs for their water supply. The right of access to a well was a valuable privilege in Bible times. If the wells in an area were blocked up, the inhabitants would die of thirst. As cities grew bigger, the problem of keeping them supplied with water became acute. Jerusalem, high in the porous limestone hills, needed a whole system of waterworks.

See also

▪ The farming year (pages 104–105)

▪ Food and drink (pages 106–107)

▪ Feasts and holy days (pages 154–155)

Mineral resources

The land of Palestine is rich in minerals. Copper was mined from very early times, with the copper mines just north of the Gulf of Aqaba in full production in King Solomon's time. Mining for iron came later, after the Hittites discovered how to smelt it. The Philistines brought the secret with them, but it was not until the time of kings David and Solomon that the Israelites were able to make their own iron tools.

The other main resources of the land are building stones, pitch, sands and clays. A variety of chemical salts are also found in the Dead Sea area, where evaporation has left them bedded in thick layers.

The snows of Mount Hermon in the north of Palestine feed the headwaters of the River Jordan. The difference in rainfall between the mountainous areas and the Jordan valley is indicated on the map (right).

Dew

In parts of Palestine where there is not much rain, the dew may play an important part in watering the land. Most of the areas with heavy dews are on the coast. The moisture comes in from the Mediterranean Sea during the summer days, then falls to the ground as dew when it is cooled at night. Some coastal areas may have dew on 200 nights each year, and it can provide as much as a quarter of their moisture.

The section below demonstrates the gradual increase in height across Palestine from west to east until it drops suddenly to the Jordan valley, climbing steeply again towards the Transjordan. The rainfall and temperature charts highlight the contrast between the hot, dry conditions of Jericho in the Jordan valley and the cooler, wetter climate of Jerusalem on the higher ground.

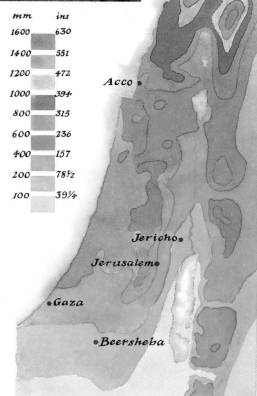

mm	ins
1600	630
1400	551
1200	472
1000	394
800	315
600	236
400	157
200	78½
100	39¾

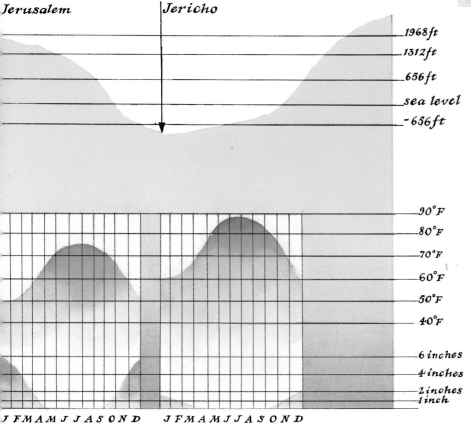

Rainfall

The amount of rainfall in Palestine generally depends upon the height of the land above sea level. There is more rain in the high mountains north of Galilee (750–1,500 mm/29–60 in per year), for example, than in the hills of Judea (500–750 mm/20–29 in). And the rainfall total lessens rapidly towards the south of the region, with less than 200 mm/8 in at Beersheba. Further south still, desert conditions apply.

Most rain comes in the winter season, beginning in about mid-September. The months of December or January have most rain, which blows in from the Mediterranean Sea for two to three days at a time, followed by brighter conditions. This pattern continues until late March or early April, when drier weather sets in. The summers are very dry, with rain unlikely to fall between the middle of June and September.

Plants and flowers

The Bible mentions many different plants and flowers, some well known; others harder to identify. Here is a selection of the most interesting and important ones.

Beans and lentils
Broad beans can be cooked as a vegetable, or dried and ground into flour. Lentils grow in a small flat pod, like a pea. Red lentils are normally made into soups and stews. Lentils can also be dried and ground into flour.

Genesis 25:34; 2 Samuel 17:28

Cereals
Cereals were an integral part of the standard diet in ancient Israel. Wheat made the best flour, and was used to make the bread offered to God by priests. Barley, which ripens before wheat and is harvested in early summer, was the food of the poorer peasants. The Bible tells of a time when Egypt's barley crop was ruined by hailstorms; the wheat, which came up later, was saved. Millet, which is rather like rye, makes the worst bread of all. It is mentioned in the Bible as food fit for a time of famine.

Exodus 9:31–32; Ezekiel 4:9

Flax
Linen cloth is made from flax, a pretty blue-flowered plant which grows about 45 cm/ 18 in high. The stem fibres of the plant are separated by steeping them in water. They can then be combed and woven like threads. The fibres are also used for string nets and lamp-wicks. Linen was used to make sails. It was also made into fine clothes in Egypt and Israel, and wrapped around dead bodies.

Joshua 2:6; Ezekiel 27:7; Mark 15:46

Papyrus
Papyrus is a sedge which grew in the marsh areas of the Nile Delta. The paper of the ancient world was made from this plant, which has mop-like flower-heads about 3 m/10 ft high. The three-cornered stems were cut into thin strips. Two layers, one at right-angles to the other, were laid out on a hard wooden surface and hammered together. These sheets of paper were then pasted end to end, to form a roll. Papyrus was also used to make boats and baskets, ropes and sandals.

Aloe
Aloe is a large plant which produces resin and oil used in perfume. The Bible records that Nicodemus brought aloe with myrrh to prepare Jesus' body for burial.

John 19:39

The ancient Egyptians cultivated myrrh and frankincense trees. This drawing, based on a mural from Hatshepsut's temple, shows trees being transported to Egypt from the Horn of Africa.

Spikenard
Spikenard, which grows in India, was used to make a sweet-smelling ointment. It was imported to Israel in Bible times in sealed alabaster jars to preserve the perfume. The Bible tells that this was the costly gift that Mary lavished on Jesus.

Mark 14:3

Frankincense
Frankincense is a gum which is collected by peeling back the bark of the frankincense-tree (*Boswellia*) and cutting into the trunk. The resin gives off a sweet scent when warmed or burned, and was used as incense in Bible times. The Bible states that frankincense was one of the gifts brought to Jesus by the wise men.

Matthew 2:1

Myrrh
Myrrh is a pale yellow gum from a shrub which grows in Somalia, Ethiopia and Arabia. It was used in Bible times as a spice and a medicine, as well as in making the holy oil for the tabernacle and temple. The Bible records that the wise men brought a gift of myrrh to Jesus when he was a baby, and that myrrh was mixed with a drink offered to Jesus as a pain-killer during his crucifixion.

Exodus 30:23–24; Matthew 2:1

Wormwood
Wormwood is the bitter-tasting absinthe, used in the Bible as a symbol of sorrow and bitterness.

Rose
The word often translated 'rose' in the Bible is not the rose as we know it, but probably the narcissus or a mountain tulip.

Isaiah 35:1;
Song of Solomon 2:1

Lily
The lily of the Old Testament may have been the wild blue hyacinth or the madonna lily (the bulb was also considered a delicacy to eat). When, in the New Testament, Jesus spoke of the 'lilies of the field', he was probably thinking of wild flowers in general, rather than one in particular. In spring the hillsides of Galilee are ablaze with brightly coloured flowers, such as the anemone, crocus poppy, narcissus and yellow chrysanthemum.

Matthew 6:28

Thistles, thorns and tares
Thistles and thorns are abundant in dry countries. In Israel there are more than 120 varieties, some growing to over 2 m/6 ft. Some, such as the milk-thistle, have beautiful flowers, but can quickly suffocate surrounding young plants. The Bible tells of how thorns were plaited into a mock crown for Jesus at his trial. The 'tares' in the New Testament story of the wheat and the weeds are darnel, which looks exactly like wheat in its early stages.

Matthew 13:24–30;
Mark 15:17

See also

- Clothes-making (pages 136–137)
- Health and healing (pages 138–139)
- Food and drink (pages 106–107)
- Priests and rituals (pages 162–163)

Cinnamon
Oil distilled from the bark of the cinnamon tree was used in Bible times to flavour food and wine.

Song of Solomon 8:2

Hyssop
In the Old Testament, hyssop was used when sprinkling the blood of sacrifices, and also on the eve of the Passover festival. The New Testament tells that, on the cross, Jesus was given vinegar in a sponge passed to him on a bunch of hyssop. Hyssop was obviously a bushy plant, and may have been different from the herb we call by the same name today.

Exodus 12:21–22;
John 19:29

Cummin and dill
Cummin seeds were used to spice meat, and also in eye medicine. Dill seeds were used to flavour bread or cakes. The Bible records that the Pharisees gave God one-tenth of everything, even their seasoning herbs such as cummin, dill and mint, but Jesus commented that they neglected much more important things: honesty, justice and mercy.

Matthew 23:23

Mustard
God's kingdom, Jesus says in the Bible, is like the tiny mustard seed which grows into a great plant. He was probably talking about the black mustard, whose seeds were grown for oil as well as flavouring in Bible times. Mustard plants usually grow to about 120 cm/4 ft high.

Matthew 13:31–32

Trees and shrubs

Trees are very important to any country's economy. They affect climate and prevent soil erosion, quite apart from their practical uses. Before industrialization, people depended on trees for food and shelter, fuel and most building projects. Here is a selection of some of the most important trees and shrubs in Palestine in Bible times.

Olive

Olives were one of the main tree-crops of ancient Israel. The trees can live to an age of several hundred years. Olives were eaten pickled, or were pressed to extract oil. Olive oil was used for cooking, as fuel for lamps and as a soothing lotion for the skin. In ancient Israel it was also used to anoint kings and priests, as a mark that they

were set apart for special work. The wood from the olive tree was carved and polished for fine work, as in Solomon's temple.

1 Samuel 10:1;
1 Kings 6:23

Fig

In Bible times, the ideal of peace and prosperity was summed up as 'everyone able to sit down under their own vine and fig-tree'. Figs are slow-growing trees, bearing fruit for about 10 months of the year. The large leaves make useful wrappings. Cakes of dried figs made excellent food and were easy to carry.

Amos 7:14; Luke 19:4

Date palm

The date palm is a tall tree with a straight trunk topped by a tuft of huge 2 m/6 ft leaves, amongst which the clusters of dates grow to provide valuable food. The palm became a national symbol of Israel, standing for victory. The Bible tells that people waved palm leaves when Jesus rode into Jerusalem.

John 12:13

Myrtle

An evergreen with fragrant leaves and sweet-scented white flowers which were used as perfume.

Oak

Many kinds of oaks grew in Israel, some of them evergreen. The wood was used for oars and for carving statues. The Bible recounts that Absalom became caught in an oak tree when fleeing from King David.

2 Samuel 18:9–10

Acacia (shittim)

The acacia is one of the few trees to grow in the Sinai desert. The Ark of the Covenant of the ancient Israelites was made from the wood of this tree.

Exodus 25:10

Tamarisk

A number of species of this softwood tree are found in desert areas in Palestine. The Bible records that Abraham planted a tamarisk tree in the desert around Beersheba.

Genesis 21:33

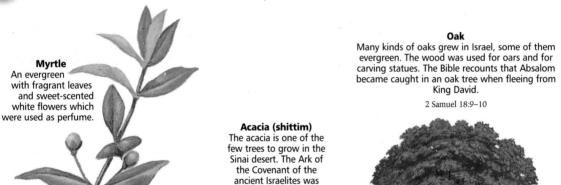

Almond

The almond was the first fruit-tree to blossom in Israel, sometimes as early as January. As well as being a favourite food, the nut also produced oil. The Old Testament records a story about an almond rod which flowers and produces fruit overnight.

Numbers 17:8

Pomegranate

Scarlet flowers contrast with deep-green leaves on this large shrub. The yellow-brown edible fruits are the size of an orange. Inside the hard rind is a juicy pulp, full of seeds. The shape of the pomegranate was copied in embroidery around the edge of the high priest's robe, and carved on the pillars in Solomon's temple.

Exodus 28:33; 1 Kings 7:20

Vine

A trailing shrub producing grapes, one of the most important of all fruit crops. Vines were planted in rows in carefully prepared vineyards on the sunny hill slopes of ancient Israel. Each spring the vines were pruned, and as the grapes ripened the owner kept a sharp look-out for intruders – animal or human – from a special watch-tower. At harvest time the grapes were picked and taken to be trodden out at the wine-press. Some were also made into raisin-cakes. The fermenting wine was stored in new skins or pottery jars to mature. The vine was a national emblem in Israel, a symbol of peace and prosperity. Jesus used it in five of his parables, and described himself as the true vine on which the branches (his followers) depend.

Matthew 9:17; John 15:1

An Egyptian wall-painting from the tomb of Nakht at Thebes (around 1420 BC) illustrates the wine-making process.

See also

■ The farming year (pages 104–105)

■ Food and drink (pages 106–107)

■ Three temples (pages 160–161)

Cedar

The beautiful, giant cedar of Lebanon once grew in great forests. Although the cedar is still the national symbol of Lebanon only a few of these trees remain, high in the mountains. In Solomon's day, King Hiram of Tyre exported vast quantities of cedar. The wood is a warm red colour, and long-lasting. It could be carved and decorated, and was used to panel Solomon's temple and palace.

1 Kings 6:15–7:12

Poplar

The white poplar has fast-growing shoots and gives a dense shade. The 'willows' of Babylon, where the exiled Israelites mourned, were probably a kind of poplar.

Psalm 137:2

Fir and pine

The wood from these evergreens which grew on the mountains and hills of Israel was used in building Solomon's temple, for ships' decks and for making musical instruments.

1 Kings 5:8; Ezekiel 27:5

Animals and birds

The Bible mentions many animals and birds by name. It can be difficult to be sure of the exact identity of some of these. Some of the more common and important ones are described here.

Deer and gazelle
These graceful animals provided the Bible writers with an image of swiftness and gentleness. Fallow and roe deer, gazelles and ibex, whose sandy colouring makes them difficult to spot, were a major source of meat in Bible times.

Song of Solomon 2:8–9

Bear
The Syrian brown bear was quite common in the hilly and wooded parts of Israel in Bible times. Bears will eat almost anything. They usually live on fruit, roots, eggs, and bees' and ants' nests. But when they are hungry they may take a lamb from a flock. The Bible tells how bears attacked a mob who were jeering at the prophet Elisha.

2 Kings 2:24

Camel
The camel referred to in the Old Testament is normally the one-humped Arabian camel, invaluable to desert nomads. It can live on poor food and can go for several days without drinking. In ordinary use it can carry a load of about 180 kg/400 lb in addition to its rider. Camels are mentioned in the Bible stories of Abraham, Jacob and Job. The Israelites were not allowed to eat camel meat.

Genesis 12:16; Job 1:3

Ass (donkey) and mule
These were the most common of all pack animals in Bible times. They were used for carrying heavy loads, and also for riding by rich and poor alike. The donkey is a descendant of the North African wild ass. The mule is cross-bred from a donkey (male) and a horse. Both ass and mule are sure-footed and can live in much rougher country than horses. The ass is the 'hero' of the Old Testament story of Balaam. And it was an ass which Jesus rode into Jerusalem on Palm Sunday, as a king coming in peace.

Numbers 22; Matthew 21:1–11

Rock hyrax
The rock hyrax (called 'coney' or 'badger' in some Bible translations) is a small, shy animal about the size of a rabbit, with neat ears and no tail. It lives in colonies in rocky places.

Proverbs 30:26

Leopard
The leopard was well known in Israel in Bible times, and was mentioned by the Israelite prophets Isaiah and Jeremiah. Its spotted coat helped it to creep up on its prey unseen, even in the open.

Isaiah 11:6; Jeremiah 13:23

Fox and jackal
These are smaller cousins of the wolf. The fox, who hunts alone, likes fruit and often damages the low vines. Jackals go about in packs, scavenging at night. The foxes in the biblical story of Samson were probably jackals.

Judges 15:4

Lion
The lion is mentioned many times in the Bible, although by New Testament times it was rare in Israel. Lions lived in the thickets of the Jordan valley, and could be a danger to flocks and to humans. Assyrian kings kept lions in pits, and enjoyed lion-hunts with their nobles. The strength and courage of the lion made it a symbol of power, so that Jesus himself is called 'lion of the tribe of Judah' in the Bible.

Daniel 6:16–24; Revelation 5:5

This Israelite clay model of a horse with a harness dates from the seventh or eighth century BC.

Wolf
Fierce and dangerous hunters which usually feed on smaller animals, but will also attack and kill deer, sheep and even cattle. The Bible speaks of cruel and evil leaders as 'wolves', and Jesus described his followers as 'sheep among wolves'.

Matthew 7:15; Luke 10:3

Horse
In Bible times horses were owned only by the rich. They were not kept in Israel until the time of King David. King Solomon, aided by Israel's geographical position, became a successful middleman, trading in chariots from Egypt and horses from Turkey (Cilicia). The horse was a 'weapon' of war and stood for power.

Joshua 11:4; Esther 6:8

Cattle
In Bible times, herds of cattle were kept to provide milk and meat, and leather from skins. The ox pulled the farmer's plough and threshing-sledge, and was harnessed to wagons and carts. Cattle were killed in the context of temple sacrifices. A farmer's wealth was reckoned by the numbers of cattle and sheep owned. Bashan, to the east of the River Jordan, was famous for its cattle.

Genesis 13:2; Leviticus 1:2

Sheep and goats
From very early times, before there was settled farming, nomads depended on their flocks of sheep and goats for milk, cheese, meat and clothes. Goatskins were the standard water-bottle. Black goat-hair was woven into strong cloth for tents. Wool from the sheep was spun and woven into warm cloaks and tunics. Sheep and goats were killed as sacrifices in the Jerusalem temple. They were well suited to rough hill pasture. Shepherds often looked after mixed flocks of sheep and goats, protecting them from wild animals and leading them to fresh grazing and watering-places.

Genesis 27:9; 4:2; Exodus 26:7

Eagles and vultures

The word usually translated 'eagle' in the Bible also includes the griffon vulture. From a distance both look alike. The Old Testament books of Isaiah and Psalms both speak of the eagle's strength and vigour. In the New Testament, the 'eagle' was the badge of the Roman legions. Matthew probably had that in mind when he described the eagles waiting for Jerusalem to fall.

Isaiah 40:31; Psalm 103:5; Matthew 24:28

Raven

The name 'raven' probably includes crows and rooks as well as ravens. Ravens are large, black, flesh-eating birds. The Bible recounts that after the flood, Noah sent out a raven to see if the land was dry. Ravens are also said to have fed Elijah in a time of famine.

Genesis 8:7; 1 Kings 17:4

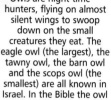

Owl

Owls are night-time hunters, flying on almost silent wings to swoop down on the small creatures they eat. The eagle owl (the largest), the tawny owl, the barn owl and the scops owl (the smallest) are all known in Israel. In the Bible the owl is pictured as the inhabitant of ruined and desolate places.

Leviticus 11:16; Isaiah 34:15

See also

- Food and drink (pages 106–107)
- Travel and transport (pages 122–123)

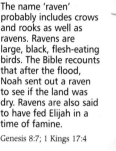

Sparrow

The word 'sparrow' is often used in the Bible to mean any small bird suitable for eating. Larks and finches as well as sparrows were often trapped or shot to be cooked and eaten. The Bible records that Jesus used the sparrow to emphasize the extent of God's love, which included even the smallest birds. So how much more must God care for people!

Matthew 10:29–31; Luke 12:6–7

Doves and pigeons

Doves and pigeons are the most common and important of all the birds of the Bible. Several kinds are native to Israel; others come as winter visitors. They were widely kept as domestic birds, for food. Poor people who could not afford to sacrifice a sheep or goat would instead offer two pigeons – which they could buy in the temple court. In the Old Testament story, it was a dove that brought back to Noah the first green leaf after the flood.

Genesis 8:8–12; Matthew 21:12

Partridge

The name 'partridge' in the Bible probably includes three kinds of partridge: the rock partridge, the desert partridge and the black partridge. All are game birds whose flesh and eggs can make a good meal. The rock partridge hides itself so well that it is more often heard than seen.

1 Samuel 26:20

Quail

The Bible records that quails provided the Israelites with meat as they journeyed from Egypt at the time of the exodus. Twice a year vast numbers of quails fly across this region, migrating north in summer, south in winter. Exhausted by the long flight, they fly low above the ground and are easily caught.

Exodus 16:13; Numbers 11:31–35

Crane

The crane is a regular migrant and winter visitor to Israel. A large grey bird with a wing-span of 2.5 m/8 ft, the crane feeds mostly on seeds and leaves.

Stork

Both white and black storks pass through Israel every year, flying north from their wintering-places in Arabia and Africa. The larger and more numerous white stork is seen most often. Storks live mostly on small animal life – snakes, fish, mice, worms and insects.

Jeremiah 8:7

The family

The family of the early Israelites was what those who live in small family units would call an 'extended family'. It consisted of not just parents and children, but grandparents, aunts, uncles and cousins – and servants, too. The Old Testament records that Abraham, for example, was able to take 318 fighting men from his own family with him into battle.

The family leader

In Old Testament times, the grandfather had complete authority over the family, not just in practical matters but in religious ones, too. When he died, his eldest son took over by right of birth.

History and change in the family

The Bible covers about 2,000 years of history, during which time there were many changes. Abraham lived a 'semi-nomadic' life. His descendants settled in Canaan, built villages and learned the skills of the Canaanite peoples. The Israelite kings introduced central control from Jerusalem, replacing the old system of village elders. Prosperity arrived, but so did forced labour, taxes, and divisions between rich and poor. Revolution split the nation in two. Invasions from Syria, Egypt, Assyria and Babylonia, a long period of exile, and later the control of the nation first by Persia, then by Greece and Rome, brought new customs and outlooks.

Religion and family life

Within the family, children were encouraged to ask questions about their religion and history. Parents taught their children God's laws, and by New Testament times they would learn parts of the Bible by heart. In earlier periods, members of the family would recite many of the stories now written down in the Bible from memory.

God's law in the family

From the very beginning, ordinary life in Israel was bound up with religious life. The two were one and could not be separated. Everything the family did was based on the Torah or Pentateuch (the first five books of the current Old Testament). The Old Testament recounts that God made a promise to Abraham, and later to Abraham's son, Isaac, and to his grandson, Jacob. In return for God's care and protection, they would follow God's rules. Those rules were spelt out in detail to later generations and came to form the basis of national life. The Ten Commandments had a central role to play in all this.

The father

When the Israelite tribes began to settle in permanent homes the normal family unit became smaller. Within this smaller unit the father had complete authority. He could, if he wished, even sell his daughter into slavery. In early Old Testament days it was possible for a father to have disobedient children put to death. He could divorce his wife without any reason and without providing for her. And he could arrange the marriages of his sons.

Respect and discipline

The Bible indicates that, for their own good, children were expected to respect their parents and pay attention to their teaching and advice. Parents who really loved their children would discipline and correct them – but not provoke them – especially when they were young. The happiness of parents and children were bound up with one another. And reverence for God was the starting-point.

Inheritance

Normally, only sons could inherit when their father died – and the eldest son in a family had a special position. He had the right to a double share of his father's property. Only if there were no sons could daughters inherit. If there were no children at all, the property passed to the closest male relative.

See also

■ The world of the patriarchs (pages 18–19)

■ God's laws in practice (pages 152–153)

■ The Torah or Pentateuch (pages 196–197)

Marriage and weddings

Many believe that the story of creation in the Old Testament book of Genesis indicates God's original plan for a man and a woman to live together for life. The reality during Bible times was often quite different, and it was not until Jesus' time that monogamy became common practice.

Arranged marriages

It was common practice for marriages to be arranged by the parents – normally within the same clan in Old Testament times, and ideally with a first cousin. Marriage to someone from another nation worshipping other gods was forbidden. The law also forbade marriage between close relatives. However, arranged marriages did not always mean that the young people had no say. The Old Testament records, for example, that Shechem and Samson both asked their parents to arrange a marriage with a particular girl. It was also possible to marry a slave or a war captive.

A civil affair

In Bible times, a marriage was a civil rather than a religious affair. At the betrothal a contract was made in front of two witnesses, which was as binding as marriage. Sometimes the couple gave one another a ring or bracelet.

Monogamy

By New Testament times the usual practice was to have only one wife – although at one time King Herod the Great had nine. It was very unusual for a man not to marry – there is no Hebrew word for 'bachelor' – and people in Palestine married very young. The legal ages for marriage were 13 for a boy and 12 for a girl.

Polygamy

From earliest times, men took it for granted that they would have more than one wife. This practice of polygamy grew until, by the time of the judges and the kings, a man could have as many wives as he could afford. No doubt, at first it made good economic sense to have more than one wife: more children meant more workers. But the time came when it cost more to keep several wives than the family gained by having more children.

The cost of marriage

Before marriage, a sum of money called the *mohar* had to be paid to the bride's father. It could sometimes be paid in part in the form of work by the man. The father seems to have been able to use any interest the *mohar* could earn, but he was not allowed to touch the *mohar* itself. This was returned to the daughter on the death of her parents, or if her husband died. The girl's father, in return for the *mohar*, gave her or her husband a wedding gift, or 'dowry'. This could be in the form of servants, land or property.

The position of women

In Old Testament times, a woman was owned by her husband and she was expected to look up to him as her master. This attitude was still the norm in New Testament times. Though women did much of the hard work, they had a low position, both in society and in the family. But the law did protect a divorced woman, and her children were taught to respect her.

See also

■ Clothing and cosmetics (pages 110–111)
■ Clothes-making (pages 136–137)
■ Genesis (pages 198–199)

The wedding

In Bible times, a wedding took place when the bridegroom had the new home ready. With his friends, he went to his bride's house in the evening. She was waiting, veiled and in her wedding dress. She wore jewellery, such as a head-band of coins, which the bridegroom had given her. In a simple ceremony, the veil was taken from the bride's face and laid on the bridegroom's shoulder. There followed a big wedding feast at the home of the bridegroom or his parents.

Divorce

A man was allowed to divorce his wife in Bible times, often for very trivial reasons. But, typically, there was a different standard for women. A wife could never divorce her husband, though under certain circumstances she could force him to divorce her.

Slave girls and concubines

The law-code of King Hammurabi of Babylon, dated about 1750 BC, records that: 'A man would not take a second wife unless the first was unable to have children. The husband was allowed a secondary wife (a concubine), or his wife might give him a slave-girl, to have children by her. The children of the slave-girl might not be sent away.' These customs seem to be reflected in the Old Testament stories of Abraham.

A new baby

The following words from the book of Psalms show how the people of Israel felt about children:
'Children are a gift from the Lord;
they are a real blessing.
The sons of a man when he is young
are like arrows in a soldier's hand.
Happy is the one who has many such arrows.'

Purification

The law required that, in order to worship God, a person had to be ritually 'clean'. Childbirth was one of the things that barred people for a time from joining in worship. In order to become 'clean' again after giving birth, a woman was required to sacrifice first a pigeon, and then a lamb. If the family was too poor to afford a lamb, the mother could offer a second pigeon instead. In New Testament times, money was put into the offering boxes of the temple to pay for these sacrifices, and the women gathered on the steps near the altar for the ceremony.

Naming the baby

In Old Testament times a baby was named at birth. The name always had a meaning. It might say something about how the baby was born, his or her character, or the family's feelings towards God. For example, in the Old Testament, the name of the prophet Elijah means 'Yahweh is God'; and Isaiah means 'God is salvation'.

Circumcision scene depicted on a wall relief in the tomb of Anach Machor in Egypt, dating from about 22 BC.

Circumcision

In Bible times it was traditional for an Israelite baby boy to be circumcised on the eighth day after birth. In many other nations, boys were circumcised when they were recognized as adult members of the clan. But as far back as the days of Abraham, circumcision on the eighth day after birth had been the physical sign of God's promise made to Abraham and his descendants for all time. This ceremony reminded them that every child in Israel was one of God's own people.

Swaddling cloths

It was customary in Bible times for a new-born baby to be washed and then rubbed over with salt which, it was believed, made the skin firm. The baby was then wrapped in 'swaddling cloths'. The mother or her helper placed the baby on a square of cloth. Then she folded the corners over its sides and feet, and wrapped bandages, often embroidered, around the whole bundle. The bandages were loosened several times a day and the skin was rubbed with olive oil and dusted with powdered myrtle leaves. This went on for several months. The wrappings made it easy for the mother to carry her baby in a woollen 'cradle' on her back. At night the cradle was hung from a beam in the house, or between two forked sticks.

Redemption

In Bible times, if a baby boy was the first-born in the family he was believed to belong to God in a special way, and he had to be 'bought back' or 'redeemed'. This practice was traced back to the time of the exodus, when all the first-born children of the Egyptians had died and God saved the first-born sons of the Israelites. The first generation of boys born after the exodus were redeemed by being dedicated to God's service. After that each family paid five pieces of silver to the priest to 'buy back' their first-born.

The Bar Mitzvah
In New Testament times, a boy became an adult on his 13th birthday. This was marked by a special ceremony called the Bar Mitzvah, which means 'son of the law'. In the months before his birthday he learned to read the passages from the Old Testament law and prophets that were to be read in the synagogue that day. He had to recite them at the service. The minister, or 'rabbi', then spoke to the boy and asked God's blessing on him.

A baby boy

It was so important to have a son in Bible times that the woman's name was changed to 'Mother of...' when her first son was born. Sons not only helped to work the family's land, but they were also needed to carry on the family name. In the earliest times, before the development of belief in life after death, people liked to think that they would live on through their children, so without children there was no future. This was why, if a man died without a child, it was the duty of his closest relative to marry the wife. Their first son would then take the dead man's name and inherit his land.

See also

▪ Clothes-making
(pages 136–137)
■ God's laws in practice
(pages 152–153)
■ New Testament religion
(pages 170–171)
■ Leviticus, Numbers, Deuteronomy
(pages 202–203)

Education

Archaeology has demonstrated that education was being developed in Bible lands from the earliest times. Yet whereas the education of the Sumerians and Egyptians, for example, was broad-ranging, that of the Israelites focused on religious affairs.

Instruction in Israel

The basic premise of education in Israel was that all knowledge comes from God. Education was not simply to satisfy human curiosity, but a means to help people to use to the full the abilities given to them by God. Thus, elementary mathematics was needed for surveying land and calculating the harvest, and for large building works. Studying the movements of the sun, moon and stars helped in working out the calendar. But central to all this were God's laws, and it was the duty of every Israelite parent to make sure that their children were taught about God.

This jar from Hazor bears an inscription in ancient Hebrew: '[belonging] to Pekah Semadar'. Pekah ben Remalyahu (i.e. Remaliah) was king of Israel in 735–733 BC; 'semadar' may refer to a type of wine.

Adult education

Education in the Bible was not only for children. Abraham was told to teach the whole of his household. Moses taught the Israelites God's law. The Israelite kings sent Levites throughout the land to teach, although the prophets complained that this duty was often done badly and was regarded as a way of making money.

Children's schools

In the Old Testament, young men had the chance to become pupils of the prophets and priests. Samuel, for example, was looked after – and presumably taught – by a priest. And the prophet Isaiah gave private teaching to a group of disciples. In later times, the religious group known as the Pharisees appear to have organized a more formal school system. Children first went to school in the synagogue, which was known as 'the house of the book'; and further education took place in 'the house of study'.

Reading and writing

Opinions differ about how many people could read and write in Old Testament times. Some think that only the nobles could. However, the Old Testament records that Joshua expected written reports on the land of Canaan. And enough other examples of ancient Hebrew writing have been found to show that there was probably widespread knowledge of the skill.

Practical skills

There were no schools as such in early Old Testament times. The children were taught at home, first by their mother, then by their father. In addition to religion and history, which was learned through stories and by question and answer, and memorized, the girls learnt home-making skills – baking, spinning, weaving – from their mother, while the boys learned a manual trade from their father. The Israelites had a saying: 'He who does not teach his son a useful trade is bringing him up to be a thief.'

In this Egyptian pen case, reed pens can be seen alongside blocks with the remains of red and black ink.

Schools in Sumer

In Sumer, there were voluntary schools to train future secretaries for work in the temples, palace and business life. The pupil's family had to pay for the schooling, and so it was usually only the privilege of the rich. Botany, geography, mathematics, grammar and literature were all studied.

Education in Egypt

In ancient Egypt schools were often attached to the temples. After the elementary course, pupils transferred to a government department, where they studied written composition, natural science and the duties of office. There was special training in letter-writing, and 'model letters' have been found. If pupils were being trained to be priests, they studied theology and medicine.

Scribes

After the Israelites returned from exile in Babylon in the sixth century BC, a specialized class of Bible scholars, known as 'scribes', came into being. The scribes taught and explained the written law of God, and they applied this law to contemporary life. Their teachings built up into large collections of rules, which were regarded as having the same authority as the Old Testament itself. At first they were taught by word of mouth, but eventually they were written down to form the 'Mishnah', in about AD 200. Jesus seems to have known some of the scribes' debates, especially the teachings of Hillel and Shammai.

The New Testament gospels and letters were all written in the Greek language. This wooden writing tablet belonged to a Greek school pupil.

Greek education

By the time of Jesus, Greek education had become world-famous. Body, mind and soul, it was thought, needed room for expression. So the syllabus included athletics, philosophy, poetry, drama, music and rhetoric. Boys would attend elementary school between the ages of 7 and 15 years, and would then go to a 'gymnasium' for a wider education. A gymnasium was established in Jerusalem in 167 BC and, along with other Hellenistic innovations of Antiochus IV, led to the Maccabean revolt.

Development of the alphabet

Picture represents	Canaanite Sinai about 1500 BC	Phoenician about 1000 BC	Old Hebrew about 700 BC	Aramaic about 500 BC	Early Greek about 600 BC	Classical Greek 5th century BC	Hebrew 1st century AD	Roman
ox								A
house						B		B
throw-stick						Γ		G
palm of hand						K		K
staff						Λ		L
water						M		M
eye						O		O
head						R		R
fish						Δ		D
man						E		E

The development of the alphabet

The earliest writing used cuneiform, hieroglyphic and related scripts, but by the second millennium BC an early form of the alphabet was invented in Canaan. Over a period of several hundred years the alphabet developed, and the letters took standard shapes. Scribes trained in Babylonian traditions at Ugarit in Syria saw the advantages of an alphabet over the other scripts. There they composed an alphabet of 30 letters in cuneiform and wrote their own language with it.

By 1000 BC the alphabet was firmly established. In Syria and Canaan the newly settled Aramaeans, Israelites, Moabites and Edomites adopted it. Soon afterwards the Greeks learned it from the Phoenicians. They made some adjustments to suit their own language, especially the use of distinguishing signs for vowels.

The Aramaean tribes of Syria spread into Assyria and Babylonia, and many were carried off captive by Assyrian kings. They took with them their form of the alphabet. Jewish exiles adopted it and popularized it in Jerusalem in preference to the older Phoenician-Hebrew form. Arab tribesmen also borrowed it, and the modern Arabic script is descended from the letters they developed.

See also

■ The Sumerians (pages 50–51)

■ The Egyptians (pages 52–53)

■ The Greeks (pages 68–69)

■ The creator-God of Israel (pages 148–149)

■ Groups and sects (pages 168–169)

■ New Testament religion (pages 170–171)

Daily work

Throughout the Bible period most families were relatively self-sufficient, owning and farming land. Men built the family home and women were responsible for spinning and weaving. Parents were expected to pass on these practical skills to their children.

Farming in Jesus' time

Farming changed little in Palestine throughout the Bible period, although in other Mediterranean countries notable progress was made. The Pharisees often referred to those with no religious education as 'people of the land', which perhaps suggests that the farmer was not held in very high regard.

By New Testament times the land was being farmed much more intensively, and it had become quite common to keep poultry. A writer of the time described the fruit of Palestine as being better than that of any other land. The fertile region of Galilee produced large quantities of flax, and probably some attempts were being made at irrigation.

The sheep fold of New Testament times consisted of a circular stone wall with a gap as an entrance. Once the sheep were safely inside the fold, the shepherd would lay across the entrance to sleep. In the Bible, Jesus describes himself as 'the gate for the sheep'.

Shepherds in Bible times often looked after mixed flocks of sheep and goats, as in this recent photograph taken in the Judean hills.

Shepherds

The life of the shepherd seems to have altered little from the time of Abraham to that of Jesus. The shepherd led the sheep and goats to food and water, knew each one, and watched over them night and day. The shepherd carried a staff to catch hold of any animal which fell, and was armed with a wooden club. Despite the rough stone enclosures which served as folds, there was constant danger from thieves and wild beasts – lions, leopards and bears (until they became extinct), wolves and hyenas, jackals, snakes and scorpions. If sheep or goats were stolen the shepherd had to repay their value; if they were attacked by wild beasts, evidence was required.

Division of labour

In Bible times, every family owned some land, and all family members pitched in to help look after it. Whilst men worked the farm or their trade, children often had outdoor jobs to do, such as looking after the vines, ploughing and threshing; and looking after any animals the family kept – usually sheep and goats.

Women were responsible for the preparation of food and clothing. Milk was often made into cheese and yoghurt. Wool was spun, woven and dyed. Two essential daily jobs were baking bread and fetching water. Bread-making was a fairly strenuous activity, involving the back-breaking effort of grinding the grain into a coarse flour, even before preparing the dough and baking it. Water collection was no simple matter, either. Very few houses had their own well or underground water-storage cistern. And so water had to be fetched from the local spring or well, and carried home in heavy water-pots on the woman's head or shoulder.

The working day ended at sunset, when the whole family gathered together for the main meal of the day.

A reliable supply of fresh water was critical for survival in Bible times, and dictated the location of cities, towns and villages.

Farm animals

The word for 'cattle' in Hebrew includes sheep, goats, oxen and asses, but not pigs. Asses were kept for carrying loads, and oxen for ploughing. Only on special occasions were oxen killed for meat.

Sheep and goats were always kept together. Sheep mainly provided wool for clothes. They were occasionally eaten as meat – in Palestine their distinctive fat tail was considered a delicacy. They also provided milk in the form of curds for the very poor. Goats were valuable for meat and milk, some of which was allowed to go sour to produce goats' milk cheese. Their hair made coarse cloth and their skins made bottles.

Every family in Palestine, even the poorest, hoped to be able to buy two lambs for the annual Passover festival. One was killed and eaten, but the other became a playmate for the children. In a poor home there was no separate shed for the animals, and the lamb often slept with the children and ate from the same dishes.

The farming family

In the main, the people of Palestine have always been farmers, although the nature of the soil, the climate and other factors made farming a life of constant toil and hardship. When the Israelites first settled in Canaan, each household was given a plot of land and also, perhaps, grazing rights on land held in common. But the Bible records that, as time passed, those who were well-off tried to 'buy out' the small farmers, and it was a constant struggle for poor people to hold on to their land.

See also

■ Animals and birds (pages 92–93)

■ The farming year (pages 104–105)

■ Food and drink (pages 106–107)

■ Crafts and trades (pages 128–129)

■ Feasts and holy days (pages 154–155)

The farming year

Some time ago, a limestone tablet was discovered dating from about the time of King Solomon, on which was written a kind of school-child's rhyme. It is called the Gezer calendar, and it shows the farmer's year at a glance.

The Gezer calendar

The two months are (olive) harvest
The two months are planting (grain)
The two months are late planting
The month is hoeing up of flax
The month is harvest of barley
The month is harvest and feasting
The two months are vine tending
The month is summer fruit

The farming year as described on the Gezer calendar.

Ploughing and planting

Ploughing and planting took place from October and November, when the summer drought was broken, until January. The plough was usually a simple wooden stake, with a handle and a point of bronze or iron. It was attached to a yoke, and drawn by one or two oxen. The farmer could hold the plough with one hand while the other held a stick for beating the oxen. Since it was light the plough could easily be lifted over any large stones. The seed – wheat, barley and flax – was scattered by hand, and then the plough was sometimes used again to cover the seed with earth.

Late planting

During the months of January to March the winter rains fell in Palestine. This was a period for planting millet, peas, lentils, melons and cucumbers.

Vines

In June, July and August the vines were pruned and tidied up. The Old Testament book of Isaiah and the New Testament gospel of Mark both provide pictures of how the vines were planted and tended. A boundary trench was dug, and posts driven in to support a hedge or fence. The young vines were planted in rows, and the branches raised up on supports. Then the pruning was done. When the fruit began to form, a shelter of branches or a stone tower was put up, and the household kept watch against thieves.

The vineyard in Bible times was enclosed by a wall to keep out wild animals. Raiding birds could be frightened away from the watchtower. Baskets of grapes were stacked up with a large heavy stone on top. Juice from the grapes then flowed into the pit below, from which large portable earthenware jars were filled.

Grain harvest

In April, May and June barley and wheat were harvested. The stalks were cut with a sickle and the bundles were tied into sheaves. These were loaded on to donkeys or carts and taken to the 'threshing-floor'. This seems to have been common property, and a centre of village life at this time of year. It was usually a rocky outcrop, or clay-covered patch, in a windy spot outside the village. Stones were put around the edge and the sheaves were spread out on the floor about a foot deep.

A threshing sledge

Threshing and winnowing grain

Threshing was carried out by beating with a stick, by driving animals round or by using a threshing-sledge. This was simply a board, or a board on wheels, with bits of stone or iron fixed to it. The stalks were chopped and the grain loosened. The farmer would then 'winnow', tossing the stalks in the air with a wooden fork or shovel. The straw was blown aside (this was used in winter to feed the animals) but the heavy grain fell back on the floor. This was probably then sifted and stored in large earthenware jars, in dry cisterns or 'silos' dug in the floor, or in 'barns'.

In this millstone olive press, the olives were placed on a grooved circular stone, which was connected to a smaller stone by means of a wooden shaft. A second shaft in the top stone enabled the millstone to be rotated, thus pressing the pulp from the olives. The pulp was then pressed under weights to obtain the oil.

Olive harvest

From September or October to November olives were picked and pressed for oil. The olives were carried in baskets to vats and, in earlier times, the oil was squeezed out by treading, or pounding with a pestle. Later, a millstone olive press was developed.

Large olive presses have been found from the time of King David, consisting of a beam which would press on the baskets of olives. The upper end had weights attached, while the lower end was fixed in a hole in the wall. The oil ran into stone vats, where it was left for some time to settle and clear.

Oxen are pulling a threshing sledge as a woman and her daughter winnow grain.

Fruit harvest

In August and September the summer fruits were harvested – figs, sycamore figs, pomegranates and grapes. Baskets of grapes were taken to small vats, whose floors sloped towards jars. The grapes were trodden to squeeze out the juice. Great numbers of these vats have been found in the 'Shephelah', the low foothills between the coastal plain and the central highlands of Palestine.

Flax harvest

In March and April the 'later rain' came, developing the grain to the point where harvesting could begin. Flax was harvested in March and April. The plant was cut with a hoe near to the ground, and the stalks were dried, ready to be made into cord and linen cloth.

See also

■ Plants and flowers (pages 88–89)

■ Trees and shrubs (pages 90–91)

■ Food and drink (pages 106–107)

■ Clothes-making (pages 136–137)

■ Feasts and holy days (pages 154–155)

Food and drink

For most people in Palestine in Bible times, there was only just enough food to live on. People were vulnerable because unreliable rainfall, drought and pests such as locusts made their crops uncertain. Famines were an expected part of normal life. Furthermore, enemies often attacked during the growing season; if the crops were destroyed, the people could not survive.

Fruit

Fruit was an important food in Bible times. Grapes were eaten fresh at harvest time, and were also dried and used as raisins. Figs, too, could also be eaten fresh or dried. Dates are not mentioned by name in the Bible, but they were certainly grown. They were also used in a special sauce called *charoseth,* made from dates, figs, raisins and vinegar, in which everyone dipped their bread at the Passover meal. Olives were also eaten – some fresh, in October, and others after pickling in salt water. Pomegranates, almonds and pistachio nuts were also available, and citrus fruits were just becoming available in New Testament times.

Vegetables

Vegetables, such as onions and leeks, melons and cucumbers, were prepared and eaten as and when they came into season. Beans, lentils and peas were dried and stored in earthenware jars. Vegetables were used to make soups. In the Old Testament book of Genesis, Esau exchanged his birthright for a bowl of red lentil soup.

Bread

Bread in Bible times was made from a variety of grains. Barley bread was probably the most common, but wheat bread was also popular.

The grain was sorted and then ground. In early Bible times this was done by rubbing the grain between a small stone and a larger one. Later the grain was ground between two small millstones. The lower one was fixed; the upper one turned round on top of it.

For each baking, 40 litres/9 gallons of flour were mixed with water or olive oil to form a dough. A piece of fermented dough, known as 'leaven', from the previous baking was kneaded into the new dough, which was left to rise. Before baking, part of the dough was put aside for the next day's 'leavening'. The bread was baked as a flat cake.

This black basalt grinding stone from Jerusalem dates from the time of King Herod. It was used to grind grain into flour.

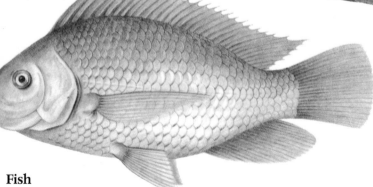

The saddle quern, common in ancient Bible lands, was used for grinding by hand. Grain was placed on the lower stone, and the upper stone was pushed backwards and forwards for grinding.

Lake Galilee supported about 25 species of fish, including this tilapia, now known as 'St Peter's fish'.

A sweet tooth

The Israelites had no sugar, and honey from wild bees was the main sweetener. Another kind of 'honey' may also have been produced by boiling dates and locust beans to make a syrup.

Fish

Fish was certainly an important food in Jesus' time. Small fish were dried and salted, and eaten with bread. Or they could be cooked over an open fire and eaten fresh, as at the breakfast Jesus prepared for his followers, recorded in the New Testament gospel of John.

Meat

People ate little meat in Bible times. Ordinary people normally ate mutton, goat's meat and birds – but only on special occasions. The wealthy ate lamb, veal and beef. Meat was normally boiled; the lamb roasted for the annual Passover festival was an exception.

Farm produce

Butter was not much used in Palestine because it would not keep in the hot weather. However, cheese and yoghurt were popular foods. And in New Testament times people kept hens and poached the eggs in olive oil.

Water

Although water was the basic liquid the Israelites used in cooking, it was not very good for drinking. Water from the local well or spring was generally safe enough, but water from the family cistern was far from safe. Even in Roman times, when water was brought to the towns by aqueduct (as it was to Caesarea and Bethlehem) or by pipeline (as it was to Jerusalem), the water was still not fit to drink. For this reason other liquids, such as goat's milk and wine, made better drinks.

See also

- Animals and birds (pages 92–93)
- Plants and flowers (pages 88–89)
- Food laws and customs (pages 108–109)
- Crafts and trades (pages 128–129)
- Genesis (pages 198–199)

This water cistern at Gibeon dates from the time of King David. The cistern is 11.3 m/37 ft in diameter and 10.8 m/35 ft deep.

Seasoning and preserving

Salt was used for seasoning food and, more importantly, for preserving it, too. There was plenty of rock salt on the south-west shores of the Dead Sea, and salt was also obtained by evaporation.

Mint, dill and cummin were used to give food the strong flavouring which everyone liked. They also helped give variety and interest to an otherwise boring diet. Rarer spices, imported from Africa and Asia, were used only by the wealthy.

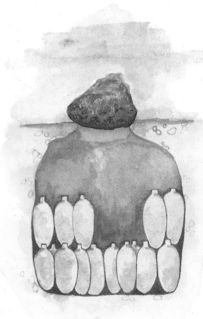

The wine cellars at Gibeon (right) contained 66 cavities for storing wine jars. By placing a large stone over the top of the cellar the ambient temperature could be kept at a constant 18°C. Each wine jar had a capacity of about 45 litres/10 gallons, and the cellar could hold up to a total of about 100,000 litres/22,000 gallons of wine.

Wine

Wine was the most common drink in Bible times. The New Testament records that Jesus provided wine for a wedding at Cana, and that he drank enough to be called a 'wine-bibber'. But people under a vow to God, or engaged on special service, sometimes gave up drinking it. Any drunkenness or excess was always condemned.

Wealthy homes in New Testament times had cellars of fine wines from all over the Mediterranean world. They were kept in narrow jars, called *amphorae*, with a pointed end, so that they could be pushed deep into earth or sand to keep the wine cool. But wine was usually stored in leather bottles, called 'wine-skins'.

This wine jar from Judea dates from the seventh century BC. The inscription reads: 'belonging to Yahzeyahu, wine of KHL'. KHL may be the name of a type of wine.

Food laws and customs

Throughout Bible times, the food laws and customs of the Israelites changed little. The religious laws regulated fairly tightly what could be eaten and how it should be prepared. Nonetheless, as in so many places today, meals were simple for the poor and more elaborate for the well-off.

Food typical of that eaten in Bible times.

Cooking

In Bible times, food was normally cooked by boiling, in a pot over a fire. Some foods were poached in oil, and bread, of course, was baked. Many vegetables were eaten raw. Lentils and beans were boiled in water or oil. Corn porridge was made with water, salt and butter.

Shopping

The town market was set up in the gateway. People selling the same goods formed groups, and normally set up their stalls together. In early Bible times, payment was by barter. But throughout most of the Old Testament period, people paid with weighed amounts of silver or, more rarely, gold. It was obviously necessary to have standard weights so that everyone knew the value, and this paved the way for coinage.

Baking bread

There were several methods of baking bread. The simplest was to scoop out a hole in the ground, make a fire in it, then remove the ash and stick the flat 'pancakes' of dough on the sides of the hole. Sometimes stones were put into the fire, and when the dough was ready for baking, the hot stones were taken out and the dough placed on them to cook. Or a large, shallow earthenware bowl was placed upside down over the fire, and the dough placed on that. Wealthier homes had a pottery oven, consisting of a beehive-shaped funnel. The fire was lit in the bottom of the funnel, and the bread was stuck on the inside towards the top. Not until Roman times was a divided oven invented, with the fire separate from the cooking area.

This woman is kneading dough ready to bake bread in the oven.

Israel's food laws

Old Testament law detailed what the Israelites may or may not eat. Only animals which chew their cud and have divided hoofs could be eaten. This ruled out the pig. Fish were allowed, but only those with fins and scales. Many birds were not to be eaten.

In New Testament times, too, a family which followed the teaching of the Pharisees was not allowed to buy or eat food which had been killed in a pagan temple as an offering. For three days before a festival they were not allowed to buy any food at all from a non-Jew.

The reason for these strict laws on diet was never explained in the Bible. They may have been a way of protecting the health of the people. They may have been intended to avoid cruelty to animals: for example, the law which required blood to be drained from a carcass before it was cooked prevented the practice of cutting a limb off a live animal for meat. Or they may have been

given for more strictly 'religious' reasons. This was certainly the reason for forbidding meat which had been offered to an idol.

Food is being offered to Egyptian gods on this relief from the temple of Seti I in Abidos.

Meals for the rich

In wealthy homes, people enjoyed elaborate food with plenty of meat. Instead of one dish, as in poorer households, there were many. A Roman-style dinner party would follow this pattern: first came the *hors d'oeuvres*, and wine mixed with honey. Next, three main courses were served on trays. After this course, pieces of food were thrown into the fire as a token 'sacrifice' to the gods. Finally, pastries and fruit were served as dessert. This was followed by drinks and entertainment.

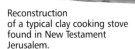

Meals for the poor

In the peasant home in Palestine, meals were very simple. There was no formal breakfast. If anything was eaten at all, it was as a snack carried and eaten on the way to work. The midday meal was usually bread and olives, and perhaps fruit. The evening meal was a vegetable stew, with a piece of bread used as a spoon to dip into the common pot. The whole family ate together for this meal, and if any important guests were present, meat might be added to the cooking-pot. The family sat on the floor to eat.

Reconstruction of a typical clay cooking stove found in New Testament Jerusalem.

Meals for the nomads

Among the nomadic, tent-dwelling people, a traveller was always welcome to stay – for three days and four hours, which was the length of time the hosts believed their food sustained their guest. Flat loaves of bread, and milk, were the basic elements of the meal. During the visit, the traveller became one of the clan. The Bible teaches the importance of hospitality. As the author of the New Testament letter to the Hebrews writes: 'Remember to welcome strangers in your homes.'

See also

Inside the home
(pages 114–115)

God's laws in practice
(pages 152–153)

Priests and rituals
(pages 162–163)

Groups and sects
(pages 168–169)

New Testament religion
(pages 170–171)

The Torah or Pentateuch
(pages 196–197)

Clothing and cosmetics

Clothing styles changed little in Palestine throughout most of the Bible period. The main differences in dress were between the rich and poor. Poor peasants owned only the woollen or goats'-hair clothes they stood up in. But rich people had clothes for winter and for summer; clothes for working and clothes for leisure; and clothes of different materials, including fine linen and even silk.

Hair fashions

Orthodox Jews today wear their hair long, according to ancient tradition.

The Israelite men normally grew their hair long, and many wore beards. They sometimes plaited their hair. At other times it was trimmed by the barber. The hair at the sides of the head, by the ears, was never cut. The Old Testament book of Leviticus forbade it as a pagan practice – a law still observed by Orthodox Jews. By New Testament times, under the influence of the Greeks and Romans, hair was worn short and many men were clean-shaven.

Women plaited, braided or curled their hair. It was often kept in place by beautiful ivory combs. In Roman times the hair was piled on top of the head and kept in place by a net. The rich had nets of gold thread.

Men's clothing

The first item of clothing a man put on was either a loincloth or a short skirt which covered him from waist to knee. Over the top of this came a calf-length shirt or tunic made of wool or linen. This was like a big sack: a long piece of material folded at the centre and sewn up the sides, with holes for the arms and a slit at the folded end for the head to go through. The tunic was usually red, yellow, black or striped.

The tunic was fastened round the waist with a girdle or belt. This was a piece of cloth, folded into a long strip to make a kind of pocket to hold coins and other belongings. If a man was rich he might have a leather belt with a dagger or an inkhorn pushed into it. When a man needed to be able to move more freely, to work, he would tuck his tunic into his belt to make it much shorter. This was called 'girding up the loins'.

Bronze mirror from Canaanite tomb at Acco. 14th century BC.

Women's clothing

Women in Palestine wore a tunic which was very similar to a man's, but was ankle-length. It was often blue, and may have been embroidered on the yoke using a traditional pattern pertaining to the village. When working, a woman could lift up the hem of her long dress and use it as a large bag, even for carrying items such as corn.

Coats

Outdoors, a rich man would wear a light coat over his tunic. This came down to his knees and was often brightly striped, or woven in check patterns. Rich people wore lightweight coats indoors as well, perhaps made from imported silk.

Poorer people wore a thick woollen coat or cloak in New Testament times. This was made from two pieces of material, often in stripes of light and dark brown, stitched together. The joined material was wrapped round the body, sewn at the shoulders, and slits were then made in the side for the arms to go through.

Footwear

Although many poor people probably went barefoot, sandals were the normal footwear in Palestine. Sandals were removed before entering someone's home and before entering a holy place. According to custom, the right sandal was always put on and taken off before the left. A man selling property took off his sandal and gave it to the buyer as a token that he gave up his right to the property.

The simplest sandals were made from a piece of hide the same size as the foot, with a long leather strap which passed between the big toe and the second toe. They were then tied round the ankle.

Make-up

In ancient Bible lands, women wore dark eyeshadow around their eyes. At first, this was to protect their eyes against the strong sunshine, but it soon became a matter of fashion. Eyeshadow was made by grinding up minerals in oil or gum with a small pestle and mortar.

Women also used lipstick and powder-puffs. They painted their toe nails and finger nails red with dye from the crushed leaves of the henna plant, and red iron oxide appears to have been used as rouge.

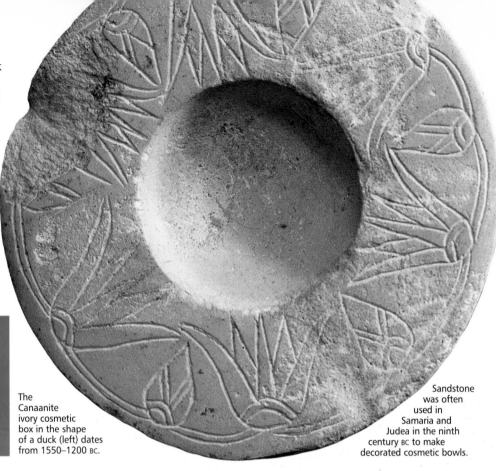

The Canaanite ivory cosmetic box in the shape of a duck (left) dates from 1550–1200 BC.

Sandstone was often used in Samaria and Judea in the ninth century BC to make decorated cosmetic bowls.

Headgear

In Palestine the sun was so hot that some covering was needed to protect the head, neck and eyes. This was usually a square of cloth folded diagonally, with the fold across the forehead. A circle of plaited wool held it in place over the head, and the folds protected the neck. A cap was sometimes worn, and a fine wool shawl or *tallith* over it, especially during prayer. Women put pads on their heads to steady the jars of water and other objects they carried.

Jewellery

Bracelets, necklaces, pendants, anklets and rings – for ears and noses as well as fingers – were all worn in Palestine on special occasions They were made from gold, silver and other metals, and set with precious or semi-precious stones, or even coloured glass. The stones were smoothed and polished, engraved and sculptured. Ivory was beautifully carved. It was used to make hair-combs, brooches and plaques, as well as vases and flasks for cosmetics.

Perfume

Oil, rubbed into the body to soothe the skin, was almost essential in the hot, dry climate of Bible lands. Perfume, added to the oil, helped to disguise body odour where there was not much water for washing. Perfume was extracted from flowers, seeds and fruit, or came from gums or resins. Many perfumes were imported into Palestine and were a luxury. Because of their cost, they were kept in very expensive bottles and containers.

See also

■ Plants and flowers (pages 88–89)

■ Inside the home (pages 114–115)

■ Crafts and trades (pages 128–129)

■ Mining and metalwork (pages 134–135)

■ Clothes-making (pages 136–137)

This jewellery dating from the 13th century BC was discovered complete with its own jewellery box at Tel Naami on the north coast of Palestine.

Tents and houses

In Bible lands there have always been 'nomads' – people who move from place to place – as well as those with settled homes. For hundreds of years Abraham's descendants lived in tents: first in Canaan, then in Egypt, then in the desert. When they conquered the Canaanites, they took over their cities – and copied their architectural style.

Stones

In the mountains, where limestone and basalt were freely available, and on the coast, where sandstone was found, roughly squared stone was used for the foundations of houses, with rough stone or brick walls nearly 91 cm/3 ft thick built on top. These thick walls were hollowed out and alcoves made for storage. Initially the walls were little more than rubble, but as iron tools became available for shaping stone more easily, the stones were roughly squared.

The central courtyard in this eighth-century BC Israelite house would have been home to the animals. Rooms were separated by solid walls or by pillars. Access to the roof was by means of a ladder or an outside staircase.

Living in tents

Nomadic peoples in Bible times lived, like the modern Bedouin, in goats'-hair tents. The black and brown striped material was woven from goats' hair after shearing time, using a loom pegged out on the ground. Wooden rings were stitched along the edge of the material and in the centre to take nine poles in three rows. The middle row of poles was about 1.8 m/6 ft high, and the two outer rows a little shorter. The tent was made by propping up a long length of goats'-hair cloth about 1.8 m/6 ft wide, and living in the area underneath it.

The area under the 'roof' was closed at the back with a screen made of goats'-hair cloth, or reeds and twigs woven together. It was then divided into two 'rooms'. One formed an open porch where visitors could be received, and the remainder was curtained off for the use of the women and for the household stores. The only adult male who could enter this part was the head of the family. Sometimes the ground under the tent was covered with woven matting, but more often it was left as bare earth. Tents were pitched in groups for protection.

Reconstruction of an Israelite house

Windows and doors

Windows were few and tiny, set high up in the wall for coolness in summer and warmth in winter. There was no glass. Instead, a lattice shutter was put across the hole to keep intruders out. Thick woollen curtains were used in the cold, wet season, to keep the weather out. At first. doors were made of woven twigs. Then, as skills developed, wood and metal were used.

Roofs

In Old Testament times, the roof was made by laying beams across the width of the walls, and laying smaller beams at right angles across them. Layers of brushwood, earth and clay were then added to the beams, and the whole structure was made firm by using a stone roller which was kept on the roof. As building skills improved, permanent upper storeys became more common. The Old Testament records that a rich woman at Shunem built on a special guest-room for the prophet Elisha. By New Testament times, tiled and pitched roofs were being built.

See also

- The exodus from Egypt (pages 20–21)
- The Israelites enter Canaan (pages 22–23)
- Inside the home (pages 114–115)
- Building and builders (pages 132–133)
- Clothes-making (pages 136–137)

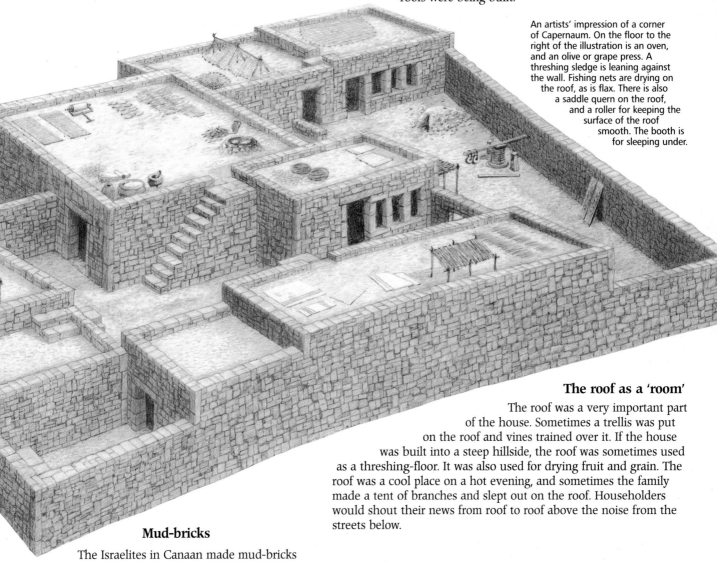

An artists' impression of a corner of Capernaum. On the floor to the right of the illustration is an oven, and an olive or grape press. A threshing sledge is leaning against the wall. Fishing nets are drying on the roof, as is flax. There is also a saddle quern on the roof, and a roller for keeping the surface of the roof smooth. The booth is for sleeping under.

The roof as a 'room'

The roof was a very important part of the house. Sometimes a trellis was put on the roof and vines trained over it. If the house was built into a steep hillside, the roof was sometimes used as a threshing-floor. It was also used for drying fruit and grain. The roof was a cool place on a hot evening, and sometimes the family made a tent of branches and slept out on the roof. Householders would shout their news from roof to roof above the noise from the streets below.

Mud-bricks

The Israelites in Canaan made mud-bricks for the walls of houses, especially those built in the plains and valleys. First, they dug a hole in the ground and filled it with water, chopped straw, palm fibre, and bits of shell and charcoal. They then trampled the mixture until they had a soft and pliable mud. This was placed in wooden moulds to make large bricks about 53 cm x 25 cm x 10 cm/21 in x 10 in x 4 in. Most bricks were laid out to dry in the hot sun, but kilns produced stronger bricks which were used for the foundations of houses.

Floors

Sometimes stone chippings were worked into the earth floor of houses in Palestine. But it was only under Greek influence, after about 300 BC, that the art of making mosaic floors was developed. Even then this was frowned on for religious reasons, and the only mosaic floors found in Israel during Bible times were in the palace of King Herod the Great at Masada and in rich houses in Jerusalem.

Inside the home

People in the East, even today, have much less cluttered homes than many in Western countries. The style, for both rich and poor, is cool and simple – with just a few mats for the floor, seating, small tables and some kind of heating for winter.

Life in the ordinary home

The floor area of ordinary houses in Bible times was divided into two rooms. The animals were brought into the lower area of the house near the door during winter. The family lived on a raised platform, farthest away from the door. The space underneath may have been used for storing tools and jars – and even keeping small animals. Cooking utensils,

Reconstruction of a rural house in Palestine, showing the bread-baking oven (the 'taboon') with earthenware pots and jars, baskets and grinding stones.

clothes and bedding were kept on the platform. During hot weather, the house was alive with insects; when the weather grew cold, it was filled with smoke from the fire. There was no real fireplace; the fire smouldered in a hole in the earth floor. If the family was wealthy enough, they warmed themselves around a brazier, but there was no chimney. When it rained hard and continuously, the roof and the walls leaked. There were no facilities for bathing.

Lamps

Because houses were so dark, one of the most important items in any household was the lamp. Throughout the Old Testament period lamps were simply pottery dishes with a lip at one side. Oil was poured into the dish and a wick laid from it to the lip. Such a lamp might stay alight for two or three hours, and then it would need refilling.

By New Testament times potters had learnt how to make lamps in moulds, completely covered over, with a small hole for the oil and a spout for the wick. This was safer and more efficient. The wicks were usually strips of flax or rag. Oil used for the lamps included olive oil and oil from other seeds and vegetables, as well as animal fat.

Development of the lamp throughout Bible times.

Furniture for the poor

Throughout Bible times the poor possessed very little by way of furniture and furnishings. The 'bed' was a thin wool-filled mattress, spread out each evening on the raised part of the floor. The whole family slept there, under goats'-hair quilts. In the morning they rolled or piled up the bed and bedding and stacked it away. The table was often simply a straw mat laid out on the raised floor. In some homes, but by no means all, there were stools to sit on.

Utensils

Every house had stone or clay storage bins in which they kept fodder for the animals as well as food stores for the family. There were special jars for storing flour and olive oil, and earthenware pots for carrying and storing water. There were cooking pots, too, and bowls for serving food. In wealthier homes, some of these utensils were made from metal.

Brooms for cleaning were made of corn stalks. They were kept with the tools needed for the family trade.

By New Testament times glass, moulded on a core, and produced in Egypt, was used. In about 50 BC, the art of glass-blowing was developed in Syria. But although this made glass cheaper, it was still beyond the reach of most people.

Glass utensils dating from Roman times.

Reconstruction of the reception hall of a wealthy home in New Testament Jerusalem.

Life in the wealthy home

From the time of King Solomon a wealthy class began to emerge in Israel, and life was much more comfortable for them. Rooms were extended around courtyards and gardens which provided shade and cool currents of air in the summer. In winter it was possible to use rooms in a warmer, sunnier position. The whole house was built on a much larger scale than poorer houses, with pillars to support roof beams. Once pillars were used it was possible to have porches and colonnades. In the Old Testament book of Amos, the prophet talks about the 'winter houses and summer houses' enjoyed by the rich.

In the time between the Old and New Testaments wealthy people even began to add special bathrooms, with tubs set into the floor. Sergius Orata is said to have invented a centrally heated bathroom, with a hot water supply, in about 70 BC! By New Testament times rich people in Palestine had houses built Roman-style, with two rectangular courtyards, one behind the other, each surrounded by rooms.

See also

- The first kings (pages 26–27)
- A brief history of Jerusalem (pages 38–39)
- Tents and houses (pages 112–113)
- Crafts and trades (pages 128–129)
- Pottery (pages 130–131)
- Three temples (pages 160–161)

Comforts of the rich

The rich had a good many comforts – including high beds, tables, chairs and couches – which were beyond the reach of poorer households in Bible times. These were often made of fine wood, carved and inlaid with bone or ivory. There were also pillows for their beds, and fine wool blankets. Extra clothes and bedding were stored in chests.

The greatest luxury of all was to be found in the temples and royal palaces. King Solomon, for example, built his palace using well-cut stone and lined his walls with cedar. King Ahab's palace at Samaria boasted beautiful carved ivory inlays and expensive furniture. Herod the Great had two palaces: a summer palace with lovely gardens at Jerusalem, and a winter palace at Jericho.

The remains of pillars which once supported the floor of the bathhouse hot room of Herod's palace at Masada.

Kings and rulers

During the long history of the Bible, the system of government and administration in Israel evolved from its beginnings as a patriarchy. Other nations had various administrative systems in place; of these, that of the Roman empire was the most sophisticated.

Israel before the kings

To begin with, the structure of authority was based on the pattern of the family, with the father as the ultimate authority, the 'patriarch', under God.

By the time of the exodus, Abraham's 'family' had grown into a nation. But the basic structure was the same. Israel was a nation of 12 family-clans. Moses, their new leader, was responsible for 'government' and settling disputes. And the people formally accepted God as their king and law maker.

In Canaan, the Israelites lived for some time as a federation of tribes united by their common ancestry and worship of one God. There were 'judges', but they had limited authority, at least until the time of Samuel. But the people wanted to have a king as other nations did. And so it was that Saul became the first king of Israel.

The seal impression on the pottery jar handle below reads: 'belonging to the king'. This example is one of about 1,200 from Judah, dating from the reign of Hezekiah in the eighth century BC. All were made from clay from the same source in the Shephelah.

Solomon divided his kingdom into 12 administrative districts, (numbered on the map), which cut across traditional tribal boundaries. This was a factor in the transfer of power from tribal elders to a centralized adminstration.

Governors and elders

King Solomon divided the land of Israel into 12 areas, each under a district-governor. The governors had to provide food from their districts for the king and his household, and they reported to a chief governor. Within these divisions, each city and the villages around it appointed its own council of elders. The exception was the capital, Jerusalem, which probably had a governor who reported direct to the king.

The kings' officials

The Bible gives three lists of officials in the administration of kings David and Solomon. Among these was the 'master of the palace', who in the early days of the monarchy may simply have managed the king's property. But he soon came to be the king's chief minister. The royal secretary was both the king's personal scribe and secretary of state. He ranked below the 'master of the palace'. The role of the 'royal herald' is not clear, but he was certainly important in the king's court. He may have kept the king aware of public opinion, as a kind of royal public relations officer.

The kings also employed military officials. The king had a personal bodyguard of regular troops, in addition to the Israelite army which could call every able-bodied man to arms. The professional troops and the conscripted army had separate commanders; both reported direct to the king.

The divided monarchy

Much of the administrative system established by kings David and Solomon was long-lasting. For example, the Old Testament records that nearly three centuries later, when Jerusalem was besieged by the Assyrians, the chief officials were still the ones in charge of the palace, the court secretary and the official in charge of the records.

'Yaazaniahu the king's slave' reads the inscription on this stone seal. It was discovered in Tel Mizpah, and dates from about the seventh century BC.

Priests and elders

After the exile in Babylon, the Jews came under the political control of various foreign powers. But, in religious matters the nation returned to the theory of 'rule by God', and maintained its identity as a religious community with its own religious laws administered by priests and elders.

The Roman empire

During the New Testament period, the Jews were living under Roman rule. Outside Italy there were two sorts of provinces in the Roman empire. The Senate kept control of the provinces where peace was established, appointing different governors, called 'proconsuls', each year. The Roman emperor took charge of the provinces which required troops to keep order. He ruled through deputies appointed for four or five years at a time: 'legates' in charge of larger areas; 'prefects' or 'procurators' in charge of smaller and more troublesome ones. Native kings were allowed to rule in some areas, as long as they complied with what Rome wanted.

Roman government

The Roman emperor's government was responsible for maintaining law and order. But it also made and maintained some of the best roads ever built, and provided local government offices, markets, baths and other public amenities. These were paid for with money raised from taxes imposed on the local people: property tax, purchase tax, customs duties – and even duties on food. The Roman censor in each area hired tax collectors to bring the money in, and people were often forced to pay far more than the required legal amount.

Roman 'free cities'

The Roman authorities allowed some cities in the empire, including Athens and Ephesus, to be self-governing. This status as a 'free city' held only as long as the peace was kept. Certain 'holy cities' also retained some control over their own affairs, including Jerusalem, where the high priest and the Jewish council, called the 'Sanhedrin', administered local affairs. But their real authority was limited by Rome. The death sentence on Jesus, for example, could be imposed only by the Roman governor.

Roman colonies

Many towns in the Roman empire became Roman colonies. They were regarded as outposts of Rome itself, and were governed, like the capital, by two magistrates. Philippi was one of several colonies featured in the New Testament.

See also

- The exodus from Egypt (pages 20–21)
- The Israelites enter Canaan (pages 20–21)
- The first kings (pages 26–27)
- The Romans (pages 72–73)
- Priests and rituals (pages 162–163)
- Old Testament history: overview (pages 204–205)

Legend:
- to Antipas
- to Archelaus
- to Philip

A Roman province

In Palestine, King Herod the Great was allowed to rule in Judea from 37 BC until his death in 4 BC. His kingdom was then divided into three areas, each ruled by one of Herod's three sons (see map, left). Antipas ruled Galilee and Perea, Philip ruled Ituraea and Trachonitis, and Archelaus ruled Judea, including Samaria and Idumea. Archelaus was unable to keep order, and in AD 6 Judea became a Roman province, governed by a 'prefect' responsible to the emperor, but supervised by the 'legate' of Syria.

Pontius Pilate was the fifth 'prefect', or 'procurator', to govern Judea. He remained there from AD 26 to AD 36.

Coins of the family of Herod
The coin at the top is of King Herod the Great, dating from 37 BC. Below, from the left, are the coins of Herod's sons: Antipas (depicting a palm branch), Archelaus (depicting grapes) and Philip (depicting the front of the temple).

Warfare

War is a dominant theme in the Old Testament. From the early days of Israel's history, every man was called to be a soldier. Under the Israelite kings, a more formal and structured army was established, but by New Testament times this had ceased to exist.

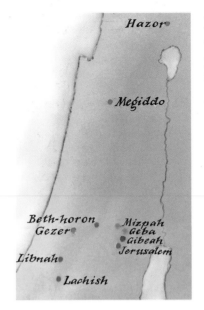

Preparations for war

It was important for an invading army to find food close to hand. This was one reason why wars often took place in spring. Surprise was also important, so war was rarely declared. Sometimes nations would provoke war by making impossible demands. Troops were gathered by blowing the ram's horn, by signals set on a hill or by sending messengers through the land.

The Israelite kings sought God's advice, usually through the prophets and priests. If the response from God was favourable, the army set out, taking with them priests and sometimes symbols of their faith, such as objects from the tabernacle. Before the battle started, the priest offered a sacrifice. King Saul sought advice through dreams and, on one occasion, consulted a medium – something that brought him into conflict with the religious leader, Samuel.

Fortresses

The Israelite kings built fortresses to protect their land (see map, left). Saul fortified his capital, Gibeah. David, in addition to work on Jerusalem, built the fortresses of Libnah, Lachish, Gezer and Beth-horon in the foothills, as a defence against the Philistines. Solomon strengthened many cities, especially Gezer, Hazor and Megiddo, guarding the strategic pass through the Carmel hills. When Israel was divided into the northern and southern kingdoms, border fortresses were established at Geba and Mizpah.

The Israelite army

King Saul established the first standing army in Israel, with 3,000 men under his direct command, but it was King David who realized the importance of the army's allegiance being given to the king in person, rather than to the nation. Under David's leadership, the general strategy and tactics of open warfare began to be more skilfully planned. The Israelites learned new military tactics and began to adopt the practice of laying siege to a city.

Canaanites equipped with iron chariots are ambushed by Israelite foot soldiers in this scene from the time of the Israelite judges.

Assyrian soldiers destroy the walls of a city in north Syria with battering rams on this bronze relief from the gates of Balawat (near Calah).

Army structure

The Bible speaks of 'fifties' and 'hundreds' with their commanders, but very little is known of the detailed organization of the army under the Israelite kings. For a long time the army was composed almost entirely of foot-soldiers – some equipped as archers or slingers, others for hand-to-hand combat. The cavalry and chariots used by the Egyptians, Philistines and Canaanites were introduced under King Solomon, but the Israelites fought mainly in the hills, where these methods were impractical.

Greek regimental markings on moulded lead slingstones (above).

The Canaanite dagger (left) dates from the 15th century BC.

The aftermath of battle

When a city was taken, it was the usual practice to kill, mutilate or enslave all adult male inhabitants. Women and children were taken captive. The walls were broken down and buildings burnt, and the soldiers were usually free to take whatever plunder they could find, though the more valuable items were claimed by the king. If a city submitted, hostages were taken and a heavy tribute demanded.

Raids and combat

Israel suffered a great deal from raiding bands of desert tribes, especially before the time of the kings. Their attacks were swift and unpredictable, and they plundered the villages, destroyed crops, and took cattle and captives.

When there was open combat, a trumpet gave the signal for attack, and sometimes there was a pre-arranged war-cry. A line of men carrying rectangular shields and long lances would advance, and then the archers would let fly a volley of arrows to cover them. When the lines met, fighting was hand to hand. Occasionally the issue was decided by contest between two or more champions.

Attack and defence

The weapons used in war depended on the type of combat. In hand-to-hand fighting, clubs, axes, and short and long swords were used. There were darts, spears and javelins for throwing. And there were many missiles, from stones and boulders to bows and arrows.

Soldiers wore armour to protect themselves, and carried a shield for defence. The Israelites appear to have used two types of shield. A small, round one was carried by the light armed infantry, and a large, rectangular one was used by the men at the front, so that the battle line presented a solid front. The shields were made of a wicker or wooden frame covered with leather, which needed regular oiling. Inside the shield was a handle for holding it.

After the exile

After the period of exile in Babylon which began to end in 539 BC, the Jews did not have an established army. This remained the case except for one short period when foreign mercenaries as well as Jews were employed as soldiers. King Herod the Great had his own forces, which were under Roman command.

See also

■ The time of the judges (pages 24–25)

■ The first kings (pages 26–27)

■ Mining and metalwork (pages 134–135)

■ Priests and rituals (pages 162–163)

■ The prophets (pages 166–167)

Superior weapons, well-developed strategy and iron discipline made Roman troops invincible for centuries.

119

Cities, towns and villages

The difference between a city or town and a village in Bible times was not its size but its defences. Villages were unwalled settlements. Cities and towns had walls around them. They were built on top of a hill, or a mound formed by the ruins of earlier towns, for defence, and they needed a good water supply close by.

Early villages

The 'village' of Old Testament times was simply an unwalled farming settlement. Villages grew up near a stream or spring that would provide water all year round. Archaeology has shown that people were farming at Jericho, using picks, axes and digging sticks, as long ago as 6000 BC. At this stage there were only villages and no towns.

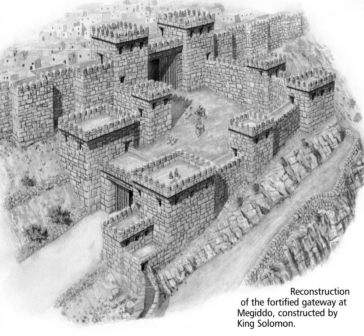

Reconstruction of the fortified gateway at Megiddo, constructed by King Solomon.

The first towns

Towns were first established some time after 4000 BC, when the invention of the bronze ploughshare led to increased food production. Towns were needed because of the struggle between settled and nomadic peoples who wanted the same water supplies. Towns were built up as larger, protected centres of civilization. In peacetime, people lived out in the villages, but when invasion threatened they gathered to the safety of the town.

Town life

The fortified gateway was the main open space in each town. In daytime the gates were noisy and crowded, bustling with life – merchants arriving; people buying and selling; elders meeting in council; others settling disputes and hearing cases. Beggars, pedlars, workers, scribes, visitors, traders and shoppers – with their asses, camels and even cattle – all gathered at the city gate.

In the bigger towns there was more space for the shopkeepers. Sometimes each trade had its own area, but there were no specially built shops. Each trader set out the goods on a stall at the side of the street. At night they were packed away. The city gates were closed and barred.

Towns in early Israel

Towns in early Israel were often very small, with about 150–250 houses and a population of about 1,000 people. Life in the towns was very cramped. Houses were poorly built, and joined up house-to-house. Where the ground sloped, houses were built one above the other. There were no real streets – just spaces between houses – and no paving. Drains were open channels. Mud and rubbish piled up outside, so that the level of the alleys was often higher than the ground-floor of the houses. Rain turned the whole mess into a swamp.

In winter, people were cooped up in the damp and filth. The summer sun helped, though the smells remained. But by then most of the people had moved away from the town to live and work in the fields. During peacetime people tended to live in villages for two-thirds of the year and in towns for the rest.

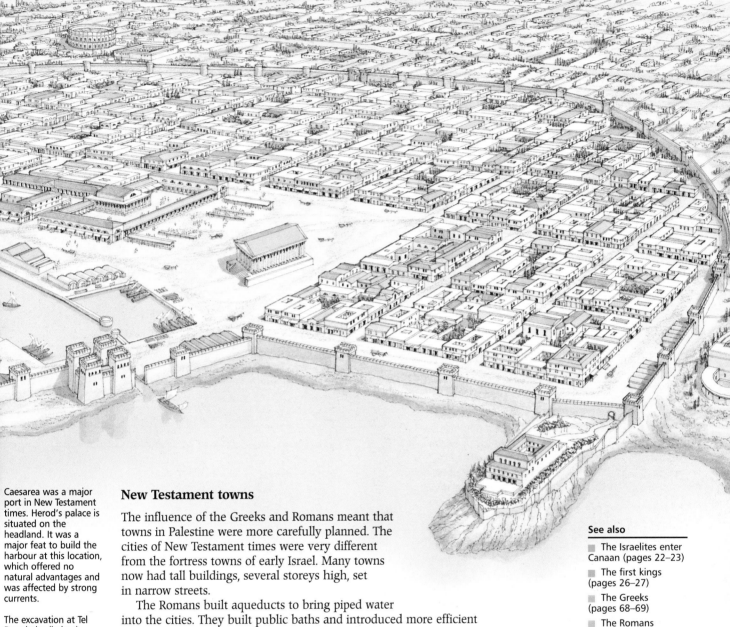

Caesarea was a major port in New Testament times. Herod's palace is situated on the headland. It was a major feat to build the harbour at this location, which offered no natural advantages and was affected by strong currents.

The excavation at Tel Beersheba (below) reveals structures from the monarchy period. In the Old Testament, Beersheba was located on the southern boundary of the land.

New Testament towns

The influence of the Greeks and Romans meant that towns in Palestine were more carefully planned. The cities of New Testament times were very different from the fortress towns of early Israel. Many towns now had tall buildings, several storeys high, set in narrow streets.

The Romans built aqueducts to bring piped water into the cities. They built public baths and introduced more efficient drainage works to take away waste water and sewage.

King Herod the Great rebuilt Samaria (renamed Sebaste) and Caesarea in the Roman style, with a main street through the centre of the city, lined with shops, baths and theatres, and crossed at right angles by smaller streets. Houses were built in blocks of four.

See also

- The Israelites enter Canaan (pages 22–23)
- The first kings (pages 26–27)
- The Greeks (pages 68–69)
- The Romans (pages 72–73)
- Building and builders (pages 132–133)
- Feasts and holy days (pages 154–155)

Landowners

When the Israelites entered Canaan, a plot of land was allocated to each of the 12 tribes. The Old Testament book of Isaiah states that each person's land was the gift of God, not to be casually bought and sold. Every 50th year was a year of jubilee, when any land which had been mortgaged to pay off a debt was to be returned to the family.

Under the Israelite kings, beginning with David and Solomon, the old equality began to break down. A new wealthy class of rulers and officials grew up.

They oppressed the poor and bought up land. Big estates took the place of small family farms. The people who had lost their land had to hire themselves out as farm labourers. The poor were very poor, and suffered great hardship.

This change in the ownership of land also led to a change in housing. In the tenth century BC, all the houses in a town or village were the same size, but by the eighth century BC some houses were bigger and better, and were grouped in a particular part of the town.

Travel and transport

The Bible describes many journeys. In the Old Testament, for example, Abraham moves into Canaan, Jacob goes to Egypt and the Israelites journey through the desert. The New Testament recounts in some detail the travels of Paul and other Christian leaders, and Jesus himself must have covered considerable distances during his public ministry.

Walking

In Bible times most journeys were made on foot. Not everybody could afford to keep a pack animal and, even if a family owned an ass, on a family journey someone would have to walk.

Carts and chariots

In Old Testament times the use of wheeled transport was limited. Carts drawn by asses or cattle were used on farms. Horse-drawn chariots were used by armies and by the rich, although the condition of the ground restricted their use.

By New Testament times first-class roads facilitated the more widespread use of chariots of various types – from the light chariots used for racing to more substantial carriages with room to seat at least two people. In the towns, where the streets were often very narrow, those who could afford it travelled in 'litters'. These litters were couches with a framework so that curtains could conceal the traveller. They rested on poles which were carried by men, or sometimes by horses.

War chariot dating from 2600 BC.

The earliest cart wheels (left) were made by slicing timber in the direction of the grain, shaping into two semi-circles and then joining them with two strips of wood.

Sailing

The great seafaring nations of the Old Testament period were the Egyptians and the Phoenicians. They built warships and trading vessels, powered by sails and oars. Israel's only successful attempt to develop a fleet of ships came during King Solomon's reign, at a time when the Phoenicians controlled the Mediterranean Sea. Indeed, it was Hiram, king of Tyre in Phoenicia, who provided Solomon with expert help in constructing a merchant fleet based at the town of Ezion-geber, at the head of the Gulf of Aqaba.

At the time of Jesus, Rome controlled the Mediterranean Sea. Corn grown in Egypt and exported from Alexandria was vital to the economic stability of the Roman Empire. State-run grain-ships carried the corn to Italy.

Roads

There were few paved roads in Palestine until the time of the Roman empire. The Romans built a system of excellent roads, connecting the provinces of the empire to Rome. The motivation behind this was to hold the empire together, to make it possible to move troops and goods, and to send imperial despatches long distances at speed. A courier on the Roman roads could cover about 120 km/75 miles a day.

Roman roads were superbly constructed, and many sections remain intact, even today. They were paved with flat stones, or with specially cut blocks of stone on top of two or three layers of foundation material. The road-builders overcame every obstacle. They built bridges over rivers and causeways through marshes, and they tunnelled through rock. Even so, the roads only went where the Romans wanted them to go. There were still many journeys that had to be made on the old 'roads', unsurfaced and worn by travellers over the centuries.

In towns, the streets were not very clean, so the Romans provided pedestrians with raised pavements and stepping-stones to allow them to avoid the dirt and mud.

This detail of a relief from the palace of King Sargon II depicts logs being transported in boats. King Solomon bought cedar wood from Lebanon to build the temple.

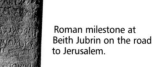

Roman milestone at Beith Jubrin on the road to Jerusalem.

Caravan convoys

Throughout Bible times, traders travelled together as a 'caravan' – a convoy of asses and camels – for company and as a protection against thieves. The caravan routes crossed Palestine in all directions. With the Mediterranean Sea to the west and the Syrian desert to the east, all traffic between Mesopotamia and Arabia, Egypt and the rest of Africa had to pass through a narrow corridor about 120 km/75 miles wide. Great cities grew up at strategic points on these routes. One of these was Palmyra, a desert city fortified by King Solomon.

See also
- The world of the patriarchs (pages 18–19)
- The journeys of Paul (pages 44–45)
- The Romans (pages 74–75)
- Trade and commerce (pages 124–125)

Ships of King Solomon's merchant fleet are moored in port.

Riding

Although the nomads of the desert kept camels, the main beast of burden throughout Bible times was the ass. The ass was domesticated long before either the horse or the camel, and was always the most popular means of general transport. Camels were used more frequently in Israel from about 1000 BC with the development of international trade, particularly the Arabian spice trade.

Horses were usually kept for war. They were expensive to feed compared with camels and asses, and could not carry as much. But by New Testament times they were often used for civilian purposes.

123

Trade and commerce

Local trade in Bible times was eventually supplemented by international trade; Palestine was well-situated for both land and sea trade routes. By New Testament times, trade and commerce were subject to strict regulations.

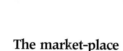

Local trade

In Old Testament times, Israelite farmers were poor. They generally produced only enough for their family's needs, and there were few things they needed that they could not make themselves. Travel and transport were difficult. So, for a long time, local trade was probably very simple. But market-places gradually developed around the gates of towns and cities. Farm produce, sheep and goats were sold there. Potters and smiths made and sold their goods, and visiting foreign merchants set up their stalls.

On this potsherd found at Tel Quasile are scratched the words 'gold of Ophir for Beth Horon, 30 shekels'. It could be a receipt for the gold.

International trade

Three factors led to Israel's involvement in international trade, especially at the time of the kings. These were the growth of 'industries' which needed imported raw materials, particularly metal-working and clothes-making; the conquest of new territories which were on the international trade routes; and the desire of the Israelite kings to create wealth and buy luxury goods.

At this time Israel exported oil and cereals, fruit, honey, nuts, aromatic gum, myrrh, wool and woollen cloth, and woven garments. The list of imports includes: tin, lead, silver, copper, timber, linen and purple-dyed cloth. Luxury items were imported by land from the east – gems, spices and gold – and by sea – ivory, apes, peacocks, precious stones, algum wood, gold and silver.

The market-place

There were seven different markets in Jerusalem in New Testament times. Those who brought goods to market paid heavy taxes, and prices were high. There was a busy trade in goods required for worship at the temple, especially animals for sacrifice. The Bible records that Jesus objected to the fact that this trade went on in the temple court. The temple was probably the most important factor in Jerusalem's commerce. Every Jew had to make payments to the temple treasury, and this no doubt helped Jerusalem to pay for imports.

The Jewish rabbis had strict rules for business deals, and there were market inspectors to see that they were carried out. Scales and weights had to be cleaned regularly. Buyers had the right to complain. And no interest was to be charged to fellow-Jews. Personal belongings could be handed over as security against a loan. But essentials such as cloaks, ploughs and millstones were not to be sold in the event of non-payment.

Sale of land

One of the earliest business deals recorded in the Bible is Abraham's purchase of a field and cave from Ephron the Hittite. From the time when the Israelites settled in Canaan, the buying and selling of land was disapproved of. People held their land in trust from God; they were not the owners. Each family had received a plot of land as its own inheritance. It should therefore remain as part of that family's property.

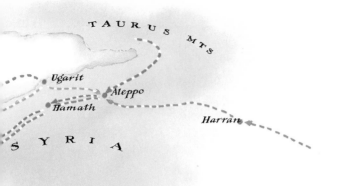

Trade routes by land and sea

Palestine stood at the junction between Asia Minor (Turkey and Syria), Egypt and Arabia. The ancient Israelites made good use of this fact, although it was nomadic desert tribes who actually carried trade goods by camel caravan. From Asia Minor they travelled over the Taurus mountains, west of the Syrian desert, through Aleppo, Hamath and Damascus to Israel (red line). From Mesopotamia they went north of the Syrian desert via Harran and Aleppo, then south into Israel (brown line). From Arabia their route (green line) was by the Red Sea shore and, at Aqaba, either north to Damascus via Moab and Gilead, north-west to Jerusalem, or west to the port of Gaza.

To the time of the Roman empire, sea transport was controlled by the Phoenicians. They travelled to the west Mediterranean, perhaps as far as Britain, and operated a coastal route (blue line) from Lebanon to Egypt, calling at places such as Ugarit, Byblos, Sidon, Tyre, Acco, Caesarea, Jaffa and ports serving the Philistine plain.

Trade in New Testament times

The long period of peace under the Romans provided ample opportunities for trade. In Palestine the profession of merchant was held in great respect, and even the priests engaged in commerce.

The range of exports and imports increased. Jewish records show that, in spite of Jerusalem's remote highland position, no fewer than 118 different kinds of foreign luxury goods were being sold there. By New Testament times the Jews were exporting increased supplies of olive oil to Egypt, which had a state monopoly, and high-grade linen. New imports included cotton, silk, other types of material, Greek wines, salted fish, spices, glass bowls, apples, cheese, baskets and slaves.

See also

■ The first kings
(pages 26–27)

■ Nations to the
north and south
(pages 76–77)

■ Crafts and trades
(pages 128–129)

■ Pottery
(pages 130–131)

■ Money, weights
and measures
(pages 126–127)

■ Mining and
metalwork
(pages 134–135)

Money, weights and measures

For many centuries, business deals in Bible lands worked on a barter system, whereby people bought and sold by exchanging goods rather than money. All kinds of items could be exchanged, from foodstuffs to cattle, metals and timber, and it was such goods that were a sign of a person's wealth.

Measuring time

Three different systems of measuring time seem to have been used in Bible times. At first, the day started at sunrise. There was a 12-month calendar of 30 days, with five extra days at the end of the year. The days of the month were marked by putting a peg into a bone plate which had three rows of ten holes.

Later, the day began at moonrise, and a whole day became 'an evening and a morning'. The evening was divided into three four-hour watches. The Romans changed this into four three-hour watches. Each new month, 28 or 29 days long, began with the moon. An extra month was added at the end of some years.

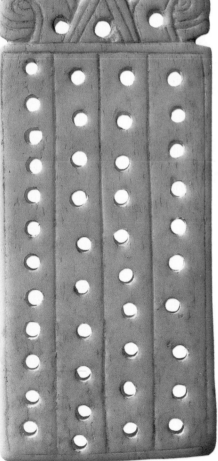

This bone tablet found at Dan is thought to be an early form of calendar.

Old Testament coins

Coinage seems to have been introduced to ancient Israel in the seventh century BC. Early coins were simply pieces of metal of a standard weight impressed with a seal. Late in the Old Testament period silver shekel pieces circulated, and the Persian kings also struck gold darics of about 130 grams.

New Testament money

Three different currencies were used in Palestine in New Testament times. There was the official, imperial money (Roman standard); provincial money (Greek standard), and local Jewish money. Money was coined in gold, silver, copper and bronze or brass. The most common silver coins mentioned in the New Testament are the Greek tetradrachma and the Roman denarius, which was a day's wage for the ordinary working person.

Roman coins

quadrans
4 quadrans = 1 as

as (bronze)
16 as = 1 denarius

denarius (silver)

25 denarii = 1 aureus

aureus (gold)

Greek coins

lepton (bronze)

128 lepton = 1 drachma

drachma (silver)
4 drachmas = 1 stater

stater (or tetradrachma) (silver)

Jewish coins

shekel
(The coin shown was minted at Tyre and may have been issued by the priests for paying the temple tax.)

Measurements of distance	New Testament stadion (furlong) 185 m/202 yd

Weights and measures

Metal – silver, copper and gold – eventually replaced other goods as the exchange 'currency' for business deals. Copper was made into discs and silver into lumps that could be weighed out. Standard weights were agreed, at first locally and later more widely.

Old Testament weights

1 gerah	approx. 0.5 gm
10 gerahs	1 bekah (approx. 6 gm)
2 bekahs	1 shekel (approx. 11 gm)
50 shekels	1 mina (approx. 500 gm)
60 minas	1 talent (approx. 30 kg)

The heavy royal shekel weighed 13 g
The heavy, double standard talent weighed 60 kg

New Testament weights

The litra (pound)	approx. 327 g
The talent	20–40 kg

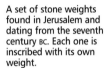

Ephah = 22 litres

(10 ephahs = 1 homer = 220 litres)

Bath = 22 litres

(10 baths = 1 homer = a 'donkey load')

Dry measures

Seah = 7.3 litres

Omer = 2.2 litres
Kab = 1.2 litres
Log = 0.3 litre

Liquid measures

Hin = 3.66 litres

Kab = 1.2 litres

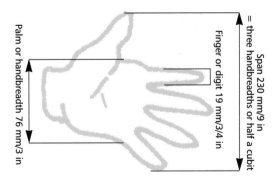

A set of stone weights found in Jerusalem and dating from the seventh century BC. Each one is inscribed with its own weight.

See also

- The Greeks (pages 68–69)
- The Romans (pages 72–73)
- The farming year (pages 104–105)
- Trade and commerce (pages 124–125)
- Mining and metalwork (pages 134–135)

Duck-shaped standardized stone weights from Mesopotamia dating from 1100–800 BC.

Measurements of length   New Testament cubit 550 mm/21.6 in; 6 cubits = 1 reed

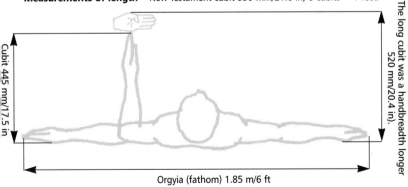

Cubit 445 mm/17.5 in

The long cubit was a handbreadth longer 520 mm/20.4 in.

Orgyia (fathom) 1.85 m/6 ft

Palm or handbreadth 76 mm/3 in

Finger or digit 19 mm/3/4 in

Span 230 mm/9 in = three handbreadths or half a cubit

Maximum travel distance permitted by Jewish law on the sabbath day: 2,000 cubits/914 m/1,000 yd

New Testament milion (mile) 1,000 paces (Roman measurement)/1,478 m/1,618 yd

Crafts and trades

In Old Testament times, Israel had few, if any, craft workers who made beautiful things for their own sake. Even when it came to making places of worship they often had to bring in foreign artists to complete the decoration. It was a poor country and skills were limited to making strictly useful objects.

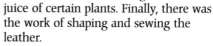

This fish hook, discovered at Bethsaida on Lake Galilee, dates from New Testament times.

Tanner's shop at Masada, Dead Sea.

Fishing

By the time of Jesus, a flourishing fishing industry seems to have developed in Palestine, based on Lake Galilee. The New Testament describes fishing people working in family groups, and often using hired helpers. They mended nets and sails, repaired boats, and often fished by night.

Bone or iron fish-hooks were used for fishing from early times. In New Testament times two kinds of nets were popular. One was a net thrown by hand from the shore. The other was a large net, called a 'dragnet', used from the boats, with floats and weights attached so that it moved vertically through the water, bringing the fish to the boats or to shallow water in smaller and smaller circles.

Leatherwork

Leather was used to make clothes, belts, footwear and other items. The complete hides of small animals were sewn together to make bottles for wine, water and milk. Leather was also used as a writing-material.

Two or three different trades may have been involved in making leather. Firstly, the animals had to be skinned. Then there was the job of tanning. In early times this may simply have been a process of drying the hides in the sun, or perhaps treating them with the juice of certain plants. Finally, there was the work of shaping and sewing the leather.

Sheepskin water bottle, with the front legs tied together as a handle for carrying.

The status of trades

Crafts were held in high regard by the Jews in New Testament times. Craft workers were exempt from the rule that everyone should rise to their feet when a scholar approached. Most of the scribes probably had a trade. The writings of the rabbis mention a nailmaker, a baker, a sandalmaker, a master builder and a tailor. But some trades were despised, for instance tanning, because it led to ritual impurity by handling skins of dead animals, and being a tax collector, because it gave scope for trickery.

Trade guilds

Trade guilds in Israel were probably established fairly early in Old Testament times, especially in the towns. Here, different crafts seem to have had special quarters. In New Testament times, trade guilds were well known in the Roman Empire. But they had to have a licence from the emperor to make sure they were not simply a cover for undesirable political activities.

See also

■ The first kings (pages 26–27)

■ The Egyptians (pages 52–53)

■ The Babylonians (pages 62–63)

□ Clothing and cosmetics (pages 110–111)

■ Trade and commerce (pages 124–125)

Ivory-carving

Ivory was imported by Israel from Africa or Syria. King Solomon probably used ivory carvings and inlay in the decorations of his temple. King Ahab built an 'ivory house' in Samaria, his capital. It is at Samaria that the largest Israelite collection of ivory has been found. Objects found consist mostly of small carvings, inlays and sculptures.

This Phoenician ivory plaque (above) has a carving of a winged sphinx. It dates from the ninth century BC.

Glass perfume bottles (right) dating from New Testament times.

Gem-cutting

The Israelites used semi-precious stones such as agate, jasper, carnelian and rock-crystal. These were cut and polished to make beads, or engraved with designs, and sometimes the owners' names, to serve as seals. The Bible mentions many different stones, although not all can be identified. Engraving stones and setting them in gold for the high priest's breastplate are described in the Old Testament book of Exodus.

Glass-making

Glass-making does not seem to have been common in Israel. Long before the Israelites entered Canaan, the Egyptians and Babylonians had discovered how to make an opaque form of glass and how to shape it over a core of sand. By New Testament times, the Romans were making transparent glass and 'blowing' it into shape. Many of the glass articles which have been found in Israel were clearly imported.

Pottery

By comparison with the products of neighbouring lands, the pottery of ancient Israel seems poor and not very artistic; it was functional rather than decorative. By the time of the Israelite kings, however, the making of pottery had developed into a minor industry, with small 'factories', mass production, some standard shapes, and trade marks.

Preparing the clay

Pottery was made from the local red clay. The potter did not alter the quality of the clay, except by mixing it occasionally with ground limestone, which was readily available. This enabled the finished pot to withstand heat, but meant that the potter had to fire the clay at a lower temperature, otherwise the limestone would decompose.

The raw clay was exposed to the sun, rain and frost to break it up and remove impurities. Then water was added and it was trampled into mud. This was skilled work; the water had to be measured and poured on evenly, and the air removed.

The potter

It is possible, especially during the time of the later Israelite kings, that several potters worked together, with their apprentices. The Old Testament also points to a royal guild of potters 'in the service of the king'. They probably produced large jars for storing produce from the king's private estates. Jars have been found with a stamp on the handles: 'Belonging to the king'. Underneath is the name of one of four cities: Hebron, Ziph, Socoh or Memshath.

Pottery from Judea dating from the sixth century BC.

Working the clay

Potters worked the prepared clay in one of three ways. First, the clay could be pressed down in a mould. Canaanite plaques were made this way, and so also were most of the lamps of New Testament times. Alternatively, the clay could be modelled freehand. In Israel the only things made in this way seem to have been toys, ovens and a few pots. Or the clay could be shaped on a wheel – the usual method of working.

The potter's wheel

The earliest type of potter's wheel was a circular disc, rotating on a vertical shaft. At about the time of the Exodus a different type came into use, with a second, larger disc, mounted below the first; this speeded the turning. Potters' wheels were probably used everywhere, but are rarely found by archaeologists. Perhaps they were usually made of wood or clay, and so have not survived. Stone wheels have been found at Megiddo, Lachish and Hazor. There is no evidence of a foot-operated wheel before 200 BC, although it was widely used in New Testament times.

Firing

The firing of the clay objects in a kiln was the ultimate test of a potter's art. Different clays needed different treatment. But the methods of firing are not known.

The potter's workshop

The whole process of producing pottery was probably carried out on one site. There had to be a water supply, wheels for shaping the clay and kilns for firing it. The potter's yard would be used for preparing the clay.

See also

■ The exodus from Egypt (pages 20–21)
■ The Canaanites (pages 56–57)
■ Food and drink (pages 106–107)
■ Games and sport (pages 140–141)

Pottery bowls and lamps

One of the main artefacts made by the potter was the bowl. This could range from a large banquet bowl with four handles, to a small cup (which rarely had handles). Bowls were used for mixing wines, serving food, cooking and so on.

Lamps were thrown in the same way as a bowl, and the rims were pinched in while the clay was still soft. Their style changed considerably during the history of Israel, but the basic design was the same. The gradual changes, at different stages, have enabled experts to use them as an indication of date.

Pottery jars

Potters in Bible times made a variety of jars and pitchers. There were jars for storing wine, water, oil and even documents. And small juglets were specially produced for perfume. Other objects made of pottery included water bottles, articles for industry and toys.

In the foreground a potter uses a wheel, while others shape pots by hand and decorate them. In the background, pots ready to be fired are stacked in a kiln.

This very fine, decorated household pottery from Jerusalem dates from New Testament times.

Decoration

The Israelites did not glaze their pottery, but they had three main ways of decorating it. They used a 'slip', whereby fine clay with a rich iron content was thinned with water and then brushed over the pot. Alternatively, they painted a line of red or black around the shoulder or middle of the jar or jug. Or they 'burnished' pots, by rubbing a tool of stone, bone or wood against the clay after drying; these areas would then shine after firing.

Building and builders

Skill in building developed slowly in Israel. As slaves in Egypt, the Israelites had made bricks for massive building projects. But when they entered Canaan in about 1230 BC they showed little interest in building. Indeed, the Israelites destroyed many Canaanite cities, and the buildings that replaced them were not at all impressive.

General building work

Building work included constructing houses and city walls, and digging wells, cisterns, water tunnels and grain silos, usually by individuals or the village community. This work would involve not only builders, but also stonemasons, carpenters and metal-workers – as well as unskilled workers.

Town walls were made of rubble or boulder masonry, sometimes plastered and strengthened by towers. The boulders were only roughly shaped, but carefully fitted together. Houses were constructed along the inside of these walls, wherever there was a space. Beyond this, there was little attempt at town planning.

Many houses had a cistern underneath to store rain water. These were dug out of solid rock and lined with slaked lime to prevent water leakage. Pools for storing water were often cut out of rock, and in several cities excavations have revealed tunnels cut to make water more accessible.

Megiddo was one of King Solomon's main fortified cities outside Jerusalem. This water tunnel was constructed to link the city with an underground cistern. It probably dates from the reign of King Ahab.

Slavery and forced labour

Some building projects needed enormous numbers of workers and, in Old Testament times, slavery was an acceptable source of labour. Prisoners-of-war were made slaves. Also, men and their families became slaves to better-off households when they were unable to meet their debts.

King David forced prisoners-of-war to work on his building projects. King Solomon organized a system of forced labour using Israelites as well. They were expected to work for the king for one month in every three. These men, with the slaves, built the roads, fortresses and temples that made Solomon famous. They looked after the king's farms and worked in his factories and mines.

The Siloam inscription, dating from the eighth century BC, was discovered in Hezekiah's tunnel. It describes the drama of digging the tunnel.

Hired workers

Slaves in New Testament times were few in number, and were not forced to do heavy work. For the most part, they were servants in the houses of the wealthy and of the court.

Workers for building projects were more usually hired by the day. When the temple begun by King Herod the Great was completed in AD 62, more than 18,000 people were thrown out of work.

The Bible contains advice to Christian slaves in the form of letters written by Paul and Peter to various church groups. These men and women lived in the wider Roman empire, where slavery was also a regular part of the economic system.

King Hezekiah's tunnel

Hezekiah's tunnel was built in about 700 BC to bring water from the Gihon spring into Jerusalem. In 1880 an interesting inscription was discovered, which describes two groups of tunnellers, 45 m/150 ft underground, about to meet in the middle after a very long route from each end. They could hear one another's picks.

'On the day of the piercing through, the stone-cutters struck through each to meet his fellow, axe against axe. Then ran the water from the spring to the pool...'

Phoenician influence

It was not until after the turn of the 10th century BC, during the time of kings David and Solomon, that real skill was used in building projects. This was probably due largely to the help and instruction of Phoenician masons and joiners, sent in a trade deal with King Hiram of Tyre. Thousands of Israelites spent seven years building Solomon's temple under Phoenician guidance. Buildings erected later, after the alliance with Phoenicia had broken down, reverted to the cruder style.

See also

■ Nations to the north and south (pages 76–77)

■ Priests and rituals (pages 162–163)

■ 1 and 2 Chronicles (pages 212–213)

Building in Jesus' time

King Herod's building programme meant that the building trade in Jesus' time had an important position in Jerusalem. Herod is said to have prepared 1,000 wagons for transporting stones, some of which may have been quarried from the caves under the city itself. Stones up to 10,000 kg/10 tons in weight were produced and moved to the buildings, possibly on rollers. Arches and vaults were constructed to a Roman pattern.

First-century Jerusalem

Jerusalem in Herod's day was a typical city of the Roman empire. Excavations have uncovered large houses built on a lavish scale, with underfloor heating and piped water. A paved Roman road in a village nearby is flanked by stone holders for torches, to serve as street lights. The houses of the poor were simple, but probably had more than one storey.

Aerial view of the fortress of Herodium in the hills south of Jerusalem. Inside the walls were a garden, a suite of baths, a dining hall and private apartments. There was a second palace at the foot of the hill.

Mining and metalwork

In the Old Testament book of Deuteronomy, Moses promises the Israelites that Canaan will be a rich land: 'Its rocks have iron in them, and from its hills you can mine copper.' These two metals were native to the area; other metals, gold, silver, tin and lead had to be imported.

Gold jewellery from Tel El-Ajul, mid second millennium BC.

Gold and silver

When the Israelites left Egypt, the Egyptians had been using gold for many centuries. The Israelites took ornaments of gold and silver with them, and they knew how to work these metals. To make solid objects, the metal was melted and poured into moulds. Gold could also be beaten into sheets in order to cover objects, or beaten into shape.

A Philistine blacksmith's forge from the time of the first kings of Israel.

Copper mining

Archaeology has shown that the desert area between the Dead Sea and the Gulf of Aqaba was being mined while the Israelites were in Egypt – and even much earlier. There is a site at Timnah, where the underground shafts penetrate for hundreds of metres in all directions and at several levels. The deeper workings are hundreds of feet below the surface, and ventilated through air channels.

Copper smelting

Some have suggested that the Israelites learned the art of smelting and working copper from the Midianites. A furnace from the time of the Old Testament judges has been found at Bethshemesh. Here copper was smelted on a small scale, and the heat was intensified, probably through pottery blowpipes or bellows. Other furnaces dating from the time of King Solomon have been found in Israel, some for treating copper, others for iron. The smiths would receive the metal, melt it in a clay pot over the fire, and then shape the articles, sometimes using stone moulds. Their main products were for army and home use: arrow-heads, lances and spear-tips, swords, daggers, axes, plough-points, chisels, needles, safety pins, tweezers, bracelets, bowls and buckets.

Copper-smelting furnace. Copper was smelted in clay crucibles on a bed of charcoal. A draught of air was supplied by a person using leather bellows.

Copper mine shaft at Timna Park, Negev.

The lost-wax method of casting complicated shapes in metal, invented in Mesopotamia in the fourth millennium BC. First, a model was made from wax. It was then covered with clay and heated so that the wax melted and ran off. The space was then filled with molten metal. When the metal cooled, the clay mould was smashed.

Copper and bronze

Copper was the most plentiful metal in early Israel. It was extracted from ore by smelting and, although the metal was rather spongy, it could be hardened and shaped by cold hammering. At some time before 2000 BC it had been discovered that if up to four per cent of tin was added, the copper was stronger and harder. Its melting-point was also lower, and it could be poured into a mould and cast into shape. The resulting metal is bronze. However, the Hebrew words for copper and bronze are the same, so it is not clear when the Israelites began to make bronze. It would certainly have been needed for the finely-shaped work of Solomon's temple – the great bronze basin, resting on twelve bronze bull-calves, and the bronze pillars whose tops were decorated with lilies and pomegranates.

Iron

The use of iron spread very slowly in Israel. Iron needed to be heated as it was being worked, and so was difficult to produce. When the Israelites entered Canaan, the Canaanites already had chariots with iron fittings and other equipment.

When the Philistines defeated the Israelites in the days of Samuel and Saul, they would not let them have blacksmiths of their own in case they made strong swords and spears. If the Israelites wanted their copper tools sharpened or repaired they had to go to the Philistines, who charged crippling prices. King David, however, had great stores of iron. He 'supplied a large amount of iron for making nails and clamps'. And, from this time on, iron objects became more plentiful.

A tang-type axehead and the mould in which it was made. This type of axe with its long narrow blade and wide edge was preferred by the Egyptians to the socket-type weapon. The rear part of the blade was inserted into a wooden haft and bound tightly to strengthen the join.

See also

■ The Egyptians (pages 52–53)

■ The Canaanites (pages 56–57)

■ Nations to the east and west (pages 78–79)

■ Warfare (pages 118–119)

■ Three temples (pages 160–161)

Clothes-making

The main materials used for making clothes were linen from flax, sheeps' wool, goats' hair and animal skins. Cotton was not used by the Israelites until they began to import it, probably after the exile from Egypt. The Israelites loved to decorate their clothes with brightly coloured fringes, borders and tassels. Gold thread was used to embroider very special clothes.

Wool

In Bible times, sheep were shorn in the spring, after being dipped. The new wool was washed, or sent to the fuller to be cleaned of natural oils. The fuller would do this by treading out the wool on a rock in water. The wool was then spread out to be dried and bleached in the sun. The fuller also worked on the newly woven cloth to shrink it, and was sometimes responsible for dyeing the wool.

Loom in a reconstructed Israelite house.

Spinning and weaving

Wool was combed, then spun into yarn. It was probably done on a simple hand spindle, although only the stone, clay and bone whorls of these have been found. Two main types of loom were used in Palestine: a vertical loom and a horizontal loom.

The weaver stood in front of the vertical loom, with the downward threads (warps) attached to a beam across the top and held down with weights. As the weaver worked, the cross-wise threads (wefts) were beaten upwards. Five or six warps could be worked on at a time, which made it possible to produce patterns. Because the weaver could move about, it was possible to make wide pieces of material. Later, a rotating beam was made for the bottom of the loom. The web (woven cloth) was begun at the bottom, and the finished cloth rolled up. This made it possible to make quite long lengths of cloth.

The horizontal loom was made of two beams, held in place by four pegs in the ground, and the weaver sat in front. The loom could be no wider than the reach of the weaver's arms, although the Egyptians seem to have had a system of two people working this loom. Both wool and linen were woven on this type of loom, and sometimes also the coarser goats' or camels' hair for thick shepherds' cloaks and for tents.

Dyeing

The colours the Bible refers to most often are blue, scarlet and purple. These may have been the basic dyes used in ancient Israel. Purple clothes were a sign of royalty and wealth. The best purple came from Tyre and was very expensive. It was made from molluscs found on the east Mediterranean coast.

Certain places in Israel became centres for dyeing. Among these were Gezer, Bethshemesh, Beth-zur and Debir. At Debir, excavations have shown that about 30 homes had rooms specially designed for dyeing. Each contained two stone vats with small openings on top.

Potash and slaked lime were probably put into the vat and dye added later, with more dye in the second vat. The wool was given two baths. The potash and lime fixed the dye, and the wool was laid out to dry. It was then ready for spinning and weaving.

This murex was boiled to release a purple dye.

One man mixes dye as another draws water from a well. In the background a kneeling woman is spinning wool while another uses a vertical loom to weave cloth.

Shaping clothes

There were two main ways of shaping a garment. If the loom was wide enough, the whole garment could be made in one piece. The weaver started at the sleeve edge and worked across to the other sleeve edge, leaving a hole for the neck. Sleeves could be as long or short as the person wanted, and the striped pattern was easy to make. When cut off, the free warps were twisted into cords which strengthened the sides. Sometimes they were left as tassels at the bottom corners.

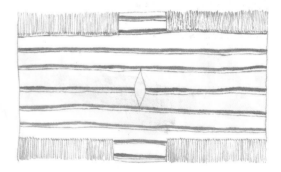

If the loom was narrow, the garment was made in three pieces; the main bodice and sleeves; the front skirt, and the back skirt. The neck opening was given a woven binding to strengthen it.

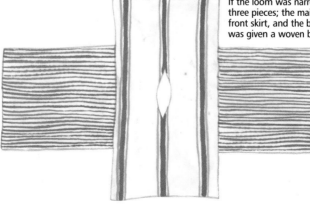

Linen

In Palestine, flax grew only on the southern coastal plain, near Jericho, and in Galilee, though in New Testament times the amount grown in Galilee was greatly increased. After the flax was cut and dried, the seeds were removed. The flax was then soaked and dried again in an oven. The fibres were separated, and then it was ready for spinning and weaving. Linen was used for making clothes and ships' sails.

See also

Plants and flowers
(pages 88–89)

Animals and birds
(pages 92–93)

Clothing and cosmetics
(pages 110–111)

Health and healing

A variety of physical and mental ailments are mentioned in the Bible, but the Israelites' general attitude to illness meant that medical skills remained relatively undeveloped: God was believed to be the only true healer.

Diseases

Even where symptoms of disease are described in the Bible, it is not always possible to be sure what diseases were involved. Some form of leprosy was fairly common. Shortage of food in times of drought, combined with the heat and poor water supply, often led to dysentery, cholera, typhoid and beriberi. The dust-filled air made blindness very common. Then there were the deaf and the disabled. The number of deaths among children was clearly quite high.

Preventative medicine

Israel's laws compensated for the Israelites' general ignorance about hygiene. To obey these laws was part of the Israelites' religious duty, but obedience clearly contributed to keeping them healthy as well.

There was one day of complete rest each week, for physical and spiritual refreshment. Certain foods could not be eaten, including pork which, in a sub-tropical climate, carried a high risk of food poisoning. Also, water had to be free from contamination. All males were required to be circumcised – an operation believed to prevent venereal disease. A man must not marry members of his own family. And careful attention must be paid to cleanliness, in daily personal habits and in sexual relationships.

Treatment of illness

Various oils and perfumes were used in personal hygiene, including myrtle, saffron, myrrh and spikenard. Olive oil and 'balm of Gilead' (a spicy resin) were swallowed or put on wounds and sores.

Certain herbs may have been used as painkillers. The New Testament, for example, talks about the 'wine mixed with a drug called myrrh' offered to Jesus on the cross. Many effective herbs must have been known, but there must also have been a good deal of superstition.

Broken arms and legs were bound up tightly, and crutches may have been used. But there is no evidence of radical surgery being done in Old Testament times in Israel, except for the discovery of three skulls in eighth-century Lachish, with holes bored in them. This kind of operation was widespread to relieve pressure or release demons.

The roots of the spikenard produced a fragrant oil which was used in personal hygiene.

Midwives

There were midwives in Israel from the very earliest times. Mothers sometimes died in childbirth, but often the midwife was very skilled. The Old Testament book of Genesis records that Tamar successfully gave birth to twins who seem to have been locked in a difficult position.

Dentists

Dentistry was practised even among the ancient Egyptians – some of the mummies have gold-filled teeth! And the Greek historian, Herodotus, recorded that in 500 BC the Phoenicians were making false teeth. There is no evidence of such a practice in ancient Israel.

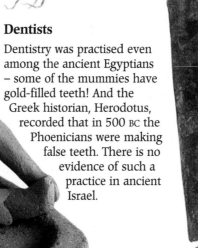

This clay figurine of a woman bathing was found at Achzib and dates from 8th–7th century BC.

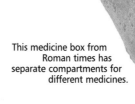

This medicine box from Roman times has separate compartments for different medicines.

Medicine in Jesus' day

In Greece, medicine and surgery had become a highly developed skill, though still mixed with a certain amount of magic. It was the Greek, Hippocrates, who laid down the principles that the life and welfare of the patient should be the doctor's first consideration; that male doctors should not take advantage of women patients, or procure abortions; and that they should not reveal confidential information. At one time, state doctors were employed, paid a salary and had to give free medical attention.

The Romans later adopted some of these practices. Surgical instruments and prescription labels have been found in excavations of Roman cities, and there was a school of medicine at Alexandria in Egypt.

In Palestine itself the rabbis required that every town should have a physician, and preferably a surgeon, too. There was always a doctor among the temple officials, whose work was to look after the priests, who worked barefoot and were naturally liable to catch certain diseases.

See also

■ The Egyptians
(pages 52–53)

■ Plants and flowers
(pages 88–89)

■ A new baby
(pages 98–99)

■ Ancient beliefs
(pages 146–147)

■ God's laws in
practice
(pages 152–153)

Tools belonging to a Roman doctor.

Attitudes to illness

The attitude to illness in Israel was always quite distinct from that of Israel's neighbours. The Mesopotamians and the Egyptians in early times regarded illness as invariably caused by the malice of evil spirits. Treatment was therefore in the hands of exorcist-priests, and involved incantations and magic alongside other methods. Israel also regarded health as a religious matter, but this was because the people firmly believed that God was all-powerful. From God came both good and evil. Health was a divine blessing. Disease was a sign that the spiritual relationship between a person and God had broken down.

Public toilets in Ephesus dating from Roman times.

Doctors

The Babylonian king, Hammurabi, drew up a code of laws in about 1750 BC, fixing doctors' fees and setting out penalties for surgeons who were careless in performing operations. The Egyptians were also practising surgery, studying anatomy by dissecting dead bodies, and writing medical and surgical notes on papyrus. But this was unthinkable in ancient Israel. The first reference to doctors in the Bible is critical: 'Asa was crippled by a severe foot disease; but even then he did not turn to the Lord for help, but to doctors.'

By the second century BC the prestige of doctors had increased. In the Deuterocanonical book 'The Wisdom of Ben Sira' it is said that, although God is the healer, this power can work through skilled people and the use of medicines. The Bible records that Jesus resisted the view that it is specific sin which causes illness. He saw disease as evidence of the power of evil in the world as a whole.

Games and sport

People in ancient Israel worked long hours and had no labour-saving tools. Nonetheless, there was time for leisure pursuits, for adults as well as children. The weekly 'sabbath' day, for example, was meant for people to rest and relax as well as to worship God. And there were special 'holidays' and festivities at the great religious festivals.

Public entertainment

In later Bible times, people began to make a living by entertaining others. This kind of entertainment became very popular in Greek times.

In Jerusalem, King Herod built a stadium for fights between gladiators – who were trained captives taken in war, or criminals – and between people and animals. He also built an amphitheatre for chariot-racing, and theatres at Caesarea and Sebaste, whose remains can still be seen.

Amphitheatre at Caesarea

Ball and target games

Marbles were popular in Bible times. They were rolled through a wall with three archways, to knock down skittles on the other side. Out of doors, hop-scotch was known, and there were throwing games with leather balls. Juggling was popular; but there seem to have been no bats or racquets. Sometimes children made a hole in the ground and had contests to see who could throw the most stones into it from a distance.

Children and adults also practised with slings and stones. A sling was made from a woollen pouch held between two strings. A stone was put into the pouch, and it was whirled round and round. When the person holding the sling released one of the two strings, the stone flew out at its target. Shooting with bows and arrows was also a pastime. There was target and distance shooting.

Athletics

The Greeks believed that exercise was necessary to maintain a healthy body. But Greek athletics were not very popular with the Jewish people in New Testament times. They found it offensive that the athletes competed naked. And the close link with Greek religion was a further obstacle.

The sporting events mentioned by Paul in his New Testament letters are all linked to the Greek games. He writes of runners competing to win a crown of laurel, pine or olive leaves. He also refers to boxing, with arms and hands bound with studded leather, so that a blow must be avoided rather than parried!

Line drawing of a discus thrower after a bronze statue by Myron (about 450 BC).

A pankration contest depicted on a Greek vase dating from 330 BC. Pankration was a form of combat in which any form of aggression was permitted except biting and gouging eyes.

Wrestling

Wrestling was a popular sport in Bible times. In Babylon people wrestled holding onto each other's belt. The Old Testament book of Genesis tells of Jacob's wrestling-match and uses the expression 'hip and thigh', which was a technical term for a wrestling throw, showing that this sport was popular in Israel too.

Board and dice games

This limestone game board with faience playing pieces was found at Beth Mirsim and dates from about 2000–1700 BC.

Draughts was played on boards of 20 or 30 squares. The boards were made of stone clay, ebony and ivory. Some of those which have been found were cut out at the back to take the pieces. Chess was played in Babylon before 2000 BC, and other games such as Ludo and Mancala were also played. What has been called the 'Royal Game' from Ur of the Chaldees seems to have been a form of Ludo. Solitaire was also played. Moves were made after throws with two kinds of dice – two-sided discs, or four-sided pyramids called teetotum. The six-sided dice we use today was not known.

People took throwing dice or 'casting lots' very seriously. The game played by the soldiers at the trial of Jesus, as recorded in the New Testament, was a dice game. As a four-sided dice was used, they moved a skittle from a central mark to positions where it could be 'robed', 'crowned' and 'sceptred', and the soldier whose move completed the 'ceremony' called 'king' and collected the stakes which had been put down.

The Greek vase (above) depicts a chariot race in progress.

This ivory gaming board, dating from about 1300 BC, was found at Megiddo.

Children's games

The Roman dice (right) found in Jerusalem are made from bone.

Children's games seem to have changed very little over the centuries. It is known, for example, that children in Bible times had toys which made a noise – such as rattles and whistles. These have been found in many places by archaeologists. Some rattles were shaped like boxes with small holes in each side; others like dolls and birds, though they were rather heavy to handle.

Girls played with dolls' houses, too. Miniature cooking pots and furniture, made out of pottery, have been found dating from between 900 and 600 BC. Some dolls had jointed arms and legs, and hair of beads and mud. They had holes in their shoulders for puppet strings.

See also

- A brief history of Jerusalem (pages 38–39)
- Hellenistic civilization (pages 70–71)
- Pottery (pages 130–131)
- Writings of the apostles: overview (pages 252–253)

Musical instruments

Music and dancing have been part of life in all cultures, as far back in history as we can go. There were three kinds of instruments in Israel – string, wind and percussion. They played together in unison rather than in harmony. And the music seems to have been strongly rhythmic rather than melodic, although there were set tunes to some of the psalms.

Wind instruments

The 'halil' was the ordinary person's hollow pipe, made of cane, wood or bone. 'Halil' means 'to bore', and describes the way the instrument was made. A reed was used in the instrument, and the player carried spare reeds about in a bag.

The 'geren' was made from the horn of an animal and was used as a trumpet. If the horn used was a ram's horn, the instrument was called a 'shofar', also translated 'trumpet' in some versions of the Bible. It was used on religious and public occasions.

The 'hazozra' was a metal trumpet, which in Bible times was made of silver. In the Old Testament book of Numbers a continuous call on two silver trumpets was the sign to gather at the tabernacle. One was sounded to call the chiefs together.

Music in worship

In Bible times, music had an important place in the worship at the temple. The Old Testament describes how King David organized the temple choir and orchestra 'to sing and to play joyful music'. In the temple the singing was often in parts – one line of a section being sung by one group, and the next sung in response by another. Dancing, too, was often part of the people's joyful expression of worship. When the sacred Ark of the Covenant was brought to Jerusalem, 'David and all the people danced with all their might to honour God'.

Pottery figurine of a female tambourine player dating from the seventh or sixth century BC.

Percussion instruments

The 'menaanim' was probably made of discs rattled along metal rods, suspended in a wooden frame. 'Meziltaim' are copper cymbals. In Bible times, they were used by Levites in the temple to mark the beginning, ending and pauses in the chapters which were sung. The 'tof' was a percussion instrument with a membrane, used to accompany singing and dancing.

Unfortunately, because the Israelites were not allowed to portray human figures in their art, we do not know exactly how these instruments were played. But pictures of similar instruments from Egypt, Assyria and Babylonia give us a fair idea. Instruments were made from a wide variety of materials – cedarwood, sandalwood, leather, gut, ivory, shell, gold and silver.

Egyptian systrum dating from about the ninth century BC.

Girls perform acrobatic dances; Necropolis of Memphis, Saqara.

Lyre

String instruments

The 'kinnor' is normally translated 'harp' in the Bible. It may have been a harp or a lyre. It was a small, eight- or ten-stringed instrument with a wooden frame, and could be carried about. It is not known if it was played simply by plucking or if a plectrum was used. The kinnor may be the instrument shown on ancient tomb-paintings at Beni-Hasan in Egypt.

The 'nebel', called a 'psaltery', was another stringed instrument in a wooden frame, played by plucking with the fingers. The word 'nebel' means a 'skin bottle' or jar, which suggests a swollen soundbox like a lute.

The Old Testament records that King David was able to play both instruments.

This bronze figurine of a female lute player was excavated in Beth-shan and dates from 700–600 BC.

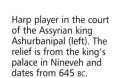

Harp player in the court of the Assyrian king Ashurbanipal (left). The relief is from the king's palace in Nineveh and dates from 645 BC.

On this vase from Vulci, which dates from about 440 BC, Melousa holds a double flute (aulos) and Musaios holds a lyre.

Egyptian musicians play at a banquet on this wall painting from the tomb of Amenennet, Tuthmosis III (1475–1448 BC) in Thebes.

See also

■ The first kings (pages 26–27)

□ Marriage and weddings (pages 96–97)

□ Mining and metalwork (pages 134–135)

■ The tabernacle (pages 158–159)

■ Priests and rituals (pages 162–163)

■ Psalms (pages 220–221)

Part 3: Picture acknowledgments

Abbreviations:

t = top, tl = top left, tc = top centre,
tr = top right,
c = centre, cl = centre left, cr = centre right
b = bottom, bl = bottom left,
bc = bottom centre, br = bottom right

Illustrations

DA = David Atkinson, GH = Gwyn Hughes,
RN = Rex Nicholls

Photographs

JA = Jon Arnold, ZR = Zev Radovan,
DT = David Townsend, Relief maps = Lion
Publishing

page
82t   Map: DA
82c   Nahal Bezet: JA
82br   Map: DA
83cr   Rock formations, Sinai desert: JA
84bl   Coastal plain: JA
84tr   Galilee: Lion Publishing/DT
84br   Jordan valley: Lion Publishing/DT
85tl   Central highlands: Lion Publishing/DT
85bl   Transjordan: ZR
85tr   'Shephelah': Lion Publishing/DT
85br   Plain of Megiddo: Lion Publishing/DT
86tr   Map: DA
86c   Waterfall, Engedi: JA
86–87b   Cross section: DA
87tl   Mount Hermon: JA
87cr   Map: DA
88tl   Barley: Nicholas Rous
88cl   Cereal basket: Lion Publishing/John
         Williams
88tc   Green corn: RN
89tr   Thistle: RN
89c   Wild flowers: Lion Publishing/DT
88–89   All other colour illustrations: Roger Kent
90   Date palm: Lion Publishing/DT
90–91   All other photographs: Lion
         Publishing/John Williams; all colour
         illustrations: Roger Kent; all black-and-
         white illustrations: Lion Publishing
92cl   Camel: Lion Publishing
92cr   Lion relief: Lion Publishing
92bl   Israelite clay horse: ZR
92–93   All colour illustrations: Mark Stewart
94–95   Main illustration: GH
96–97   Main illustration: GH
97bc   Hammurabi's law-code: ZR
98bl   Circumcision scene: ZR
98–99   Main illustration: GH
99cl   Bar Mitzvah: Lion Publishing/DT
100cl   Jar from Hazor: ZR
100c   Egyptian pen case: Ashmolean
         Museum, Oxford
101t   Wooden writing tablet: Lion
         Publishing/Collection Ashmolean
         Museum, Oxford
101b   Development of the alphabet: Joshua
         Smith

102t   Sheep fold: RN
102c   Flocks: Lion Publishing/DT
102cl   Ploughing: GH
102b   Village well: ZR
103   Main illustration: GH
104tl   Gezer calendar: ZR
104tr   Farming year: DA
104cl   Planting seed: GH
104b   Vineyard: RN
104–105 Main illustration: GH
105tl   Threshing sledge: ZR
105tr   Millstone olive press: JA
106tr   Bread: RN
106tr   Black basalt grinding stone: ZR
106cr   Woman grinding corn: Ashmolean
         Museum, Oxford
106bl   Fish: RN
107t   Water cistern, Gibeon: JA
107cl   Salt formations, Dead Sea: JA
107cr   Wine cellar: Joshua Smith
107b   Wine jar: ZR
108tr   Food: Lion Publishing/DT
108–109 Main illustration: GH
109tr   Relief depicting offerings: ZR
109cr   Reconstruction of a cooking stove: ZR
110tr   Orthodox Jew: JA
110cl   Canaanite bronze mirror: ZR
110br   Sandals: ZR
111c   Duck-shaped cosmetics box: ZR
111tr   Sandstone cosmetics bowl: ZR
111br   Jewellery: ZR
112t   Israelite house: Nick Talbott
112bl   Tent: GH
113tl   Reconstruction of Israelite house: JA
113c   Corner of Capernaum: RN
114tr   Reconstruction of a rural house: ZR
114cl   Development of lamps: Joshua Smith
114–115 Reconstruction of a wealthy home:
         Nick Talbott
115tc   Glass utensils: ZR
115br   Bath-house hot room, Masada: JA
116tc   Seal impression on jar handle: ZR
116tr   Map: DA
116b   Stone seal and its impression: ZR
117cl   Roman amphitheatre, Aspendos: JA
117bl   Map: DA
117br   Coins: Photo Lion Publishing/
         Collection Ashmolean Museum, Oxford
118tc   Map: DA
118b   War chariots: GH
118–119 Canaanite dagger: ZR
119t   Relief from gate at Balawat: ZR
119cl   Lead slingstones: ZR
119br   Roman soldier: Martin Sanders
120cl   Reconstruction of gateway at
         Megiddo: Nick Talbott
120–121t Reconstruction of Caesarea:
         Stephen Conlin
121bl   Tel Beersheba: ZR
122tc   War chariot: ZR
122c   Cart wheels: Joshua Smith
122bl   Relief of logs being transported: ZR
122bc   Roman milestone: ZR
123   Main illustration: GH

124cl   Clay tablet: ZR
124–125t Map: DA
124–125b Market scene: GH
126bl   Bone tablet: ZR
126br   Coins: Photo Lion Publishing/
         Collection British Museum
127tr   Stone weights: ZR
127b   Duck-shaped weights: ZR
128cl   Fish hook: ZR
128tr   Sheepskin water bottle: ZR
128c   Tanner's shop, Masada: JA
128b   Fishing boats: GH
129l   Phoenician ivory plate: ZR
129r   Glass perfume bottles: ZR
130l   Pottery from Judea: ZR
130–131 Main illustration: GH
131bl   Decorated household pottery: ZR
132cl   Water tunnel: Sonia Halliday
         Photographs/Jane Taylor
132bc   Siloam inscription: ZR
132–133t Main illustration: GH
133bc   Herodium: Comstock UK 1998
134t   Gold jewellery: ZR
134b   Blacksmith: GH
135tr   Copper smelting furnace: Joshua Smith
135cr   Casting metal: Joshua Smith
135cl   Copper mine shaft: JA
135bc   Tang-type axe-head: ZR
136bl   Spinning loom: JA
136–137t Main illustration: GH
137tr   Murex: ZR
137br   Shaping clothes: Joshua Smith
138tc   Spikenard: RN
138bl   Clay figurine: ZR
138br   Medicine box: ZR
139c   Tools of a Roman doctor: ZR
139b   Roman public toilets: JA
140tr   Amphitheatre at Caesarea: ZR
140bl   Discus thrower: Lion Publishing
140bc   Greek vase: Photo © Michael
         Holford/ Collection British Museum
140–141c Greek vase: © The British
         Museum, by courtesy of the Trustees
141tl   Limestone game board: ZR
141cr   Ivory gaming board: ZR
141bl   Roman dice: ZR
142c   Pottery figurine: ZR
142bl   Depiction of acrobatic dances: ZR
142r   Egyptian sistrum: Photo © Michael
         Holford/ Collection British Museum
143tl   Lyre: RN
143cl   Relief depicting harp player: ZR
143c   Bronze figurine: ZR
143tr   Greek vase: © The British Museum,
         by courtesy of the Trustees
143b   Wall painting depicting Egyptian
         musicians: ZR

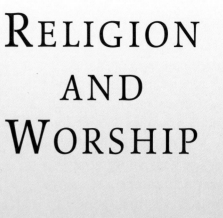

RELIGION
AND
WORSHIP

Ancient beliefs

From the earliest times, people have felt the need to worship, or pay respect to, someone or something greater than themselves. In every age people have tried to describe and picture a powerful 'god' or 'gods', or have sought out – often unconsciously – a substitute for these gods.

This wall painting from the tomb of Horemheb in Thebes depicts Horemheb offering ointments to the Egyptian god Osiris.

Offerings and sacrifices

Ancient peoples took offerings to their gods for many reasons. Some were almost a bribe, seeking a favour from a god; others gifts of gratitude given after a fortuitous event. And because people believed that the gods showed their annoyance by causing illness and misfortune, they brought special sacrifices to the gods to placate them. The worshippers confessed their faults before their gods, and asked for forgiveness and pardon.

Ancient gods

Ancient peoples usually pictured their gods as being like humans or animals, with particular powers and characteristics to match. Leading gods and goddesses were like human kings and queens. The lesser gods were their 'families' and 'court officials'. And the gods acted like human beings: they loved, hated, fought, and punished and rewarded one another and the creatures under their control.

Ancient religion

For the Israelites and their Old Testament neighbours, religion touched all areas of life. The sun, storms, earth, sea and other natural elements were treated as powers in themselves, or as the work of superhuman beings – the gods. Under the influence of the prophets, the Israelites came to believe in just one all-powerful and unique God.

Sacred places

From earliest times, certain places were thought to be 'sacred' – places where people believed that a god lived or where they might meet the god. Some of these places were private ones, but most were 'temples' where many people worshipped.

Divination

The practice of divination to determine the will of the gods was common in the ancient Middle East. Several methods were used, including: hepatoscopy, or divination by the liver; hydromancy, or divination by mixing liquids; and necromancy, or communication with the dead.

Magic

Ancient literature records that magic was employed both by human beings and by the gods. In the Babylonian creation story, the *Enuma Elish,* the god of wisdom kills his father after reciting a magic spell. The Old Testament prohibited the use of magic by the Israelites, although instances are recorded where the Israelites disregarded this command.

Creation beliefs

Ancient peoples thought of themselves as having been created by one, some or all of their gods. The fact that they had to work to provide food for their own families made them believe that they had been created by the gods in order to feed them, too. So they put a helping of their own meals on one side, or they prepared a special meal, for the god.

Rock-carved inscriptions discovered at Caesarea Philippi indicate that worship of the Greek god Pan continued into the third century AD.

A group of Sumerian votive statuettes from the temple to the god Abu in ancient Ashnunak, dating from about 2900–2600 BC. Carved out of limestone, alabaster and gypsum, these statuettes would have been offered or consecrated in fulfilment of a vow.

Telling the future

The gods of ancient times were unpredictable, and therefore people could have no certainty about the future. They were ready to listen to anyone who made out a good case for having a message from the gods. So there were prophets and fortune tellers, witches and magicians, as well as priests in most societies.

The role of the priests

Priests often held great power as agents or spokespersons for the gods. They could say whether or not a god was pleased, and could decide what offerings were necessary. In many cases, priests were able to influence the affairs of the nation by claiming to speak a god's mind.

Assyrian temple servant.

Statuettes of the Egyptian gods Isis, Osiris and Horus, dating from 950 BC.

Idolatry

Ancient peoples created statues of their gods in human or animal forms, and these were sometimes worshipped. This practice was so widespread throughout the Middle East that it was difficult for the Israelites to extricate themselves from it, despite strict instructions to do so in Old Testament law. The use of such idols remained commonplace in Greek and Roman religion, and the early Christian church had to tackle issues related to idolatry even in New Testament times.

See also

■ Egyptian religion and beliefs (pages 54–55)

■ The Canaanites (pages 56–57)

■ Babylonian religion and beliefs (pages 64–65)

■ Death and the afterlife (pages 164–165)

The creator-God of Israel

The ancient Israelites lived amidst peoples whose belief in multiple gods involved the practice of idolatry, magic and divination. The Israelites' belief in one God – an all-powerful God who played an active part in their corporate and individual lives – was quite different, and often led to misunderstanding.

A God for all people

The Israelites sometimes misunderstood the nature of God's involvement in their history. They believed that they were God's 'favourites'. And yet the Old Testament prophets knew that God's purposes were much broader than this. God's purpose was the salvation of all nations – Yahweh, the God of Israel, was to be the God of all people.

Figurine of the Canaanite goddess of love and war, Astarte, dating from 1300–1000 BC.

Who is God?

The Israelites took God's existence for granted, and the Old Testament never directly tackles the question 'Who is God?'. But it does, in places, ask some searching questions about God, and does not assume easy answers to life's issues and problems. Indeed, at times of difficulty in the history of the people of Israel, they sometimes questioned whether their exclusive worship of a single God was contributing to their decline. But time and time again, the Israelites came back to the reality and power of their creator-God, though it was not until after the exile that they were ready to categorically deny that other gods could exist.

A God above nature

Most religions in the ancient Middle East were means of explaining and controlling the world of nature as it affected people's lives. But the Israelites believed that their God was above nature, not a part of nature. God might be described in imagery derived from natural phenomena, such as light or fire, but could never be identified with the forces of the natural world.

Statuette of the Canaanite weather god, Baal, from the first century AD.

A functional God

The ancient Israelites never attempted to dissect or to analyse God. The world of abstract thought was quite foreign to their way of thinking. Instead of defining God metaphysically, by asking what God is made of, they defined God functionally, by exploring God's relevance to human life and experience.

An invisible God

The God of the Israelites differed greatly from the gods of other ancient peoples. Firstly, the Israelites' God was 'invisible'. Whereas other nations created images of their gods in the form of humans or animals, the Old Testament strongly forbade such practice by the people of Israel.

'You [God] have been a refuge for the poor, a refuge for the needy in his distress, a shelter from the storm and a shade from the heat.' (Isaiah 25:4)

Describing God

The Old Testament writers refer to God not as a force or an abstract will, but very much as a person. They describe God in many different ways. God can be depicted in terms of close personal and family relationships – as a loving parent, a step-parent or a spouse. And God is portrayed as both male and female. The book of Deuteronomy, for instance, states: 'You deserted the Rock, who fathered you; you forgot the God who gave you birth.' Here, God is the divine parent: both male and female. And frequently, God is described as a ruler and as the ultimate king.

Coin of the Seleucid king Antiochus IV Epiphanes, who elevated himself to the status of a god. The title 'Epiphanes' adopted by the king means 'the outshining of God'.

'For the Lord your God is a consuming fire…' (Deuteronomy 4:24)

See also

- The Canaanites
(pages 56–57)

- The practice of prayer
(pages 174–175)

- Jesus the teacher
(pages 182–183)

- Exodus
(pages 200–201)

A personal God

The Old Testament makes clear that God is intimately interested in the world and its inhabitants, and is not remote from people and their needs. Numerous Old Testament stories tell of God in discussion with people – even undergoing a change of mind as a result. God related to Israel as a nation, but was also personally concerned for individuals.

An active God

The Old Testament indicates that God was active in all areas of the life of the people of Israel, both as a nation and as individuals. Indeed, the Old Testament story depicts God in control of the very history of the Israelites. From the beginning, the nation of Israel was proactively selected to be God's own people. But the Israelites were expected to return God's love with obedience, and their prosperity or decline was seen to be related to their faithfulness to God.

Israel's faith

The religion of the people of Israel has a long history, beginning with God's promise to Abraham recorded in the Old Testament book of Genesis. Throughout this period, God made a series of promises, or covenants, to key individuals – Abraham, Isaac, Jacob – and the different facets of God's nature were revealed.

Yotvata oasis, Arava valley, Negev.

A God who can be known

The Old Testament story of Abraham sets out one of the most basic beliefs of the ancient Israelites. This was the certainty that God was a real personality and that human beings – individually or as a group – could know God.

Abraham's faith

The starting-point of Israel's religion was the day when God spoke to Abraham, telling him to leave his land and his family home and go to a new country. On that day, the Bible shows God promising to make Abraham the founder of a great nation. Abraham 'put his trust in Yahweh, and because of this Yahweh was pleased with him and accepted him.' Abraham moved to the 'promised land' of Canaan, building an altar and worshipping God in all the places he stayed.

A living God in action

In rescuing the Israelites from Egypt to keep the promises made to their ancestors, God demonstrated reliability. And as they were led through the unknown wilderness, with their need for food and water met, and constantly restored in spite of their rebellions, this was an indication of a living God in action.

Jacob and the nation of Israel

The history of Israel as a nation began with Abraham's grandson, Jacob, and his 12 sons, from whom the 12 tribes of Israel were descended. 'I am the Lord, the God of Abraham and Isaac,' God said to Jacob. 'I will give to you and to your descendants this land... I will be with you and protect you wherever you go, and I will bring you back to this land. I will not leave you until I have done all that I have promised to you.'

Famine came. Jacob and his family followed Jacob's son, Joseph, into Egypt. Their descendants remained there for centuries. But God's promise still held. This family and nation were God's people. When the Egyptians made slaves of them and they cried out for help, God heard.

The 'promised land': The Jerusalem hills near Ein Kerem.

The Ark of the Covenant is surrounded by menorah and other ceremonial objects on this mosaic floor of the 4th–5th century AD synagogue in Tiberias.

Moses and the law

The Old Testament recounts that one day, in the desert, God spoke to Moses. 'I am sending you to the king of Egypt,' God said, 'so that you can lead my people out of his country'. Moses needed to know how he could describe God to the people. And so Moses learned God's personal name, Yahweh ('the Lord'), meaning 'I am' or 'I will be who I will be'. This showed two things: God was unchanging and completely reliable; and God was always alive, active and creative. It was the knowledge of this God that Moses brought to his people.

The prophets

The Old Testament prophets' greatest contribution to Israel's faith was their constant challenge to the people to be be faithful to what they knew of the God of the exodus period. The prophets spoke to the conscience of Israel, warning of impending disaster, but also offering hope and God's promise for a new future, if only the people would turn from their wrongdoing.

The city of Arad in the Negev was the site of an Israelite sanctuary at the end of the ninth century BC. The photograph shows the remains of the Holy of Holies.

The discipline of God

Many Israelites saw the exile only as a disaster. But those who saw it as God's judgment on a disobedient people could also see the exile as a time of purification. They realized that they would only survive by keeping themselves separate from other nations, and by insisting on renewed obedience to God's law.

See also

■ The world of the patriarchs
(pages 18–19)

■ The exodus from Egypt
(pages 20–21)

■ Two kingdoms
(pages 28–29)

■ The prophets
(pages 166–167)

■ Genesis
(pages 198–199)

■ Exodus
(pages 200–201)

This ostracon from Arad, dating from the sixth century BC, is inscribed with the words 'Beth Yahw'h' ('house of Yahweh').

The grandeur of God

During the time of David and Solomon, a new sense of the grandeur of God can be seen in the temple and its worship, and in the psalms sung in the temple, hailing Yahweh as a 'mighty God, a mighty king over all the gods'. Along with the solemnity of the temple worship went a strong sense of joy: 'The Lord is king! Earth, be glad! Rejoice, you islands of the seas!'

The time of the kings

During the time of the Old Testament kings, Israel became an independent state for the first time. The Israelites were impressed by the pomp and splendour of kingship, but they recognized that the dignity of their earthly kings was only a shadow of the greatness of the Lord, the King of kings.

The time of the exile

During the exile, the Israelites came to recognize, in a way they had never needed to before, just how much they and their God were connected. Unless they saw themselves as the people of God, Israel was no different from any other nation on earth, and could be wiped off the map as easily as many nations had been in the course of history.

God's laws in practice

The Old Testament laws are summed up in the Ten Commandments given through Moses at Mount Sinai. These were addressed to the whole nation of Israel and to every Israelite as an individual. They were not primarily rules for worship or religious occasions; they covered every aspect of life.

Two copies

The Bible records that the Ten Commandments were written on two stone tablets. This probably means two copies. When a written covenant was made in the ancient world, it was common practice for each party making the covenant to have a copy of its contents. If the covenant was between two nations, for instance the Hittites and the Egyptians, the two copies would be kept far apart, in the temple of a god of each land.

In Israel, though, the covenant was between God and the people. Both copies of the Ten Commandments were kept in the Ark of the Covenant. This was kept in the inner sanctuary of the temple, and was the visible throne of Israel's invisible God – a distinctive sign of God's presence.

The purpose of the law

The law was intended to be a guide to good relationships – with God and with other people. In it, God tells the Israelites how they are to live, for their own good and well-being.

The Hebrew word which is usually translated 'law' (*torah*) actually means 'guidance' or 'instruction'. These laws were never intended to be a long list of dos and don'ts to make life a burden. The law reflects God's character – holiness, justice and goodness – and expresses God's will. It gives to people the practical guidance they need in order to obey God's command to 'Be holy, as I am holy.'

The Ten Commandments

Worship no god but me.

Do not make for yourselves images of anything in heaven or on earth or in the water under the earth. Do not bow down to any idol or worship it, because I am the Lord your God and I tolerate no rivals. I bring punishment on those who hate me and on their descendants down to the third and fourth generation. But I show my love to thousands of generations of those who love me and obey my laws.

Do not use my name for evil purposes, because I, the Lord your God, will punish anyone who misuses my name.

Observe the Sabbath and keep it holy. You have six days in which to do your work, but the seventh day is a day of rest dedicated to me. On that day no one is to work – neither you, your children, your slaves, your animals, nor the foreigners who live in your country. In six days I, the Lord, made the earth, the sky, the sea, and everything in them, but on the seventh day I rested. That is why I, the Lord, blessed the Sabbath and made it holy.

Respect your father and your mother, so that you may live a long time in the land that I am giving you.

Do not commit murder.

Do not commit adultery.

Do not steal.

Do not accuse anyone falsely.

Do not desire another man's house; do not desire his wife, his slaves, his cattle, his donkeys, or anything else that he owns.'

The fourth of the Ten Commandments forbade working on the sabbath day. This law applied to all people and also to working animals.

The 'Book of the Covenant'

The first major collection of supplementary laws is found in the Old Testament book of Exodus. It contains moral, civil and religious laws. Instructions about worship are followed by laws dealing with the rights of slaves; murder and injury to human life; theft and damage to property; social and religious duties; and justice and human rights. At the end there are instructions for the three great religious festivals: Passover, Firstfruits and Weeks.

Supplementary laws

In any society, detailed rules and laws are always necessary. For the Israelites, the basic laws of the Ten Commandments needed to be expanded. The Old Testament contains many 'case-laws' which supplemented the Ten Commandments. Some of these laws were similar to those of other nations. There are three major collections of laws.

Aspects of the law reminded Israelites that they had once been slaves in Egypt, and that God had rescued them from slavery. For example, anyone who acquired a fellow Israelite as a worker was to regard this person not as a slave, but as a hired hand. After seven years, the worker should be released from duty, with a good supply of food and livestock.

See also

■ The exodus from Egypt (pages 20–21)

■ Priests and rituals (pages 162–163)

■ New Testament religion (pages 170–171)

■ Exodus (pages 200–201)

■ Leviticus, Numbers, Deuteronomy (pages 202–203)

The Old Testament book of Deuteronomy lists which animals people were permitted or forbidden to eat, according to the law. Animals which were allowed as food included those which chewed cud and had split hoofs, such as sheep, cattle and deer. Pigs did not fall into this category, and were classified as 'unclean'.

The 'holiness' laws

The Old Testament book of Leviticus contains the second important collection of supplementary laws. These mainly concern how the Israelites should worship God, the rituals connected with the tabernacle and temple. But they also deal with everyday behaviour. The keynote of the teaching is the command to the Israelites: 'Be holy, because I, the Lord your God, am holy'.

Deuteronomy

The third collection of detailed supplementary laws is set down in the form of a sermon by Moses, in the Old Testament book of Deuteronomy. This book covers many of the same matters as the books of Exodus and Leviticus. It includes frequent encouragements to keep God's law, and warnings of the consequences if the people disobey.

Modern-day orthodox Jews with a scroll containing the law at the Western Wall in Jerusalem.

The law contained instructions for growing and harvesting crops. Reapers were instructed not to reap to the edges of a field or to go through the field a second time. Any gleanings must be left for the poor and landless. Crops could be planted for six consecutive years, but on the seventh year the land must be left fallow for the soil to recover. God promised that the harvest on the sixth year would be sufficient to provide food for the following year as well.

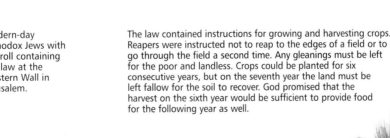

Feasts and holy days

From the earliest times, the Israelites kept fasts and festivals as part of their religion and way of life. Festivals were times of thanksgiving to God for harvests, occasions for remembering outstanding events in Israel's history, and opportunities for great rejoicing and feasting.

Seasonal influences

Israel's main religious festivals were connected with the seasons and the farmer's year in Canaan. They were held in spring, early summer and autumn. On each occasion the Israelites were expected to go to their local shrine and present their offerings to God. After the seventh century BC these 'pilgrim' festivals were held only in Jerusalem. By the time of Jesus, the city's normal population of 40,000 or so was swollen to about 150,000 by the pilgrims who came for the annual Passover festival.

The practice of fasting

People fasted as a sign of genuine repentance. During the time of fasting they did not eat or drink. Fasting and prayer often went together. During a fast, some people would tear their clothes, dress in coarse sackcloth, throw dust and ashes on their heads, and leave their hair uncombed and their bodies unwashed. But the Old Testament prophets and, later, Jesus made it plain that these outward signs of fasting were not enough. A real change of heart was what mattered most.

Regular fast days

Old Testament law required the Israelites to set apart one day in the year for a national fast: the Day of Atonement, which was the 'tenth day of the seventh month' (end of September/beginning of October). During the exile in Babylon, special fasts were also held in the fifth and seventh months to mourn the destruction of the temple and the murder of Gedaliah, the governor of Judah. After the exile, two other regular fasts were held: in the tenth month, to remember the start of the siege of Jerusalem, and in the fourth month, marking the final capture of the city. Fasts were also kept by the nation and by individuals at times of special need.

See also

▢ The farming year
(pages 104–105)

◼ Annual festivals
(pages 156–157)

◼ Jesus the prophet
(pages 186–187)

'Celebrate the Feast of Harvest with the firstfruits of the crops you sow in your field. Celebrate the Feast of Ingathering at the end of the year, when you gather in your crops from the field.' (Exodus 23:16)

Jubilee year

The law said that in every 50th year – the year after seven 'sabbatical' years – land and property (except for town houses) were to be returned to their original owners, slaves were to be set free, debts cancelled and the land allowed to lie fallow. The jubilee law may have proved too difficult to keep, and eventually it was seen as a future Golden Age that only God could introduce. This was the 'year' of God's favour promised by Isaiah, and announced by Jesus.

Sabbatical year

Just as every seventh day was to be a day of rest, so every seventh ('sabbatical') year was 'to be a year of complete rest for the land, a year dedicated to the Lord'. Obviously the whole land could not lie fallow at the same time. Probably each field lay fallow every seventh year after it was first sown. Anything which did grow in this year could be harvested free by the poor. This arrangement was intended to remind the Israelites that the land was not their own. It was 'holy' (belonging to God). Also, each seventh year, all Israelite slaves were to be set free and all debts cancelled.

New moon

The day of the new moon signalled the beginning of each month. Trumpets were blown and special sacrifices were made. The arrival of the new moon was understood as a reminder that God had created an orderly world. No work was done on this day, but there were special meals and religious teaching.

The sabbath

The sabbath was Israel's most distinctive festival. Other nations had harvest festivals and new moon rituals, but only Israel had the sabbath, which cut across the rhythm of the seasons.

Every seventh day was set aside for rest. This was the 'sabbath' and it belonged to God. On this day, people were to remember all that God had done, especially in rescuing them from slavery in Egypt. 'If you treat the Sabbath as sacred,' God said through the prophet Isaiah, 'and do not pursue your own interests on that day; if you value my holy day and honour it by not travelling, working or talking idly on that day, then you will find the joy that comes from serving me.'

By New Testament times, keeping the sabbath had become so complicated with rules and regulations that Jesus had to remind people that 'the Sabbath was made for the good of people; people were not made for the Sabbath.'

Annual festivals

The sabbath and most of the great festivals of the Jewish religion were kept from the very earliest period of Israel's history. But two major festivals began to be observed much later – Purim, from the the fifth century BC, and Hanukkah, from the second century BC.

Weeks/Pentecost

(seven weeks)

TAMMUZ

SIVAN

AB

IYYAR

ELUL

May *June* *July* *August*

April *September*

NISAN

March *October*

TISHRI

February *November*

January *December*

ADAR

MARCHESVAN

Firstfruits

Passover Unleavened Bread

New Year Trumpets

Day of Atonement

Tabernacles/Bo...

Purim

SHEBAT

KISLEV

TEBET

Dedication/Lights

Passover

Passover (also called Unleavened Bread) was one of the most important annual festivals. It took place on the evening before the 14th of Nisan. On that night every family sacrificed a lamb. This was a reminder of the first such sacrifice, which took place just before the exodus from Egypt. On that occasion God 'passed over' the Israelite houses where the blood of the lamb had been sprinkled on the door-posts and lintel, and spared the lives of their firstborn.

Unleavened bread, made quickly and without yeast, was eaten at the Passover meal and all through the following week. This, too, was a reminder of the hurried preparations made when the Pharaoh finally allowed the Israelites to leave Egypt. It also recalled the first bread baked from new corn, four days after the Israelites entered Canaan.

The Passover was always held in the home, but by New Testament times it was the main 'pilgrim' festival celebrated in Jerusalem. Even then, it was still a family-based celebration, and pilgrims would hire their own rooms for the purpose – as Jesus and his disciples did. It remains one of the most important Jewish festivals today.

Trumpets

The beginning of every month, as well as every festival, was signalled by a blast of trumpets. But on the first day of the seventh month the trumpets sounded for a special celebration. It was a day for rest and worship, more important even than the sabbath. It marked out the seventh month as the most solemn month in the year. After the exile, Trumpets was treated as a religious New Year festival (*Rosh Hashanah*).

Weeks

Weeks was the main harvest festival. At the end of the grain harvest the priest offered two loaves of bread made from the new flour, along with animal sacrifices. This took place 50 days (or seven weeks plus one day) after Passover and the start of the harvest. The festival later came to be known as Pentecost, from the Greek word meaning 'fiftieth'. It was a time of great rejoicing and thanksgiving for God's gifts at harvest.

Hanukkah

Hanukkah, or Dedication, commemorated the cleansing and re-dedication of the temple by Judas Maccabaeus in 164 BC, after it had been defiled by the Seleucid ruler, Antiochus IV Epiphanes. It was also called 'Lights' because each evening lamps were placed in houses and synagogues.

Purim

Purim was an excited and noisy celebration, and was traditionally connected with the story of how the Israelites were saved from massacre during the reign of the Persian king Ahasuerus, told in the Old Testament book of Esther. Purim means 'lots', and the name refers to the lots cast by the king's chief minister to decide on which day he should massacre the Jews.

Day of Atonement

On the Day of Atonement (*Yom Kippur*) the whole nation of Israel confessed their sin and asked for God's forgiveness and cleansing. The high priest, dressed in white linen, first offered a sacrifice for his own sin and the sin of the priests, and then offered another sacrifice for the sin of the people.

This was the only day in the year when the high priest went into the 'holy of holies' – the inner, most sacred part of the temple. There he sprinkled blood from the sacrifice. Then he took a goat, known as the 'scapegoat', and, after laying his hand on its head, sent it off into the desert as a sign that the people's sins had been taken away.

Firstfruits

This ceremony was held on the last day of the Passover festival. During the ceremony, the first sheaf of the barley harvest was presented to God.

Ingathering

Ingathering, also known as Tabernacles, Booths and Shelters, was the most popular and joyful of all the festivals. It was held in the autumn when all the fruit crops had been harvested. The celebrations included camping out in gardens and on roof-tops in tents or huts made from the branches of trees. These tents were a reminder of the time when Israel had lived in tents in the desert.

See also

■ The exodus from Egypt (pages 20–21)

■ The farming year (pages 104–105)

■ Food and drink (pages 106–107)

■ Priests and rituals (pages 162–163)

■ Leviticus, Numbers, Deuteronomy (pages 202–203)

■ Esther (pages 214–215)

The tabernacle

The Old Testament describes the tabernacle as the centre of Israelite religious life after the exodus, though descriptions of it were based on the later temple in Jerusalem. The tabernacle was also called the 'tent of meeting' (between God and the people) and 'the dwelling place' (of God).

Carving of the Ark of the Covenant.

The tabernacle

The Old Testament describes the tabernacle as a large tent made by the Israelites to a design given to Moses by God at Mount Sinai. It was the place where they worshipped God on the journey from Egypt to Canaan. It stood at the centre of the camp, with the Levites' tents around it on all four sides. Behind them were the tents of the 12 tribes of Israel, three tribes on each side.

The holy of holies

Inside, the tabernacle was divided into two rooms. The smaller one, furthest from the door, was called the 'holy of holies' or 'the most holy place'. Only the high priest was allowed to enter the 'holy of holies', and then only once a year, on the Day of Atonement. A linen curtain separated this from the larger room, which was called 'the holy place'. The entrance to it was covered by another embroidered linen curtain.

The Ark of the Covenant

The Ark of the Covenant was a rectangular box, measuring about 115 x 70 x 70 cm/4 x 2 x 2 ft. It was made of acacia wood overlaid with gold, and was carried by poles pushed through rings at the four lower corners. It traditionally contained the two tablets of the Ten Commandments, a golden pot of manna and Aaron's rod which blossomed overnight. The lid was of gold, and at both ends were the figures of two cherubim with wings spread out as a sign of God's protection.

The Ark of the Covenant stood in the 'holy of holies'. It was thought of as the place where God was invisibly enthroned, because God said, 'I will meet you there, and from above the lid between the two winged creatures I will give you all my laws for the people of Israel.' It was sometimes carried into battle, as a symbol of God's protection. The fact that on one occasion it was captured by the Philistines showed it had no power of its own. It was also a focus for processions in the temple at Jerusalem.

During the early period of Israel's settled life, the Ark of the Covenant and the tabernacle were kept at Shiloh. When David established his capital in Jerusalem, he placed the Ark there as a symbol of the legitimacy of his rule.

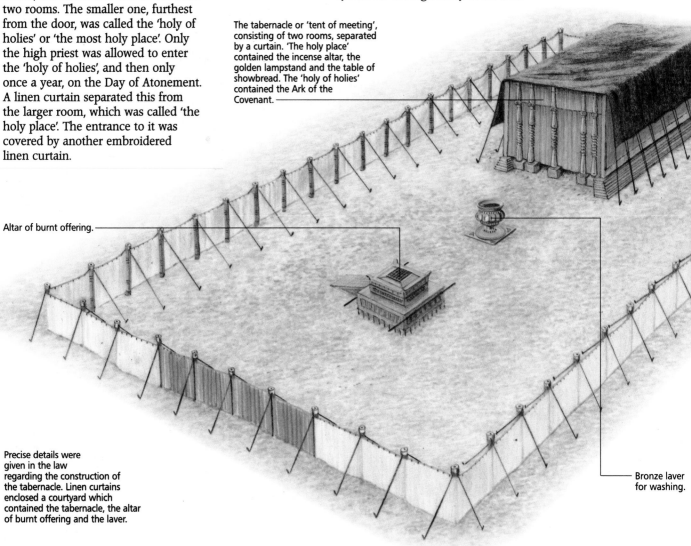

The tabernacle or 'tent of meeting', consisting of two rooms, separated by a curtain. 'The holy place' contained the incense altar, the golden lampstand and the table of showbread. The 'holy of holies' contained the Ark of the Covenant.

Altar of burnt offering.

Precise details were given in the law regarding the construction of the tabernacle. Linen curtains enclosed a courtyard which contained the tabernacle, the altar of burnt offering and the laver.

Bronze laver for washing.

Table of showbread

The table of showbread, also called the bread of presence, was a gold-overlaid table that stood in the holy place. On each sabbath, 12 new loaves – one for each tribe of Israel – were placed as an offering on the table of showbread.

Courtyard

The tabernacle stood in the western part of a courtyard about 50 x 25 m/150 x 75 ft in size. The courtyard itself was enclosed by a screen of linen curtains. There was an entrance on one side, with a curtain of embroidered linen drawn across it.

Screen of linen curtains surrounding courtyard.

Selection of stone carved decorated spoons, possibly used for plugging bottles of anointing oil, dating from 1200–800 BC.

The incense altar

In the holy place, in front of the curtain which screened the holy of holies, stood a small altar on which incense was burnt each morning and evening. It was made out of acacia wood, overlaid with gold. It had a horn at each corner, and rings were attached to two of the sides to make it easy to carry.

Altar of burnt offering

Sacrifices of lambs, bulls, goats and other animals were made on the altar of burnt offering. This altar, like several objects in the tabernacle, was made of wood overlaid with bronze. It was about 2.5 m/7 ft square and 1.5 m/4 ft high. Halfway up the altar was a ledge on which it seems the priests stood to make their sacrifices. The altar may have been filled with earth, or it may have been empty and used like an incinerator.

The golden lampstand

The seven-branched golden lampstand (the menorah) was the only source of light in the tabernacle. It was hammered out of one piece of gold, weighing 30 kg/66 lb or more, and decorated with flowers and buds, like almond blossom.

Tabernacle design

The tabernacle was supported by a frame of acacia wood. It was about 14 m/45 ft long, 4 m/13 ft wide and 5 m/15 ft high. Four types of coverings were draped over this frame. First came linen curtains, decorated with blue, purple and scarlet tapestry which could be seen inside the tabernacle. Next came a set of curtains made of goats' hair. These were a little longer than the linen curtains, and one of them formed the door of the tent. On top of these curtains was a weatherproof covering, made of rams' skins, dyed red. Finally, there was another waterproof covering made from the skin of another animal, translated in the Bible as 'badger', 'porpoise' or simply 'fine leather'.

Laver

The laver was a large bronze basin on a bronze base. It was used by the priests for washing their hands and feet each time they were about to enter the tabernacle or offer a sacrifice.

See also

- The exodus from Egypt (pages 20–21)
- God's laws in practice (pages 152–153)
- Three temples (pages 158–159)
- Priests and rituals (pages 162–163)

The table of showbread was fitted with rings and poles for carrying, as it was considered too sacred to be touched.

Three temples

Three temples were central to the Israelites during their long history: Solomon's temple; the second temple; and Herod's temple.

Solomon's temple

Solomon's temple was not large by today's standards, but it must have been the largest building the Israelites had constructed up to that time. It measured about 9 x 27 m/30 x 87 ft and was 13.5 m/43 ft high. Built at Jerusalem, Solomon's temple became the centre of worship for the kingdom of Judah.

Design of Solomon's temple

Solomon's temple was very similar in layout to the pattern of temples in other nations. The priests entered the temple through a large porch. Then came the main room, the 'holy place'. In it stood the incense altar, the table of showbread and five pairs of lampstands. The inner room was the 'holy of holies', and was probably approached by steps from the holy place. The holy of holies contained the Ark of the Covenant, together with two cherubim made of olivewood overlaid with gold.

The walls of each room in the temple were panelled with cedar, carved with flowers, palm-trees and cherubim, and overlaid with gold. No stonework could be seen from inside the building. The holy place was dimly lit by high windows and by the lampstands. But the holy of holies had no windows and so was completely dark.

Herod's temple

In 19 BC King Herod the Great began work on a new temple at Jerusalem. He wanted to win favour with his subjects and to impress the Roman world with his splendid building. It was not completed until AD 62, long after Herod's reign had ended. Built on the same plan as Solomon's temple, this third temple was by far the grandest. It was twice as high as Solomon's temple, and covered with so much gold that it was a dazzling sight in the bright sun.

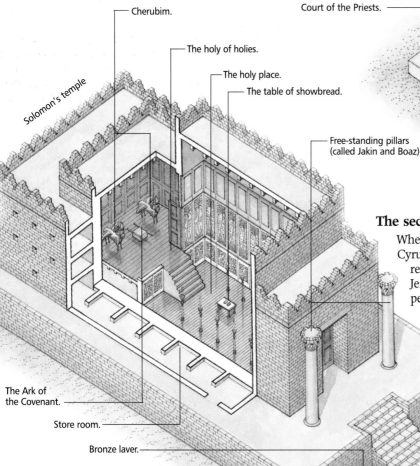

Cherubim.

The holy of holies.

The holy place.

The table of showbread.

Court of the Priests.

Solomon's temple

Free-standing pillars (called Jakin and Boaz).

Herod's temple

The Ark of the Covenant.

Store room.

Bronze laver.

The second temple

When the Persian king Cyrus allowed the Jews to return from Babylon to Jerusalem in 8 BC, he gave them permission to rebuild Solomon's temple. He also returned some of the gold and silver objects which Nebuchadnezzar had taken from the temple. They began work straight away, but soon became discouraged. Only after the prophets Haggai and Zechariah had spurred them on was the second temple completed, in 515 BC.

Although it stood for 500 years very little is known about the second temple. It almost certainly followed the plan of Solomon's temple, but was not nearly so splendid. When the Seleucid ruler Antiochus IV (175–164 BC) defiled it by offering sacrifices of pigs to his own gods, his action led to the Maccabean revolt. Three years later the temple was re-dedicated – the event commemorated at the festival of Dedication.

Destruction of Solomon's temple

Solomon's temple was destroyed by Nebuchadnezzar of Babylon when he captured the city of Jerusalem in 587 BC. Its remaining bronze, gold and silver furnishings were taken to Babylon.

This inscription, written in Greek, forbids entry by non-Jews into the sanctified area of the temple.

The sanctuary, consisting of the holy place separated by a curtain from the holy of holies.

Temple courts

A covered cloister ran right round the outer courtyards of Herod's temple. The main entrance was from the south, and led to the Court of the Gentiles. Anyone could enter this part of the temple. But notices in Greek and Latin forbade non-Jews to enter the inner court of the temple. The result of breaking this rule was likely to be death. The next court was the Court of the Women. This was as far as women were allowed to go into the temple itself. Men could go further, into the Court of Israel, and they could even enter the Court of the Priests for a procession round the altar at the festival of Tabernacles.

See also

■ From exile to return (pages 34–35)

■ A brief history of Jerusalem (pages 38–39)

■ Mining and metalwork (pages 134–135)

■ Priests and rituals (pages 162–163)

The domed ceiling of the Huldah gateway, one of the entrances into Herod's temple.

Temple platform, Herod's temple.

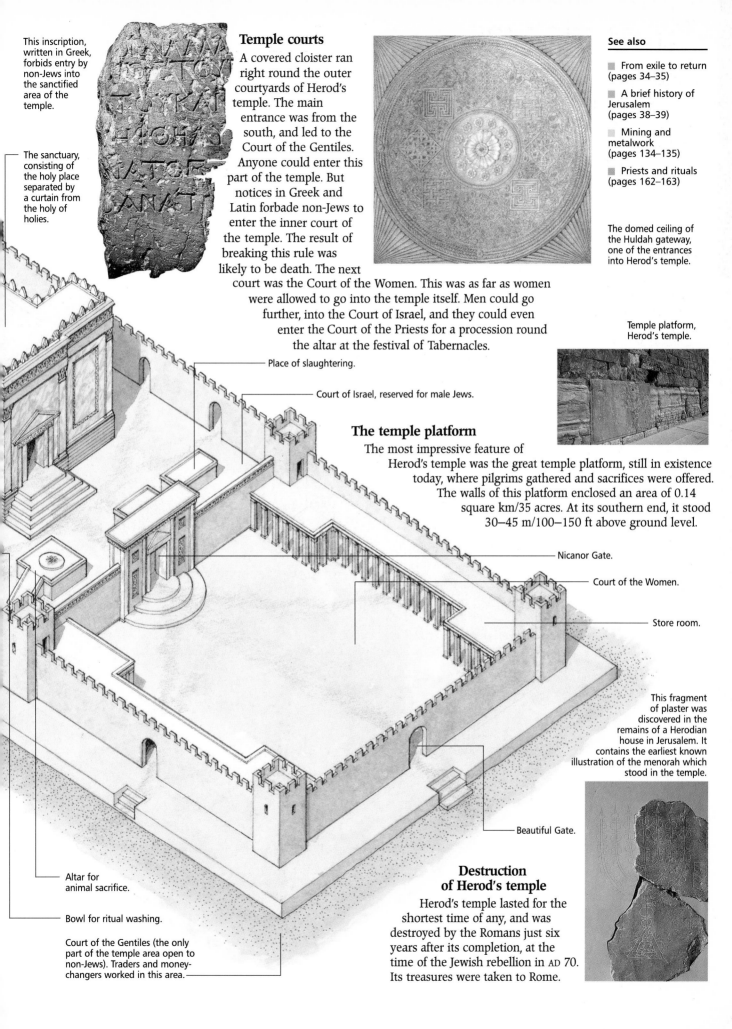

Place of slaughtering.

Court of Israel, reserved for male Jews.

The temple platform

The most impressive feature of Herod's temple was the great temple platform, still in existence today, where pilgrims gathered and sacrifices were offered. The walls of this platform enclosed an area of 0.14 square km/35 acres. At its southern end, it stood 30–45 m/100–150 ft above ground level.

Nicanor Gate.

Court of the Women.

Store room.

This fragment of plaster was discovered in the remains of a Herodian house in Jerusalem. It contains the earliest known illustration of the menorah which stood in the temple.

Beautiful Gate.

Altar for animal sacrifice.

Bowl for ritual washing.

Court of the Gentiles (the only part of the temple area open to non-Jews). Traders and money-changers worked in this area.

Destruction of Herod's temple

Herod's temple lasted for the shortest time of any, and was destroyed by the Romans just six years after its completion, at the time of the Jewish rebellion in AD 70. Its treasures were taken to Rome.

Priests and rituals

Priests in ancient Israel were in charge of sacrifice and offerings, among other duties. Sacrifice was an ancient practice, and was taken for granted as part of religious observance in the Old Testament. Kings and other key community leaders could offer sacrifices, as well as priests.

The first priests

The Old Testament's instructions for priests are placed alongside descriptions of the tabernacle in the Torah. Aaron and his four sons were regarded as the forerunners of all priests. Detailed rules were given regarding duties, rituals and even clothing. The priests were to be supported by offerings from the people, including a share of the meat from the sacrifices.

The Levites

Aaron was a member of the tribe of Levi, which gave the Levites a special position, consecrated to God and set apart from the other Israelite tribes for religious duties. There were too many Levites for them all to serve as priests. Those who could not show direct descent from Aaron performed ancillary duties in the temple. The Levites did not own any land and were supported by the other tribes by means of tithing, whereby one-tenth of all harvests and livestock were given to God.

Duties of the priests and Levites

The duties of the priests and Levites were mostly connected with the temple sacrifices and worship. But they also had a number of other duties, such as blessing the people and delivering oracles to identify God's will on difficult issues. The priests and Levites were also responsible for teaching the *torah*.

Burnt-offering

In the practice of burnt-offering, whole animals, except for the skin, were sacrificed. The animals had to be in perfect condition. The worshippers placed their hands on the animals to show that the animals were sacrifices for their own shortcomings. The blood of the animal was sprinkled on the altar as a further sign that the life of the animal given in death had been dedicated to God.

Peace-offering

The ritual of the peace-offering was similar to that for the burnt-offering, except that here only the fat – which the Israelites considered the best portion – was burnt on the altar, and the meat was eaten by the worshippers and their families. Since God also shared in the sacrifice, it was also thought of as a friendship meal with God.

Animal sacrifice

In Old Testament times, animal sacrifice was understood in many different ways. It was often used as an expression of repentance through which a worshipper could make peace with God.

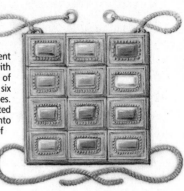

The high priest wore a breastplate set with 12 different precious stones, each engraved with the name of one of the 12 tribes of Israel. On each shoulder were six stones, also representing the 12 tribes. When the high priest was anointed with oil, it flowed from his head onto his shoulders, and was symbolic of God's blessing flowing over the tribes of Israel.

Incense featured in the religious ceremonies of many of Israel's neighbours as well as in the Israelites' worship of God. This decorated Canaanite pottery stand from the 11th century BC was used to hold a bowl for burning incense.

Grain-offering

A grain-offering was an offering of flour, baked cakes or raw grain, together with oil and frankincense. It was a good-will offering to God. Part of the grain-offering – a 'memorial portion' – was burnt on the temple altar. The grain-offering was also a way of asking God to 'remember' the worshipper for good, as well as a contribution to the priests' food supply.

See also

■ Kings and rulers (pages 116–117)

■ Ancient beliefs (pages 146–147)

■ Feasts and holy days (pages 154–155)

■ Groups and sects (pages 168–169)

This inscription reads 'To the House of Trumpeting'. It was discovered near the south-western corner of the temple mount, and is presumed to have been located on the tower of Herod's temple where the priest stood when blowing the shofar to announce the onset of the Sabbath.

Every year on the Day of Atonement the high priest made two sacrifices: first, he sacrificed a bull for his own sin and the sin of the priests, and then he sacrificed a goat for the sin of the people. He then laid his hands on the head of a second goat – the 'scapegoat' – symbolically transferring the sin of the people to the goat. The scapegoat was then released into the desert.

Sin-offering

A sin-offering was a sacrifice given when a person had sinned against someone else or against God. This sin brought ritual defilement that needed to be cleansed. The blood of the sacrifice was sprinkled as a sign that the defilement had been removed through the death that had taken place. Some of the sacrifice was taken as food for the priest; when the worshipper saw the priest eat the meat without being harmed it was regarded as a sign that God had accepted this act of repentance.

Death and the afterlife

From early Old Testament times, the Israelites believed that the body and soul were one, and that death brought the death of the entire 'self'. It was only later in their history that they began to speculate on the possibility of life after death.

Typically, tombs in New Testament times had two rooms: one containing ossuaries used for storing the bones of the dead and, beyond that, another room with a shelf on which the embalmed body of a more recently deceased person was laid. A circular millstone set in a groove covered the entrance of the tomb.

Sheol

In the early days of the Old Testament, the Israelites believed that when people died, they went down to the place of the dead – called *sheol* – deep in the earth. All people – good or bad – were believed to go to *sheol*.

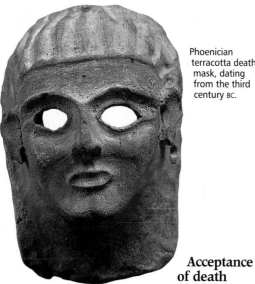

Phoenician terracotta death mask, dating from the third century BC.

Acceptance of death

Throughout the Old Testament, death was seen both as a natural part of life and an intrusion. Death at the end of a long and fruitful life was accepted, and consolation taken from having many children, the continuation of the family name and a proper burial. If death cut short life in its prime, or if there were no remaining children, death was seen as an intrusion – or a curse.

The afterlife

The ancient Israelites believed that the dead continued to play an active part in the living world. As in neighbouring nations, many people in Israel practised necromancy, or communication with the dead via a medium. This practice was strongly condemned by the prophets, but they were unable to stamp it out.

Resurrection

Following the exile in Babylon, Jewish beliefs about death and the afterlife began to change. The Old Testament book of Daniel indicates a belief in resurrection, though there were many ideas as to what this might entail, and even into New Testament times there was considerable debate. The Pharisees believed in resurrection, for example, but the Sadduccees did not.

New Testament beliefs

The New Testament indicates that Jesus' teaching presupposed a belief in resurrection. And after Jesus' own death and resurrection, Christians were convinced that there would be life after death – and death lost its power to terrify. When the missionary Paul was facing possible death, he wrote: 'What is life? To me, it is Christ. Death then will bring more. I very much want to leave this life and be with Christ.'

The bones of a deceased person were transferred to an ossuary about one year after death.

These tombs in the Kidron valley, Jerusalem, were constructed by wealthy families in the first and second centuries BC.

Funeral customs

In ancient Palestine, a quick burial was necessary because of the hot climate. When a person died, the eyes were closed, and the body was washed and wrapped in strips of cloth. The body was not placed in a coffin, but was carried on a wooden stretcher to the burial-place.

Family and friends made a great show of mourning: weeping, wailing, wearing uncomfortable clothes, walking barefoot, putting ashes on their heads, tearing their clothes and shaving off their beards. Sometimes professional mourners were hired to add to the wailing. Mourning normally lasted for seven days, but it lasted longer for an important person – 70 days for Joseph and 30 days for Moses, for example. A time of fasting went with the time of mourning. But there was a funeral feast which often took place at the tomb.

Coffins and mummy of an Egyptian official from the city of Thebes, dating from 828–712 BC.

Burial

The people of Israel often buried their dead in caves. Some caves were large enough for all the members of a family, but if necessary they could be enlarged to form corridors with shelves cut out of the rock on which the bodies could be placed. In New Testament times a large circular stone was sometimes set in a groove and rolled across to cover the opening of burial caves. Because the number of caves was limited, bones were often removed and stored in chests of wood or stone called 'ossuaries'.

Rich people often had tombs specially constructed, with a stairway leading down through the solid rock to the burial chamber. A slab of stone was put at the entrance with a boulder against it. The poor were buried in shallow graves in open ground. A row of stones was placed round the body and the spaces in between were filled up with small stones and earth. A slab of stone was then put on the top. All graves were painted white to warn people not to touch them: any contact with the dead made a person ritually 'unclean'.

See also

■ Ancient beliefs (pages 146–147)

■ Jesus the saviour (pages 190–191)

The prophets

The work of the priests continued throughout the history of Israel, but the Old Testament prophets began to appear only with the establishment of institutions of national life. The messages of the prophets were generally concerned with particular times and places.

Messengers

The prophets are best understood as messengers. Their speeches often began with the words 'God says' or 'God spoke'. This is the way a messenger in the ancient world would begin a message from someone important. The prophets were called by God to hear God's plans and messages, and to transmit them to the Israelites.

Sometimes the prophets saw visions; sometimes they preached sermons; sometimes they used parable, poetry or drama to speak to the Israelites. They all speak differently about how they actually received their messages. But they were completely convinced that what they said came from God.

Challengers

The prophets were usually against the mainstream of opinion. When all seemed well, they attacked the evils of their society and predicted its doom. When their people were pessimistic, they prophesied hope. They brought these disturbing, challenging words from God because God's call had broken into their own lives and changed them drastically.

The message of the prophets

The message of the prophets looked to the past, recalling Israel to obedience; to the present, dealing with the crisis of faith in which the Israelites found themselves; and to the future, because they believed that God was committed to Israel. This commitment might mean the destruction of Israel for a time, but it would end in rebuilding and hope.

The Hebrew prophets conveyed God's warnings and promises to his people using powerful images, such as Jeremiah's shattered pottery, Ezekiel's valley of dry bones and Zechariah's golden lampstand.

The 'first prophet'

The prophets first emerged as a group in the time of Samuel, who has been described as 'the last of the judges and first of the prophets in Israel'. Samuel is best remembered for the fact that he, like many of the prophets, was the one through whom God's choice of a king was made known. He anointed Saul, and later David, as God's chosen rulers.

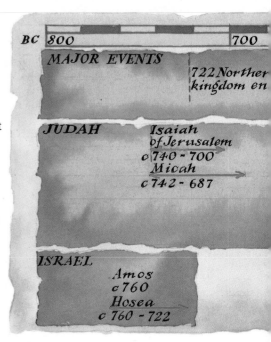

BC 800		700
MAJOR EVENTS		722 Northern kingdom en
JUDAH	Isaiah of Jerusalem c 740 - 700 Micah c 742 - 687	
ISRAEL	Amos c 760 Hosea c 760 - 722	

Before the exile

The pre-exilic prophets – people like Amos and Hosea in Israel, and Jeremiah in Judah – warned that judgment was inevitable. Social injustice, corruption and unfaithfulness to God were rife. The prophets called on their people to repent, but they were forced to realize that the people were often in no mood to do so.

Teachers

The prophets were also teachers calling Israel back to obey God's laws. One of their favourite themes was that the people should return to the original faith of their forebears.

Early prophets

At the time of the earliest prophets, the Philistines were the main threat to Israel. The enthusiasm of these early prophets for Israel's God strengthened the people's determination to be free and independent. But it was not until the middle of the ninth century BC that prophecy came to the fore with the work of Elijah and Elisha.

Later prophets

The period from the eighth to the fifth centuries BC is known as the 'classical' period of prophecy. The crisis behind this new period of prophecy was the changing political scene that led first to the exile of Israel after its capital, Samaria, was captured by the Assyrians in 721 BC, and then to the exile of Judah after Jerusalem had been destroyed by the Babylonians in 586 BC.

The message of the 'later prophets' of this era centres on the exile. Some looked ahead to it; others reflected on its meaning. And the prophets encouraged the nation to rebuild itself out of the disaster.

See also

- Two kingdoms (pages 28–29)
- The Babylonian invasion (pages 32–33)
- From exile to return (pages 34–35)
- The prophets: overview (pages 222–223)

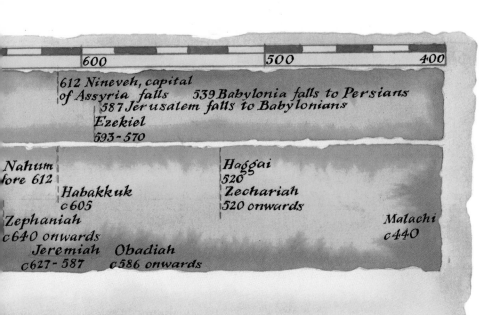

612 Nineveh, capital of Assyria falls   539 Babylonia falls to Persians
587 Jerusalem falls to Babylonians
Ezekiel 593–570

Nahum before 612
Habakkuk c605
Zephaniah c640 onwards
Jeremiah c627–587   Obadiah c586 onwards
Haggai 520
Zechariah 520 onwards
Malachi c440

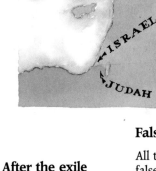

During the exile

Once Judah as well as Israel had gone into exile, some, at least, began to realize that they had deserved this punishment. From this time on, the prophets were able to stir up hope. Ezekiel, for example, foresaw a day when the nation, lifeless as a heap of dead bones, would begin to live again as the spirit of God breathed new life into the people. He looked forward to the rebuilding of the temple and a new settlement of the land.

After the exile

After the first exiles had returned to Judah, a new generation of prophets was needed to meet a different crisis of disillusionment and despair. If Haggai and Zechariah had not encouraged the people to work on rebuilding the temple, it would never have been completed. At this period the restoration of regular worship became a priority.

False prophets

All through Israel's history there were false prophets who claimed that their messages came from God, when in fact they did not. Although a prophet might begin preaching with 'God says', this was no guarantee that it really was a word from God. This problem was so widespread that the Torah had rules dealing with it. A prophet who predicted something which did not happen was a false prophet. And if the message led people away from God's laws it was a false message.

Groups and sects

A number of religious groups or sects developed in Palestine in the last centuries before Jesus was born. Most Jews did not belong to any sect, though those who did were widely admired.

The Hasidim (the 'pious ones')

The Hasidim was not an organized sect, but was the name given to those Jews who resisted the inroads of Hellenism into Jewish life and culture. In the second century BC some of them joined the Maccabees in the armed struggle against the Greek rulers. Others were pacifists. All certainly were faithful followers of God's law, and groups like the Pharisees and Essenes arose among people like this.

The Pharisees

The Pharisees were a strict religious sect whose origins are uncertain, but probably go back to the second century BC. They were ordinary people – not priests – who kept closely to God's law, and were constantly updating the old traditions to match new circumstances. They often extended the way the laws applied, adding extra rules to serve as 'a fence around the law'. By keeping these other rules, people would be in less danger of disobeying the actual law of God.

Although the Pharisees were the largest Jewish sect in the time of Jesus, there were only about 6,000 of them. They were very pious, but could also despise those who did not, or could not, follow their way of life.

The Pharisees were a very pious group, and their dress reflected this. They wore a phylactery on the forehead, which contained four pieces of parchment, each bearing a passage of scripture. Another phylactery, containing one sheet of parchment, was strapped to the left arm.

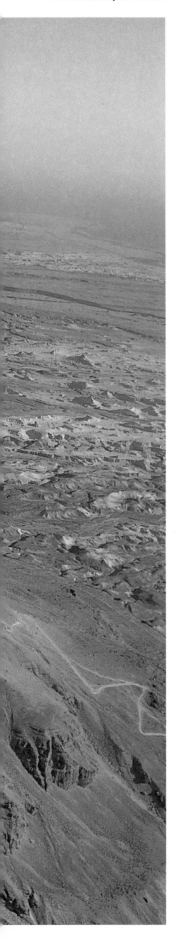

Caves at Qumran, probably home to a community of Essenes.

The Essenes

The Essenes were a smaller and more exclusive sect than the Pharisees, never numbering more than a few thousand. They had grown up in the second century BC as a protest movement – against Greek influence on the Jewish religion; against corrupt kings; and against the growing carelessness among Jewish people about keeping God's law. They were even stricter than the Pharisees, whom they denounced as 'givers of easy interpretations'. They were so alienated from Jewish society that many of them opted out of it and went to live in monastic communities. But they always looked for better things, and expected they would play an important part in the Messianic Age, when it came.

The community at Qumran, the people who wrote the Dead Sea Scrolls, probably belonged to the Essene movement.

The fortress of Masada was a scene of tragedy for the Zealots. During a revolt against Rome in AD 66–73, a band of Zealots held Masada for a brief period. The Romans were forced to raise a vast siege ramp in order to recapture the fortress but, on breaking through the walls, they discovered that the Zealots – more than 900 men, women and children – had joined in a suicide pact in order to avoid being captured.

The 'Temple scroll' from Qumran.

The Zealots

This was the group that kept alive the spirit of Judas Maccabaeus – the guerrilla leader who had succeeded in overcoming the forces of Antiochus IV in the second century BC. They refused to pay taxes to the Romans, and held themselves ready for the war that would bring in God's kingdom. During the New Testament period, they engineered several revolts. One of these was ended only by the Roman destruction of Jerusalem in AD 70.

Ritual bath, Qumran.

The scribes

The scribes were not a sect or a political party, but were professional experts in the Old Testament law. They were also called lawyers or teachers (rabbis). They interpreted the law and applied it to everyday life.

See also

- Education (pages 100–101)
- God's laws in practice (pages 152–153)
- Priests and rituals (pages 162–163)
- Jesus the prophet (pages 186–187)

The Sadducees

This group was smaller than the Pharisees, but more influential. Most Sadducees were members of the families of priests. They supported the Hasmonean high-priest kings, and later the Roman rulers. Unlike the Pharisees, they saw no reason for updating the old traditions, and the only part of the Old Testament they regarded as authoritative was the Torah itself.

New Testament religion

Festivals, sacrifices, synagogue services, prayer and fasting were basic to Jewish religious life. Judaism also affected other aspects of daily life.

In the temple

In New Testament times the temple was still at the heart of Jewish religious life. Crowds of pilgrims went there for the great annual festivals. It was also a centre for religious teaching. And the priests serving in the temple still carried out the rites and sacrifices of ancient Israel.

Temple rituals

In the temple, each day began with the recitation of Bible passages and prayers. The chief rituals were the morning and evening sacrifices. Then the priests would address the worshippers with the words of the ancient blessing from the Old Testament book of Numbers:

May the Lord bless you and take care of you;
May the Lord be kind and gracious to you;
May the Lord look on you with favour and give you peace.

Hymns were sung by the temple choirs, but sometimes the people joined in, especially in the torchlight procession at the festival of Tabernacles.

One of the Jewish motifs carved in the synagogue at Capernaum is the Star of David.

This synagogue at Capernaum in Galilee replaced the one that stood in Jesus' time.

Food laws

The Old Testament law identified a wide range of animals that were not to be used for food. There were also strict regulations about how animals for food should be killed so as to avoid eating blood. Meat produced according to this Jewish law is nowadays known as *kosher*.

In the home

At home every Jew was expected to pray the 'Eighteen Benedictions' each morning, afternoon and evening. Each benediction begins, 'Blessed are you, O Lord, king of the universe.' They all praise God – for the promise of a redeemer or the resurrection of the dead, or the gift of repentance, or healing the sick, and so on.

Before every meal the father of the household said a blessing: 'Blessed are you, our God, king of the universe: you create the fruit of the vine' (or 'you bring forth food from the earth'; or 'you create the fruit of the tree').

Tithes and taxes

Each year a 'tithe', or tenth, of one's produce was paid to the temple for the upkeep of the priests. A second tax was used for a sacrificial meal, in which the worshipper's family shared at one of the festivals. A third tax was used to help the poor.

Uncleanness

Many things made a person ritually 'unclean', and so unable to take part in worship. These included regular things such as menstruation, as well as more unexpected things like touching a dead body or a grave and eating meat with blood in it. In all these circumstances there were rituals through which 'cleanness' could be regained.

In the synagogue

Synagogues first began during the exile, when there was no temple and the Jews were far away from Jerusalem. By the time of Jesus, most Jews normally met together on the sabbath at the local synagogue. The service at the synagogue was mainly for readings from the Bible (usually a passage from the Law and one from the Prophets) and prayers.

The synagogue served as the local school and as the centre for local government, as well as for worship. Every synagogue had a chest, called an 'ark', in which the scrolls of God's law were kept. The leaders sat in front of the ark, facing the people. Men and women sat separately.

This stone seat from Galilee was carved from a single block of basalt in about AD 100. The inscription reads: 'May Yudan Son of Ishmael who made this hall and its staircase be remembered for good. As his reward, may he have a share with the righteous!'

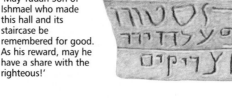

The synagogue service

The synagogue service began with the *Shema*, from the Old Testament book of Deuteronomy: 'Hear, O Israel, the Lord our God is one Lord; and you shall love the Lord your God with all your heart, and with all your soul, and with all your might.' The Bible passages were read in Hebrew. But since most Jews in Palestine at the time of Jesus spoke Aramaic, an interpreter gave a verse-by-verse translation and explanation. Sometimes there was also a sermon.

See also

- Food laws and customs (pages 108–109)
- God's laws in practice (pages 152–153)
- Feasts and holy days (pages 154–155)
- Jesus the teacher (pages 182–183)
- The gospels and Acts: overview (pages 242–243)

The synagogue at Capernaum stood at the centre of this town which is mentioned many times in connection with Jesus' ministry.

The earliest Christians

The earliest Christian worship comprised elements of Jewish forms of worship. Over time, however, in addition to implementing rites specifically commanded by Jesus, such as the Lord's supper, Christians moved away from certain Jewish customs.

Temple and synagogues

The earliest Christians were all Jews, so it is not at all surprising that they drew very much on their Jewish background for their forms of worship. They continued to worship at the Jerusalem temple, adding a special Christian meal. But Christians came to see that the temple sacrifices were no longer necessary, because Jesus' death was believed to be the final once-for-all sacrifice for sin.

Gentile Christians never attended temple worship, though Jewish believers resident in Jerusalem continued to do so. And for several decades many Jewish Christians continued to attend the synagogues. The Jewish synagogue service – with its Bible reading, prayer and sermon – formed a model for some early Christian services.

A new life

Christian baptism could be regarded as a 'washing' from sin. It appears that in baptism, people were plunged beneath a pool or river, and the New Testament explains that when the person being baptized disappears beneath the water and then reappears, he or she has undergone a symbolic death, burial and resurrection. Thus, in baptism Christians share in the death and resurrection of Jesus and receive a new life.

The remains of Peter's house at Capernaum.

These plaster fragments (probably from the second and third centuries AD) are based on numerous pieces discovered during excavation of Peter's house at Capernaum. Some 131 inscriptions, mainly in Greek and Aramaic, were found, including the names of Jesus and Peter. One inscription is a prayer which reads: 'O Lord Jesus Christ help … and …' (the two missing names are indecipherable).

Creeds and hymns

The New Testament church was a community which believed certain basic truths. These beliefs were expressed not only in the New Testament writings, but also in worship, often sung as hymns.

Some of the early Christian creeds were very simple and short. 'Jesus is Lord' was the basic one. These were probably words each new convert spoke. Some creeds contain two or three statements of faith. 'There is one God, and there is one mediator between God and humankind, namely Christ Jesus who was himself human'; 'one Lord, one faith, one baptism'.

At times, New Testament writers quote early Christian statements of faith. The following words from the New Testament book of Timothy form a creed in the style of a hymn:

[Christ] appeared in a body,
was vindicated by the Spirit,
was seen by angels,
was preached among the nations,
was believed on in the world,
was taken up in glory.

An even more detailed confession of the person and work of Jesus was used by Paul in the New Testament book of Philippians. The hymn ends with the confession of the new convert: 'all will openly proclaim that Jesus Christ is Lord.'

This mosaic of loaves and fishes at Tabgha, Galilee, symbolizes the miracle performed at this place by Jesus, as recorded in the New Testament.

The Lord's supper

Jesus instituted this communal meal at Passover time, at the last supper shared with his disciples before his death. At Passover, the Jewish people looked back to their ancestors' escape from slavery in Egypt, and looked forward to the coming kingdom of God. The Lord's supper looks back to the death of Jesus, and it looks forward to the time when he will come back again.

Throughout the New Testament period, the Lord's supper was an actual meal, shared in the homes of Christians. It was only much later that the Lord's supper was moved to a special building, and Christian prayers and praises that had developed from the synagogue services and other sources were added to create a grand ceremony.

Baptism

Jesus' followers also baptized those people who joined them. This practice also had a Jewish background. In the time between the Old and New Testaments, people who became converts to the Jewish religion were baptized, or immersed in water — usually a river — as a sign of cleansing. John the Baptist also baptized many people as a sign of their repentance and their inner cleansing by God.

See also

■ The birth of Christianity (pages 42–43)

■ The earliest churches (pages 46–47)

■ The practice of prayer (pages 174–175)

■ Jesus the saviour (pages 190–191)

Bread and wine

Bread and wine are central to the Lord's supper. Jesus' death was understood as a sacrifice that sealed a new covenant between God and all people. The wine is a token of the blood, or the death, of Jesus. The wine also points to the future kingdom of God. As Christians shared the bread, they identified it with 'the body of Christ', emphasizing Jesus' continued presence with them.

Prayer

As well as the private prayers of individuals, the New Testament often mentions groups of Christians praying together. These prayers were spontaneous, but they were full of the spirit and language of the Old Testament.

Wall painting of the Lord's Supper from the Greek Chapel, catacomb of Priscilla.

The practice of prayer

Prayer throughout the Bible is seen as a dialogue between God and people. People believed that prayer actually made a difference to their lives. And prayer led to a closer relationship with God.

Prayer in the Old Testament

The Old Testament records dozens of prayers in the form of prose, some brief, and some longer and more formal. These are the prayers of individuals to God in times of need. During the time of the exile in Babylon, daily prayer became vitally important to the Jews, who were unable to go to the temple. In addition to these prayers, the Old Testament also contains more structured, formal psalms and public prayers.

The Psalms

The Old Testament book of Psalms is the largest collection of prayer-poems in the Bible. They encompass the full breadth of human emotion. Some Psalms are joyful and are songs of praise to God. Others are heavy-laden with distress and sorrow.

'"My name will be great among the nations, from the rising to the setting of the sun. In every place incense and pure offerings will be brought to my name, because my name will be great among the nations," says the Lord Almighty.' (Malachi 1:11)

Jesus' teachings about prayer

Jesus taught his followers that prayer should not be used to impress others; praying in groups was fine, but prayer should also be a private affair. Prayer should be simple, not overly long or eloquent. Jesus also taught that people should be persistent in prayer, knowing that their prayers are heard by God – but they should not expect immediate answers.

The New Testament records that Jesus told a story to people who were confident of their own goodness. He contrasted the attitude of a self-righteous Pharisee with that of a penitent tax collector as they both came to pray. The tax collector approached God in humility and begged for God's mercy. This was the man, Jesus said, who went home at peace. 'For everyone who exalts himself will be humbled, and he who humbles himself will be exalted.'

See also

■ Jesus the teacher (pages 182–183)

■ The earliest Christians (pages 172–173)

■ Psalms (pages 220–221)

Prayer and the early Christians

The New Testament records many instances when Jesus prayed, and it is evident that he prayed at each of the decisive moments in his life. The early Christians followed Jesus' example. For example, they prayed regularly, regarding the selection of leaders, for courage in times of persecution, and for the success of the missionary work of Paul and Barnabas. Indeed, the early Christian church was characterized by prayer.

Words in New Testament prayer

Some of the original words of early Christian prayer appear untranslated in the New Testament.

Marana tha. These two Aramaic words mean 'Our Lord, come!' Early Christians used them to address Jesus, calling him by the same name, 'Lord', that Jews had reserved for God alone.

Abba. This word was used by Jesus himself in addressing God. It is an informal Aramaic word meaning 'dear father'. Children would use it to speak to their own fathers, though some religious people would have thought it an irreverent way to speak to God. But Jesus' relationship with God was so close that he felt free to use this family word, and encouraged his disciples to do the same.

Amen. This is a Hebrew word which was used in the temple and synagogue services at the end of prayers. It means, 'It is sure' or 'There is no doubt about that.'

'The grace'

Many Christians over the centuries have used the following words from 2 Corinthians as a blessing: 'May the grace of the Lord Jesus Christ, and the love of God, and the fellowship of the Holy Spirit be with you all.'

The Lord's Prayer

The New Testament records that Jesus taught his followers the Lord's Prayer when they asked him how to pray.

Our Father in heaven,
hallowed be your name,
your kingdom come,
your will be done,
on earth as in heaven.
Give us today our daily bread.
And forgive us our sins
as we forgive those who sin
*   against us.*
Lead us not into temptation,
but deliver us from evil.

Part 4: Picture acknowledgments

Abbreviations:
t = top, tl = top left, tc = top centre,
tr = top right,
c = centre, cl = centre left, cr = centre right
b = bottom, bl = bottom left,
bc = bottom centre, br = bottom right

Illustrations

DA = David Atkinson, GH = Gwyn Hughes,
RN = Rex Nicholls

Photographs

JA = Jon Arnold, ZR = Zev Radovan,
Relief maps = Lion Publishing

page
146*t*   Wall painting: © Mary Jellisse, The Ancient Art and
         Architecture Collection
146–147*b* Sumerian votive statuettes: Courtesy of the Oriental
         Institute of the University of Chicago
147*tc*   Rock-carved inscriptions: ZR
147*c*   Assyrian temple servant: Lion Publishing
147*cr*   Statuettes of Egyptian gods: The Ancient Art and
         Architecture Collection
148*tr*   Figurine of Canaanite goddess: Ashmolean Museum, Oxford
148*c*   Statuette of Baal: Sonia Halliday Photographs
148*bc*   Cave: JA
148–149*b* Main illustration: Linda Smith
149*tc*   Coin of Antiochus IV: ZR
150*tc*   Yotvata oasis: JA
150*b*   Jerusalem hills: JA
151*tl*   Ark of the Covenant mosaic: ZR
151*c*   Israelite temple, Arad: JA
151*br*   Ostracon: ZR
152–153*b* Orthodox Jews: JA
153*tl*   Donkey: RN
153*tc*   Slaves: Lion Publishing
153*c*   Pigs: RN
153*b*   Crops: RN
154*b*   Man: Martin Sanders
154–155 Main illustration: Linda Smith
156   Annual festivals: DA
156   Trumpeter: Martin Sanders
157   Main illustration: GH
158*tc*   Ark of the Covenant: RN
158*b*   Tabernacle: RN
159*t*   Incense shovels: ZR
159*b*   Table of showbread: RN
160*bl*   Solomon's temple: Stephen Conlin
160–161 Herod's temple: Stephen Conlin
161*tl*   Greek inscription: ZR
161*tc*   Domed ceiling: RN
161*cr*   Temple platform: Lion Publishing/David Townsend
161*br*   Plaster fragment: ZR
162   Main illustration: Martin Sanders
163*tl*   Incense stand: ZR
163*tr*   Breastplate: RN
163*br*   Inscription: ZR
164*tc*   Tombs: Joshua Smith
164*cl*   Phoenician terracotta death mask: ZR
164–165 Coffins and mummy: Ashmolean Museum, Oxford
165*tl*   Herod's family tomb: JA
165*tr*   Ossuary: RN

165*c*   Tombs, Kidron valley: RN
166–167 Timeline: DA
167*bl*   Map: DA
168*bl*   Pharisee: Lion Publishing/Mark Astell
168–169 Fortress of Masada: Comstock UK 1998/Ted Spiegel
169*tc*   Caves at Qumran: JA
169*cr*   'Temple Scroll' from Qumran: ZR
169*br*   Ritual bath: Lion Publishing/David Townsend
170*cl*   Star of David carving: RN
170–171 Synagogue, Capernaum: JA
171*cr*   Carved stone seat: RN
171*br*   Synagogue, Capernaum: ZR
172*bl*   Mosaic: JA
172*c*   Peter's house, Capernaum: ZR
172*r*   Plaster fragments: RN
173*c*   Pottery: ZR
173*b*   Wall painting: Lion Publishing/© Benedettine di Priscilla
174–175*b* Main illustration: Linda Smith
175*t*   Pharisee and tax collector: GH

THE LIFE
AND
TEACHING
OF JESUS

The Jesus of history

For 2,000 years, Jesus Christ has been the central character of human history. The date is calculated from the time of his birth, and more than two billion people still worship him as God. But it is not just Christians who have admired him. Mahatma Gandhi, the founder of modern India, took much of his inspiration from Jesus, and the Qur'an commends him as a person with unique insights into the nature of God.

Who was Jesus?

Who was Jesus? And what can be known about him? There can be no doubt that Jesus did actually exist, and that from about AD 27–30 he was a wandering teacher in rural Palestine, who was crucified by the Romans and then believed by his followers to have risen from the dead. The Jewish historian Josephus, who was not a Christian, described him in these words: 'About this time arose Jesus, a wise man, if indeed it be lawful to call him a man. For he was a doer of wonderful deeds, and a teacher of those who gladly receive the truth. He drew to himself many both of the Jews and the Gentiles…' It is in the four gospels of the New Testament – Matthew, Mark, Luke and John – that the most detailed descriptions of Jesus' life and teaching are preserved.

The landscape around the Palestinian town of Bethlehem, Jesus' birthplace.

Just one story about Jesus' childhood appears in the Bible. When Jesus was 12 years old he went to Jerusalem with his family to celebrate the festival of Passover. When his family left to return home, they inadvertently left Jesus behind. After three days, they found Jesus in the temple courts, engrossed in debate with the religious teachers.

'The Finding of the Saviour in the Temple', William Holman Hunt (1827–1910)

Jesus' childhood

The New Testament gospels preserve stories about Jesus' birth – the first Christmas – but then record remarkably little about his childhood. This apparent omission prompted later generations to produce their own imaginary accounts of what Jesus was like as a youth. From the second century and later, several such stories survive, with exotic titles such as *The Gospel of the Nativity of Mary, The History of Joseph the Carpenter* and *The Childhood Gospel of Thomas.* These 'gospels' contain obviously legendary stories, mostly concerned with proving that Jesus had miraculous powers even as a child – powers which they claim he used to bring embarrassment both to his family and to the religious establishment. But such accounts are no more than fabrication, written later by committed believers in an effort to satisfy their own curiosity and to enhance Jesus' reputation.

The significance of the wise men's gifts to the infant Jesus was profound. Gold, the ancient world's most precious metal, represented Jesus' kingship. Frankincense, commonly burnt as incense in worship, was a symbol of prayer and indicative of Jesus' role as 'priest', bringing the people closer to God. Myrrh, which was commonly used to embalm the dead, pointed to the grim reality that Jesus would have to give up his life.

'The Adoration of the Magi', Hieronymous Bosch (c. 1450–1516)

Jesus' family background

Jesus was not the only child in his family. Brothers and sisters are mentioned in the New Testament gospels, as is his mother Mary. His father Joseph, however, never features beyond Jesus' birth, which has led some to speculate that he may have died before Jesus began his public ministry.

Some members of Jesus' family may have been Pharisees, which would explain why he often singled them out for special criticism, as the religious group of which he had most first-hand experience. Certainly, the Pharisees drew most of their support from the kind of middle-class family in which Jesus grew up. And James, one of Jesus' brothers who later became leader of the Christian church in Jerusalem, appears throughout the New Testament as a very conservative individual, who placed great value on his traditional Jewish religious heritage.

Events in the life of Jesus

	Matthew	Mark	Luke	John
Announcement of the birth of John the Baptist			1:5–23	
Announcement of the birth of Jesus	1:18–24		1:26–38	
Jesus' mother Mary visits Elizabeth			1:39–56	
Birth of John the Baptist			1:57–79	
Birth of Jesus	1:25		2:1–39	
Visit of the shepherds			2:8–20	
Visit of the wise men	2:1–12			
Escape to Egypt and return to Nazareth	2:13–23			
Jesus' boyhood visit to the temple in Jerusalem			2:41–50	
John the Baptist's preaching	3:1–12	1:1–8	3:1–18	1:19–28
Jesus' baptism	3:13–17	1:9–11	3:21–22	1:29–34
The temptation of Jesus	4:1–11	1:12–13	4:1–13	
The first Passover festival				2:13–25
Meeting with Nicodemus				3:1–21
Meeting with Samaritan woman				4:1–42
John the Baptist imprisoned	14:3–5	6:17–20	3:19–20	
Jesus rejected in Nazareth			4:16–30	
Call of the disciples Andrew, Simon, James and John	4:18–22	1:16–20	5:1–11	
Call of Matthew (Levi)	9:9–13	2:13–17	5:27–32	
The second Passover festival				5:1–47
The 12 disciples chosen	10:2–4	3:13–19	6:12–16	
The Sermon on the Mount	5:1–7:28		6:20–49	
The 12 disciples sent out	10:1–11:1	6:6–13	9:1–6	
Death of John the Baptist	14:1–12	6:14–29	9:7–9	
The third Passover festival			6:1–71	
Peter acknowledges Jesus as the Christ	16:13–20	8:27–30	9:18–21	
Jesus foretells his death and resurrection	16:21–28	8:31–9:1	9:22–27	
The transfiguration of Jesus	17:1–13	9:2–13	9:28–36	
The 70 disciples sent out			10:1–20	
Jesus at Jerusalem at the festival of Tabernacles				7:1–52
Jesus with Martha and Mary			10:38–42	
Jesus in Jerusalem at the festival of Dedication				10:22–39
Last visit to Jerusalem	20:17–28	10:32–34		
In Jericho			19:1–10	
Bartimaeus	20:29–34	10:46–52		
Triumphal entry into Jerusalem	21:1–11	11:1–11	19:28–44	12:12–16
Judas' betrayal and rulers' plots	26:1–5,14–16	14:1–2, 10–11	20:19, 22:1–6	11:45–57
Passover/Last Supper	26:17–29	14:12–25	22:7–38	13:1–20
Gethsemane	26:36–46	14:32–42	22:39–46	
Jesus arrested	26:47–56	14:43–52	22:47–53	18:2–12
Jesus' trial by Annas and the synagogue council	26:57–27:1	14:53–15:1	22:54–71	18:13–24
Peter's denial of Jesus	26:69–75	14:66–71	22:54–62	18:15, 25–27
Jesus before Pilate	27:2–30	15:1–19	23:1–25	18:28–19:15
Jesus crucified and buried	27:31–66	15:20–47	23:26–56	19:16–42
Resurrection and resurrection appearances over a 40-day period	28:1–15	16:1–8, 9–14	24:1–49	20:1–21:23
The ascension of Jesus into heaven		16:19–20	24:50–53	

See also

■ In the steps of Jesus
(pages 40–41)

■ Groups and sects
(pages 168–169)

■ The gospels and
Acts: overview
(pages 242–243)

Jesus' education

Jesus was not a writer; all his teaching was delivered orally. But he was not illiterate. Indeed, he probably knew three languages – Hebrew, Aramaic and Greek – and he came from a middle-class family where he would have had good educational opportunities.

Jesus' occupation

The gospels use the Greek word *tekton* to describe the occupation of Jesus' father Joseph, and though generations of Christian artists have depicted Joseph as a humble 'carpenter' spending his life making wooden implements for a rural economy, that would have been only a small part of his business. In a village like Nazareth, Joseph would, in effect, have been the local builder, skilled in many trades.

It was a good time to be a builder in Galilee. During the time when Jesus was growing up, Herod Antipas was in the middle of a vast redevelopment of the town of Sepphoris, just a few kilometres from Nazareth, as well as the building of Tiberias on the western shore of Lake Galilee. Projects such as these must have created enormous employment opportunities for skilled craftspeople. Sepphoris was completed shortly before Jesus began his teaching ministry: perhaps he and some of his first disciples had lost their jobs at that time.

Jesus the leader

When John the Baptist began challenging his people, Jesus was immediately attracted. John modelled himself on the Old Testament prophet Elijah, adopting the same dress, diet and style. He also linked the social and political problems of the day with the moral and spiritual disobedience of individuals, and he invited people to be baptized as a sign of their willingness to change. This was, in fact, a familiar ceremony through which non-Jewish people could be admitted to the Jewish faith. But Jesus shared his vision, and had no hesitation in offering himself to be baptized.

Jesus' baptism

Jesus' baptism set the scene for all that was to follow. In describing it, the New Testament gospels use two quotations from the Old Testament to show how the priorities of his entire mission were established at this time. A reference to the coming Messiah from the book of Psalms is placed alongside another reference, from the book of Isaiah, to God's 'servant, who would suffer on behalf of other people'. Jesus was to be the Messiah – but not in a traditional way. He would do God's will through suffering and service, not by military might and coercion.

The River Jordan was the place where John the Baptist baptized those who wished to change their relationship with God.

Jesus' temptation

The gospels all describe a series of temptations at the very start of Jesus' public work. By dealing with these temptations, Jesus' basic aims and objectives were clarified and understood.

The temptation to make stones into bread. The Old Testament spelled out that the coming Messiah was expected to feed hungry people, and Jesus certainly cared about those who were starving. But to establish a reputation on this basis would have denied the very essence of what God was calling him to do – and he dismissed the idea with a reference to the Old Testament book of Deuteronomy.

The temptation to prove that he had special powers by jumping from a high tower at the temple in Jerusalem. A prophecy from the Old Testament book of Malachi seemed to suggest that the Messiah would do this. Maybe Jesus should try it, just to prove that God really was on his side? He was not afraid of the miraculous and the supernatural, but he knew that his message was

not to become just a publicity stunt – and again he quoted the Old Testament to back up his judgment.

Was he to be a military leader, the kind of Messiah figure most people were expecting? Jesus was offered all the kingdoms of the world, in exchange for worshipping the devil. But God's idea of community was not the imposed unity of a military dictatorship, which was the devil's way of doing things. Jesus knew that, and he rejected this temptation too – but it kept coming back to him throughout his life.

The New Testament gospels of Matthew and Luke depict Jesus in dialogue with the devil in person. But these questions, and others like them, kept on being raised by ordinary people throughout Jesus' ministry.

Jesus' message

Jesus' message was simple: 'The right time has come, and the kingdom of God is near! Turn away from your sins and believe the Good News.' Some would be attracted by the thought that God's 'kingdom' might replace the Roman empire with an autonomous Jewish state once more. Others were excited by the spiritual possibilities of people changing their lifestyles and finding new directions. But most were just fascinated by Jesus, and wanted to be with him. This was how Simon and his brother Andrew came to be disciples, as did two other brothers, James and John – not to mention countless others whose names we do not know.

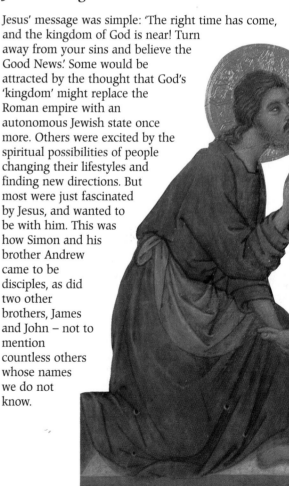

Jesus' radical approach challenged those who were content with the *status quo*. Jesus was not afraid to associate with those who were reviled by society. Here, Jesus calls Matthew – the tax-collector – to be his disciple.

The Calling of St Matthew, Caravaggio (c. 1571–1610)

Jesus' disciples

The disciples needed to learn many things – about Jesus, about God, about themselves, and about the world and its possibilities. But that would be a long process, and the thing that Jesus valued most of all was their simple enthusiasm for a better way of being. Being a disciple did not involve any fancy religious rituals. Nor were they required to sever all ties with their previous friends. Jesus left them the space to do whatever they were happy with at that stage of their relationship to him. The same personal openness characterized all his relationships, and attracted people of all sorts – though it eventually brought him into conflict with the religious authorities of his day.

See also

■ In the steps of Jesus (pages 40–41)
■ New Testament religion (pages 170–171)
■ Zechariah, Malachi (pages 234–235)
■ Mark (pages 244–245)
■ Luke (pages 248–249)

Jesus taught his followers about the nature of leadership. By washing the disciples' feet, he graphically demonstrated that to be a leader was to be a slave. 'Now that I, your Lord and Teacher, have washed your feet, you also should wash one another's feet.'

'Christ Washing the Disciples' Feet', Duccio di Buoninsegna (1278–1318)

Jesus the teacher

Many teachers in biblical times expected their followers to learn by rote. But Jesus gave people freedom to think for themselves, and encouraged them to work out what God was saying to them personally. He taught using proverbs and riddles, visual images and poetry.

The kingdom of God

When Jesus spoke of 'the kingdom of God', he was referring to God's way of doing things – and that could come into being whenever people adopted God's values and standards. This is why he could say 'the kingdom of God is within you…' But to do things God's way, people needed to recognize their own need of God. Entering 'the kingdom' began with trusting God just as children trust their parents. Religious people often found this too challenging, but the marginalized and oppressed identified with Jesus' message.

Lost and found

Three parables in the gospel of Luke follow a theme of something lost, then found. **The lost sheep** is found because the shepherd cares and goes out in search of the wanderer. **The lost coin** comes to light as its owner diligently sweeps through her entire house. **The lost son**, who finds himself living in poverty in a hostile environment, recognizes that he needs to go home, where he is welcomed with open arms by his father. But even so, he finds himself at the centre of a controversy. In this case, the son himself knows his own weakness, and is ready enough to accept his parent's generosity. Too ready, in the opinion of his brother, who like so many finds it hard to accept that anyone should get something for nothing. Yet, Jesus said, God is exactly like that generous parent!

'Blessed are the poor in spirit, for theirs is the kingdom of heaven.' So began Jesus' teaching to his disciples on a mountainside in Galilee. The Sermon on the Mount sets out clearly Jesus' expectations for his followers, who are, he says, the 'salt of the earth' and the 'light of the world'.

'The Sermon on the Mount',
Fra Angelico (c. 1387–1455)

The importance of the world

Jesus taught that this world is important to God, and he often used the beauty of nature as a picture of what it was like to be a disciple. In the gospel of Matthew, Jesus encourages his followers to trust God in the same open-ended way as birds trust their maker.

The importance of the disciples

Jesus taught that the disciples should make a difference. They were to demonstrate and proclaim God's kingdom in all they did. That even meant copying God's own extraordinary generosity. The gospel of Mark recounts that Jesus told a rich man, 'Sell what you own, and give the money to the poor.' And if a passing Roman soldier forced them to carry his bags for one mile (a common experience in occupied Palestine), disciples should go for two, turning the other cheek, and returning good for evil. These were all quite absurd notions – but the kind of moral absurdity in which God takes delight. For without such magnanimity on God's part, who could ever hope to be a part of God's kingdom?

See also

■ In the steps of Jesus (pages 40–41)

■ Mark (pages 244–245)

■ Matthew (pages 246–247)

The parables of Jesus

	Matthew	Mark	Luke
The lamp under a bowl	5:14–16	4:21–22	8:16, 11:33
Houses built on rock and sand	7:24–27	6:47–49	
New cloth sewn on an old garment	9:16	2:21	5:36
New wine poured in old wineskins	9:17	2:22	5:37–38
The sower and the different soils	13:3–9, 18–23	4:3–8, 13–20	8:5–8, 11–15
The mustard seed	13:31–31	4:30–32	13:18–19
The wheat and the weeds	13:24–30, 36–43		
The yeast in the dough	13:33		13:20–21
Hidden treasure	13:44		
The priceless pearl	13:45–46		
The drag-net	13:47–50		
The lost sheep	18:12–14		15:4–7
The two debtors (the unforgiving servant)	18:23–25		
The workers in the vineyard	20:1–16		
The two sons	21:28–32		
The wicked tenants	21:33–44	12:1–9	20: 9–16
The invitation to the wedding; the man with no wedding clothes	22:2–14		
The fig tree as herald of summer	24:32–33	13:28–29	21:29–31
Ten bridesmaids	25:1–13		
The talents (Matthew); pounds (Luke)	25:14–30		19:12–27
The sheep and the goats	25:31–46		
Seed-time to harvest		4:26–29	
The creditor and the debtors			7:41–50
The good Samaritan			10:30–37
The friend in need			11:5–10
The rich fool			12:16–21
The alert servants			12:35–40
The faithful steward			12:42–48
The fig tree without figs			13:6–9
The places of honour at the wedding feast			14:7–14
The great banquet and the reluctant guests			14:16–24
Counting the cost			14:28–33
The lost coin			15:8–10
The lost son			15:11–32
The dishonest steward			16:1–8
The rich man and Lazarus			16:19–31
The master and the servant			17:7–10
The persistent widow and the unrighteous judge			18:2–8
The Pharisee and the tax collector			18:10–14

'Love your neighbour'

Jesus taught that affirming and valuing others was essential. The gospel of Mark says that Jesus reiterated the traditional advice that people should love their neighbours as themselves; one of his most striking parables – the good Samaritan – was designed to answer the question, 'Who is my neighbour?' Jesus also expected that the quality of the relationships between the disciples themselves would attract others to God's kingdom.

Jesus' parables

Jesus loved using parables – stories that would entertain, and also help people reflect on life and its meanings and possibilities. The parables have sometimes been treated as if they were encoded messages, with every detail representing something else – usually something abstract and theological. But they were just simple stories, with one key message: that God's love is not something to be earned by being 'religious', but is freely available to everyone.

Jesus the healer

The gospel of Luke records that John the Baptist sent from his prison cell to ask Jesus whether he really was the expected Messiah. This was Jesus' answer: 'Go back and tell John what you have seen and heard: the blind can see, the lame can walk, the lepers are made clean, the deaf can hear, the dead are raised to life, and the good news is preached to the poor.'

Ancient superstition?

People in the Western world over the past 200–300 years have sometimes dismissed the miracle stories of the New Testament as the ignorance and superstition of ancient people. But as the 20th century has progressed, this opinion has become much less credible than it once seemed. The chauvinistic attitude that presumed all ancient people were either fools or frauds has been exposed as simple arrogance, for there is plenty of evidence to show that ancient people were no more gullible or naive than their modern counterparts. Furthermore, the more science has discovered, the more mysteries there are about many things, including illness and how it is cured.

People in Bible times were not taken aback by Jesus' work as a healer. Indeed, Jesus' reputation went before him, and wherever he travelled he was followed by crowds asking for his healing touch. The gospel of Matthew records: 'People brought all their sick to him and begged him to let the sick just touch the edge of his cloak, and all who touched him were healed.'

'Jesus Healing the Sick', Rembrandt van Rijn (1606–69)

Miracles and signs

The New Testament gospels emphasize that Jesus proclaimed God's kingdom through deeds as well as words, and John describes the miracles of Jesus as 'signs', showing the reality of God's presence for all who wanted to see. The gospel of Mark says that when Jesus sent the disciples out, he told them to do the same: 'As you go, proclaim the good news, "The kingdom of heaven has come near." Cure the sick, raise the dead, cleanse the lepers, cast out demons...' Jesus' teaching and Jesus' miracles were just two sides of the same coin.

The New Testament writers record at least two occasions on which Jesus provided food for thousands of people from a starting point of a few fish and loaves of bread.

Healing miracles

No one at the time of Jesus was surprised that Jesus was a healer. The New Testament records that Jesus himself referred – apparently in a positive manner – to other people who were casting out demons, and he expected his own disciples to exercise the same sort of ministry. Both Jewish and Roman literature of the day contain stories of healing miracles of various sorts.

The rational versus the spiritual

As Western peoples have increased their knowledge of other cultures, it has become more obvious that rationalism, with its insistence on 'logical' explanations of cause and effect, is only one way of looking at the world. Many non-Western cultures, comprising the majority of the world's people, hold a belief in a spiritual world that is beyond what Westerners normally see and understand. It is only an outmoded and defensive form of intellectual and cultural imperialism that will question this. If anyone doubts that, they need only look around at the way the New Age movement has put the miraculous and the supernatural very firmly back onto the Western agenda.

A distinctive approach

The distinctive thing about Jesus' miracles is not so much what he did, but when he did it – and to whom. The kind of people Jesus healed – the deaf, dumb and lame – do not feature at all in contemporary stories of Jewish healers.

The Old Testament book of Isaiah indicated that concern for such people was a sign of the coming kingdom of God. This coincidence would not be lost on those who were suspicious of Jesus' intentions. Nor would it escape their attention that the circumstances in which Jesus cured people often infringed Jewish laws. The New Testament records that Jesus healed people on the Sabbath day, traditionally a day of rest for the Jews. Jesus also healed those who were considered 'non-people' so far as Jewish ritual purity was concerned: people of the wrong racial origins; people who lived in the wrong kind of places; and people who by any definition were ritually impure.

Care and concern

Jesus' miracles communicate the same underlying basic theme as his spoken message. Just as Jesus taught in words and attitudes that God loves all kinds of people, so his miracles often involved the outcasts of society. His declaration of God's care and concern was not just talk; it demanded action. Moreover, as the gospel of Mark spells out, healing and forgiveness went hand in hand, and faith also was required of those who would be healed. Indeed, at least one story in the New Testament gospel of Mark implies that the absence of faith could be a hindrance to the work of healing.

See also

- Health and healing (pages 138–139)
- Feasts and holy days (pages 154–155)
- Luke (pages 248–249)
- John (pages 250–251)

Jairus, a synagogue ruler, pleads with Jesus to heal his dying daughter, but by the time they reach the family home it appears to be too late. When Jesus announces that the girl is 'not dead, but asleep', the gathered crowd laughs at him. Yet minutes later, the Bible tells, the girl gets up and walks around.

'The Raising of Jairus' Daughter', George Percy Jacomb-Hood (1857–1927)

The miracles of Jesus

Healing miracles	Matthew	Mark	Luke	John
Leper	8:2–4	1:40–44	5:12–14	
Centurion's servant	8:5–13		7:1–10	
Peter's mother-in-law	8:14–15	1:30–31	4:38–39	
Possessed man	8:28–34	5:1–15	8:27–35	
Paralysed man	9:2–7	2:3–12	5:18–25	
Woman with a haemorrhage	9:20–22	5:25–34	8:43–48	
Two blind men	9:27–31			
Man who was dumb and 'possessed'	9:32–33			
Man with a withered hand	12:10–13	3:1–5	6:6–10	
Man who was dumb, blind and 'possessed'	12:22			
Canaanite woman's daughter	15:21–28	7:24–30		
Boy with epilepsy	17:14–18	9:17–29	9:38–43	
Bartimaeus and another blind man	20:29–34	10:46–52	18:35–43	
Deaf and dumb man		7:31–37		
Man who was 'possessed', synagogue		1:23–26	4:33–35	
Blind man at Bethsaida		8:22–26		
Woman who was bent double			13:11–13	
Man with dropsy			14:1–4	
Ten lepers			17:11–19	
Malchus' ear			22:50–51	
Official's son at Capernaum				4:46–53
Sick man, pool of Bethsaida				5:1–9
Man born blind				9

Command over the forces of nature	Matthew	Mark	Luke	John
Calming of the storm	8:23–27	4:37–41	8:22–25	
Walking on the water	14:25–31	6:48–51		6:19–21
Feeding 5,000 people	14:15–21	6:35–44	9:12–17	6:5–13
Feeding 4,000 people	15:32–38	8:1–9		
Coin in the fish's mouth	17:24–27			
Fig-tree withered	21:18–22	11:12–14, 20–26		
Catch of fish			5:1–11	
Water turned into wine				2:1–11
Another catch of fish			21:1–11	

Bringing the dead back to life	Matthew	Mark	Luke	John
Jairus' daughter	9:18–19, 23–25	5:22–24, 38–43	8:41–42, 49–56	
Widow's son at Nain		7:11–15		
Lazarus				11:1–44

Jesus the prophet

Jesus enjoyed enormous popularity, especially among ordinary people. But the religious establishment came to see him as a threat. He spent too much time with those who were regarded as outcasts – tax collectors, prostitutes, lepers – and seemed to challenge the accepted standards of decent people.

*'The Woman Taken in Adultery',
Giovanni Guercino (1591–1666)*

A people's man

Jesus was certainly not uneducated. He was able to read the scriptures in Hebrew, which not everyone could do, and he had no difficulty engaging in the kind of theological arguments going on among the Jewish rabbis. But he had never been formally trained to be a religious teacher – and, in any case, he had no time for bookish religion. He was unashamedly a populariser, his teaching was immediate and direct, and easily captivated people's imagination. This made him a favourite with the crowds, but such an unconventional style was bound to make the religious establishment nervous.

Challenging Old Testament law

Jesus challenged and disregarded some significant aspects of the traditional Old Testament law. Conflict over keeping the Sabbath day as a day of rest surfaced at the very beginning of his ministry, and remained a controversial issue. Observance of the Sabbath was enshrined in the Ten Commandments but, for those who knew how, it was not difficult to get round it – and they did. The same thing had happened with procedures for washing and eating food, designed to ensure ritual purity.

On some occasions, Jesus challenged the establishment's ways of doing things more directly – for example, when he took a whip and drove the merchants and bankers out of the temple. Or when a woman caught in the very act of committing adultery was brought to him, and he refused to endorse the death sentence for her – something that was clearly laid down in the law; at the same time he insinuated that her accusers had sinned at least as much as she had. By questioning such things, Jesus must have known he was challenging some central aspects of conventional religious practice. It inevitably ensured that those who saw themselves as guardians of the old traditions would regard him as nothing more than a dangerous heretic.

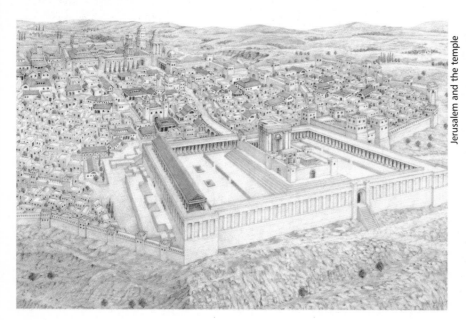
Jerusalem and the temple

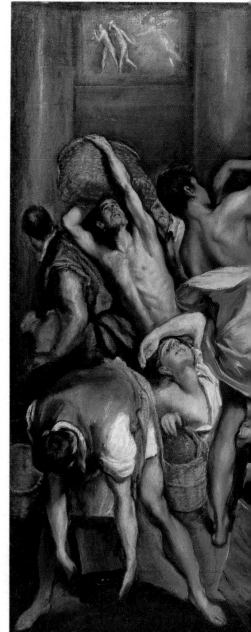

Challenging the Pharisees

The Pharisees especially disliked Jesus. Their teachings were not so very different from what Jesus himself was saying. But they were often morally overbearing, giving the impression that they were the only ones who could ever truly know God. To them, Jesus' talk of a God with a special concern for the marginalized and the outcast made little sense, and was bound to lead to conflict.

Jesus directly challenged tradition by questioning the many rules and regulations with which the Pharisees had surrounded the religious law. These rules had been put in place for a perfectly good reason: to update an ancient code of conduct and to apply it to the changed circumstances of a much later generation.

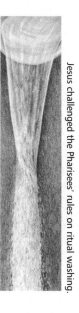

Jesus challenged the Pharisees' rules on ritual washing.

But they had become so complex and demanding that there was no chance of ordinary people ever being able to keep them all. Only the well-off had that option open to them.

As a result, the degree to which a person observed these rules had become a means of social division within the community. Those like the Pharisees, who were scrupulous in keeping all the rules, looked down on others as second-class citizens, and despised them as spiritually corrupt and inferior. For Jesus to suggest that God would welcome such people challenged not only theological perceptions, but also questioned the very structure of society itself.

See also:

◻ Trade and commerce
(pages 124–125)

◻ God's laws in practice
(pages 152–153)

◻ Groups and sects
(pages 168–169)

◻ Mark
(pages 244–245)

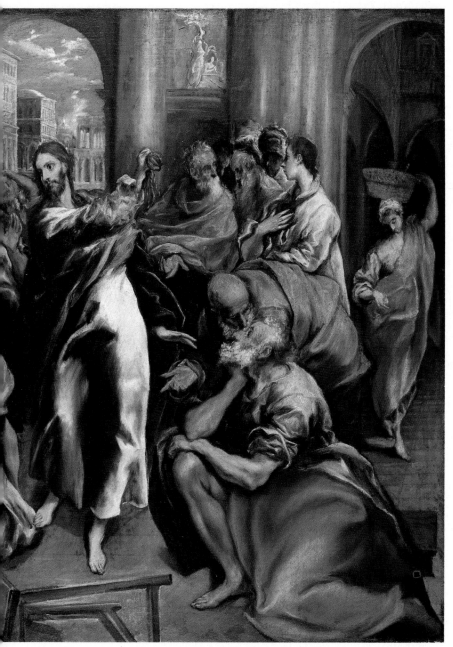

A special relationship

Jesus did and said things that seemed to be making grand claims for himself. Although he rarely claimed to be the Messiah outright, he did on occasion imply as much. For example, the gospel of Luke records that Jesus read from the Old Testament book of Isaiah and claimed that 'This passage of scripture has come true today, as you heard it being read!' In the gospel of Mark, Jesus offers to forgive sins and is found casting out demons – both of these hinting at some special relationship with God.

Moving towards a showdown

The growing opposition of the religious establishment to Jesus was in strong contrast to the developing commitment of his disciples. The religious experts claimed to know all the answers, but it was among ordinary people that Jesus found most faith. As Jesus questioned and challenged the accepted opinions, he both attracted and repelled, and it was only a matter of time before the opposition to him would become overwhelming, and the conflict would move towards a showdown in Jerusalem.

Jesus was not afraid to challenge the traditions of the religious establishment. Driving the traders and merchants out of the temple, Jesus taught: 'Is it not written: "My house will be called a house of prayer for all nations"? But you have made it "a den of robbers".' Hearing of Jesus' actions, the Bible records, 'the chief priests and the teachers of the law began looking for a way to kill him.'

'Christ Driving the Traders from the Temple',
El Greco (1541–1614)

Jesus the convict

About half of the New Testament gospel of Mark deals with just the final week of Jesus' life, so these few days are obviously central to understanding his entire ministry. They were a time of increasing tension between Jesus and the religious authorities, culminating in his arrest, trial and crucifixion.

'Hosanna! Blessed is he who comes in the name of the Lord! Blessed is the coming kingdom of our father David! Hosanna in the highest'! These were the words, the Bible records, which greeted Jesus on his final visit to Jerusalem.

Sixth-century gospel illumination from the cathedral library at Rossano, Italy

Entry to Jerusalem

Most of Jesus' ministry was spent in the region of Galilee, but he was determined to make one last effort to share his message in the spiritual capital of the nation, Jerusalem. Jesus made a dramatic entry to the city – riding on a donkey. The significance of this would not be lost on Jesus' companions, for it was widely expected that the Messiah would ride in procession on a stallion up to the temple, and that would be the signal for the revolution that would get rid of the hated Romans once and for all.

This was Passover week, and Jerusalem was full of visitors. Some of them formed an honour guard along Jesus' route, just as if they were the regular retinue of an oriental monarch. Others laid their clothes on the beast to make a saddle, throwing their coats in the roadway as Jesus passed by. They tore down palm branches, and joined in an enthusiastic rendition of some words from the book of Psalms. The Psalm chosen was one of the 'Hallel' psalms which were a common feature of Passover celebrations,

and would be in the minds of many people that week. In greeting Jesus with the cry 'Hosanna' (meaning 'Lord save us'), and acclaiming him as 'the one who comes in the name of the Lord', the crowd were consciously welcoming the king to their capital. Yet unlike the Messiah of legend and mythology, Jesus did not arrive on a war horse, but on a donkey. Nor did he take the temple by storm: instead he took a quiet look round, then returned to Bethany to spend the night in private. The themes of majesty and suffering, first evoked at his baptism, came together again, and would remain central to the events of this week.

Jesus' arrest

As Jesus continued to teach in Jerusalem, it was not long before he had provided enough evidence to allow formal action to be taken against him – and his popular support began to dwindle. Even one of his own disciples – Judas Iscariot – deserted him, and when Jesus emerged after taking a meal with the other disciples, Judas was waiting for him in the Garden of Gethsemane, ready to betray him to his enemies. Probably Judas was still hoping for a military Messiah to lead the last crusade against the hated Romans. If Jesus really was the Messiah, then handing him over to them might goad him into action – and if not, then he deserved to die anyway.

Jesus was arrested almost before the other disciples knew what was happening. He was dragged off to the

home of Caiaphas, the high priest, where an informal enquiry was held by the Jewish Council to sift through the evidence that might be used in making out a case against Jesus in the court that mattered, where the Roman governor Pontius Pilate would be the judge.

Gethsemane

The Bible records that Pilate was amazed when Jesus refused to answer the charges before him. To the question 'Are you the king of the Jews?', he simply replied 'Yes, it is as you say.' And Jesus' fate was sealed when the crowds called to Pilate: 'Crucify him!'

'Ecco Homo', Antonio Ciseri (1821–91)

The final straw

When Jesus returned to the temple in Jerusalem and threw the money-changers out, condemning them in words first used by Jeremiah to announce God's judgment on the people centuries before, those with a sense of history got the message. The religious leaders felt they had to take action. His entry into Jerusalem with a large crowd, followed by this behaviour, must mean Jesus was planning a revolution.

Jesus before Pilate

Pontius Pilate was already in Jerusalem because it was Passover time. He had no interest in Jewish religious matters, and it made no difference to him if Jesus was blaspheming God, as was being alleged. But three other accusations were also made: that Jesus misled the people; that he forbade paying taxes to Caesar; and that he claimed to be a king. Pilate could see that Jesus had certainly upset the religious establishment. But was he really guilty of any crime under Roman law? A weak and indecisive man at the best of times, Pilate was faced with an impossible choice, and when Jesus' accusers suggested that Pilate would be no friend of Caesar's if he let Jesus go, Pilate really had little choice. It was either his career or Jesus' life – and so he reluctantly condemned Jesus to death.

See also

■ A brief history of Jerusalem (pages 38–39)

■ In the steps of Jesus (pages 40–41)

■ Annual festivals (pages 156–157)

■ Mark (pages 244–245)

Jesus the saviour

As Jesus met with his disciples for their last evening meal together, he took some familiar foods – bread and wine – and blessed them in traditional Jewish fashion. This was the Passover season, when the whole nation gathered in family groups to celebrate God's covenant with their ancestors. As he spoke with the disciples, Jesus looked backwards to that, but he went on to say that the meal his group was sharing would be the start of a totally new chapter in God's dealings with the world. For he was about to die, and through his suffering a 'new covenant' would come into being.

The awfulness of Jesus' death by crucifixion was compounded by the abuse heaped upon him. A crown of thorns was placed on his head, he was stabbed in the side of the body, and a sign above his cross mocked: 'Here is Jesus, king of the Jews.' People insulted him: 'He saved others, but he can't save himself... He trusts in God. Let God rescue him now.' But when Jesus gave up his last breath, the Bible recounts, an earthquake struck the land and those who were guarding Jesus 'were terrified, and exclaimed, "Surely he was the Son of God!"'

'Crucifixion',
Diego Velasquez (1599–1660)

The New Testament gospel of Mark states that Jesus was crucified at Golgotha. Some believe this skull-shaped rock formation could be the place.

Jesus' crucifixion

Crucifixion was a Roman punishment – more a form of torture than of execution, for it could take days to die this way. But for Jesus' followers, it became a symbol of great hope and new life.

Jesus might have been put to death on a cross, but his death – and, more especially, what followed later – meant that his disciples found new inspiration for their own living, and felt that they had been brought close to God in a special way.

Jesus' resurrection

The New Testament accounts all insist that, after three days, Jesus rose again from the dead – and this fact was to become the central motif of Christian faith. Whenever the story of Jesus was told, his resurrection was an intrinsic part of it. Nor was this merely a fairy-tale ending to what would otherwise be a tragic story; lists of those who had seen the risen Jesus could be produced, and were. It is sometimes suggested that these earliest disciples were hallucinating. But the account of Paul is especially significant in this connection. For not only is it the earliest to have been written, but he was a man with extensive psychic experience, and he was certain that whatever he saw when he met the risen Jesus was not a vision.

An empty tomb

The New Testament stories also record that Jesus' tomb was empty. How did this happen? It is hard to imagine the disciples would have stolen the body, and then founded their faith on a self-conscious lie – especially when they were prepared to die for their belief that the resurrection really did happen. It is equally unlikely that if Romans or Jews removed the body for some reason, they would not have produced it to squash the stories of Jesus' resurrection. The disciples unquestionably believed that Jesus was alive. The exact meaning of the resurrection can be explained in many different ways, but it stands at the centre of Christian faith.

See also

- Annual festivals (pages 146–147)

- Death and the afterlife (pages 164–165)

- The earliest Christians (pages 172–173)

- Luke, Acts of the Apostles (pages 248–249)

- John (pages 250–251)

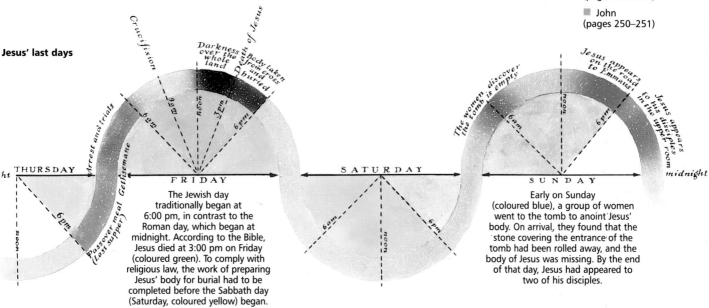

Jesus' last days

The Jewish day traditionally began at 6:00 pm, in contrast to the Roman day, which began at midnight. According to the Bible, Jesus died at 3:00 pm on Friday (coloured green). To comply with religious law, the work of preparing Jesus' body for burial had to be completed before the Sabbath day (Saturday, coloured yellow) began.

Early on Sunday (coloured blue), a group of women went to the tomb to anoint Jesus' body. On arrival, they found that the stone covering the entrance of the tomb had been rolled away, and the body of Jesus was missing. By the end of that day, Jesus had appeared to two of his disciples.

The Bible records that Jesus' disciple, Thomas, needed physical evidence to be convinced that Jesus was still alive. 'Unless I see the nail marks in his hands and put my fingers where the nails were, and put my hand into his side, I will not believe it', he said. When Jesus appeared to the disciples again, he invited Thomas to do just that.

'The Incredulity of St Thomas', Giovanni Guercino (1591–1666)

Jesus' ascension

The story of Jesus ends with his ascension, which marked the point at which the regular resurrection appearances finally ceased. In one sense, Jesus could have been described as exalted into the presence of God from the time of the crucifixion. Presumably the ascension stories marked a particular occasion when he left the disciples in a dramatic, memorable way, after which they saw him no more.

The 'Son of Man'

Today most people no longer think of the universe in the way that ancient people did, as a kind of three-tiered construction with the earth sandwiched in the middle between heaven and hell. The New Testament itself is not concerned with the spatial dimensions of Jesus' ascension. Instead, it centres on the conviction that Jesus himself had returned to be exalted in glory with God. This had been implied from the very beginning through the title 'Son of Man' which Jesus regularly used to describe himself, for in the Old Testament book of Daniel this character received 'authority, honour and royal power'.

One way of understanding Jesus' crucifixion is to think of it as his final battle with the forces of evil, and his resurrection as the proof that he has triumphed. The ascension then becomes a demonstration that this victory was absolute. Not only that, but the historical Jesus of Nazareth has now become the cosmic Christ, the one who will heal all the dysfunction in the entire universe, bringing order out of chaos and harmony out of conflict, as the natural world is redeemed, and people are empowered to live at peace with nature and in community with one another.

Part 5: Picture acknowledgments
Abbreviations:
t = top, tl = top left, tc = top centre, tr = top right,
c = centre, cl = centre left, cr = centre right
b = bottom, bl = bottom left, bc = bottom centre, br = bottom right

Illustrations
RN = Rex Nicholls

Photographs
JA = Jon Arnold

page
178*c*   Landscape around Bethlehem: JA
178*t*   'The Adoration of the Magi', *c.* 1510 by Hieronymus Bosch (*c.* 1450–1516) Prado,
Madrid/Bridgeman Art Library, London/New York
178*b*   'The Finding of the Saviour in the Temple', 1854–60 by William Holman Hunt
(1827–1910) Birmingham Museum and Art Gallery/Bridgeman Art Library,
London/New York
179*br*   Carpenter's work bench: RN
180*tc*   River Jordan at Degany: JA
180*l*   Pebbles: RN
180*b*   Temple: RN
180–181*b* Maesta: 'Christ Washing the Disciples' Feet', 1308–11 by Duccio di
Buoninsegna (*c.* 1278–1318) Museo dell'Opera del Duomo, Siena/Bridgeman Art
Library, London/NewYork
181*tl*   'The Calling of St Matthew', *c.* 1598–1601 by Michelangelo Merisi da Caravaggio
(1571–1610) Contarelli Chapel, S. Luigi dei Francesi, Rome/Bridgeman Art Library,
London/New York
182*t*   Oil lamp: RN
182*b*   'The Sermon on the Mount', 1442 (fresco) by Fra Angelico (Guido di Pietro)
(*c.* 1387–1455) Museo di San Marco dell'Angelico, Florence/Bridgeman Art Library,
London/New York
183*t*   Purse and coins: RN
183*b*   Wheat: RN
184*c*   'Jesus Healing the Sick', Rembrandt van Rijn (1606–69): Courtesy of The Victoria
and Albert Museum
184*b*   Loaves and fish: RN
185   'The Raising of Jairus' Daughter' by George Percy Jacomb-Hood (1857–1927)
Guildhall Art Gallery, Corporation of London/Bridgeman Art Library, London/New York
186*tl*   'The Woman Taken in Adultery' by Guercino (Giovanni Francesco Barbieri)
(1591–1666) Dulwich Picture Gallery/Bridgeman Art Library, London/New York
186*bl*   Jerusalem and the temple: RN
186–187 'Christ Driving the Traders from the Temple', El Greco (1541–1614): © National
Gallery, London
188*cl*   Sixth-century illumination showing Palm Sunday: Scala, Florence
188*br*   Gethsemane: RN
188–189 'Ecco Homo' by Antonio Ciseri (1821-91) Galleria d'Arte Moderna,
Florence/Bridgeman Art Library London/New York
189*t*   Crown of thorns: RN
190*t*   'Crucifixion' by Diego Rodriguez de Silva y Velasquez (1599–1660) Prado,
Madrid/Bridgeman Art Library, London /New York
190*bl*   Golgotha: JA
191*t*   Jesus' last days: David Atkinson
191*c*   Folded grave clothes: RN
191*b*   'The Incredulity of St Thomas' by Giovanni Guercino (1591–1666): Scala, Florence

THE BIBLE
BOOK
BY
BOOK

Part 6

Understanding the Bible

The Bible's individual books were produced over many centuries, by different writers, addressing different audiences, in varying styles of writing and language.

The books of the Bible illustrated here follow the order found in most editions of the Bible in use today. In the following pages the books are arranged in their probable order of composition.

Books of the Old Testament

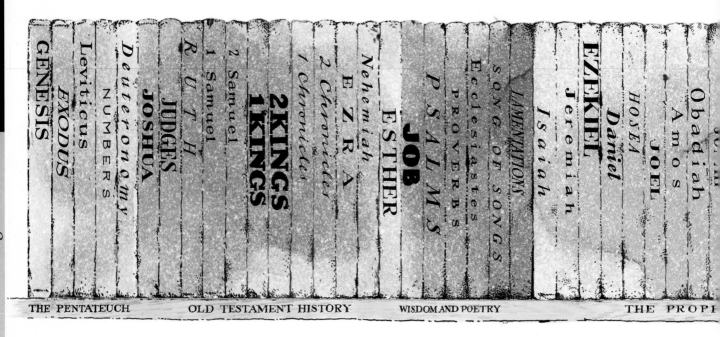

GENESIS · EXODUS · Leviticus · NUMBERS · Deuteronomy · JOSHUA · JUDGES · RUTH · 1 Samuel · 2 Samuel · 1 KINGS · 2 KINGS · 1 Chronicles · 2 Chronicles · EZRA · Nehemiah · ESTHER · JOB · PSALMS · PROVERBS · Ecclesiastes · SONG OF SONGS · LAMENTATIONS · Isaiah · Jeremiah · EZEKIEL · Daniel · HOSEA · JOEL · Amos · Obadiah

THE PENTATEUCH   OLD TESTAMENT HISTORY   WISDOM AND POETRY   THE PROPH...

The Old Testament

As the literary archive of the nation of Israel, these books came together gradually, across a period of many centuries. It was only after the exile in Babylon that the Jews began reflecting on the status of the various books, and by about 400 BC the five 'books of Moses' were accepted as authoritative scripture, with the 'former prophets' and 'latter prophets' recognized along with them by the early second century BC. The precise make-up of 'the writings' was more open for some time, and was complicated by the production of new books written in Greek during this period. It was not until late in the first century AD that Jewish scholars met at Yavneh to draw up a list of the 39 books which would constitute the original Hebrew Bible, referred to by Christians today as the Old Testament.

Text and interpretation

Because of the history and nature of its text, understanding the Bible inevitably involves more than just reading it. It is not a book of religious philosophy, and every one of its component parts had its own original context. In approaching any particular passage it is important to pay attention to three aspects of the text: time and place, purpose and genre.

TIME AND PLACE

The historical origin of a passage is significant: a piece written during the time of the Israelite kings is going to have different concerns from one written during the Roman occupation of Palestine, and one originating in the Babylonian exile will differ from one written centuries later in Italy or Greece. Events in the wider world at the time will be relevant to a proper understanding.

PURPOSE

What was a particular author trying to achieve? A storyteller has different concerns from a historian, and a law-maker is not the same as a psychic visionary. A piece of literature written to correct mistaken beliefs is going to require a different kind of approach than a letter written to encourage friends in time of hardship. Understanding an author's purpose can be difficult, because the only evidence for it is what they have written – and there is a tendency to interpret the writing in terms of what we imagine its purpose to have been. But it is still worth making the effort.

GENRE

There are many clearly identifiable distinctive forms of literature in the Bible: history, law, fiction, visions, poetry, gospels, letters, worship materials, philosophy and ethics, and faith stories. No particular genre is more 'true' than any other: all in their different ways bear witness to the Bible's essential message. But in order to understand any passage with clarity, we need first to identify its genre, and then ask the kind of questions that apply to that kind of writing. Expecting fiction or poetry to be like history, for example, would be pointless.

By exploring the passage in this way, understanding what it meant for its

The New Testament

The New Testament was quite different. All its books were written over less than 100 years, and were in regular use by the Christian churches from the very beginning. About AD 150, Marcion left the church at Rome and declared that he had a new understanding of the Christian message, based on his own selection of sacred books, most of which the main church leaders did not regard as authentic compositions of the apostles. This forced them in turn to create their own lists of those writings that could be regarded as authentic. In doing so they did not actually endow these books with authority, but merely confirmed the existing practice of the churches in reading and valuing them. Eventually, in AD 397 the Council of Carthage issued a definitive list containing the 27 books of the New Testament.

Books of the New Testament

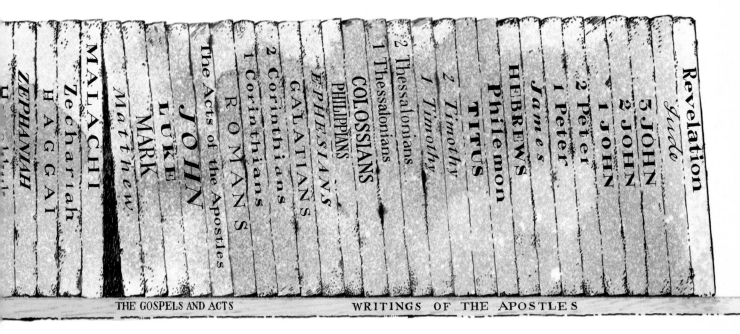

THE GOSPELS AND ACTS   WRITINGS OF THE APOSTLES

original readers and how it was used from one generation to another, we can probe its significance for today's world with greater confidence. It should never be forgotten, however, that readers come with their own questions. For centuries, no one ever thought of asking what the Bible had to say about slavery, or the relationships of women and men, because patriarchy and slavery were taken for granted as part of everyday life. This is why the Bible needs to be interpreted afresh for each generation. One of its most amazing characteristics is the way in which it provides resources for addressing new issues. This is largely because of its nature as story. Stories rarely give universal answers, but they always direct attention to the right questions – and in the case of the Bible, that always comes down to questions about the ultimate meaning of life, which are also questions about God.

Deuterocanonical books (see pages 240–243)

The Torah or Pentateuch

The first five books of the Bible: Genesis, Exodus, Leviticus, Numbers and Deuteronomy. In the original Hebrew Bible, and throughout the history of Judaism, they are known as the *Torah,* a word meaning 'guidance' or 'instruction'. They constituted the section of the original Hebrew Bible known as the Law. By the beginning of the Christian era, they had been translated into Greek, and this is the origin of the term 'Pentateuch', meaning 'the five scrolls'.

The Hebrew term gives a clue to their real significance, for these books set out the underlying worldview on which the Bible's faith was founded. They deal with fundamental issues such as the nature of God, the nature of people, and the relationships between God, people and the natural world. They also include the traditional legends told by Hebrew people to help them understand their own heritage and their place in God's plan for humankind. These themes give consistency to what might otherwise look like a miscellaneous collection of stories and laws.

Genesis

In Hebrew, this book was known by its first phrase: 'In the beginning'. The Greek title, 'Genesis', means the same thing. It consists of a collection of stories about beginnings, starting with the creation of the world, then moving on to well-loved tales of the traditional founders of the Hebrew nation: Abraham, Sarah, Rachel, Isaac and Joseph, and their families.

Exodus

The Greek title of this book aptly indicates its story-line, for the word 'exodus' just means 'the way out'. At the start of the book, the ancestors of Israel are enslaved in a foreign land – by the end of it they are on their way to a new land, led by Moses who orchestrated their escape from the tyranny of Egypt and its rulers. They do not immediately find a new home to settle, and the book depicts them wandering around in the Sinai desert for many years, during which time they received laws for living which would equip them for the settled life which lay before them. The Ten Commandments are recorded in the book of Exodus, but most of its laws relate to worship and other ritual matters.

Leviticus and Numbers

These books contain regulations to cover every imaginable aspect of the life that Israel later enjoyed in Palestine. Social laws, food laws, rules for judges and other community leaders – they are all here, and more besides. In addition, there are descriptions of the regular festivals in Israel's faith, and instructions on how they should be celebrated.

Deuteronomy

This book continues much of the social legislation of Leviticus and Numbers, but also has a major concern for the worship of Israel at its one central sanctuary. In the context of these early stories, this is depicted as a tent of worship used on the journey from Egypt to Palestine, though much of what is spelled out here is more obviously related to a later period when Solomon's temple in Jerusalem was the most significant place of worship.

Author

These books came together in the same way as most national archives do, with a long history of compilation as traditional stories that inspired later generations were valued and repeated, and then written down to be preserved for the future. Though some elements within them might go back to the earliest period, many of the laws also evolved over several centuries. Some of them deal with situations that did not exist at the time of Moses, covering the role of the king (there was no king at this time), procedures for agriculture (Moses' generation were nomads), and the life of the Jerusalem temple (not built until Solomon's reign, 970–930 BC). No doubt these materials were gathered together over a long period of time, before eventually reaching their present form about the time of the exile in Babylon (587–539 BC).

Literary form

This part of the Bible contains more diverse forms of writing than almost any other. The earliest sections of Genesis, which deal with enduring issues of human life by telling equally timeless stories, are obviously a different kind of literature from the many laws contained in Leviticus and Numbers, while the stories of the Hebrew ancestors are different again. Intermingled with all these we find poetry, ethical instructions, guidelines for worship, and much more. Though being so different, these five books are all telling one story, and throughout their pages there is a strong message that this is God's world, and God is at work in it, involved in the natural environment, as well as in the lives of individuals and nations.

View from Mount Sinai, Egypt.

Genesis

This is the book of beginnings: the beginning of the world, a new beginning after a great flood, the beginning of the Hebrew nation.

Key contents

THE BEGINNING OF THINGS
(CHAPTERS 1–11)
The world, people and God
(chapters 1–3)
From Adam to Noah (chapters 4–5)
Noah and the great flood
(chapters 6–10)
The tower of Babel (chapter 11)

ABRAHAM AND HIS FAMILY
(CHAPTERS 12–50)
Abraham, Isaac, Esau and Jacob
(chapters 12–36)
Joseph and his brothers
(chapters 37–45)
Jacob and his family in
Egypt (chapters 46–50)

'Creation of Adam', Michelangelo Buonarroti
(1475–1564)

Message

Genesis 1–11 contains traditional faith stories that provide the foundation for the entire Bible. They indicate the importance of the natural world to God, and the role of people as part of nature, which they are intended to nurture and preserve. The perfect state for the world to be in is one where people, God, animals and plants live in peace with each other – something that humans in particular have difficulty in accepting, because they feel a need to control everything else. That path leads to disaster, as the harmony of all things is broken. Hope for a better way of being still runs through the entire narrative, as a new start is made with Noah, then later with Abraham. There is debate among scholars as to whether the Abraham stories introduce historical narrative in the strict sense. It is certainly difficult to place them on a chronological time scale. Either way, their message is clear, as they highlight the constancy of God even in the face of much human failure.

'Adam and Eve banished from Paradise' (detail), Tommaso Masaccio (1407–28)

Key characters

Adam and Eve, Cain and Abel, Noah, Abraham, Sarah, Hagar, Ishmael, Lot, Isaac, Rachel, Leah, Rebekah, Jacob, Esau, Joseph and his brothers (the 12 sons of Jacob, from whom the 12 tribes of Israel traditionally traced their origin).

Key stories

God's blessing of nature and people, and their struggle with sin (Genesis 1–3)
Noah and his family saved from the flood (Genesis 6–10)
God makes a promise to Abraham (Genesis 12)
Abraham's family (Genesis 12–25)
Isaac (Genesis 21–28, 35)
Jacob (Genesis 25–50)
Joseph (Genesis 30, 37–50)

ABRAHAM

The Abraham story begins in the city of Ur on the River Euphrates, then moves to Harran several hundred miles to the north-west, thence to Canaan. Motivated by the dream of a permanent home for his descendants, Abraham moved from place to place with his flocks and herds. He is depicted as a person of great faith, trusting God's promise, building altars and worshipping wherever he goes. At the same time, he struggles constantly with crisis, and makes many mistakes. During a time of famine, he sold his wife Sarah as a prostitute to the king of Egypt. Later, when Sarah was still infertile, and they were both very old, he had a son (Ishmael) by Sarah's servant-woman, Hagar – whom he rejected once Sarah became pregnant and gave birth to the child – Isaac – who then became the true heir of his family. Isaac himself only narrowly escaped being murdered by his father, when God intervened as he was trussed up ready to be sacrificed on a stone altar on a mountain-top. The Bible never whitewashes any of its characters, and Abraham eventually emerges as a striking illustration of the way that God brings healing and wholeness into even the most painful circumstances.

Genesis 11:31–32; 12:1ff; 17:1–8; 21:1–3; 22:1–14; Romans 4:1–3; Hebrews 11:8–19; James 2:21–23

Family tree: Terah to the 12 tribes of Israel

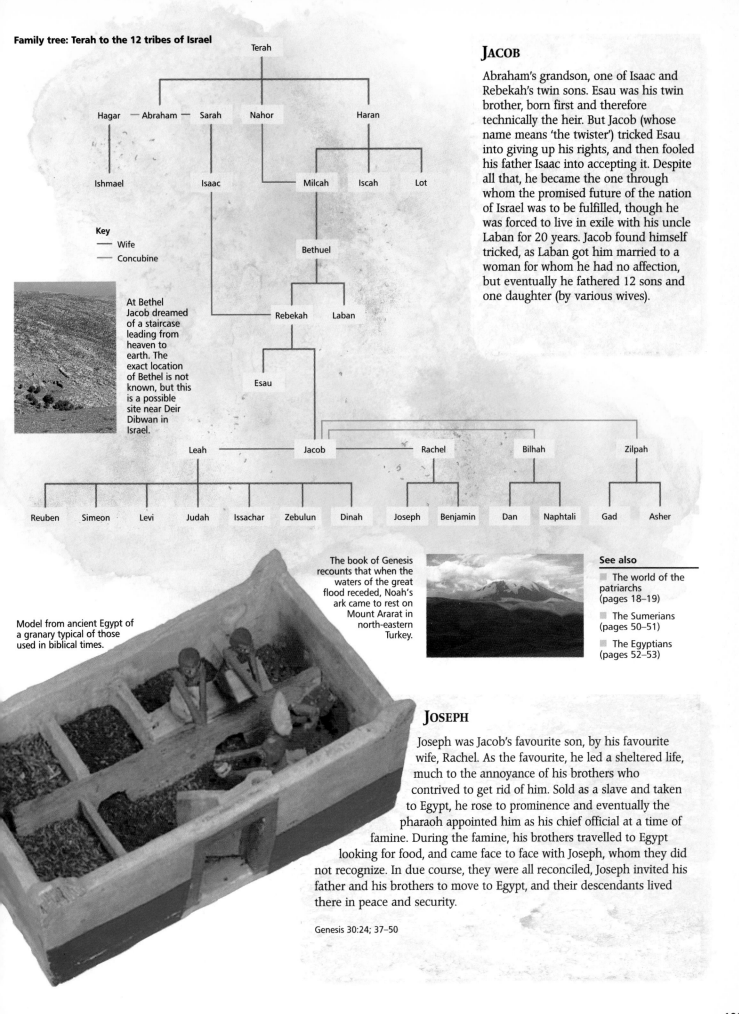

Terah

Hagar — Abraham — Sarah   Nahor   Haran

Ishmael   Isaac   Milcah   Iscah   Lot

Key
— Wife
— Concubine

Bethuel

At Bethel Jacob dreamed of a staircase leading from heaven to earth. The exact location of Bethel is not known, but this is a possible site near Deir Dibwan in Israel.

Rebekah   Laban

Esau

Leah — Jacob — Rachel   Bilhah   Zilpah

Reuben Simeon Levi Judah Issachar Zebulun Dinah   Joseph Benjamin   Dan Naphtali   Gad Asher

JACOB

Abraham's grandson, one of Isaac and Rebekah's twin sons. Esau was his twin brother, born first and therefore technically the heir. But Jacob (whose name means 'the twister') tricked Esau into giving up his rights, and then fooled his father Isaac into accepting it. Despite all that, he became the one through whom the promised future of the nation of Israel was to be fulfilled, though he was forced to live in exile with his uncle Laban for 20 years. Jacob found himself tricked, as Laban got him married to a woman for whom he had no affection, but eventually he fathered 12 sons and one daughter (by various wives).

The book of Genesis recounts that when the waters of the great flood receded, Noah's ark came to rest on Mount Ararat in north-eastern Turkey.

See also
- The world of the patriarchs (pages 18–19)
- The Sumerians (pages 50–51)
- The Egyptians (pages 52–53)

Model from ancient Egypt of a granary typical of those used in biblical times.

JOSEPH

Joseph was Jacob's favourite son, by his favourite wife, Rachel. As the favourite, he led a sheltered life, much to the annoyance of his brothers who contrived to get rid of him. Sold as a slave and taken to Egypt, he rose to prominence and eventually the pharaoh appointed him as his chief official at a time of famine. During the famine, his brothers travelled to Egypt looking for food, and came face to face with Joseph, whom they did not recognize. In due course, they were all reconciled, Joseph invited his father and his brothers to move to Egypt, and their descendants lived there in peace and security.

Genesis 30:24; 37–50

Exodus

The title means 'exit' or 'departure'. The key story of this book tells how God empowered Moses to rescue the people of Israel from what by this time had become enforced slavery in Egypt.

This wall painting from the temple of Beit El-Wali depicts the Egyptian Pharaoh Ramesses II in battle against the Nubians.

Key contents

ISRAEL ESCAPES FROM SLAVERY IN EGYPT
(CHAPTERS 1–15)
Slaves in Egypt (chapter 1)
Moses' early years (chapters 2–4)
Aaron and pharaoh (chapters 5–11)
Escape, Passover, and crossing the sea (chapter 12–15)

DESERT JOURNEY TO MOUNT SINAI (CHAPTERS 16–18)

COVENANT WITH GOD AT MOUNT SINAI, AND FOR A NEW NATION (CHAPTERS 19–24)

INSTRUCTIONS FOR BUILDING A TENT FOR WORSHIP (TABERNACLE), AND RULES FOR ITS OPERATION (CHAPTERS 25–40)

The setting

The events of Exodus take place in the Nile Delta of Egypt, and in the Sinai peninsula.

Literary form

The book of Exodus contains two quite distinct types of

writing: stories and laws. There has been much debate as to whether the stories can be placed in a historical context and, if so, how. Those who regard the story of the exodus as a historical event argue about whether it involved the whole nation of Israel, or just one section of

Key characters

Moses, his brother Aaron and sister Miriam; Pharaoh, the king of Egypt.

View across the River Nile to Luxor, Egypt.

Key stories

Rescue of the baby Moses (Exodus 2)
Moses and the burning bush (Exodus 3)
The ten plagues (Exodus 7–12)
The first Passover (Exodus 12)
Crossing of the 'sea of reeds' (Exodus 14)
The Ten Commandments (Exodus 20)
God and Israel make a covenant (Exodus 23–24)
Worship of the golden calf (Exodus 32)
Building of a tent for worship (Exodus 36)

the Israelites, while others claim that what is known of the archaeology of late bronze age Palestine seems to imply that what later became 'Israel' was always a part of the native population of Canaan at this time. Either way, there can be no doubt that the stories are told in Exodus primarily for the purpose of establishing the moral and religious basis on which the nation was meant to operate. Those who want to date these events chronologically would place them sometime in the period 1325–1225 BC.

Meaning and message

The book of Exodus begins to set out the social implications of the Bible's world view. God is not described here in religious abstractions, but in relation to the everyday needs of ordinary people. Justice for the oppressed and marginalized are at the heart of this vision, as God sees those who are suffering, hears their cry, and initiates action to change things. In response to this, the escaping slaves are invited to live by the same standards and values, and to signify their acceptance first by entering into a solemn covenant with God, and then by expressing this not only in worship but also in the way they structure their own society. This is why in the book of Exodus laws about ritual actions are found alongside basic ethical teaching and rules for the establishment of a just nation. The point of it all is simple: because God is concerned with justice for those who are exploited, those who follow God's way should have the same concerns. The rest of the Bible shows how difficult it was to live up to this ideal, but it was always central to the ethos of the nation, and formed a major part of the message of the later prophets.

MOSES

Moses was the leader who freed the Israelites from slavery in Egypt and led them through the desert to the borders of Canaan. Born of Israelite parents in Egypt, Moses was adopted into the Egyptian royal family, but as an adult reacted against the unfair treatment of his own people. Driven into exile and working as a shepherd in the desert, he had an experience of God speaking to him through a desert bush which flamed but did not burn up. Inspired by this, he returned to Egypt and demanded freedom for his people. Eventually, the slaves escaped, hotly pursued by pharaoh's army, but they were aided by a miraculous crossing of the 'sea of reeds'.

Once in the desert, Moses took the people to Mount Sinai, and there delivered to them the Ten Commandments and various instructions for building a tent of worship, called the tabernacle. After much wandering around in the desert, moving from one oasis to another, the people arrived at the border of the land they were to settle: Canaan. By now many of the original slaves had died, and Moses himself handed on the leadership to Joshua before he himself died. As the law-giver, he became a key figure in later Jewish tradition, and also features in the New Testament as a pivotal Old Testament character.

Exodus 2 – Deuteronomy 34; Luke 9:28ff.

The oasis of Paran in southern Sinai. The Bible states that the Israelites travelled through Paran after the exodus.

See also

■ The exodus from Egypt (pages 20–21)

■ The Egyptians (pages 52–53)

■ The creator-God of Israel (pages 148–149)

■ Israel's faith (pages 150–151)

'Israel in Egypt', Edward John Poynter (1836–1919)

Leviticus

This book consists of laws relating to matters of ritual purity, and includes dietary regulations as well as instructions for the conduct of worship. It takes its name from the Levites, the traditional tribe of priests in ancient Israel.

Key contents

LAWS ABOUT OFFERINGS AND SACRIFICES (CHAPTERS 1–7)

REGULATIONS FOR THE APPOINTMENT AND CONDUCT OF PRIESTS (CHAPTERS 8–10)

LAWS ABOUT HYGIENE, FOOD AND RITUAL CLEANSING (CHAPTERS 11–15)

THE DAY OF ATONEMENT (CHAPTER 16)

THE REGULAR FESTIVALS OF FAITH (CHAPTERS 17–27)

This phylactery dates from the first century AD.

Key themes

The unexpected combination of regulations for food and personal hygiene with rules for the conduct of worship emphasizes the Bible's commitment to seeing faith as part of a total lifestyle, affecting all aspects of daily existence, and not just what went on in places of worship. Sacrifice – of both animals and plants – played a central part in Old Testament worship, as a symbolic way of breaking down the barriers between God and people, and expressing the essential unity of all things in the whole cosmos.

Key passage

Love your neighbour as yourself. (Leviticus 19:18)

The Israelites caught quails as food in the desert. This Egyptian wall painting from the tomb of Nefermaat shows a man snaring birds.

Numbers

This book contains more stories of the Israelite people during their nomadic period in the Sinai peninsula, after the exodus, along with further rules for priests. Its title is taken from the two censuses that are recorded in the book.

Key contents

MOVING ON FROM MOUNT SINAI (CHAPTERS 1–9)
A national census (chapter 1)
Lists of the tribes (chapter 2)
More rules for priests and Levites (chapters 3–8)
Passover celebration (chapter 9)

FROM MOUNT SINAI TO MOAB (CHAPTERS 10–21)

EVENTS IN MOAB: STORIES OF BALAAM AND BALAK (CHAPTERS 22–32)

JOURNEY'S END (CHAPTERS 33–36)

Key stories

Miriam's punishment (Numbers 12)
The 12 spies and their report (Numbers 13)
Complaints, rebellion and 40 years of wandering (Numbers 14)
Leadership challenges (Numbers 16–17)
A plague of poisonous snakes (Numbers 21)
Balaam and his ass (Numbers 22)
Joshua becomes the leader (Numbers 27)

Key characters

Moses and Aaron, Caleb and Joshua, Balaam and Balak.

Key passage

May the Lord bless you and keep you; may God's gracious face shine upon you; may the Lord's face turn towards you, and give you peace. (Numbers 6:24–26).

Key theme

The book of Numbers emphasizes the faithfulness of God and the disobedience of the people: faithfulness will lead to success, but disobedience leads to catastrophe. This is one of the central messages of the entire Old Testament, and is especially prominent in the messages of the prophets and the later books of national history.

Deuteronomy

The name of this book means 'the second law', and most experts believe that is what it is: a book of regulations compiled for use in the temple at Jerusalem in the time of King Josiah of Judah (640–609 BC). In keeping with the tradition that all law went back to Moses, however, it is located here in the form of further reflections on how the Israelites should live as they entered Canaan.

'The Scapegoat', William Holman Hunt (1827–1910)

Apis, the sacred bull worshipped in Memphis by the ancient Egyptians.

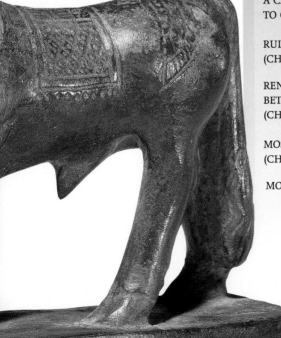

'And Moses made a serpent of brass' (Numbers 21:9). This bronze snake dates from about the 12th century BC.

AARON

Aaron was the elder brother of Moses and Miriam, and a loyal supporter of Moses' initiatives at the exodus. At Mount Sinai, Aaron made a golden calf for the people to worship in Moses' absence, though he subsequently became high priest in charge of Israel's worship, and was regarded by all later generations as the ancestor of all priests. According to the story, he died before the Israelites entered Canaan and his son Eleazar became high priest after him.

Exodus 4:14; 5–12; 28:1; 32:1; Numbers 20:23–29

See also

■ Food laws and customs (pages 108–109)

■ God's laws in practice (pages 152–153)

■ Annual festivals (pages 156–157)

■ Priests and rituals (pages 162–163)

Key stories

The 12 spies (Deuteronomy 1)
Desert journeys (Deuteronomy 2)
The Ten Commandments (Deuteronomy 5)
Joshua's appointment (Deuteronomy 31)
Moses' death (Deuteronomy 34)

Key passages

Love the Lord your God with all your heart, with all your soul, and with all your strength.
(Deuteronomy 6:4–6)
People cannot live on bread alone, but need every word that God speaks.
(Deuteronomy 8:3)

Key themes

Deuteronomy provides a bridge between the books of the Law in the original Hebrew Bible and the history books that follow it. Indeed, in some ways it is better understood not as part of the Law, but as the preface to the history books known as the 'Deuteronomistic history' (Deuteronomy – 2 Kings). It certainly sets out the great theme that motivated the editors of these books: obedience to God brings blessing, while disobedience leads to disaster. This insight in turn owed a great deal to the prophets as they sought explanations for Israel's troubled history.

Key contents

MOSES REVIEWS EVENTS ON THE JOURNEY FROM MOUNT SINAI (CHAPTERS 1—4)

A CALL FOR RENEWED OBEDIENCE TO GOD'S LAWS (CHAPTERS 5—26)

RULES FOR LIFE IN THE LAND (CHAPTERS 27—28)

RENEWAL OF THE COVENANT BETWEEN GOD AND PEOPLE (CHAPTERS 29—30)

MOSES' LAST INSTRUCTIONS (CHAPTERS 31—33)

MOSES' DEATH (CHAPTER 34)

Old Testament history: overview

A significant portion of the Old Testament consists of history books, relating from different perspectives the story of Israel from the earliest times through to the Babylonian exile and beyond. These books fall neatly into two clearly distinct sections: the 'Deuteronomistic history' (Joshua, Judges, 1–2 Samuel and 1–2 Kings) and the 'history of the chronicler' (1–2 Chronicles, together with Ezra and Nehemiah).

Old Testament history is largely dominated by the relationships between Israel and the various international superpowers of the day: Egypt, Syria, Assyria and Babylon. Though they were inspired by the vision of a divine promise that they would be a great nation, the reality for the people of Israel was very different. Whether struggling to establish their own state in the midst of a Canaanite culture, or trying to repel the inroads of invaders, their national achievements never quite managed to live up to their expectations. The various historical accounts of the Old Testament were written both to document and to explain these thwarted ambitions.

The 'Deuteronomistic history'

This consists of the books from Joshua to 2 Kings, with the book of Deuteronomy as a kind of theological preface to them. Using the concept of a covenant between God and the people, the book of Deuteronomy sets out the terms and conditions of this covenant. The following books then explore how and why the covenant came to be ignored by the people, leading to the Israelites' national downfall, first at the hands of the Assyrians (722 BC), then at the hands of the Babylonians (587 BC).

This collection of books includes material drawn from many ancient sources. But as a complete unit it was probably compiled sometime during the exile in Babylon, but before the Persians came to power and defeated the Babylonians (539 BC). It would be natural to preserve the nation's stories at a time like this, and also to reflect on them to see what had gone wrong.

This analysis is presented in the form of speeches at key points in the narrative, pointing out that obedience to God's laws led to success, and disobedience led to failure (see Joshua 23; 1 Samuel 12; 2 Samuel 7; 1 Kings 8:22–53). It was not God, but the people, who had failed to keep the bargain entered into at Mount Sinai, and that was the root cause of the disasters they had suffered. But all was not lost, for even in what seemed like a hopeless situation, God's promises still held firm, and if the people were ready to change their ways, the promises made to Abraham could still come true. This prospect is clearly spelled out in Deuteronomy 4:27–31, which refers to the exile (a sure indication that this book was part of the national self-examination of that period), while the entire history ends on an optimistic note, with the release of Jehoiachin (the former king of Judah) from prison in Babylon (2 Kings 25:27–30).

The 'history of the chronicler'

When King Cyrus of Persia defeated the Babylonians (539 BC), he allowed the Jewish exiles to return to their homeland. Not all wished to do so, but those who did managed to rebuild a temple in Jerusalem under the leadership of Zerubbabel (520–515 BC). Over the next century or so they were followed by others, culminating in major efforts under Ezra and Nehemiah to re-establish a powerful Jewish state that would be run along the lines of the traditional laws of God.

The books of 1–2 Chronicles were issued at this time, to encourage the people in this task. These books mention the edict of King Cyrus (2 Chronicles 36:22–23), so they must be later than 539 BC, but it is difficult to determine their date more exactly. The closing words of 2 Chronicles are repeated in the first paragraph of Ezra, which suggests some obvious connection between them, though the books of Ezra and Nehemiah are quite different in character. Whereas

1–2 Chronicles presents a carefully worded, polished account, Ezra and Nehemiah contain a collection of apparently disconnected stories. They are no less valuable for that, as they have every appearance of having been written almost at the same time as the events they describe, which would place these two books around 400 BC. Maybe the book of Chronicles was written slightly earlier than that, and Ezra and Nehemiah were intended to continue and update the ongoing story.

Historical stories

The books of Esther and Ruth are quite different from the great history books, and contain two stories about women whose faithfulness to God and their people were recorded as examples for later generations to follow. In their different ways, they both highlighted the theme that faithfulness was the way to ensure God's purposes for the nation would be fulfilled.

View of the old city of Jerusalem from the Church of the Redeemer.

Joshua

This book tells the story of the Israelite occupation of Canaan, under the leadership of Joshua, the successor to Moses.

Time-span

About 1230–1200 BC

Main characters

Joshua; also Rahab and Caleb.

Key events

The two spies (Joshua 2)
Crossing the Jordan (Joshua 3)
Battle of Jericho (Joshua 6)

Key passages

Be strong and courageous. (Joshua 1:5–9)
As for me and my household, we will serve the Lord. (Joshua 24:15)

Key theme

Joshua presents a picture of a successful capture of major Canaanite cities by the Israelite forces, who appear as a unified and disciplined army. The one exception, at the city of Ai, highlights the overall Deuteronomic theme that disobedience leads to disaster, while obedient faithfulness ensures triumph. By the end of the book of Joshua, Canaan has been subdued, and the covenant between God and the people is renewed. There is archaeological evidence of radical change in Canaanite culture in the period about 1400–1200 BC, and indications that some of the cities mentioned in Joshua were indeed conquered at this time. But the reasons for this are unclear, and other evidence shows that the real struggle for land continued long after this.

JOSHUA

Joshua became leader of the Israelites after Moses' death. His name means 'God is salvation'. Joshua appears first as one of the 12 spies sent to see the lie of the land while Israel was still in the desert.

Exodus 17:9ff.; Numbers 13–14; Joshua

Some of the pillars of the Canaanite 'high place' at Gezer. The town was situated close to the main road between Egypt and Mesopotamia, and so was of strategic value. The Bible records that Joshua defeated the king of Gezer, but did not take the town.

Key contents

SUCCESS AND FAILURE IN BATTLE (CHAPTERS 1–12)
Across the River Jordan (chapters 1–5)
The conquest of Jericho and its consequences (chapter 6–7)
Defeat at Ai (chapter 8)
Campaign in the south (chapters 9–10)
Campaign in the north (chapters 11–12)

THE LAND DIVIDED AMONG THE TRIBES
(CHAPTERS 13–21)

THE EASTERN TRIBES AND JOSHUA'S FAREWELL
(CHAPTERS 22–24)

Ram's horn trumpet

Ivory plaque from Megiddo, dating from about 1300–1200 BC. It depicts a ruler, probably the king of Megiddo, sitting on his throne surrounded by attendants and inspecting prisoners.

Judges

This book contains stories of various local heroes, or 'judges', at roughly the same period as the narratives in Joshua.

Key contents

VARIOUS BATTLES BETWEEN CANAANITES AND ISRAELITES (CHAPTERS 1–2)

STORIES OF THE 'JUDGES' (CHAPTERS 2–16)
Othniel, Ehud and Shamgar (chapter 3)
Deborah and Barak (chapters 4–6)
Gideon (chapters 6–8)
Abimelech tries to become king (chapter 9)
Tola, Jair and Jephthah (chapters 10–12)
Samson (chapters 13–16)

MORE STORIES OF VIOLENCE AND WARFARE (CHAPTERS 17–21)

The judges and their opponents

Judge	*Opponent(s)*
Othniel of Judah	Cushan-Rishathaim of Mesopotamia
Ehud of Benjamin	Eglon of Moab
Shamgar	the Philistines
Deborah (Ephraim) and **Barak** (Naphtali)	Jabin (a Canaanite king) and Sisera (his commander)
Gideon of Manasseh	the Midianites and Amalekites
Tola of Issachar	
Jair of Gilead	
Jephthah of Gilead	the Ammonites
Ibzan of Bethlehem	
Elon of Zebulun	
Abdon of Ephraim	
Samson of Dan	the Philistines

Key theme

Judges depicts a more gradual conquest of Canaan than the book of Joshua, with local leaders negotiating treaties with other ethnic groups (Judges 1:27–36), and fighting isolated battles against a variety of opponents. The main emphasis is on tribal groups, though there is a strong sense of unity between the various tribes, focused around their worship of God and their common commitment to the covenant. The general impression is of a fragmented and demoralized people enduring much hardship as they tried to establish their own nation within this land.

GIDEON

The Bible tells of how Gideon selected 300 men, and armed them with only an empty pitcher, a flaming torch and a trumpet. Operating in three groups, they surprised the Canaanites at night, creating panic among the enemy, who turned on each other and then fled, with the Israelites in pursuit.

Judges 6:11–23; 36–39; 7:1–23

See also

■ The Israelites enter Canaan
(pages 22–23)

■ The time of the judges
(pages 24–25)

■ The Canaanites
(pages 56–57)

■ The lands of the Bible
(pages 82–83)

DEBORAH

Deborah was the only woman among the judges. Along with Barak, she defeated the Canaanite general Sisera. The 'Song of Deborah' which celebrates this victory (Judges 4) is considered to be one of the most ancient pieces of poetry in the Bible.

Judges 4 5

View across the Jezreel plain from Mount Tabor, the site of the defeat of the Canaanite army by Deborah and Barak.

SAMSON

Samson was set aside at birth as a Nazirite, as a sign of which his hair was never to be cut. As an adult, he developed great physical strength, the secret of which was his long hair. He single-handedly battled against the Philistines, but fell in love with a Philistine woman, Delilah. When Delilah discovered the secret of Samson's strength, she had his hair cut while he slept. Samson was blinded and imprisoned by the Philistines, but as his hair grew longer his strength began to return. When he was chained to a Philistine temple to amuse a crowd he saw an opportunity to take revenge. He prayed and heaved with all his might, and demolished the building, killing himself and the Philistines in the process.

Judges 13–16

1 and 2 Samuel

The story of Israel from the period of the judges through to the reign of King David.

According to the Bible, God transformed David's life as the simple shepherd boy became a great king.

Key contents

SAMUEL'S BIRTH AND LEADERSHIP (CHAPTERS 1–7)

SAUL BECOMES ISRAEL'S FIRST KING (CHAPTERS 8–10)

SAUL LOSES POPULAR SUPPORT (CHAPTERS 11–15)

DAVID IS CHOSEN AS THE NEXT KING (CHAPTER 16)

DAVID FIGHTS GOLIATH (CHAPTER 17)

DAVID THE OUTLAW (CHAPTERS 18–30)

SAUL AND JONATHAN ARE KILLED
(CHAPTER 31 – CHAPTER 1)

DAVID BECOMES KING OF JUDAH (CHAPTERS 2–4)

DAVID KING OF ALL ISRAEL (CHAPTERS 5–7)

VARIOUS BATTLES (CHAPTERS 8–10)

DAVID'S ADULTERY WITH BATHSHEBA (CHAPTERS 11–12)

FAMILY TROUBLES AND POLITICAL DISTURBANCES (CHAPTERS 13–20)

DAVID'S LATER YEARS (CHAPTERS 21–24)

Saul (1050—1010)   David (1010—970)   Solomon (970—930)

Kings of the united monarchy

Shiloh was the Israelite town in which Joshua had set up the tabernacle and the Ark of the Covenant.

SAUL

Saul was the first king of Israel, from the small tribe of Benjamin. He lacked the resources and support needed to deal firmly with the Philistines (who, like Israel, were invaders of the land seeking to establish their own state). Once Saul rejected the advice of religious leaders such as Samuel, his days were numbered. David was a more attractive character, and his popularity only increased Saul's sense of isolation. The stories of the two are carefully interwoven, as David appears not only as Saul's rival but also as his personal musician, helping Saul cope with his depression. Saul becomes a tragic figure, turning for help to a medium before killing himself in despair at the loss of his power.

1 Samuel 8–31; 2 Samuel 1ff.

Family tree: King David's wives and children

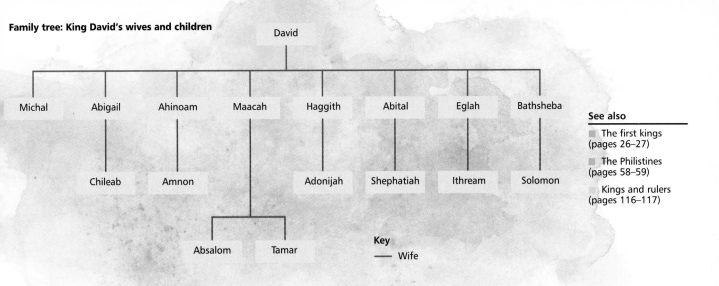

David

- Michal
- Abigail — Chileab
- Ahinoam — Amnon
- Maacah — Absalom, Tamar
- Haggith — Adonijah
- Abital — Shephatiah
- Eglah — Ithream
- Bathsheba — Solomon

Key
—— Wife

See also

■ The first kings
(pages 26–27)

■ The Philistines
(pages 58–59)

□ Kings and rulers
(pages 116–117)

Time-scale and setting

Israel is still struggling to gain control over the land, until David eventually establishes secure boundaries and creates the conditions for stability and prosperity. These stories can be placed in a clear historical context, during the period 1075–975 BC.

Key passages

Hannah's prayer and Samuel's birth
(1 Samuel 1–2)

The child Samuel hears God's voice
(1 Samuel 3)

Capture and return of the Ark of the Covenant (1 Samuel 4–6)

David's friendship with Jonathan
(1 Samuel 18–20)

David's lament for Saul and Jonathan
(2 Samuel 1)

God's promise to David's family
(2 Samuel 7)

Nathan's story of the poor man's lamb
(2 Samuel 12)

David's victory song (2 Samuel 22)

Key themes

Saul and David are both judged by their attitude to the ancient covenant between God and the people. When they trust in God and uphold covenant values they are successful. Departing from this ideal leads to disaster. Behind this judgment is the notion that the Israelite kings only have authority when it is delegated to them from God. Much of the narrative is taken up with showing how and why David's family came to inherit the kingship in Jerusalem on a permanent basis. By the time the books were finally edited, the promise made to David through Nathan was an important symbol of the coming Messiah.

DAVID

Unlike Saul, David understood the need for unity among the tribal factions in Israel, and set about establishing a power base that would be rooted in more than personal popular appeal. Instead of relying on local volunteer armies, he set up his own full-time fighting force, captured the city of Jerusalem and placed the Ark of the Covenant there – ensuring that the people's religious commitment would also be a commitment to him as king. In the process, he transformed the political structure of the nation, and ensured the continuation of his family's reign long after his own death. David was a multi-faceted person: a great musician and poet, a good father, a faithful friend – as well as an adulterer and, eventually, a murderer, who still managed to survive when he admitted his wrongdoing and sought forgiveness. But even in his own family there was discontent with his centralization of power, and two of his sons (Absalom and Adonijah) plotted against him at different times.

1 Samuel 16–1 Kings 2; 1 Chronicles 11–29

'David and Jonathan', Giovanni Battista Cima da Conegliano (1459–1518)

1 and 2 Kings

These books begin with Israel's golden age, the reign of Solomon (970–930 BC), then document the rise and fall of the two kingdoms of Israel and Judah, covering the period 975–587 BC.

Key passages

Solomon's wisdom
(1 Kings 3)
Building and dedication of the temple (1 Kings 6–8)
Queen of Sheba
(1 Kings 10)
Elijah and the widow at Zarephath (1 Kings 17)
Elijah and the prophets of Baal (1 Kings 18)
Elijah and the 'still, small voice' (1 Kings 19)
Naboth's vineyard
(1 Kings 21)
Elijah and the fiery chariot
(2 Kings 2)
Elisha and the woman from Shunem (2 Kings 4)
Naaman (2 Kings 5)
Jezebel's death (2 Kings 9)
Assyria takes Samaria
(2 Kings 17–18)
Destruction of the Jerusalem temple (2 Kings 25)

Key theme

King Solomon's autocratic style created resentment, and when his successor Rehoboam resisted reform the kingdom of Israel divided into the 10 northern tribes (Israel) and the two southern tribes (Judah).

Judah remained faithful to the line of King David, while Israel sought to reinstate a way of life that would more closely reflect the way the Israelite tribes had lived in the desert prior to entering Canaan.

With the Ark of the Covenant and the temple still in Jerusalem, Israel needed its own alternative shrines of national unity – something that inevitably led to the inclusion of elements of Canaanite worship. The north was politically unstable, with only the family of King Omri able to establish anything like a dynasty, and by 722 BC its people were taken into exile by the Assyrians. Attention then focuses on Judah, which itself succumbed to Babylonian power with the destruction of Jerusalem in 587 BC. The history writers connect the crisis for both nations with the fact that most of the kings were too eager to adopt alien religious practices.

Key contents

SOLOMON SUCCEEDS DAVID (CHAPTERS 1–2)

SOLOMON'S REIGN (CHAPTERS 3–11)
Solomon's reputation (chapters 3–4)
The temple in Jerusalem (chapters 5–8
Trade and other projects (chapters 9–10)
Solomon's death (chapter 11)

THE DIVIDED KINGDOM (CHAPTER 12–2 KINGS CHAPTER 17)
The northern tribes rebel (chapters 12–14)
Kings of Israel and Judah (chapters 14–16)
Stories of Elijah (chapters 17–19)
Ahab of Israel (chapters 20–22)
Judah and Israel (chapter 22–2 Kings chapter 1)
Stories of Elisha (chapters 2–8)
Kings of Israel and Judah (chapters 8–16)
Assyria destroys Israel (chapter 17)

JUDAH (CHAPTERS 18–25)
Hezekiah and Assyria (chapters 18–20)
Manasseh and Amon (chapter 21)
Josiah's reforms (chapters 22–23)
Last kings of Judah (chapter 24)
Babylon destroys Jerusalem (chapter 25)

Soon after King Solomon's death the Egyptian pharoah Shishak invaded Judah and plundered the temple. This gold armlet, belonging to Shishak's son, may well have been made from gold from the temple.

Kings of Israel

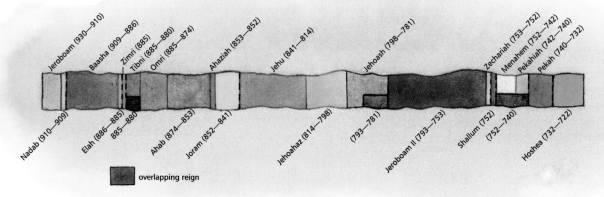

Jeroboam (930–910)
Baasha (909–886)
Zimri (885)
Tibni (885–880)
Omri (885–874)
Ahaziah (853–852)
Jehu (841–814)
Jehoash (798–781)
Zechariah (753–752)
Menahem (752–742)
Pekahiah (742–740)
Pekah (740–732)

Nadab (910–909)
Elah (886–885)
885–880
Ahab (874–853)
Joram (852–841)
Jehoahaz (814–798)
(793–781)
Jeroboam II (793–753)
Shallum (752)
(752–740)
Hoshea (732–722)

overlapping reign

Panel from the black obelisk of King Shalmaneser III, dating from about 825 BC. It depicts Israelite porters paying tribute to the Assyrian king.

See also

■ Two kingdoms (pages 28–29)

■ The rise of Assyria (pages 30–31)

■ The Babylonians (pages 62–63)

■ The prophets (pages 166–167)

JEROBOAM I

Jeroboam I was the first ruler of the northern kingdom of Israel (930–910 BC). To displace the people's loyalty to Jerusalem and its temple, he established shrines at Dan and Bethel, and placed golden bulls in them – like the Ark of the Covenant in Jerusalem, to serve as visible thrones for the invisible God. But the bull was also a symbol of the Canaanite fertility god, Baal, and the writers of 1 Kings traced all Israel's later problems back to this.

1 Kings 11:26–14:20

REHOBOAM

Rehoboam was the son and heir of Solomon, but he was a weak king whose intransigence over taxation and slavery led to the revolt that divided the kingdom of Israel.

1 Kings 11:43–14:31; 2 Chronicles 9:31–12:16

King Hazael of Damascus, who fought against Jehu and Jehoahaz of Israel, had furniture decorated with ivory plating, including this figure discovered in a Syrian palace. In 841 and 837 BC Hazael also fought against the Assyrian king Shalmaneser III. Thirty years later, the ageing king submitted to Assyrian power.

Bronze ring inscribed with the words 'Ahab King of Israel'.

AHAB AND JEZEBEL

Ahab was the seventh king of Israel (874–853 BC). His father Omri left him a flourishing state and a new capital, Samaria. He married Jezebel, a Canaanite princess, and allowed the worship of Baal to flourish, while adopting a grand lifestyle which the prophet Elijah denounced as incompatible with the values of the covenant with God. Jezebel outlived Ahab, and soon after his death Jehu led a revolution, in the course of which Jezebel suffered a violent death, which the history writers saw as just retribution for her corrupt religious practices.

1 Kings 16:29–34; 18; 19:1–2; 21; 22; 2 Kings 9:30–37

ELIJAH AND ELISHA

Elijah was a fierce prophet who adopted an ascetic lifestyle modelled on the hardships experienced by those Israelite slaves who crossed the desert with Moses. He called on Ahab and Jezebel to return to the values of those days and to create a culture to reflect God's will. Outlawed and victimized, Elijah challenged the prophets of the Canaanite storm god Baal to a show of strength which ended in his triumph and the death of the opposition. Like other prophets, Elijah was a political activist, and plotted to replace Ahab's house with Jehu, whom he hoped would be more faithful to the covenant. Elisha, his pupil, continued his work after his death.

1 Kings 17 – 2 Kings 9; 13:14ff

1 and 2 Chronicles

These books cover events recorded in 2 Samuel and Kings, but from the perspective of exiles returning to Jerusalem from Babylon, and their forebears in the kingdom of Judah.

Key passages

The Ark of the Covenant arrives in Jerusalem (1 Chronicles 15–16)
David's hymn of praise and commendation of Solomon (1 Chronicles 29)
Solomon dedicates the new temple (2 Chronicles 5–7)
Hezekiah rededicates the temple (2 Chronicles 29)

Impression of a seal inscribed with the words 'Shema, servant of Jeroboam'. It was found in Megiddo and may refer to King Jeroboam II of Israel.

Key themes

The books of Chronicles begin with the story of creation, but pay most attention to the reigns of kings David and Solomon, the time when the temple was built, and worship in the temple. The returning Jewish exiles are encouraged to rebuild the ruined temple and restore its worship. David and Solomon's failures never feature here, nor is the kingdom of Israel mentioned – maybe to discourage the returning exiles from relating to the descendants of the northerners who still lived in and around Jerusalem.

Key contents

VARIOUS FAMILY TREES (CHAPTERS 1–9)

DAVID (CHAPTERS 10–29)
Saul's death (chapter 10)
David's achievements (chapters 11–21)
David and the temple (chapters 22–29)

SOLOMON (CHAPTERS 1–9)
Wisdom and wealth (chapter 1)
Building the temple (chapters 2–7)
International relations (chapters 8–9)

KINGS OF JUDAH (CHAPTERS 10–36)
Revolt under Rehoboam (chapter 10)
Rehoboam to Asa (chapters 11–16)
Jehoshaphat's reforms (chapters 17–20)
Jehoram to Ahaz (chapters 21–28)
Hezekiah's reforms (chapters 34–35)
The end of Judah and Jerusalem (chapter 36)

'The Visit of the Queen of Sheba to King Solomon', Edward John Poynter (1836–1919)

SOLOMON

Solomon was the son of David and Bathsheba. He was Israel's most successful king. Solomon inherited peace, and kept a strong army to maintain it. He made treaties with many surrounding nations, frequently marrying into other royal families, and established his kingdom as a major trading and industrial nation. His considerable wealth helped finance the building of the temple in Jerusalem, using materials and skilled workers from other cultures. He also built palaces for himself and his many wives, and funded much of this expansion by harsh taxation of his subjects. Those who could not pay were forced into hard labour, and by the end of his reign he had little support. The Old Testament history books portray him as a man who put his own convenience before the values of God's laws and covenant.

1 Kings 1–11; 1 Chronicles 22:5–23:1; 1 Chronicles 28 – 2 Chronicles 9

Kings of Judah

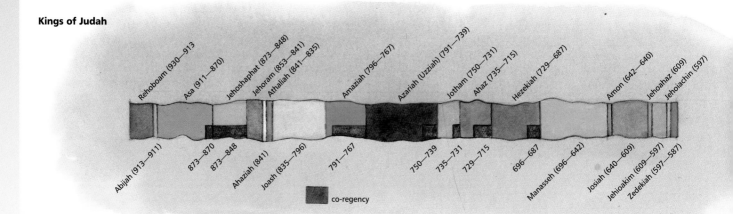

Rehoboam (930—913)
Asa (911—870)
Jehoshaphat (873—848)
Jehoram (853—841)
Athaliah (841—835)
Amaziah (796—767)
Azariah (Uzziah) (791—739)
Jotham (750—731)
Ahaz (735—715)
Hezekiah (729—687)
Amon (642—640)
Jehoahaz (609)
Jehoiachin (597)

Abijah (913—911)
873—870
873—848
Ahaziah (841)
Joash (835—796)
791—767
750—739
735—731
729—715
696—687
Manasseh (696—642)
Josiah (640—609)
Jehoiakim (609—597)
Zedekiah (597—587)

co-regency

JOSIAH

Crowned king of Judah as a child of eight, Josiah (640–609 BC) reigned during the last years of the Assyrian empire, and was able to throw off foreign rule. As part of this, he reinstated worship in the temple in accordance with the regulations of Deuteronomy, leading the nation in a covenant renewal ceremony pledging faithfulness to their ancestral traditions.

2 Kings 21:24–23:30; 2 Chronicles 33:25–35:27; Jeremiah 22:15–16

Hazor was an ancient Canaanite town which was extensively rebuilt under kings Omri and Ahab. The three-aisled colonnaded hall was probably built by King Ahab as a storehouse.

HEZEKIAH

Hezekiah, king of Judah in 729–687 BC, saw the possibility of relaxing the Assyrian grip on his economy, and re-asserted his nation's independence by removing Assyrian religious symbols, withholding taxes and strengthening the army. His hopes were short-lived, and the Assyrian king Sennacherib besieged Jerusalem. The siege was lifted without the city being taken, and the writers of both Kings and Chronicles saw this as evidence of Hezekiah's obedience to the faith traditions of his people, and identified him as one of the reforming kings.

2 Kings 18–20; 2 Chronicles 29–32; Isaiah 36–39

This seal dates from the sixth century BC and is inscribed 'to Pedaiah son of the King'. This name is mentioned in the Bible (1 Chronicles 3:18) as one of the sons of King Jehoiakim of Judah.

Ezra

The returning Jewish exiles rebuild the temple and rediscover their ancient laws.

Key contents

EXILES RETURN WITH ZERUBBABEL (CHAPTERS 1–2)

THE TEMPLE IS REBUILT (CHAPTERS 3–6)
Beginning the work (chapter 3)
Local opposition and Persian support (chapter 4)
Rebuilding continues (chapters 5:1–6:12)
The new temple is dedicated (chapters 6:13–22)

MORE EXILES RETURN WITH EZRA (CHAPTERS 7–10)
Stories from the journey (chapters 7–8)
Racial concerns (chapters 9–10)

Time-scale and setting

Jewish exiles returned from Babylon to Jerusalem over a long period of time, and found their temple in ruins and the land occupied by people of mixed race, including some who never went into exile, and descendants of the population of the original northern kingdom of Israel. The stories in Ezra span the years from about 538 to 428 BC.

Key themes

This book belongs with the books of Chronicles, and continues the same themes – with an additional concern for ethnic purity in order to ensure the continued survival of the Jewish people, and their rejection of other religious influences.

EZRA

A religious teacher who returned from Babylon to Jerusalem either before or shortly after Nehemiah. He found a rebuilt temple, but no enthusiasm for following the Mosaic laws, and little sense of national identity. He inaugurated a programme of ethnic cleansing, and sought to apply the law to the new circumstances. In Jewish tradition, he is identified as one of those responsible for editing the Old Testament books.

Ezra 7–10; Nehemiah 8–10

Nehemiah

Key contents

NEHEMIAH RETURNS TO JERUSALEM (CHAPTERS 1–7)
Nehemiah receives bad news and prays for Jerusalem (chapter 1)
The return (chapter 2)
Rebuilding the walls (chapters 3:1–7:3)
Lists of returned exiles (chapters 7:4–73)

RELIGIOUS REFORMS (CHAPTERS 8–10)
Ezra calls for change (chapter 8)
Prayer of repentance and confession (chapter 9:1–37)
Renewing the covenant (chapters 9:38–10:39)

NEHEMIAH AS GOVERNOR (CHAPTERS 11–13)
Lists: people and officials (chapters 11:1–12:26)
Dedicating new walls (chapters 12:27–43)
Nehemiah's reforms (chapters 12:44–13:31)

NEHEMIAH

Nehemiah was a Jewish cupbearer in the Persian royal court who for twelve years from 445 BC was governor of Judah, and started rebuilding Jerusalem. This work raised morale and prepared the way for Ezra's subsequent religious reforms.

Nehemiah 1–13

Key passages

Nehemiah's prayer (Nehemiah 1)
The people's prayer of confession (Nehemiah 9)

See also
■ Two kingdoms (pages 28–29)
■ From exile to return (pages 34–35)
■ Three temples (pages 160–161)
■ The prophets (pages 166–167)

Ruth

The story of Ruth is set in the time of the judges. It tells how Elimelech, a native of Bethlehem, migrated to Moab at a time of famine. He was accompanied by his wife, Naomi, and his two sons, both of whom married Moabite women. The father and the two sons all died in Moab, and Naomi decided to return to her own people in Bethlehem. Ruth, her Moabite daughter-in-law, insisted on going with her. On their return, the two women found themselves living in poverty, and Ruth as a foreigner had other additional pressures to cope with. In due course Ruth met Boaz, who was a distant relative of her first husband's family. Moved by her loyalty to Naomi, Boaz fulfilled his family duty and married her, even though Ruth was not an Israelite. As a result, Ruth, a Moabite woman, became the great-grandmother of King David.

Key theme

At the time Ruth was written, ethnic purity was being enforced among the returning exiles. Many existing mixed marriages between Jews and non-Jews were being deliberately broken up, and there was increasing hostility against people of other races. A story about a foreigner who married into an Israelite family, and then became a key ancestor of such a central Old Testament character as David, would have formed a powerful protest against the racial exclusiveness of the day.

Boaz ——— Ruth

Obed

Jesse

Key
——— Wife

Eliab | Abinadab | Shammah | Nethanel | Raddai | Ozem | Zeruiah | David | Abigail

Time-scale

Ruth is included in the Writings, the latest section of the original Hebrew Bible, which suggests that it was written after the Babylonian exile. Its opening sentence confirms this with its statement that it all took place: 'Long ago, in the days before Israel had a king'. Like other parts of the Old Testament, it might easily have been compiled using more ancient materials, but as it stands it is probably the product of the age of Ezra and Nehemiah.

RUTH

Ruth was from Moab, and therefore not an Israelite. However, her commitment to her Israelite mother-in-law, Naomi, earned her the respect of Naomi's extended family, and Ruth was subsequently welcomed as a full member of the nation of Israel. Indeed, she became a central figure in the nation's history, because her son Obed turned out to be the grandfather of King David, and ultimately one of the forebears of Jesus.

Ruth 1–4

Esther

Esther, an attractive Jewish woman, became queen to the Persian king Xerxes (485–464 BC) and uncovered a plot to have all the Jews in the Persian empire exterminated. Haman, the king's leading politician, was the instigator of the plot, and when the king learned what was going on, Haman was executed and Esther's Jewish guardian, Mordecai, was promoted to high office in his place.

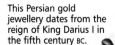

This Persian gold jewellery dates from the reign of King Darius I in the fifth century BC.

ESTHER

Esther is one of very few female heroes of the Old Testament. A Jewish orphan among the exiles in Persia, she was brought up by her relative Mordecai. When the Persian king Xerxes divorced his wife Vashti for her refusal to be used as a sex toy, Esther became the new Persian queen, though she concealed the fact that she was Jewish. Unbeknown to the royal court, therefore, she became a potential victim when a plan to exterminate all Jews was announced. By a mixture of charm and cunning, Esther managed to turn the tables, and the enemies of the Jewish people died while the Jews survived, even improving their social standing in the process.

Esther 1–10

The tomb of the Persian king Xerxes I near Persepolis. Four generations of Persian kings were buried in tombs carved out of the rockface.

Time-scale and setting

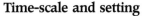

As one of the Writings, the book of Esther occurs in the latest section of the original Hebrew Bible, though it is difficult to be more precise about its likely time of composition. The story is set in Susa, the royal residence of the Persian empire, to the west of the capital Persepolis, during the years when many Jews were returning to Jerusalem from exile in Babylon.

Key theme

The story of Esther and her relationship with a non-Jewish state is told with great imagination and flair. It is the one book of the entire Old Testament where God is never mentioned at all, although an argument can be made that God worked through Esther to save the Jews from annihilation. Various additions were later made to the book, inserting the name of God, and highlighting the role of dreams and visions in Esther's experience. These supplements are found among the Deuterocanonical books.

Its theme is God's faithfulness in preserving the Jewish people even at times of great danger, and in particular against the destructive schemes of foreign rulers. This was a major concern throughout later Jewish history. In later Jewish observance, the book of Esther was used to explain the origin of the Feast of Purim.

See also

■ The time of the judges
(pages 24–25)

■ From exile to return
(pages 34–35)

■ The Persians
(pages 160–161)

This winged lion with a ram's head and griffins' claws is from the palace of Darius I in Susa. It dates from about 500 BC.

Wisdom and poetry: overview

Wisdom books

The books of Job, Proverbs and Ecclesiastes are collectively known as 'wisdom books'. The historical books are constantly searching for the meaning of life in the grand movements of nations and people, and see God primarily at work on the stage of international politics. The wisdom books are quite different – more reflective and more personal, though still asking the same questions about God's relationships to the world of nature and the lives of people. In many ways they are the philosophy books of the Bible, tackling the great issues that have perplexed people in all times and places: the book of Job asks why innocent people suffer, while the book of Ecclesiastes enquires whether life has any meaning. The book of Proverbs contains advice on appropriate behaviour within a wide range of personal relationships.

STYLE AND CHARACTER

The style and character of the wisdom books owes much to Israel's interaction with the thinking of other nations over a long period – beginning with the reign of King Solomon and running right through to the time of the Greek empire of Alexander the Great (333–323 BC). In the ancient world, the pursuit of 'wisdom' involved many different skills. Royal courts employed full-time scholars, whose interests ranged from diplomacy to specialist knowledge of botany and zoology.

The wisdom books are strongly creation-centred, using imagery from the world of nature to spell out God's character and purpose. They do, however, share the strong commitment to social justice found in the Old Testament Law (the books of the Pentateuch). But whereas the Pentateuch affirms the essential equality of all people on the basis of God's direct revelation, the wisdom books make the same claims by drawing attention to the way the world is made. The wisdom writers apply these lessons to everyday life in the home and at work, rather than concerning themselves with religious institutions like the temple.

ORIGIN

In Jewish tradition, the wisdom books were linked to the name of King Solomon, but with their timeless message it is difficult to date them exactly. As they are part of the Writings in the original Hebrew Bible, they presumably reached their present form only after the exile in Babylon.

Poetry books

Much of the Old Testament is written in poetry, including not only the book of Psalms, the Song of Solomon and the book of Lamentations, but also most of the messages of the prophets, as well as the books of Job and Proverbs. Poems are also to be found in some of the history books, and some of the first parts of the Old Testament to be remembered and written down were probably poems such as the Song of Miriam and the Song of Deborah.

POETIC STYLE

Different languages have their own poetic conventions, and in Hebrew the key feature of poetry was not its metric form, but its parallelism. In its simplest form, 'synonymous parallelism', the second line of a typical poetic couplet would repeat the ideas of the first line, though using different words. For example, Psalm 24:3:

Who has the right to go up the Lord's hill?

Who may enter God's holy temple?

In another form, 'antithetic parallelism', the same point could be made by having the first half of a couplet expressing things positively, and the second line putting it in a negative way. For example, Proverbs 10:7:

Good people will be remembered as a blessing,

but the wicked will soon be forgotten.

There are many other more subtle and complex forms of Hebrew poetry, as well as other literary devices that are regularly found in wisdom and poetry books of the Old Testament. The book of Job is written in the form of a play, with dialogue between Job and his various friends. Riddles and parables also form a part of creative literary style, and the acrostic was another favourite. This is a longer poem, in which each stanza or section begins with a different letter of the alphabet, starting with the first letter and working through to the end. Psalm 119 is the longest and most outstanding example, but Proverbs 31:10–31 uses the same technique in more abbreviated form.

THEMES

Much of the Old Testament's poetry is about God, whether in the challenging social messages of the prophets, or in the celebratory praise of the Psalms. The Song of Solomon is a love poem, written by two lovers, while much of the commonsense advice of a book like Proverbs is probably in poetic form just because it would be easier to remember that way. But running through all this literature is an emphasis on the fact that God is to be a part of the whole of life. For these Bible writers, faith was not something to be limited to what went on in obviously religious places such as temples, nor was God's activity restricted to the great events of national history, but could be found just as easily in the world of nature, and in human relationships.

Lake Galilee from Golan Heights, Israel.

Job

A dramatic story about a good man who lost everything and struggled hard to find God in his sufferings.

'Satan smiting Job with boils', William Blake (1757–1827)

Key contents

JOB, TESTED BY THE ADVERSARY (SATAN), MEETS WITH DISASTER (CHAPTERS 1–2)

DISCUSSION BETWEEN JOB AND THREE FRIENDS (CHAPTERS 3–31)
Complaints against God (chapter 3)
Job questions God (chapters 4–14)
Do wicked people really prosper? (chapters 15–21)
Job, condemned by friends, insists on his innocence (chapters 22–31)

ELIHU'S FALSE PICTURE OF A REMOTE, UNCARING GOD (CHAPTERS 32–37)

GOD'S GREATNESS IS REVEALED (CHAPTERS 38:1–42:6)
God in creation (chapters 38–41)
Job's response (chapter 42:1–6)

JOB IS BLESSED ONCE AGAIN (CHAPTER 42: 7–16)

Key passages

I know that my Redeemer lives (Job 19:25)
Hymn in praise of wisdom (Job 28)

Message and literary form

The prologue and epilogue are in prose; all the rest is poetry. The prose sections preserve an old story about an upright person who lost all his wealth and health, while the poetry explores the question of undeserved suffering. Job's friends present the conventional view, that great suffering must be the product of wrongdoing, but Job denies this and blames God for his suffering. His questions never receive an answer, but as God is revealed in the splendour of nature, Job finds himself making a response of worship and fresh commitment, reassured that God cares for him even in the midst of hardship and pain.

Time-scale

The original story could date from almost any period, but concern for cosmic order and mention of the signs of the zodiac (Job 38:31–32) suggest that the book of Job was written after the time of the exile in Babylon.

Job's suffering causes him to question God's justice, but this falls into perspective as Job sees God's hand in the wonders of nature. The photograph is of a sunrise over Mount Sinai.

Proverbs

Sayings from Israel's wisdom teachers, with a simple message: doing good will lead to prosperity and success.

Key contents

IN PRAISE OF WISDOM (CHAPTERS 1–9)

WISE SAYINGS (CHAPTERS 10–29)
Proverbs of Solomon (chapters 10:1–22:16)
Thirty wise sayings (chapters 22:17–24:21)
Additional sayings (chapters 24:22–33)
Hezekiah's collection of sayings (chapters 25–29)

MORE WISE SAYINGS (CHAPTERS 30–31)
Wisdom of Agur (chapter 30)
Sayings of King Lemuel's mother (chapter 31:1–9)
Poem on the ideal wife (chapter 31:10–31)

Time-scale and setting

The title connects the book with King Solomon, whom Jewish tradition identified with the wisdom tradition in Israel. But since King Hezekiah (729–687 BC) features, it cannot have been written before his time. More likely, its final editing was not completed until around the third century BC, though the kind of practical advice contained in it is so universal that it is impossible to be more precise about its origins.

Key passages

The fear of the Lord is the beginning of wisdom. (Proverbs 1:7)
Trust in the Lord with all your heart. (Proverbs 3:5–6)

Key themes

The kind of advice found in the book of Proverbs is common to many cultures: instructions about good manners, relationships between parents and children, work situations and so on. Some parallels exist in ancient texts from Egypt (Proverbs 22:17–25:7) and Ugarit (Proverbs 25:2–7), but the book of Proverbs is firmly rooted in Israel's covenant tradition. In spite of many metaphors drawn from the world of nature, this is firmly set in the context of the belief that nature itself is under God's control, and a part of God's purposes. Wisdom itself is here elevated to a cosmic principle, the agent through which God created all things (Proverbs 8:22–31) – an important idea that was later used by the early church to explain the significance of Jesus, and which in subsequent centuries came to form an important part of Christian theologies of creation and of the relationship between female and male images of God.

Ecclesiastes

The book of Ecclesiastes ponders a timeless question: why does life often seem meaningless?

See also
■ From exile to return (pages 34–35)
■ Education (pages 100–101)
■ The prophets (pages 166–167)

Author and time-scale

The Hebrew title of Ecclesiastes is *Koheleth* ('someone who speaks to the community'), identified as 'David's son, king in Jerusalem' – that is, King Solomon, who was well-known for his wisdom. It was once widely believed that Ecclesiastes was written by Solomon. However, most biblical scholars now believe the book was written long after Solomon's time.

Key passages

There is a time for everything. (Ecclesiastes 3:1–8)
Remember your creator while you are young (Ecclesiastes 12:1–2)

Key themes

Unlike the book of Proverbs, Ecclesiastes has a very pessimistic outlook. Far from being a book of faith, it is a testimony to great doubt. Though the author is clearly part of a believing community, he finds it hard to make sense of life, or to see much meaning in the repetition of traditional religious dogmas. If there is fulfilment in life, it is likely to be found through hard work, which brings its own reward. Yet it is still worth believing in God, and even if this

'I saw that all labour and all achievement spring from [a person's] envy...' writes the author. 'This too is meaningless, a chasing after the wind.'

does not always seem to bring immediate rewards, participation in the life of God's people is the key to ultimate happiness.

Orange orchard in blossom at Banyas, Golan. 'There is a time for everything, and a season for every activity under heaven,' remarks the writer of Ecclesiastes.

Psalms

The book of Psalms is a collection of hymns, prayers and poems expressing every kind of emotion, designed for use in a variety of corporate and personal contexts.

Time-scale and setting

The book of Psalms as it now stands was compiled for use in the temple in Jerusalem rebuilt after the exile in Babylon, but the individual pieces were written over a long period from at least 1000 BC onwards. Some of them clearly refer to life in Israel under kings David and Solomon, while many more originate from the time when the nation was divided into the two kingdoms of Israel and Judah. It is often thought that various earlier collections can be identified by reference to the names associated with them in their subtitles (David, Sons of Korah, Sons of Asaph and others). Jewish tradition depicts King David as the author of the Psalms, and while he cannot have been responsible for them all, there is no reason to imagine he did not make a contribution to some of the earlier pieces.

Key contents

The Psalms were originally arranged in five sections: Psalms 1–41, Psalms 42–72, Psalms 73–89, Psalms 90–106 and Psalms 107–150. Each section concluded with words of praise. The most useful way to group the Psalms, however, is by literary type, and several major categories can easily be identified: hymns of praise to God (for example, Psalms 40, 92, 116 and 138); community laments (for example, Psalms 44, 74, 80 and 83); personal laments (for example, Psalms 13 and 71), sometimes including confessions (for example, Psalms 51 and 130); personal thanksgivings (for example, Psalms 30, 92 and 116); covenant renewal liturgies (for example, Psalms 50, 76, 89, 105 and 114); and royal enthronement psalms (for example, Psalms 2, 20, 45, 72 and 110).

Desert flowers, Petra, Jordan

Key themes

The Psalms are all very diverse, so it is impossible to make generalizations about them. But a very large number of them originated in temple worship at different stages of Israel's history. Many of these are not just hymns, but more comprehensive liturgies, showing the richness of worship with processions, dance, music and interactive responses. Some themes are recurrent. Central concerns are God's power over the forces of evil (for example, Psalm 29), the exodus (for example, Psalm 68), the temple as a sign of God's presence (for example, Psalm 48), the fall of Jerusalem and the exile in Babylon (for example, Psalms 79 and 137), and the return from exile (for example, Psalm 51). Some express the faith of all Israel, while others are individual and deeply personal. But all of them reveal a realistic attitude to life's hardships, combined with unshakeable faith in God.

Key Psalms

The heavens declare the glory of God (Psalm 19)
The Lord is my shepherd (Psalm 23)
God is our refuge and strength (Psalm 46)
A plea for forgiveness (Psalm 51)
Come, let us praise the Lord (Psalm 95)
A psalm of God's goodness (Psalm 103)
God our protector (Psalm 121)
Lord, you have searched me and you know me (Psalm 139)

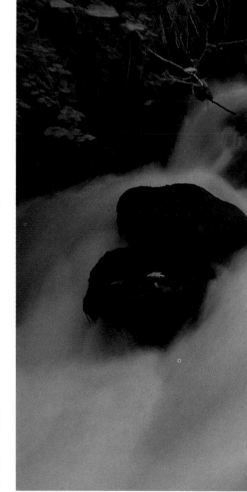

'You care for the land and water it;
you enrich it abundantly
The streams of God are filled with water
to provide the people with corn,
for so you have ordained it.
You drench its furrows and level its ridges;
You soften it with showers and bless its crops.'
Psalm 65:9–10

The Song of Songs

A collection of erotic love poetry, in which a woman and her lover celebrate their sexual relationship.

Author and time-scale

King Solomon is mentioned several times in the Song of Songs, but there is no obvious connection between him and this book. Those passages which refer to him rather suggest he was not the author, and the presence of both Persian and Greek words points to a much later date, no earlier than the rise of the Persian empire in 539 BC. Being more precise is virtually impossible. Some features suggest an earlier origin, while there is evidence of similar poetry from other nations long before the time of Solomon. Probably, like much of the Old Testament, this is an anthology of poetry of different origins collected together by an editor after the exile in Babylon.

Key theme

The songs are about the wonder of physical love. Their inclusion here underlines the way in which biblical faith related to the whole of life: God is the creator of all things, sexuality included, and so a book of love poems was no more out of place than the story of God's actions in history, or the account of the Ten Commandments given to Moses at Mount Sinai.

Lamentations

This book consists of five poems. The first four are written as acrostics based on the letters of the Hebrew alphabet. They all express the people's anguish at the destruction of Jerusalem by the Babylonians. Their writer seems to have witnessed the city's fall in 587 BC and to be one of those who was not transported to Babylon, but was left behind to eke out a miserable existence among the ruins of the land.

Key theme

The poems are laments. It is bad enough that Jerusalem has fallen and its people have suffered. Worse still is the reason: God has apparently given up the people and handed them over to suffering because of their unfaithfulness. But there is still a ray of hope, as the writer expresses confidence in God's unfailing mercy (Lamentations 3:21–27).

See also

■ The Babylonian invasion
(pages 32–33)

■ From exile to return
(pages 34–35)

■ The practice of prayer
(pages 174–175)

The prophets: overview

People called prophets feature throughout the Old Testament story. The Hebrew word for prophet, *nabi*, meant a person who was taken over by some kind of spiritual power, and as a consequence had the ability to mediate God's will to others. This sometimes takes place through strange acts, but most characteristically the Hebrew prophets were speakers, bringing curse and blessing, and challenging their rulers when they departed from the lifestyle and values demanded by God's covenant with the people.

The first prophets

Early prophets were people like Elijah, Elisha and Nathan, but the prophets whose words are preserved in the Old Testament began to appear from about the eighth century BC onwards. At a time when the northern kingdom of Israel and its southern counterpart Judah were both struggling to survive in the face of threats from their more powerful neighbours, the prophets served as the religious and moral conscience of their nations, reminding both kings and people of the solemn promises their forebears had made, and the need to take seriously the commitments that were enshrined in the covenant relationship between them and their God. Prophets came from all social classes: Isaiah was a member of the royal family of Judah; Amos and Micah were peasant farmers. Some prophets seem to have worked from religious shrines, along with priests.

Books of the prophets

This section of the Old Testament contains 16 books which preserve the messages delivered by these fierce advocates of Israel's faith. Of these, the four longest are often referred to as the 'major prophets': Isaiah, Jeremiah, Ezekiel and Daniel. The remaining 12 shorter books are the 'minor prophets': Hosea, Joel, Amos, Obadiah, Jonah, Micah, Nahum, Habakkuk, Zephaniah, Haggai, Zechariah and Malachi.

Time-scale and setting

The books of the prophets are not in any chronological order. Collectively they document the careers of prophets that spanned the whole of Israel's history.

Some (Amos and Hosea) were active during the last days of the kingdom of Israel, as the threat from Assyria became more powerful. Others (Isaiah and Micah) spoke to the situation in the kingdom of Judah at about the time of Israel's destruction (722 BC), while many others sought to challenge the nation during the dark days that eventually culminated in Jerusalem's destruction by the Babylonian king Nebuchadnezzar (587 BC). These include Zephaniah, Nahum and Habakkuk, as well as Jeremiah, whose ministry extended into the time of the exile in Babylon. Other prophets during the exile were Ezekiel and Isaiah of Babylon. After the return of the Jews from exile came Haggai, Zechariah, Obadiah, Joel and Malachi. The book of Daniel is more difficult to place historically, and has a different style from the rest. This has led some scholars to conclude that the book probably belongs in the period of the Maccabean revolt in the mid-second century BC. Others hold to the view that the book was composed by the prophet himself in the sixth century BC.

Style of the prophets

The prophets rarely made long speeches. Instead, they usually gave short messages that were easy to remember – often in the style of poetry. They were also story-tellers and mime artists, but they were not generally writers. On one occasion the prophet Jeremiah instructed his friend Baruch to write his messages down and then read them out in the streets of Jerusalem. But more often, the followers of the prophets passed their teachings on by word of mouth for a long time before they wrote them down.

The prophets and God

All the prophets were conscious of having some special form of insight into the will of God. They delivered their messages as if God was speaking in person, often prefacing them with 'This is what Yahweh says ...' or ending with 'this is the word of Yahweh.' They had unusual experiences which they ascribed to being called by God (for example, Isaiah 6, Jeremiah 1 and Ezekiel 1–3), and claimed the direct inspiration of God's Spirit. Some of them had visions, out-of-body experiences and other spiritual encounters.

Key themes

The prophets all lived through times of turmoil and crisis for their people. Things were changing very fast, as one world empire succeeded another – each of them bringing new challenges for the Israelites. In particular, expressing allegiance to new political overlords often involved placing statues of their gods and goddesses in Israel's places of worship. How could the people remain faithful to God and yet survive in this political reality? How could the old ways be applied to new situations? And why were they at the mercy of their enemies, anyway, when they were supposed to be God's chosen people? These were the key issues addressed by the prophets. Their answer was simple, and came to be enshrined in the works of the history writers who followed them: the nation must remain faithful to their roots, upholding God's laws, and trusting God to keep them safe and bring all the promises to fulfilment.

Nahal Zin from Midreshet Ben Gurion, Israel.

Amos

The prophet Amos was a native of the town of Tekoa, in Judah, but he delivered his messages in the northern kingdom of Israel, in Bethel and probably also in Samaria. Though there was great prosperity in the land, there was little social justice for the disadvantaged. Amos saw this as a direct violation of the covenant law, and denounced the corrupt lifestyles of the rich, warning that judgment and destruction were inevitable.

Key passage

Let justice roll on like a river, righteousness like a never-failing stream (Amos 5:24)

'Woe to those who lie upon beds of ivory…' (Amos 6:4). The 'beds of ivory' Amos refers to are couches decorated with ivory inlays, upon which guests sprawled during pagan festivities. This scene of a cow suckling her young calf was carved by Phoenicians and comes from such a couch. It dates from the eighth century BC.

Key themes

It seemed to the people of Jeroboam's kingdom that nothing could go wrong. They had peace and security, and growing wealth. All around them were the signs of prosperity: new buildings, comfortably furnished homes and places of worship that were hardly big enough to contain all who wanted to attend. The rich believed they were prosperous because they were very religious, but Amos saw things differently. The rich had amassed so much wealth only by disregarding the fundamental values of their traditional faith. They had forgotten their own national origins, as slaves in Egypt, and instead of having special care for the poor, they exploited them at every opportunity. In this light, all their cosy worship was mere hypocrisy, and Amos denounced it as objectionable to God. Instead of filling the streets with the blood of their many animal sacrifices, they should be saturating the land with justice and fairness, for that was most truly what God required.

Amos was a realist, and could see that no one would listen. Thrown out of the main sanctuary in Bethel, he issued scathing denunciations against the priests and people, assuring them that 'the day of the Lord' would not be long in coming – and that it would bring judgment. The grand buildings would be destroyed, and the people would be taken off into exile – something that happened not long afterwards, when the Assyrians invaded the land and captured the capital Samaria.

'He asked me, "Amos, what do you see?" "A plumb line," I answered. Then he said, "I am using it to show that my people are like a wall that is out of line…"' (Amos 7:8)

The prophet Amos warned of the impending destruction of Israel if the people did not repent. Here, Israelite prisoners are shown on an Assyrian relief.

Time-scale

Amos' work can be dated quite precisely, to the reign of Jeroboam II, probably towards the end of that period, maybe around 750 BC. It was one of the few settled periods during the short existence of the northern kingdom of Israel, with enemies defeated and nothing to inhibit economic growth.

Hosea

The book of Hosea has a completely different feel from Amos's harsh messages of doom and judgment. This prophet was a very sensitive person, whose own experience of rejection and hurt in his personal life gave him a unique insight into the way he believed God must have felt when Israel rejected the covenant and neglected God's love.

Time-scale and setting

Hosea began his work after Amos, though still during the reign of Jeroboam II. He continued for the next 20 years, during which six weak kings reigned, and at the end of which Samaria was taken by the Assyrians in 722 BC.

'I will be to the people of Israel like rain in a dry land. They will blossom like flowers; they will be firmly rooted like the trees of Lebanon. They will be alive with new growth, and beautiful like olive trees. They will be fragrant like the cedars of Lebanon.'
(Hosea 14:5–6)

Key themes

The book begins with the story of Hosea's marriage to a woman named Gomer. She left him to go and live with another man, and eventually ended up as a prostitute, offered for sale in the public market-place. There, Hosea found her, and was so moved by her plight that he paid for her freedom and took her back to live in his own home.

Figurine of the Canaanite fertility goddess Astarte, dating from the 13th century BC.

This experience then becomes the key to Hosea's understanding of Israel's relationship to God. The people have acted like the unfaithful Gomer, leaving the covenant relationship with God in favour of illicit relations with the Canaanite fertility religion and its nature gods (whose worship often involved sacred prostitution and other sexual acts). Just as Hosea's own broken marriage led to pain for him and his three children, so Israel has caused pain to God, and the breakdown of the special relationship promised to their ancestor Abraham. But like Hosea, God was still in love with these people, and would do anything to see their relationship restored. The prospect of destruction by the armies of Assyria was already looming large, but there was still a chance of avoiding this pain, if the people changed their ways and returned to the true worship of God. If not, then they would suffer the consequences of their action. But God would never give up Israel, any more than Hosea had been able to abandon his own wife – a message that became increasingly poignant, as one crisis followed another.

Key passages

God's love for Israel
(Hosea 11:1–4)
God's promise of blessing
(Hosea 14:4–9)

See also

■ The creator-God of Israel
(pages 148–149)

■ Israel's faith
(pages 150–151)

■ The prophets
(pages 166–167)

Isaiah

The book of Isaiah is the longest book in the Bible, containing prophetic comments on events from about 740 BC to 530 BC, all related to the kingdom of Judah, its downfall, exile and restoration.

Key contents

THE THREAT FROM ASSYRIA (CHAPTERS 1–39)

God's message for Judah and Jerusalem (chapters 1–5)

Isaiah's vision (chapter 6)

The kingdom, present and future (chapters 7–12)

Judgment on the nations (chapters 13–23)

God's final judgment and victory (chapters 24–27)

Future judgments and blessing (chapters 28–35)

The contemporary crisis (chapters 36–39)

MESSAGES FOR THE EXILES IN BABYLON (CHAPTERS 40–55)

On the brink of freedom (chapters 40–48)

God's servant and the redemption he brings (chapters 49–55)

THE RETURNED EXILES (CHAPTERS 56–66)

A call for repentance and promise of restoration (chapters 56–59)

Glory to come (chapters 60–62)

Judgment on Edom (chapters 63:1–6)

A prayer for God's people (63:7–64:12)

New heavens and a new earth (chapters 65–66)

Time-scale and setting

Two quite specific settings can be identified within the book of Isaiah. The career of Isaiah of Jerusalem is very precisely dated, beginning in the year that King Uzziah of Judah died and continuing through the reigns of Jotham, Ahaz and Hezekiah (approximately 750–687 BC). Throughout this period, the dominant superpower of the region was Assyria, and Isaiah lived through the fall of the northern kingdom of Israel and saw his own nation of Judah seriously threatened by the expansion of Assyrian power. With the fall of Samaria, there was no way Judah could escape subservience to Assyria, and Isaiah found himself giving political advice to both Ahaz and his successor Hezekiah, sometimes recommending resistance, at other times proposing collaboration with the Assyrians – and always insisting on

This inscription from the first century AD reads: 'Hither were brought the bones of Uzziah, King of Judah. Do not open.'

faithfulness to the covenant with God.

By the sixth century BC, Assyrian domination had been replaced by the Babylonians, and they were the ones who finally destroyed Judah in 587 BC, taking its leading citizens off into exile in Babylon itself. Babylonian dominance was short-lived, and when King Cyrus of Persia became a serious alternative, the Jewish exiles had high hopes of a return to their own land. This is the situation addressed in Isaiah 40–55, where Cyrus is named as God's agent for change, and the fall of Babylon is expected any day. Many scholars believe that the prophetic messages in these chapters were written by one of a continuing group of Isaiah's disciples. The messages in chapters 55–66 could also be by this unknown author, but seem to relate to the period of disillusionment following the return of the first exiles, but before the arrival of Nehemiah and Ezra. However this book came to be written, it is clear that its messages have a unity and coherence that can be traced back to the work of Isaiah who prophesied in Jerusalem from about 740 BC.

The relentless advance of the Assyrian forces attacking Lachish is conveyed on this relief. As archers bombard the city with arrows, captured prisoners are executed. The prophet Isaiah was alive when the Assyrians brought the northern kingdom of Israel to an end, and was living in Jerusalem when their armies threatened the city.

See also

■ The rise of Assyria (pages 30–31)

■ The Babylonian invasion (pages 32–33)

■ The prophets (pages 166–167)

Lachish was held siege by King Sennacherib in 701 BC. This fragment of a Hebrew letter records the fate of one of the Hebrew prophets.

Key themes

One theme runs throughout the entire book, presented in the story of Isaiah's call to be a prophet (chapter 6), and repeated and reinforced in many subsequent passages. The whole collection focuses on God's power and majesty, greater than any other force in the whole world. The affairs of all nations are in God's control, and judgment is inevitable for those who ignore God's purposes – including Judah. Still, God's overall purpose is for wholeness throughout the entire creation, and Israel's special covenant relationship is misunderstood when interpreted as racial exclusiveness: in reality, it was to be the doorway to peace and blessing for all nations.

Key passages

The Assyrian war machine (Isaiah 5:26–30)
Isaiah's vision and God's call (Isaiah 6)
Immanuel (Isaiah 7:13–16)
'To us a child is born' (Isaiah 9:2–7)
The coming king: the branch from Jesse (Isaiah 11:2–9)
We have a strong city (Isaiah 26: 1–9)
The desert will rejoice: God's highway (Isaiah 35)
Comfort, comfort my people (Isaiah 40:1–31)
The servant of the Lord (Isaiah 42:1–4, 49:1–6, 50:4–9, 52:13–53:12)
Messenger of peace (Isaiah 52:7–12)
Come all you who are thirsty (Isaiah 55)
Good news to the poor (Isaiah 61:1–4)
New heavens and earth (Isaiah 65:17–25)

'Streams of water will flow through the desert; the burning sand will become a lake, and dry land will be filled with springs.' (Isaiah 35:6–7)

Structure

There are strong reasons for supposing that Isaiah 1–39 and 40–55 were separate, even though closely related. Firstly, chapters 40–55 never mention Isaiah at all, whereas chapters 1–39 contain several stories about him.

Chapters 40–55 have a distinctive style and language; they are the most sophisticated Hebrew writing in the whole Bible and, in place of the short sayings found in chapters 1–39, they consist of extended poetic celebrations of God's power in creation and history. Furthermore, chapters 40–55 clearly state that the fall of Jerusalem is in the past and that the fall of Babylon is imminent, and Cyrus is named as the new king of Persia.

Micah

Micah was one of the eighth-century prophets, along with Amos, Hosea and Isaiah of Jerusalem. As a hill-country farmer, his message was born out of his own experience of the injustices of poverty and exploitation.

Key contents

THE SIN OF JUDAH AND ISRAEL (CHAPTERS 1–3)

RESTORATION AND PEACE (CHAPTERS 4–5)

CALLING PEOPLE BACK TO THEIR ROOTS IN THE COVENANT (CHAPTERS 6:1–7:7)

REPENTANCE AND HOPE (CHAPTER 7:8–20)

Time-scale and setting

Micah operated during the reigns of Jotham, Ahaz and Hezekiah, commenting on circumstances in both Judah and (until its fall in 722 BC) Israel.

Key passages

God's reign of peace
(Micah 4:1–4)
A king from Bethlehem
(Micah 5:2–4)
A call for justice
(Micah 6:6–8)

Key themes

Like Amos, Micah had no time for formal religious worship as a substitute for justice and fair play. He looked back in Israel's history long before the establishment of the temple to see what had motivated faith in the earliest times, and argued that authentic spirituality should result in structures that would promote social justice. There would be little hope for those who had so perverted their inherited faith that they were able to exploit the poor without any conscience. God's judgment would be so severe that even the temple itself would be obliterated – though beyond the destruction, God's promises would still stand.

Zephaniah

Zephaniah is said to have been a descendant of king Hezekiah, and he lived at a time when Assyrian power over Judah was beginning to weaken.

Key contents

THE DAY OF JUDGMENT (CHAPTERS 1:1–2:3)

DOOM FOR THE NATIONS (CHAPTER 2:4–15)

HOPE FOR THE FAITHFUL REMNANT (CHAPTER 3:1–13)

A SONG OF JOY (CHAPTER 3:14–20)

Time-scale and setting

The messages of Zephaniah relate to the reign of King Josiah of Judah (640–609 BC). The first two chapters probably come from early in this period (640–622 BC), and the third one from after 612 BC, when Josiah's efforts to reform worship had been largely thwarted. Since there is a reference to return from the exile in Zephaniah 3:20, the book was presumably edited into its present form at a later date.

'Your land by the sea will become open fields with shepherds' huts and sheep pens. The people of Judah who survive will occupy your land. They will pasture their flocks there and sleep in the houses of Ashkelon. The Lord their God will be with them and make them prosper again.'
(Zephaniah 2:6–7)

Key themes

Zephaniah repeats some familiar themes: God's judgment on the people for neglecting their covenant faith, adopting foreign values and lifestyles, and generally ignoring their religious commitments. But he goes on to ask how such prophecies of judgment and destruction fit in with messages of hope for the future. He suggests that judgment will be a way of purifying the nation, burning away their pride and complacency. But only a small minority (a 'remnant') of the people will trust in God and be saved.

Nahum

Nahum belongs to the end of Josiah's reign, around the time when the Assyrian capital Nineveh was overcome by the Babylonians and Medes (612 BC).

Key themes

The book of Nahum describes the collapse of Nineveh in such vivid language (Nahum chapters 2–3) that many believe it was an eyewitness account of the event. The book has nothing to say about Judah as such: all its focus is on Nineveh, as an example of a nation that over-reached its power, not recognizing that God is the Lord of all the nations – indeed, of the whole of history.

The form of this book suggests that it may have been compiled as a liturgy for use in the temple in Jerusalem to celebrate the collapse of Assyrian power and to remind the worshippers of God's great power.

Key passages

Living by faith (Habakkuk 2:4)
The Lord is in the holy Temple; let everyone on earth be silent in God's presence. (Habakkuk 2:20)

Habakkuk

No personal details are known about Habakkuk, but he tackles a perennial question: how can God allow wicked people to prosper? What fairness is there in Judah being punished for relatively minor transgressions by people like the Babylonians, who regularly commit major atrocities and seem to get away with it?

Habakkuk affirms his trust in God: even if the fig tree does not bud and there are no grapes on the vine, he will still rejoice in God. (Habakkuk 3:17)

Time-scale and setting

The content of the book indicates that it belongs after Babylon had defeated Egypt at the Battle of Carchemish (605 BC) and before the first invasion of Jerusalem in 597 BC. Its messages are therefore slightly later than Nahum, and during the reign of Jehoiakim (609–597 BC). Habakkuk must have been roughly contemporary with Jeremiah.

Key contents

WHY DO EVIL PEOPLE PROSPER? (CHAPTER 1)

GOD'S ANSWER (CHAPTER 2)

A PSALM OF PRAISE (CHAPTER 3)

Key theme

The book opens with a debate between Habakkuk and God, centred on the question of why God does not intervene to stop the extreme suffering inflicted on the people by conquerors such as the Assyrians and Babylonians. The answer is that these other powers will themselves be punished for their cruelty. That is little comfort for those actually suffering, but the book of Habakkuk eventually resolves it in a way similar to Job's wrestling with suffering, with a magnificent poem in praise of God's love and glory, reassuring its readers that God is in control and can be trusted.

See also

■ Two kingdoms (pages 28–29)

■ The rise of Assyria (pages 30–31)

■ The Babylonian invasion (pages 32–33)

■ The prophets (pages 166–167)

'Their horses are faster than leopards, fiercer than hungry wolves. Their horsemen come riding from distant lands; their horses paw the ground.' (Habakkuk 1:8)

Jeremiah

This book belongs to the reigns of Judah's last five kings, including the events leading up to the fall of Jerusalem. A sensitive man, Jeremiah struggled with the message of judgment that he brought to the people.

Time-scale and setting

Jeremiah was born into a priestly family in Anathoth, near Jerusalem, and was called to be a prophet in 627 BC. His ministry therefore began during good times for Judah, during the reign of Josiah (640–609 BC), and continued through the reigns of Jehoiakim (609–597 BC), Jehoiachin (597 BC) and Zedekiah (597–587 BC). This was a period of great uncertainty for Judah, as Assyria was displaced by the Babylonians, and the mood swings in Jerusalem went from optimism to despair. These proved to be the final days of independence in Judah, and by the end of Jeremiah's lifetime the temple had been destroyed and the leading citizens of Jerusalem taken into exile in Babylon, with no obvious prospect of the renewal of national life and institutions.

'Then the Lord said to me, "Go down to the potter's house, where I will give you my message." So I went there and saw the potter working at his wheel. Whenever a piece of pottery turned out imperfect, he would take the clay and make it into something else. Then the Lord said to me, "Haven't I the right to do with you the people of Israel what the potter did to the clay? You are in my hands just like the clay in the potter's hands.'
(Jeremiah 18:1–6)

Key contents

JEREMIAH'S CALL TO BE A PROPHET (CHAPTER 1)

POETIC REFLECTIONS ON ISRAEL'S HISTORY (CHAPTERS 2–6)

SERMONS AND CONFESSIONS (CHAPTERS 7–24)
… relating to Jehoiakim (chapters 7–20)
… at the time of Zedekiah (chapters 21–24)

STORIES AND MESSAGES OF CONFLICT (CHAPTERS 25–45)
Pronouncements against the nations (chapter 25)
Jeremiah's personal predicament (chapters 26–28)
Letters to exiles in Babylon and to Shemaiah (chapter 29)
Hope of return and a new beginning (chapters 30–33)
Selected events from Jeremiah's life (chapters 34–45)

GOD WILL JUDGE THE NATIONS (CHAPTERS 46–51)

THE FALL OF JERUSALEM (CHAPTER 52)

Key passages

Jeremiah's call (Jeremiah 1:1–19)
Blessed are those who trust (Jeremiah 17:5–8)
The deceitful human heart (Jeremiah 17:9)
Jeremiah's complaint (Jeremiah 20:7–18)
The false and the true prophet (Jeremiah 23:15–32)
The new covenant (Jeremiah 31:31–34)

'Then the Lord told me to break the jar in front of
those who had gone with me and to tell them that
the Lord Almighty had said, "I will break this people
and this city, and it will be like this broken clay jar
that cannot be put together again…"'
(Jeremiah 19:10–11)

See also

■ The Babylonian
invasion
(pages 32–33)

■ From exile to return
(pages 34–35)

■ The prophets
(pages 166–167)

'The prophet Jeremiah
lamenting the destruction
of Jerusalem',
Rembrandt van Rijn (1606–1669)

The prophet Jeremiah

Most Old Testament prophets are known through
their messages, with little information about them
as people. Jeremiah is one of the exceptions. In
this book, there are many insights into his
character and personality, and the creativity
with which he communicated his message. He
comes across as a deeply spiritual person, full of
confidence in what he has learned of God,
and with strong convictions about the need
for his nation to return to the values of the
covenant laws with their roots in the days
following the exodus. Yet he is also a person
with an acute sense of his own inadequacy
for the task, who struggles to come to terms
with the harsh message he has been given,
and even doubts whether he has truly been
called by God at all. His artistic temperament reveals
itself in the many creative ways he uses to get
through to the people. He is not only a speaker, but a
writer and poet as well. Nor is he a purely word-
based communicator: several key stories show him as
a silent mime artist, an actor or a clown, using all the
skills at his disposal to get his message across.

This bulla is
inscribed: 'belonging to
Berechyahu son of
Neriyahu the scribe'. The
Bible refers to Baruch,
short for Berechiah, son of
Neriah, as a prophet and
Jeremiah's faithful
secretary
(Jeremiah 36:4 and 36:8).

Key themes

It is not possible to read the book of Jeremiah through from beginning to
end and find one consistent line of argument. The various messages and
stories are organized neither thematically nor chronologically, and messages
relating to the early part of Jeremiah's life are regularly found alongside
passages from his final years. The book itself seems to be organized
according to the literary style of the various materials.

But the dominant theme is obvious. This was a period of
enormous upheaval in the life of Judah, with political
uncertainty and social unrest, and Jeremiah seeks to set all this
in the context of the covenant between God and the people,
asking what future there could now be for the promises made
by God to Abraham and his successors. There was much popular
optimism, and a naive belief that because the temple was in
Jerusalem, the city's security would be guaranteed. Jeremiah
points out that trust in such material expressions of God's
presence was pointless if the deeper challenge of covenant
faith was being ignored.

To cling on to God's promises of protection while
continuing in disobedience to God's commands was
worthless. Jeremiah consistently warned that Jerusalem
would be destroyed – and at one stage was put in prison for
saying so. But he also expressed a firm faith in the future, even
demonstrating it by investing in property in Judah not long before the final
Babylonian invasion. Yet he was clear that when it came, the return from
exile would not be a renewal of what was there before, but would require a
radical change on the part of the people – something he described as a new
covenant which would become part of the hearts and minds of God's people
in a way that the original one had not been.

Ezekiel

The visions and prophecies of Ezekiel came to him while an exile in Babylon, between 593 and 571 BC.

'I felt the powerful presence of the Lord, as God's spirit took me and set me down in a valley where the ground was covered with bones.' (Ezekiel 37:1)

Key contents

EZEKIEL'S CALL (CHAPTERS 1–3)

MESSAGES FOR JERUSALEM (CHAPTERS 4–24)
An acted parable of Jerusalem's fall (chapters 4–5)
The end has come (chapters 6–7)
Jerusalem's guilt (chapters 8–11)
Parables, allegories and prophecies (chapters 12–17)
Individual responsibility (chapter 18)
Israel's rebellion (19:1–20:44)
Fire and sword (20:45–21:32)
Israel's doom and Jerusalem's destruction (chapters 22–24)

PROPHECIES AGAINST OTHER NATIONS (CHAPTERS 25–32)

HOPE FOR THE FUTURE (CHAPTERS 33–39)
The prophet as watchman (chapter 33:1–20)
Jerusalem's fall (chapter 33:21–33)
The sins of rulers and their people (chapter 34)
Invective against Edom (chapter 35)
Restoration (chapter 36)
Can dry bones live again? (chapter 37)
Against Gog (chapters 38–39)

A NEW TEMPLE (CHAPTERS 40–48)
Plans for building and worship (chapters 40–42)
God's glory in the temple (chapter 43:1–12)
Rules for temple and priesthood (chapters 43:13–44:31)
Rules for the land, rulers, and festivals (chapters 45–46)
A stream flowing from the sanctuary (chapter 47:1–12)
The land and the tribes (chapters 47:13–48:35)

Key passages

Ezekiel's call and vision of God's glory (Ezekiel 1–3)
Personal responsibility: 'The soul who sins will die' (Ezekiel 18)
The prophet's role as a watchman (Ezekiel 33:1–20)
God as shepherd of the people (Ezekiel 34:11–16)
God's gift of a new heart (Ezekiel 36:22–32)
Vision of the valley of dry bones (Ezekiel 37)
The life-giving river flowing from the temple (Ezekiel 47:1–12)

Key themes

The book of Ezekiel opens on the plains of Babylon, with Ezekiel seeing a mighty vision of God. Many of Ezekiel's messages denounce Israel's faithlessness, and declare God's judgment. In keeping with his interest in ritual matters, there is an emphasis here on impurity and idolatry (in contrast to Jeremiah's emphasis on morality). He recognizes that Jerusalem could not be saved from destruction, and yet the messages given after its capture show a strong note of hope. God's power will be shown as the people are brought back home and a purified worship is re-established in a new temple.

Time-scale and setting

Ezekiel gives precise dates: he was taken from Judah to Babylon in the first deportation (597 BC), and became a prophet a few years later (593 BC). His messages continued after the fall of Jerusalem (587 BC), when more Jewish exiles arrived in Babylon. The first section of the book contains messages concerning events and people in Jerusalem. Some think he visited his homeland at this time, but since the whole book is full of psychic experiences, it is more likely that this was through extra-sensory perception, astral projection or something similar.

The prophet Ezekiel attacked the leaders of Judah who oppressed the people, and likened them to shepherds who took care only of themselves and not of the flock.

Ezekiel the prophet

Ezekiel belonged to a family of priests, which explains his special interest in the details of worship and ritual purity. He had many visions and spiritual experiences and, like Jeremiah, communicated his message through the use of mime and drama, as well as words.

Daniel

The book begins with stories about Daniel, a young Jew exiled in Babylon who rose to prominence through his innate talents and faithfulness to God's law. It continues with dramatic visions of the future. Mostly written in Hebrew, with chapters 2:4–7:28 in Aramaic, the official language of the Persian empire.

See also
■ From exile to return (pages 34–35)
■ The Babylonians (pages 62–63)
■ The Persians (pages 66–67)
■ Three temples (pages 160–161)
■ Priests and rituals (pages 162–163)
■ The prophets (pages 166–167)

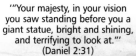

'"Your majesty, in your vision you saw standing before you a giant statue, bright and shining, and terrifying to look at."'
(Daniel 2:31)

Key theme

Both parts of the book of Daniel serve the same purpose: to inspire and encourage people at a time of great persecution. The stories of Daniel himself show it was possible to win through by staying faithful to God, while the visions use dramatic images to assure their readers that, though things might seem out of control, God had not abandoned them, and their cruel oppressors would soon be destroyed.

Key passages

Shadrach, Meshach and Abednego in the fiery furnace (Daniel 3)
Belshazzar's feast (Daniel 5)
Daniel escapes the lions (Daniel 6)
Daniel's prayer (Daniel 9:1–19)

Time-scale and setting

The stories about Daniel are set in the sixth century BC, and highlight the pressures put on the Jewish exiles to abandon their traditional lifestyle and faith. In spite of threats to their lives, Daniel and his friends resist, and are presented as an example to all subsequent generations who may be tempted to give up their distinctive beliefs and national identity. The visions, however, refer to a later time when Palestine was ruled by the Seleucid king Antiochus IV Epiphanes (175–163 BC), and specifically to the events of the Maccabean period when Jewish people were suffering horrendous persecution for their faith (167–164 BC). The book must have been compiled at this time, incorporating the older traditional stories.

'Belshazzar's Feast',
John Martin
(1789–1854)

Haggai

Haggai brought messages of encouragement for the second wave of exiles returning to Jerusalem led by Zerubbabel (a diplomat and member of Judah's royal family) and Joshua (a priest).

Key contents

ENCOURAGEMENT TO REBUILD THE RUINED TEMPLE (CHAPTER 1)

REFLECTIONS ON THE FUTURE SPLENDOUR OF THE TEMPLE (CHAPTER 2:1–9)

PROMISES OF BLESSING FOR THE OBEDIENT (CHAPTER 2:10–19)

A MESSAGE FOR ZERUBBABEL (CHAPTER 2:20–23)

Time-scale and setting

Haggai gives precise dates, indicating that he began speaking to the people in 520 BC, during the reign of King Darius I (522–486 BC). This particular group of exiles had built grand homes for themselves, but work on the temple in Jerusalem – an essential focus for effective national identity – had so far been neglected. A refurbished temple – albeit on a less grand scale than the one built by King Solomon, which it replaced – was completed by 516 BC, so Haggai's messages all relate to the four years leading up to this.

Key passage

The danger of economic inflation (Haggai 1:6)

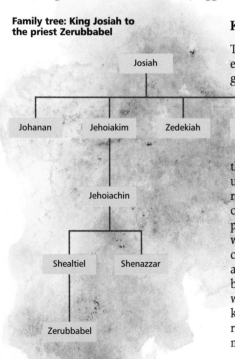

Family tree: King Josiah to the priest Zerubbabel

- Josiah
  - Johanan
  - Jehoiakim
  - Zedekiah
  - Jehoahaz
- Jehoiachin
  - Shealtiel
  - Shenazzar
- Zerubbabel

Zechariah

Zechariah is identified as a colleague of Haggai in the Old Testament book of Ezra. The book of Zechariah contains his messages, supplemented by later material.

Key contents

A NEW AGE IS BEGINNING (CHAPTERS 1–8)
Introduction (chapter 1:1–6)
Eight visions (chapters 1:7–6:8)
  Horses (chapter 1:7–17)
  Horns (chapter 1:18–21)
  Measuring line (chapter 2:1–13)
  High priest (chapter 3:1–10)
  Lampstand (chapter 4:1–14)
  Flying scroll (chapter 5:1–4)
  A woman (chapter 5:5–11)
  Four chariots (6:1–8)
Messages for civil and religious leaders (6:9–8:23)

PART 2: ISRAEL AND THE NATIONS (CHAPTERS 9–14)
Poetic assurances of Judah's future (9:1–11:3)
Prose warnings of coming judgment (11:4–14:21)

The Assyrian royal cavalry relief from the king's palace in Nineveh, dating from the seventh century BC. Zechariah looked forward to a time when a sense of God's holiness would be evident everywhere. Even the bells on horses would be inscribed with the words 'Holy to the Lord'.

Key themes

This period was one of mixed emotions for the returning exiles: great elation at being back home, with high hopes for the future; yet depression bordering on despair at the state of disrepair of their once-beautiful city and the uphill struggle that would be required to restore it. Haggai challenged the people to get their priorities right, and to place the worship of God ahead of their own comfort. Zerubbabel had been appointed governor by the Persians, but because of his royal ancestry there was speculation that he might become king of a new Jewish kingdom. Haggai refers to him in terms later used of the messiah (Haggai 2:23).

Malachi

Time-scale and setting

Much of the book of Zechariah relates to the same situation as Haggai, but the second part of it (chapters 9–14) is so different that it is believed by most scholars to come from a later period, possibly the third century BC.

Key passages

Victory through God's Spirit (Zechariah 4:6)
The king is coming! (Zechariah 9:9)

Key themes

The book of Zechariah is in two distinct sections, with chapters 1–8 repeating the same themes as Haggai, and clearly related to the same circumstances. Zechariah, however, presents this message in a very different way, through a series of visions of another world which, like that which Ezekiel saw, was full of elaborate depictions of God's character and purposes, mediated largely through angels. Like Haggai, Zechariah identifies Zerubbabel as a key figure in the nation's restoration, though here Joshua the priest is the one who receives a crown, maybe suggesting that functions previously attached to the king were now to be carried out by the priests. The remaining chapters, however, present a vision for the future that goes well beyond what could realistically be expected to happen politically in Jerusalem. This vision develops into a major hope for a new age of love and justice inaugurated by a messianic figure, and taking in the whole world and all its people, not just the Jews. This continues the theme of the arrival of God's new order, but in a way more typical of later apocalyptic writings.

The book of Malachi consists of messages delivered in Jerusalem after the rebuilding of the temple.

> ### Key contents
>
> GOD'S LOVE FOR ISRAEL (CHAPTER 1:1–5)
>
> WORTHLESS SACRIFICES (CHAPTERS 1:6–2:9)
>
> BROKEN PROMISES (CHAPTER 2:10–16)
>
> GOD'S JUDGMENT (CHAPTERS 2:17–3:5)
>
> THE IMPORTANCE OF TITHES (CHAPTER 3:6–12)
>
> GOD'S PROMISE OF MERCY (CHAPTERS 3:13–4:6)

Time-scale and setting

Malachi prophesied after the rebuilt temple was completed (515 BC), and therefore after Haggai and Zechariah, but before the arrival of Nehemiah (445 BC). His messages highlight the hardships endured by the people at this time, and their loss of national pride and religious commitment.

Key passages:

God's messenger (Malachi 3:1)
I will open the windows of heaven (Malachi 3:10)
The sun of righteousness will rise (Malachi 4:2)

Key themes

The temple was operational once more, but the spiritual realities it was supposed to symbolize were not being taken seriously. Priests were neglecting their duties, and magical practices had been incorporated into the worship of God, leading in turn to social corruption and exploitation of the poor by the rich. Men were abandoning their Jewish wives in favour of women from the racially mixed population around them (the very people who had tried to prevent the rebuilding of the temple). Malachi urged the people to return to their covenant roots, otherwise more judgment would surely follow. But obedience would lead to blessing.

'The angel who had been speaking to me came again and roused me as if I had been sleeping. "What do you see?" he asked. "A lampstand made of gold," I answered. "At the top is a bowl for the oil. On the lampstand there are seven lamps, each one with places for seven wicks…"' (Zechariah 4:1–2)

See also

■ From exile to return (pages 34–35)

■ Three temples (pages 160–161)

■ The prophets (pages 166–167)

Joel

A ruinous plague of locusts is seen as a sign of the coming final 'day of the Lord' when God's judgment will be even more devastating than any natural disaster. In light of this, Joel calls the nation to repent, and anticipates the possibility of future prosperity.

Joel called for God's people to repent; the alternative, he said, would be a crushing of the people by a vast army. These bronze decorations from the palace of the Assyrian king Shalmaneser III (858–824 BC) depict scenes of his campaigns.

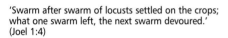

'Swarm after swarm of locusts settled on the crops; what one swarm left, the next swarm devoured.' (Joel 1:4)

Key contents

A PLAGUE OF LOCUSTS (CHAPTER 1)

THE COMING DAY OF THE LORD (CHAPTER 2:1–17)

FUTURE FERTILITY (CHAPTER 2:18–32)

ORACLES AGAINST THE NATIONS (CHAPTER 3)

Key passage

I will pour out my Spirit on all people (Joel 2:28–29)

Time-scale and setting

Virtually nothing specific is known about Joel or when he wrote. But since the book speaks of Israel scattered among the nations (Joel 3:2), it must obviously be later than the exile in Babylon. Possibly it relates to the same period as Malachi (515–445 BC).

Meaning and message

The immediate occasion of Joel's messages is famine, caused by a plague of locusts. This was clearly also a time of more general despondency among the people, frustrated with the slow progress towards the rebuilding of their city and renewal of national life. Joel calls for a time of repentance, warning that the locusts could be a sign of worse to come, because God could not ignore unrepented sin. His vision of God's Spirit being poured out on the whole world features in the New Testament to explain the events of the Day of Pentecost.

Obadiah

The book of Obadiah is the shortest book in the Old Testament. It is a poem deploring the advantage that the Edomites had gained out of the disaster that befell Judah at the hands of the Babylonians. This book probably belongs to the same period as Joel, and assured the people that better times were on the way.

View of the mountains of Jordan across the Arava valley in Negev.

Jonah

The book of Jonah tells the story of a reluctant prophet with a racist attitude who believed that God could be interested only in his own people. Through his adventures, he eventually realizes his mistake, and acknowledges that God's mercy is extended to all.

See also

■ The Babylonian invasion (pages 32–33)

■ Nations to the east and west (pages 78–79)

■ Israel's faith (pages 150–151)

■ The prophets (pages 166–167)

The story

A prophet named Jonah is called by God to take a message to Nineveh, capital of the Assyrian empire. Not surprisingly, perhaps, Jonah is resistant to the idea and heads in the opposite direction (the Assyrians were, after all, sworn enemies of Israel). The ship he travels on is hit by a huge storm, Jonah is thrown overboard and swallowed by a giant fish which subsequently disgorges him onto a beach. Recognizing God's hand in this, Jonah makes for Nineveh, delivers his message – and is both surprised and dismayed when its inhabitants not only listen to him, but act on what he says, changing their ways and thereby avoiding God's judgment. As the prophet sits under a shady plant reflecting on this, the hot sun withers the plant, much to Jonah's consternation, whereupon God points out that his compassion would be better directed towards the Ninevites.

Time-scale and setting

A prophet called Jonah is mentioned briefly in 2 Kings 14:25, about the time of Amos, but since the book of Jonah contains none of the messages delivered by its hero, it is impossible to make any direct connection. The narrative itself is typical of traditional stories in many cultures, and could therefore belong to any period.

The book itself seems to have been written after the fall of Nineveh to the Babylonians (612 BC), and some Aramaic terminology places it even later, in the Persian period. Maybe it was written after the return from exile, following the reforms of Ezra which laid great emphasis on racial exclusiveness.

Key themes

The book of Jonah is clearly a story with a message. Like Job, it may even have been intended to be acted out as a drama: there is certainly a lot of striking dialogue in its pages. Whatever the ultimate origin of the basic story, in terms of its purpose, it is attractive to place it alongside the book of Ruth, which also combines a traditional story with the theme of God's love for all humankind. Throughout the history of Israel, there had always been a tendency for people to imagine that the promises made by God to Abraham endowed their nation with special privilege. The prophets repudiated that view, and saw Israel's calling in more universal terms, emphasizing that the revelation Israel had received imposed a particular responsibility to share the good news with others. In the difficult days following the return from exile, an increasingly narrow racial exclusiveness emerged, aimed at preserving ethnic purity. Like Jonah, these people would go to any lengths to avoid engaging with people of other races, preferring that non-Jews should be destroyed rather than given the opportunity to repent. This book takes that attitude and turns it on its head.

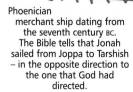

Phoenician merchant ship dating from the seventh century BC. The Bible tells that Jonah sailed from Joppa to Tarshish – in the opposite direction to the one that God had directed.

Between the Testaments: overview

A new empire

Persian rule in Palestine lasted for 200 years, and was replaced by a very different kind of empire. In 333 BC, Alexander the Great defeated the Persian king Darius III Codomannus. This young warrior from Macedonia reigned in person for only 10 years after this, but by the time Alexander died in 323 BC his empire stretched from Greece to Pakistan, and was easily the most extensive empire that part of the world had ever seen. On Alexander's death, his empire was divided among his four leading generals, each of whom founded a separate dynasty. Judah – or Judea as it was now to be called – came under the jurisdiction of Ptolemy, who established his rule in Egypt.

From about 323 BC until 198 BC, the Jews came under the jurisdiction of these Greek rulers based in Egypt. But Ptolemy had not been the only one of Alexander's generals with an eye on Judea. Seleucus, one of the others, who established his own kingdom based at Antioch in north Syria, was constantly looking for an opportunity to take Judea and Lebanon out of the control of Egypt, and incorporate them into his own realm. After more than a century of skirmishing, the matter was finally decided in 198 BC, when the Seleucid ruler Antiochus III defeated Scopus, the general of Ptolemy V, at the battle of Paneon. From now until 63 BC (when the Romans took over Palestine), the Jews would be subject to Greek overlords.

Hellenism and Judaism

Alexander the Great had set out to build a different kind of empire than the Assyrians, Babylonians and Persians. They had mostly been concerned with military conquest, and were satisfied as long as defeated nations paid them whatever taxes they demanded. But Alexander saw his work as a kind of cultural crusade on behalf of his Greek homeland. He was convinced that Greek ways of doing things were the best there could possibly be, and therefore everyone in the whole world should adopt them. Wherever he went, he insisted that people learned the Greek language and adopted Greek customs. He built new cities on the Greek pattern, and exported customs such as the Greek athletic games and theatre. By this time, there were Jewish communities all around the Mediterranean area (for only a minority of the exiles ever returned permanently to Judea). For the most part, they were happy to be a part of this prosperous new culture, and found their own ways of preserving their cultural identity through the development of local places of worship,

called synagogues. The Jews of Alexandria translated their ancient scriptures from Hebrew into Greek.

But the Jews in Judea had a hard time, especially with the accession of Antiochus IV Epiphanes (175–164 BC). Up to this point, the Greek rulers of Palestine had generally been tolerant of the religious scruples of their subjects, and Antiochus III (223–187 BC) even reduced their taxes and gave them a grant for the running of the temple. But money worries forced his successor to adopt a tougher policy. And in the meantime, a power struggle among the Jews themselves had led to the emergence of two competing factions: the Tobiads, who wanted to stick rigidly to traditional Jewish ways, and the Oniads, who were happy to adopt this new Hellenistic culture, even when it meant abandoning time-honoured values.

Cultural conflict

Things came to crisis point when Antiochus IV found his wider financial base being eroded, and ransacked the treasures of the Jerusalem temple. He became fanatically obsessed with a desire to bring Jewish culture fully in line with his own Hellenistic lifestyle, and banned some of the most distinctive aspects of Jewish religion, including circumcision, reading of the Law and keeping the Sabbath. He also gave the temple over to worship of the Greek god Zeus, and opened its holiest places to the whole population of the land, including non-Jews. He embarked on a fierce policy of Hellenization throughout Judea, sending his troops to every town and village to construct altars to Greek gods, and forcing local priests to offer sacrifices on them using pigs, which were unclean animals to the Jews. Resistance was cruelly put down, until a priest called Mattathias killed a Seleucid soldier, and signalled the start of the resistance movement now known as the Maccabean Revolt. This was in 167 BC, and within three years Mattathias and his five sons,

led by Judas (who was given the nickname 'Maccabi', or 'the hammerer', the origin of the word 'Maccabean'), had reduced the Seleucid army to a shambles, and rededicated the temple to its rightful purpose. Following this, Judea enjoyed a period of relative political independence, ruled by Judas' family (the Hasmoneans) until the Roman general Pompey took Jerusalem in 63 BC.

View of the Parthenon Acropolis, Athens, Greece.

The Deuterocanonical books

All Christian Bibles include the 39 books of the original Hebrew Bible. Some contain others, variously referred to as the Apocrypha or Deuterocanonical books, which were never part of the Hebrew Bible, but which entered the Christian scriptures through the Greek translation, the Septuagint, and other ancient versions. Most were originally written in Greek.

This coin bears the stamp of a menorah. It comes from Jerusalem and dates from 40 BC.

The Deuterocanonical books

Tobit
Judith
Additions to Esther
Wisdom of Solomon
Wisdom of Ben Sira
Baruch
The Letter of Jeremiah
Additions to Daniel:
  Prayer of Azariah
  Susanna
  Bel and the Dragon
1–2 Maccabees
1–2 Esdras
Prayer of Manasseh
Psalm 151
3–4 Maccabees

Judith and Tobit

These are traditional stories designed to encourage later generations of Jews to maintain faithful religious observance. Tobit can be dated around 200 BC, while Judith reflects the time when the Hasmoneans were ruling Palestine (about 100 BC).

The book of Tobit is set in Nineveh during the reign of the Assyrian king Shalmaneser V (727–722 BC). Tobit upholds traditional values, especially by ensuring that other Israelite exiles receive a proper burial after their death. When illness and other afflictions befall him and his family, their faithfulness to God ensures a supernatural deliverance.

The book of Judith is set in Judea after the return from the Babylonian exile, and concerns the resistance of the inhabitants of the town of Bethulia to a foreign general named Holofernes. Details of the story are taken variously to refer to Assyrians, Persians and Babylonians, but the core of it lies in Bethulia's resistance, inspired and led by Judith, a courageous widow, who distracts Holofernes by her beauty, and then when he is drunk decapitates him and takes his head back to the elders of the town.

Additions to Bible books

The Greek versions of the books of Esther and Daniel both have material not contained in the original Hebrew text. In the case of Esther, this includes prayers and stories highlighting her great piety, and the risks she took by remaining faithful to her people. The additions to Daniel consist of a long prayer attributed to the victims of Nebuchadnezzar's fiery furnace, together with the stories of Bel and the Dragon, and Susanna. Like the stories of Daniel himself, they emphasize God's care for those who are faithful in the face of persecution.

Baruch and the Letter of Jeremiah

These short writings purport to be by Jeremiah and his scribe, Baruch, and seem to have been originally written in Hebrew. The Letter of Jeremiah contains a poem denouncing trust in idols, while Baruch (which is a mixture of poetry and prose) calls Israel to return to the traditional spiritual disciplines of prayer and obedience to the law. Both date from the mid-second century BC.

The Decapolis was an alliance of 10 towns to the east of the River Jordan, one of which was Gerasa (Jerash) in present-day Jordan.

Wisdom books

The Wisdom of Solomon is a sophisticated Greek composition, showing the combination of traditional Hebrew ideas with Stoic and Platonic thought-forms that is also found in the writings of Philo of Alexandria (born about 20 BC). The personification of Wisdom found in Proverbs is developed further, and here Wisdom becomes a female person who mediates the purposes of God to the world. Probably written in Alexandria in the first century BC.

The Wisdom of Jesus Ben Sira (called Ecclesiasticus in the Latin Bible) is an older work, certainly written before the time of Antiochus IV, maybe around 180 BC. Translated from Hebrew, its contents and style are not too different from the book of Proverbs, with other sections praising various past heroes of the faith.

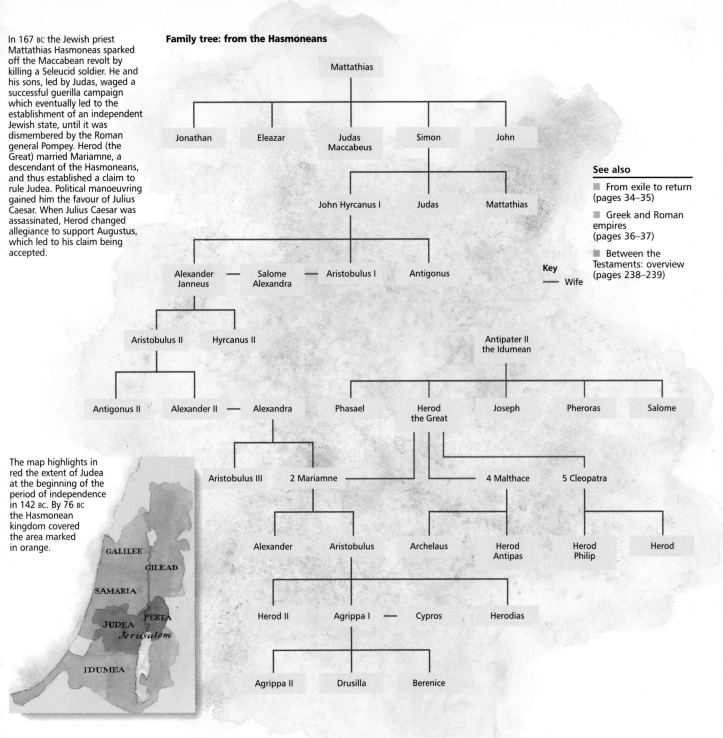

Family tree: from the Hasmoneans

In 167 BC the Jewish priest Mattathias Hasmoneas sparked off the Maccabean revolt by killing a Seleucid soldier. He and his sons, led by Judas, waged a successful guerilla campaign which eventually led to the establishment of an independent Jewish state, until it was dismembered by the Roman general Pompey. Herod (the Great) married Mariamne, a descendant of the Hasmoneans, and thus established a claim to rule Judea. Political manoeuvring gained him the favour of Julius Caesar. When Julius Caesar was assassinated, Herod changed allegiance to support Augustus, which led to his claim being accepted.

See also

■ From exile to return (pages 34–35)

■ Greek and Roman empires (pages 36–37)

■ Between the Testaments: overview (pages 238–239)

Key
— Wife

Mattathias

Jonathan — Eleazar — Judas Maccabeus — Simon — John

John Hyrcanus I — Judas — Mattathias

Alexander Janneus — Salome Alexandra — Aristobulus I — Antigonus

Aristobulus II — Hyrcanus II

Antipater II the Idumean

Antigonus II — Alexander II — Alexandra — Phasael — Herod the Great — Joseph — Pheroras — Salome

Aristobulus III — 2 Mariamne — 4 Malthace — 5 Cleopatra

Alexander — Aristobulus — Archelaus — Herod Antipas — Herod Philip — Herod

Herod II — Agrippa I — Cypros — Herodias

Agrippa II — Drusilla — Berenice

The map highlights in red the extent of Judea at the beginning of the period of independence in 142 BC. By 76 BC the Hasmonean kingdom covered the area marked in orange.

GALILEE
GILEAD
SAMARIA
PEREA
JUDEA
Jerusalem
IDUMEA

Poems

Manasseh was one of the kings most reviled in the Old Testament history books because of his acceptance of religious practices alien to Israelite tradition. The Prayer of Manasseh depicts him repenting of this, as a result of which God pardons his wrongdoing. Probably written in the first century AD to encourage a generation facing demands to worship Roman emperors as divine.

Psalm 151 is found in Hebrew in the Dead Sea Scrolls, and is a poem recounting David's reflections on his encounter with Goliath.

1–2 Esdras

1 Esdras retells the story of the nation of Judah from the days of Josiah to the time of Ezra, and was written in 150–100 BC.

2 Esdras is quite different, and consists of apocalyptic visions reflecting events during the second and third centuries AD.

1–2 Maccabees

These books tell the story of the Maccabean revolt, 1 Maccabees covering the period 175–135 BC, and 2 Maccabees dealing with 176–161 BC. Compiled during the first century BC from earlier sources.

3–4 Maccabees

3 Maccabees is set in Egypt during the reign of Ptolemy IV (221–204 BC), and depicts faithful Jews risking their lives by defying royal decrees that are incompatible with the Old Testament Law. Written in the first century BC, in the same novelistic style as Esther, Daniel, Jonah, Tobit and Judith.

4 Maccabees is a philosophical reflection on the value of undeserved suffering, influenced by Plato and Stoic thinkers, written early in the first century AD.

The gospels and Acts: overview

The four gospels (Matthew, Mark, Luke and John) contain stories of the life and teaching of Jesus, but they are obviously not biographies. They say virtually nothing about Jesus' childhood or youth, preferring instead to give extensive accounts of the last week of his life. The Acts of the Apostles was written by the author of Luke's gospel, as a second volume which would take the story on from the death and resurrection of Jesus, into the early years of the Christian church.

The four gospels

Many things about Jesus are never mentioned in the gospels. There are no descriptions of what he looked like or what kind of personality he had. All four of them put together do not even document every day of the three years or so with which they are most concerned. The gospel writers' main concern was to share the Christian message with others, and they used the stories of Jesus as a way of doing that. The information they include was determined by its relevance to this one purpose which they all shared. This has important consequences for our understanding of their narratives

All four of the gospels are selective accounts: both Luke (Luke 1:1–4) and John (John 20:30; 21:25) specifically say that they omitted a lot of other information that was available to them.

The gospels contain more than just simple stories: they present mature reflection on the meaning of Jesus, and tell their readers what is worth believing about him. They also tell us something about their authors' interests and concerns: they each made distinctive selections of material, and comparing their procedures can help in understanding their message.

Historical perspective

It has sometimes been suggested that the gospels do not present an accurate picture of Jesus as he really was, and their writers' evangelizing purposes are often supposed to be evidence for that. But their interpretation and application of the material is no more than any competent historian would be expected to provide. The fact that the early church happily preserved four different accounts of Jesus'

life and teaching shows that they had no doubts about their authenticity or usefulness. In any case they were all written within a generation of the events they describe. Stories about Jesus must have been communicated orally by his followers from the very earliest days, and the materials out of which the gospels were compiled had been circulating by word of mouth long before they were written down. As the Christian church expanded throughout the Roman empire, the need for literature grew enormously, and with the deaths of those people who actually knew Jesus it was more important than ever to preserve their memories for the future.

By the time the gospels were written, the church had spread extensively into non-Jewish culture, yet there is scarcely any mention at all of non-Jewish, or Gentile, concerns in the gospels. Even within 10 years of Jesus' death, there were fierce arguments about whether Gentile converts should observe the Old Testament laws on practices such as circumcision and eating certain foods – yet none of these features anywhere in the gospels. Christians were soon applying elevated titles to Jesus – Son of God, Christ/Messiah, Saviour – but in the gospels, the most frequent term is 'Son of Man'. And everywhere there are signs of Palestinian culture and the Aramaic language. These features, and others like them, suggest that the gospel writers had a conscious concern for historical accuracy, which was not overridden by their other theological purposes.

Acts of the Apostles

Like the gospels, the book of Acts was also written as 'history with a purpose', and shares many of the same characteristics. It is a selective account, and does not document the deeds of anything like all the apostles. The first few chapters contain stories of people such as Peter and John, who were leading disciples of Jesus. The focus then moves to Paul, who was a second-generation convert to Christianity, and most of the book deals with his endeavours to take the Christian message around the major towns and cities of the eastern Roman empire.

Luke portrays himself as a writer of history, and there is no reason to doubt the accuracy of what he writes. But there are other purposes running through this work. Luke is at pains to point out that Christianity is the fulfilment of Judaism – and, therefore, deserves the legal status that Judaism enjoyed within the Roman empire. He emphasizes repeatedly that Christians are not a threat to the peace of the empire, but are loyal subjects – even though, at the time he was writing, they were refusing to worship the emperor as a god. And at all times, he presents the story of the early church as an example to be followed by the Christians of his own day.

View over Tiberias, Lake Galilee, Israel.

Mark

The book of Mark was almost certainly the earliest of the gospels to be written. Mark is short, fast-moving and action-packed.

Key contents

Author and time-scale

Early traditions associate this gospel with John Mark, claiming that he gathered much of his material from the preaching of Peter. The book itself was written in Rome, probably between AD 60 and AD 70, and was later used as a source of information by both Matthew and Luke.

Key events

John the Baptist prepares the way (Mark 1:1–8)
Jesus' baptism and temptation (Mark 1:8–13)
The 12 disciples (Mark 3:13–19)
Feeding the 5,000 (Mark 6:30–43)
The transfiguration (Mark 9:2–13)
The triumphal entry to Jerusalem (Mark 11:1–11)
The last supper (Mark 14:1–26)
Jesus' arrest, trial and death (Mark 14:27–15:20)
The resurrection (Mark 16:1–8)

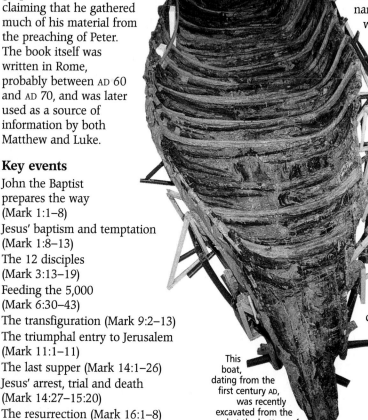

This boat, dating from the first century AD, was recently excavated from the mud at the bottom of Lake Galilee.

Key passages

The good news in a nutshell (Mark 1:14–15)
I will make you fish for people (Mark 1:16–20)
Forgiving sins: the paralysed man (Mark 2:1–12)
Choosing the 12 (Mark 3:13–19)
Who is the greatest in God's kingdom? (Mark 9:33–37)
Let the little children come (Mark 10:13–16)
The rich young man (Mark 10:17–31)
A ransom for many (Mark 10:42–45)
Moneychangers chased from the temple (Mark 11:15–17)
The greatest commandment (Mark 12:28–34)

Key themes

Mark's gospel has a strong sense of urgency about it. The whole narrative is made up of short sections, linked together with words like 'and' or 'immediately'. Jesus too is presented as a man of action, constantly on the move, declaring the imminent arrival of God's kingdom. The disciples by contrast are very slow to understand who Jesus is and to respond to him in appropriate ways – not least because Jesus seems to speak in riddles, avoiding using Messianic terminology and always speaking of the enigmatic figure he calls 'the Son of Man'. Mark uses this to encourage his readers in their own Christian faith: if they find themselves with as much doubt as faith, then they are no different even from those original followers of Jesus whom they so admired.

Mark also presents Jesus himself as a very human figure, and emphasizes how he could be angry on occasions, and if the conditions of trust in him were not there, he was sometimes unable to perform miracles. He experiences the full range of human emotions – something that some early Christians found hard to reconcile with his position as Son of God. This kind of unease eventually surfaced as a major issue in the community to which the letters 1–3 John were written, but Mark might also be correcting an early move in this direction in the church at Rome.

JOHN THE BAPTIST

By the time of Jesus, apocalyptic speculation expected one of the old prophets to return to herald the arrival of the Messiah. John is depicted as this prophet, sent by God to prepare people for the coming of Jesus, the Messiah. His lifestyle (in the desert), clothes (rough camel's hair), and diet (locusts and wild honey) are all reminiscent of the prophet Elijah (whom Malachi had specifically identified in this role).

Mark's gospel says nothing of John's background, but Luke contains stories about his birth. Like several Old Testament heroes, John was born to his parents, Zechariah and Elizabeth, at a time in life when it would normally have been impossible to conceive children. John's special significance is highlighted by the appearance of an angel to announce his birth, and by his being Jesus' own cousin. His early life was spent in the desert of Judea, which has prompted speculation that he may have had some connections with the Essenes, an ascetic sect associated with the monastery at Qumran (home of the Dead Sea Scrolls). They shared some characteristics with John: looking for the Messiah and ensuring their personal purity by repeated washings. But John's baptism was once-for-all, and was available for anyone who wished to change their lifestyle. Along with many others, Jesus was baptised by John before beginning his own ministry.

John was later imprisoned for his outspoken criticism of the lifestyle of King Herod and his family. From prison he sent some of his disciples to Jesus to ask if he really was the person they were expecting. 'Tell John how I heal the sick and preach good news to the poor,' Jesus answered. Then he told the crowds, 'John the Baptist is more than a prophet. He is greater than anyone who has ever lived.' Not long after this, Herod's wife tricked him into having John beheaded.

Luke 1; 3; 7:18ff.; Matthew 3; 11; 14:1–12; Mark 1; 6

Herod's family tomb, Jerusalem

See also

■ In the steps of Jesus
(pages 40–41)

■ New Testament religion
(pages 170–171)

■ The life and teaching of Jesus
(pages 178–191)

■ John
(pages 250–251)

'The Entry into Jerusalem', Ambrogio Bondone Giotto (circa 1266–1337)

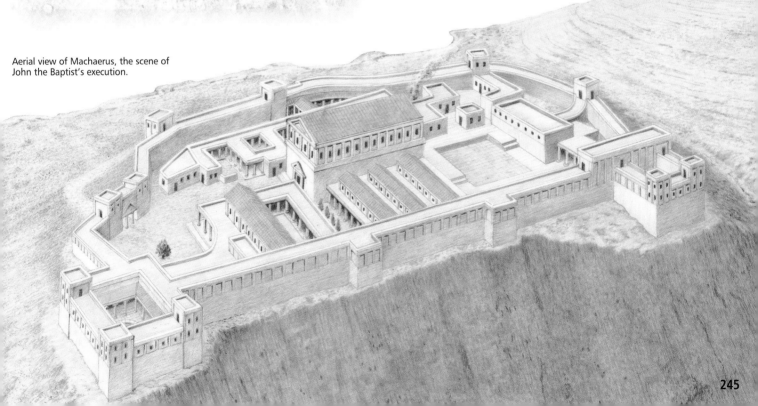

Aerial view of Machaerus, the scene of John the Baptist's execution.

Matthew

This gospel shows particular interest in the concerns of Jewish Christians, and more than any other stresses Old Testament prophecies which were fulfilled in Jesus, who is depicted as the Messiah long expected by the Jews.

Lake Galilee from the Mount of Beatitudes

Key contents

JESUS' BIRTH (CHAPTERS 1–2)

A NEW WAY OF LIVING (CHAPTERS 3–7)
Baptism and temptations
(chapters 3–4:11)
Jesus begins his work
(chapter 4:12–25)
Sermon on the Mount (chapters 5–7)

DISCIPLESHIP (CHAPTERS 8–10)
Healing and teaching
(chapters 8–9:34)
Mission (chapters 9:35–10:42)

**THE KINGDOM OF HEAVEN
(CHAPTERS 11–13)**
John the Baptist's messengers
(chapter 11:1–19)
Teaching and religious arguments
(chapters 11:20–12:50)
Parables (chapter 13)

THE CHURCH (CHAPTERS 14–18)
Teaching and miracles
(chapters 13:53–16:12)
Peter's declaration (chapter 16:13–28)
The transfiguration (chapter 17)
Relationships among disciples
(chapter 18)

**MOVING TOWARDS THE CRISIS
(CHAPTERS 19–25)**
Teaching and healing
(chapters 19–20)
Jesus in Jerusalem (chapters 21–22)
Denunciations of the Pharisees
(chapter 23)
Visions of the end times
(chapters 24–25)

JESUS' LAST DAYS (CHAPTERS 26–28)
The last supper (chapter 26:1–30)
Arrest and trials
(chapters 26:31–27:26)
Crucifixion (chapter 27:27–56)
Burial and resurrection
(chapters 27:57–28:15)
The great commission
(chapter 28:16–20)

Key events

Jesus' birth (Matthew 1)
Jesus' baptism (Matthew 3)
The temptation of Jesus (Matthew 4)
The transfiguration (Matthew 17)
Jesus' entry into Jerusalem (Matthew 21)
Trials and crucifixion (Matthew 26–27)
Jesus' resurrection (Matthew 28)

Key passages

SERMON ON THE MOUNT (MATTHEW 5–7)
Beatitudes (Matthew 5:3–12)
Love your enemies (Matthew 5:43–48)
Lord's Prayer (Matthew 6:9–13)
First things first (Matthew 6:25–34)
Ask, seek, knock (Matthew 7:7–11)
The narrow gate (Matthew 7:13–14)
The two houses (Matthew 7:24–27)

COME TO ME AND REST
(MATTHEW 11:28–30)
PETER AND THE KEYS OF THE KINGDOM
(MATTHEW 16:13–20)

PARABLES OF THE KINGDOM:
The sower (Matthew 13:1–23)
Wheat and weeds (Matthew 13:24–30)
Mustard seed and yeast
(Matthew 13:31–43)
Treasure and pearl (Matthew 13:44–46)
Fishing net (Matthew 13:47–50)
Bridesmaids (Matthew 25:1–13)
Three servants (Matthew 25:14–30)
Sheep and goats (Matthew 25:31–46)
The great commission
(Matthew 28:16–20)

Donkey at the Mount of Olives, Jerusalem.

Key themes

Matthew's gospel was placed first in the New Testament because it has a lot to say about the church, with a lot of liturgical and ethical material which made it particularly suitable for instructing new converts. It also makes an explicit link between the Old Testament and the New, presenting Jesus as the fulfilment of all the original Hebrew scriptures, often referring to specific Old Testament passages and indicating their relevance to the life and teaching of Jesus.

PETER

Peter was a member of a Galilean fishing family, and a leader among Jesus' disciples. His name is variously given in the New Testament as Simon, Cephas (Aramaic) and Peter (Greek), the latter two meaning 'rock' – a reference to the central position he came to hold in the church. Peter was with Jesus in all the crucial events of his ministry, though after Jesus' arrest he denied knowing him. Of all the disciples, he is the one of whom most is recorded, and one of the few New Testament characters of whom we have anything like a personality profile.

On the Day of Pentecost Peter proclaimed Jesus as the risen Messiah, and some 3,000 people became Christians. His initial ministry was restricted to Jews, but later he travelled throughout the Roman empire much as Paul did. He is identified with the writing of the letter of 1 Peter, and he died in Rome during Nero's persecution in the mid-60s AD – crucified, like Jesus, but upside down.

Matthew 4:18–19; 10:2; 14:28–33; 16:13–23; 17:1–9; 26:30ff.; Mark 1:16–18, 29–31; 5:37; John 1:40–42; 18:10–11; 20:2–10; 21; Acts 1–15; Galatians 1–2; 1 Peter

The wilderness of the Judean desert

See also

■ In the steps of Jesus (pages 40–41)

■ New Testament religion (pages 170–171)

■ The life and teaching of Jesus (pages 178–191)

Time-scale and setting

Matthew's gospel appears first in the New Testament, but it was not the earliest gospel to be written. Matthew is, in effect, a revised and much expanded version of Mark's gospel, though it also contains other material that is also found in Luke, as well as some teaching that is unique to Matthew. It is for these reasons that the first three gospels are referred to as 'synoptics': they are basically different versions of the same materials. References in Matthew's gospel suggest that it was written after AD 70, when the Romans destroyed Jerusalem and its temple, though by the early second century it was widely known and attributed to Matthew, a tax-collector and one of Jesus' disciples. It was probably written between AD 80 and AD 90, for a Christian community which either saw itself as a reforming synagogue within Judaism, or which had recently broken with its Jewish roots.

JUDAS ISCARIOT

Judas Iscariot was the disciple who betrayed Jesus. His motives are unclear, but probably related to his hopes that Jesus would lead a rebellion against the Romans: 'Iscariot' means 'dagger man', suggesting that he was a Zealot. When Jesus turned out to be a different kind of messiah, Judas betrayed him – either out of frustration or in an effort to force him into armed resistance to the authorities. He later regretted his action, returned the money he had been paid for the betrayal and committed suicide.

Matthew 10:4; 26:14ff.; 27:3ff.; John 12:4–6; 13:21–30; Acts 1:18–19

Luke

Luke's gospel was written for 'Theophilus' ('lover of God'), a rich Roman – or possibly a pseudonym for all Christians. It was certainly written for Gentiles.

Key passages

The angel's message to Mary (Luke 1:26–38)

Mary's song: the Magnificat (Luke 1:46–55)

Zechariah's prayer (Luke 1:68–79)

Shepherds and angels (Luke 2:8–20)

Simeon's song: Nunc Dimittis (Luke 2:29–32)

The Spirit of the Lord is upon me (Luke 4:16–21)

The good Samaritan (Luke 10:25–37)

Mary and Martha (Luke 10:38–42)

The rich fool (Luke 12:13–21)

The great feast (Luke 14:15–24)

The prodigal son (Luke 15:11–32)

The Pharisee and tax-collector (Luke 18:9–14)

A blind beggar (Luke 18:35–43)

Zacchaeus (Luke 19:1–10)

The walk to Emmaus (Luke 24:13–35)

Author and time-scale

Luke's gospel was written by Luke, a Gentile companion of the missionary Paul, incorporating material from Mark's gospel, it was probably written in about AD 85.

Key contents

(CHAPTERS 1:1–4)

JOHN THE BAPTIST AND JESUS (CHAPTERS 1:5–4:13)
Birth and childhood (chapters 1:5–2:52)
John's ministry (chapter 3:1–20)
Jesus' baptism and temptations (chapters 3:21–4:13)

GALILEE (CHAPTERS 4:14–9:50)
Nazareth and Capernaum (chapter 4:14–41)
Teaching, healing, calling disciples (chapters 4:42–6:16)
Discipleship (chapter 6:17–49)
Miracles and teaching (chapters 7:1–9:17)
Peter's faith, and the transfiguration (chapter 9:18–50)

TRAVELLING TO JERUSALEM (CHAPTERS 9:51–19:27)
Starting out (chapter 9:51–62)
The mission of 72 disciples (chapter 10:1–24)
Teaching and controversy (chapters 10:25–11:54)
Warning and reassurance (chapters 12:1–13:17)
Parables (chapters 13:18–18:14)
Jesus and people (chapters 18:15–19:10)
Parable of the gold coins (chapter 19:11–27)

IN JERUSALEM (CHAPTERS 19:28–23:58)
Entry to the city and temple (chapter 19:28–48)
Religious disputes (chapters 20:1–21:4)
Future hopes (chapter 21:5–38)
The last supper (chapter 22:1–38)
Arrest and trials (chapters 22:39–23:25)
Crucifixion and burial (chapter 23:26–49)

RESURRECTION (CHAPTER 24)

MARY

Mary was Jesus's mother and the wife of Joseph, a general builder in Nazareth. Throughout the stories of Mary's pregnancy, there are hints of the tragic end her child would suffer. Little is recorded anywhere about Jesus' home life, but despite mixed feelings on the part of others in the family, Mary remained faithful to Jesus to the end and features in the book of Acts as a leader in the early church.

Matthew 1:18–25; 2:11; 13:55; Luke 1–2; John 2:1–11; 19:25–27; Acts 1:14

'The Last Supper', Leonardo da Vinci (1454–1519)

Acts of the Apostles

The book of Acts covers the period from Jesus' ascension into heaven to the missionary Paul's arrival in Rome.

Via Sacra, Forum, Rome. Paul saw Rome as a strategic city for the spread of the Christian message throughout the Roman empire.

See also
- The birth of Christianity (pages 42–43)
- The journeys of Paul (pages 44–45)
- The earliest churches (pages 46–47)
- The earliest Christians (pages 172–173)

Key contents

WAITING FOR THE SPIRIT (CHAPTER 1)
Jesus' ascension (chapter 1:1–11)
Judas' replacement (chapter 1:12–26)

THE GOSPEL IN JERUSALEM (CHAPTERS 2:1–8:3)
Day of Pentecost (chapter 2:1–42)
A snapshot of church life (chapter 2:43–47)
Peter and John (chapters 3:1–4:31)
Life in the early church (chapters 4:32–6:7)
Stephen's martyrdom (chapters 6:8–8:3)

THE GOSPEL INTO PALESTINE (CHAPTERS 8:4–9:31)
Samaria (chapter 8:5–25)
Philip (chapter 8:26–40)
Saul's conversion (chapter 9:1–31)

MISSION AMONG GENTILES (CHAPTERS 9:32–12:34)
Lydda and Joppa (chapter 9:32–43)
Peter's vision and Cornelius's conversion (chapters 10:1–11:18)
Antioch (chapter 11:19–30)
Persecution (chapter 12:1–24)

THE WIDER EMPIRE (CHAPTERS 13–28)
Paul and Barnabas (chapters 13–14)
Debates on Jews and Gentiles (chapter 15:1–35)
Paul, Silas and Timothy (chapters 15:36–18:23)
Paul in Ephesus (chapters 18:24–21:16)
Paul's arrest and imprisonment (chapters 21:17–26:32)
Voyage to Rome (chapters 27:1–28:15)
Paul in Rome (chapter 28:16–31)

Antioch in Pisidia, a stopping point on Paul's missionary journeys.

Key passages

The heart of Peter's great sermon (Acts 2:22–24)
Snapshot of the first believers (Acts 2:43–47)
The believers' shared life (Acts 4:32–35)
Stephen's speech in his own defence (Acts 7:1–53)
The church at Antioch (Acts 11:19–26)
The jailer at Philippi (Acts 16:22–34)
Paul in Athens (Acts 17:22–31)
Paul's farewell to the elders at Ephesus (Acts 20:17–38)
Paul's defence before Agrippa (Acts 26:1–29)

Author and time-scale

The Acts of the Apostles was written by Luke, who used his personal travel diary in some sections of the book. Acts may have been written shortly after the last events it describes (in the mid-60s AD).

A Roman grain ship, possibly the type of vessel which took Paul from Caesarea towards Rome.

Key themes

Luke strongly emphasizes the roots of Christianity in Judaism – something that in Acts becomes an apologetic to the Roman empire for the legitimate status of Christianity. But from the start, Luke also stresses that the Gentile mission was part of God's original intention. In line with this, he also underlines the gospel's appeal to people on the fringes of society, including the economically deprived as well as women and children. The deep spirituality of Luke's writings focuses around prayer and the work of the Holy Spirit.

PAUL (SAUL)

Paul, formerly known as Saul, was a Jewish rabbi and Roman citizen who became a Christian as a result of a remarkable conversion experience on the road to Damascus, where he was going to persecute Christians. He later engaged in the work of the church at Antioch, which became his home base for a series of journeys around the Mediterranean, in the course of which he established Christian communities in many major cities and wrote the letters now in the New Testament. Paul's strategy was to visit Roman provincial capitals, which were easily reached by the regular trade routes, and from where his converts could take the message into outlying areas. His policy of accepting Gentiles without requiring them to observe the Jewish law aroused much opposition, and led to his arrest in Jerusalem, and eventually his trial before the emperor Nero and his execution in Rome.

Acts 7:58–8:1; 9–28; the letters of Paul

John

Iohn's gospel is quite different from the synoptic gospels (Matthew, Mark and Luke). It gives its own distinctive angle on Jesus, designed to draw its readers towards faith in him as the Messiah and Son of God.

Author, time-scale and setting

John's gospel is traditionally regarded as the work of John the disciple of Jesus. The gospel appears to be written by the same person as the New Testament letters 1, 2 and 3 John, which identify their author as 'the elder', giving rise to the suggestion that this was a different John, albeit still associated with the church at Ephesus – and for whose existence there is some evidence. The way Old Testament concepts and Hebrew words are carefully explained suggests that the gospel was originally compiled for a Jewish readership, then revised for a Hellenistic context, though probably by the same author as there is no discernible stylistic variation. It is certainly independent of the synoptic gospels, though no less historically reliable, and displays clear knowledge of Jerusalem at the time of Jesus. Some date John's gospel as early as AD 45, but a date around AD 90 is more likely.

Eastern wall of temple mount and stairway, Jerusalem.

JOHN THE APOSTLE

Like his father Zebedee and his brother James, John was a fisherman. He was probably a follower of John the Baptist before Jesus called him to become his disciple. Jesus nicknamed John and James 'sons of thunder' because they were quick-tempered. One of three disciples who were especially close to Jesus, John was present at all key events in the gospels. Tradition identifies him with 'the disciple whom Jesus loved', who in John's gospel lay alongside Jesus at the last supper and was entrusted with the care of Mary by Jesus at the crucifixion.

With Peter, John became a leader of the earliest church in Jerusalem, and was still in the city 14 years after Paul was converted. Tradition depicts him living in Ephesus to a great age, and also as the John who wrote the book of Revelation. Three New Testament letters also bear his name, though again none of them identify their author specifically with John the apostle.

Matthew 4:21ff.; 10:2; 17:1ff.; Mark 3:17; 5:37; 10:35ff.; 14:33; Luke 9:49ff.; John 19:26–27; Acts 3–4; Galatians 2:9

Key contents

JESUS AS DIVINE WORD (CHAPTER 1:1–18)

THE SEVEN SIGNS (CHAPTERS 1:19–12:50)
John the Baptist and Jesus' first disciples (chapter 1:19–51)
Sign 1: Water into wine (chapter 2:1–12)
Debates over faith (chapters 2:13–3:36)
A woman by a well (chapter 4:1–41)
Sign 2: Healing an official's son (chapter 4:42–54)
Sign 3: The pool of Bethesda (chapter 5:1–9)
More religious arguments (chapter 5:10–47)
Sign 4: Feeding the 5,000 (chapter 6:1–15)
Sign 5: Walking on water (chapter 6:16–21)
The bread of life (chapter 6:22–71)
The Feast of Tabernacles (chapters 7–8)
Sign 6: A man born blind (chapter 9)
The good shepherd (chapter 10:1–21)
More arguments and sign 7: Lazarus raised (chapters 10:22–11:57)
Entry into Jerusalem (chapter 12)

THE UPPER ROOM AND GARDEN OF GETHSEMANE (CHAPTERS 13–17)
Footwashing (chapter 13:1–20)
Teaching for disciples (chapters 13:21–16:33)
A prayer by Jesus (chapter 17)

ARREST, TRIALS, CRUCIFIXION AND BURIAL (CHAPTERS 18–19)

RESURRECTION (CHAPTERS 20–21)
The empty tomb (chapter 20:1–10)
Jesus meets Mary Magdalene (chapter 20:11–18)
Jesus and Thomas (chapter 20:19–31)

JESUS COMMISSIONS PETER (CHAPTER 21)

The Antonia Fortress may have been the site of Jesus' trial before Pontius Pilate.

Key passages

In the beginning was the Word (John 1:1–18)
You must be born again (John 3:1–8)
God so loved the world (John 3:16–17)
The bread of life (John 6:35–40)
Streams of living water (John 7:37–39)
The light of the world (John 8:12)
The truth will set you free (John 8:31–32)
Before Abraham was born, I am (John 8:56–58)
The good shepherd (John 10:1–16)
The resurrection and the life (John 11:23–27)
The seed must die (John 12:24–26)
The way, the truth and the life (John 14:1–7)
The true vine (John 15:1–8)
The comforter is coming (John 16:5–15)
Feed my sheep (John 21:15–19)

The Via Dolorosa in Jerusalem is traditionally the route believed to be that taken by Jesus to his place of execution.

Olive trees at Gethsemane, Jerusalem

'The Raising of Lazarus', Ambrogio Bondone Giotto (c. 1266–1337)

See also

■ In the steps of Jesus
(pages 40–41)

■ New Testament religion
(pages 170–171)

■ The life and teaching of Jesus
(pages 178–191)

Key themes

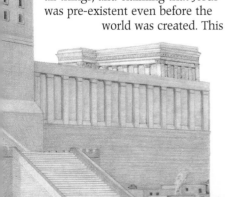

The opening chapter of John's gospel sets the ministry of Jesus in a cosmic context, identifying him with the divine 'word' (Greek *logos*) at the centre of all things, and claiming that Jesus was pre-existent even before the world was created. This description of Jesus owes much to the wisdom tradition within the Old Testament and later Judaism (where wisdom had been God's agent of creation), as well as to Greek philosophy. It is typical of this writer to bring together these two worlds of thought, arguing that while Jesus was certainly the Jewish Messiah, his coming was also the fulfilment of the wider Hellenistic spiritual search.

Whereas in the synoptic gospels Jesus' Messianic identity only appears gradually, in John it is obvious from the start, and the seven 'signs' (miracles) and seven sayings ('I am' sayings) make explicit claims for Jesus' divine origin.

Other differences between John and the other gospels include the setting (the synoptic gospels place Jesus mainly in Galilee; John places Jesus in Jerusalem), and the style of teaching (parables in the synoptic gospels, longer conversations and theological discourses in John, though there are still very many extended metaphorical uses of language in John).

Writings of the apostles: overview

Less than 20 years after Jesus' crucifixion, thriving churches were found in all the major cities of the Roman empire. Many New Testament books were written to encourage the development and understanding of their faith. Most were letters sent by Christian leaders to their converts, often in answer to specific questions they had been asked, and most of the letters were associated with the ministry of Paul.

The books

THE GENERAL LETTERS	THE LETTERS OF PAUL		THE LETTERS OF JOHN
James	Galatians	Philippians	1 John
Hebrews	1 Thessalonians	Colossians	2 John
1 Peter	2 Thessalonians	Philemon	3 John
Jude	1 Corinthians	Ephesians	
2 Peter	2 Corinthians	1 Timothy	OTHER BOOKS
	Romans	2 Timothy	Revelation
		Titus	

Writing and sending letters

Not everyone in the Roman empire was literate, but letters were still a good way to communicate. Culturally, the Romans were the heirs to the Hellenizing policies of Alexander the Great, and though they had their own language (Latin), its use was largely restricted to official business within government circles. Greek was the language of everyday commerce, and even when it existed alongside other local languages (as with Aramaic in Palestine) it was widely understood throughout the empire. This was a great advantage to early Christian missionaries, for it meant they could use one language to communicate everywhere they went. There was a postal system of sorts in the Roman empire, though letters were often entrusted to friends, who could also give a verbal commentary when they delivered them to their recipients. With the ease of travel provided by the system of Roman trade routes, it is no wonder that letters became so popular and useful in the Christian churches.

Understanding ancient letters

Ancient letters were written in a more or less fixed style, and the New Testament letters follow this style. The writer's name came first, followed by that of the recipient, and this was followed by a greeting. Then came a thanksgiving for the recipient's health, as well as an appreciation of their personal qualities. The main subject matter followed this, with personal news and greetings from mutual friends. Some form of verification was then given in the form of a note in the sender's own handwriting (the main letter would be written by a

professional scribe). Finally, there would be a word of farewell.

New Testament letters

Paul's letters in particular follow the traditional style very closely. By comparing the way Paul uses language, it has been possible to identify his letters as very personal communications: the sort of letters that would be sent from one family member to another, rather than less personal, business-style letters. Six New Testament letters were addressed to individuals (Philemon, 1–2 Timothy, Titus and 2–3 John), with the remainder being sent to churches.

Some other New Testament books follow the formal letter style less closely, and for that very reason may not have been real letters, even though they have been traditionally described that way (the book of Hebrews is a particularly striking example).

Meaning and message

Whatever their literary form, all these New Testament books present the same challenges to their modern readers. They were all written to address specific concerns, but for the most part these books themselves are the only evidence we have as to the nature of the debates to which they related. In some cases, for example Paul's correspondence with the church at Corinth, we know for certain that letters had been sent to him asking particular questions, to which 1 Corinthians was his answer. But these other letters have not been preserved, and Paul never explicitly spells out their contents, which creates real problems of interpretation. Reading the New Testament letters is like listening to only one half of a phone conversation, and to work out what was being said on the other end requires painstaking research along with a good deal of imagination.

Collecting the writings

The collection of the apostles' writings must have begun almost when they were first written. Paul recommended two of his churches to exchange the separate letters he had sent them (Colossians 4:16), and by the time 2 Peter was written many, if not all, of Paul's letters had clearly been gathered together and were regarded as of equal value alongside the Old Testament, being read in the course of regular worship (2 Peter 3:15–16).

Other literary forms

The book of Revelation begins with letters written to seven churches in Asia Minor, all of which address contemporary issues in the same way as Paul did. But most of this book has a different form altogether. It is a collection of visions, very similar to the apocalyptic material contained in the Old Testament book of Daniel, and served much the same purpose.

The book of Hebrews is also distinctive, and consists of a dense exposition of the Old Testament books of Exodus, Leviticus and Numbers, explaining how their ritual laws relate to Christian beliefs about Jesus – and, like Revelation, encouraging Christians at a time of persecution.

View from Acro Corinth, Greece.

James

This is a totally practical letter about the importance of a high standard of conduct. It has echoes of the teaching of Jesus, as well as the Old Testament book of Proverbs.

This painting from first-century AD Pompeii depicts a man with a papyrus scroll, and his wife holding hinged writing tablets and a metal stylus.

Key contents

DEEDS NOT WORDS (CHAPTER 1)

THE NEED TO AVOID SOCIAL PREJUDICE (CHAPTER 2:1–13)

FAITH AND ACTIONS (CHAPTER 2:14–26)

AVOIDING HURTFUL WORDS (CHAPTER 3:1–12)

HEAVENLY WISDOM (CHAPTER 3:13–18)

GOD'S STANDARDS AND VALUES (CHAPTERS 4:1–5:6)

PATIENCE AND PRAYER (CHAPTER 5:7–20)

Golden earring from the ancient city of Memphis. James warned his readers against showing favouritism towards wealthier members of the church.

Time-scale and setting

The letter's greeting reveals little about either its author or its readers. James was an exceedingly common name, so the author could have been absolutely anyone. But he was presumably someone reasonably well-known in the church, and ancient tradition identified him as James the brother of Jesus – someone who was not a disciple during Jesus' lifetime, but who soon rose to prominence as leader of the church in Jerusalem. Some sections of the book seem to reflect an early stage in the life of the church, with no sign of later arguments about Jewish and Gentile Christians, and much of its imagery only makes sense in the context of rural Palestine. But it is written in exceedingly elegant Greek, showing knowledge of Greek literature – and what it says about 'faith and works' (2:14–26) seems to refer to arguments such as Paul used in Romans 3:28 (written about AD 57). A date of around AD 60 seems reasonable.

Bronze horse bit from Luristan dating from 800–700 BC. Although small in size, a bit is used to control a large animal. James points out that the human tongue – such a small part of the body – can do infinite damage if not kept under control.

Key passages

Hearing and doing (James 1:22–25)
Faith without works is dead (James 2:26)
The wisdom that comes from God (James 3:17–18)
Prayer, anointing and healing (James 5:14–16)

Key themes

The letter covers many aspects of practical Christian living, emphasizing that Christian belief relates to every area of life. Readers are encouraged to show integrity and to avoid double standards. Intellectual belief is not enough: it needs to make a difference in everyday behaviour. Several Old Testament characters are held up as examples of this – Abraham, Rahab, Job and Elijah – but there are also many echoes of Jesus' teaching and the Sermon on the Mount.

Hebrews

The book of Hebrews claims that Jesus was the complete fulfilment of all the Old Testament scriptures, and had a unique personal relationship to God.

The writer of the book of Hebrews states that Jesus, through his death and resurrection, is far superior to any angel.

'The Flight into Egypt' (detail), Giotto di Bondone (c.1266–1337)

Key contents

JESUS IS THE CULMINATION OF GOD'S REVELATION (CHAPTER 1:1–3)

THE UNIQUENESS OF JESUS (CHAPTERS 1:4–10:39)
Greater than the angels (chapter 1:4–14)
Gateway to salvation (chapter 2)
Superior to Moses (chapters 3:1–4:13)
Greater than Aaron (chapters 4:14–7:28)
Jesus' unique covenant and sacrifice (chapters 8–10)

FAITH AND PERSEVERANCE (CHAPTERS 11–12)
Old Testament heroes of faith (chapter 11)
Endure God's discipline (chapter 12:1–11)
The kingdom that cannot be shaken (chapter 12:12–29)

FINAL EXHORTATION, PRAYER AND GREETINGS (CHAPTER 13)

Key passages

Jesus Christ, God's final revelation (Hebrews 1:1–3)
Our sympathetic High Priest (Hebrews 3:14–16)
Christ's one great sacrifice for all time (Hebrews 10:11–14)
By faith (Hebrews chapter 11)
Jesus, the author and perfecter of faith (Hebrews 12:1–3)
Jesus Christ, the same yesterday and today and forever (Hebrews 13:8)
The great shepherd (Hebrews 13:2–21)

See also

■ Three temples (pages 160–161)

■ Groups and sects (pages 168–169)

■ New Testament religion (pages 170–171)

■ The earliest Christians (pages 172–173)

Key themes

The book of Hebrews is very difficult to understand without a detailed knowledge of the Old Testament. Not only does it contain detailed references to the worship of ancient Israel, but it singles out little-known characters such as Melchizedek for particular consideration. Many of its special concerns were also found among Jewish sects, such as the Essenes who wrote the Dead Sea Scrolls. But there are also traces of Greek philosophical concepts. These two world-views had been brought together just before the time of Jesus by Philo, a Jewish philosopher in Alexandria, and Hebrews echoes many of his themes.

The main message is clear: Christians who may be tempted to return to Judaism in order to avoid persecution would be denying their faith, for Jesus had already brought the Old Testament to its fulfilment in such a way that it no longer had any relevance or validity. Jesus is greater than any of the Old Testament institutions, in fact he has fulfilled everything that they foreshadowed, and more besides.

Author, time-scale and setting

The book of Hebrews never even hints at its author's identity, though it seems to indicate it was written by a second-generation Christian to people living in Rome. It has no connection with Paul, and is totally different from his letters in both style and ideas – nor are there any reliable ancient traditions about its author. One of its major themes is that the coming of Jesus has rendered the Jewish temple redundant, but there is no mention of its physical destruction in AD 70, which would have clinched the author's argument. Nor is there any indication of a complex form of church organization. These facts, and the nature of its readers' sufferings, suggest a date of about AD 64, towards the start of the emperor Nero's persecution of Christians. Its readers were Christians who were tempted to return to Jewish ritual practices, presumably in an effort to avoid suffering by claiming the legal protection given by the Roman empire at this time to Jews, but not to Christians.

This section of one of the Dead Sea Scrolls is part of a commentary applying the words of the seventh-century BC prophet Habakkuk to the writer's own time.

1 Peter

The first letter of Peter encourages Christians to stand firm in the face of persecution.

This palindrome (that is, a phrase which reads the same backwards as forwards) was discovered engraved on wall plaster at Cirencester, England. There are a number of ways of interpreting the palindrome which would have been understood by Christian readers. One is to read the central word 'TENET' across and down; this forms the shape of a cross and transmits the message 'HE [the creator/Christ] HOLDS'. The discovery of the same palindrome in the ruins at Pompeii demonstrates that this system was in use before AD 79.

Author, time-scale and setting

1 Peter was referred to as early as AD 96 in 1 Clement, a letter sent from the church in Rome to the Christians at Corinth. Ancient tradition identifies its author with Peter, the disciple of Jesus, and there are good reasons for believing this. Much of its language echoes the teaching of Jesus, as well as the preaching of Peter as recorded in the early chapters of Acts. It was written from Rome (referred to in code language as 'Babylon' in 1 Peter 5:13), to Christians in what is now western and northern Turkey. We have no knowledge of Peter ever visiting this area, though he did spend some time travelling in much the same way as Paul. The recipients were being persecuted, and references to the nature of their ordeal suggests a time in the early stages of Nero's persecution, therefore earlier than AD 64.

Key themes

Peter has much to say about Christians being the true inheritors of the promises contained in the Old Testament, originally made to the Jewish people. The whole letter is full of Old Testament passages which are explicitly applied to the life and belief of the

church. In the face of suffering, Peter's readers are encouraged to remember Jesus, whose life centred around suffering which was not destructive, but redemptive. In the same way, the suffering of believers can become the crucible in which faith is purified. At the same time, Peter is concerned that the values exemplified in Jesus' life should be put into practice in everyday living, and gives instructions for the way Christians should behave, with one another as well as in relation to the wider community.

Corner of temple platform, Jerusalem. Peter quotes the prophet Isaiah, likening Jesus to a chosen and precious cornerstone.

Nero was Roman emperor during AD 54–68. When a fire destroyed over half of Rome in AD 64 he blamed the Christians, sparking off a brief but fierce period of persecution. Some Christians were used as human torches to illuminate a garden party.

Jude

The brief letter from Jude deals with a threat from false teachers, and encourages its readers to resist them. In doing so, it draws on Old Testament stories of how God had punished people for unfaithfulness in the past, and threatens the same fate to Christians who refuse to change their ways.

Author, time-scale and setting

The exact circumstances addressed by Jude's letter are unclear. The heresy is described in very general terms, though the general tone of the work suggests a period when the church had developed a fixed organizational structure, and a clear understanding of the difference between 'heresy' and 'orthodoxy'. The author is said to be a brother of James, and presumably therefore the same Jude who was Jesus' brother (Mark 6:3; Matthew 13:55), but it is more likely to have been written towards the end of the first century AD. One of the distinctive features of Jude is the way it happily quotes from Jewish apocalyptic books that were never part of either the Jewish or Christian scriptures (Assumption of Moses and Apocalypse of Enoch). The passage in Jude 4–16 is closely parallel to 2 Peter 2:1–8, which many believe to have been based on it.

'Angel Standing in Storm', J.M.W. Turner (1775–1851)

2 Peter

This letter was written to combat some who taught that morality does not matter for Christians, and that Jesus Christ would not return.

Key contents

THE IMPORTANCE OF KNOWING GOD (CHAPTER 1)

FALSE TEACHERS (CHAPTER 2)

THE CERTAINTY OF CHRIST'S RETURN (CHAPTER 3)

Author, time-scale and setting

The writer announces himself as Simon Peter, and some sections have struck readers as authentic accounts from Peter himself. But the style and content is completely different from 1 Peter. Moreover, 2 Peter 2:1–8 seems to be based on Jude's letter, and there are other signs of a later date, including the reference to Paul's letters as already being 'scripture' (2 Peter 3:15–16). 2 Peter was probably the last New Testament book, written at the end of the first century AD, maybe by a group of Peter's disciples who not only valued his heritage but also incorporated some reminiscences originating with the apostle himself.

Key theme

Like Jude, 2 Peter opposes mystics who laid more emphasis on their own experiences than the facts of the Christian message. They seem to have believed that their personal spiritual exploits superseded more primitive hopes for the physical return of Jesus and a literal resurrection of the dead – neither of which had happened anyway. To this, 2 Peter replies that no one could predict such things, because God's time schedule is quite different from the way humans operate – and the delay in Jesus' second coming is a sign of God's mercy and patience.

'But the day of the Lord will come like a thief. The heavens will disappear with a roar; the elements will be destroyed by fire, and the earth and everything in it will be laid bare.'
2 Peter 3:10

See also

■ The earliest churches (pages 46–47)

■ The earliest Christians (pages 172–173)

■ Acts of the Apostles (pages 248–249)

Galatians

This letter was written to establish Paul's authority as a genuine apostle of Jesus, and to contradict the idea that non-Jews needed to convert to Judaism before they could become Christians.

Key contents

Author, time-scale and setting

No one has ever doubted that Paul wrote the letter to the Galatians – in either AD 48 (which would make it the earliest of his letters) or about AD 56, depending on what 'Galatia' means. If 'Galatia' refers to the Roman province of Galatia itself, then Paul's letter could have been sent to the churches of Lycaonia (Lystra, Derbe and Iconium) shortly after he established them in the mid-40s AD. If 'Galatia' is an ethnic term referring to people resident around Ankara (much further north), then the later date is appropriate. Either way, the context is clear: conservative Jewish Christians ('Judaizers') had infiltrated Paul's congregations, insisting that Gentiles convert to Judaism before being acceptable as Christians, and casting doubt on Paul's credentials as a true apostle. Since Paul had never mentioned any of this to them, his converts were understandably confused: some were getting circumcised, and all needed some reassurance.

Marble head of the Greek god Zeus, excavated at Dor.

Key passages

Living by faith (Galatians 2:19–21)
All one in Christ Jesus (Galatians 3:28)
God sent the Son (Galatians 4:4–5)
Freedom (Galatians 5:1)
The fruit of the spirit (Galatians 5:22–23)

Key themes

Jewish people preserved their ethnic distinctiveness by continuing to eat only kosher food, keeping the Sabbath, upholding Old Testament moral standards and maintaining the practice of circumcision. So when Paul allowed Gentiles to join the church without requiring any of these things, trouble was inevitable. In response, Paul goes back to the roots of Hebrew faith and argues that, since these laws were not as old as Abraham, they had only a limited application, and with the coming of Christ were now irrelevant.

The hills of Lycia from Antalya in modern Turkey. The southern part of Galatia meets the sea near Lycia.

1 Thessalonians

Paul wrote this letter to encourage Christians in Thessalonica, to help them come to terms with the unexpected death of some of their number.

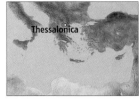
Thessalonica

Key contents

GREETING (CHAPTER 1:1)

THANKSGIVING AND FURTHER ENCOURAGEMENT (CHAPTERS 1:2–3:13)

PRACTICAL CHRISTIAN LIVING (CHAPTER 4:1–12)

TEACHING ON THE SECOND COMING OF CHRIST (CHAPTERS 4:13–5:11)

FINAL INSTRUCTIONS AND GREETINGS (CHAPTER 5:12–28)

Author, time-scale and setting

Paul, Silas and Timothy visited Thessalonica, capital of Macedonia in northern Greece, during their second missionary journey. It was a short visit, because they were forced out by local opposition. By the time Paul reached Athens he was desperate to hear how things were going, and he sent Timothy, who brought good news during Paul's stay in Corinth (AD 50 or 51). He wrote this letter in response.

Key passages

A new allegiance (1 Thessalonians 1:9–10)
Paul's mission strategy (1 Thessalonians 2:1–12)
Raising the dead (1 Thessalonians 4:15–18)
The blessing (1 Thessalonians 5:23–24)

Key themes

1 Thessalonians was written about six months after these people became Christians, and Paul expresses his pleasure at the progress they had made in both understanding their faith and putting it into practice. His main message to them is one of praise and encouragement to continue as they had begun. One important question had arisen: what was the fate of those who died before the second coming of Christ? Paul alludes to Jesus' own teaching about this, and discourages pointless speculation, but assures his readers that the dead will rise – and advises them to be constantly ready for Jesus' return, whenever it might be.

The arch of Galerius straddled the Ignatian Way, a major Roman road, as it passed through Thessalonica. Thessalonica was the principal city of Macedonia during the time of Alexander the Great.

2 Thessalonians

The Thessalonian Christians misunderstood what Paul wrote in his first letter about Christ's second coming, and this second letter informs them more fully about what is to come.

Key contents

GREETINGS AND COMMENDATION OF THE THESSALONIAN CHRISTIANS (CHAPTER 1)

DAYS OF EVIL WILL PRECEDE CHRIST'S RETURN (CHAPTER 2:1–12)

PAUL REASSURES HIS READERS (CHAPTERS 2:13–3:5)

ADVICE ON PRACTICAL CHRISTIAN LIVING (CHAPTER 3:6–15)

PERSONAL POSTSCRIPT (CHAPTER 3:16–18)

Excavations of a Roman agora in Thessaloniki, Greece.

Key themes

Forged letters had appeared, claiming that Christ had already returned, and Paul responds by detailing some of the events that would surround the return of Christ: the arrival of an antichrist figure, and social upheavals. Some Christians were so caught up by future speculation that they stopped working and expected others to fund them. Paul condemns that, and stresses that even Christian belief is worthless if it has no practical outworking in everyday life.

See also

■ The journeys of Paul (pages 44–45)

■ The earliest churches (pages 46–47)

■ The earliest Christians (pages 172–173)

■ Acts of the Apostles (pages 248–249)

1 Corinthians

In this letter Paul responds to news and questions from the church he had founded at Corinth.

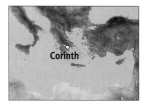
Corinth

Key contents

Paul remarked that the Christian life which did not display love was nothing more than a noisy gong or cymbal.

Time-scale and setting

Paul worked in Corinth for 18 months during AD 50–51, but he was in Ephesus when he received the news that provoked this letter. It was not the first letter he wrote to the Christians at Corinth, but forms part of a more extensive correspondence between AD 54 and 57, as follows:

News from Corinth
Letter 1 (mentioned in 1 Corinthians 5:11)
More news, and questions from Corinth
Letter 2 (1 Corinthians)
Paul visits Corinth (threatened in 1 Corinthians 4:21; reported in 2 Corinthians 2:1; 12:14; 13:1)
Letter 3 (mentioned in 2 Corinthians 2:4)
More news (2 Corinthians 7:15–16)
Letter 4 (2 Corinthians)

1 Corinthians seems to have had little effect, hence Paul's visit to Corinth and further letters. Eventually Titus reported to Paul that the Corinthians had taken his appeals to heart, and 2 Corinthians is a more relaxed letter – at least up to chapter 9. But chapters 10–13 present another vigorous defence of his authority. Some believe that 2 Corinthians is in fact an anthology of the other letters, which otherwise would be presumed lost, with letter 1 being 2 Corinthians 6:14–7:1, letter 3 being 2 Corinthians 10–13, and letter 4 being 2 Corinthians 1–9.

Key passages

The message of Christ crucified
(1 Corinthians 1:18, 23–25)
We are God's building
(1 Corinthians 3:10–15)
I have become all things to all people
(1 Corinthians 9:19–22)
This is my body: the bread and the wine
(1 Corinthians 11:23–25)
You are the body of Christ, each one a part (1 Corinthians 12:27–31)
If I speak in the tongues of mortals and of angels, but have not love
(1 Corinthians 13:1–13)
The truth of Christ's resurrection
(1 Corinthians 15:20–21)
Death, where is your sting?
(1 Corinthians 15:51–57)

Paul instructed the Christians at Corinth how to eat the Lord's supper. The bread was to represent the broken body of Christ, and the wine his blood.

Key themes

Corinth stood at the junction of many trade routes, and was a thoroughly cosmopolitan city with a great mixture of cultures and lifestyles. When Paul took the gospel there, even those who became Christians understood it in different ways, depending on their background and origins. They included Jews and Gentiles, and a variety of religious traditions, ranging from the conservative and traditional to the mystical and philosophical. What some regarded as acceptable behaviour was gross immorality to others, and this was the root of most of the problems Paul had to address. Coupled with an attitude of spiritual superiority among more than one group, chaos and division were threatening to engulf the young Christian community.

2 Corinthians

This letter documents Paul's struggles with his apparent inability to bring order out of chaos in one of his largest churches.

Key passages

The letter kills, but the Spirit gives life (2 Corinthians 3:5–6)
Growing more like Jesus (2 Corinthians 3:17–18)
Whoever is in Christ becomes a new creation (2 Corinthians 5:17–21)
God loves a cheerful giver (2 Corinthians 9:6–10)
Paul's hardships (2 Corinthians 11:16–33)
Taken up to the third heaven (2 Corinthians 12:1–10)
The grace (2 Corinthians 13:14)

Key themes

This letter has many echoes – conscious and unconscious – of the Old Testament prophet Jeremiah who, like Paul, struggled with the pain of ministry, while experiencing a strong sense of God's calling. Frustrated by his inability to convince the Corinthians of the need to follow his previous advice, and angered by their claim that he was more impressive in writing than in person, Paul repeatedly explores the nature of human weakness, and returns constantly to the theme that effective ministry can be exercised only through the empowerment of God's Holy Spirit. He takes comfort from the fact that Jesus himself suffered, and challenges his readers to abandon their mistaken identification of human power with the work of God.

Large terracotta storage jars from Jerusalem, dating from Roman times. Paul wrote to the Corinthians that God gives them spiritual treasure, but yet 'we who have this spiritual treasure are like common clay pots, in order to show that the supreme power belongs to God, not us' (2 Corinthians 4:7).

Temple of Apollo at Corinth, Greece.

See also

■ The journeys of Paul
(pages 44–45)

■ The earliest churches
(pages 46–47)

■ The earliest Christians
(pages 172–173)

■ The Acts of the Apostles
(pages 248–249)

Romans

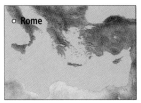
○ Rome

P aul's letter to the Romans has been one of the most influential of all the New Testament books, and down through the centuries it has inspired many of the greatest Christian leaders. In it, Paul sets out some of the key elements in his understanding of Christian faith.

Key passages

The power of the gospel (Romans 1:16–17)
God's grace meets human need (Romans 3:23–24)
Justified through faith (Romans 5:1)
Wages of sin and gift of life (Romans 6:23)
The new life of freedom (Romans 8:1–2)
Nothing can separate us from the love of God in Christ (Romans 8:35–39)
A living sacrifice – the true offering (Romans 12:1–2)

Time-scale and setting

No one has ever doubted that Paul wrote this letter: it has all the hallmarks of his way of expressing himself, and his characteristic concerns about Gentile and Jewish Christians.

Towards the end of his dealings with the church at Corinth, Paul paid a visit to that city and stayed for about three months. During this period, he wrote this letter to the Christians in Rome, which dates it to AD 57. Romans is the only letter he wrote to a church that neither he nor his co-workers had founded, and he goes to some pains to emphasize that he was not wishing to interfere. It is unclear exactly who did first take Christianity to Rome, but the fact that this city was the capital of the Roman empire gave it a strategic importance unlike any other. At the point of writing, Paul was planning to return to Jerusalem to present the Christians there with the collection of money he had been taking among his own churches in Greece and Asia Minor. Then he would head for Rome, before extending his mission further west into Spain.

This was a crucial moment in his ministry. He had recently come through a series of painful experiences, especially in Galatia and Corinth, and his message had been both contradicted and misunderstood. He knew he needed to clarify his own thoughts on what had become matters of controversy. He was also aware that his reputation in both Jerusalem and Rome had been tarnished by his opponents, who had given what he regarded as a false account of his teachings, especially in regard to his attitude over the Jewish law. He wrote the letter to the Romans to spell out a balanced account of these matters. This was

Key contents

GREETING, PRAYER AND INTRODUCTION (CHAPTER 1:1–15)

THE GOOD NEWS OF JESUS CHRIST (CHAPTERS 1:16–8:39)
Brief statement of the theme (chapter 1:16–17)
Humankind's need for God (chapters 1:18–3:20)
God's gift of salvation (chapters 3:21–4:25)
The centrality of faith (chapter 5)
The work of the Holy Spirit (chapters 6–8)

GOD'S PLAN FOR ISRAEL (CHAPTERS 9–11)

THE CHRISTIAN WAY OF LIFE (CHAPTERS 12:1–15:13)
The shared Christian life (chapter 12)
Duties to the state and to other people (chapter 13)
Questions of Christian conscience (chapters 14:1–15:13)

CLOSING WORDS AND GREETINGS (CHAPTERS 15:14–16:27)
Paul's reason for writing (chapter 15:14–33)
Greetings and instructions (chapter 16:1–24)

A CLOSING PRAYER OF PRAISE (CHAPTER 16:25–27)

how he would defend himself to the more conservative Jewish Christians in Jerusalem – and hopefully the letter itself would undermine the opposition in Rome before he arrived in the city.

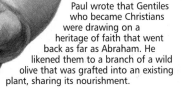
Paul wrote that Gentiles who became Christians were drawing on a heritage of faith that went back as far as Abraham. He likened them to a branch of a wild olive that was grafted into an existing plant, sharing its nourishment.

Key themes

Romans is not a comprehensive account of the whole of Paul's theology. It says nothing about the second coming of Christ or the end times, and very little about the church. It is entirely related to Paul's understanding of the promises given to ancient Israel through Abraham, and how Gentile believers in Christ could become full members of God's covenant people without needing to convert to Judaism first. These questions were especially important in Rome, because the church itself seems to have consisted of a series of separate house churches, and there is some evidence to suggest they were divided theologically in relation to this question. In tackling it, Paul repeats all the arguments he put forward in Galatians, though he includes in addition a much longer section showing that the inclusion of Gentiles did not displace the promises to the Jews, but would actually be a means of them being fulfilled.

Some of Paul's opponents had questioned how his Gentile converts could have acceptable moral standards if they did not obey the Old Testament laws, and Paul also tackles this matter more fully by pointing out that, though Christians did not need the law – not even the Ten Commandments – the maintenance of God's standards would be assured by the work of the Holy Spirit in their lives.

Like some of Paul's other letters, Romans falls neatly into two halves: in the first part, Paul deals with theological issues, and then in the second section he applies all this to practical matters and shows how belief ought to relate to the way Christians live.

See also

■ The journeys of Paul
(pages 44–45)

■ The earliest churches
(pages 46–47)

■ Israel's faith
(pages 150–151)

■ The earliest Christians
(pages 172–173)

■ Acts of the Apostles
(pages 248–249)

Via Sacra, Roman forum, Rome, Italy

Philippians

Paul wrote this letter to thank his friends in Philippi for supporting his ministry.

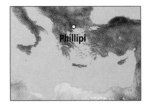

Key contents

GREETING AND THANKSGIVING (CHAPTER 1:1–11)

NEWS AND FUTURE HOPES (CHAPTER 1:12–26)

FOLLOWING JESUS' EXAMPLE (CHAPTERS 1:27–2:18)

TIMOTHY AND EPAPHRODITUS (CHAPTER 2:19–30)

PAUL'S PRIORITIES (CHAPTER 3)

INSTRUCTIONS, AND THANKS FOR A GIFT (CHAPTER 4:1–20)

FINAL GREETINGS (CHAPTER 4:21–23)

Time-scale and setting

The city of Philippi was home to retired Roman soldiers and civil servants, and the first place in Europe Paul established a church. Epaphroditus had visited Paul in prison, bringing a gift from the Philippian Christians, and this letter was Paul's response – written either about AD 62 during his final imprisonment in Rome, or in about AD 55 from prison in Ephesus.

Key passages

To live is Christ (Philippians 1:20–24)
A hymn praising Christ (Philippians 2:5–11)
Running the race (Philippians 3:12–14)
God's peace (Philippians 4:4–7)
Whatever is true (Philippians 4:8)

Key themes

Paul wrote to the Philippians in order to thank them for the gift they had sent him, and to commend Epaphroditus to them. But he used the opportunity to express his affection for this church and his delight in its spiritual progress. He seems to have sensed that his own death might be near, yet his spirit is undaunted and the words 'joy' and 'rejoice' occur many times. The prospect of death encourages him to reflect on life's priorities.

This Roman crypt in Philippi, Greece, may have been the place of Paul's imprisonment.

Colossians

Paul wrote to the Colossians to correct false ideas about the identity of Jesus.

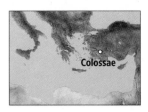

Key contents

GREETING AND THANKSGIVING (CHAPTER 1:1–8)

THE COSMIC CHRIST (CHAPTERS 1:9–2:10)

ERRORS IN THE CHURCH (CHAPTER 2:11–19)

NEW LIFE IN CHRIST (CHAPTERS 2:20–4:6)

FINAL GREETINGS (CHAPTER 4:7–18)

The Lysus valley, looking towards Colossae, Turkey.

Time-scale and setting

The church in Colossae was founded by Epaphras, one of Paul's converts in nearby Ephesus. Paul wrote in response to concerns expressed by Epaphras, who was with him in prison – either as a visitor or under arrest himself. As with Philippians, the date depends on where Paul was imprisoned at the time.

Key passages

A hymn in praise of the cosmic Christ (Colossians 1:15–20)
You have been raised with Christ (Colossians 3:1–4)
Whatever you do, it is Christ you are serving (Colossians 3:23–24)

Key themes

Speculation in Colossae about how Jesus related to spiritual entities worshipped in the mystery religions led Paul to reflect on Jesus' significance in cosmic terms. He affirms that, whatever spiritual powers there might be, Jesus is more powerful than them all. Greek philosophy had insisted that the spiritual world could have no contact with the material, and some in Colossae accepted this and were adopting ascetic practices to try to put down their bodies so that their spirits might be set free. Paul condemns this, and denies that there is any separation between the two, because Jesus was both fully divine and yet also fully human.

Philemon

T his brief letter from Paul was addressed to Philemon, a leader of the church at Colossae.

Key theme and setting

Onesimus, one of Philemon's slaves, had absconded, but met Paul in prison, and became a Christian. Under Roman law, the penalty for a runaway slave could be death. But Paul sent him back to Philemon and wrote this warm letter inviting his master to set him free so he could return to help Paul.

Onesimus himself may have carried this short letter, along with Colossians, from Paul's prison to Colossae. Some think he was the one who first gathered Paul's letters together, which is why this personal note was included.

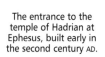

In New Testament times, although slaves were not generally ill-treated, they were considered the property of their masters. This Roman slave-badge reads 'Seize me if I should try to escape and send me back to my master.'

The entrance to the temple of Hadrian at Ephesus, built early in the second century AD.

Ephesians

I n this letter Paul celebrates the unity which Christ brings to all creation.

Ephesus

Key contents

INTRODUCTION (CHAPTER 1:1–2)

GOD'S GREAT PLAN OF UNITY (CHAPTERS 1:3–3:21)
The unity of creation and the fullness of Christ (chapter 1:3–23)
Life in Christ (chapter 2:1–10)
Jews and Gentiles made one (chapter 2:11–22)
Paul's role in announcing God's plan (chapter 3:1–13)
A prayer (chapter 3:14–21)

CHRISTIANS' SHARED LIVES (CHAPTERS 4:1–6:20)
Life in the body of Christ (chapter 4:1–16)
Practical Christian living (chapters 4:17–5:20)
Household relationships (chapters 5:21–6:9)
The armour of God (chapter 6:10–20)

FINAL GREETINGS (CHAPTER 6:21–24)

See also

■ The journeys of Paul (pages 44–45)

■ The earliest churches (pages 46–47)

■ The earliest Christians (pages 172–173)

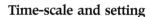

Diana was a fertility symbol and the patron goddess of Ephesus. The silversmiths of the city made small models of the goddess, and feared that the spread of the Christian message would damage their trade.

Time-scale and setting

Ephesians is different from Paul's other letters, and the best ancient manuscripts omit the words 'at Ephesus' in the opening sentence. Surprisingly, it has no specific references to events or people in the Ephesian church, even though Paul knew it well. Some think it was a circular letter sent to several churches, and written while Paul was a prisoner in Rome around AD 62. Others believe that its style and contents are so different from Paul's other letters that it must have been written long after his death by one of his admirers.

Key passages

Saved by God's grace, through faith (Ephesians 2:8–10)
Paul's prayer for love (Ephesians 3:14–21)
Reaching the stature of Christ (Ephesians 4:12–16)
Put on the full armour of God (Ephesians 6:10–17)

Key themes

Ephesians covers similar ground to Colossians, but without the immediate local references found there. This is a more discursive, reflective treatment of the way all things find their unity in Christ – including the church, the races (Jews and Gentiles) and the extended family of the Roman household, as well as the entire cosmos.

The pastoral letters   1 Timothy

Paul's letters to Timothy and Titus are known as the 'pastoral letters'. Timothy and Titus were both associates of Paul in his missionary work, and others who were Paul's co-workers are also referred to in these letters.

Timothy was taken on as a colleague by Paul when still a shy young man. In this letter he appears in the demanding role of leader of the church in Ephesus, facing the challenge of false teaching and internal dissension within the Christian community.

Time-scale and setting

The pastoral letters appear to have been written while Paul was in prison, but it is difficult to fit them into the framework of his ministry as we know it from the book of Acts, and as it can be inferred from Paul's other letters. This difficulty led some second-century church leaders to imagine that the letters must have been written after Paul's final imprisonment in Rome – assuming that he was released after his trial before Nero, and went on to the further travels he had originally intended after visiting Rome. But there is no evidence for this, and it is now widely assumed that these letters were written some time after Paul's death, perhaps incorporating materials extracted from other, shorter letters he wrote on more personal matters.

They certainly assume a more bureaucratic form of church structure than was in existence in Paul's day, with Timothy and Titus occupying positions more like the role of later clergy, and formal qualifications for appointment to church offices spelled out quite precisely. This is a definite shift away from the more informal networks of leaders mentioned in Paul's undisputed letters, whose status seems to depend not on appointment to an office, but is related to their spiritual discernment, as well as their natural skills and talents.

Some of Paul's favourite words still appear here, but are used in different ways. For example, 'faith' is not so much a matter of personal trust in Christ, but indicates a fixed body of Christian beliefs, handed on from one generation to another. Other key themes, such as the hope of Christ's return, are also more muted here, while there are several technical terms that Paul never used but which were popular two or three generations later. For all these reasons, there is widespread agreement that these letters must have been written near the end of the first century AD, by an admirer of Paul who wanted to update and reinterpret his teaching for the needs of a different age.

Key contents

GREETING (CHAPTER 1:1–2)

FALSE TEACHING (CHAPTER 1:3–11)

PAUL AND TIMOTHY (CHAPTER 1:12–20)

PRAYER AND WORSHIP (CHAPTER 2)

LEADERSHIP IN THE CHURCH (CHAPTER 3)

HOW TO COUNTER FALSE TEACHING (CHAPTER 4)

SERVING PEOPLE OF ALL KINDS (CHAPTERS 5:1–6:2)

REAL WEALTH (CHAPTER 6:3–10)

PERSONAL INSTRUCTION (CHAPTER 6:11–21)

Key passages

Christ Jesus came into the world to save sinners
(1 Timothy 1:15–16)
Godliness with contentment is great gain (1 Timothy 6:6)
The love of money is a root of all kinds of evil (1 Timothy 6:10)

Key themes

The pastoral letters have always been especially valued by those who occupy officially appointed positions in the churches. There is no trace of anything resembling the later concept of ordained ministry in Paul's earlier letters or the book of Acts, but 1 Timothy gives close, practical attention to the character required for Christian ministry and instructions on how to conduct relationships with different groups of people in the churches. The writer also highlights the ministry of teaching as the best way to maintain the purity of church life.

Timothy was leader of the church at Ephesus when Paul wrote to him. This splendidly ornate entrance was part of the Library of Celsus at Ephesus.

2 Timothy

On death row, Paul reflects on his own experiences as a way of encouraging Timothy to persevere in the Christian ministry.

Key contents

GREETING (CHAPTER 1:1–2)

I THANK GOD (CHAPTER 1:3–18)

A WORKER FOR JESUS CHRIST (CHAPTER 2)

TROUBLED TIMES AHEAD (CHAPTER 3)

FINAL INSTRUCTIONS AND GREETINGS (CHAPTER 4)

Painting of the vase given as a prize at the Panthenon games, 500–480 BC. Paul reminds Timothy that the winner of a race has to compete according to the rules.

Key passages

The Spirit God has given (2 Timothy 1:7)
The inspired Scriptures (2 Timothy 3:15–17)
I have fought the good fight (2 Timothy 4:6–8)

Key themes

This letter repeats the same themes as the other pastoral letters, though with a growing sense of hostility to the church in the wider culture. The work of Christian leaders in this context needs to be focused on helping church members to believe the correct things and behave properly, rather than trying to convert those outside.

Titus

Titus was the leader of the church on Crete, needing similar advice to Timothy in the face of the same challenges.

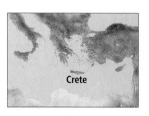

Crete

Key contents

GREETING (CHAPTER 1:1–4)

THE KIND OF LEADER THE CHURCH NEEDS (CHAPTER 1:5–16)

THE QUALITIES OF A TEACHER (CHAPTER 2)

PRACTICAL CHRISTIAN LIVING (CHAPTER 3:1–11)

FINAL INSTRUCTIONS (CHAPTER 3:12–15)

See also

■ The journeys of Paul (pages 44–45)

■ The earliest churches (pages 46–47)

■ The earliest Christians (pages 172–173)

■ The Acts of the Apostles (pages 248–249)

Key passage

The gospel in miniature (Titus 3:4–7)

Key themes

Like 1 Timothy and 2 Timothy, this letter is primarily concerned with the character of Christian clergy and the practical conduct of their ministry. At the heart of these mundane instructions, the author has inserted one of the most comprehensive summaries of Paul's message, maybe in the apostle's own words (Titus 3:4–7).

Examples of Roman writing instruments. The wooden pen-case with quill pens was discovered in Egypt with remains of black ink in its well. The hanging bronze ink pot was recovered from the River Tiber.

1 John

This letter was written to Christians who were arguing about Christian doctrine, especially matters related to beliefs about Jesus.

Author, time-scale and setting

The letters of John are clearly related to the gospel of John: similar themes keep occurring, and the language and style are the same. They are widely believed to have been composed by the same author, and sent to the same Christian community. Neither letters nor gospel give any unambiguous indication of their author, apart from his self-designation as 'elder' in 2 and 3 John. This term was very widely applied in the early church, though Papias in the early second century AD refers to an 'elder John' in Ephesus (the likely origin of these books). Some take this to indicate a second- or third-generation Christian leader, though Papias applies the same term to some of Jesus' original disciples. There is a tradition that John the apostle lived to a great age in Ephesus and penned these letters towards the end of his life. Whoever was their author, there is no doubt that they belong at the very end of the first century, as the topics with which they deal did not become problematic until then. They are all to be dated sometime between AD 90 and 100. It is difficult to say with certainty which order the various books were written in, but its contents may imply that 2 John was first, followed by 1 John, with 3 John and John's gospel slightly later, as a more extensive way of addressing the situation. Stylistically, 1 John is quite different from Paul's letters, and though it refers to particular people and episodes it is more like a sustained theological argument than a real letter.

John encouraged his readers to walk in the light, as God is in the light. This oil lamp dating from New Testament times depicts a menorah.

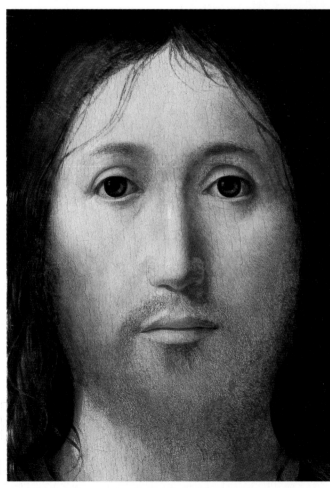

John wrote as one who knew Jesus personally.

'Christ blessing',
Antonello da Messina
(active 1456, died 1479)

Key contents

THE THEME STATED (CHAPTER 1:1–4)

LIGHT AND DARKNESS (CHAPTERS 1:5–2:17)

TRUTH AND FALSEHOOD (CHAPTERS 2:18–4:21)

FAITH IN CHRIST (CHAPTER 5:1–12)

CLOSING INSTRUCTIONS (CHAPTER 5:13–21)

Key passages

Walking in the light (1 John 1:5–10)
God's love and ours (1 John 4:7–12)
Life through God's Son (1 John 5:10–12)

Key themes

John's gospel has much more to say than the synoptic gospels on the topic of beliefs about Christ (Christology), and this is a major theme of 1 John also. The church being addressed was suffering serious divisions as a result of arguments about whether Jesus was both human and divine. This question originated from the Greek idea that the worlds of matter and spirit were completely separate from and incompatible with one another – thereby making it impossible for anyone, including Jesus, to be part of both worlds at one and the same time. The troublemakers addressed in 1 John were arguing that the spiritual Christ had only seemed to be human, entering into Jesus of Nazareth at the baptism and departing before the crucifixion. That way they avoided the notion that God could either become human or suffer. As a consequence, they argued that Christian faith should focus on the spiritual Christ, not on the human Jesus – and communication with the spirit world could come only through mystical experiences of the sort they were having, and which in their opinion marked them out as superior to other Christians whose faith was more earth-bound. These people came to be known as 'Docetists' (from the Greek word meaning 'to seem').

1 John challenges these views by arguing that true Christian faith is firmly rooted

2 and 3 John

These books both follow the stylistic form of real Greek letters, and belong to different stages of an ongoing argument.

Key themes

2 John addresses 'the elect lady and her children', which in this context is probably a way of saying 'the church and her members'. It warns against accepting false teachers coming in from outside. The general nature of this warning suggests it might have been the first letter written, and when it was ignored the more extended theological treatment of 1 John became necessary. Both 1 John and 3 John refer to groups who had left the church, or started their own rival gatherings, so things only seem to have got worse. There is no indication in the New Testament as to what the eventual outcome was.

John talks much about living in the light and the truth. Here the artist has reversed the roles of Jesus and Pontius Pilate, portraying Pilate standing in the light as he asks his prisoner the question: 'What is truth?'

'What is truth?', Nicolai N. Ge (1831–1894)

See also

■ The earliest churches
(pages 46–47)

■ The earliest Christians
(pages 172–173)

■ John
(pages 250–251)

in the belief that in Jesus God became a real human person, as well as remaining divine. And furthermore, Christians must live as Jesus did, demonstrating true openness and love in all their relationships. The Docetists were failing on both counts. These points are not made in a linear, logical way, and the author moves in and out of different aspects of the argument, in much the same way as a musical composer might have a central theme which is explored through different variations. In the process, he picks up many of the favourite key words and phrases of his opponents, and reinterprets them in the light of his own understanding of true Christianity.

'We love because God first loved us. If we say we love God, but hate our brothers and sisters, we are liars. For people cannot love God, whom they have not seen, if they do not love their brothers and sisters, whom they have seen. The command that Christ has given us is this: all who love God must love their brother or sister also.'
(1 John 4:19–21)

Revelation

This book is completely different from anything else in the New Testament. Its powerful visions celebrate God's final victory over all the forces of evil, and have inspired many great artists through the centuries.

This statue of the Roman emperor Domitian Promulgator was discovered in Seville, Spain.

Author and time-scale

According to Irenaeus, Bishop of Lyons, writing in about AD 180, this book was written towards the end of the reign of the Roman emperor Domitian (AD 81–96). There is no reason to doubt this: Revelation was obviously written at a time when Christians were undergoing fierce persecution, which seems to have included the demand to worship the emperor as divine – all of which happened under Domitian. We can therefore date the book to about AD 95 or 96.

Deciding on the book's author is less straightforward. He identifies himself only as 'John', and some second-century traditions link him with John the apostle. At the time the book was written, the author was on the island of Patmos in the Aegean Sea, presumably as a prisoner doing hard labour in the quarries there. There is no evidence that John the apostle ever suffered this fate. Nor are there any obvious literary connections between Revelation and the gospel or letters of John, whose style and language is quite different. At the same time, some themes are common, notably the description of Jesus as 'the Word', found only in Revelation and John's writings. One of the churches addressed in Revelation is Ephesus, and some believe this city was home to an extensive school of Christian thinkers inspired and established by John the apostle. Maybe different members of this group were responsible for all these books.

Sardis

Laodicea

Key passages

Christ in glory (Revelation 1:12–18)
Christ at the door (Revelation 3:20)
God enthroned (Revelation 4)
The four horsemen (Revelation 9:13–21)
Hymn of the victors (Revelation 15:2–4)
A new heaven and a new earth (Revelation 21)
The bright morning star (Revelation 22:16–17)

The acropolis at Pergamum.

Roman agora at Smyrna

Letters to the seven churches

The first section of Revelation is quite different from the remainder of the book, and consists of letters to churches located in the same area of Asia Minor: Pergamum, Thyatira, Sardis, Smyrna, Ephesus, Philadelphia and Laodicea. But they are letters with a difference, written as if coming from the risen Christ though addressing specific concerns in each of these cities. Each letter shows close knowledge of local issues, and the different challenges faced by Christians in these various places. In each case, they are encouraged to remain faithful to the gospel, and not to be diverted from their task of calling others to follow Jesus.

The visions

This is the major part of the book, and serves the same purpose as the letters, though in a more cryptic way. These visions belong to the tradition of apocalyptic writing that became popular in Judaism in the years following the Maccabean conflict. As with the Old Testament book of Daniel, so here there is much symbolism and the use of secret code language. The identity of the beast with the number 666 has been much debated, though it probably referred to one of the Roman emperors, maybe Nero ('Babylon' is certainly a code word for the Roman empire).

Suffering Christians are encouraged by the message that this world in which evil seems to reign is not the only world, nor is it the most significant. What God is doing – sometimes unseen and unheralded – is the key to the meaning of life and the future of the world. When viewed from God's perspective, even the present violent suffering looks different. The days of evil are already numbered as a result of

Jesus' death and resurrection, and the visions contain a series of vivid pictures depicting how God will finally crush those wicked forces that now seem to have the upper hand. The details of the visions are not meant to be understood individually, but are rather part of the graphic portrayal of their overarching message: that God's sovereign power has encouraged and sustained persecuted Christians throughout history, and however much power the persecutors may seem to have, their days are ultimately numbered. The final picture is of Christ victorious, his people vindicated, and all evil destroyed, and the book closes with a powerful description of heaven, where those who are faithful will enjoy God's presence forever and all pain and evil have been vanquished.

See also

■ Greek and Roman empires (pages 36–37)

■ The earliest churches (pages 46–47)

■ Daniel (pages 232–233)

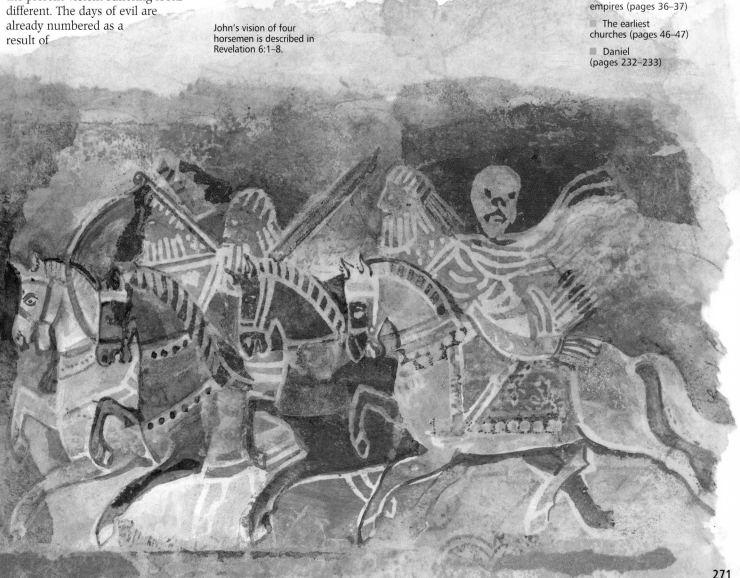

John's vision of four horsemen is described in Revelation 6:1–8.

271

Part 6: Picture acknowledgments

Abbreviations:
t = top, tl = top left, tc = top centre, tr =
top right, c = centre,
cl = centre left, cr = centre right
b = bottom, bl = bottom left,
bc = bottom centre, br = bottom right

Illustrations

DA = David Atkinson,
GH = Gwyn Hughes, RN = Rex
Nicholls, JS = Joshua Smith,
LS = Linda Smith

Photographs

JA = Jon Arnold, ZR = Zev Radovan,
DT = David Townsend,

page

194–195*c* Main illustration: DA

195*br* Illustration: DA

196–197 View from Sinai: JA

197*tr* Sistine Chapel ceiling:
'Creation of Adam', 1510 by
Michelangelo Buonarroti
(1475–1564) Vatican Museums
and Galleries, Vatican City,
Italy/Bridgeman Art Library,
London/New York

198*c* 'Adam and Eve banished
from Paradise' *(detail)* by
Tommaso Masaccio (1401–28)
Brancacci Chapel, Santa Maria del
Carmine, Florence, Italy/
Bridgeman Art Library, London

199*cl* Bethel: JA

199*cr* Mount Ararat: ZR

199*bl* Model granary: Ashmolean
Museum, Oxford

200*tr* Wall painting: ZR

200*bl* River Nile: JA

200–201*b* 'Israel in Egypt', 1867 by
Sir Edward John Poynter
(1836–1919) Guildhall Art
Gallery, Corporation of
London/Bridgeman Art Library,
London/New York

201*l* Oasis of Paran, ZR

202*cl* Phylactery: ZR

202*bl* Egyptian painting:
Ashmolean Museum, Oxford

202–203*b* Apis: Ashmolean
Museum, Oxford

203*tr* Bronze snake: ZR

203*cl* 'The Scapegoat' by William
Holman Hunt (1827–1910) Lady
Lever Art Gallery, Port Sunlight/
Bridgeman Art Library, London/
New York Board of Trustees:
National Galleries on Merseyside

204–205 Jerusalem: JA

206*t* Ivory plaque: ZR

206*bl* 'High place', Gezer: Lion
Publishing/DT

206*r* Ram's horn trumpet:RN

207*cr* Jezreel plain: JA

208*tr* Shepherd: GH

208*cr* United monarchy: Roger
Kent/Matt Buckley

208*br* Shiloh: ZR

209*br* 'David and Jonathan' by
Giovanni Battista Cima da
Conegliano (*c.* 1459–1518):
© National Gallery, London

210*cr* Gold armlet: Lion
Publishing/David Alexander

210*b* Kings of Israel: Roger
Kent/Matt Buckley

211*tl* Panel: ZR

211*cr* Bronze ring: ZR

211*bc* Hazael: Musee du Louvre,
Photo R.M.N., Chuzeville

212*tc* Seal: ZR

212*b* Kings of Judah: Roger
Kent/Matt Buckley

212*c* 'The Visit of the Queen of
Sheba to King Solomon' by
Sir Edward John Poynter:
(1836–1919) Superstock Ltd

213*cl* Hazor: Lion Publishing/DT

213*bl* Seal: ZR

214*tr* Hills of Moab: JA

214–215*b* Winged lion: Photo:
AKG/Erich Lessing/Collection
Musee du Louvre

215*c* Gold jewellery: Photo ©
Michael Holford/Collection
British Museum

215*cr* Tomb of King Xerxes: ZR

216–217 Lake Galilee: JA

218*tl* Illustrations of the Book
of Job: 'Satan Smiting Job with
Boils', 1825 by William Blake
(1757–1827) Private Collection/
Bridgeman Art Library,
London/New York

218*br* Mount Sinai: JA

219*cr* Rowing boat: JA

219*br* Orange orchard: JA

220*tr* Desert flowers: JA

220–221*b* Stream, Banyas: JA

221*cr* Stone fragments: RN

222–223 Nahal Zin: JA

224*tc* Panel from couch: ZR

224*bl* Prisoners: Lion Publishing

224*br* Plumb line: LS

225*tr* Illustration: LS

225*b* Astarte: ZR

226*c* Inscription: ZR

226–227*b* Main illustration: LS

227*tl* Lachish relief: ZR

227*tr* Record: ZR

228*c* Illustration: LS

229*tc* Fig tree: JA

229*b* Illustration: LS

230–231 Main illustration: LS

231*tl* 'The Prophet Jeremiah
Lamenting the Destruction of
Jerusalem' by Rembrandt van
Rijn (1606–69): Rijksmuseum
Amsterdam

231*b* Bulla: ZR

232*tr* Illustration: LS

232*bc* Sheep: JA

233*bl* Illustration: LS

233*br* 'Belshazzar's Feast', 1820
by John Martin (1789–1854)
Christie's Images/Bridgeman Art
Library, London/New York

234*tr* Assyrian relief: ZR

234–235 Illustration: LS

236*tr* Bronze decoration: ZR

236*bl* Illustration: LS

237*cl* Mountains of Jordan: JA

237*bl* Phoenician merchant ship:
Lion Publishing

238–239 Acropolis: JA

240*tr* Coin: Lion Publishing/
Collection British Museum

240*bl* Gerasa: Sonia Halliday
Photographs/Jane Taylor

241*cl* Map: DA

242–243 Lake Galilee: JA

244*tr* Lake Galilee: ZR

244*bc* Boat: ZR

245*tr* Herod's family tomb: Lion
Publishing/DT

245*cr* 'The Entry into Jerusalem'
c. 1305 (fresco) by Ambrogio
Bondone Giotto (*c.* 1266–1337)
Scrovegni Chapel, Padua/
Bridgeman Art Library,
London/New York

245*b* Machaerus: RN

246*l* Lake Galilee: JA

247*tr* Donkey: JA

247*cl* Judean desert: ZR

247*bl* Gethsemane: JA

248*b* 'The Last Supper' by
Leonardo da Vinci: Superstock Ltd

249*t* Via Sacra, Rome: JA

249*c* Roman grain ship: Lion
Publishing/Mark Astle

249*bl* Antioch, Pisidia: Sonia
Halliday Photographs

250*c* Temple: JA

250–151*b* Antonia Fortress: RN

251*tl* Grapes: Roger Kent

251*tr* Via Dolorosa: JA

251*cl* 'The Raising of Lazarus'
c. 1305 by Ambrogio Bondone
Giotto (*c.* 1266–1337) Scrovegni
Chapel, Padua/Bridgeman Art
Library, London/New York

251*cr* Olive trees: JA

252–253 View from Acro
Corinth: JA

254*tl* Painting: Scala, Florence

254*tr* Golden earring: ZR

254*b* Bronze horse bit:
Ashmolean Museum, Oxford

255*tr* 'The Flight into Egypt'
(detail) by Giotto di Bondone
(*c.* 1266–1337): Superstock Ltd

255*br* Dead Sea Scroll: ZR

256*tc* Palindrome: Corinium
Museum, Cirencester

256*cr* Temple platform: Lion
Publishing/David Townsend

256*bc* Nero: JA

257*bl* 'Angel Standing in Storm'
by J.M.W. Turner (1775–1851):
Superstock Ltd

258*tr* Map: JS

258*c* Zeus: ZR

258*b* Hills of Lycia: JA

259*tc* Map: JS

259*cr* Agora, Thessaloniki: JA

259*br* Arch of Galerius: Lion
Publishing/Mark Astle

260*tc* Map: JS

260*tr* Cymbal: RN

260*bc* Bread and wine: RN

260–261*bl* Temple of Apollo,
Corinth: JA

261*bl* Storage jars: ZR

262*tc* Map: JS

262*bc* Olive branch: Roger Kent

262–263*b* Via Sacra, Rome: JA

264*t* Maps: JS

264*c* Lysus valley: JA

264*bc* Roman crypt, Philippi: JA

265*tr* Map: JS

265*cl* Slave badge: Lion
Publishing/Pauline O'Boyle

265*cr* Diana: Lion
Publishing/Mark Astle

265*br* Temple of Hadrian: Lion
Publishing/Simon Bull

266*bc* Library of Celsus,
Ephesus: JA

267*cl* Vase: Photo © Michael
Holford/Collection British
Museum

267*b* Roman writing
instruments: RN

268*c* Oil lamp: Ashmolean
Museum, Oxford

268*bc* 'Christ Blessing' by
Antonella da Messina
(active 1456; died 1479):
© National Gallery, London

269*tl* 'What is Truth?' (Christ
and Pilate) 1890 by Ge (Gay),
Nikolai Nikolaevich (1831–94)
Tretyakov Gallery, Moscow/
Bridgeman Art Gallery, London/
New York

269*br* Illustration: GH

270*tl* Domitian: The Ancient Art
and Architecture Collection

270*cl* Sardis: JA

270*c* Laodicea: JA

270*c* Map DA

270*bl* Acropolis, Pergamum: JA

270*bc* Roman agora, Smyrna: JA

271*b* Four horsemen: LS

Old Testament Israel

Maps of Israel

Scale:
0 10 20 30 40 km
0 5 10 15 20 25 miles

Abel-beth-maacah

Tyre

Dan

MAACAH

Kedesh

BASHAN

Ramah

Merom

Hazor

Chinnereth

GALILEE

Sea of Chinnereth

Ashtaroth

Gath-hepher

Edrei

Endor

Lo-debar

Shunem

Ramoth-gilead

Dor

Jezreel

Megiddo

Taanach

Beth-shan

GILEAD

Ibleam

Sharon

Dothan

Mediterranean

Sea

Abel-meholah

River Jordan

Samaria

Tirzah

Jabesh-gilead

Succoth

Mahanaim

Shechem

Penuel

Shiloh

Aphek

ISRAEL

Adam

Joppa

Bethel

AMMON

Jazer

Upper/Lower
Beth-horon

Mizpah

Ai

Michmash

Rabbah

Gezer

Gibeon

Geba

Gilgal

Aijalon

Gibeah

Shittim

Ekron

Sorek

Anathoth

Jericho

Heshbon

Timnah

Jerusalem

Libnah

Eshtaol

Kiriath-jearim

Ashdod

Zorah

Bethlehem

Makkedah

Adullam

Ashkelon

Azekah

Keilah

Tekoa

Ataroth

Mareshah

Kiriathaim

Lachish

Beth-zur

Dibon

Gaza

Eglon

Hebron

Aroer

Engedi

*Salt
Sea
(Sea
of the
Arabah)*

PHILISTIA

Maon

MOAB

Gerar

Ziklag

JUDAH

Arad

Beersheba

Ar

Hormah

Ziph

Kir-hareseth

NEGEV
DESERT

274

New Testament Israel

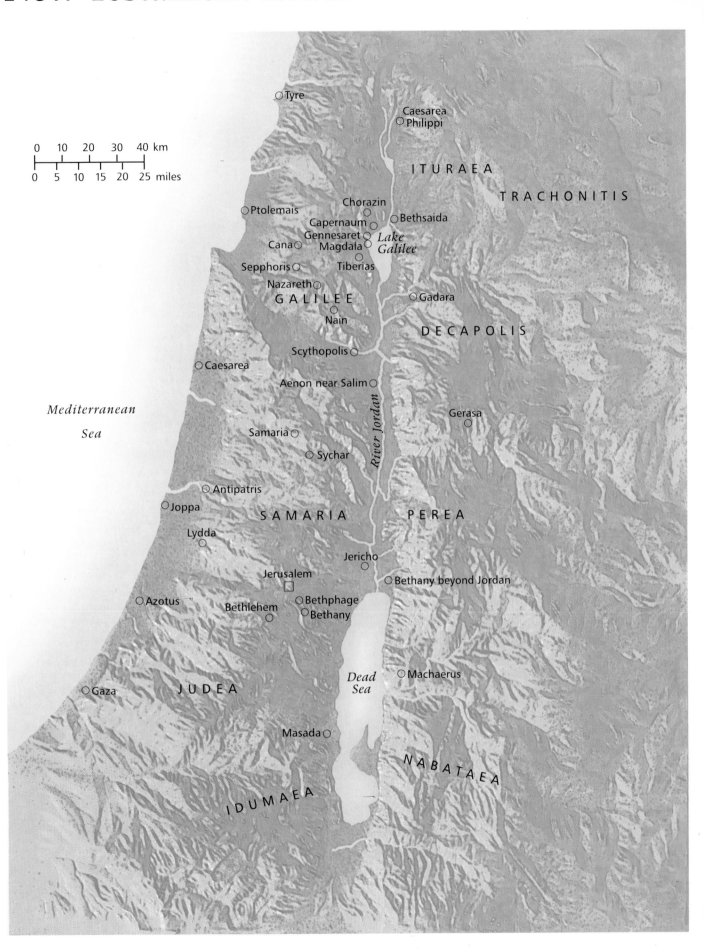

Tyre

Caesarea
Philippi

ITURAEA

TRACHONITIS

0 10 20 30 40 km
0 5 10 15 20 25 miles

Ptolemais

Chorazin
Capernaum
Gennesaret
Cana
Magdala
Sepphoris
Nazareth
Tiberias

Bethsaida

Lake Galilee

GALILEE
Nain

Gadara

DECAPOLIS

Scythopolis

Caesarea

Aenon near Salim

River Jordan

Gerasa

Mediterranean Sea

Samaria

Sychar

Antipatris
Joppa

SAMARIA

PEREA

Lydda

Jericho

Jerusalem

Bethany beyond Jordan

Azotus

Bethphage
Bethlehem
Bethany

Machaerus

Gaza

JUDEA

Dead Sea

NABATAEA

Masada

IDUMAEA

People

Aaron
See Aaron, page 203.

Abednego
The Babylonian name given to Azariah, one of three Jewish exiles chosen for special service by King Nebuchadnezzar of Babylon. He and the two others (Shadrach and Meshach), encouraged by Daniel, courageously refused to eat the court food because, even in a foreign country, they were determined to obey the Israelite food-laws. Later they refused to bow before an idol the king had set up. All three were thrown into a blazing furnace. But the Bible tells that God protected them, and they came out unharmed. The king was most impressed. 'No other God can do what this one does', he said.
Daniel 1–3; The Prayer of Azariah 1:68

Abel
Adam and Eve's second son, brother of Cain. The Old Testament records that Abel became a shepherd when he grew up, and offered a lamb to God as a sacrifice. This pleased God. But Cain was jealous because God did not accept his gift of fruit, and he killed his brother. The New Testament praises Abel as a person of great faith, and indicates that is why his offering was more acceptable than his brother's.
Genesis 4:1–8; Hebrews 11:4

Abiathar
The son of Ahimelech the priest in the days of the Israelite king Saul. When David subsequently became king, Abiathar was made joint high priest with Zadok. But after David's death he conspired to put Adonijah on the throne, instead of Solomon, and was banished.
1 Samuel 22:20ff; 2 Samuel 8:17; 15:24ff; 1 Kings 1–2

Abihu
See Nadab.

Abigail
The wife of Nabal, who later married King David. See Nabal.

Abijah
The son of King Jeroboam I of Israel. He died as a child.
1 Kings 14

Abijah/Abijam
Son of King Rehoboam of Judah; he reigned for

three years, about 908–905 BC.
1 Kings 15; 2 Chronicles 13

Abimelech
1. Because he was afraid for his life, Abraham pretended that his wife, Sarah, was only his sister. Abimelech, king of Gerar, wanted to make her his wife, but when he realized Abraham was trying to trick him, he called his bluff.
Genesis 20
2. A son of Gideon who killed his brothers in order to become king himself.
Judges 8:31ff; 9

Abiram
He joined with Korah and Dathan in leading a rebellion against Moses. See Korah.
Numbers 16

Abishag
A young woman from Shunem who nursed King David in his old age.
1 Kings 1–2

Abishai
A nephew of King David, brother of Joab, and one of the king's generals.
1 Samuel 26:6–12; 2 Samuel 10:9–10; 16:9, 11–12; 18:2

Abner
A first cousin of King Saul and commander of his army. When Saul was killed, Abner put Ish-baal, Saul's son, on the throne. This led to war between the tribes who accepted Ish-baal and the tribe of Judah, where David reigned. Angry at the way he was being treated, Abner eventually defected to support David as king of the whole of Israel. He was subsequently murdered by David's army commander, Joab, whose brother he had killed.
1 Samuel 14:50; 2 Samuel 3

Abraham/Abram
See Abraham, page 198.

Absalom
A favourite son of King David. He rebelled against his father and plotted to become king himself. David's men defeated Absalom's army in the forest of Ephraim. Absalom, escaping on a mule, was caught by his long hair in the branches of an oak tree, and while he was hanging there Joab, David's general, killed him, much to the king's displeasure.
2 Samuel 15–19

Achan
When the Israelites conquered Jericho,

Achan disobeyed the orders not to steal goods from the city. He helped himself to items of gold and silver, and fine clothes for himself. According to the writer of Joshua, this action led to the Israelites being defeated in their next battle.
Joshua 7–8

Achish
A king of Gath, one of the cities of the Philistines. On two occasions he protected David when he was being pursued by King Saul.
1 Samuel 21; 27–29

Adam
Adam appears in the Old Testament as the first man (in Hebrew, his name just means 'humankind'), living in the idyllic paradise known as the Garden of Eden. Here, he was given responsibility for acting as God's representative in caring for all other life.

Adam's partner in the Garden was Eve – the woman – and like him she was 'created in the image of God'. The two of them lived together in a relationship of mutual openness, to one another and to God, enjoying the fruits of the earth. It was only when they decided to assert their independence of the loving provision of God that disaster struck. Symbolized by the taking of fruit from a tree that was forbidden to them, Adam and Eve destroyed the lifestyle that they enjoyed. Their insistence on being able to live a good life without taking account of God's will is at the root of what the Bible calls sinfulness – something that all other generations of humankind has suffered from. As a consequence of their wrongdoing, Adam and Eve's open relationship with God was destroyed, and their own family life suffered too, with pain and death spoiling all that they had.
Genesis 1:26–27; 2–5:5

Adonijah
The fourth son of King David. When David was old, and the elder brothers were dead, Adonijah tried to seize the throne. But David had promised his wife Bathsheba that her son

Solomon would succeed him. Adonijah's attempt failed. David forgave him but once Solomon was king he lost no time in having Adonijah executed to secure his own position.
1 Kings 1–2

Agabus
A Christian prophet from Jerusalem who told the church at Antioch that a great famine was coming. Later he also warned Paul that he would be imprisoned if he went to Jerusalem.
Acts 11:27–30; 21:7–14

Ahab
See Ahab, page 211.

Ahasuerus
Hebrew form of the name of a Persian king, who was almost certainly Xerxes I (485–464 BC). He features in the Old Testament book of Ezra, and probably also in the book of Esther – though the form of his name there leads some to connect the Hebrew Ahasuerus not with Xerxes I, but with Artaxerxes II (404–359 BC). Another king of the same name appears in the book of Daniel as father of Darius the Mede.
Esther; Ezra 4:6; Daniel 9:1

Ahaz
King of Judah about 732–716 BC (co-regent from 735 or earlier). He is condemned for the corrupting of temple worship, introducing rites that included even the sacrifice of his own son. Ahaz was defeated when Israel and Syria launched a combined attack on Judah. Rejecting the prophet Isaiah's advice, he appealed to the Assyrian King Tiglath-pileser III for help but by doing so became his subject.
2 Kings 15:38ff; 2 Chronicles 27:9ff; Isaiah 7

Ahaziah
1. The son of Ahab and Jezebel. He was king of Israel after Ahab but only for a short time (about 852 BC). The Old Testament history writers condemn him for continuing the lifestyle and religious apostasy of his father.
1 Kings 22:40ff; 2 Kings 1; 2 Chronicles 20:35–37
2. A king of Judah, the son of Jehoram (841 BC). He and his uncle, King Jehoram of Israel, with whom he had made an

alliance, were murdered by Jehu.
2 Kings 8:24ff; 2 Chronicles 22:1–9

Ahijah
A prophet from Shiloh. Ahijah tore his dress into 12 pieces before King Jeroboam I to show how Solomon's kingdom would be divided. He told Jeroboam to take 10 of these pieces, because he would be the one to rule 10 of the 12 tribes of Israel.
1 Kings 11:29ff; 14

Ahimaaz
A son of Zadok, the high priest. He risked his life as a spy for King David during Absalom's rebellion.
2 Samuel 17:17ff; 18

Ahimelech
The priest at the sanctuary of Nob who helped David when he was escaping from King Saul. He gave David bread from the altar, and Goliath's sword. When Saul discovered this he had Ahimelech, his fellow priests and everyone at Nob put to death.
1 Samuel 21–22

Ahithophel
King David's trusted adviser who turned traitor and supported Absalom in his rebellion. When Absalom ignored his advice Ahithophel committed suicide.
2 Samuel 15:12–17:23

Alcimus
A Jewish high priest during the time of the Maccabees, who aligned himself with the Seleucid ruler Demetrius in order to safeguard his own position. By making false accusations against Judas Maccabeus he provoked several battles, including one in which Judas lost his life. The Old Testament writers thoroughly disapproved of his actions, which were a betrayal of all that Judaism was supposed to represent, both morally and religiously.
1 Maccabees 7:1–25; 9:1–57; 2 Maccabees 14:1ff

Alexander
1. Son of Simon of Cyrene, the man who carried Jesus' cross.
Mark 15:21
2. A member of the high priest's family and one of the Jewish leaders in Jerusalem.
Acts 4:6
3. A Jew who tried to speak to the crowd

during the silversmiths' riot at Ephesus. See Demetrius.
Acts 19:33
4. A Christian who lost his faith, at least for a time.
1 Timothy 1:20
5. A coppersmith who was bitterly opposed to Paul and the gospel. Paul warned Timothy against him.
2 Timothy 4:14

Alexander Balas
A Seleucid king, who claimed to be the son of Antiochus IV, though there is some doubt about this. He promised to give the Maccabees military backing, in exchange for their support, but was eventually deposed because of his selfishness and incompetence. He was a devious ruler, though the Jews never condemned him, not least because they gained a measure of independence during his reign.
1 Maccabees 10:1–11:19

Amasa
King David's nephew, chosen by Absalom to lead his rebel army. After Absalom's defeat, David pardoned Amasa and made him commander of his own army in place of Joab. In revenge Joab murdered him.
2 Samuel 17:25; 20

Amaziah
1. The son of King Joash of Judah, who came to the throne when his father was assassinated. Amaziah (796–767 BC) was a good man, but victory over Edom went to his head. He challenged Israel and lost. He introduced elements of Edomite religion in preference to the messages of the prophets. The people plotted against him and eventually he was murdered at Lachish.
2 Kings 12:21–14:21; 2 Chronicles 24:27ff.
2. A priest at Bethel who opposed the prophet Amos.
Amos 7:10ff

Amnon
The eldest son of King David. He raped Tamar, his half-sister, and in revenge Absalom had him killed.
2 Samuel 3:2; 13

Amon
King of Judah after Manasseh, his father (642–640 BC). Amon is condemned in the Old

Testament for his promotion of alien religious practices. After a reign of only two years he was murdered by the palace servants.
2 Kings 21:18–26; 2 Chronicles 33:20–25

Amos
One of the first of the Israelite prophets whose messages are preserved in the Old Testament. Amos lived in the eighth century BC, and started life as a shepherd and grower of fig trees at Tekoa, a hill village in Judah. His ministry, however, took place mostly at Bethel in the kingdom of Israel. This was the location of one of King Jeroboam I's main shrines, dominated by the golden statue of a calf. Here Amos bore witness to a message of justice and judgement in the face of much oppression and greed, denouncing the way that cheating traders tried to make up for their dishonesty by offering sacrifices to God. Amaziah, the priest at Bethel, who was in the pay of the king of Israel, told Amos to pack up and take his message back to Judah. But Amos continued to warn the people of Israel of judgment and exile if they did not repent.
Amos 1:1; 7:10–15

Ananias
1. Ananias and his wife, Sapphira, gave the apostles only part of the money they received from the sale of land, though they pretended to give it all. As a consequence, they both died unexpectedly – something that was seen as God's judgment on their dishonesty.
Acts 5:1–11
2. A Christian who lived in Damascus. After Saul (Paul) met the risen Christ on the road to Damascus, he was unable to see for three days. Ananias, a local Damascus Christian, visited him, baptized him, and his sight was restored.
Acts 9:10–19
3. A religious official involved with the trials of Paul by the Sanhedrin council and, later, before the Roman governor Felix.
Acts 23:2–3; 24:1

Andrew
One of Jesus' original 12 disciples. Andrew and his brother Simon Peter were fishing people from Bethsaida on Lake Galilee. In John's gospel,

John the Baptist identifies Jesus to Andrew as the 'Lamb of God', and Andrew later brought his brother Peter to hear Jesus' teaching. Other stories tell how, when they were fishing, Jesus called both brothers to follow him. Andrew brought the boy with the loaves and fishes to Jesus when he fed 5,000 hungry people. When some Greek visitors to Jerusalem were looking for Jesus, Andrew and Philip told him about them. And Andrew was with the other disciples in Jerusalem after Jesus' ascension.
John 1:35–42; Matthew 4:18–19; 10:2; John 6:6–9; 12:22; Acts 1:13

Anna
An woman prophet who was in the temple when Joseph and Mary took Jesus there as a baby to carry out the rituals related to childbirth and have him circumcised. Together with her companion Simeon, she expressed hopes that Jesus would be the Saviour and Messiah of his people.
Luke 2:36–38

Annas
A senior religious official in Jerusalem, who was involved in the arrest and trials of Jesus.
Luke 3:2; John 18:13–24

Antiochus III (the Great)
Seleucid ruler of Palestine in the early second century BC, who managed to extend his kingdom into some eastern parts of Egypt. His daughter Cleopatra married Ptolemy of Egypt. He also seized parts of Asia Minor, and forcibly removed thousands of Jews to live in exile there.
Daniel 11:10–19; 3 Maccabees 1:1–7

Antiochus IV Epiphanes
The most notorious of all the Seleucid rulers of Palestine (175–164 BC), who forced the Jewish population to adopt Greek ways of life and worship. He plundered the Jerusalem temple, and turned it into a shrine in honour of Zeus. He also believed he was himself divine. All these actions provoked resistance, and eventually led to the Maccabean revolt, in which his sophisticated armies were defeated by bands of Jewish guerrillas.
1 Maccabees 1:10–6:17; 2 Maccabees 5:1–7:42; 9:1–29

Apollos
A Jew from Alexandria in Egypt, who went to Ephesus in Asia Minor, and taught in the synagogue after Paul's visit there. As a result of the teaching he heard from Paul's friends Aquila and Priscilla, he became a Christian and later was involved with the church at Corinth in Greece.
Acts 18:24–28; 19:1; 1 Corinthians 16:12

Aquila
A Jewish Christian who was a friend of Paul. Aquila and his wife, Priscilla (or Prisca), were forced to leave Italy when the Roman emperor Claudius expelled the Jews from Rome (AD 48). Like Paul they were tentmakers and for a time Paul stayed with and worked with them in Corinth. When Paul travelled to Ephesus, Aquila and Priscilla went with him (see Apollos). Later, Aquila and Priscilla moved back to Rome. In both places Christians met in their home.
Acts 18:1–3, 18–26; Romans 16:3; 1 Corinthians 16:19; 2 Timothy 4:19

Araunah/Ornan
A man from Jerusalem who sold his threshing-floor to King David, on which David constructed an altar for sacrifice, in an effort to rid Israel of a vicious plague. The plague was successfully stopped, and according to tradition the temple was later built on this same site.
2 Samuel 24:16–25; 1 Chronicles 21:18–30

Archelaus
See Herod.

Aretas
An Arabian king whose capital was Petra (in present-day Jordan), whose domains included Damascus at the time of Paul's conversion. Paul escaped the unwelcome attention of Aretas' governor in Damascus by escaping over the city walls in a basket.
2 Corinthians 11:32

Aristarchus
A Macedonian Christian, a friend and co-worker of Paul. He was with Paul when the Ephesian silversmiths started a riot, and accompanied Paul on his final trip to Jerusalem, then later to Rome. When Paul was in prison in Rome he stayed with him.
Acts 19:29ff; 20:4; 27:2; Colossians 4:10

Artaxerxes
Name of several kings of Persia. Ezra and Nehemiah probably returned to Jerusalem from exile in Babylon during the reign of Artaxerxes I (464–423 BC).
Ezra 4:6–7

Asa
The son of Abijah and third king of Judah. He reigned for 41 years (about 911–870 BC). When Asa became king he tried to reform temple worship in Jerusalem. He won a great victory when a huge Cushite army led by Zerar attacked Judah.
1 Kings 15:8ff; 2 Chronicles 14:1ff

Asahel
A nephew of King David. Asahel was one of David's bravest soldiers and commander of a large division of the army.
2 Samuel 2:18ff; 23:24

Asaph
A Levite who is connected with the musical traditions of the Jerusalem temple, and whose descendants are said to have formed the nucleus of a later temple choir. He is also named as inspiration for several of the psalms of the Old Testament.
1 Chronicles 15:17ff; 25:1ff; 2 Chronicles 29:30; 35:15

Athaliah
The only woman to rule over Judah (841–835 BC). Her reign was noteworthy for her cruelty in murdering all the royal children except the baby Joash, who escaped only by being hidden by his aunt. When Joash was seven, he was crowned king as a result of a palace coup, in the course of which Athaliah was killed.
2 Kings 11:1–16; 2 Chronicles 22:10–23:21

Augustus Caesar
The first Roman emperor, successor to Julius Caesar. He ruled from 31 BC to AD 14. Jesus was born during his reign.
Luke 2:1

Azariah
Best-known of several Azariahs is the king of Judah (791–739 BC), also called Uzziah. The Bible depicts him as a good king, strong and powerful, and politically astute. In later life he was forced to live in isolation, due to a severe skin disease, which was viewed as a divine punishment for his

failure to purify the temple worship completely. His son, Jotham, was acting king for much of his reign.
2 Kings 14:21ff; 2 Chronicles 26

Baasha
A man from the tribe of Issachar who seized the throne of Israel from Nadab, son of Jeroboam, and ruled from about 909–886 BC.
1 Kings 15:16ff

Bacchides
Governor of the eastern boundaries of the Seleucid territory during the reign of Demetrius I, Bacchides became a key opponent of the Maccabean struggle for Jewish independence, though he later shifted his allegiance to Jonathan, the Maccabean king. He was a scheming ruler, who managed to install Alcimus as high priest in Jerusalem for a while, before it became prudent for him to shift his support to Jonathan Maccabee, following a defeat in battle.
1 Maccabees 7:1–25; 9:1–57; 2 Maccabees 8:30–36

Balaam
A Mesopotamian seer who was summoned by Balak, king of Moab, to curse the Israelites at the time of their desert wanderings. They had just defeated the Amorites and Balak was afraid his country would suffer the same fate. At first Balaam refused to go and meet the Moabites, but then he later agreed. The Bible story tells how Balaam's ass was stopped by an angel, who warned Balaam to say only what God told him. As a result, instead of cursing the Israelites, Balaam blessed them three times. He later attempted to bring about the Israelites' downfall and gain the reward he had been promised, by encouraging them to worship non-Israelite gods. He was killed when the Israelites attacked the Midianites.
Numbers 22–24; 31

Balak
A king of Moab who reigned at the time when the Israelites were waiting to conquer Canaan. See Balaam.
Numbers 22:2–24:5

Barabbas
A political prisoner in Judea at the time of Jesus' arrest. The Roman governor, Pilate, apparently believing Jesus to be innocent of

any crime, though reluctant to let him go, tried to pass responsibility to the crowds in Jerusalem by asking if they would prefer to see Barabbas or Jesus set free. Predictably, the mob asked for Barabbas, and so the weak-willed Pilate released him and Jesus was crucified.
Matthew 27:15–26

Barak
An Israelite from Naphtali chosen by Deborah, the judge and prophet, to recruit a large army to fight Jabin, a Canaanite king of the time. Barak's men won a great victory for Israel which ended 20 years of domination by this powerful ruler.
Judges 4–5

Barnabas
The nickname ('son of encouragement') of a Jewish Christian, born in Cyprus, who became a member of the church at Jerusalem. He was generous and warm-hearted, and sold his land to give the money to poor Christians. When Paul reached Jerusalem after his conversion most Christians were understandably suspicious of his motives. But Barnabas welcomed Paul and introduced him to the apostles. When later the Jerusalem church sent Barnabas to Antioch to help the predominantly Gentile church, he sent to Tarsus for Paul to join him in this work.

Barnabas and Paul set out together from Antioch on their first missionary journey and took John Mark, Barnabas' cousin, with them. On their return they reported to an important meeting of church leaders in Jerusalem. The two men later disagreed about whether Mark should be allowed to join them for a second trip. So Barnabas went back to Cyprus with Mark while Paul went on to Asia Minor. Barnabas and Paul continued to be good friends and in his letters Paul commends him warmly.
Acts 4:36; 9:27; 11:22ff; 12:25ff; 15; 1 Corinthians 9:6; Galatians 2

Bartholomew
Named as one of the 12 apostles, though absolutely nothing more is known of him. Some identify him as the same person as Nathaniel, the man whom Philip

brought to Jesus (though nothing is known of him either).

Matthew 10:3; Acts 1:13

Bartimaeus
A blind man healed by Jesus.

Mark 10:46–52

Baruch
A loyal friend of Jeremiah, the prophet during the last days of Jerusalem, just before the Babylonians captured the city in 587 BC. Baruch wrote down some of Jeremiah's prophetic messages, and read them out in the streets and the royal courts. He stayed with Jeremiah after Jerusalem was destroyed, even when he was forced to go to Egypt. One of the Deuterocanonical books bears his name.

Jeremiah 36; 43:6

Barzillai
A loyal supporter of King David. He fed David and his men when they were in hiding at Mahanaim during Absalom's rebellion.

2 Samuel 17:27ff; 19:31–39

Bathsheba
Wife of Uriah the Hittite, raped by King David and then taken by him to be one of his own wives. See David.

2 Samuel 11–12;1 Kings 1–2

Belshazzar
Ruler of Babylon, killed when Babylon was captured in 539 BC by the Persians and Medes. He had been acting king, ruling in the absence of his father Nabonidus. The Bible story describes a grand banquet during which he was frightened by a disembodied hand writing on the wall of his dining-hall. Daniel was called to translate the words, which turned out to be a warning that Belshazzar's kingdom had failed to find God's approval, and would be overthrown, with Belshazzar losing his life in the process. That very night the Persian army took the city by surprise.

Daniel 5

Belteshazzar
A Babylonian name given to Daniel. See Daniel.

Benaiah
The best-known of several men of this name is the captain of King David's bodyguard who remained loyal when Adonijah tried to seize the throne. Benaiah played a leading part in proclaiming Solomon king, and became commander of his army.

2 Samuel 8:18; 1 Kings 1–2

Benhadad
Name of three kings of Syria, probably meaning 'son of Hadad' (the Syrian storm-god). Benhadad I (about 900–860 BC) helped Asa, king of Judah, against Israel. Benhadad II (about 860–843 BC) was an enemy of Ahab, king of Israel. Benhadad III (about 796–782 BC) went to war against Israel in the time of Elisha, the prophet. The Israelites escaped the clutches of the Syrians several times in answer to Elisha's prayers, in the course of which it was revealed to Elisha that Benhadad would die at the hands of his servant, Hazael.

1 Kings 20; 2 Kings 6–8

Benjamin
Youngest son of Jacob and Rachel. His mother died at his birth, which ensured that, with his brother Joseph, he would become one of his father's most favourite sons. Their jealous half-brothers sold Joseph into Egypt. Later, when the brothers were in Joseph's power in Egypt, he tested them to see if they would be equally cruel to Benjamin. But the brothers were changed men. They refused to leave Benjamin behind in Egypt, even to save themselves. One of the 12 tribes of Israel was subsequently named after Benjamin.

Genesis 35:18–20; 43–45

Bernice
The sister of Herod Agrippa II. See Herod Agrippa II.

Acts 25:13ff

Bezalel
A skilled craft worker in charge of making the tabernacle when the Israelites were in the desert.

Exodus 35:30ff

Bildad
One of Job's three friends who talked to him in his suffering.

Job 2:11, etc.

Bilhah
Rachel's servant, who became the mother of Dan and Naphtali (two of the ancestors of the Israelite tribes).

Genesis 29:29; 30:3–7

Boaz
Hero of the Old Testament book of Ruth. Boaz was a rich and generous farmer in Bethlehem who married Ruth and became the great-grandfather of King David.

Ruth 2–4

Caesar
The title of Roman emperors in New Testament times. Augustus reigned when Jesus was born. Tiberius reigned after him. Peter and Paul were probably martyred when Nero was Caesar. Jesus sometimes used the word 'Caesar' to mean 'the ruling power', without reference to a particular emperor.

Mark 12:14–17; Luke 2:1; 3:1; Acts 25

Caiaphas
High Priest in Jerusalem AD 18–36. At the trial of Jesus he and his father-in-law, Annas, found Jesus guilty of blasphemy and sent him to Pilate for further trial and sentence. Caiaphas also features in Acts as an opponent of the first Christians.

Matthew 26:3, 57ff; Luke 3:2; John 18:13ff; Acts 5:17ff

Cain
Eldest son of Adam and Eve, who killed his brother Abel and as punishment lived the rest of his life as a nomad. See Abel.

Genesis 4; 1 John 3:12

Caleb
One of the spies sent by Moses to find out about Canaan and the people who lived there. According to the Old Testament, of the 12 spies who reported on what they had seen, only Caleb and Joshua believed that it would be possible to conquer the land. Because of their confidence in God, Caleb and Joshua were allowed to settle in Canaan, unlike all the other Israelites born in Egypt, who died in the desert.

Numbers 13–14; Joshua 14:6ff

Canaan
Son of Ham, who gained notoriety because of his disrespect for Noah, his grandfather.

Genesis 9:18–27

Cephas
See Peter.

Chedorlaomer
A king of Elam.

Genesis 14

Claudius
The fourth Roman emperor. Claudius reigned in AD 41–54. During this time the famine predicted by the Christian prophet Agabus took place. Towards the end of his reign Claudius forced all Jews to leave Rome.

Acts 11:28; 18:2

Claudius Lysias
A commander of the Roman garrison at

Jerusalem who rescued Paul when an angry crowd of Jews was about to kill him. Claudius Lysias arrested Paul and, following agreed procedures on religious matters, allowed the Jewish council (the Sanhedrin) to question him. When the session ended in chaos, and he heard about a plot to murder Paul, Claudius Lysias sent him to Caesarea to be tried by Felix, the Roman governor.

Acts 21:31–23:30

Clement
A Philippian Christian who shared in Paul's work.

Philippians 4:3

Cleopas
The New Testament records that on the day of Jesus' resurrection Cleopas and a friend were walking from Jerusalem to Emmaus. They had thought Jesus was the Messiah, and were puzzled about his death and the report that he was alive again. A man joined them. As he explained the Old Testament passages about the Messiah it was as if 'a fire burned within them'. At Emmaus, Cleopas and his friend (presumably his wife) invited the stranger to join them in their home for a meal. As he asked God's blessing on the food and broke bread they realized it was Jesus. They went to Jerusalem at once to share the news with the other disciples.

Luke 24:13–53

Cornelius
A Roman army centurion stationed at Caesarea. He had adopted the Jewish faith as a 'God-fearer' (an adherent rather than a full convert). In a dream, an angel told Cornelius to send for Peter, who was at Joppa at the time (see Peter). Though Peter was reluctant to go (Cornelius was a Gentile, and a soldier), at Cornelius' house Peter found a crowd of the soldier's friends and relatives eagerly waiting to hear him. They believed and were baptised, and are one of the first groups of non-Jewish converts to Christianity to be mentioned in the book of Acts.

Acts 10

Crescens
A friend of Paul. Crescens was with Paul when he was a prisoner in Rome but left him to

go and work in Galatia.

2 Timothy 4:10

Crispus
Chief official of the Jewish synagogue in Corinth, southern Greece. He and his family were converted to Christianity and baptized by Paul.

Acts 18:8; 1 Corinthians 1:14

Cushan-rishathaim
A king of Mesopotamia who dominated life in Canaan for a period during the time of the judges.

Judges 3:7–10

Cyrus
The Persian king who captured Babylon in 539 BC. Cyrus allowed the Jews exiled in Babylon to return to Jerusalem to rebuild their temple. He sent back with them the treasures removed from the temple by Nebuchadnezzar and gave them a substantial sum of money to help with the work. Some passages in the book of Isaiah identify Cyrus by name as God's appointee to bring about freedom for the Jewish captives. Some of the stories about Daniel seem to be set in the context of Cyrus's reign.

Ezra 1:1–6:14; Isaiah 44:28ff; Daniel 6:28

Daniel
Best-known of several Old Testament Daniels is the upper-class Jew who was taken captive to Babylon, probably in his teens. At the court of King Nebuchadnezzar, Daniel and his three friends, Shadrach, Meshach and Abednego, were trained to be counsellors to the king. The Bible records that Daniel was determined still to observe the traditional religion of his people, and so refused the rich food that was available to him, preferring instead the simple diet allowed by Old Testament food-laws.

God gave Daniel great wisdom. Twice he was able to tell Nebuchadnezzar the meaning of strange dreams. Daniel later explained to king Belshazzar the writing that appeared on his dining-room wall, warning that his kingdom was about to be overthrown. That same night Belshazzar was killed and the Persians captured Babylon. They made Daniel an important

official, but other leaders were jealous of his power and plotted his downfall. In other stories, Daniel resists worshipping an idol called Bel, and succeeds in killing a fierce dragon that was also being worshipped as divine by the Babylonians. For all these things, he was eventually thrown into the lions' den, but was saved when an angel appeared to calm the beasts. The Old Testament book of Daniel also contains dreams and visions explaining how God would never lose control of things, no matter how strong the powers of evil might sometimes seem to be.

Daniel; Bel and the Dragon 1–42

Darius
1. Darius the Mede is named in the Old Testament book of Daniel as ruler after Belshazzar, though a person of that name is not otherwise known from contemporary records. Some speculate that Cyrus may have made Darius ruler of Babylon, or may even have used the name Darius himself.

Daniel 5:31ff

2. Darius I of Persia (522–486 BC), who encouraged the Jews to finish rebuilding the temple.

Ezra 4:5; Haggai 1:1; Zechariah 1:1

3. Darius II of Persia (423–408 BC), mentioned in the Old Testament book of Nehemiah.

Nehemiah 12:22

Dathan
Joined with Korah and Abiram in leading a rebellion against Moses. See Korah.

Numbers 16

David
See David, page 209.

Deborah
See Deborah, page 207.

Delilah
A Philistine woman with whom Samson had a romantic affair, and by whom he was eventually betrayed. See Samson.

Judges 16

Demas
A Christian who was with Paul when he was a prisoner in Rome, though he later left and went off to Thessalonica.

Colossians 4:14; 2 Timothy 4:10

Demetrius I (Soter)
A member of the Seleucid royal family, who was sent by his

own relatives as a hostage to Rome, but managed to escape and became king of Syria (162–151 BC). This was at the time that the Maccabees had just asserted Jewish independence, something which he fiercely opposed. He succeeded in having Judas Maccabee killed, but he himself lost his life in a power struggle with Alexander Balas, his brother.

1 Maccabees 9:1; 10:46–50

Demetrius II (Nicator)
The son of Demetrius I, who had two separate terms of office during the second century BC, interrupted by a period of captivity at the hands of the Medes. He was unpopular with the Jews, who conspired against him in alliance with the Romans, but Simon Maccabee eventually came to an accommodation with him.

1 Maccabees 10:67–11:59; 14:1–3; 15:1

Demetrius
1. A silversmith in Ephesus who made souvenirs at the temple of Diana (Artemis). He feared that if Paul's preaching was successful, there would be less demand for these models, and so he encouraged others in the same business to riot.

Acts 19:24ff

2. A Christian mentioned in John's third letter, of whom everyone spoke well.

3 John 12

Diana
Roman goddess of the moon and hunting, called Artemis by the Greeks. Her magnificent temple at Ephesus was one of the wonders of the ancient world.

Acts 19

Dinah
The daughter of Jacob and Leah raped by Shechem, son of a Hivite king. In revenge Dinah's brothers killed Shechem and the people from his city.

Genesis 34

Dionysius
A member of the Areopagus, an influential group of thinkers in Athens who concerned themselves with philosophical and religious affairs. Dionysius became a Christian after hearing what Paul had to say about Jesus.

Acts 17:34

Diotrephes
A proud and awkward church leader who refused to accept John's authority.

3 John 9–10

Doeg
An Edomite who was King Saul's chief herder. He was at Nob when Ahimelech the priest fed and armed the escaping David. Doeg betrayed Ahimelech, and then carried out the executions Saul ordered.

1 Samuel 21:7; 22:9ff

Dorcas/Tabitha
A Christian from Joppa who helped the poor by making clothes for them. On her death, her friends sent for Peter, and her resuscitation followed.

Acts 9:36–41

Drusilla
The youngest daughter of Herod Agrippa I and wife of the Roman governor Felix. See Felix.

Acts 24:24

Ebed-melech
An Ethiopian who was one of King Zedekiah's palace officials (sixth century BC). He was instrumental in securing Jeremiah's safety, in return for which he was promised that he himself would survive the destruction of Jerusalem.

Jeremiah 38; 39:16–18

Eglon
A king of Moab in the time of the judges. He defeated Israel and captured Jericho, keeping the Israelites subject for 18 years. He was murdered by Ehud.

Judges 3:12–26

Ehud
A left-handed Israelite from the tribe of Benjamin. Ehud thought up a cunning and daring plot to kill King Eglon of Moab, who had oppressed part of Israel, including the eastern section of the land belonging to Ehud's tribe, for 18 years. With Eglon dead, Ehud gathered an army to defeat the Moabites and free his people.

Judges 3:15–30

Elah
The best-known man of this name in the Old Testament is the son of King Baasha. Like most kings in this period of Israel's turbulent history, Elah was a weak man, and reigned for less than two years (886–885 BC), before being murdered while drunk by Zimri, a general in his army.

1 Kings 16:8–14

Eleazar
1. The most important of several Eleazars was Aaron's third son. Eleazar's two elder brothers were killed, so he was regarded as Aaron's natural successor. The work of the Levites and general supervision of Israelite worship are described as his responsibility.

Exodus 6:23; Leviticus 10; Numbers 3ff; Joshua 14, etc.

2. The fourth son of Mattathias, and brother of Judas Maccabeus. He died in a battle at Beth-zechariah as he was trying to bring down an elephant bearing a Seleucid king.

1 Maccabees 2:5; 6:32–47

Eli
A judge and priest in Israel. Samuel's mother (see Hannah) took her son to Eli to be trained in the shrine at Shiloh. Eli is portrayed as a weak man, whose two sons, Hophni and Phinehas, were out of control and were both eventually killed in a battle against the Philistines. In the same conflict, the Ark of the Covenant was captured, and when Eli heard of this disaster he collapsed and died.

1 Samuel 1–4

Eliab
Jesse's eldest son, the brother of David.

1 Samuel 16:6ff; 17:13, 28

Eliakim
The most important person of this name was the son of Hilkiah, King Hezekiah's chief palace official. When King Sennacherib of Assyria threatened to besiege Jerusalem Hezekiah sent Eliakim, along with Shebna and Joah, to deal with the Assyrian envoys.

2 Kings 18:18ff; Isaiah 36–37:6

Eliashib
A high priest in the time of Nehemiah who helped rebuild the walls of Jerusalem.

Nehemiah 3:1; 13:4–9

Eliezer
Abraham's leading servant, and potential heir until Abraham had a son. It was presumably Eliezer who was trusted with the task of going to Mesopotamia to choose a wife for Isaac.

Genesis 15:2

Elihu
The angry young man in the Old Testament story of Job, whose understanding of Job's suffering was that it could only be as a result of great wrongdoing on Job's part.

Job 32–37

Elijah
A prophet who lived in Israel during the reign of King Ahab. The Old Testament records that Ahab and his foreign queen, Jezebel, inaugurated the worship of non-Israelite deities, and persecuted Israel's own prophets. Invoking the authority of Israel's God, Elijah announced a coming drought, but then was overcome by self-doubt and went into hiding by a brook in the Kerith ravine. There, wild birds brought him food, then when the brook itself dried up, he moved on to Zarephath in Sidon and lodged with a widow and her household. She shared what looked like the last of her food with Elijah, but the supply of flour and oil was miraculously preserved until the famine was over. When the widow's son died, he was revived in answer to Elijah's prayer.

In the third year of the drought Elijah returned to Ahab. The king accused him of causing Israel's troubles. 'I'm not the troublemaker,' Elijah replied. 'You are – you and your father before you – because you have disregarded Yahweh's commands and chosen to worship other gods.' He told Ahab to send the prophets of Baal and Asherah to Mount Carmel. There Elijah challenged them to prove that their god was real. If Baal could set fire to their sacrifice then the people would worship him; but if Yahweh sent fire to burn up Elijah's sacrifice, that would prove this was the true God. The prophets of Baal danced, prayed and cut themselves all day, but nothing happened. When Elijah prayed, the fire fell and burnt his sacrifice. All the people shouted, 'Yahweh, he is God.' The priests of Baal were killed – and that same day the drought ended.

Jezebel was furious when she heard all this. Elijah fled south into the desert to save his life, and was again afflicted by a loss of self-confidence. He felt alone and near to despair. But he was assured that God still had work for him to do: he was to anoint a new king and train

Elisha to take over his work.

In another story, Ahab had his poorer neighbour Naboth killed in order to seize his vineyard. Elijah warned the king in God's name that he could expect his whole family to suffer divine punishment. Ahab was later killed in battle, but Elijah enjoyed God's protection, and when his work was finished, he was taken off to heaven in a chariot of fire.

Later. the prophet Malachi wrote of a character like Elijah returning to usher in the age of the Messiah. The New Testament describes John the Baptist in ways reminiscent of Elijah's dress and lifestyle, and also depicts Elijah appearing alongside Moses at the time of Jesus' transfiguration.

1 Kings 17 – 2 Kings 2; Malachi 4:5-6; Luke 9:28ff

Elimelech
See Naomi.

Eliphaz
One of Job's three friends who came to him in his suffering.

Job 2:11ff

Elisha
See Elisha, page 211.

Elizabeth
Wife of Zechariah, a priest. Elizabeth was unable to have children, but then in her old age she became the mother of John the Baptist. Mary, Jesus' mother, was a relative of Elizabeth and visited her before their two babies were born. Elizabeth identified Mary's child as the long-awaited Messiah.

Luke 1

Elkanah
Best-known of several men of this name is Samuel's father, the husband of Hannah. See Hannah.

1 Samuel 1

Elymas/Bar-Jesus
A Jewish magician and soothsayer at the court of Sergius Paulus, Roman governor of Cyprus at the time when Paul and Barnabas visited. Elymas was afraid of losing his job if Sergius Paulus became a Christian, but his opposition to Paul and Barnabas only resulted in him being temporarily struck blind – something that convinced Sergius Paulus there must be something in what Paul and Barnabas were saying.

Acts 13:6–12

Enoch
A descendant of Adam's son, Seth, who the Bible says lived in such close friendship with God that instead of dying he was 'taken away' by God.

Genesis 5:22; Hebrews 11:5

Epaphras
A Christian who founded the church at Colossae. Epaphras visited Paul when he was in prison in Rome and gave him news about the Colossian Christians. As a result Paul wrote his letter to them.

Colossians 1:7–8; 4:12; Philemon 23

Epaphroditus
A Christian from the church at Philippi. When Paul was in prison in Rome, members of the Philippian church sent Epaphroditus to Rome with a gift.

Philippians 2:25–30; 4:18

Ephraim
The younger of Joseph's two sons, born in Egypt. Though therefore relatively insignificant, the tribe which traced its descent from him later became an important one. Indeed, Israel as a whole was occasionally called 'Ephraim' by the prophets. This prominence was traced to the fact that the original Ephraim was adopted by Jacob, his grandfather, and singled out to receive a greater blessing than Manasseh, his elder brother.

Genesis 41:52; 48

Erastus
1. An assistant of Paul who went with Timothy to work in Macedonia, while Paul stayed on in Asia Minor.

Acts 19:22; 2 Timothy 4:20

2. The city treasurer at Corinth. Erastus was a Christian and sent his greetings to the church in Rome. This name appears on a Latin inscription found at Corinth, as the donor of a pavement to the city, and many believe it was the same person as one the New Testament mentions.

Romans 16:23

Esarhaddon
Son of Sennacherib. He became king of Assyria (681–669 BC) when his father was murdered. Manasseh, king of Judah, was one of many minor kings who were subject to Esarhaddon.

2 Kings 19:37; Ezra 4:2

Esau
The (elder) twin brother of Jacob; son of Isaac and Rebekah. The Old

Testament tells that he became a hunter, and understood so little about the covenant promises of God that he was willing to allow Jacob to take over the rights of the elder son in return for food. When Jacob exploited this, and persuaded their father Isaac to go along with this, Esau was angry and knew he had been tricked. Afraid of what he might do, Jacob left home.

In the years that Jacob was away, Esau settled in the area around Mount Seir and became rich. When they met again Esau greeted his brother warmly and accepted his gift of livestock. Esau went back to Seir and was regarded as the ancestor of the Edomite people, while Jacob went into Canaan, to become the ancestor of Israel. But despite their apparent reconciliation, there was continued trouble between their descendants.

Genesis 25:21ff.; 27–28:9; 32–33; Hebrews 12:16–17

Esther
See Esther, page 215.
Esther

Eunice
Mother of Timothy.
Acts 16:1; 2 Timothy 1:5

Eutychus
A young child, member of the Christian community in Troas. His main claim to fame is that he fell from a third-floor window as Paul was speaking with the church – though when this happened Paul went down and revived him.
Acts 20:7–13

Eve
The first woman, and Adam's partner. With him, she asserted her independence of God by eating the fruit of the 'tree that gives knowledge', heralding the disruption of life as God had intended it to be, symbolized by their exclusion from the idyllic Garden of Eden. Genesis names three sons of Eve: Cain, Abel and Seth.
Genesis 2:18–4:2; 4:25

Evil-Merodach
King of Babylon 562–560 BC, otherwise known as Amel-Marduk. When he came to the throne he released King Jehoiachin of Judah from prison in Babylon.
2 Kings 25:27–30; Jeremiah 52:31–34

Ezekiel
One of the most significant Old Testament prophets.

Ezekiel was the son of a priest called Buzi and seems to have lived in Jerusalem until Nebuchadnezzar invaded the city in 597 BC. Along with King Jehoiachin and other important citizens he was then taken captive to Babylon. There he was allowed to have his own house and lived in a settlement of Jewish exiles at Talabib on the River Chebar. After about four years he felt called by God to be a prophet. Until Jerusalem was completely destroyed in 587 BC his main message was a call to repentance. The Jews had disobeyed God and must seek forgiveness. After the Babylonians had overthrown Jerusalem Ezekiel looked forward to the day when God would allow the Jews to rebuild the city and God's temple. His messages and lifestyle were characterized by extensive psychic insights: as well as visions and dreams, he also had regular out-of-body experiences and engaged in astral travel, apparently being able to see what was going on in Jerusalem even while living in Babylon, hundreds of miles away.
Ezekiel 1:1–3; 20:33–37; 36:26–33; 43:1–5, etc.

Ezra
See Ezra, page 213.

Felix
The Roman governor before whom Paul was brought for trial at Caesarea. He kept Paul in prison for two years, hoping for a bribe.
Acts 23:24; 24:1–27

Festus
The Roman governor of Palestine after Felix. He listened carefully to Paul and called him to defend himself before King Herod Agrippa II and Bernice. All three agreed that Paul was innocent of any significant crime, but since Paul had already appealed to Caesar, they dispatched him to Rome for a full trial.
Acts 25–26

Gabriel
One of the leading archangels in Jewish religious thought at and before the time of Jesus. Gabriel appears twice to Daniel, first to tell him the meaning of a dream and later to predict what was going to happen to the city of Jerusalem. Gabriel also announces the births of John the

Baptist to Zechariah, and of Jesus to Mary.
Daniel 8:16; 9:21; Luke 1:11–20, 26–38

Gad
Seventh son of Jacob, who gave his name to the tribe of Gad.
Numbers 32

Gaius
1. A Macedonian Christian who was with Paul on his third missionary journey. Gaius was dragged into the amphitheatre during the Ephesian silversmiths' riot. See Demetrius.
Acts 19:29
2. A Christian from Derbe who travelled with Paul to Jerusalem.
Acts 20:4
3. One of the few Christians Paul baptized at Corinth.
1 Corinthians 1:14
4. The Christian friend to whom John addressed his third letter.
3 John 1

Gallio
Brother of the famous Roman philosopher Seneca, and proconsul of Achaia during either AD 51–52 or 52–53. In this position, he was based at Corinth, where Paul was brought before him by some members of the Jewish community who were concerned about the success of his preaching. However, Gallio refused to get involved in arguments about religion, and as a result Paul was able to continue his work. Gallio is particularly important because his proconsulship fixes a fairly exact date for Paul's work in Corinth, and from that much of the rest of the chronology of Paul's life can be dated (and, therefore, much of the New Testament).
Acts 18:12–17

Gamaliel
A famous Pharisee, one of Paul's rabbinic teachers, and a member of the religious council, the Sanhedrin. When the apostles were arrested and questioned, some of this council wanted to put them to death. But Gamaliel advised caution. 'Leave them alone!' he said. 'If what they have planned and done is of human origin, it will disappear, but if it comes from God, you cannot possibly defeat it.'
Acts 5:34ff.; 22:3

Gedaliah
Best-known of several Gedaliahs is the man appointed governor of

Judah by King Nebuchadnezzar of Babylon after he had captured Jerusalem. After seven months he was murdered by Ishmael, a member of the original Judahite royal family. Many of those Jews still living in Judah were afraid that the Babylonians would treat this murder as rebellion, and fled to Egypt.
2 Kings 25:22–26; Jeremiah 39:14–41:18

Gehazi
Servant of the prophet Elisha. When the Syrian general Naaman came to Elisha seeking a cure for his leprosy, Gehazi took the gift which the prophet had refused. He covered up his deceit by lying to Elisha, and subsequently became a leper himself. He continued as Elisha's servant and commended Elisha's accomplishments to King Jehoram.
2 Kings 4–5; 8:4ff.

Gershon
Levi's eldest son. Gershon and his descendants formed one of the three groups of Levites.
Exodus 6:16–17; Numbers 3:17ff.

Geshem
An influential Arabian who tried to stop Nehemiah rebuilding the walls of Jerusalem.
Nehemiah 2:19; 6:1ff.

Gideon
See Gideon, page 207.

Gog
Described in the Old Testament book of Ezekiel as the ruler of Magog and the prince of Meshech and Tubal. There Gog represents enemies from the north over whom Israel wins a great victory. In the New Testament book of Revelation Gog and Magog become symbols for all the forces of evil that are opposed to God, and are finally defeated in the last great battle between God and evil.
Ezekiel 38–39; Revelation 20:7–9

Goliath
The 3-m/10-ft Philistine giant from Gath who was killed by David using only a sling-shot. Not only did this lead to a rout of the Philistine army, but it brought David to prominence as a possible future king of Israel.
1 Samuel 17

Gomer
The wife of the prophet Hosea. See Hosea.
Hosea 1–3

Gorgias
One of Antiochus IV's generals, soundly defeated by Judas' forces in the Battle of Emmaus.
1 Maccabees 3:38; 4:1–25; 2 Maccabees 10:14–23; 12:32–37

Habakkuk
A prophet to Judah who lived at the end of the seventh century BC, the time of Jeremiah. The Chaldaeans were becoming more and more powerful, and Habakkuk found it hard to understand how God could use such a wicked nation to punish Judah. The answer came that God would one day judge all who were proud and wicked, including Judah's enemies.
Habakkuk

Hadadezer/Hadarezer
A king of Zobah in Syria. Three times King David defeated Hadadezer's troops. After the third defeat the people of Zobah became David's subjects.
2 Samuel 8–10; 1 Chronicles 18–19

Hagar
Servant to Sarah, wife of Abraham. The Old Testament records that Abraham had sex with her when it seemed as if Sarah's infertility meant that he would have no children to carry on the family line and inherit the promises made by God. When Hagar became pregnant, the jealous Sarah oppressed her until she was forced to flee into the desert. There, she was reassured by an angel that her son Ishmael would still be the founder of a great nation, even though he was rejected by Abraham.

When Sarah did give birth to her own son, Isaac, the story tells of rising tension between the two boys until eventually Sarah gave Abraham an ultimatum to get rid of Hagar and her son. The two of them were forced to travel through the desert until they were near death, but just as they were about to give up an angel again appeared, directed them to a well and repeated the promise about Ishmael.
Genesis 16; 21

Haggai
A prophet who probably returned from exile in Babylon to Jerusalem in the party led by Zerubbabel. His message recorded in the Old Testament book of

Haggai, was given in 519 BC. Haggai was concerned to find that the people had built houses for themselves and were living in comfort while the temple was still in ruins. He urged the people to rebuild it, for only by putting their faith in God could they expect to succeed.
Haggai

Ham
Noah's second son.
Genesis 5:32; 6:10; 10:6–20

Haman
The chief minister of King Ahasuerus of Persia. He is the villain of the book of Esther, locked in a power struggle with Mordecai (a Jew), and eventually plotting to get rid of not only him but all the Jewish people in Persia. When Queen Esther revealed his plot to the king, the tables were turned and Haman himself was put to death.
Esther 3–9

Hanamel
A cousin of Jeremiah. When Jerusalem was about to be captured by the Babylonians Hanamel wanted to sell a field he owned. Jeremiah bought the field to show his belief that one day Judah would no longer be ruled by Babylon and it would be worth owning land again.
Jeremiah 32

Hanani
Best-known of several Hananis is the man who travelled to Susa to tell Nehemiah that Jerusalem was still in ruins, even though the Jewish exiles had returned. When Nehemiah had rebuilt the walls of Jerusalem he made Hanani governor.
Nehemiah 1:2; 7:2

Hananiah
A prophet who opposed Jeremiah. His message was one of optimism and confidence, trying to convince the people that they would be free of Babylonian rule after only a short time. Jeremiah on the other hand saw the Babylonian invasion as part of God's judgment on his nation, and believed they needed to learn important moral and spiritual lessons before they could hope for improving fortunes.
Jeremiah 28

Hannah
The wife of Elkanah and mother of Samuel.

Hannah was childless, and while on pilgrimage to the shrine at Shiloh she vowed that if she had a son she would devote him to the service of God at Shiloh. Samuel was born, and while still a small child Hannah handed him over to Eli, the priest of Shiloh. Hannah's wonderful prayer of thanks for Samuel's birth is one of the greatest poetic pieces in the Old Testament, and many of its themes were echoed in Mary's song of praise to God as she awaited the birth of Jesus. Hannah became the mother of three other sons and two daughters.
1 Samuel 1–2

Hasideans
This Hebrew term means 'people devoted to the Law', and though they probably existed earlier it was only at the time of the Maccabean struggle against the Seleucids that they emerged into prominence. They at first gave their support to the revolt, but after the temple had been rededicated they refused to recognize the Maccabees' successors (Hasmoneans) as legitimate heirs to the priesthood there. Some of them may have left Jerusalem at this time, maybe settling at the site of Qumran by the Dead Sea. Some of their concerns were also taken up by the later religious group, the Pharisees.
1 Maccabees 2:42; 7:13; 2 Maccabees 14:6

Hasmoneans
The family name of the people otherwise known as Maccabees (a term that was originally a nickname applied to Judas, one of their leaders in the revolt against Antiochus IV, 167–164 BC). After their successful defeat of the Seleucid king, they took control of the priesthood in the temple at Jerusalem, then later became kings of an independent Jewish state, over which they ruled until the Roman general Pompey invaded Palestine in the first century BC.
2 Maccabees 8:1–10:9

Hazael
An officer at the court of Benhadad II, supported as king of Syria by a prophetic message from Elisha. Elisha wept when he saw in a vision what Hazael would do to the Israelites. Hazael killed Benhadad and seized the throne. He made war

against the kings of Israel and Judah.
1 Kings 19:15–17; 2 Kings 8ff.

Heliodorus
An official of Seleucus IV (Philopater). He was sent to pillage the Jerusalem temple, but when he got there was attacked by a horse rider wearing shining golden armour, and two other men who appeared miraculously. He was rescued only by the intervention of the high priest.
2 Maccabees 3:1–4:14

Herod
1. Herod the Great. Son of Antipater, who was made ruler of Judea by Julius Caesar in 47 BC. Antipater then appointed Herod to be governor of Galilee. After the death of his father and brother Joseph, who was governor of Jerusalem, the Romans gave Herod the title 'king of the Jews', and he reigned in that capacity from 37 to 4 BC. Herod was a good king, and began the building of a completely new temple in Jerusalem. But his people suspected his motives, and disliked his family. He was not a Jew by birth, and murdered members of the Jewish Hasmonaean family whom he saw as a threat to the throne. He features in the New Testament as the king who ordered the murder of all children in Bethlehem under two years old at the time of Jesus' birth, and certainly had a reputation for ruthless cruelty. He murdered not only his opponents, but also most of his own family, and after his death his kingdom was divided amongst his three surviving sons: Archelaus, Antipas and Philip.
Matthew 2; Luke 1:5
2. Archelaus, called Herod the Ethnarch, ruled Judea from 4 BC to AD 6. When Mary and Joseph returned with Jesus from Egypt and heard that Archelaus was ruler of Judea they decided to settle in Galilee instead. Archelaus treated the Jews and Samaritans so cruelly that they complained to the Romans, who sent him into exile.
Matthew 2:22
3. Antipas, called Herod the Tetrarch, ruled Galilee from 4 BC to AD 39. This is the king who imprisoned John the

Baptist and, as a result of a rash promise, agreed to his wife's request to have John beheaded. Pilate later invited Antipas to hear the case against Jesus, because he came from Galilee. But Antipas was bright enough to see a trap, and after deriding Jesus he sent him back to be dealt with by Pilate.
Matthew 14; Mark 6; Luke 23:7ff.
4. Agrippa I, was son of Aristobulus and grandson of Herod the Great. He became ruler of Galilee, Judea and Samaria. To try and placate the wider population, he persecuted the Christians with some enthusiasm. He killed James, the son of Zebedee, and imprisoned Peter. Luke, the writer of the New Testament book of Acts, records that Agrippa's death in AD 44 as a result of his pride.
Acts 12
5. Agrippa II was the son of Agrippa I. When he went to Caesarea to visit the Roman governor, Festus, he heard Paul's case. His verdict was that Paul could have been released if he had not appealed to Caesar.
Acts 25:13–26:32

Herodias
The wife of Herod Antipas. Antipas married Herodias while Philip, her first husband, was still alive. It was John the Baptist's condemnation of this behaviour that motivated Herodias to want him beheaded.
Matthew 14; Mark 6; Luke 3:19

Hezekiah
See Hezekiah, page 213.

Hilkiah
Best-known of several Hilkiahs is the high priest who lived in the reign of King Josiah of Judah. During renovations in the temple, he highlighted an old scroll containing Judah's historic faith in God – a discovery which gave fresh impetus to a wide-ranging reform not only in the worship at the temple but also in national life.
2 Kings 22–23; 2 Chronicles 34

Hiram
1. A king of Tyre who was a friend of kings David and Solomon. He sent cedar-wood from Lebanon to Jerusalem for the building of David's palace and later for Solomon's temple.

2 Samuel 5:11; 1 Kings 5; 9–10
2. A craftsman sent by King Hiram to help King Solomon to build his palace and the temple.
1 Kings 7

Hophni and Phinehas
Eli's two sons, priests at Shiloh. They showed open contempt for Israel's religious traditions, even taking the Ark of the Covenant into battle against the Philistines. When it was captured and they were both killed, it was regarded as appropriate punishment for such disregard of the covenant laws.
1 Samuel 2:12ff.; 4

Hosea
A prophet in the northern kingdom of Israel, from the time of Jeroboam II until just before the Assyrians captured Samaria in 722 BC. The book of Hosea shows how Hosea used his own unhappy experience of marriage as a picture of the way Israel's relationship to God had been corrupted. Just as Hosea desperately wanted to get things right with his wife, so God was also promising that 'I will bring my people back to me. I will love them with all my heart'.
Hosea

Hoshea
The last king of Israel. Hoshea got the throne by killing King Pekah. He was defeated by King Shalmaneser V of Assyria and as a result had to pay him tribute. When Hoshea rebelled he was imprisoned by Shalmaneser. Three years later Samaria, the capital of Israel, was captured and the people taken away to Assyria.
2 Kings 17

Huldah
A female prophet who lived in the reign of King Josiah. When Hilkiah the priest wanted advice about the correct interpretation of an ancient scroll of God's law, he turned to Huldah for advice.
2 Kings 22:14ff.; 2 Chronicles 34:22ff.

Hushai
A trusted friend of King David. During Absalom's rebellion Hushai pretended to go over to Absalom's side, and became an informer to David. His devious behaviour won extra time for David and enabled him to escape by informing David's

spies of Absalom's plans.
2 Samuel 15:32–17:15

Hymenaeus
A man who Paul dismissed from the church because of disagreements over belief that were weakening the faith of other Christians.
1 Timothy 1:20; 2 Timothy 2:17

Isaac
Son of Abraham and Sarah, born when they were both too old to expect to have children naturally. As a youth he had a privileged position, as the son who would inherit the family's wealth, and eventually he became embroiled in the controversies surrounding Abraham's older son Ishmael by another woman, Hagar. Abraham is presented throughout the Bible story as a person of great faith, the most striking evidence of which is said to be his willingness to murder Isaac. Just as he is about to do this in a religious ritual, an angel steps in to stop him.

At the age of 40, Isaac married Rebekah, a woman chosen for him from Abraham's family living in the ancestral home in Harran. They have twin sons, Esau and Jacob, and the divine blessing passed on from Abraham to Isaac is to be given to one of them. This was to be the oldest (Esau), but Jacob managed to trick the aged and blind Isaac to give him the blessing instead. Jacob was forced to leave home to escape the consequences of his deceit, but returned several years later in time to see his father before he died.
Genesis 21–22; 24–28:9; 35:27–29

Isaiah
A prophet who lived in Jerusalem in the reigns of Uzziah, Jotham, Ahaz and Hezekiah. He was related to the royal family of Judah, which gave him easy access to the king's court. He was called to his prophetic work as a result of a grand vision received by him in the temple, and the story of this is one of the Old Testament's most striking passages.

Isaiah's wife was also a prophet, and they had two sons whose names were selected to symbolize the prophet's message to the nation. At this period, Judah was in constant danger of attack from the powerful

Assyrian army. On one occasion when Jerusalem was besieged Isaiah encouraged King Hezekiah to trust God and not surrender. At this time, Isaiah's message gave the people of Judah hope. But he also believed they could not escape the consequences of their long-term rejection of the Old Testament laws, and so would have to suffer defeat at the hands of their enemies. But in time even these same enemies would themselves come under divine judgment, and the people of Judah could look forward to better times and a new start.
2 Kings 19–20; Isaiah

Ish-baal/Ishbosheth
One of King Saul's sons. When Saul was killed by the Philistines, Ish-baal was crowned as his successor by Abner, the commander of Saul's army. He reigned over the majority of the nation, while David was king only of his own tribe of Judah. For two years there was civil war, but when Ish-baal was murdered by two commanders of his army, David was able to become king of both sections of the nation.
2 Samuel 2–4

Ishmael
Son of Abraham and Hagar. See Hagar.
Genesis 16; 21

Israel
The name given to Jacob after he had wrestled all night with an otherwise unidentified divine messenger by the River Jabbok. Israel means 'the one who strives with God'. The 12 tribes tracing their descent from Jacob were often known as the children of Israel.
Genesis 32:22ff; 35:9

Issachar
Son of Jacob and Leah, who gave his name to one of the 12 tribes of Israel.
Genesis 35:23

Ithamar
Aaron's youngest son. In the Old Testament Ithamar is the priest who supervised the making of the tabernacle, giving direction to two groups of Levites and being founder of an important family of later priests.
Exodus 6:23; 38:21; Numbers 3ff.; 1 Chronicles 24:1

Ittai
A man from Gath who was leader of a band of

600 Philistine soldiers, but gave his loyalty to David in his struggle with the rebellious forces associated with his son Absalom. As a reward David made Ittai commander of one-third of his army.
2 Samuel 15, 18

Jabin
1. King of Hazor defeated and killed by Joshua.
Joshua 11:1–11
2. Canaanite king of Hazor, defeated by Barak and Deborah.
Judges 4

Jacob
See Jacob, page 199.

Jael
A woman from the nomadic Kenite tribe, and hero of the struggle of Barak and Deborah against the forces of Jabin of Hazor. After Sisera, commander of the Canaanite army, had lost his battle against the Israelites he took refuge in Jael's tent, where she murdered him as he slept by piercing his head with a tent peg. In one of the greatest pieces of Hebrew poetry in the Bible, Deborah praises this action by Jael.
Judges 4; 5:24–27

Jairus
Leader of the synagogue in Capernaum who asked Jesus to heal his 12-year-old daughter. Though the mourning rituals had already started by the time Jesus reached Jairus' house, to the amazement of her parents, Jesus revived her and returned her to her family.
Mark 5:22ff.

James
1. The son of Zebedee and a disciple of Jesus. Like his brother John, James made his living by fishing. They loved a good argument, and Jesus affectionately referred to these two brothers as 'children of thunder'. Along with Peter and John, James was one of the inner circle of three special disciples, who played a special part in Jesus' ministry. He was one of the first disciples to give his life for his faith, being put to death under Herod Agrippa I in about AD 44.
Matthew 4:21ff.; 17:1ff.; Mark 5:37; 10:35ff.; Acts 12:2
2. Another disciple, described variously as the son of Alphaeus, and 'James the younger'. Apart from this, nothing more is known of him.

Matthew 10:3; Mark 15:40; Acts 1:13
3. A brother of Jesus who became a disciple only after Jesus' death and resurrection. Paul seems to imply that this was as a result of a personal appearance of the risen Jesus to him. He soon became the leader of the church in Jerusalem, perhaps because of his essentially conservative outlook – though the Jewish historian Josephus records that he was stoned to death by even more conservative people in AD 62.
Matthew 13:55; Acts 12:17; 1 Corinthians 15:7; James

Japheth
One of Noah's three sons.
Genesis 5:32; 9:18ff.; 10:1ff.

Jason
1. High priest in Jerusalem, 174–171 BC. He was a fierce advocate of the Seleucid policy of thoroughgoing Hellenization of Jewish life, but not enthusiastic enough for some – and he was deposed by more radical elements. Following a disastrous attempt to regain control by military means, in which he showed extreme cruelty, he was forced to spend the rest of his life in exile.
2 Maccabees 4:7–22; 5:1–14
2. A Christian with whom Paul and Silas stayed when they were in Thessalonica. A person of the same name is mentioned by Paul in Romans, and they may well have been the same though there is no way of being certain.
Acts 17:5–9; Romans 16:21

Javan
Grandson of Noah, son of Japheth, Javan is named as the ancestor of a group of peoples, probably including those who lived in Greece and Asia Minor in early times. The name itself seems to be used in later parts of the Old Testament to indicate Greece or Greek people.
Genesis 10:2; 1 Chronicles 1:5; Isaiah 66:19; Ezekiel 27:13

Jeduthun
A Levite who is connected with music and singing in the temple worship during the reigns of kings David and Solomon.
1 Chronicles 16:41–42; 25; 2 Chronicles 5:12

Jehoahaz
1. King of Israel in 814–798 BC, succeeding Jehu, his father. The Old Testament history

writers condemn him as an apostate king who corrupted true faith. He was defeated by Hazael and Benhadad, kings of Syria.
2 Kings 13:1ff.
2. Son of Josiah and king of Judah for only a matter of months in 609 BC, before being captured and taken prisoner to Egypt by the Egyptian pharaoh Neco.
2 Kings 23:31–34

Jehoiachin
King of Judah for three months in 597 BC. He was taken prisoner to Babylon by Nebuchadnezzar, and lived there in exile. Years later a new king of Babylon recognized him by giving him a privileged place in his own royal court.
2 Kings 24:8–16; 25:27ff.; 2 Chronicles 36:9–10; Jeremiah 52:31ff.

Jehoiada
The most important person of this name was a leading priest in Jerusalem during the reigns of Ahaziah, Athaliah and Joash. Jehoiada was married to Jehosheba, sister of King Ahaziah, and on his death Athaliah, the queen mother, seized the throne and gave orders for all remaining members of the royal family to be killed. Jehoiada hid his infant nephew Joash, one of Ahaziah's sons, and six years later he made Joash king. In the process, Athaliah herself was killed, and Jehoiada ruled as regent until Joash was old enough to govern the country.
2 Kings 11–12; 2 Chronicles 23–24

Jehoiakim
Son of Josiah and king of Judah in 609–597 BC. He was made king by the Egyptian pharaoh Neco, and had to pay taxes to Egypt. In the process of ensuring the survival of his kingdom, Jehoiakim reversed most of the religious reforms of his father's reign. He had no time for dissidents and when messages from Jeremiah were delivered to him, he had no hesitation in burning the scrolls on which they were written. The influence of Egypt was short-lived, and when Jehoiakim tried to break free of Babylonian domination, his days were numbered.
2 Kings 24:1–7; 2 Chronicles 36:4–8; Jeremiah 22:18ff.; 26; 36

Jehoram/Joram
1. Son of King Ahab. Jehoram was king of Israel in 852–841 BC, after the death of his brother, King Ahaziah. He discontinued the worship of Canaanite gods and goddesses which had so incensed the prophets of his father's day, but did not carry through his promised reforms. He was murdered by Jehu, who wiped out all Ahab's remaining descendants.
2 Kings 3; 8–9
2. King of Judah 851–841 BC (co-regent from 853 BC) after his father Jehoshaphat. The prophet Elijah warned that he would die from a terrible disease because he had massacred his six brothers and did nothing to encourage faithfulness to the Old Testament law.
2 Kings 8:16ff.; 2 Chronicles 21

Jehoshaphat
The son of King Asa who was king of Judah in 873–848 BC (co-regent from 875 BC). The Old Testament history writers approve of him as a good king who rejected foreign gods and tried to ensure his people honoured their own religious faith. He reformed the legal system, appointing judges in the major towns. But his downfall began when he made the mistake of forming an alliance with King Ahab, and found himself drawn into Israel's wars.
1 Kings 22; 2 Kings 3; 2 Chronicles 17–21:1

Jehosheba/Jehoshabeath
The sister of King Ahaziah of Judah, wife of Jehoiada, the priest. See Jehoiada.
2 Kings 11:1–3; 2 Chronicles 22:11–12

Jehu
A commander in the army of King Jehoram of Israel. He was king in 841–814 BC, nominated by the prophet Elisha with a mandate to annihilate the descendants of Ahab and Jezebel in revenge for their disregard of the prophetic messages. He carried this task through with such enthusiasm that his violence was later condemned for its sheer inhumanity by the prophet Hosea. Later in his reign King Hazael of Syria invaded Israel. Shalmaneser III of Assyria includes Jehu in a list of subject kings. Jehu may have asked

Assyria to help him defeat Syria.
2 Kings 9–10

Jehudi
A court official in Jerusalem who read the scroll containing Jeremiah's messages aloud to King Jehoiakim.
Jeremiah 36

Jephthah
One of the judges of early Israel for six years. Distinguished for murdering his own daughter, in fulfilment of a vow that if he had success in battle he would kill the first living thing he saw and offer it as a religious sacrifice.
Judges 11–12

Jeremiah
A prophet in Judah in about 627–590 BC. He was the son of a priest, and felt a call to be a prophet when he was still young. For years the people of Judah had dismissed the prophets and their messages, and disregarded the religious laws of their nation. Jeremiah warned them that unless they changed their ways their land and city would be captured, and the people taken away to Babylon. But God would forgive them and rebuild their country if they turned back to God. 'I will make a new covenant with the people of Israel… I will put my law within them and write it on their hearts.' Still the people refused to listen, and Jerusalem fell to the Babylonian king Nebuchadnezzar. Jeremiah was able to stay on in Judah even after this, but his own people forced him to go to Egypt after the murder of the governor of Judah and he probably died there.
2 Chronicles 35:25; 36:12, 21–22; Jeremiah

Jeroboam I
See Jeroboam I, page 211

Jeroboam II
Became king of Israel after his father, Joash, and reigned for 41 years, in 793–753 BC. He reconquered land which Israel had lost and during his reign the country became wealthy. Israel grew confident and careless. Neither king nor people took notice of the warnings of the prophets, Hosea and Amos. They continued to amass wealth for themselves, and created an unjust society which was unworthy of the covenant between God and their nation.
2 Kings 14:23–29; Amos 7

Jerubbaal
Another name for Gideon.

Jesse
Grandson of Ruth and Boaz, and father of King David.
1 Samuel 16–17

Jesus
See The Life and Teaching of Jesus, pages 176–191.

Jesus ben Sira
Author of the book known as the Wisdom of Ben Sira (or Ecclesiasticus). He was a Jew living in Egypt sometime in the early second century BC, though he was in close contact with Jerusalem, and probably ran an educational establishment there. He was well-versed in the traditions of his own people, but had also travelled extensively and was familiar with the wisdom teachings of many other nations.
Wisdom of Ben Sira

Jethro/Reuel
A Midianite priest and father-in-law of Moses. When Moses brought the Israelites to Sinai, Jethro came to see him, bringing Moses' wife and sons. He advised Moses to choose capable assistants who could share the burden of leadership.
Exodus 2:16ff.; 3:1; 4:18–19; 18

Jezebel
See Jezebel, page 211.

Joab
King David's nephew and commander of his army. He was fearless but violent. Joab helped David become king of all the tribes of Israel. He remained loyal to David during Absalom's rebellion, but later gave his backing to Adonijah's revolt. After David's death King Solomon had Joab executed for his part in that revolt and to avenge the murders of Abner and Amasa, two other army leaders.
2 Samuel 2–3; 10–11; 14; 18–20; 24; 1 Kings 1–2; 1 Chronicles 11ff.

Joanna
The wife of an official of Herod Antipas, who became a regular follower of Jesus after she was healed by him. As a woman of some wealth, she gave regular financial support to Jesus and his disciples. After the crucifixion, she was one of the women who found Jesus' tomb empty.
Luke 8:1–3; 24:10

Joash/Jehoash

1. Son of King Ahaziah, made king of Judah when he was only eight years old. As an infant, his life was saved by his uncle Jehoiada, a priest. In the early part of his 40-year reign (835–796 BC) he was guided by Jehoiada. He is praised by the Old Testament historians for his many religious reforms, though after Jehoiada's death he went back on some of them and murdered Zechariah, Jehoiada's son. He stripped gold from the temple to appease the invading Syrians. Joash was murdered by his own officials. See Jehoiada.
2 Kings 11–12; 2 Chronicles 24

2. King of Israel for 16 years (798–781 BC) after King Jehoahaz, his father.
2 Kings 13–14

Job

Hero of the Old Testament book of Job. Job was a man of outstanding goodness, who lost his wealth, his 10 children and his health in a series of inexplicable disasters. In spite of this he refused to take his wife's advice and curse God. Three friends who came to visit him were convinced that Job's troubles were his own fault. But he knew that this was untrue, and as he struggles to come to terms with all that has happened to him he eventually finds new direction in a fresh awareness of God's sovereign power and wisdom. In the end he finds healing and his fortunes are restored.

Joel

A post-exilic prophet; the son of Pethuel. The book of Joel describes a plague of locusts and a terrible drought, which are understood from God to the people who had returned to Judah from exile in Babylon. While calling for repentance, Joel also spoke of a coming new age when those who remained faithful to God would find a new prosperity in life.
Joel

Johanan

A Jewish leader who stayed in Judah after Jerusalem was captured by King Nebuchadnezzar of Babylon. Johanan warned Gedaliah, governor of Judah, about the plot to murder him. Afterwards, against Jeremiah's advice, he led the people to Egypt.
Jeremiah 40–43

John the apostle

See John, page 250.

John the Baptist

See John the Baptist, page 245.

Jonah

A prophet whose story is set in the eighth century BC, during the ascendancy of Assyria. Jonah receives divine instructions to go to the Assyrian capital city, Nineveh, to speak out against the wickedness of the people there and give them a chance to change their ways. Instead he took a ship to Tarshish, in the opposite direction. A storm blew up and Jonah knew intuitively that this was because he had run away from God. He told the crew to throw him overboard. When they did this the storm died down. Instead of drowning, Jonah was swallowed by a huge fish which later disgorged him onto a beach.

Given a second chance, Jonah went straight to Nineveh and delivered his message. He was well received, and the whole nation, from the king down, fasted and prayed to God, and the city was spared. But Jonah was angry that God could so easily forgive the story of Israel's enemies, and the story concludes with him struggling to come to terms with this.
Jonah

Jonathan

Eldest son of King Saul and an intimate friend of David. He was a brave warrior and distinguished himself in several battles against the Philistines. Although Jonathan knew David might become king in his place he was a loyal friend and saved him even from being killed by his father, Saul. Jonathan and Saul died in the same battle against the Philistines. David's lament in praise of Jonathan is one of the Old Testament's outstanding poems.
1 Samuel 13–14; 18–20; 23:16–18; 31:2; 2 Samuel 1

Jonathan

A son of Mattathias, the priest who first resisted the Hellenization policies of Antiochus IV. After the death of his brother Judas, Jonathan became leader of the Maccabean forces.
1 Maccabees 9:23–12:53

Joseph

1. See Joseph, page 199.

2. Husband of Mary, the mother of Jesus. Joseph's family home was in Nazareth, a small village of Galilee, where he operated a building business in which he was presumably joined by Jesus. Apart from the stories of Jesus' birth, and the account of one episode in which Joseph and Mary went on pilgrimage with Jesus when he was 12 years old, Joseph is never mentioned in the stories of Jesus' life and teaching. It is widely supposed that he may have died before Jesus was grown up. That may indicate he was much older than Mary, but equally building construction can be dangerous work, and he may have died in an accident.
Matthew 1–2; Luke 1:27

3. Joseph of Arimathaea. A member of the religious Sanhedrin council in Jerusalem, and evidently a secret admirer, if not disciple, of Jesus. After the crucifixion he arranged for Jesus' body to be buried in the brand-new tomb he had prepared for himself.
Luke 23:50–53; John 19:38–42

Joshua

1. See Joshua, page 206.

2. High priest immediately after the return from exile in Babylon. He started rebuilding the temple, but the work was slow and difficult. The prophets Haggai and Zechariah helped to enthuse the people, and the temple was sufficiently repaired to be back in use again.
Haggai; Zechariah 3

Josiah

See Josiah, page 213.

Jotham

King of Judah in 750–731 BC, after his father King Uzziah. He began to reign while his father was still alive but suffering from leprosy. Jotham is regarded in the Old Testament as a good king, faithful to God's covenant with the people. He fortified Judah and defeated the Ammonites.
2 Kings 15:32–38; 2 Chronicles 27:1–6

Judah

The fourth son of Jacob and Leah. Judah persuaded his brothers to sell Joseph to passing traders on their way to Egypt, instead of killing him. Jacob's last words to Judah promised him a future kingdom.
Genesis 29:35; 37:26–27; 38; 49:9–10

Judas/Jude

1. Judas, the son of James, is listed as one of Jesus' 12 disciples. He is mentioned as present at Jesus' ascension.
Luke 6:16; Acts 1:13

2. One of Jesus' brothers. It is not clear whether, like James, he became a follower of Jesus after his death, but he was not a disciple during Jesus' lifetime.
Matthew 13:55; John 7:5; Acts 1:14

3. See Judas Iscariot, page 247.

Judas Maccabeus

Third son of Mattathias, instigator of the Jewish revolt against Antiochus IV. He was a skilled guerrilla fighter, and defeated the superior Seleucid forces in less than two years. The name 'Maccabeus' was originally a nickname, meaning 'the hammerer'.
1 Maccabees 3:1–9:22; 2 Maccabees 8:1–36; 10:10–15:36

Judith

A courageous widow of the town of Bethuliah, under siege by Holofernes, the general of King Nebuchadnezzar of Babylon, who had sent him with a large army to punish Judah. Just as the elders of her town were thinking about giving up their resistance, Judith gained access to the Babylonian camp and, because she was an attractive woman, succeeded in getting into Holofernes' tent. Throughout the time she was there, she insisted on following Jewish food and other laws scrupulously, waiting for the moment when she could get rid of Holofernes. One night, as he lay drunk in his tent, she managed to decapitate him with his own sword, and returned to her own people with his head in a bag. The army fled, and her town was saved.
Judith 1:1–11:25

Julius

A Roman centurion in charge of Paul on his voyage to Rome to be tried before Caesar.
Acts 27:1, 3, 42–44

Keturah

Abraham's second wife.
Genesis 25:1ff.

Kish

A wealthy man from the tribe of Benjamin; the father of Saul, first king of Israel.
1 Samuel 9:1ff.

Kittim

One of the sons of Javan in the Genesis 'table of the nations', and so the name of Cyprus and of its early city of Kition.
Genesis 10:4; 1 Chronicles 1:7; Numbers 24:24; Isaiah 23:1, 12; Jeremiah 2:10; Ezekiel 27:6

Kohath

A son of Levi and grandfather of Moses. His descendants were known as the Kohathites and formed one of the three groups of Levites.
Exodus 6:16ff.; Numbers 3:17ff.

Korah

1. A Levite who led a rebellion against Moses and Aaron. He did not see what right they had to be leaders and was angry because the people had not reached Canaan quickly enough. Korah and his collaborators never reached Canaan, something which the Old Testament links with their rejection of Moses as a leader with divine authority.
Numbers 16

2. A son of Levi, whose descendants are mentioned as singers in the temple.
1 Chronicles 6:37; Psalms 44–49

Laban

The brother of Rebekah, Isaac's wife. He lived in Harran and welcomed his nephew Jacob when he was forced to leave home after his treachery against Esau. Laban had two daughters – Leah and Rachel – and Jacob agreed to work for Laban for seven years to earn the right to marry Rachel. But Laban tricked him into marrying Leah instead, and forced him to work for a second seven years for Rachel. Jacob in turn outwitted Laban and as a result his flock of sheep and goats became larger and stronger than his uncle's. When Laban discovered that Jacob had secretly left for Canaan he chased after him, but after a divine warning in a dream Laban was persuaded to be reconciled to Jacob, and they each agreed to go their own way.
Genesis 24:29ff.; 29–31

Lamech

1. A descendant of Cain, noteworthy for a particularly brutal attitude to vengeance.
Genesis 4:18ff.

2. Son of Methuselah, and father of Noah.
Genesis 5:28–31

Lazarus

1. Brother of Martha and Mary, residents of Bethany. All three were friends with Jesus, and when Lazarus became ill his sisters sent for Jesus. Jesus' arrival was delayed until after Lazarus was dead. (See Martha.) But when Jesus went with the weeping women to the tomb, he surprised everyone by ordering the stone to be rolled away from the entrance, and then calling in for Lazarus to come out. When Lazarus does so, it becomes a turning point in the entire narrative in John's gospel, with some religious leaders deciding to join forces with Jesus, while other opponents became even more convinced of the need to get rid of him.
John 11–12:11

2. The name of the beggar in Jesus' story of the rich man and the beggar at his gate.
Luke 16:19–31

Leah

Elder daughter of Laban, married to Jacob through Laban's trick. She and Jacob had six sons and a daughter.
Genesis 29:16–33:7

Levi

1. Third son of Jacob and Leah, and ancestor of the Levites, whose traditional role was related to the worship in the temple.
Genesis 29:34; 34:25ff.; 49:5ff.; Numbers 3:5–20

2. See Matthew.

Lot

Abraham's nephew. He went with Abraham from Harran to Canaan but they parted after their employees quarrelled. Lot settled in Sodom, where he was rescued from a variety of dangerous situations. When Sodom met its end in a fireball, Lot managed to escape with his life, but his wife was caught in the disaster and reduced to a 'pillar of salt'.
Genesis 11:31–14:16; 19

Lud

Lud, a son of Shem, gave his name to a people known later as the Lydians. They lived in the west of Asia Minor around Sardis.

Luke

A doctor by profession, and the only Gentile writer of the New Testament. He wrote the gospel of Luke and the

Acts of the Apostles. He was a friend of Paul and travelled with him on some of his journeys, so he was able to describe at first-hand some of the things Paul said and did. He sailed to Rome with Paul and stayed with him while he was a prisoner there. He may have been one of Paul's rich sponsors, subsidizing the cost of his extensive travels and using his own contacts to ensure the Christian message was heard by significant people.

Colossians 4:14; 2 Timothy 4:11; Philemon 24

Lydia

A dealer in purple cloth who came from Thyatira in Asia Minor. She heard Paul preach in Philippi (Macedonia) was convinced by his message and became a Christian.

Acts 16:14–15, 40

Lysias

A Seleucid military leader, given charge of his realm by Antiochus IV while he was fighting the Parthians. Lysias fought several battles against the Maccabees, either in person or through his generals Ptolemy, Nicanor and Gorgias.

1 Maccabees 3:32–4:35; 6:55; 2 Maccabees 11:1–38

Malachi

Malachi's book is the last in the Old Testament, though he was not the latest Old Testament prophet (about mid-fifth century BC). At the time when he lived, the temple had been rebuilt after the return from exile but its operations were being neglected as people concentrated on building houses for themselves and generally preferred to re-establish social structures rather than religious ones. Malachi (whose name means 'my messenger') warned the people against trying God's patience, and forecast doom and disaster would once more come upon them if they paid no attention to his message.

Malachi

Manasseh

1. Joseph's elder son who was adopted and blessed by Jacob. His descendants formed the tribe of Manasseh.

Genesis 41:51; 48:1ff

2. King of Judah for 45 years (696–642 BC) after his father, King Hezekiah. Manasseh is unreservedly condemned in the Old Testament as

the most wicked of all the kings, a ruler who led the nation astray by introducing unacceptable forms of worship into the Jerusalem temple and making too many political compromises with the Assyrians. The account in 2 Chronicles describes his later repentance, something that is elaborated in the later version of the Prayer of Manasseh.

2 Kings 21:1ff; 2 Chronicles 33:1–20; Prayer of Manasseh 1–15

Manoah

Samson's father.

Judges 13; 14:3

Mark

The writer of the New Testament gospel of Mark. His exact identity is not completely indisputable, but there was a John Mark who lived in Jerusalem, and whose mother, Mary, was leader of a church that met in her house. Mark later went with Paul and Barnabas, his cousin, to Cyprus on Paul's first missionary journey. He left them halfway through and Paul refused to take him when they set out again. Instead Mark returned to Cyprus with Barnabas. Later Paul and Mark were together in Rome, and Paul wrote of him as a loyal friend and helper. Peter also knew him, and described him as 'my son Mark' and, by tradition, it was Peter who gave Mark much of the story of Jesus told in Mark's gospel.

Mark 14:51; Acts 12:12; 25; 13:13; 15:36ff; Colossians 4:10; 2 Timothy 4:11; Philemon 24; 1 Peter 5:13

Martha

The sister of Mary and Lazarus. She lived with them at the village of Bethany, close to Jerusalem. Jesus often visited their home. She is presented as the pragmatic housekeeper, who had little interest in discussions about religion, and who resented her sister Mary's insistence in taking part in them (something that would have been reserved for men in those days).

Luke 10:38–42; John 11:20ff

Mary

1. See Mary, page 248.
2. Sister of Martha. She lived in Bethany with her sister and brother Lazarus and loved to listen to Jesus. Just before Jesus' death she anointed him with precious oil and wiped

his feet with her hair.

Luke 10:38–42; John 11; 12:3ff

3. Mary Magdalene became a disciple of Jesus as a result of being healed by him. The New Testament tells that she was the first person to see Jesus after the resurrection, and the one who ran to tell the news to the other disciples.

Mark 16:9; Luke 8:2; 24:10; John 20:1ff

4. Mary, mother of James and Joseph. She was present at the crucifixion and was one of the group of women who found Jesus' tomb empty on the resurrection morning. This Mary is possibly the same person as 'the other Mary' and Mary, wife of Clopas.

Matthew 27:56, 61; 28:1; John 19:25

5. Mary, the mother of John Mark. The first Christians met in her house in Jerusalem.

Acts 12:12

Mattathias

A priest of Modein, not far from Jerusalem, who refused to offer sacrifices in honour of Antiochus IV, and thereby sparked off the Maccabean revolt against Greek domination of the Jewish people. He allowed his men to fight even on the Sabbath day, so that the Hellenistic forces could not surprise them. His son, Judas, took over the struggle from him, and was the one who saw the campaign through to an effective completion.

1 Maccabees 2:1–70

Matthew

One of the 12 disciples, and traditionally the writer of the New Testament gospel of Matthew. Matthew, also called Levi, was a tax collector before he became a follower of Jesus.

Matthew 9:9; 10:3; Luke 5:27–32

Matthias

Chosen after the death of Judas Iscariot to take the traitor's place as one of the 12 disciples of Jesus.

Acts 1:21–26

Melchizedek

A king and priest at Salem (Jerusalem), who met and blessed Abraham after a battle. In the New Testament, he becomes a symbol for Jesus, who also could be described as 'king' and 'priest'.

Genesis 14:18–20; Psalm 110:4; Hebrews 5:4–10; Hebrews 7:1–28

Menahem

One of the last kings of Israel (752–742 BC). When King Shallum had reigned for only one month Menahem killed him and seized the throne for himself. During his reign Tiglath-Pileser III of Assyria invaded Israel, and he was forced into accepting Assyrian domination. Since this inevitably included the adoption of Assyrian religious symbols and practices, he is roundly condemned in the Old Testament history books.

2 Kings 15:14–22

Menelaus

A scheming high priest in the time of Antiochus IV. When the high priest Jason sent him to take tribute to Antiochus, Menelaus offered a larger amount if he could be made the high priest instead. In the event, he got the post, but never paid up. He tried to build up his own power base, interfering with other neighbouring states, and eventually convincing Antiochus he should be taken seriously. When Antiochus saw through him, he had him executed by being thrown into a tower of ashes.

2 Maccabees 4:23–50; 13:1–8

Mephibosheth

The son of Jonathan, David's close friend, and grandson of King Saul. When David became king he gave Mephibosheth a place at the palace and servants to wait on him.

2 Samuel 4:4; 9; 16:1ff; 19:24–30; 21:7

Merab

A daughter of King Saul. Saul promised David he could marry her, but gave her to another man instead.

1 Samuel 14:49; 18:17ff

Merari

One of Levi's sons. His descendants, the Merarites, formed one of the three groups of Levites.

Exodus 6:16ff; Numbers 3

Merodach-Baladan

A king of Babylon (otherwise known as Marduk-apla-iddina II, 721–710 BC) who sent messengers to King Hezekiah in Jerusalem, hoping to encourage him to join forces with Babylon to oppose the Assyrians.

Isaiah 39

Meshach

See Abednego.

Methuselah

Remembered as the oldest person mentioned in the Bible. The Old Testament states that he died in the year of the great flood, aged 969 years.

Genesis 5:22–27

Micah

A prophet who lived in the eighth century BC. He was active at roughly the same time as Isaiah, Amos and Hosea. Micah lived in a village in the lowlands of Judah but his message was for people in Samaria, the capital of Israel, as well as those in Jerusalem. He predicted that both cities would be destroyed because of the evil and harsh treatment of the poor which the leaders allowed to continue. A century later, Jeremiah reminded the people of Micah's words.

Jeremiah 26:18–19; Micah

Micaiah

A prophet who lived in the reign of King Ahab. When Ahab planned to fight a battle against the Syrians he asked many prophets if he was going to win. Four hundred predicted that he would have success, and only Micaiah foretold defeat. Ahab was angry at this answer and threw Micaiah into prison, but his prediction came true.

1 Kings 22

Michael

An archangel described in Daniel as the guardian of the Jewish people.

Daniel 10:21; 12:1; Jude 9; Revelation 12:7

Michal

King Saul's younger daughter and one of David's wives. She helped David to escape from Saul and saved his life, but Saul gave her to another man.

1 Samuel 14:49; 18:20ff; 25:44; 2 Samuel 3:13–16; 6:16ff

Miriam

Sister of Moses and Aaron. The Old Testament tells that she watched over her baby brother Moses in the reed basket until he was found by the daughter of the Egyptian pharaoh. After the Israelites had escaped from Egypt, Miriam led them all in singing and dancing for joy. Later she quarrelled with Moses, because she was jealous of him as leader. For a short time thereafter she suffered a terrible skin disease, but was miraculously healed. Miriam died at Kadesh before the Israelites

reached Canaan.

Exodus 2:4, 7–8; 15:20–21; Numbers 12; 20:1

Moab

A son of Lot and traditional ancestor of the nation of Moab.

Genesis 19:36–37

Mordecai

Esther's cousin and guardian. Mordecai was a Jew who lived in Susa, capital of Persia. When he heard about a plot to kill all his people he persuaded Esther, then wife of the Persian king Ahasuerus to plead for their lives. Mordecai afterwards became the king's chief minister.

Esther

Moses

See Moses, page 201.

Naaman

A Syrian general who went to the prophet Elisha looking to be cured of his leprosy.

2 Kings 5

Nabal

A rich sheep farmer who lived near Carmel. David, then an outlaw, protected Nabal's land. At sheep-shearing time, when David asked for supplies, Nabal rudely refused. Abigail, Nabal's wife, heard that David's men were about to attack. Without telling her husband she packed up a large amount of food and wine and pleaded with them to spare her husband's life. The raid was called off, but when Nabal heard, he collapsed – and died soon afterwards.

1 Samuel 25

Naboth

Owner of a vineyard in Jezreel next to King Ahab's palace. When Ahab tried to buy the vineyard from Naboth, he refused to sell, pointing out that under the covenant laws there was meant to be no such thing as private property in Israel. Naboth, like everyone else, held the land in trust from God, and for the next generations. The king was far from happy, though recognised the truth of what Naboth was saying. Ahab's wife Jezebel, though, was from a different culture, and to her all this made no sense at all. If the king wanted the vineyard, he would have it. Jezebel set up two false witnesses to claim that Naboth had cursed God and the king. He was found guilty and stoned to death. Ahab got his vineyard – but the prophet Elijah came soon afterwards to condemn his actions, and to announce the coming of disaster to his own family.

1 Kings 21

Nadab

1. Aaron's eldest son. He became a priest but died unexpectedly – a fate attributed to the way he and Abihu, his brother, had dishonoured their office.

Exodus 6:23; Leviticus 10

2. Son of Jeroboam I, he became king of Israel in 910 BC, and was assassinated and succeeded by Baasha almost immediately.

1 Kings 14:20; 15:25–28

Nahor

1. The father of Terah and grandfather of Abraham.

Genesis 11:22–25

2. Abraham's brother.

Genesis 11:26–29; 22:20ff; 24:10ff.

Nahum

A prophet from Elkosh, probably in Judah, of whom nothing is known apart from the book that contains his messages. These were delivered just before Nineveh, capital of Assyria, was captured by Babylon in 612 BC. Nahum said that Nineveh would be destroyed because of its cruelty to other nations.

Nahum

Naomi

The mother-in-law of Ruth. Naomi and her husband Elimelech came from Bethlehem. They had two sons, Mahlon and Chilion. The family moved to Moab because of a famine. There Mahlon and Chilion married Moabite girls. After her husband and sons had died, Naomi returned to Bethlehem and Ruth (one of the Moabite wives) insisted on going with her. Following the customs of the day, Boaz, a distant male relative, saw it was his duty to marry Ruth – and did so, even though she was of a different race. Their son turned out to be King David's grandfather – something which the writer of the Old Testament book takes to be a legitimization of such mixed marriages.

Ruth

Naphtali

The fifth son of Jacob; founding father of the tribe of Naphtali.

Genesis 30:8; 49:21

Nathan

Best-known of several Nathans is the prophet who lived in King David's reign. Nathan was the king's confidant and conscience on several occasions – most notably, confronting him with his rape of Bathsheba and subsequent murder of her husband, Uriah. During David's final days, it was Nathan, along with Zadok the priest, who anointed Solomon to be the next king.

2 Samuel 7; 12; 1 Kings 1; 1 Chronicles 17

Nathanael

One of Jesus' disciples. He is mentioned only in the New Testament gospel of John, but some believe he was the same person as the disciple known in the other gospels as Bartholomew. Nathanael heard about Jesus through Philip.

John 1:45ff; 21:2

Nebuchadnezzar/Nebuchadrezzar

King of Babylon in 605–562 BC. He was the son of Nabopolassar who conquered the Assyrian empire. Nebuchadnezzar led his father's army against the Egyptians and defeated them at Carchemish in 605 BC. Babylon gained control of the countries which had been subject to Egypt, including Judah. For three years Judah paid tax to Babylon. But in 597 BC King Jehoiakim rebelled, and Nebuchadnezzar attacked Jerusalem. He took Jehoiachin, who was now king, prisoner to Babylon along with the most important citizens. Nebuchadnezzar put Zedekiah on the throne in Jerusalem, but then when he rebelled he besieged the city, and it finally fell and was destroyed in 587 BC. More of the people were taken into exile in Babylon, and Judah's days as an independent state were finished.

2 Kings 24–25; 2 Chronicles 36; Jeremiah 21:2–52:30; Ezekiel 26:7ff.; 29:18ff.; 30:10; Daniel 1–4

Nebuzaradan

The captain of King Nebuchadnezzar's guard. Nebuzaradan was responsible for sending the people of Judah into exile in Babylon after Nebuchadnezzar had captured Jerusalem. He burned down the temple and reduced the city to ruins. However, he carried out

Nebuchadnezzar's command to treat Jeremiah kindly and let him stay in Judah.

2 Kings 25; Jeremiah 39ff.

Neco

See Pharaoh.

Nehemiah

See Nehemiah, page 213.

Nicanor

One of three Seleucid generals dispatched by Antiochus IV's governor Lysias to subdue the Maccabean revolt. His troops suffered a serious defeat, and he escaped only by wearing disguise as he fled to Antioch. He was nominated governor of Judea, but was unable to subdue Judas Maccabee, and it was only a matter of time before he was killed in battle. His final humiliation came after death, as his body was displayed in public in Jerusalem.

1 Maccabees 3:38; 7:26–50; 2 Maccabees 8:9–36; 14:15–36; 15:1–37

Nicodemus

A Pharisee and a member of the religious council, the Sanhedrin. The New Testament records that he came to talk to Jesus secretly, at night. 'No one can see the kingdom of God,' Jesus said, 'without being born again.' Nicodemus did not understand what he meant then, but later he spoke up for Jesus when the Pharisees wanted to arrest him. After Jesus' crucifixion Nicodemus brought spices to embalm his body.

John 3:1–20; 7:50ff.; 19:39–42

Noah

The Old Testament presents Noah as a good man at a time of great evil and violence. Things in the world were so corrupt that it was to be annihilated altogether through a great flood. Thanks to instructions from God, Noah and his family survived, by building a large boat. It made no sense to those who watched, but when the rains came, Noah, his wife, his three sons and their wives, went on board together with pairs of every kind of living creature. The boat floated until the flood went down, when it came to rest on a mountain. After the flood Noah received an assurance that there would never again be such a flood that would destroy all living things. The rainbow was the sign of that promise.

Stories like this were preserved in many nations of the ancient world. The distinguishing feature of the story of Noah is not so much what happened, as the moral basis on which it is founded. Unlike the Babylonian flood stories, in which the gods play around with the destiny of humans for their own fun, in the Old Testament the destruction comes as a direct consequence of evil behaviour, and Noah is saved because of his desire to be good.

Genesis 6–9; 1 Peter 3:20

Obadiah

1. A steward in charge of King Ahab's household. When Queen Jezebel gave orders for all God's prophets to be killed, Obadiah hid 100 of them in caves and fed them until the danger was over. He risked his life again when Elijah asked him to arrange a meeting with Ahab.

1 Kings 18

2. A prophet, probably from Judah, who spoke out against the nation of Edom. Apart from the book containing his messages, nothing else is known of him. He condemns Edom bitterly for refusing to help their neighbours in an emergency. This seems to refer to the time when Jerusalem was destroyed by Babylon in 587 BC. If so, it places Obadiah sometime in the fifth century BC.

Obadiah

Obed

The son of Ruth and Boaz and grandfather of King David.

Ruth 4:13ff.

Obed-Edom

A Philistine in whose house the Ark of the Covenant was placed for a time by King David, after Uzzah's death.

2 Samuel 6; 1 Chronicles 13

Og

King of Bashan, a land east of the River Jordan. The Israelites, led by Moses, defeated Og and captured his 60 fortified cities. The land of Bashan was given to the half tribe of Manasseh.

Numbers 21:32ff.; Deuteronomy 3; Joshua 22:7

Omri

Commander of the army of King Elah of Israel. His fellow officers made him king when they heard that Zimri had murdered Elah. Omri was a strong and vigorous king, and

reigned 885–874 BC. He chose Samaria as his new capital – a good site at the top of a steep hill and easily defended. Omri lost one of his cities to Syria but conquered Moab. As a result Moab paid a heavy tax to Israel each year. In spite of his political success, he is condemned by the Old Testament historians as one of the kings who corrupted Israel's faith – and encouraged his son, Ahab, to do the same.

1 Kings 16:15–28; 20:34

Onesimus

A slave who belonged to Philemon, a Christian convert of Paul's who lived in the city of Colossae. Onesimus had met up with Paul in prison (in either Ephesus or Rome), having run away from his master. During this time, Onesimus became a Christian. Paul wrote the letter to Philemon asking him to forgive Onesimus and accept him as a brother-Christian – and also to set him free so he could work full-time with Paul in his missionary endeavours. There is no record of how he was received by Philemon, though presumably this small letter would not have been included in the New Testament if things had not worked out as Paul hoped. A person by the name of Onesimus was bishop of the church in Ephesus at the end of the first century, and some think this was the same person. Some also believe it was Onesimus who first gathered together all the letters of Paul – and that explains why this essentially personal little note was included along with the others.

Colossians 4:9; Philemon

Onesiphorus

A Christian who helped Paul when he was at Ephesus. He later encouraged Paul by visiting him when he was in prison at Rome.

2 Timothy 1:16ff.; 4:19

Onias

The family name of a group of priests during the Hellenistic period, who accommodated themselves to the Greek rulers of Palestine over several generations. One of them, Onias III, established a temple at Heliopolis in Egypt, in about 168 BC.

2 Maccabees 4:1–34

Ornan

See Araunah.

Orpah

A Moabite girl who married one of Naomi's sons.

Ruth 1

Othniel

One of the judges in Israel. Othniel opposed the worship of Canaanite deities, and as a result gained victory over Cushan-Rishathaim, king of Mesopotamia.

Joshua 15:16–17; Judges 3:7–11

Pashur

A priest in charge of the temple in Jeremiah's time. He had Jeremiah thrown into the stocks because he had said Jerusalem would be destroyed.

Jeremiah 20:1–6

Paul (Saul)

See Paul (Saul), page 249.

Pekah

A captain in King Pekahiah's army who seized the throne of Israel (740–732 BC). He is dismissed as an evil king who introduced and encouraged the worship of alien gods and goddesses. Pekah made an alliance with King Rezin of Syria and both countries invaded Judah. King Ahaz of Judah appealed to Tiglath-Pileser III of Assyria for help. As a result the Assyrians invaded Israel and captured several cities. Shortly after this Pekah was murdered by Hoshea.

2 Kings 15:25–16:5; 2 Chronicles 28:5–6

Pekahiah

King of Israel after Menahem, his father, in 742–740 BC. Pekahiah allowed the Israelites to continue worshipping idols. He was assassinated in the second year of his reign by Pekah, a captain in his army.

2 Kings 15:22–26

Peter

See Peter, page 247.

Pharaoh

Title of the kings of Egypt. Several pharaohs are mentioned in the Old Testament including:

1. The pharaoh visited by Abraham.

Genesis 12:10ff.

2. The pharaoh who made Joseph his chief minister.

Genesis 40ff.

3. The pharaoh who was forced to let Moses lead the Israelites out of Egypt, according to some Ramesses II, who built great store cities.

Exodus 5ff.

4. The pharaoh who sheltered Hadad after David defeated the Edomites.

1 Kings 11

5. The pharaoh who gave Solomon his daughter in marriage.

1 Kings 9:16

6. Shoshenk. He encouraged Jeroboam to lead the 10 tribes in revolt against King Solomon's unpopular son, Rehoboam. Later he raided Jerusalem and took away the temple treasure.

1 Kings 11:40; 14:25–26

7. So, who was asked by King Hoshea of Israel to form an alliance against Assyria.

2 Kings 17:4

8. Tirhakah led his army against Assyria during the reign of King Hezekiah. The Assyrian army had to abandon its attack on Jerusalem to meet the Egyptian forces.

2 Kings 19:9; Isaiah 37:9

9. Neco, 610–595 BC. He killed King Josiah of Judah at the Battle of Megiddo. For four years Neco made Judah pay tribute to him, but then he was himself defeated by Nebuchadnezzar of Babylon at the battle of Carchemish (605 BC). After that Judah was in Babylon's power. Neco spent his later years defending Egypt and trying to strengthen his country.

2 Kings 23:29ff; 24:7; 2 Chronicles 35:20–36:4

10. Hophra, 587–570 BC. He supported King Zedekiah's rebellion against Nebuchadnezzar of Babylon.

Jeremiah 37:5; 44:30; Ezekiel 17:15ff; 29:2

Philemon

A Christian friend of Paul who lived in Colosse. Philemon was the master of the runaway slave, Onesimus, and the leader of the church at Colosse, which met in his house.

Philemon

Philip

1. One of the 12 disciples of Jesus. He came from the lakeside town of Bethsaida in Galilee, the home town of Peter and Andrew. The stories about Philip are all in John's gospel. There, he was the one who introduced Nathanael to Jesus. Faced with a crowd of 5,000 hungry people, Jesus tested Philip's faith. 'Where can we buy enough bread to feed all these people?' he asked.

Philip was wondering where the money would come from. But Jesus fed them all from five small loaves and two fish. At the last supper, when Jesus said, 'No one goes to the Father except by me', Philip questioned the meaning of that. 'Whoever has seen me,' Jesus answered, 'has seen the Father.'

Matthew 10:3; John 1:43–46; 6:5–7; 12:21–22; 14:8–9; Acts 1:13

2. Son of Herod the Great. His wife, Herodias, left him to marry his half-brother, Herod Antipas. John the Baptist was beheaded because he condemned this marriage.

Mark 6:17

3. Another son of Herod the Great, brother of Antipas and Archelaus. He became ruler of Ituraea.

Luke 3:1

4. Philip the evangelist. One of seven men set aside as administrators in the church at Jerusalem. When the Christians in Jerusalem were being persecuted, he fled to Samaria, where he preached and healed many people. A meeting with an Ethiopian diplomat who was travelling from Jerusalem to Gaza ended with this man becoming a Christian and being baptized by Philip. Philip obviously had a widely spread itinerant ministry, all along the coast of Palestine, and seems to have been joined by his family in this work (his four daughters are singled out for special mention as being significant prophets). Some 20 years later Paul stayed at Philip's home in Caesarea.

Acts 6:1–6; 8; 21:8–9

Phinehas

1. The son of Eleazar and grandson of Aaron. A fanatic for religious and racial purity, he took stern action to keep Israel to their covenant obligations – as a result of which he was promised that he and his descendants would always be priests.

Exodus 6:25; Numbers 25; 31:6; Joshua 22:13ff; Judges 20:28

2. One of Eli's two sons. See Hophni and Phinehas.

Phoebe

A Christian woman who was one of Paul's favourite co-workers. She was one of the leaders in the church at

Cenchreae near Corinth in Greece.

Romans 16:1–2

Pilate

Roman governor in Judea in AD 26–36. He was cruel and unpopular with the Jewish people. Above all, he was a weak character, who would do anything to keep the peace. When Jesus was brought to him to be tried, he was unwilling to take responsibility, and tried to pass the buck to others, until he realized his actions could provoke a riot, which would draw his incompetence to the attention of the emperor. So the easiest course of action – which he took – was to condemn Jesus to death.

Matthew 27; Mark 15; Luke 3:1; 13:1; 23; John 18–19

Potiphar

Egyptian official who bought Joseph as a slave. See Joseph.

Genesis 37:36; 39

Priscilla

See Aquila.

Publius

A leading citizen of the island of Malta, when Paul and the others sailing with him to Rome were shipwrecked there.

Acts 28:7ff.

Pul

See Tiglath-pileser.

Quirinius (Cyrenius)

Roman governor of Syria at the time of the census which brought Mary and Joseph to Bethlehem for the birth of Jesus.

Luke 2:2

Rachel

The daughter of Laban, for whom Jacob worked seven years without pay. After Laban tricked him into marrying her less attractive sister Leah, Jacob worked a further seven years to get Rachel. For many years Rachel was childless; then Joseph was born. She died giving birth to a second son, Benjamin.

Genesis 29–30; 35:18–20

Rahab

A prostitute who lived in a house on the wall of Jericho. Two spies sent by Joshua ended up in her house, and were given protection by her. In return the spies promised to save Rahab and her family when they captured Jericho. Rahab's name features in the list of Jesus' ancestors in Matthew's gospel.

Joshua 2; 6; Matthew 1:5; James 2:25

Raphael

One of the Jewish archangels, the angel of healing, who was sent in the guise of a relative (Azariah) to remove the haze from the eyes of Tobit and to restrain the demon Asmodeus, so that Sarah, the daughter of Raguel, could marry Tobit's son Tobias.

Tobit 5:11–6:18; 12:1–22

Razis

An elder in Jerusalem during the Maccabean period, who committed suicide in a particularly spectacular and gory manner rather than allow himself to be captured by the Seleucid general Nicanor.

2 Maccabees 14:37–46

Rebekah

The wife of Isaac and mother of Esau and Jacob. Rebekah grew up in Harran, the city where Abraham lived on his way to Canaan. Her father was Abraham's nephew. When Abraham decided it was time for Isaac to marry he sent Eliezer, his chief steward, back to Harran to find a suitable wife. The first person who came to the well where he was resting his camels was Rebekah. With her family's blessing Rebekah set off for Canaan. Isaac is said to have loved her on sight.

For 20 years Isaac and Rebekah tried to have a son. Then twin boys – Esau and Jacob – were born. Home-loving Jacob was Rebekah's favourite; Isaac preferred Esau, the hunter. When Isaac was old and nearly blind Rebekah helped Jacob to trick his father into giving him the elder son's blessing which rightfully belonged to Esau, who was born first. To save him from the consequences of his action, Rebekah sent Jacob to her brother Laban in Harran.

Genesis 24; 25:19–26:16; 27

Rehoboam

See Rehoboam, page 211.

Reuben

Eldest son of Jacob and Leah. He tried to save Joseph's life when his brothers plotted to kill him. Years later he offered his own two sons as hostages to guarantee Benjamin's safety. Reuben was founding father of the tribe named after him.

Genesis 29:32; 37:21–22; 42; 49:3

Reuel

Another name for Jethro.

Rezin

The last king of Syria. Rezin made an alliance with King Pekah of Israel. When Rezin and Pekah attacked Judah, King Ahaz appealed to the Assyrian King Tiglath-pileser III for help. Tiglath-pileser captured Damascus, the capital of Syria, and killed Rezin.

2 Kings 15:37–16:9; Isaiah 7:1ff

Rezon

A man from Zobah who became king of Syria. Rezon made trouble for King Solomon throughout his reign.

1 Kings 11:23–25

Rhoda

Servant girl at the home of John Mark's mother in Jerusalem who answered the door when Peter was released from prison.

Acts 12:12ff.

Rizpah

One of King Saul's concubines.

2 Samuel 3:7; 21

Ruth

See Ruth, page 214.

Salome

One of the leading women among Jesus' disciples. Salome was present at the crucifixion, and three days later was one of the women who took spices to the tomb to embalm the body – and found it had gone. Some believe that Salome was the wife of Zebedee, and the mother of James and John.

(Matthew 27:56); Mark 15:40; 16:1

Samson

See Samson, page 207.

Samuel

The son of Elkanah and Hannah whose work bridged the gap between the judges and the prophets in early Israel. Before his birth, Samuel's mother had been longing for a child, and made a vow that if she had a son he would be dedicated to the service of the shrine at Shiloh, where she regularly went on pilgrimage. While staying in the house of Eli, the priest at Shiloh, Samuel received a message intimating that Eli's family would be punished because of his sons' wickedness.

When Eli died, Samuel faced a difficult situation. Israel had been defeated by the Philistines and the people felt it might make more sense to join forces with them. That would have involved the

abandonment of their ancestral life – the very thing that Samuel regarded as the cause of all their troubles. Samuel exercised a strong influence in Israel, but it became clear that further advance would depend on good leadership. People wanted a king – something Samuel resisted at first, but then he came to see it could be the way forward, and anointed Saul the Benjaminite. He showed himself to be a good strategist, but less concerned about religious observance, and it was not long before Samuel was encouraging Saul's rejection, and the appointment of David in his place.

1 Samuel 1–4; 7–16; 19:18ff; 25:1

Sanballat

A Samaritan governor who tried to stop Nehemiah rebuilding the walls of Jerusalem.

Nehemiah 2:10, 19; 4; 6; 13:28

Sapphira

See Ananias.

Sarah

Abraham's wife; the mother of Isaac. She must have been an attractive woman, and a stronger person than her husband, who twice tried to encourage other men to have sex with her, pretending she was his sister instead of his wife, to protect his own skin. Depressed by her failure to give Abraham the son he wanted, Sarah encouraged him to have sex with her maid Hagar, and Ishmael was born. Abraham and Sarah were both old when an angel told Abraham that Sarah would have a son. At first she laughed at the idea, but in due course Isaac was born. He was to be Abraham's true heir, which involved Sarah in some unpleasant jealousies with Hagar and her son Ishmael. At her death, she was buried in a cave near Hebron, which is still revered today.

Genesis 11–12; 16–18:15; 20–21

Saul

See Saul, page 208.

Seleucid

A dynasty of Greek kings, who ruled Palestine and Syria from the time of the death of Alexander the Great until the Romans took over Palestine in the first century BC. Some of them respected the Jews' traditional lifestyle and religious traditions, but it was one of the Seleucid kings, Antiochus IV, who provoked the Jewish revolt under the Maccabeans, which effectively led to the end of Seleucid control over Judea.

Seleucus IV (Philopator)
The son of the Seleucid king Antiochus III, and brother of Antiochus Epiphanes. He sent his chief minister, Heliodorus, to rob the temple in Jerusalem, but Heliodorus eventually assassinated him, and he was succeeded by Antiochus.
Daniel 11:20; 2 Maccabees 3:1–8

Sennacherib
King of Assyria in 705–681 BC. He strengthened the Assyrian empire, and dealt decisively with subject nations that were tempted to resist his rule. After Hezekiah of Judah refused to pay tax, Sennacherib attacked Jerusalem. Although he had already captured several cities in Judah, Isaiah encouraged Hezekiah not to surrender, and Jerusalem was saved. With the Egyptian army threatening action from the south and an inexplicable plague striking his own forces, Sennacherib returned to Nineveh, where he was murdered by two of his sons.
2 Kings 18–19; 2 Chronicles 32; Isaiah 36–37

Sergius Paulus
Roman governor of Cyprus, who received Paul and Barnabas on their arrival, and expressed considerable interest in religious affairs. See Elymas.
Acts 13:7ff.

Seth
Third son of Adam and Eve, born after Cain had murdered Abel.
Genesis 4:25ff.

Shadrach
See Abednego.

Shallum
1. The son of Jabesh; he murdered King Zechariah and made himself king of Israel, 752 BC. Shallum reigned for only one month before being in turn assassinated by Menahem.
2 Kings 15:10–15
2. A son of King Josiah, usually known as Jehoahaz. See Jehoahaz.
1 Chronicles 3:15; Jeremiah 22:11

Shalmaneser
Name of several kings of Assyria. Shalmaneser V (727–722 BC) defeated King Hoshea of Israel and made him pay tax to Assyria every year. When Hoshea rebelled, Shalmaneser besieged Samaria, capital of Israel. After three years Samaria fell and the Israelites were exiled to Assyria.
2 Kings 17

Shamgar
One of the lesser-known judges in early Israel, who engaged in battles against the Philistines.
Judges 3:31; 5:6

Shaphan
Best-known of several men of this name is one of King Josiah's important officials. He helped to supervise the temple repairs and reported to Josiah the finding of an scroll which led to significant reforms.
2 Kings 22; 2 Chronicles 34

Shebna/Shebnah
One of King Hezekiah's most important officials, sent to negotiate with King Sennacherib's representatives.
2 Kings 18–19; Isaiah 22:15–25; 36–37

Shechem
The son of King Hamor, a Hivite king. Shechem raped Dinah, Jacob's daughter. See Dinah.
Genesis 34

Shem
Noah's eldest son, who is credited with being the ancestor of several 'Semitic' nations, the group of people to which the Hebrews belonged.
Genesis 6–10

Sheshbazzar
Sheshbazzar led the Jewish exiles back to Jerusalem when King Cyrus of Persia allowed them to return to rebuild the temple. Cyrus handed over to him some of the treasures Nebuchadnezzar had taken from the temple in Jerusalem before he destroyed it. Sheshbazzar laid the foundations of the new temple.
Ezra 1:8ff; 5:14ff

Shimei
A man from the tribe of Benjamin, and a relative of King Saul. During Absalom's rebellion Shimei cursed David and accused him of murdering Saul.
2 Samuel 16:5ff; 19:16–23; 1 Kings 2:8–9

Sihon
An Amorite king whose land lay on the east side of the River Jordan. Moses asked Sihon to allow the Israelites to travel through his land to reach Canaan. Sihon refused and attacked Israel, and was defeated.
Numbers 21

Silas
A leader of the church at Jerusalem who travelled with Paul on his second missionary journey, in place of Barnabas. At Philippi (Macedonia) Paul and Silas were beaten and thrown into prison. After an earthquake shattered the prison the jailer and his family all became Christians. Silas stayed in the nearby town of Berea while Paul went south to Athens, but joined him again in Corinth. He probably appears in some of the New Testament letters as Silvanus (the Latin form of his name, Silas being Greek). Silvanus was involved in the writing of 1 Peter, and it is reasonable to imagine he may well also have helped Paul with his letter writing. Paul sends greetings from Silvanus in his two letters to the Thessalonians.
Acts 15:22–17:15; 18:5; 2 Corinthians 1:19; 1 Thessalonians 1:1; 2 Thessalonians 1:1; 1 Peter 5:12

Simeon
1. Second son of Jacob and Leah. When Simeon and his brothers went to Egypt to buy corn, he was left behind as a hostage to make sure they brought Benjamin with them next time. As with the rest of Jacob's sons, one of the 12 tribes of Israel was named after him.
Genesis 29:33; 34:25ff; 42:24ff; 49:5
2. An old man who had been told by God that he would not die until he had seen the Messiah. In the temple he took the baby Jesus in his arms and praised God. His prayer is known as the Nunc Dimittis.
Luke 2:22–35
3. A teacher at the church in Antioch. He was probably an African, though nothing more is known about him.
Acts 13:1–2

Simon
1. Simon Peter. See Peter.
2. One of the 12 disciples of Jesus. He had been a member of the Zealots, an extreme Jewish nationalist group pledged to drive out the Romans.
Matthew 10:4; Acts 1:13

3. A brother of Jesus.
Matthew 13:55
4. A leper who invited Jesus to his house in Bethany. While Jesus was there, a woman anointed his head with expensive perfume. The same story appears in Luke, with Simon identified as a Pharisee.
Matthew 26:6; Mark 14:3; Luke 7:40ff
5. Simon of Cyrene, who was ordered to carry Jesus' cross.
Matthew 27:32
6. Simon Magus, a magician at Samaria who tried to buy the disciples' power.
Acts 8:9–24
7. A leather worker with whom Peter stayed in Joppa.
Acts 9:43ff
8. The second son of Mattathias. Like his brothers, he was involved in the defeat of the Seleucid king Antiochus IV, playing a key role in battles at Beth-zur and Joppa. He eventually became leader, and was the one who secured Jewish independence through negotiation with Demetrius II. He also made alliances with Rome and Sparta, which strengthened his position politically. His son-in-law assassinated him.
1 Maccabees 2:65; 13:1–16:17

Sisera
Captain of the army of Jabin, king of Hazor. He had under his command 900 iron chariots, and was for that reason a particularly formidable opponent for early Israel. Sisera's army was defeated by Deborah and Barak, and though he escaped from the battlefield on foot, he was killed by a woman called Jael when he took refuge in her tent.
Judges 4–5

Solomon
See Solomon, page 212.

Sosthenes
Appointed chief official of the synagogue at Corinth when Crispus, the previous ruler, became a Christian. Sosthenes was beaten up after a group of Jews had failed to persuade Gallio, the Roman governor of Achaia, to condemn Paul. There is no specific evidence. but it seems likely that he became a Christian, and is the same Sosthenes mentioned by Paul in writing to the Corinthian church.
Acts 18:17; 1 Corinthians 1:1

Stephanas
Stephanas and his family were the first people to become Christians in Achaia (southern Greece). They were amongst the few Christians whom Paul baptized personally at Corinth.
1 Corinthians 1:16; 16:15ff

Stephen
A Greek-speaking Jew, and the first Christian mentioned in the book of Acts to die for the faith. Stephen was one of seven men chosen by the apostles to administer funds to support widows in the church at Jerusalem. But most of what we know of him shows him not as an administrator, but a speaker of some reputation. He was arrested and brought before the religious council (the Sanhedrin). In his speech, he questioned some of the most deeply held beliefs of the Jewish faith, including the central place of the temple and its worship. At the end of his speech, it was inevitable that he would be found guilty of religious blasphemy. The punishment for this under old Jewish laws was death by stoning and, though this was illegal under Roman rule, a mob took the law into its own hands and executed him there and then on the spot. Paul, who at that time was working out his own attitude towards the Christians, guarded the coats while others put Stephen to death.
Acts 6 and 7

Susannah
A beautiful young Jewish woman living in exile in Babylon, married to Joakim. When two elders of the Jewish community attempted to seduce her, she dismissed their advances, but they still claimed she had had sex with them, and was therefore an adulterer under the Old Testament law. She was duly tried and condemned to death, but then Daniel intervened and pointed out not only that the proper procedures had been ignored, but also that the witnesses were untrustworthy. She was acquitted – and her accusers suffered the death penalty themselves. This is one of several Old Testament stories illustrating the rigour with which faithful Jewish exiles stuck to the moral

principles of their faith, even in trying circumstances.
Susanna 1 – 64

Tabitha
See Dorcas.

Tamar
1. The daughter-in-law of Judah and mother of his twin sons.
Genesis 38
2. David's daughter, raped by Amnon, her half-brother.
2 Samuel 13

Terah
Father of Abraham. He set off from Ur with Abraham, intending to go to Canaan. Instead he settled at Harran and died there.
Genesis 11:27–32

Theophilus
The person to whom Luke addressed the New Testament gospel of Luke and the Acts of the Apostles. He knew something about Christianity but Luke wanted him to have a much fuller explanation. The name 'Theophilus' means 'friend of God'.
Luke 1:3; Acts 1:1

Theudas
Leader of a band of 400 rebels. When he was killed, his men scattered and the movement died out. Gamaliel quoted this example when the apostles were on trial. The movement Jesus had started would similarly come to nothing unless God was behind it.
Acts 5:34ff.

Thomas
One of the 12 disciples of Jesus. He was a twin, though we have no idea who his twin was. In John's gospel, Thomas asks some key questions. At the last supper, it is in response to his enquiry that Jesus describes himself as 'the way, the truth and the life.' Thomas was not with the disciples when Jesus appeared to them after his resurrection. He said he that would not believe Jesus was alive again unless he saw and touched the scars. A week later, Thomas saw Jesus for himself. 'My Lord and my God,' he said. Tradition places Thomas as the first missionary to India.
John 11:16; 14:5–7; 20:24ff; 21:1–14; Acts 1:12–14

Tiberius
Emperor of Rome in Jesus' lifetime. He ruled in AD 14–37. In the New Testament gospels he is simply referred to as 'Caesar'.
Luke 3:1

Tiglath-pileser

Tiglath-pileser III (Pul) was king of Assyria in 745–727 BC. He increased Assyrian power by going to war against smaller nations. Israel was one of the countries he invaded. King Menahem paid Tiglath-pileser a large sum of money to preserve his own position as king of Israel. After King Pekah of Israel and King Rezin of Syria had attacked Jerusalem, Tiglath-pileser responded to Ahaz of Jerusalem's appeal for help by capturing Damascus and several cities in northern Israel. Ahaz and Judah then became subject to Tiglath-pileser.

2 Kings 15:29; 16:7ff.; 2 Chronicles 28:16ff.

Timothy

A Christian from Lystra who was a friend and helper of Paul. His mother was a Jewish Christian, and his father was Greek. Paul chose Timothy to help him while he was on his second missionary journey. After Paul had left Thessalonica Timothy went back to encourage the persecuted Christians there. Later Paul sent him from Ephesus to Corinth to teach the Corinthian Christians. Timothy became leader of the church at Ephesus. He often lacked confidence and needed Paul's encouragement. But he was always loyal and faithful. The two letters to Timothy are full of advice on the leadership of the church.

Acts 16:1–3; 17:13–15; 1 Corinthians 4:17; 1 Thessalonians 1:1; 3:1–6; 1 and 2 Timothy

Tirhakah

See Pharaoh.

Titus

A Gentile Christian who was a friend and helper of Paul. Titus was with Paul on one of his visits to Jerusalem and probably travelled with him quite often. For some time Titus worked with the Christians at Corinth. He smoothed over the bad feeling between the Corinthian church and Paul. When Titus rejoined Paul and told him how much better things were, Paul wrote the second letter to the Corinthians. Titus went back to Corinth with this letter and helped organize a collection there for needy Christians in Judea. He

later went to work with the church in Crete.

1 Corinthians 16:10; 2 Corinthians 2:13; 7:13ff.; 8; 12:18; Galatians 2; 2 Timothy 4:10; Titus

Tobiah

An Ammonite who tried to force Nehemiah to stop rebuilding the walls of Jerusalem.

Nehemiah 2:10ff.; 4; 6; 13

Tobit

A Jew taken to exile in Assyria by Shalmaneser in the eighth century BC, and who committed himself to keeping his ancestral traditions, especially giving money to the poor, and ensuring that Jewish people had a decent burial. Returning home one night, ritually unclean from handling the dead, he slept in the open courtyard, where a bird's dropping fell into his eyes and blinded him. After being blind for four years, he prayed for God's help, and the angel Raphael came to his assistance, and his own life and that of his family were eventually transformed.

Tobit 1:1–14:15

Trophimus

A Christian from Ephesus who joined Paul in some of his travels.

Acts 20:4; 21:29; 2 Timothy 4:20

Trypho

An untrustworthy ruler of Syria from 142 to 138 BC, who began life as a soldier in Alexander Balas' army before seizing the throne for himself. He tricked the Maccabean king Jonathan and imprisoned him at Ptolemais, refusing to release him even when a ransom had been paid – and eventually managing to get Jonathan murdered. He himself was deposed as king, and committed suicide.

1 Maccabees 11:38–59; 12:39–53; 13:31; 15:10–37

Tychicus

A friend and helper of Paul, probably from Ephesus. It is almost certain that he went with Paul to Jerusalem because he had been chosen by the churches of Asia Minor to take the money they had collected for needy Christians in Judea. Tychicus was with Paul while he was in prison. Paul trusted him and appears to have sent him to Colossae and Ephesus.

Acts 20:4; Ephesians 6:21–22; Colossians 4:7–9; 2 Timothy 4:12; Titus 3:12

Uriah

1. A Hittite soldier in King David's army, and husband of Bathsheba. David raped his wife Bathsheba, and then arranged for Uriah to be sent to the front line, to ensure he would be killed and so to allow David to marry his wife.

2 Samuel 11

2. A priest in Jerusalem, who was implicated in King Ahaz's redesigning of the temple to a pattern that would suit his Assyrian overlords.

2 Kings 16:10ff.

3. A prophet at the time of Jeremiah, killed by King Jehoiakim because he spoke out against the people of Judah.

Jeremiah 26:20ff.

Uriel

One of the four archangels in Jewish thought (the others being Michael, Gabriel and Raphael). The name means 'flame of God' and Uriel appears as a divine messenger to Noah, Enoch and Ezra.

Enoch 9:1; 2 Esdras 4:1; 5:20; 10:28

Uzzah

One of the men who helped King David take the Ark of the Covenant from Kiriath-jearim to Jerusalem. He drove the cart on which it was placed, and died as a result of trying to steady the ark with his hand.

2 Samuel 6:3–7

Uzziah

See Azariah.

Vashti

Wife of the Persian king Ahasuerus, divorced when she refused to show off her beautiful body before his drunken guests.

Esther 1

Zacchaeus

A tax collector who lived in Jericho, and who features in the Bible as a small man who needed to climb a tree in order to see Jesus. Not expecting to be noticed, Jesus nevertheless addressed him, challenged his lifestyle and asked if he could pay him a personal visit. As a result of this meeting with Jesus, Zacchaeus was a changed man.

Luke 19:1–10

Zadok

In King David's reign Zadok and Abiathar were the most important priests. At the end of David's reign Abiathar supported Adonijah's claim to the throne. Zadok crowned Solomon

as the new king and was made high priest.

2 Samuel 15:24ff.; 17:15; 19:11; 1 Kings 1:7, 32ff.; 2:35

Zebedee

The father of Jesus' disciples James and John.

Matthew 4:21–22

Zebulun

A son of Jacob and Leah. Ancestor of one of the 12 tribes of Israel.

Genesis 30:19–20; 49:13

Zechariah

1. Zechariah, king of Israel, reigned for only six months and was then murdered by Shallum (752 BC).

2 Kings 14:29; 15:8–12

2. A prophet and priest born during the Jewish exile in Babylon. His first message was given in 519 BC and is recorded in the Old Testament book of Zechariah. By that time the Jews who had returned from exile in Babylon had lost heart and given up rebuilding the temple. Zechariah encouraged them to carry on with this work and promised a bright future.

Ezra 5:1–2; Nehemiah 12:16; Zechariah

3. A priest: the husband of Elizabeth and father of John the Baptist. Zechariah and Elizabeth were both old, and when an angel announced to him that they would have a son, he could not believe it. He was unable to speak until John was born.

Luke 1:5, 59

Zedekiah

1. Last king of Judah, 597–587 BC, though really only a puppet as he was appointed by King Nebuchadnezzar of Babylon. When Zedekiah rebelled, it was inevitable that Nebuchadnezzar would besiege Jerusalem. After several months the city was captured and destroyed, and Zedekiah himself was blinded and taken prisoner to the city of Babylon.

2 Kings 24–25; 2 Chronicles 36:10ff.; Jeremiah 21; 32; 34; 37–39

2. A false prophet who lived in the reign of King Ahab.

1 Kings 22; 2 Chronicles 18

Zephaniah

A Judahite prophet during the reign of King Josiah. Little is known of him, apart from the messages recorded in the book of Zephaniah, though he seems to have been descended from King Hezekiah. He warned people in Judah of God's coming judgment if they

continued to worship foreign deities in disregard of the demands of the covenant. Injustice would be punished – but for those who returned to their traditional faith there would be a bright future.

Zephaniah

Zerah

An Ethiopian who led a large army against the troops of King Asa of Judah. Zerah's army was wiped out by the people of Judah.

2 Chronicles 14:9–14

Zerubbabel

Grandson of King Jehoiachin and a leader of the exiles who returned from Babylon to Judah in about 537 BC. He became governor of Judea and worked alongside Joshua, the high priest. Under their leadership the foundations of the temple were laid. The work was difficult and spasmodic, but eventually the task was finished when the prophets Haggai and Zechariah managed to instil a degree of enthusiasm into the people.

Ezra 2:2; 3–5; Haggai; Zechariah 4

Ziba

Servant of King Saul. After the death of Saul and Jonathan, Ziba told King David that Jonathan's disabled son, Mephibosheth, was still alive.

2 Samuel 9; 16:1–4; 19:17ff.

Zilpah

Leah's servant and one of Jacob's wives. She was mother of Gad and Asher, two of his 12 sons.

Genesis 29:24; 30:9–13

Zimri

Commander in the Israelite army. Zimri killed King Elah and reigned as king of Israel for seven days (886 BC). He was overthrown by Omri.

1 Kings 16

Zipporah

Wife of Moses and daughter of Jethro, the man who gave Moses a home when he escaped from Egypt. She was the mother of Moses' two sons.

Exodus 2:16–22; 4:24–26; 18:2–4

Zophar

One of Job's three friends who famously tried to comfort him in his time of suffering.

Job 2:11

Places

Abana
Now called Barada, 'cool'. One of two rivers which flow through Damascus in Syria. When the prophet Elisha sent a message to the Syrian general Naaman that he needed to bathe in the River Jordan to be healed of his leprosy, Namaan expressed surprise that the muddy Jordan should be more efficacious than the clear, fast-flowing waters of the rivers Abana and Pharpar.
2 Kings 5:12
See map page 274

Abel-beth-maacah
A town in the north of Israel, near Lake Huleh. It was one of those border towns that changed hands between the Arameans of Damascus and the Israelites on several occasions.
2 Samuel 20; 1 Kings 15:20; 2 Kings 15:29
See map page 274

Abel-meholah
The place to which a Midianite army fled after being surprised by Gideon's small unarmed force. The home-town of the prophet Elisha.
Judges 7:22; 1 Kings 19:16
See map page 274

Abilene
The region north-west of Damascus, governed by Lysanias in New Testament times.
Luke 3:1

Accad
Name of a region and a city in ancient Babylonia, connected in the Bible with Nimrod.
Genesis 10:10

Achaia
The Roman province of this name covered what is now southern Greece. Its capital city was Corinth.
Acts 18:12

Achor
This is the place where Achan was killed after bringing disaster on his people. Its name means 'Valley of Trouble', and in Hebrew it would also sound quite similar to the word 'Achan'.
Joshua 7:24

Adam
The place where the book of Joshua located the landslide that blocked the flow of the River Jordan and enabled the Israelites led by Joshua to enter the land of Canaan. Earth tremors still occasionally cause

the high clay banks to collapse at the same spot, even today.
Joshua 3:16
See map page 274

Admah
One of a group of five cities, of which Sodom and Gomorrah are best-known, now probably submerged under the southern end of the Dead Sea. The kings of these cities formed an alliance and rebelled against four northern kings in Abraham's time. In the battle that followed, Abraham's nephew Lot was taken captive.
Genesis 10:19; 14:2

Adramyttium
A port near Troy on the west coast of modern Turkey. A ship from Adramyttium took the missionary Paul and his fellow prisoners on the first stage of their journey to Rome.
Acts 27:2

Adullam
David, on the run from King Saul and fearing King Achish of Gath, took refuge in a cave here. His family and a group of 400 outlaws joined him and, while he was there, three of David's bravest soldiers risked their lives to bring him water from the well at Bethlehem, which at the time was held by the Philistines.
1 Samuel 22:1; 2 Samuel 23:13
See maps pages 26, 274

Aenon near Salim
The place where John the Baptist baptized his followers.
John 3:23

Ahava
The name of a canal and a region in Babylonia where the priest Ezra assembled the second party of returning Jewish exiles. Here they fasted and prayed for protection on their 1,448-km/900-mile journey to Jerusalem.
Ezra 8:15, 21, 31

Ai
The name means 'the ruin', and features in the Old Testament as the place where Joshua's army was beaten after its victory at Jericho. This is explained by reference to the story of Achan, who secretly stole goods for himself from the ruins of Jericho. Once he had been unmasked and punished, a second attack on Ai led to a

successful outcome for Joshua and his forces.
Joshua 7 and 8
See map page 274

Aijalon
An Amorite town included in the heritage allotted to the Israelite tribe of Dan, but then given to the Levites. Much later it is mentioned as one of King Rehoboam's fortified arsenals.
Joshua 19:42; 21:24; Judges 1:35; 2 Chronicles 11:10
See map page 274

Aijalon
A valley through which an important trade route passed, near to the town of Aijalon. This is the place where Joshua fought a great battle against the Amorites, and 'the sun stood still' until he was successful.
Joshua 10
See map page 274

Alexandria
A strategic Egyptian seaport on the Nile Delta founded by Alexander the Great. The famous Pharos lighthouse stood at the harbour entrance. Alexandria was the capital of Egypt under the Ptolemies, and remained a great centre of learning and trade throughout New Testament times.
In Roman times there was a huge trade in grain, which the Romans grew in Egypt, then loaded into ships at Alexandria to be taken to Rome to feed its growing population economically. The city had a 'museum' of arts and sciences, and a famous library containing thousands of papyrus scrolls. It was also home to one of the largest Jewish communities anywhere in the ancient world, with many more Jewish people here than in Jerusalem. In Alexandria, the Hebrew scriptures were translated into Greek – the Septuagint version. Apollos, who became an important teacher in the early church, came from Alexandria.
Acts 6:9; 18:24; 27:6; 28:11
See maps pages 36, 47

Ammon, Ammonites
A state on the east of the River Jordan whose capital was Rabbah (modern Amman).
See maps pages 27, 28, 274

Amphipolis
A town on Paul's route through Macedonia

(what is now northern Greece) on his second missionary journey.
Acts 17:1

Anathoth
A town 4 km/3 miles north of Jerusalem traditionally belonging to the Levites. The birthplace of the prophet Jeremiah.
Joshua 21:18; Jeremiah 1:1
See map page 274

Antioch in Pisidia
A city in the heart of Asia Minor (modern Turkey) visited by Paul and Barnabas on their first missionary journey. As in many places, they took their message first to the local Jewish synagogue, but then when Gentiles accepted their message the religious leaders stirred up trouble and had Paul and Barnabas thrown out of the city. But their work was effective, and when they revisited the city two or three years later, there was a well-established Christian community there.
Acts 13:14–52
See maps pages 45, 47

Antioch in Syria
Modern Antakya, on the Syrian border of Turkey. The most famous of 16 cities with this name, founded by one of Alexander the Great's generals in honour of his father. Antioch, on the River Orontes, had its own sea-port. Under the Romans it became the capital of the province of Syria and third largest city of the Roman empire, renowned for its culture. Like most such cities in the east of the empire, it had a large Jewish community.
After the death of Stephen, the first Christian mentioned in Acts to die for his beliefs, persecuted Christians fled the 483 km/300 miles from Jerusalem to Antioch. This was the start of one of the largest and most active of the early Christian churches. Many local people, including a large number of Gentiles, became Christians. The missionaries Paul and Barnabas worked there together for over a year before going on their missionary travels, and Antioch remained Paul's home church for the rest of his life. The ancient city was levelled

by an earthquake in AD 526.
Acts 11:19–26; 13:1; 15:35
See maps pages 37, 43, 45, 47

Antipatris
The ancient town of Aphek rebuilt by King Herod and named in honour of his father, Antipater. When Paul's life was threatened he was taken under escort from Jerusalem to Caesarea on the coast, spending a night on the journey at Antipatris.
Acts 23:31

Aphek
The place where the Philistines camped before the battle in which they captured the Ark of the Covenant from the Israelites. Centuries later, Aphek was rebuilt as Antipatris by Herod the Great.
1 Samuel 4:1
See maps pages 26, 274

Ar
Capital of Moab, on the River Arnon. One of the cities untouched by the Israelite tribes after the exodus, as it was the heritage of the Moabites, who were their own relatives (traditionally the descendants of Lot).
Numbers 21:15; Deuteronomy 2:9; Isaiah 15:1

Arabah
The rift valley of the River Jordan, stretching from Lake Galilee in the north to the Dead Sea ('the Sea of Arabah') in the south, thence to the Gulf of Aqaba on the Red Sea.

Arad
A Canaanite city in the Negev captured and occupied by the Israelites. Excavations at Tell 'Arad have revealed an Israelite temple and fortresses.
Joshua 12:14
See map page 274

Aram, Aramaeans
A generic term to describe various states in southern Syria, especially Damascus.

Ararat
The mountain country where, in the Genesis story, Noah's ark came to rest after the great flood subsided. The area, called Urartu in Assyrian inscriptions, is Armenia, on the borders of present-day Turkey and Georgia. Mount Ararat itself is an extinct volcano nearly 5,214 m/17,000 ft high.
Genesis 8:4; Jeremiah 51:27
See maps pages 28, 29

Areopagus
'The hill of Ares' (for Romans, 'Mars hill', Mars being the Latin name of the Greek god Ares), situated north-west of the Acropolis in Athens, and from which the Council of the Areopagus (which originally met there) took its name.
Acts 17

Argob
Part of the kingdom of Og in Bashan, east of the River Jordan. Part of the territory of the half-tribe of Manasseh, and a fertile region with many strong towns.
Deuteronomy 3; 1 Kings 4

Arimathea
The home of Joseph, a secret admirer of Jesus, in whose new rock-tomb the body of Jesus was placed after he was crucified.
Matthew 27:57; Mark 15:43
See map page 275

Arnon
A river which flows into the Dead Sea from the east (now Wadi Mujib). It formed the border between the Amorites and Moabites, and remained the southern border of territory allotted to the Reubenites.
Numbers 21:13–14; Deuteronomy 2:24, 3:12–16; Isaiah 16:2

Aroer
A town on the north bank of the River Arnon, east of Jordan. The southern limit of the Amorite kingdom and later of the Israelite tribe of Reuben. Under Moabite rule from the time of Jehu to the prophet Jeremiah's day. Also the name of a town in the Negev, south of Beersheba.
Deuteronomy 2:36; 2 Kings 10:33
See map page 274

Ashdod
One of five Philistine strongholds in Old Testament times. When the Philistines captured the Ark of the Covenant they took it to the temple of their god Dagon at Ashdod. The next morning the statue of Dagon was flat on its face; on the following day it was broken into pieces. Later, Ashdod fell to King Uzziah of Judah. In New Testament times the city (by now called Azotus and separated from Judea) was restored by the Roman Gabinius

and given to Salome, Herod's sister, by the emperor Augustus.

1 Samuel 5; 2 Chronicles 26:6; Isaiah 20:1; 1 Maccabees 9:15; 10:83; 11:4; Acts 8:40

Ashkelon

An ancient city on the coast of Israel, between Jaffa and Gaza, one of the main strongholds of the Philistines. Samson made a raid on Ashkelon, killing 30 men to pay what he owed in a bet. In the centuries that followed, Ashkelon was ruled in turn by Assyria, Babylonia and Tyre. Herod the Great, ruler of Palestine at the time Jesus was born, was born at Ashkelon.

Judges 1:18; 14:19; 1 Samuel 6:17; Jeremiah 47:5–7
See maps pages 24, 274

Ashtaroth/Ashteroth-karnaim

A city east of the River Jordan, named after the Canaanite mother-goddess. Captured by Chedorlaomer in Abraham's time, it later became a capital of King Og of Bashan. One of the cities allotted to the Levites.

Genesis 14:5; Deuteronomy 1:4; 1 Chronicles 6:71
See map page 274

Asia

Originally the western part of Asia Minor (modern Turkey), which included a number of important Greek city-states. Later the Roman province of Asia, including the whole west coast, with its capital city at Ephesus. Much of Paul's missionary work took place in this region.

Acts 2:9; 19:10; Revelation 1:4, 11

Assos

The sea-port in the north-west of modern Turkey from which Paul sailed on his last journey to Jerusalem.

Acts 20:13

Assyria, Assyrians

An important country in north Mesopotamia. Assyria was a great power from the ninth to the seventh century BC.

Ataroth

A town east of the River Jordan, allocated to the Israelite tribe of Reuben.

Numbers 32:3; 34
See map page 274

Athens

The capital of Greece, with a long history, emerging into particular prominence from the sixth century BC. The city was at the height of its greatness in the fifth century BC when its most famous public buildings,

including the Parthenon, were built. Athens was then a model democracy and centre of the arts, attracting actors, writers, sculptors, historians, philosophers and scientists from all over Greece. In 86 BC the city was besieged and stripped by the Romans. Although it lost its power and wealth as a centre of trade Athens was still effectively the intellectual centre of the Roman empire when Paul visited it during his second missionary journey.

Acts 17:15–34
See maps pages 44, 47

Attalia

Modern Antalya, a port of Pamphylia on the south coast of modern Turkey, used by Paul on his first missionary journey.

Acts 14:25
See map page 45

Azekah

Joshua pursued the Amorites to this town; it was later a fortified border city of Judah.

Joshua 10:10; Jeremiah 34:7

Babel

Archetypal image of urban living, no doubt based in the Genesis story on life in ancient Babylon. The plan of its people to construct a grand city on the plain of Shinar (Sumer) in the 'land of the two rivers' (Mesopotamia), together with 'a tower that would reach to heaven' becomes a symbol for human pride and self-confidence – all of which comes to nought when their language is confused so they could no longer understand one another.

Genesis 10:10; 11:1–9

Babylon

A city on the River Euphrates, 80 km/50 miles south of modern Baghdad. After the defeat of Assyria in 612 BC Babylon became the capital of a powerful empire extending from the Persian Gulf to the Mediterranean Sea.

The city covered an extensive area on both banks of the River Euphrates. Both the inner and outer city were protected by double brick walls 3–7 m/11–25 ft thick. Eight great gates led to the inner city, and there were 50 temples. The 'hanging gardens' of Babylon were one of the wonders of the ancient world. These were terraces on different

levels laid out with palms and many other trees and plants, providing colour and shade in a flat land.

In 539 BC the Persians, under Cyrus, took the city. Herodotus, the Greek historian, describes how they diverted the River Euphrates and marched along its dried-up bed to enter the city. From that time on, Babylon fell into decline. Nothing remains of the city today other than a series of widely scattered mounds.

Genesis 10:10; 2 Kings 24:1; 25:7–13; Isaiah 14:1–23; Daniel 1–6
See maps pages 31, 33, 34, 36

Bashan

A fertile region east of Lake Galilee, famous for its cattle, sheep and strong oak trees. King Og of Bashan was one of the opponents met by the Israelite tribes following the exodus, and his land was subsequently allotted to the tribe of Manasseh.

Deuteronomy 3; Psalm 22:12; Isaiah 2:13
See map page 274

Beersheba

The southernmost town to belong to the Israelites, on the edge of the Negev Desert and on the trade route to Egypt. The well (*be'er*) which gave the town its name is connected by the Old Testament to Abraham, and most of the stories of Abraham and his family take place in and around Beersheba. Beersheba is also mentioned in connection with Elijah and Amos. The phrase 'from Dan to Beersheba' became a common way to speak of the whole land, from north to south.

Genesis 21:14, 30–32; 26:23–33; 1 Kings 19:3; Amos 5:5
See map page 19

Beroea

A city in Macedonia (northern Greece), 80 km/50 miles from Thessalonica, visited by Paul in the course of his second missionary journey.

Acts 17:10–15; 20:4
See map page 45

Bethany

A village about 3 km/2 miles from Jerusalem, beyond the Mount of Olives and on the road to Jericho. Home to Mary, Martha and Lazarus in the New Testament, and a favourite retreat for Jesus.

Matthew 26:6–13; Luke 10:38–42; 24:50; John 11; 12:1–9
See map page 275

Bethel

A place 19 km/12 miles north of Jerusalem and given its name (meaning 'house of God' by Jacob following his dream of a staircase from heaven to earth. It also features in the stories of the Israelite occupation of Canaan in the days of the judges.

Later, when the kingdom divided to become the separate realms of Israel and Judah, King Jeroboam of Israel set up a major shrine at Bethel, so that people could worship there instead of at Jerusalem. The prophets condemned this, regarding its worship as idolatrous. After the Israelite exile, Bethel was settled by Assyrians. After Judah's exile in Babylon, some of the returning settlers moved into Bethel.

Genesis 28:10–22; Judges 1:22–26; 20:18; 1 Kings 12:26–30; 2 Kings 2; 17:28; Nehemiah 11:31
See maps pages 19, 28, 29, 274

Bethesda/Bethzatha

A large pool in Jerusalem, sheltered by five porches in the time of Jesus, and rediscovered by archaeologists in the twentieth century in the north-east of the city. The pool was fed by a spring which bubbled up from time to time. Sick people gathered there, believing that the first to get into the water after this bubbling would be healed. Jesus healed a man here who had been ill for 38 years.

John 5:1–15

Beth-horon (Upper and Lower)

These two towns controlled the Valley of Aijalon and the ancient trade route which passed through it. Invading armies regularly took this route throughout Bible times: Philistines, Egyptians and Syrians as well as the forces of Israel.

Joshua 16:3–5; 10:10; 1 Samuel 13:18; 1 Maccabees 3:16–26; 9:39
See maps pages 22, 274

Bethlehem

'The house of bread', 8 km/5 miles south-west of Jerusalem, in the Judean hills. Rachel's tomb is here, and the story of Ruth also ends here. Bethlehem was David's birthplace, and the place where he was first acclaimed as king. The prophet Micah spoke of a coming leader being born in

Bethlehem, and the New Testament connects this with Jesus' birth in the city.

Genesis 35:19; Ruth; 1 Samuel 16; Micah 5:2; Matthew 2; Luke 2
See maps pages 26, 40, 275

Bethphage

A village near Bethany, on or near the Mount of Olives, on the east side of Jerusalem. The place from which Jesus sent two disciples to commandeer a mount for his entry to the city of Jerusalem.

Matthew 21:1; Mark 11:1; Luke 19:29
See map page 275

Bethsaida

A fishing town on the north shore of Lake Galilee, near the River Jordan. The home of Jesus' disciples, Philip, Andrew and Peter, and setting for some of Jesus' healings and teaching.

John 1:44; Mark 8:22; Matthew 11:21
See maps pages 27, 275

Beth-shan

An ancient city in northern Palestine where the valley of Jezreel slopes down to the west bank of the River Jordan. A stronghold of Canaanite culture always resistant to Israelite infiltration. After Saul and Jonathan were killed by the Philistines on Mount Gilboa, their bodies were fixed on the walls of Beth-shan, but were later rescued and buried by men from Jabesh-gilead. In New Testament times Beth-shan was known by the Greek name Scythopolis, and became one of the 10 cities of the Decapolis – the only one west of the River Jordan. The modern town of Beisan stands close to the mound of the old site.

Joshua 17:11, 16; Judges 1:27; 1 Samuel 31:10–13; 2 Samuel 21:12; 1 Kings 4:12
See maps pages 27, 274

Bethshemesh

A town about 19 km/12 miles west of Jerusalem, allotted as the heritage of the Israelite priests. It was near the borders of Philistine territory in the early period, and when the Ark of the Covenant was returned by the Philistines, this is where it came to rest. Later Jehoash, king of the northern kingdom of Israel, defeated and captured Amaziah, king of Judah, at Bethshemesh.

Joshua 21:16; 1 Samuel 6:9–21; 1 Kings 4:9; 2 Kings 14:11–13
See maps pages 28, 274

Bethulia

The home city of Judith. Its location is described in great detail, opposite Esdraelon and near to the plain of Dothan, on a hilltop overlooking a valley, surrounded by mountains and near to some springs of water. But in spite of this, there is no agreement on its exact location, though some have argued that it must be another name for Shechem.

Judith 4:6; 6:10–7:32; 8:11; 21; 24; 10:10; 13:10–14

Beth-zechariah

A small settlement to the north of Beth-zur, in the coastal hills west of Jerusalem. It was the scene of one of the few battles in which the Maccabean forces were defeated by Antiochus IV's army, something that was attributed to his use of elephants crazed by being fed grape and mulberry juice.

1 Maccabees 6:32–47

Beth-zur

A city of Judah, 6 km/4 miles north of Hebron, connected to the family of Caleb. Later it was one of 15 cities fortified by King Rehoboam. Later still, its inhabitants joined Nehemiah in rebuilding Jerusalem. It had a high vantage point, and was the scene of one of the great Jewish victories during the time of the Maccabean revolt.

Joshua 15:58; 1 Chronicles 2:45; 2 Chronicles 11:7; Nehemiah 3:16; 1 Maccabees 4:26–34; 6:7, 31, 49–50; 9:52; 14:7; 2 Maccabees 11:1–5
See map page 274

Bithynia

A Roman province in the north-west of Asia Minor (Turkey). One of the places that Paul was 'forbidden by the Holy Spirit' to visit, though its inhabitants are included in the address of 1 Peter. It was a significant Christian centre, and the church there is mentioned in a letter written by the Roman governor Pliny to the emperor Trajan in the early second century AD.

Acts 16:7; 1 Peter 1:1
See map page 43

Bozrah

An ancient city in Edom, south-east of the Dead Sea, about 128 km/80 miles south of modern Amman in Jordan. A place identified as home to many false prophets.

Genesis 36:33; 1 Chronicles 1:44; Isaiah 34:6; 63:1; Jeremiah 49:13, 22; Amos 1:12
See map page 274

Caesarea

A Mediterranean port built by Herod the Great and named in honour of the Roman emperor Augustus. Statues of the emperor stood in a huge temple dedicated to him and to Rome. Traders on their way from Tyre to Egypt passed through Caesarea, and it was an important distribution centre for inland as well as sea trade.

In the New Testament Caesarea was home to Philip, and also of Cornelius, the Roman centurion who sent for Peter to explain the Christian faith to him. Paul used the port several times on his travels. It was the home base of the Roman governors of Judea, which is why Paul was taken there for trial before Felix after his arrest in Jerusalem. Paul spent two further years in prison at Caesarea before sailing from there to Rome and the emperor's court.

Acts 8:40; 21:8; 10; 11; 9:30; 18:22; 23:33–26:3
See maps pages 40, 43, 5, 47, 275

Caesarea Philippi

A town at the foot of Mount Hermon and close to the main source of the River Jordan. The ancient town of Baal-gad, called Paneas by the Hellenistic rulers of Paneas (Baal and Pan both being nature gods). Herod the Great built a marble temple here dedicated to Augustus Caesar, and Herod's son Philip later renamed the town Caesarea. Thence it became known as Caesarea Philippi ('Philip's Caesarea') to distinguish it from the port of the same name. Its ancient name still survives today in the modern town of Banias.

See maps pages 31, 275

Calah

An ancient city of Mesopotamia on the River Tigris, later a leading city of the Assyrian empire. Excavations at the site, now Nimrud in Iraq, have unearthed inscriptions and ivory carvings which throw light on the times of the kings of Israel.

Genesis 10:11–12
See map page 41

Cana

A village in Galilee, and the place where Jesus turned water into wine at a wedding. During another visit to Cana, Jesus healed the son of

an official from Capernaum. Nathanael, a leading disciple in John's gospel, came from Cana.

John 2:1–12; 4:46–53; 21:2
See maps pages 41, 275

Canaan

A general term for the whole of Syria and Palestine in the early Old Testament period, but especially relating to the coastal area around Phoenicia. Both the Old Testament and Canaanite traditions trace the name back to their original forebear, Canaan.

Genesis 10:15–19; Numbers 13:29; Joshua 5:1, 11:3; Judges 1:27ff
See maps pages 18, 21

Capernaum

An important town on the north-west shore of Lake Galilee at the time of Jesus. There may have been an army post here. It was Jesus' home base while he was teaching in Galilee. Matthew the tax-collector lived there, as also did a Roman army officer whose servant was healed. Many of Jesus' miracles took place at Capernaum.

Mark 1:21–34; 2:1–11; Luke 7:1–10; 10:13–16
See maps page 41, 275

Caphar-salama

Probably modern Khirbet Selma, some 10 km/6 miles north-west of Jerusalem. Site of a battle between Judas Maccabee and Nicanor, in which the Jewish forces were victorious.

1 Maccabees 7:31

Cappadocia

A Roman province in the east of Asia Minor (modern Turkey). Jewish pilgrims from Cappadocia were among those who heard Peter's address in Jerusalem on the day of Pentecost, and Christians in Cappadocia were among those to whom 1 Peter is addressed.

Acts 2:9; 1 Peter 1:1

Carchemish

An important Hittite city from early times, on the River Euphrates. The ruins now lie on the border between Turkey and Syria. When the Egyptian pharaoh Neco went to attack Carchemish, Josiah, the king of Judah, made a needless attempt to oppose him, and was defeated and killed in the plain of Megiddo. In 605 BC Neco himself was defeated at Carchemish by Nebuchadnezzar, king of Babylon.

2 Chronicles 35:20; Isaiah 10:9; Jeremiah 46:2
See map page 32

Carmel

A mountain range which juts into the Mediterranean Sea close to the modern port of Haifa. The ancient city of Megiddo guarded one of the main passes through the hills some miles inland. On Mount Carmel (535 m/1,740 ft at the highest point) the Israelite prophet Elijah challenged the prophets of Baal to a contest. His disciple and successor Elisha also seems to have made a base there.

1 Kings 18:19–46; 2 Kings 2:25; 4:25
See maps pages 28, 29, 274

Caspin

A heavily defended town captured in the Maccabean period by Judas, with considerable loss of life among its inhabitants. Also called Chaspho, it is the modern Khisfin, which lies about 14 km/9 miles to the east of the Sea of Galilee.

1 Maccabees 5:26, 36; 2 Maccabees 12:13

Cenchreae

The eastern port of Corinth (on the Aegean Sea), from which Paul sailed to Ephesus.

Acts 18:8; Romans 16:1
See map page 47

Chaldea

South Babylonia; Abraham's family home, and a land that impinged on Israel and Judah throughout their histories. In addition to its original specific reference, it is variously used in different Old Testament passages to refer to the whole of Babylonia, to its people, and its culture.

Genesis 11:28; Isaiah 13:19, 23:13, 43:14, 47:1–5; Ezekiel 23:23; Daniel 3:8, 9:1; Acts 7:4

Charax

Its name means 'fortress', but its location is otherwise unknown. It must have been somewhere in the hills east of Galilee, and was one of the places where Judas defeated Seleucid forces.

2 Maccabees 12:17

Chebar

A canal running from the River Euphrates in Babylonia (modern Iraq); in the Old Testament the location of some of the prophet Ezekiel's most distinctive visions.

Ezekiel 1:3; 10:20; 43:3

Cherith, Kerith

A desert stream east of the River Jordan. The place where Elijah took refuge during years of drought and famine in

the reign of King Ahab of Israel.

1 Kings 17:3–7
See map page 274

Chinnereth, Kinnereth

The Old Testament name for Lake Galilee, occurring in various descriptions of the boundaries of lands belonging to Israel and other nearby kingdoms.

Numbers 34:11; Deuteronomy 3:17; Joshua 11:2; 1 Kings 15:20
See map page 274

Chorazin

A town near Capernaum, on a hill above Lake Galilee, now a deserted ruin. Jesus was concerned that his message made little impact there.

Matthew 11:21; Luke 10:13
See map page 275

Cilicia

A region in the south of Asia Minor (modern Turkey) which became a province of the Roman empire in 103 BC. Tarsus, the birthplace of Paul, was the capital city. Behind it, running north-east, lay the wild Taurus mountains, cut through by an impressive pass known as the Cilician Gates.

Acts 21:39; 22:3; 23:34
See map page 43

Colossae

A city in the Lycus Valley, in the Roman province of Asia (part of modern Turkey). It stood just a few miles from Laodicea, on the main road east from Ephesus. The Christian message reached Colossae through the work of Epaphras, one of Paul's converts in Ephesus. Paul seems never to have visited the city, though he wrote a letter to the Colossian Christians.

Colossians 1:2
See maps pages 45, 47

Corinth

An old Greek city destroyed by the Romans in 146 BC and rebuilt by them 100 years later. Corinth stood on the narrow neck of land connecting Greece with the southern peninsula, between the Aegean and Adriatic seas. In a day when sailors never liked to leave sight of land, it was in a good position for attracting trade, as it had two harbours (one on each sea).

The town drew people of many nationalities. It was dominated by the 'Acro-corinth', the steep rock on which the acropolis and a temple to

Aphrodite (goddess of love) was built. Temple prostitutes and a large mobile population helped to give Corinth a reputation for every kind of sexual behaviour imaginable. Paul stayed in Corinth for 18 months, on his second missionary journey. During that time he founded a church to which he later wrote his most extensive correspondence (1 and 2 Corinthians).

Acts 18
See maps pages 44, 47

Crete

A mountainous island in the eastern Mediterranean Sea. The 'Cherethites', who formed part of King David's bodyguard, probably came from Crete. Much earlier, from before 2000 BC until after 1400 BC, the Minoan civilization flourished on the island. It is believed to have been the original home of the Philistines, before they settled in Palestine.

In the New Testament, pilgrims from Crete were in Jerusalem on the Day of Pentecost. Paul's ship called at the island on the way to Rome, and the letter to Titus is addressed to a leader of the church there.

Genesis 10:14; Deuteronomy 2:23; Jeremiah 47:4; Amos 9:7; Acts 2:11; 28:7–14; Titus 1:5, 12–13
See map page 44

Cush

A land in Africa (probably modern Sudan) named after the grandson of Noah. Occasionally translated 'Ethiopia' in modern Bible versions, though not definitely identical with the modern state of that name.

Genesis 10:6–8; Isaiah 11:11; 18:1

Cyprus

A large island in the eastern Mediterranean Sea. The Old Testament terms 'Elishah' and 'Kittim' may refer to Cyprus and Cypriots, respectively. In the New Testament Cyprus features as the home of Barnabas. It was the first place Paul and Barnabas visited when they set out to take the Christian message to the non-Jewish world. Here they met the governor, Sergius Paulus, and his court psychic adviser Elymas. Barnabas later returned to Cyprus with Mark.

Acts 4:36; 13:4–12; 15:39; 27:4
See map page 45

Cyrene

A Greek city on the north coast of Africa, in

modern Libya. An otherwise unknown Simon from Cyrene was forced by the Romans to carry Jesus' cross. Jewish pilgrims from Cyrene were among those present in Jerusalem on the Day of Pentecost, and other Cyrenians seem to have been involved in the work of the church at Antioch.

Matthew 27:32; Mark 15:21; Acts 2:10; 6:9; 11:20; 13:1
See map page 42

Dalmatia

A Roman province on the east coast of the Adriatic Sea, now part of Bosnia, mentioned in the New Testament as the location of Titus' ministry.

2 Timothy 4:10

Damascus

The capital of Syria. Damascus was already established from the earliest Old Testament period and is often mentioned in its pages. It was the centre of one of the smaller kingdoms of the area that, like Israel and Judah, were always struggling to retain their independence in the face of the superpowers located in Mesopotamia and Egypt. King David captured the city, but it soon regained its independence. It features in the story of Elisha as the home of Naaman, who came to the prophet looking for healing.

Isaiah predicted the destruction of Damascus. After a series of attacks the Assyrians captured the city in 732 BC, carried away its treasures and many of its people, and reduced its power. From 64 BC to AD 33 Damascus was a Roman city, and it was on the road there that Paul had his encounter with the risen Jesus that was to change his life. Even then, it was already home to a sizeable Christian population.

Genesis 14:15; 15:2; 2 Samuel 8:5; 1 Kings 20:34; 2 Kings 5; 8:7–15; Isaiah 17; Acts 9
See maps pages 29, 30, 31, 43, 45, 47

Dan

The land of the tribe of Dan, and a town (Laish) in the far north of Israel. Dan was the northern-most city of Israel, and the expression 'from Dan to Beersheba' came to mean 'from one end of the land to the other'. When the kingdom was divided, Jeroboam I established two great shrines to serve as alternatives to the temple in Jerusalem. One was at Bethel (in the south of his territory), and the other at Dan.

Joshua 19:40–48; 1 Kings 12:25–30
See maps pages 23, 28, 274

Decapolis

An association of 10 Greek towns gave this region its name (Decapolis means 'the ten cities'). An area south of Lake Galilee, mostly east of the River Jordan. In New Testament times, home mostly to non-Jews, many of whom were nonetheless attracted by Jesus and his teaching. Jewish Christians later fled to Pella, one of the towns in the Decapolis, at the time of the final war with the Romans (AD 66–70).

Matthew 4:25; Mark 5:1–20; 7:31–37
See maps pages 41, 275

Dedan

The city of Dedan (now Al-'Ula) was an important trading centre in the area of Midian.

Isaiah 21:13; Jeremiah 25:23; 49:8; Ezekiel 27:20

Derbe

A city in Lycaonia, in southern Asia Minor (modern Turkey), where Paul preached on his first and second missionary journeys. Probably one of the towns to which Paul's letter to the Galatians was sent.

Acts 14:20–21; 16:1
See maps pages 45, 47

Dibon

A Moabite town east of the Dead Sea and 5.5 km/4 miles north of the River Arnon. Listed as one of the towns captured for the tribes of Gad and Reuben at the time of the entry into Canaan, though it changed hands many times during the Old Testament period.

Numbers 21:30; 32:34; Isaiah 15:2
See map page 274

Dok

The place where Simon Maccabee was killed and two of his sons were also murdered. Probably to be identified with the modern settlement of 'Ain Duq, to the north-west of Jericho.

1 Maccabees 16:15

Dor

A Canaanite town, Dor is listed as a member of the northern alliance of kings opposed to Joshua. The town was allocated to the Israelite tribe of Manasseh, which had to be content to share it with its original Canaanite population. It continued to hold a significant place into New Testament times.

Joshua 11:1–15; Judges 1:27; 1 Kings 4:11; 1 Maccabees 15:11–13, 25
See map page 274

Dothan

A town on the route from Beth-shan and Gilead to Egypt. The place where Joseph was sold by his brothers to slave traders. At a later period, Elisha was rescued from the surrounding Syrian army here.

Genesis 37:17–28; 2 Kings 6
See maps pages 19, 29, 274

Ebal

A rocky mountain in Samaria, opposite the wooded height of Mount Gerizim, close to ancient Shechem and modern Nablus. A place of challenge and covenant renewal in the time of Joshua.

Deuteronomy 11:29; 27; Joshua 8:30, 33
See maps pages 22, 274

Ecbatana

One-time capital of the Median empire, which was later taken over by the Persians under Cyrus. It is referred to in several later Old Testament books.

Ezra 6:6–12; Tobit 5:6; 6:10; 7:1; Judith 1:1–6

Eden

The archetypal symbol of perfect human existence as God intended it to be. The Old Testament records Eden as the garden God made, in the beginning, as a place for his people to live in. After they had disobeyed him, God sent Adam and Eve out of the Garden of Eden. Two of the rivers in the garden were the Tigris and the Euphrates.

Genesis 2:8–14

Edom/Seir

The mountainous land south of the Dead Sea, traditional home of Esau's descendants.

Genesis 32:3, 36:20–21; Numbers 24:18
See maps pages 18, 21, 8

Edrei

Site of a battle between Israel and the army of Og, king of Bashan (modern Der'a, on the Syrian frontier with Jordan).

Numbers 21:33; Deuteronomy 1:4; 3:1, 10; Joshua 12:4; 13:12, 31
See map page 274

Eglon

One of a group of Amorite cities listed among Joshua's conquests. Believed to be probably Tell el-Hesi near Lachish, in the Shephelah, the low hill-country west of Jerusalem.

Joshua 10:3; 15:39
See map page 22

Egypt

A fertile and powerful land to the south of Israel, prominent throughout the history of the Old Testament as one of the two major superpowers in the region (Mesopotamia being the other). Egypt plays a key role in the story of the exodus.

Genesis 46; Exodus 1–14
See maps pages 18, 20, 31, 33, 36, 43

Ekron

One of the five main cities of the Philistines. It is listed as part of the territories of the tribe of Judah, but the Philistines retained firm control over it. It is mentioned in the Old Testament story of the Philistine capture of the Ark of the Covenant, and the oracle of its god Baal-zebub was later consulted by the Israelite King Ahaziah. By New Testament times, 'Beelzebub' (which originally was a Hebrew term of mockery, meaning 'lord of the flies') had come to be used as a name for the devil.

Joshua 15:11, 45–46; Judges 1:18; 1 Samuel 5:10–6:17; 7:14; 17:52; 2 Kings 1:3–6; Amos 1:8
See map page 274

Elah

A valley south-west of Jerusalem which played a central role in the early battles between Israel and the Philistines. This is where David fought the Philistine champion Goliath.

1 Samuel 17:2
See map page 274

Elam

The country east of Babylonia whose capital was Susa.

Genesis 14:1; Ezra 4:9; Isaiah 11:11; 21:2; Jeremiah 25:25; Acts 2:9
See maps pages 31, 33

Elasa

The place where Judas Maccabee met his death in battle against Syrian forces. Near to Beth-horon, in an area where many battles took place in Biblical times.

1 Maccabees 9:5

Elath/Ezion-geber

A settlement at the head of the Gulf of Aqaba on the Red Sea. Mentioned in the itinerary of the Israelite journey from Egypt to Canaan, but most significant much later as the home base for King Solomon's Red Sea trading fleet. King Jehoshaphat later tried unsuccessfully to revive this trade, and the town eventually came under Edomite control.

Numbers 33:35–36; Deuteronomy 2:8; 1 Kings 9:26–27; 22:48; 2 Kings 16:6
See map page 21

Emmaus

Two towns of this name feature in the biblical literature, and there is no certainty about the exact location of either of them. One was the place where Judas defeated the Syrian general Gorgias during the Maccabean period, and this one appears to have been a sizeable town – perhaps modern Amwas, some 32 km/20 miles west of Jerusalem in the valley of Aijalon. The other was obviously a much smaller village, and nearer to Jerusalem, and was the scene of one of Jesus' appearances after the resurrection. Tradition has identified this one with the modern El-Qubeibeh.

1 Maccabees 4:1–25; Luke 24:13
See map page 275

En-dor

A place in northern Israel, near Mount Tabor, significant in the Old Testament as the place visited by King Saul on the night before his last battle. He went there to consult a psychic in an effort to get in touch with the spirit of the dead Samuel, to take his advice. The advice he received condemned him for consulting a medium, and announced his own impending death. The next day, in a battle at nearby Mount Gilboa, Saul and his son Jonathan were both killed.

1 Samuel 28
See map page 274

Engedi

A spring to the west of the Dead Sea where David hid from King Saul.

Joshua 15:62; 1 Samuel 23:29
See maps pages 26, 274

En-rogel

A well on the south side of Jerusalem, near where the Hinnom valley joins the Kidron valley. The place where Adonijah, one of King David's sons, had himself anointed king for his father's death, in an unsuccessful attempt to secure the kingdom for himself instead of it going to Solomon, David's own choice.

1 Kings 1:9

Ephesus

The capital city of the Roman province of Asia (what is now western Turkey). Ephesus stood at the end of one of the great caravan trade routes through Asia, at the mouth of the Cayster river. The temple to Artemis (Diana) at Ephesus was one of the seven wonders of the ancient world, four times the size of the Parthenon at Athens.

There had been a settlement at Ephesus since before the 12th century BC. But by New Testament times it was a significant city, both strategically and architecturally. One amphitheatre alone could hold 25,000 people, and the city's total population may have been as large as one-third of a million. It had a substantial Jewish community, and became an important centre for early Christians, too. Paul visited the city, spending two years there at one stage of his life. His friends Aquila and Priscilla also moved to live at Ephesus, and Timothy seems to have had a long association with the church in this city. The letter to the Ephesians and one of the letters to the seven churches addressed in Revelation were addressed to Christians here, and there is an ancient tradition regarding Ephesus as the home of the apostle John.

Acts 18:19; 19; 20:17; 1 Corinthians 15:32; 16:8–9; Ephesians 1:1; 1 Timothy 1:3; Revelation 2:1–7
See maps pages 45, 47

Ephraim

The land assigned to the Israelite tribe of Ephraim.

Joshua 16:4–10
See maps pages 23, 274

Ephrathah

Another name for Bethlehem.

Genesis 48:7; Ruth 4:11; 1 Samuel 17:12; Micah 5:2

Erech

One of the great Sumerian cities, in southern Babylonia, about 64 km/40 miles north-west of Ur.

Genesis 10:10; Ezra 4:9

Eshcol

A valley near Hebron, whose name means 'a cluster of grapes'. When Moses sent spies into Canaan they returned with samples of the fruit of the country, including a huge bunch of grapes from this valley.

Numbers 13:23–24; 32:9; Deuteronomy 1:24

Eshtaol

A place about 16 km/10 miles west of Jerusalem, on the borders of the land belonging to the Israelite tribe of Dan. It features in the Old Testament story as the home district of Samson, where he grew up and from where he was first moved to go out against the Philistines in the lowlands to the west.

Joshua 15:33; 19:41; Judges 13:24–25; 16:31; 18
See map page 274

Ethiopia

See Cush.

Euphrates

One of the greatest rivers of the world, some 1,931 km/1,200 miles long, rising in eastern Turkey and flowing south-east to the Persian Gulf. It played such a strategic role in ancient times that the Old Testament sometimes refers to it simply as 'the river'. Over the centuries, its course through the Babylonian plains has moved west, leaving many of the ancient cities which once stood on its banks now 5–6 km/3–4 miles to the east. It has rightfully been regarded as the cradle of civilization, and features in the Old Testament as one of the boundary rivers of the Garden of Eden.

Genesis 2:14; 15:18; Revelation 9:14; 16:12

Fair Havens

A small port on the south coast of Crete, visited by Paul's ship on his final voyage to Rome. The centurion Julius, who was in charge of the prisoners, together with the owner and captain of the ship decided they would prefer a more attractive harbour in which to spend the winter, a decision which led to the ship being caught in a violent storm, before being wrecked on Malta.

Acts 27:8–12

Gad

The land of the tribe of Gad. Part of the traditional Amorite kingdom, east of the River Jordan (south Gilead).

Joshua 13:8–13
See map page 274

Galatia

The ancient kingdom of Galatia was in the north of Asia Minor along the

southern shore of the Black Sea, settled in the third century BC by the Gauls, who established three separate territories here. By Roman times, this traditional territory of those who could be called ethnic Galatians had been included in the Roman province of Galatia, which was more extensive, and included other major cities further to the south, including Pisidian Antioch, Iconium, Lystra and perhaps Derbe – all of them visited by Paul during his first missionary journey. There has been much debate about the destination of Paul's letter to the Galatians: was it written to the Christians in these southern cities of the Roman province of Galatia, or to people in the traditional heartlands of the ancient Galatian kingdom? There is no unequivocal statement in the New Testament that Paul actually visited ethnic Galatia, though there are some hints to that effect, and opinion is divided on the subject.
Acts 13–14; 16:6; 18:23; Galatians 1:1
See maps pages 43, 45

Galilee
The name of a region and a large lake in northern Israel, mentioned occasionally in the Old Testament, but of special interest because it was the home area of Jesus and most of his disciples. It was surrounded on three sides by other nations – and strongly influenced by them. In New Testament times it was often referred to as 'Galilee of the Gentiles', and the people here were familiar with the Greek language as well as the traditional Hebrew of Judaism, and the Aramaic which was spoken in the home. Most of Galilee is hilly, but the land falls steeply to 210 m/682 ft below sea level around the lake.
At the time of Jesus several major roads of the Roman empire crossed the region of Galilee. Farming, trade and the lakeside fisheries were the main industries. Many of the towns and villages mentioned in the New Testament gospels were in Galilee, including Nazareth (where Jesus grew up), Capernaum, Cana and Bethsaida. The lake, which is liable to

sudden fierce storms as the wind funnels through the hills that ring it round, is also a focal point in the gospel stories.
1 Kings 9:11; 2 Kings 15:29; Isaiah 9:1; Luke 4:14; 5:1; 8:22–26; John 21; Acts 9:31
See maps pages 41, 275

Gath
One of five Philistine strongholds in Old Testament times. Best known as the home of Goliath, the Philistine giant defeated by David. David himself later escaped to Gath when he was on the run from King Saul, and later still his son Absalom enlisted the help of forces from Gath in his own unsuccessful bid for power. The city was subject to the kingdom of Judah for some time and eventually fell to the Assyrians in the eighth century BC.
Joshua 11:22; 1 Samuel 5, 17:4; 21:10–22:1, 27; 2 Samuel 15:18; 2 Kings 12:17; 2 Chronicles 11:8; 26:6
See map page 26

Gath-hepher
A place in Galilee on the borders of the lands of the tribes of Zebulun and Naphtali. Birthplace of a prophet named Jonah, though it is unclear whether this is the same person as the hero of the book of Jonah. Not far from the location of Nazareth, childhood home of Jesus many centuries later.
Joshua 19:13; 2 Kings 14:25

Gaza
One of five Philistine strongholds in Old Testament times, on the coastal plain. The city appears in the Old Testament in the stories of Joshua, as a town that he conquered and then lost again. It also features in the story of Samson, as the place where he was imprisoned and finally died when he brought about the collapse of a great building.
The town occupied an important location on the trade route to Egypt. It was conquered by King Hezekiah of Judah, and later by the Assyrian armies and the Egyptian pharaoh. In the New Testament, Philip was on the road from Jerusalem to Gaza when he met a travelling African and spoke to him about Jesus.
Joshua 10:41; Judges 16; 1 Samuel 6:17; 2 Kings 18:8; Jeremiah 47; Acts 8:26
See maps pages 24, 36, 274

Geba
Modern Jeba', opposite Michmash, 10 km/6 miles north of Jerusalem. A city belonging to the Israelite tribe of Benjamin. King Saul's army camped here in front of his capital at Gibeah when the Philistines held Michmash. Later Geba became the northern limit of the southern kingdom of Judah, and was heavily fortified by King Asa. Like Michmash, it was on the route of the Assyrian approach to Jerusalem, and was resettled after the exile.
Joshua 18:24; 21:17; 1 Samuel 13:16; 1 Kings 15:22; 2 Kings 23:8; 1 Chronicles 6:60; Isaiah 10:29; Ezra 2:26; Nehemiah 7:30; Zechariah 14:10
See map page 274

Gebal
An ancient Phoenician city, often known by its Greek name Byblos. It was on the coast of modern Lebanon, north of Berytus (Beirut). It is mentioned in the book of Joshua, and later supplied craft workers for the construction of Solomon's temple in Jerusalem.
Joshua 13:5; 1 Kings 5:18; Psalm 83:9; Ezekiel 27:9

Gennesaret
A fertile valley to the north-west of the Sea of Lake Galilee. The term also appears as a name for the lake itself.
Mark 6:53; Luke 5:1
See map page 275

Gerar
A place in the Negev between Beersheba and Gaza linked to stories about Abraham and Isaac.
Genesis 20:1, 26:1
See map page 274

Gerizim
The 'mountain of God's blessing' in Samaria, opposite Mount Ebal. Gerizim later became the sacred mountain of the Samaritans, and the place where they built a temple whose site can still be identified today.
Deuteronomy 11:29, 27; Joshua 8:33; John 4:20
See map page 274

Geshur
A region and town in southern Syria. One of King David's wives came from here, and their son, Absalom, fled to Geshur after he had killed his half-brother Amnon in revenge for the rape of his sister Tamar.
Joshua 12:5; 2 Samuel 3:3; 13:38

Gethsemane
A garden across the Kidron valley from Jerusalem, close to the

Mount of Olives. A favourite quiet place for Jesus and his disciples, and the site of his betrayal to the Romans by the renegade disciple Judas Iscariot.
Matthew 26:36–56; Mark 14:32–51; Luke 22:39; John 18:1–12

Gezer (Gazara)
A Canaanite town mentioned in the campaign of Joshua. It was in the low hills, on the road from Joppa (on the coast) to Jerusalem. Gezer belonged to Egypt for a while until one of the pharaohs gave it to his daughter, King Solomon's wife. Solomon fortified the town, with Hazor and Megiddo. Its military significance lasted all through Old Testament times, and it was still a fortress in the Maccabean period, when it was known as Gazara. There have been many interesting archaeological finds here, including the 'Gezer calendar', a schoolchild's jottings dating from the 10th century BC and outlining the operations of the agricultural year at that time.
Joshua 10:33; 1 Kings 9:15–17; ; 1 Maccabees 9:52; 13:43–48; 14:7; 15:35; 16:19–21; 2 Maccabees 10:32
See map page 274

Gibeah
A hill-top town 4 km/3 miles north of Jerusalem, which became famous as the home and capital city of King Saul. The site is at Tell el-Ful, overlooking the suburbs of Jerusalem.
Judges 19:12–20:48; 1 Samuel 10:26; Isaiah 10:29
See maps pages 26, 274

Gibeon
A town about 10 km/6 miles north-west of Jerusalem. Early Israel made a treaty with its inhabitants, though this was later broken by Saul. David's forces fought the supporters of Saul's son Ish-baal at the pool of Gibeon, in order to decide which of the two men should be king. The Ark of the Covenant is associated with Gibeon, and King Solomon worshipped at the shrine there. At a later period, its inhabitants joined Nehemiah in rebuilding the walls of Jerusalem.
Archaeologists have discovered a huge pit at Gibeon, with a stairway leading down to water. Inside it there were handles of a great many storage jars, each one inscribed with the name

'Gibeon' and the owner's name. The town seems to have been an important centre for wine-making in the seventh century BC.
Joshua 9; 2 Samuel 2:12–29; 20:8, 21; 1 Kings 3:4; 1 Chronicles 21:29; Nehemiah 3:7
See maps pages 22, 274

Gihon
A name variously applied to one of the four rivers flowing out of the Garden of Eden, and also to a spring at the foot of the hill on which the first city of Jerusalem stood. At that time it was the main source of water for the city. Solomon was anointed king of Israel at this spring by the command of his father David, to forestall the attempt of his rival Adonijah to seize the throne. The Gihon spring water was vitally important to the safety of the city and at a later stage King Hezekiah cut a tunnel to bring the water right through the hill and inside the walls. This tunnel still exists, and the water surfaces at the Pool of Siloam within the city boundaries.
Genesis 2:13; 1 Kings 1; 2 Chronicles 32:30, 33:14
See map page 39

Gilboa
A mountain and range in the north of Palestine, overlooking the deep valley of Jezreel which runs down to the River Jordan. The location of King Saul's last stand against the Philistines, in which he and three of his sons were all killed.
1 Samuel 28:4; 31:1, 8; 2 Samuel 1; 21:12; 1 Chronicles 10:1, 8
See maps pages 27, 274

Gilead
A large area east of the River Jordan, extending north from the Dead Sea. The tribes of Reuben, Gad and Manasseh each occupied part of Gilead. The region was good grazing-land, famous for its flocks and herds. It was also famous for a gum or spice known as the 'balm' of Gilead, which was used to heal wounds and also as a cosmetic. Jair, Jephthah and the prophet Elijah all came from Gilead.
Genesis 37:25; Joshua 17:1; Judges 10:3; 11; 1 Kings 17:1; Song of Songs 4:1
See maps pages 25, 274

Gilgal
A place between Jericho and the River Jordan. An ancient river crossing, connected to the Israelite conquest of Canaan, Gilgal was also the site of an important shrine. It is

mentioned in the stories of the prophets Elijah and Elisha, while Hosea and Amos both castigated its worship as mere hypocrisy.
Joshua 4:20; Judges 3:19; 1 Samuel 7:16; 10:8; 2 Samuel 19:15; 2 Kings 2:1; 4:38–41; Hosea 4:15; Amos 4:4
See maps pages 22, 274

Gomorrah
One of five cities probably now beneath the southern end of the Dead Sea, violently destroyed in ancient times. Together with its neighbouring city Sodom, Gomorrah is regularly cited as an example of the kind of judgment that could follow disregard for the covenant and its values.
Genesis 14; 19; Isaiah 1:9–10; Ezekiel 16:48–58; Matthew 10:15

Goshen
A fertile area of the eastern Nile Delta in Egypt. Traditional home of Jacob and his family, it was a good place for the nomadic herders to settle.
Genesis 45:10; Exodus 8:22
See maps pages 18, 20

Gozan
Israelites from Samaria were taken captive to Gozan by the Assyrians. The town is modern Tell Halaf on the River Khabur in north-east Syria.
2 Kings 17:6; 19:12

Great Sea
The Bible often uses this name for the Mediterranean Sea.

Greece
The conquests of Alexander the Great brought Israel (and the rest of the eastern Mediterranean lands) under Greek control. The influence of Greek civilization, culture and thought was strong in the centuries preceding Jesus' birth and in New Testament times.
Daniel 11; John 12:20; Acts 6; 17; 18

Habor
The River Khabur in north-east Syria; a tributary of the River Euphrates. The town of Gozan was on the River Habor.
2 Kings 17:6

Hamath
Modern Hama, on the River Orontes in Syria. In Old Testament times Hamath was an important town, the capital of a small kingdom, and on a main trade-route from Asia Minor south towards Israel and Egypt.

Hamath Pass, some distance to the south, was often regarded as the northern limit of Israel's territory. In the reigns of David and Solomon, Israel had a peace treaty with King Toi of Hamath. The town fell to the Assyrians and many of its people were moved into Israel. First Pharaoh Neco (before the Battle of Carchemish) and then King Nebuchadnezzar of Babylon made it their headquarters for a time.

Joshua 13:5; 2 Samuel 8:9–11; 1 Kings 8:65; 2 Chronicles 8:4; 2 Kings 17:24; 18:34

Harod

The spring where Gideon chose his fighting force by watching how the volunteers drank from the stream. The 300 who showed their alertness by stooping and lapping the water were chosen. The place was in northern Palestine, probably by a stream which flows down the valley of Jezreel.

Judges 7:1–8

Harran

A town in what is now south-east Turkey, on the River Balikh, a tributary of the River Euphrates. The place where Abraham's father, Terah, settled after leaving Ur, and where Jacob worked for Laban. Harran was on the main road linking Nineveh with Aleppo in Syria, and further south to the port of Tyre. It was fortified by the Assyrians as a provincial capital. For three years after the fall of Nineveh it was Assyria's capital city. Then in 609 BC it fell to the Babylonians.

Genesis 11:31; 12:4–5; 29:4; 2 Kings 19:12; Ezekiel 27:33

Hazor

A Canaanite city in the north of Israel, featuring in early stories of conquest by Joshua, then Deborah and Barak. King Solomon rebuilt and fortified Hazor, along with Megiddo and Gezer. In the eighth century BC the Assyrians destroyed the city.

An upper and a lower city have been uncovered, which seem to have accommodated as many as 40,000 people. The lower part was destroyed in the 13th century BC. A city gate and wall from Solomon's time match others of the same design at Megiddo and Gezer. Hazor is mentioned in Egyptian

and Babylonian texts, and in the Amarna Letters, as well as in the Bible itself.

Joshua 11; Judges 4; 1 Kings 9:15; 2 Kings 15:29

See maps pages 23, 24, 30, 274

Hebron

A town high in the Judean hills (935 m/3,040 ft above sea level). The old name for Hebron was Kiriath-arba. A place associated with the stories of Abraham and his family. Moses' 12 spies also visited it, and it was allocated to Caleb. It also appears as a city of refuge, and one of the Levites' towns. It was David's capital before he captured Jerusalem. Absalom staged his rebellion from Hebron. Much later, after the exile, Jews returned to live there.

Genesis 13:18; 23; 35:27; 37:14; Numbers 13:22; Joshua 14:6–15; 2 Samuel 2:1–4; 15:9–10; Nehemiah 11:25

See maps pages 19, 21, 22, 24, 26, 274

Hermon

A mountain on the Lebanon/Syria border. It is more than 2,750 m/9,000 ft high. Also known as Sirion in the Bible, Mount Hermon is topped with snow almost all the year round. The melting snow and ice form a major source of the River Jordan. Mount Hermon is close to Caesarea Philippi and may be the 'high mountain' where, according to the New Testament, Jesus' disciples saw him 'in his glory'.

Joshua 12:1; Psalms 42:6; 133:3; Matthew 17:1

See maps pages 41, 275

Heshbon

A town east of the River Jordan which belonged first to Moab, then to the Amorites, and then to the Israelite tribes of Reuben and Gad. It was prosperous for a while at the time of Isaiah and Jeremiah.

Numbers 21:25–30; 32:37; Isaiah 15:4; Jeremiah 48:2

See map page 274

Hierapolis

A city in the Roman province of Asia, now in western Turkey. Paul mentions the Christians at Laodicea and Hierapolis in his letter to nearby Colossae. Over the centuries the hot-water springs at Hierapolis (modern Pamukkale) have petrified to form amazing waterfalls of stone.

Colossians 4:13

See map page 47

Hinnom

The name of a valley on the south side of Jerusalem, forming the boundary between the Israelite tribes of Judah and Benjamin. Here the kings Ahaz and Manasseh set up a shrine for the god Molech, and offered children (including their own) in sacrifice. The shrine was destroyed by King Josiah. The prophet Jeremiah denounced the evil of this place. Later, rubbish from the city was burned in the valley of Hinnom, and the constant smoke and flames became a convenient image of hell ('Gehenna', meaning 'Valley of Hinnom').

Joshua 15:8; 18:16; 2 Kings 23:10; 2 Chronicles 28:3; 33:6; Jeremiah 7:31; 19:2; 32:35

See map page 39

Horeb

Another name for Mount Sinai.

Hormah

The exact site of this town in southern Canaan is not certain, but it features in the stories of early conflict between Israelites and Canaanites at Hormah, and was later given to the tribe of Judah.

Numbers 14:39–45; 21:3; Joshua 15:30

Ibleam

A Canaanite town in the north of Israel, about 14 km/10 miles south-east of Megiddo. The place where Jehu killed King Ahaziah of Judah.

Joshua 17:11–12; 2 Kings 9:27; 15:10

See map page 274

Iconium

Present-day Konya in south-central Turkey. When Paul visited here, it was a city in the Roman province of Galatia.

Acts 13:51; 14:1-6, 19–22; 2 Timothy 3:11

See maps pages 45, 47

Idumea, Idumaea

The Greek name for what the Old Testament calls Edom. By New Testament times many Idumeans had settled west of the River Jordan, in the dry country in the south of Palestine. King Herod the Great was an Idumean. The New Testament records that people came from this area to see Jesus in Galilee.

Mark 3:8

See maps pages 117, 275

Illyricum

The Roman name of a land stretching along the eastern shore of the Adriatic Sea. It covered much the same area as

modern Croatia and Bosnia, and south into Dalmatia. Paul mentions it as the furthest west he had travelled until the time he went to Rome, though there is no New Testament account of Paul's work there.

Romans 15:19

Israel

The land occupied by the 12 Israelite tribes. After King Solomon died and his kingdom was divided, the name 'Israel' came to refer to the northern part of the land, with the southern part (which included Jerusalem) being called Judah.

See maps pages 28, 274

Issachar

Land belonging to the Israelite tribe of Issachar, south of Lake Galilee and west of the River Jordan.

Joshua 19:17–23

See map page 274

Ituraea

A name mentioned only in the New Testament gospel of Luke, when the author dates the time when John the Baptist began to preach. Herod Philip was then ruler of Ituraea and Trachonitis. The Ituraeans were probably the descendants of the Old Testament people called Jetur, centred in the hills west of Damascus, north of the head-waters of the River Jordan.

Luke 3:1; compare 1 Chronicles 5:19

See map page 275

Jabbok

Now the Zerqa, a river that flows into the River Jordan from the east between the Dead Sea and Lake Galilee. Jacob wrestled with an angel beside the River Jabbok. Adam – site of a landslide that allowed Israelites to cross the river Jordan easily into Canaan – stands at the confluence of the Jabbok and the Jordan. The river is also mentioned in the Bible as a boundary.

Genesis 32:22–30; Numbers 21:24; Deuteronomy 3:16; Judges 11:13

See maps pages 19, 25, 274

Jabesh-gilead

A town on the east of the River Jordan, mentioned in the Old Testament as a source of wives for Benjaminite men. King Saul answered an appeal for help when Jabesh-gilead was besieged by the Ammonites, and men from this town later risked their lives to remove Saul's dead body

from Bethshan.

Judges 21; 1 Samuel 11; 31:11–13

See maps pages 27, 274

Jazer

An Amorite town east of the River Jordan, famous for its vines, part of the territory of the Israelite tribe of Gad.

Numbers 21:32; Joshua 13:25; 1 Chronicles 26:31; Isaiah 16:8–9

See map page 274

Jebus

An early name for Jerusalem.

Jericho

A town west of the River Jordan, 250 m/820 ft below sea level, about 8 km/5 miles from the northern end of the Dead Sea. Jericho's fresh-water spring makes it an oasis in the surrounding desert – the 'city of palm trees'. The town was in a well-fortified position, guarding the fords of the River Jordan, which explains its strategic role in the stories of the Israelite entry into Canaan.

At the time of the judges Ehud killed King Eglon of Moab at Jericho. At the time of the prophets Elijah and Elisha it was the home of a large group of prophets. After the return from exile, people from Jericho helped to rebuild the walls of Jerusalem. In the New Testament, Jericho was the place where Jesus gave Bartimaeus his sight and where Zacchaeus became a changed man. The story of the good Samaritan is set on the road from Jerusalem to Jericho.

Jericho has a very long history covering thousands of years. The first town was built here as early as 8000 BC, though there are signs of human settlement there for almost 2,000 years before that – making it the oldest known continuously-inhabited city in the world.

Joshua 2; 6; Judges 12:13; 2 Kings 2; Nehemiah 3:2; Mark 10:46; Luke 19:1–10; 10:30

See maps pages 21, 22, 23, 274, 275

Jerusalem

Captured by David and made into his capital city, Jerusalem then became the religious and political centre of the nation, especially with the building of a new temple there by King Solomon. When the kingdom was divided in two, it remained as the capital of the southern kingdom of Judah, and

to this day is still one of the world's most famous – and disputed – cities. Jerusalem stands high in the Judean hills with no access by sea or river. The ground drops steeply away on all sides except the north. To the east, between Jerusalem (with its temple) and the Mount of Olives, is the Kidron valley. The Hinnom valley curves around the city to the south and west. A third, central valley – the Tyropoean valley – cuts right into the city, dividing the temple area and city of David from the 'upper', western section.

Genesis 14:18; Joshua 15:63; 2 Samuel 5; 1 Kings 6; Psalms 48; 122; 125; 1 Kings 14:25–26; 2 Kings 12:18; 18:13–19:36; 20:20; 25; Ezra 5; Nehemiah 3–6; Luke 2; 19:28–24:49; John 2:23–3:21; 5; 7:10–10:42, etc.; Acts 2; 15

See maps pages 22, 23, 26, 28, 29, 32, 33, 34, 37, 38, 40, 43, 45, 47, 274, 275

Jezreel

A town in the north of Israel and the plain in which it stood, close to Mount Gilboa. Saul camped at the spring in the valley of Jezreel before the battle of Gilboa. King Ahab of Israel had a palace at Jezreel, and his queen, Jezebel, met a gory death here.

1 Samuel 29:1; 1 Kings 18:45–46; 21; 2 Kings 8:29; 9:30–37

See maps pages 25, 29, 274

Joppa

The only natural harbour on the coast of Israel south of the Bay of Acre (Haifa); modern Jaffa, close to Tel Aviv. Joppa was the port for Jerusalem, 56 km/35 miles away. The town has a long history and was mentioned in about 1400 BC in the Egyptian Amarna Letters. In the story of Jonah, Joppa is the port from which the prophet set sail for Tarshish (Spain). In the New Testament, it is mentioned as the location of an early Christian community, and centre of significant missionary work among Gentiles.

2 Chronicles 2:16; Jonah 1:3; Acts 9:36–43; 10

See maps pages 47, 274

Jordan

The main river of Israel, constantly referred to in the Bible. The River Jordan flows from Mount Hermon in the far north, through Lake Huleh and Lake Galilee to the Dead Sea. It is 120 km/75 miles from Lake Huleh to the Dead Sea, but the river winds about so much that it is more than twice that length.

The name 'Jordan' means 'the descender'. It flows through the deepest rift valley on earth. Lake Huleh is 71 m/230 ft above sea level. Lake Galilee is 210 m/682 ft below sea level, and the north end of the Dead Sea is 397 m/1,290 ft below sea level. The northern part of the Jordan valley is fertile; the southern end approaching the Dead Sea is desert, but dense jungle grows on the banks. The main tributaries of the River Jordan are the Yarmuk and Jabbok rivers, both of which join it from the east. Many smaller tributaries dry up completely through the summer.

The river Jordan features in many significant Bible stories, including the entry of the people of Israel into Canaan, David's escape at the time of Absalom's revolt, the work of the prophets Elijah and Elisha, and the ministry of John the Baptist.

Joshua 3; 2 Samuel 17:20–22; 2 Kings 2:6–8, 13–14; 5; Jeremiah 12:5; 49:19; Mark 1:5, 9
See maps pages 19, 23, 24, 25, 29, 40, 274, 275

Judah
The Judean hills south of Jerusalem and the desert bordering the Dead Sea. The land belonging to the Israelite tribe of Judah. Later the name of the southern kingdom, with Jerusalem as its capital.

Joshua 15; 1 Kings 12:21, 23
See maps pages 23, 26, 28, 34, 274

Judea
The Greek and Roman name for Judah. Usually it refers to the southern part of the country, with Jerusalem as capital. But it can be used as a name for the whole land, including Galilee and Samaria. The 'wilderness of Judea' is the desert west of the Dead Sea.

Luke 3:1; 4:44
See maps pages 40, 43, 274

Kadesh-barnea
An oasis and settlement in the desert south of Beersheba. It is mentioned in the campaign of Chedorlaomer and his allies at the time of Abraham. According to the Old Testament, it was near Kadesh-barnea that Hagar saw an angel. After the escape from Egypt, most of Israel's

years of desert wandering were spent in the area around Kadesh-barnea. Miriam died there, and Moses brought water out of the rock. From Kadesh-barnea he sent spies into Canaan. It is later mentioned as a point on the southern boundary of Israel.

Genesis 14:7; 16:14; Numbers 13:26; 20:14; 33:36; Deuteronomy 1:19–25, 46; Joshua 10:41; 15:23
See map page 21

Kedesh
A Canaanite town in Galilee conquered by Joshua and given to the Israelite tribe of Naphtali. It was the home of Barak. Kedesh was one of the first towns to fall to the Assyrians when the Assyrian king Tiglath-pileser III invaded Israel from the north (734–732 BC).

Joshua 12:22; 19:37; Judges 4; 2 Kings 15:29
See map page 274

Keilah
A town about 11 km/8 miles north-west of Hebron. The Old Testament records that David saved it from a Philistine attack and stayed there, escaping from King Saul.

Joshua 15:44; 1 Samuel 23; Nehemiah 3:17–18
See maps pages 26, 274

Kidron
The valley which separates Jerusalem and the temple from the Mount of Olives. For most of the year the valley is dry. The Gihon spring, whose water King Hezekiah brought inside the city walls through the Siloam tunnel, is on the west side of the Kidron valley.

David crossed the Kidron valley when he left Jerusalem at the time of Absalom's rebellion. Asa, Hezekiah and Josiah, kings who reformed the nation's worship, destroyed foreign religious artefacts in the Kidron valley. Jesus and his disciples crossed the valley many times on their way to the Garden of Gethsemane.

2 Samuel 15:23; 1 Kings 15:13; 2 Chronicles 29:16; 2 Kings 23:4; John 18:1
See map page 39

King's Highway
The main route north to south along the heights east of the River Jordan, between Damascus and the Gulf of Aqaba.

Numbers 20:17; 21:22; Deuteronomy 2:27

Kir, Kir-hareseth
The name of an unknown place where the Syrians were exiled.

An important fortified town in Moab.

2 Kings 16:9; Amos 1:5; 2 Kings 3; Isaiah 16:7–12
See map page 274

Kiriath-arba
An earlier name for Hebron.

Kiriath-jearim
A hill town a few miles east of Jerusalem, and one of the towns of the Gibeonites who, according to the Old Testament, tricked Joshua into signing a peace treaty. Location of the Ark of the Covenant for 20 years before King David installed it in his new capital of Jerusalem.

Joshua 9; 1 Samuel 6:20–7:2; Jeremiah 26:20; Nehemiah 7:29
See map page 274

Kiriathaim
A town east of the Dead Sea given to the Israelite tribe of Reuben. It was later taken by the Moabites.

Joshua 13:19; Jeremiah 48:1–25; Ezekiel 25:9
See map page 274

Kishon
A small stream which flows across the plain of Megiddo and into the Mediterranean Sea just north of Mount Carmel. Features in the story of Barak when heavy rain raised its water level so high that the surrounding ground turned to mud and bogged down Sisera's chariots, giving Israel victory. The prophet Elijah killed the prophets of Baal by the River Kishon after the contest on Mount Carmel.

Judges 4; 5:21; 1 Kings 18:40
See maps pages 25, 274

Kue/Coa
A region from which King Solomon obtained horses. It was in the eastern part of Cilicia, in the south of modern Turkey.

Lachish
An important fortified town about 48 km/30 miles south-west of Jerusalem. Lachish has a long history. The Old Testament records that the king of Lachish joined with four other Amorite kings to fight Joshua. Solomon's son, King Rehoboam, later rebuilt Lachish as a defence against the Philistines and Egyptians.

King Amaziah of Judah fled to Lachish for safety, though not for long. When the Assyrian king

Sennacherib attacked Judah he besieged Lachish, cutting Jerusalem off from possible help from Egypt. Lachish fell, and Sennacherib had the siege pictured on the walls of his palace at Nineveh. Archaeologists have also discovered at Lachish a mass grave from this time, holding 1,500 bodies.

The Babylonian army attacked Lachish at the time of the final siege of Jerusalem (587 BC), the final days of which are documented in a series of messages written on broken pottery, known as the Lachish Letters. When the city fell it was burned by the Babylonians, and though it was resettled after the exile, it was never again an important place.

Joshua 10; 2 Chronicles 11:5–12; 2 Kings 14:19; 18:14–21; Isaiah 36–37; Jeremiah 34:7; Nehemiah 11:30
See maps pages 22, 274

Laodicea
A city in the Lycus valley of present-day western Turkey (the Roman province of Asia in New Testament times). Laodicea stood at the junction of two important main roads. It grew prosperous from trade and banking. The region produced clothes made of glossy black wool, and also medicines. Water for the town was piped from springs some distance away and arrived lukewarm. These features of life there are all reflected in the letter to the church at Laodicea contained in the New Testament book of Revelation. Paul's letter to the Colossians mentions a letter he had written to Laodicea, and encourages the two churches to exchange letters. The origins of the church there are uncertain, though it could have been started in much the same way as the church in Colossae, as converts Paul won in Ephesus moved out into the surrounding area taking the Christian message with them.

Colossians 2:1; 4:13–16; Revelation 1:11; 3:14–22

Lebanon
Lebanon in the Old Testament was famous for its forests, especially its great cedar trees. The Bible refers also to the snows of Lebanon, and to the country's fertility. All kinds of fruit grow

on the coastal plain and lower hill slopes: olives, grapes, apples figs, apricots, dates and all kinds of green vegetables.

The great Phoenician ports of Tyre, Sidon and Byblos were all on the coast of Lebanon and prospered as international trading centres. King Solomon sent to the king of Tyre for cedar and other wood from Lebanon to build the temple and royal palace at Jerusalem.

1 Kings 5:1–11; Hosea 14:5–7; Ezra 3:7; Psalm 72:16; Isaiah 2:13; 14:8; Ezekiel 31

Libnah
A fortified lowland town not far from Lachish, taken by Joshua. In the reign of King Jehoram of Judah, Libnah rebelled. The town survived a siege by the Assyrian King Sennacherib when plague hit his army.

Joshua 10:29–30; 2 Kings 8:22; 19:8, 35
See maps pages 22, 274

Lo-debar
A place in Gilead, east of the River Jordan, home of Mephibosheth, Jonathan's son, until King David brought him to his court.

2 Samuel 9; 17:27
See map page 274

Luz
The older name for Bethel.

Lycia
A small, mountainous land in the south-west of Asia Minor (Turkey). The ports of Patara and Myra, at which the missionary Paul landed, were in Lycia.

Acts 27:5
See map page 43

Lydda
A town about 16 km/10 miles inland from Joppa, known as Lod in Old Testament times. Connected with the ministry of Peter in the New Testament.

Acts 9:32–35, 38
See maps pages 47, 275

Lystra
A remote city in the Roman province of Galatia. Paul and Barnabas went on to Lystra after rough treatment at Iconium on the first missionary journey. As a result of a miraculous healing, Paul was acclaimed as an incarnation of Hermes (messenger of the Greek gods) and his companion Barnabas was believed to be Zeus (the chief god in the Greek pantheon). Paul was subsequently

stoned and left for dead by his enemies, though a Christian community was founded there, and Paul later returned to visit them on his second journey.

Acts 14:6–20; 16:1–5
See maps pages 45, 47

Maacah
A small Aramaean state to the south-east of Mount Hermon, mentioned in the story of King David's campaigns as home to one of his warriors.

Joshua 12:5; 2 Samuel 10; 23:34
See map page 274

Macedonia
What is now northern Greece, with its capital in Thessalonica. The Roman province of Macedonia included Philippi and Beroea as well as Thessalonica.

Paul crossed the Aegean Sea from Troas after seeing a vision of a Macedonian man asking for his help. Three of Paul's letters (Philippians, and 1 and 2 Thessalonians) are addressed to Macedonian Christians. They gave generously to his relief fund for Christians in Judea, and several of them became his regular co-workers.

Acts 16:8–17:15; 20:1–6; 2 Corinthians 8:1–5; 9:1–5
See maps pages 36, 42

Machpelah
Location of the graves of Abraham, Sarah, Isaac, Rebekah and Jacob, the sites of which were later restored and commemorated in a shrine built there by Herod the Great, which can still be seen today.

Genesis 23; 25:9; 49:30; 50:13

Mahanaim
A place in Gilead, east of the River Jordan and near the River Jabbok. Jacob saw angels here, just before the reunion with his brother Esau. For a short time it was the capital of King Saul's son Ish-baal, then later it served as King David's headquarters during Absalom's rebellion. One of King Solomon's district officers was based at Mahanaim.

Genesis 32:2; 2 Samuel 2:8–10; 17:24–29; 1 Kings 4:14
See map page 274

Makkedah
Site of a struggle between Joshua and five Amorite kings, this town was subsequently allocated to the tribe of Judah.

Joshua 10:10; 16; 15:41
See maps pages 22, 274

Malta

The modern name of an island in the central Mediterranean Sea, between Sicily and the north coast of Africa. Its ancient name was Melita, and Paul's ship was wrecked here during his final voyage as a prisoner to Rome. Those on board were rescued, and entertained by the island's inhabitants for a full winter before sailing on to Italy.
Acts 28:1–10
See map page 44

Mamre

A place near Hebron, location of several key episodes in the stories about Abraham and Isaac.
Genesis 13:18; 14:13; 18; 23:17; 35:27

Manasseh

The land belonging to the Israelite tribe of Manasseh. West Manasseh was the hill country of Samaria as far west as the Mediterranean Sea. East Manasseh was the land east of central Jordan.
Joshua 13:29–31; 17:7–13
See maps pages 23, 274

Maon

A town in the hills of Judah, home to Nabal, the husband of Abigail. David stayed here twice when he was an outlaw from King Saul.
Joshua 15:55, 1 Samuel 23:24–25; 25
See maps pages 26, 274

Mareshah

A town in the low hills nearly 32 km/20 miles south-west of Jerusalem. Fortified by Rehoboam, and in the time of King Asa the scene of a victory over the Cushite army. The prophet Micah foretold disaster for Mareshah.
Joshua 15:44; 2 Chronicles 11:8; 14:9–12; 20:37; Micah 1:15
See map page 274

Media

North-west Iran. Media came under Assyrian control, and some Israelites were taken into exile there by Sargon II in 716 BC. The Medes helped the Babylonians to overthrow the Assyrians, then later they were subdued by Cyrus, though there were subsequent revolts against Persian rule.
Genesis 10:2; 2 Kings 17:6; 18:11; Jeremiah 51:11,28; Isaiah 13:17; Daniel 6:8,15; 9:11; 11:1; Esther 1:19; 1 Maccabees 14:1–3; Acts 2:9
See map page 31

Megiddo

An important Old Testament city on the edge of the plain of Jezreel, guarding the main pass through the Carmel hills. About 32 km/20 miles from modern Haifa. So many battles took place here that the New Testament uses the name symbolically for the site of the great last battle of all time: Armageddon ('the hill of Megiddo').

Megiddo first appears in the account of the Israelite conquest of Canaan, following which it is included in lists of territory belonging to the tribe of Manasseh. King Solomon chose Megiddo to be one of his main fortified cities. King Ahaziah of Judah died at Megiddo after being wounded by Jehu's men. So too did King Josiah, attempting to stop the advance of Pharaoh Neco of Egypt. The site has been extensively excavated, with 20 main levels of settlement identified on a mound now 21 m/70 ft high and covering, at the top, an area of more than 10 acres. The earliest settlement goes back to before 3000 BC. Excavation has uncovered, among other things, a Canaanite 'high place'; the city's water supply system; a fortified gateway built to the same pattern as others at Gezer and Hazor; a hoard of carved ivory objects; and a series of stables (probably from King Ahab's time).
Joshua 12:21; Judges 1:27-28; 5:19; 1 Kings 9:15; 2 Kings 9:27; 23:29; Revelation 16:16
See maps pages 30, 32, 274

Memphis

The ancient capital of Egypt, on the River Nile not far south of modern Cairo. The pyramids at Giza are also near to Memphis. The city remained important for many centuries, up to the time of Alexander the Great. Several of the Old Testament prophets refer to Memphis when they condemn Israel's trust in Egypt.
Isaiah 19:13; Jeremiah 2:16; 46:14; Ezekiel 30:13
See maps pages 31, 33

Mesopotamia

The land between the River Tigris and the River Euphrates. The centre of some of the earliest civilizations – including the Sumerians, Babylonians and Assyrians – Mesopotamia included such famous cities as Ur, Babylon and Nineveh.

Harran and Paddan-aram where, according to the Old Testament, some of Abraham's family settled, are in Mesopotamia. It is named as the home of Balaam, the prophet sent to curse the Israelites, and also appears in the book of Judges.

The New Testament states that people from Mesopotamia were in Jerusalem on the Day of Pentecost, and heard Peter and the disciples speak to them in their own languages.
Genesis 24:10; Deuteronomy 23:4 and Numbers 22; Judges 3:8, 10; Acts 2:9

Michmash

A place about 11 km/7 miles north-east of Jerusalem, at a village still called Mukhmas. It was separated from Geba by a deep valley, but an important route, 'the passage of Michmash' crossed an easy part of the valley. The Old Testament records that the Philistines invaded Israel and camped in force at Michmash, threatening King Saul's capital at Gibeah. Jonathan and his armour-bearer surprised the Philistine garrison by climbing across from Geba at a steep place down the valley, and in the panic which followed Saul defeated the Philistines. Michmash was on the route by which the Assyrians approached Jerusalem from the north. It was reoccupied after the exile.
1 Samuel 13–14; Isaiah 10:28; Ezra 2:27; Nehemiah 7:31; 11:31
See maps pages 274

Midian

Part of Arabia, east of the Gulf of Aqaba. When Moses fled for his life from Egypt after killing an Egyptian overseer, this is where he went. There he married a Midianite wife before returning to Egypt to help free the Israelite slaves. The people of this region feature in the story of Gideon, who faced an army of camel-riding invaders from Midian.
Genesis 25:1–6; Exodus 2:15–21; Judges 6

Miletus

A sea port on the west coast of modern Turkey. Paul stayed at Miletus on his way to Jerusalem at the end of his third missionary journey. To save time, the elders from the church at Ephesus came to meet

him there and heard his farewell message.
Acts 20:15–38; 2 Timothy 4:20
See maps pages 45, 47

Mitylene

The most important city and port on the Greek island of Lesbos, off the west coast of Asia Minor (Turkey). Paul stopped there overnight on his last voyage to Jerusalem.
Acts 20:14

Mizpah/Mizpeh

The name (meaning 'watchtower') of a number of different places. The Old Testament records that when Jacob and Laban made a peace agreement they called the place Mizpah. A Mizpah in Gilead (perhaps the same as Ramoth-gilead) features in the story of Jephthah, one of the judges. The most important Mizpah is a town a few miles north of Jerusalem, and plays a major role in the stories of Samuel and the anointing of Saul as king. Later, King Asa of Judah fortified the town. After Jerusalem fell to the Babylonians the governor, Gedaliah, lived at Mizpah.
Genesis 31:44–49; Judges 10:17; 11; 20:1; 1 Samuel 7:5–16; 10:17; 1 Kings 15:22; 2 Kings 25:23
See maps pages 24, 274

Moab

The country east of the Dead Sea. The land is a 900-m/3,000-ft plateau intersected by deep gorges. Ruth was a native of Moab, though it mostly appears in the Old Testament as a country that was often at war with Israel, and whose practices were regularly denounced by the prophets.
Judges 3:12–30; Ruth 1; 2 Samuel 8:2; 2 Kings 3; Isaiah 15
See maps pages 21, 26, 28, 29, 274

Modein

The home and burial place of the Maccabean leaders, and the place where they first resisted Antiochus IV's orders to offer sacrifice. The remains of the ancient town are close to the modern village of Medieh, in the Shephelah roughly halfway between Beth-horon and Lydda.
1 Maccabees 2:1, 15–26; 70; 2 Maccabees 13:9–17

Moreh

The hill a few miles north-west of Mount Gilboa where the Midianites camped before Gideon's attack.
Judges 7:1
See map page 274

Moresheth/Moresheth-gath

The home town of the prophet Micah, probably near Mareshah in the low country south-west of Jerusalem.
Jeremiah 26:18; Micah 1:1, 14
See map page 274

Moriah

Name of the mountain to which Abraham went to sacrifice his son, Isaac, later identified by 2 Chronicles as the site on which Solomon's temple was built in Jerusalem – a claim disputed by the Samaritans, who believed that Abraham's place of sacrifice was not Jerusalem, but Mount Gerizim.
Genesis 22:2; 2 Chronicles 3:1

Mount of Olives/Olivet

An 830-m/2,700-ft hill overlooking Jerusalem and its temple area from the east, across the Kidron valley. In Jesus' day it was planted with olive trees.

King David passed this way when he fled from Jerusalem at the time of Absalom's rebellion. King Solomon built an altar for the worship of foreign gods on the Mount of Olives. Later, during the exile, the prophet Ezekiel saw the dazzling light of God's glory leave Jerusalem and move to the Mount of Olives. The prophet Zechariah foresaw God, on the Day of Judgment, standing on the mount, which would then split in two.

In the New Testament chiefly connected with Jesus, who rode in triumph into Jerusalem from the Mount of Olives. Seeing the city from the Mount, he wept over its fate. When he stayed at Bethany on his visits to Jerusalem he must have walked into the city round the shoulder of the Mount of Olives. The Garden of Gethsemane, where he prayed on the night of his arrest, was on its lower slopes, and it is also identified as the site of his ascension.
2 Samuel 15:30; 2 Kings 23:13; Ezekiel 11:23; Zechariah 14:4; Luke 19:29, 37, 41–44; 21:37; 22:39; Acts 1:12
See maps pages 39, 274, 275

Myra

A port in Lycia, in the south-west of modern Turkey, where the Paul and his party changed ships on his voyage to Rome. Myra was a regular port of call for the corn fleet which

carried grain to Rome from Egypt.
Acts 27:5

Mysia

A land in the north-west of Asia Minor (Turkey), forming part of the Roman province of Asia. Paul came to this district during his second missionary journey but, according to the New Testament, was constrained by divine intervention from crossing the border from Asia into Bithynia. He passed through Mysia, travelling west, and came to Troas before he had a clear idea of where he should go next.
Acts 16:7–8

Nain

A town near Nazareth in Galilee, scene of the resuscitation of a widow's son.
Luke 7:11
See maps pages 41, 275

Naphtali

Land belonging to the Israelite tribe of Naphtali, in Galilee.
Joshua 19:32–39
See maps pages 23, 274

Nazareth

A town in Galilee, the home of Jesus' parents, Mary and Joseph. Jesus grew up in Nazareth but made his base in Capernaum when he began his public work, and only occasionally returned to Nazareth thereafter.

Like most towns in Galilee, Nazareth was close to a number of important trade routes, and so was in much closer contact with the wider Hellenistic world than was the case for many Judean towns in the New Testament period.
Luke 1:26; Matthew 2:22–23; Luke 2:39, 51; Mark 1:9; Matthew 4:13; Luke 4:16–30; John 1:45–46
See maps pages 41, 275

Neapolis

The port for Philippi, in Macedonia, now Kavalla in northern Greece. This was the place where Paul first set foot in Europe, in answer to a visionary call for help from Macedonia. He later sailed from here on his last voyage to Jerusalem.
Acts 16:11; 20:6

Nebo

A mountain east of the north end of the Dead Sea, in Moab. The Old Testament tells how, before he died, Moses climbed Mount Nebo and saw the whole of the 'promised land' of Canaan spread out

297

before him. The exact location of it is disputed, and it is variously identified with Jebel en Neba (to the north-east of the Dead Sea and from which it is possible to see as far north as Mount Hermon, as well as the Dead Sea and the Negev), and Jebel Osha, a mountain of similar size but further north.

Deuteronomy 32:48–52; 34:1–5

See maps pages 21, 274

Negev, Negeb

A dry scrubland and desert area in the far south of Israel. The Negev merges with the Sinai desert on the way to Egypt. Mentioned as a stopping place in several early Old Testament stories.

Genesis 20:1; 24:62; Numbers 13:17; 21:1; Isaiah 30:6

See map page 274

Nile

The great river of Egypt on which the country's whole economy depended. The River Nile flows from Lake Victoria in the heart of Africa, about 5,632 km/3,500 miles to the Mediterranean Sea. The fertile valley of the Nile (never more than about 19 km/12 miles wide in Upper Egypt) is flanked on either side by desert. Every year the river flooded its banks in spring, leaving behind a layer of fertile mud. Crops would grow wherever the water reached. Too high a flood meant destruction; too low a flood, starvation. The river was also a useful means of transporting goods from one part of the country to another. About 19 km/12 miles north of modern Cairo the River Nile divides into a western and an eastern branch. Between them is the flat marshy land known as the Nile Delta.

The River Nile plays a prominent part in the various stories about Israel in captivity in Egypt, featuring in the dreams of the pharaoh at the time of Joseph, as well as being the place where Moses was hidden in a basket in the hope of preventing his premature death. Its water is polluted by one of the subsequent plagues, and the river was often mentioned by the later prophets.

Genesis 41:1–36; Exodus 1:22; 2:3–10; 7:17–25; 8:1–15; Isaiah 18:2

See maps pages 18, 20

Nineveh

An important city in Assyria, notably in King Sennacherib's reign. The Bible links its foundation to Nimrod the hunter. The site certainly has a very long history, going back to about 4500 BC. From about 2300 BC the city had a temple to the goddess Ishtar.

Nineveh grew in importance from about 1250 BC onwards, as Assyria's power increased. Several Assyrian kings had palaces there. Sennacherib undertook a great deal of rebuilding and other work. Reliefs carved on the walls of his new palace there depict his many victories, including the siege of Lachish in Judah. At Nineveh, too, archaeologists discovered a clay prism (the Taylor Prism) which describes how King Hezekiah was 'shut up like a bird' in Jerusalem. King Ashurbanipal added to Nineveh's greatness. Whole libraries of inscribed tablets, including the *Epic of Gilgamesh* (containing a flood story) and the creation epic (*Enuma Elish*), have been discovered at his palace and in the temple of Nabu. Nineveh fell to the Babylonians in 612 BC.

This is also the city to which the reluctant Jonah was sent; and against which Nahum issued some damning condemnations.

Genesis 10:11; 2 Kings 19:36, Jonah 1:2; 3; Nahum 1:1; Luke 11:30

See maps pages 31, 33

Nob

In trying to escaped from King Saul's attempts to kill him, David received help from the priest Ahimelech at Nob – something that resulted in a massacre of the priests there when Saul heard of it. Much later, Isaiah spoke of the Assyrians using Nob as their base camp before advancing on Jerusalem. It seems that Nob was a strong place close to the city, perhaps at Mount Scopus, north of the Mount of Olives. There was still a settlement at Nob when Nehemiah was rebuilding Jerusalem.

1 Samuel 21–22; Isaiah 10:32, Nehemiah 11:32; compare Matthew 12:4; Mark 2:26; Luke 6:4

See maps pages 26, 274

Olives

See Mount of Olives.

On

An ancient city in Egypt, famous for its worship of the sun-god Re. Joseph married the daughter of the priest of On, and they had two sons, Ephraim and Manasseh. On is mentioned later in the prophets, once by its Greek name 'Heliopolis' ('city of the sun').

Genesis 41:45, 50; 46:20; Ezekiel 30:17; compare Isaiah 19:18; Jeremiah 43:13

Ophir

A country famous for its gold, though its location is unclear: southern Arabia, East Africa and India are all equally plausible.

1 Kings 9:28; 2 Chronicles 8:18; Job 22:24; Psalm 45:9; Isaiah 13:12

Orthosia

A town to the north of Tripolis in Phoenicia. This is where the Syrian Trypho fled in an attempt to save his life after being defeated by Antiochus VII.

1 Maccabees 15:37

Paddan-aram

The area around Harran in north Mesopotamia. The place to which Abraham sent his servant to find a wife for Isaac from the branch of his family which had settled there. Jacob later fled from Esau to his uncle Laban, who was living at Paddan-aram.

Genesis 25:20; 28:2

Pamphylia

A region on the south-west coast of modern Turkey. The town of Perga, visited by Paul, was in Pamphylia. Jewish pilgrims from this region were in Jerusalem and heard Peter's speech on the Day of Pentecost.

Acts 2:10; 13:13

See map page 43

Paphos

A town in the south-west of Cyprus. According to the New Testament, Paul visited Paphos on his first missionary journey. Here he met the governor of the island, Sergius Paulus, and his psychic adviser, Elymas.

Acts 13:4–13

See map page 47

Paran

A desert area south of Kadesh-barnea, where Hagar's son Ishmael grew up. Also mentioned in connection with the movements of the Israelites after the exodus, as the place from which they sent spies into Canaan.

Genesis 21:20; Numbers 10:12; 12:16; 13:1–16

Patmos

An island off the west coast of modern Turkey. A prison island in Roman times, where convicts would work in the quarries. One of them was the Christian leader John, who had a series of visions while there which are recorded in the Book of Revelation.

Revelation 1:9

Penuel/Peniel

A place near the River Jabbok, east of the River Jordan, site of Jacob's wrestling with an angel.

Genesis 32:22–32

See map page 274

Perga

A city of Pamphylia just inland from Antalya (Attalia) on the south coast of modern Turkey. Paul visited Perga on arrival from Cyprus on the first missionary journey, and again when he returned to the coast.

Acts 13:13; 14:25

See maps pages 45, 47

Pergamum

The first administrative capital of the Roman province of Asia (west Turkey). The first temple to be dedicated to Rome and the Emperor Augustus was built at Pergamum in 29 BC. Pergamum was renowned for its devotion to Zeus, Athena and Dionysus, and it also boasted a centre of healing connected with the temple of Asclepius. Pergamum was one of the seven churches to which the letters in the New Testament book of Revelation were addressed.

Revelation 1:11; 2:12–16

Persia

The country which overthrew Babylon to establish an empire which then continued until the conquests of Alexander the Great. The Old Testament story of Daniel is set in Babylon at the time when the city was taken by the army of the Persians. Cyrus, king of Persia, allowed the Jews and other exiles to return to their homelands. The book of Esther also tells the story of a Jewish woman who became queen to the Persian King Xerxes I (Ahasuerus).

Daniel 5:29–30; 6; 8:20; 10:1; Ezra 1:1–11; Esther 1

See map page 33

Pharpar

See Abana.

Philadelphia

A city in the Roman province of Asia (modern Alashehir, in western Turkey). Philadelphia was one of the seven churches of Asia to which the letters in the New Testament book of Revelation were addressed.

Revelation 1:11; 3:7–13

See map page 47

Philippi

A city 12 km/8 miles inland from Neapolis on the coast of Macedonia, named after Philip of Macedon. Philippi was annexed by the Romans in 168 BC. It was the site of a famous battle of Antony and Octavian (Augustus) against Brutus and Cassius in 42 BC. Some years later, Octavian made Philippi a Roman colony, which ensured for its people rights and privileges similar to those they would have enjoyed in Rome itself – a status that ensured its popularity with retired army chiefs and other significant Roman officials.

Paul visited Philippi on his second missionary journey, after seeing a vision of a Macedonian man appealing to him for help. The Christian church at Philippi thereby became the first in Europe to be mentioned in the book of Acts (though almost certainly a church already existed before that in Rome, and probably other places as well). Paul and Silas were illegally imprisoned here but later released with an apology when they made it known that they were Roman citizens. The letter to the Philippians was written to the church at Philippi, probably during Paul's final imprisonment in Rome.

Acts 16:6–40; 20:6; Philippians 1:1; 1 Thessalonians 2:2

See maps pages 45, 47

Philistia

The land of the Philistines, on the coast of Palestine.

See maps pages 26, 28

Phoenicia

A small state on the coast of Syria, north of Israel. Its chief towns were Tyre, Sidon and Byblos.

See map page 41

Phoenix

The destination for which Paul's ship to Rome was heading when it was caught in a violent storm and wrecked. Delayed by the wrong winds, the ship was still only at the south coast of Crete when the summer sailing season ended, and at Fair Havens the majority decided to try to reach Phoenix (modern Finika), which was the safest harbour on that coast, and there to spend the winter.

Acts 27:12

Phrygia

A land in the centre of Asia Minor (modern Turkey). Most of it was in the Roman province of Asia, but Paul visited the smaller district which belonged to the province of Galatia. The main cities of this district were Pisidian Antioch and Iconium. Three other Phrygian cities are mentioned by name in the New Testament: Laodicea, Colossae and Hierapolis.

Acts 16:6; 18:23; Colossians 1:1; 4:13; Revelation 3:14–22

See map page 45

Pisgah

One of the peaks of Mount Nebo.

See map page 274

Pisidia

A mountainous inland area off the south coast of modern Turkey. Paul passed through this remote and dangerous region on his first missionary journey, en route from Perga to Antioch.

Acts 13:14; 14:24

Pithom

One of the Egyptian pharaoh's two store cities, identified as being built by Israelite slave labour. It lay east of the Nile Delta in Egypt.

Exodus 11:1

Plains of Moab

The place east of the River Jordan opposite Jericho where, according to the Old Testament, the Israelites gathered before they crossed into Canaan.

Numbers 22:1; 35:1; Joshua 13:32

Pontus

The ancient name of the Black Sea, and so of the land along its south coast. This became a Roman province, stretching along most of the northern coast of Asia Minor. This was one of the territories to which 1 Peter was addressed. The Christian message may have reached Pontus very early, as Jewish visitors

from there were in Jerusalem on the Day of Pentecost.
Acts 2:9; 18:2; 1 Peter 1:1
See map page 43

Ptolemais

The Greek name of an ancient city on the coast of northern Israel; Old Testament Acco. Paul sailed here from Tyre on his last visit to Jerusalem, and spent a day with the Christians. The city is now again known by its early name Akko (Acre), but has lost much of its importance since the growth of modern Haifa nearby.
Judges 1:31; Acts 21:7
See map page 275

Put

An African country, precise identity disputed, but widely believed to have been a part of Libya.
Genesis 10:6; Jeremiah 46:9; Ezekiel 27:10; 30:5; 38:5
See maps pages 45, 47, 275

Puteoli

The port near Naples in Italy where Paul landed on his way to Rome as a prisoner. The town is now called Pozzuoli.
Acts 28:13
See map page 46

Raamses/Rameses

Egyptian city near the coast on the east side of the Nile Delta. Pharaoh Ramesses II had a palace here. Earlier this was the northern capital of the Hyksos Dynasty, Avaris. The book of Exodus names Raamses as one of the supply centres constructed by Israelite slave labour, and identifies it as the starting point for the exodus from Egypt.
Exodus 1:11
See map page 20

Rabbah

The capital city of the Ammonites, sometimes also called Rabbath-Ammon. It is mentioned in several Old Testament stories, as the location of the 'iron bed' (sarcophagus) of Og, king of Bashan, and part of the territory of the Israelite tribe of Gad (though it was occupied by the Ammonites until King David's general Joab captured it). When David later fled from his rebellious son Absalom he received help from the city of Rabbah, but later on its inhabitants are denounced by some of the prophets, who looked forward to its destruction.

The city later took the Greek name Philadelphia, and became one of the 10 cities of the Decapolis, though the name of its ancient Ammonite inhabitants is preserved in its modern name, Amman.
Deuteronomy 3:11; Joshua 13:25; 2 Samuel 11:1; 12:26–31; 17:27; 1 Chronicles 20:1–3; Jeremiah 49:2; Ezekiel 21:20; 25:5; Amos 1:14
See map page 274

Ramah

A Hebrew name meaning 'height', and used of several towns on hills. Two of these are important in the Old Testament story. One was at Er-Ram, 8 km/5 miles north of Jerusalem. In early times, this was the home of the judge Deborah, and later it was a border town between Judah and Israel, which changed hands between the two nations on several occasions. Isaiah depicted the Assyrians approaching Jerusalem by way of Ramah, then at a later period when Jerusalem fell to the Babylonians, Jeremiah was set free at Ramah. The place was resettled after the exile in Babylon. Rachel's tomb was said to have been near Ramah, and Jeremiah spoke of her weeping for her children. In the New Testament, Matthew refers to this prophecy about Ramah in his account of what happened after Jesus' birth.

The second Ramah was about 19 km/12 miles further north-west. It was probably the birthplace and home of the prophet Samuel, and may have been the same as New Testament Arimathea. It was also called Ramathaim-Zophim.
Judges 4:5; 19:13; 1 Samuel 1:1; 2:11; 1 Kings 15:17, 22; 2 Chronicles 16:1, 6; Jeremiah 31:15; 40:1; Isaiah 10:29; Ezra 2:26; Nehemiah 11:33; Matthew 2:18
See maps pages 26, 274

Ramoth-gilead

A city of refuge east of the River Jordan which changed hands several times in the wars between Israel and Syria. It may be the same as Mizpah in Gilead, and so the home of Jephthah at the time of the judges. The Old Testament mentions it as the base of one of Solomon's 12 district governors. Later, King Ahab of Israel was killed in battle, and Jehu was anointed king here.
Joshua 20:8; Judges 11; 1 Kings 4:13, 22; 2 Kings 9:1–10
See maps pages 28, 274

Red Sea

The sea dividing north-east Africa from Arabia. In the Old Testament, it seems to be designated by a Hebrew term that properly means 'sea of reeds'. Most of these references (for example in the exodus story) clearly relate to an area of lakes and marshes (called the Bitter Lakes) between the head of the Gulf of Suez and the Mediterranean Sea (the Suez Canal area), though the term seems to have been used more loosely for the Gulf of Suez and the Gulf of Aqaba, and maybe therefore by inference for the Red Sea proper (which was further to the south).
Exodus 13; Numbers 33:10; Deuteronomy 1:40

Rephaim

A valley south-west of Jerusalem, where King David fought and defeated the Philistines.
2 Samuel 5:18

Reuben

Land belonging to the Israelite tribe of Reuben, traditionally located east of the Dead Sea.
Joshua 13:15–23
See maps pages 23, 274

Rhegium

A port on the toe of Italy, on the Strait of Messina opposite Sicily; the modern city of Reggio di Calabria. Paul's ship called in here on his voyage to Rome.
Acts 28:13
See map page 44

Riblah

A town in Syria on the River Orontes. King Jehoahaz of Judah was taken prisoner at Riblah by Pharaoh Neco of Egypt. Later, King Nebuchadnezzar of Babylon had his headquarters here, and King Zedekiah, the last king of Judah, was taken to him at Riblah for sentence following rebellion.
2 Kings 23:33; 25:6–7

Rome

Capital of the Roman empire; on the River Tiber in Italy. The traditional date for the founding of Rome is 753 BC.

In New Testament times over a million people from all parts of the empire lived in Rome, most of them in crowded multi-storey housing. The emperor and his government provided subsidies and public entertainments to keep the masses happy. The city attracted wealth and people from all over the empire. Travel was easy by the network of Roman roads from every part of the empire, and there was a busy trade in foodstuffs and in luxury goods through the nearby port of Ostia. In Rome the emperors built some of the most magnificent public buildings any city has ever possessed. Jews from Rome were in Jerusalem on the Day of Pentecost and heard Peter's message. The origins of the church in Rome are unknown, though there is no reason to question the ancient tradition that Peter was one of its founders and key apostles. There was certainly a strong network of home churches there long before Paul visited the city. Aquila and Priscilla, two of Paul's closest friends and co-workers, were forced to leave Rome, probably when the emperor Claudius expelled all the Jews from his capital. At the end of his life, Paul was in Rome under guard for two years and during that time is believed to have written letters to Christians in some other places. Paul met his death here, beheaded in the course of the persecution of Christians begun by the emperor Nero in AD 64, and Peter was also martyred here in the same period. The book of Revelation paints a lurid picture of life in this city, describing in detail its opposition to the Christian faith, and portraying it as the 'great Babylon', drunk with the blood of the martyrs.
Acts 2:10; 18:2; 19:21; 28:14–30; Romans 1:7, 15; 16; 2 Timothy 1:16–17; Revelation 17:5–18
See maps pages 44, 46

Salamis

A commercial centre on the east coast of Cyprus. A number of Jews lived here and, according to the New Testament, when Paul visited the town he preached in synagogues.
Acts 13:5
See map page 47

Salt Sea

The Old Testament name for the Dead Sea, given because the water contains very heavy deposits of salt. See Arabah.

Samaria/Sebaste

Capital of the northern kingdom of Israel. The city was on the main north-south trade route through Israel and was built on top of a hill so that it could easily be defended. The work of building the city was started in about 875 BC by King Omri, and was continued by his son Ahab, who added a new palace. So much carved ivory was used to decorate the palace that it became known as the 'ivory house'. Over 500 pieces of ivory, some decorated with gold leaf, have been recovered from the ruins of the palace. It was often used by the Old Testament prophets as a symbol for what they regarded as decadent religious practices and lifestyles – for which, they believed, the city would be destroyed.

The Syrians attacked and besieged Samaria many times, but it was the Assyrians who finally captured the city in 722 BC. Its people were exiled to Syria, Assyria and Babylonia, and replaced by colonists from different parts of the Assyrian empire. When Samaria fell, the kingdom of Israel ceased to exist, and the whole area (not just the city) became known as Samaria.

By New Testament times the city of Samaria had been rebuilt by Herod the Great and renamed Sebaste (Greek for 'Augustus'). It became a centre for the later Samaritans, a group of uncertain origin who were despised and hated by orthodox Jews in New Testament times. Jesus' actions in travelling through their land and staying with them surprised many, including some of his own disciples, though after his crucifixion this work was continued by his followers, notably Philip, Peter and John. A small group of Samaritans still live in Nablus and Jaffa and worship on Mount Gerizim.
1 Kings 16:24, 32; Isaiah 8:4; Amos 3:8; 2 Kings 6:8–7:17; Luke 17:11; John 4:1–43; Acts 8:5–25
See maps pages 28, 29, 30, 31, 40, 47, 275

Sardis

A city in the Roman province of Asia (modern Turkey) situated at the point where two main trade routes met. In Roman times there were thriving dyeing and woollen industries here. One of the seven letters to churches in Asia, in the New Testament book of Revelation, was addressed to the Christians at Sardis. Like the other letters in that book, it analyses the city's spiritual state by reference to its physical characteristics. The church is condemned for living in the past instead of concentrating on the present and future – an attitude typical of the city as a whole. It had been the capital of the kingdom of Lydia and at one time was ruled by Croesus, whose wealth was legendary – though not hard to come by, as gold was easily obtained from a river which flowed close to the city. Indeed, the first gold and silver coins seem to have been minted at Sardis.
Revelation 1:11; 3:1–6
See map page 47

Seir

Another name for Edom.

Sela

Capital of Edom. The name means 'rock' or 'cliff' and was given to this fortress city because it was built on a rocky plateau high up in the mountains of Edom. In about 300 BC the Nabataeans took Sela and carved the city of Petra (the Greek word for 'rock') out of the rocky valley at the foot of the original settlement.
2 Kings 14:7; Isaiah 16:1; 42:11

Seleucia (Seleucia Pieria)

One of several cities named after Seleucus. Seleucia Pieria was the port of Antioch in Syria. It was built by, and named after, the first Seleucid king. It features in the New Testament as the port from which Paul and Barnabas set sail for Cyprus on their first missionary journey.
Acts 13:4
See map page 37

Senir

Another name for Mount Hermon. It is also used to describe a nearby peak and sometimes the whole range of mountains.
Deuteronomy 3:9; Song of Solomon 4:8; 1 Chronicles 5:23; Ezekiel 27:5

Sepharvaim

A unidentified town lying somewhere in the region of Syria that was captured by the Assyrians. People from here were taken to Samaria after the Israelite people had been sent into exile.
2 Kings 17:24, 31; 18:34

Sharon

The coastal plain of Israel. It extends from Joppa to Caesarea – about 80 km/50 miles – and is about 16 km/10 miles wide. Today the plain is a rich agricultural area. In Bible times few people lived here. The land was used as pasture for sheep, but much of it was left in its natural state of thick scrub. The woman in the Song of Solomon refers to herself as a 'rose of Sharon', one of the many beautiful wild flowers which grew on the plain.

1 Chronicles 27:29; Song of Solomon 2:1
See map page 274

Sheba

A country in south-west Arabia, now the Yemen. Sheba became a wealthy land by trading spices, gold and jewels with the Mediterranean world. The Old Testament mentions an unnamed 10th century BC queen of Sheba who visited King Solomon to test his wisdom. The remains of a great dam and a temple to the moon-god Ilumquh have been discovered at Marib, once the capital of Sheba.

Psalm 72:15; Isaiah 60:6; 1 Kings 10:1–10; 13

Shechem

An ancient Canaanite town which became an important religious and political centre for the Israelites, in the hill-country of Ephraim, near Mount Gerizim. It features in many of the stories about Abraham and Jacob.

Shechem plays a particular part in the story of Joshua, as the place where he gathered all his people together to renew the covenant, and also to incorporate within it people of other races. In the time of the judges, its violent culture led the inhabitants of the town to give Gideon's son Abimelech money from the temple of Baal-berith so that he could pay to have his 70 brothers killed. Abimelech then made himself king of Shechem but the people soon turned against him – and in revenge he destroyed the town.

Also at Shechem, after the death of King Solomon, 10 of the Israelite tribes rejected his son Rehoboam, and Jeroboam, the first king of the new northern kingdom, adopted it as his capital. Shechem

survived the fall of Israel to the Assyrians, and later became a significant Samaritan city, with its own temple.

Genesis 12:6–7; 33:18–35:4; 37:12–18; Joshua 24; Judges 9; 1 Kings 12
See maps pages 19, 22, 23, 28, 29, 274

Shiloh

An early centre of Israel's worship, location of the Ark of the Covenant. Its annual pilgrims' festival plays a central role in the story of the childless couple Hannah and Elkanah, who eventually devoted their son Samuel to the service of this shrine under the care of Eli the priest.

Shiloh was destroyed in about 1050 BC, probably by the Philistines. Many years later, the prophet Jeremiah warned that the temple in Jerusalem would be destroyed just as the place of worship at Shiloh had been. But it seems that some people lived on the site of Shiloh, at least until the time of the exile.

Joshua 18:1; Judges 21:19; 1 Samuel 1–4; Jeremiah 7:12; 41:5
See maps pages 24, 25, 28, 274

Shinar

Another name for Sumer.

Shittim

A place on the plains of Moab, across the Jordan from Jericho, also known as Abel-shittim ('field of acacias'). It is listed as a temporary camp for Israel in the stories of their conquest of Canaan, and may be the location indicated in the story of Balaam, the psychic who was brought in by the king of Moab tried to curse them. Also mentioned as the place where Joshua was chosen as Moses' successor; and from which two men were sent to spy out Jericho.

Numbers 25:1; 22–24; 26, 27:12–23; Joshua 2; 3:1; Joel 3:18
See map page 274

Shunem

A place in the valley of Jezreel, in northern Israel (modern Solem). The Philistines' base camp for the battle on Mount Gilboa when Saul and Jonathan were killed. Elisha was the guest of a woman of Shunem, and he restored her child to life. Abishag, David's female companion in his old age, was also a Shunnamite. The young woman called a 'Shulammite' in the Song

of Solomon may have come from the same place.

Joshua 19:18; 1 Samuel 28:4; 1 Kings 1–2; 2 Kings 4:8–37; Song of Solomon 6:13
See map page 274

Shur

A desert area in the north-west part of the Sinai peninsula. Traders followed the 'Way of Shur' across the desert towards Egypt, a route which features in the Old Testament account of Hagar's flight from her mistress Sarah, and also later in the account of the journey of the Israelite slaves who escaped from Egypt.

Genesis 16; Exodus 15:22–25
See map page 21

Siddim

A valley (probably now submerged at the southern end of the Dead Sea), site of a battle between Chedorlaomer, king of Elam, and a group of other kings – the battle in which Lot was taken prisoner, and later rescued by Abraham.

Genesis 14

Sidon

A Phoenician port on the coast of modern Lebanon. Many skilled craft workers were based in Sidon. Carved ivory, gold and silver jewellery and beautiful glassware were among its exports. Each Phoenician city was virtually self-governing.

Sidon was often singled out in the Old Testament as a melting-pot of cultures and religions, and many of the problems of both Israel and Judah were said to stem from its syncretistic way of life. This was no doubt largely due to the influence of Jezebel, wife of King Ahab of Israel, and daughter of a king of Sidon – who incurred the particular anger of the prophets, notably Elijah and Elisha. Sidon was captured, in turn, by the Assyrians, the Babylonians and the Persians. Later it came under Greek and Roman control.

In the time of Jesus most of the inhabitants of Sidon were Greek. Many travelled to Galilee to hear him preach. Jesus also visited Sidon and the neighbouring city of Tyre. He compared Chorazin and Bethsaida, two towns in Galilee, with Tyre and Sidon, saying how much more readily the non-Jewish cities would have responded to him. Paul

stopped at Sidon on his journey to Rome and stayed with friends in the city.

Judges 1:31; 10:12; 6; 1 Kings 16:31; Isaiah 23:1–12; Ezekiel 28:20–24; Luke 6:17; Mark 7:24–31; Matthew 11:20–22; Acts 27:3
See maps pages 45, 47

Siloam

A pool, originally underground, which was one of Jerusalem's main sources of water. The water in the pool came through a tunnel from the Gihon Spring outside Jerusalem. When the Assyrians threatened to besiege Jerusalem King Hezekiah knew that in order to survive the city must have its own water supply, and gave orders for the tunnel's construction. It is 538 m/1,750 ft long, cut through solid rock.

The New Testament tells of Jesus healing a man who had been blind all his life by first putting clay on his eyes and then sending him to wash in the Pool of Siloam. The tower of Siloam, also mentioned in the gospels, probably stood on the slope of Mount Zion, above the pool.

2 Kings 20:20; John 9:1–12; Luke 13:4

Simeon

The land allotted to the Israelite tribe of Simeon, in the Negev, the southernmost part of Canaan.

Joshua 19:1–9; compare Joshua 15:20–32
See maps pages 23, 274

Sinai

A mountain in the Sinai peninsula and the area of desert around it. Significant as the place where the Ten Commandments were delivered, though its exact location is uncertain. It was probably one of two peaks – Gebel Musa or Ras es-Safsafeh – in the south of the peninsula.

Exodus 19–32
See map page 21

Smyrna

A port serving one of the main trade routes across Asia. It is now the city of Izmir in modern Turkey. In New Testament times it was a beautiful city with many splendid public buildings. One of them was the temple built in honour of the emperor Tiberius, which was a major focus for emperor worship. One of the letters to the seven churches in the New Testament book of Revelation is addressed

to the Christians at Smyrna.

Revelation 1:11; 2:8–11
See map page 47

Sodom

In Genesis, Lot's adopted home, which was suddenly destroyed, along with its neighbour Gomorrah. The site of Sodom is traditionally located at the southern end of what is now the Dead Sea.

Genesis 13:8–13; 14; 19

Sparta

An ancient city in southern Greece, which declined in influence from the fifth century BC onwards. But by Maccabean times it had achieved an independent status under the Romans, and was a natural ally for the Hasmoneans as they sought to maintain their own independence from the Syrians. There was a Jewish settlement there from as early as the second century BC.

1 Maccabees 14:16–23; 2 Maccabees 5:9

Succoth

An Egyptian town, mentioned in the story of the exodus and the ensuing journey of the slaves.

Exodus 12:37; 13:20; Numbers 33:5–6

Succoth

A town in the Jordan valley which became part of the territory of Gad. Featured in stories about Jacob and Esau. In the time of the judges the people of Succoth refused to provide Gideon and his army with food while he was fighting the Midianites. When Gideon was victorious he returned and punished the town officials.

Joshua 13:24, 27; Genesis 33:12–17; Judges 8:4–16
See map page 274

Susa

Capital of the Elamite empire until King Ashurbanipal of Assyria destroyed the city in 645 BC and exiled its inhabitants to Samaria. Under the Medes and Persians it once again became an important city. King Darius I built a splendid palace here. The ruins, in modern Iran, can still be seen.

The royal court at Susa is the setting for the Old Testament story of Esther. It was here, too, that Nehemiah acted as royal cup-bearer. The city was later captured by Alexander the Great.

Ezra 4:9–10; Esther 1:2; Nehemiah 1:1
See maps pages 31, 33, 34, 36

Sychar

A Samaritan town close to Jacob's well, where Jesus met and talked to a Samaritan woman who had come to draw water. It is modern Askar, to the north of Jacob's well and on the eastern slope of Mount Ebal.

John 4:1–42
See maps pages 40, 275

Syene

A place on the southern border of Egypt (modern Aswan). In the Old Testament, Isaiah pictured dispersed Jews returning to Jerusalem from as far away as Syene. Papyrus documents found here record activities of Jewish settlers in about 450 BC (the Elephantine Papyri).

Isaiah 49:12; Ezekiel 29:10; 30:6

Syria

In the Old Testament, Syria was the land occupied by the Aramaeans to the north and north-east of Israel. The capital of Syria was Damascus. In the New Testament Syria was a Roman province whose capital was Antioch on the Orontes.

See maps pages 28, 29, 33, 37, 43, 45

Taanach

A Canaanite city on the edge of the valley of Jezreel. Barak's battle with Sisera is located near here, and it is also listed as one of the cities of the Levites.

Joshua 12:21; 21:25; Judges 5:19; 1 Kings 4:12
See map page 274

Tabor

An 550-m/1,800-ft steep-sided mountain rising from the Plain of Jezreel. According to the Old Testament, the place where Barak gathered his army at the time of the judges.

Judges 4; Psalm 89:12; Hosea 5:1
See maps pages 24, 25, 274

Tahpanhes

An Egyptian town in the east part of the Nile Delta, to which the prophet Jeremiah was taken after the fall of Jerusalem. He presumably spent the rest of his life there.

Jeremiah 43:5–10; Ezekiel 30:18

Tarshish

Probably Tartessus in Spain, certainly in the opposite direction from Nineveh, as this is the destination for which Jonah set sail in order to avoid taking his message to the Assyrian capital. A source of

silver, tin, iron and lead.
Jonah 1:3; Isaiah 23:6; Jeremiah 10:9; Ezekiel 27:12

Tarsus
A town on the Cilician plain 16 km/10 miles inland from the south coast of modern Turkey. It was part of the Persian empire, though from the beginning of its existence it had a large Greek element in the population. Reorganized in the Seleucid period; its large Jewish population probably began to settle at this time. By New Testament times its population was around half a million, and it was an important centre of culture and learning. This where Paul was born, presumably into an influential Jewish family since he inherited from them all the privileges of Roman citizenship. He returned there briefly after becoming a Christian, but spent most of the rest of his life elsewhere.
2 Maccabees 4:30-36; Acts 9:11; 21:39; 22:3; 9:30; 11:25–26
See maps pages 45, 47

Tekoa
A town in the Judean hills about 10 km/6 miles south of Bethlehem. Mentioned in the stories of King David, but chiefly significant as the original home of the prophet Amos.
2 Samuel 14:2; Amos 1:1
See map page 274

Teman
Part of Edom, and a place with a long wisdom tradition which was home to Job's friend Eliphaz.
Jeremiah 49:7; Job 2:11

Thebes
The ancient capital city of upper Egypt, on the River Nile about 531 km/330 miles south of modern Cairo. Two great temples of the God Amun (Karnak and Luxor) mark the site. From about 1500–1000 BC, when Amun was the official god of the Egyptian empire, wealth and treasures poured into Thebes. But despite the city's remoteness it fell to the Assyrian king Ashurbanipal in 663 BC. Thebes (No-Amon) is mentioned along with other Egyptian cities in the oracles of Jeremiah and Ezekiel.
Nahum 3:8–10; Jeremiah 46:25; Ezekiel 30:14–19

Thessalonica
The chief city of Macedonia (northern Greece), on the Ignatian Way, the main Roman road to the East. Thessalonica (now Thessaloniki) is still a major city, and Paul visited here on his second missionary journey. His two letters to the Thessalonian Christians were written within a few months of his departure.
Acts 17:1–9; 20:4; 27:2; Philippians 4:16; 1 Thessalonians 1:1; 2 Thessalonians 1:1; 2 Timothy 4:10
See maps pages 45, 47

Thyatira
A city in the Roman province of Asia (now Akhisar in west Turkey). Thyatira was a manufacturing centre for dyeing, clothes-making, pottery and brasswork. Lydia, a business woman from Thyatira engaged in cloth trade, became a Christian when she met Paul at Philippi. The actual origin of the church there is unknown, but one of the seven letters of the book of Revelation was addressed to it.
Acts 16:14–15; Revelation 1:11; 2:18–29
See map page 47

Tiberias
A spa town on the west shore of Lake Galilee. It was founded by King Herod Antipas and named after the Roman emperor Tiberius. It was a non-Jewish town, and there is no record that Jesus ever went there. Tiberias is still a sizeable town today, unlike all the other lakeside places mentioned in the Gospels.
John 6:23
See maps pages 41, 275

Tigris
The second great river of Mesopotamia. The River Tigris rises in the mountains of eastern Turkey and flows for more than 2,250 km/1,400 miles, joining the River Euphrates 64 km/40 miles from its mouth on the Persian Gulf. The Tigris floods in spring and autumn. The great Assyrian cities of Nineveh, Calah and Ashur were all built on the banks of the Tigris. The Bible mentions it as one of the four rivers of Eden.
Genesis 2:14; Daniel 10:4

Timnah
A town on the northern boundary of Judah, variously held by Israelites and Philistines. The home of Samson's wife.
Joshua 15:10; 19:43; Judges 14:1; 2 Chronicles 28:18
See maps pages 24, 274

Timnath-serah, Timnath-heres
A town in the hill country of Ephraim, north-west of Jerusalem. Traditionally regarded as the personal heritage of Joshua, and site of his tomb.
Joshua 19:50; 24:30; Judges 2:9
See map page 274

Tirzah
A town in northern Israel, noted for its beauty. Listed among the conquests of Joshua, and subsequently home to Jeroboam I, and the first capital of the northern kingdom of Israel, until King Omri moved the centre of government to his new city of Samaria. The site of Tirzah is Tell el-Far'ah about 11 km/7 miles north-east of Shechem (Nablus).
Joshua 12:24; 1 Kings 14–16; 2 Kings 15:14, 16; Song of Solomon 6:4
See map page 274

Tishbe
Presumably home of Elijah, who is referred to as 'the Tishbite'. It was in Gilead, east of the Jordan, perhaps at al-Istib, just to the north of the river Jabbok.
1 Kings 17:1; Tobit 1:2

Tob
A region south of Damascus, where Jephthah lived as an outlaw. The people of Tob helped the Ammonites against David.
Judges 11:3; 2 Samuel 10:6

Topheth
An altar in the valley of Hinnom particularly connected with child sacrifice, evidently destroyed in the course of King Josiah's reforms.
2 Kings 23:10; Jeremiah 7:31; 19:6, 11–14

Trachonitis
A district linked with Ituraea. Together they made up the territory ruled by Herod Philip at the time when John the Baptist began his preaching. Trachonitis was a rocky volcanic area, the haunt of outlaws, east of Galilee and south of Damascus.
Luke 3:1
See map page 275

Tripolis
An important Phoenician seaport to the north of Byblos. How and when it was founded is unknown, but it features in the Biblical narrative at the time of the Hasmoneans as an independent city-state.
2 Maccabees 14:1

Troas
A port about 16 km/10 miles from Troy, in what is now north-west Turkey. Paul used this port a number of times on his travels, and it was here that he had his vision of a Macedonian calling for help. On a later visit to Troas he restored the child Eutychus who had fallen from an upstairs window during a church meeting.
Acts 16:8–12; 20:5–12; 2 Corinthians 2:12; 2 Timothy 4:13
See maps pages 45, 47

Tyre
An important port and city-state on the coast of Lebanon. Tyre had two harbours, one on the mainland, the other on an off-shore island. In about 1200 BC the Philistines plundered Sidon, the other important Phoenician port 32 km/20 miles or so to the north. From that time on Tyre became the leading city, and its 'golden age' was during the time of kings David and Solomon. At this period, King Hiram of Tyre supplied wood and skilled workers to build the temple at Jerusalem, and trade of all kinds flourished. Tyre's own specialities were glassware and fine-quality purple dye made from local sea-snails.

King Ahab of Israel married the daughter of the king of Tyre, Jezebel. The city is often mentioned in the Old Testament book of Psalms and by the prophets, who condemned Tyre's pride and self-indulgent luxury. In the ninth century BC Tyre came under pressure from the Assyrians. The city paid heavy tribute in return for a measure of freedom. In the same year as the fall of Samaria, Sargon II of Assyria captured Tyre. When Assyria lost power Tyre became free and prosperous again. For 13 years (587–574 BC), King Nebuchadnezzar of Babylon besieged the city. In 332 BC Alexander the Great managed to take the island port by building a causeway from the mainland.

In New Testament times Jesus paid a brief visit to the area.
2 Samuel 5:11; 1 Kings 5; 9:10–14; 16:31; Psalm 45:12; Isaiah 23; Ezekiel 26; Matthew 15:21; Luke 6:17; Acts 21:3
See maps pages 36, 41, 45, 47, 274, 275

Ur
A famous city on the River Euphrates in south Babylonia (modern Iraq). According to the Old Testament, the home of Abraham's family before they moved north to Harran. The site of Ur had been occupied for several thousand years before it was finally abandoned in about 300 BC. Excavations have uncovered thousands of inscribed clay tablets documenting the city's history and life. The royal graves (about 2600 BC) contained many treasures and examples of beautiful craftsmanship: gold weapons, an inlaid mosaic gaming-board, the famous mosaic standard showing scenes of peace and war, and many other things. Ruins of a great stepped temple tower (ziggurat) still remain.
Genesis 11:28–31

Uz
The home country of Job, probably in the region of Edom and Arabia.
Job 1:1

Zarephath/Sarepta
A small town that belonged to Sidon, later to Tyre, and a place where the prophet Elijah stayed during a time of drought.
1 Kings 17:8–24; Luke 4:26
See maps pages 29, 274

Zeboiim
One of a group of five early cities, of which the most famous are Sodom and Gomorrah. Zeboiim was also the name of a valley near Michmash, in the desert north-east of Jerusalem, the site of a Philistine raid in the days of Saul.
Genesis 14:2, 8; Deuteronomy 29:23; 1 Samuel 13:18

Zebulun
Land belonging to the Israelite tribe of Zebulun, in Galilee.
Joshua 19:10–16
See maps pages 23, 274

Ziklag
A town in the south of Judah, given by King Achish of Gath to David at the time when he was running away from King Saul. David recovered the captives taken by the Amalekites after they had raided the town.
Joshua 15:31; 1 Samuel 27:6; 30:1
See maps pages 26, 274

Zin
An area of desert south of Kadesh-barnea where, according to the Old Testament, the Israelites camped after the exodus.
Numbers 13:21; 20:1; 27:14

Zion
A name for the fortified hill which King David captured from the Jebusites to make it his capital, Jerusalem. The name is often used in the Psalms and by the prophets, particularly with reference to the religious significance of the city.
2 Samuel 5:7; Psalms 2:6; 65:1; Isaiah 8:18; 41:27; Jeremiah 31:6

Ziph
A town belonging to the Israelite tribe of Judah, in the hills south-east of Hebron. David hid from King Saul in the desert near Ziph, and Jonathan came to encourage him here. But the men of Ziph betrayed him to Saul, and he moved to Maon and Engedi. Later, Ziph was one of the places fortified by King Rehoboam. The site is still called Tell Zif.
Joshua 15:55; 1 Samuel 23:14–29; 2 Chronicles 11:9
See map page 274

Zoan/Tanis
An ancient Egyptian town in the north-east of the Nile Delta. From about 1100 to 660 BC Zoan was the capital of Egypt.
Numbers 13:22; Isaiah 19:11

Zoar
One of five cities probably at the southern end of the Dead Sea. Lot fled to Zoar at the time when Sodom and the others were destroyed.
Genesis 13:10; 14:2, 8; 19:18–30

Zobah
An Aramaean kingdom defeated by King David; located between Damascus and Hamath.
2 Samuel 8:3; 10:6; 1 Kings 11:23

Zorah
Birthplace of Samson.
Judges 13:2; 16:31

Subjects

Angel
The word 'angel' means 'a messenger'. In the Bible it is used of the supernatural beings who surround the throne of God. Angels are also referred to as 'children of God', 'heavenly beings', 'heavenly powers' and the 'servants of God'. Their work is to serve God. In heaven they worship God, and on earth they act as God's messengers and help people.

The phrase 'the angel of the Lord' is often used in the Old Testament as a way of describing how God sometimes came to people in human form, to give them a special message. The 'angel of the Lord' is also God's agent of judgment. Angels and archangels feature strongly in the Deuterocanonical books, and by the New Testament period several archangels were identified by name. In the New Testament, one of them (Gabriel) brought news of Jesus' birth, while angels took care of Jesus after he spent 40 days in the wilderness.
Genesis 16:7–14; 22:11–12; 31:11; Judges 6:11–21; 13:3–21; 1 Kings 22:19; Psalm 103:20–21; Daniel 12:1; Job 1:6; Tobit 12:11–22; Matthew 1:20; 4:11; Luke 1:26–38; 15:10; Hebrews 1:14, and many other places

Apostle
The word means 'a person who is sent' – a messenger or representative. In the New Testament it is mainly used to refer to Jesus' 12 disciples, to Paul and to other Christians who were involved in missionary work.
Luke 6:12–16; Acts 1:12–26; 14:1–4; 1 Corinthians 15:5, 7; Galatians 1:1; 2:7, 8

Ascension
The ascension refers to the time when according to the New Testament, Jesus returned to heaven. It was after Jesus' resurrection; he had visited his disciples regularly over a period of 40 days and on this occasion he gave them what was to be his final message on the Mount of Olives. As they watched, the Bible records, the disciples saw Jesus 'taken up to heaven... and a cloud hid him from their sight'.
Luke 24:50–53; John 16:5–15; Acts 1:6–11; Hebrews 1:3; 4:14–16; 7:24–26

Atonement
The people who wrote the Bible were concerned with one problem above all others: how can men and women enjoy friendship with God? They recognized that people were separated from God because of sin, and that humans' basic need is to be made 'at one' with God. This is the meaning of the word 'atonement'.

In Old Testament times, sacrifices were offered for many purposes, but one key reason was in order to atone for people's sin. Some Old Testament writers express dissatisfaction with the sacrificial system, and looked for God to deal with the problem of sin in some final way. The prophet Isaiah wrote of the coming of God's servant to solve this problem: 'All of us were like sheep that were lost, each of us going our own way. But the Lord made the punishment fall on him, the punishment all of us deserved.'

In reflecting on the significance of Jesus' death, the New Testament picks up this sacrificial imagery from the Old Testament, and sees the crucifixion as the fulfilment of Old Testament faith, and the complete, final sacrifice that would atone for human sin. Hebrews has much to say along these lines, while the gospels describe the curtain hanging in the temple as being torn from top to bottom when Jesus died, declaring that from now on the sacrificial system was finished, and through Jesus people could enjoy direct access to God. Jesus had atoned for the sin of the world.
Genesis 4; Leviticus 16; Isaiah 53; Mark 10:45; 15:34, 38; John 3:14–17; 2 Corinthians 5:14–21; Ephesians 2:14; Hebrews 7:26–9:28; 10:19–20

Baptism
In New Testament times people were 'baptized' when they became Christians. They publicly declared their new faith by going through a simple ceremony of 'washing in water'. The New Testament writer Paul explained this as a symbolic re-enactment of and sharing in the death and resurrection of Jesus. It symbolized a complete break with the past, a removal of sin, and the start of a new life lived in the power given by Jesus Christ himself.
Matthew 28:19–20; Mark 1:1–8; Acts 2:38–41; Romans 6:3–11

Blood
The New Testament often describes the death of Jesus by the phrase 'the blood of Christ'. The background to this unusual phrase is in the Old Testament, where the word 'blood' is used in a number of distinctive ways.

When blood is shed a person's life is over: 'The life is in the blood.'

Life is the gift of God, so no one must shed another's blood.

The blood of animals was shed in sacrifice, and represented the animal's life poured out in death.
Genesis 9:4–6; Deuteronomy 12:15–16, 20–28; Ephesians 1:7; Hebrews 10:19–22; 1 Peter 1:18–19

Body
In the Bible the word 'body' is often used to represent the whole person, or the 'self'. The New Testament places great importance on the physical body. The body, for example, is the temple of the Holy Spirit, and people's 'bodies' are to be used for God's glory. The missionary Paul used the image of the human body to highlight the character of the Christian church. People, he wrote, are like the different parts which make up a body: there is great diversity among the various parts, but each of them has an indispensable role in the life of the whole.

The New Testament also uses the phrase 'resurrection body' to indicate the new form humans will have after being raised by God after death. Unlike the Greek philosophers, the early Christians were not embarrassed by the body, and did not see it merely as a container for the soul. They used the term in writing of life after death, which they clearly regarded as a full, continued life for the whole person, not merely some disembodied existence as a spirit.
Romans 12:1; 4–5; 1 Corinthians 6:15–20; 12:12–30; 15:35–49; Ephesians 4:15–16

Call
Throughout the Bible, God is portrayed as a God who calls people and speaks directly to them. In the Old Testament, the story of the nation of Israel begins with the call of Abraham. It tells that the Israelites were God's people – not because they had earned the right to this, but because God decided to 'call' them. In the New Testament, Jesus called people to follow him and to respond to his teaching. The early church did the same.

In both Old and New Testaments the personal nature of God's call to people is often emphasized. God called people to specific tasks: Abraham, Moses, Deborah, Isaiah, Jeremiah, Esther, Judith and many others. The missionary Paul was 'called to be an apostle', and to travel abroad to preach the gospel.
Genesis 12:1; Exodus 3; 1 Samuel 3; 16; Isaiah 6; Jeremiah 1:4–10; Ezekiel 1–3; Hosea 11:1; Matthew 11:28–30; Mark 1:20; 2:14; Acts 2:39; 9; 13:1; Romans 1:1; 1 Corinthians 7:15; 1 Thessalonians 4:7; 2 Thessalonians 2:13–14; 1 Timothy 6:12; 1 Peter 2:21

Church
The church is the community of those who believe in Jesus. In the Old Testament, only the Israelites were regarded as God's special people, but the New Testament transforms that by affirming that all those who believe in Jesus – whatever their race – are now God's chosen people, the 'church'.

In the New Testament the word for church referred both to a local group of Christians and to all Christians throughout the world. It always referred to people, never to a building. Indeed, for several generations Christians had no purpose-built meeting places. There was no organization of the local church comparable with what we know today. Some churches had leaders, who could be called 'elders' or 'bishops', and they would teach and support the members. But many others had no 'official' leaders, and special gifts, such as preaching or healing or caring for others, were exercised by different members.

The missionary Paul taught that Jesus is the head of the church, and that no Christian stands alone but is part of the whole: 'Though we are many, we are one body in union with Christ, and we are all joined to each other as different parts of one body.'
Matthew 16:18; Acts 2:42–47; 4:23–25; 13:1; Romans 12:5; 1 Corinthians 11:13–34; 12:1–11; 12–28; Ephesians 4:11–16; Colossians 1:18; 1 Timothy 2–3; Titus 1:5–9; Revelation 19:5–9

Circumcision
Circumcision is a minor operation to cut away the loose skin covering the end of the penis. It is practised by people in many different cultures, and in Old Testament times all baby boys were circumcised on the eighth day after birth as a sign that they belonged to God's people. Over time the sign came to be more important than what it represented, and the Old Testament prophets often reminded people that this external sign alone was not enough – it should be matched by love of other people and obedience to God. The New Testament makes a similar point. 'True circumcision', or membership of the people of God, is really a matter of what people believe and how they behave.
Genesis 17; Jeremiah 9:25–26; Luke 2:21; Romans 2:25–29; Galatians 5:2–6; Philippians 3:2–3; Colossians 2:11–15

Covenant
A covenant is a form of agreement. Most covenants mentioned in the Bible are between God and people, but there are also 'person-to-person' covenants in the Old Testament. The Bible itself is arranged into two major 'covenants' in the old and the new – more commonly known as the Old and the New Testaments.

Covenants recorded in the Old Testament include the one made between God and Moses on Mount Sinai, when the Ten Commandments were given to Israel as the basic rules for living. This covenant formed the basis of Israel's religion. A covenant was also made with all people when Noah was promised that God would never again destroy the earth with a flood.

The New Testament speaks of a new covenant between God and people, inaugurated by the death and resurrection of Jesus. Jesus himself spoke of this at the last supper: 'This cup is God's new covenant, sealed with my blood.' The New Testament compares the old and new covenants, suggesting that the new was both the goal and the fulfilment of all that had gone before.
Genesis 9:1–17; 12:1–3; 15:7–21; Exodus 19:3–6; 20:1–17; Jeremiah 31:31–34; 1 Corinthians 11:25; Hebrews 8:13; 10:4

Creation
The Bible teaches that everything was made by God, and that God continues to maintain creation. It has nothing to say about which scientific theory of creation is most likely to be true – unsurprising, since it was never intended to be a book of science. Its purpose is to tell about God, and about God's dealings with humans and the world they live in.

The Old Testament book of Genesis tells that God created the world, plants and animals – and placed people at the centre of creation to take care of it. The world as God created it was a delightful place in which to live, especially since the man and the woman enjoyed a free and open relationship with God, 'made in the image of God'. The first perfection of creation was lost, though, when people chose to disregard God's values and standards. But the Bible continues to speak of God as creator, stating that God cares for people and provides for all creation.

New Testament writers mention a 'new creation', beginning with the life, death and resurrection of Jesus, and the gift of the Holy Spirit to his disciples. Christians already know something of this new creation and one day they will be fully part of it, when the universe spoiled by sin is completely transformed so as to reflect God's will.
Genesis 1–3; Job 38–42:6; Psalms 8; 33:6–22; 104; Isaiah 40:21–26; Matthew 6:25–33;

Acts 14:15–18; Romans 1:18–23; 8:18–23, Colossians 1:15–20; Hebrews 1:1–3; Revelation 21–22

Cross

The cross has come to be the universal symbol of the Christian faith, reminding people of the most astonishing and important event in the story of Jesus of Nazareth. To be executed like a common criminal was not part of the common expectations of the Messiah, and on that account many found it impossible to accept that Jesus could possibly be at the centre of God's purposes. Yet to the early Christians the cross had a deep meaning, and represented new hope and new life, as well as forgiveness for sin. The missionary Paul was quite sure that the cross was all-important – so much so that he wrote to the Christians at Corinth: 'While I was with you, I made up my mind to forget everything except Jesus Christ and especially his death on the cross.'

The New Testament makes it clear that Jesus died on the cross not because of his own wrong-doing (the charges against him were false), but in the place of all people. Through his death, men and women can be reconciled both to God and to each other. In the cross God defeated all the powers of evil.

The cross is also presented as a dramatic symbol of the sort of life Christians ought to live. Jesus called disciples to 'take up the cross' and follow him, to live a life of self-sacrifice. They must give up their own claims over their lives, and live in the power of the new life which God could give. Paul understood this in his own experience: 'I have been put to death with Christ on his cross, so that it is no longer I who live, but it is Christ who lives in me.'

Romans 5:6–11; 1 Corinthians 1:18–2:5; Galatians 2:20; Ephesians 2:16–18; Colossians 2:14–15; 1 John 4:7–10

Death

The Bible recognizes the fact that death comes to everyone: all humankind 'is like a puff of wind; their days are like a passing shadow'. Yet death can also be seen as something evil that strikes a note of terror in the hearts of all people.

The Bible makes a close connection between death and sin. According to the Old Testament book of Genesis, death is part of the judgment that comes to Adam after his disobedience. The New Testament writer Paul regards death as the inevitable consequence of the presence of sin in the world. The New Testament often speaks of people as being physically alive, but 'spiritually dead because of disobedience and sins'.

Some Bible passages describe Jesus' death on the cross as the point at which he took the ultimate consequences of sin on himself, and his resurrection as a demonstration that the power of death had been defeated. The 'eternal life' made available by faith in Jesus is a sharing in this, as believers are redeemed from spiritual death into a new life which will be consummated at the end of the age when physical death, 'the last enemy', will also be overcome.

Genesis 3:19; Deuteronomy 30:15, 19; Psalms 55:4; 144:4; Matthew 7:23; Romans 6:23; 1 Corinthians 15:21, 26; 2 Corinthians 5:1–10; Ephesians 2:1; Hebrews 2:14–15

Election

The New Testament records Jesus' words: 'You did not choose me; I chose you.' They sum up the Bible's teaching on election, or choice.

The Old Testament tells of how God chose people. For instance, God chose Abel and not Cain; Isaac and not Ishmael; Jacob and not Esau; Joseph and not his brothers. They were not chosen for their own goodness or greatness. Moses told the people of Israel: 'Do not say to yourselves that God brought you in to possess this land because you deserved it.' But those who accepted the challenge of God's election were expected to obey God and give their lives to God's service.

Deuteronomy 7:7–8; 9:4–5; John 15:16; Romans 9:18–29; 1 Peter 2:9

Faith

In the New Testament the missionary Paul explains that a person can find a right relationship with God not through good deeds, but only through faith

or believing. 'Faith' means having confidence and trust in God, depending wholly on what God has already done for people through Jesus. This life of dependence on God goes right back to the beginning of God's dealings with humans, as Paul demonstrates when he traces it back to the patriarch Abraham.

Some later New Testament books also refer to 'the faith', meaning the basic teaching about Jesus on which people's trust is grounded.

John 1:12; 3:16; 5:24; Romans 1:17; 5:1; 10:9–10; Galatians 3; Ephesians 2:8–9; 1 John 5:1–5. See also Genesis 15:6; Psalm 37:3–9; Proverbs 3:5–6; Jeremiah 17:7–8; Habakkuk 2:4; 1 Timothy 3:9; 5:8; Hebrews 11; James 2

Fall, the

The Bible's underlying worldview regards human suffering and sin as a reflection of the fact that the whole of creation has 'fallen' from the condition of original perfection that God intended it to have. The faith-stories of the early chapters of Genesis explain this.

The story of Adam and Eve depicts the dramatic 'fall' of men and women from the high place they once had as friends of God in the context of God's creation. People were always intended to be at peace with the world of plants and animals, and living in open relationships with God and each other. But when the primeval couple thought they could go it alone, and replace God's values with their own judgments, they found themselves cut off from God, who was their only source of true satisfaction. As a result of this rebellion (or 'fall'), the whole of creation is suffering. The universal nature of the fall then determines the cosmic scope of the redemption that the Bible talks about – which extends not just to people, but to plants, animals and all that is in the entire universe.

Genesis 1–3; Romans 1:18–32; 5:12–19; 7:14–25

Fellowship

Fellowship can be described as the 'sharing' companionship which is at the heart of Christian experience. The Bible regards people as 'made in God's image', intended to live in

'fellowship' with God. The power of sin corrupted this friendship, but in the new society described by Jesus, effected by his death, resurrection and the gift of the Spirit, there is the possibility of these broken relationships being restored.

In the New Testament, Jesus pictures the closest possible 'sharing' between himself and his followers. 'I am the vine,' he said, 'and you are the branches.' But Christians are not just individuals joined to Christ, they also share a new life with fellow-Christians and with Christ himself. 'We are all joined to each other', and the hallmark of Christian 'fellowship' is love.

John 13:34–35; 15:1–17; Acts 2:44–47; 4:32–37; Romans 12:4–13; 15:25–27; 1 John 1:3

Flesh

The word 'flesh' in the Bible is often used to refer to people as physical beings – 'mortal flesh'. In this sense it can be used to show the weakness of people in contrast with the strength of God. In the New Testament, when Jesus' disciples fell asleep in the Garden of Gethsemane he told them to watch and pray: 'the spirit is willing, but the flesh is weak'.

New Testament writers like Paul can use the word 'flesh' metaphorically, referring to a way of living that ignores, or even opposes, God's standards – and contrasting that with life 'in the Spirit', life as God intended it to be. Until the final renewal of all things, even Christians can find themselves struggling with these two options.

Psalm 78:39; Isaiah 40:5; Mark 14:38; Romans 7:13–25; 8; Galatians 5:16–4

Forgiveness

Though the Bible has much to say about human alienation from God, and its consequences, the keynote of its message is that God loves people and delights to forgive them. 'If you kept a record of our sins, who could escape being condemned? But you forgive us, so that we should stand in awe of you.' Those who sincerely want to live by God's standards can be sure of God's acceptance and forgiveness.

Exodus 34:6–7; Psalms 51; 130:3–4; Isaiah 1:18; 55:6–7;

Hosea 14; Matthew 6:12–15; 26:26–28; Luke 7:36–50; Acts 2:38; Ephesians 4:32; 1 John 1:9

Freedom

The concept of freedom plays a large part throughout the Bible. In the New Testament Jesus described his work thus: 'The Spirit of the Lord is upon me… he has sent me to proclaim liberty to the captives.'

Many had hoped the Messiah would come to free the people from Roman rule. But Jesus had other priorities: releasing people from moral failure into the possibilities of renewed living by God's standards, in God's kingdom. This was the underlying message of not only his spoken words, but his exorcisms and healings as well.

Paul expanded on this in the light of Jesus' own death and resurrection, identifying this moral and spiritual freedom as God's own gift to those who would receive it – not something enshrined in rules and regulations, but an empowerment through God's Spirit to enable people to serve God and others, while at the same time finding true fulfilment for themselves.

Matthew 11:28; Mark 3:22–27; Luke 4:18; 13:10–16; John 8:31–36, 41–44; Romans 1:1; 6; 6:16–23; 8:2, 21; Galatians 3:28; 5:1, 13; James 1:25; 2:12; 1 Peter 2:16

Future destiny

Apart from the certainty of judgment at the second coming of Jesus, the Bible says very little about what happens after death. The Old Testament writers generally expected a continued existence in *sheol*, a place of rest and silence when the blessing of life had been taken away. But as time went on people began to understand more clearly that God had a glorious future in store for them beyond *sheol*. Job and Daniel both express confidence about the future: Job speaks about ultimately seeing God, while Daniel expects the dead to live again.

By New Testament times, *Hades* had become the equivalent of *sheol*. Peter, writing of the death of Jesus, noted that David 'spoke about the resurrection of the Messiah when he said, "he was not abandoned in the world of the dead [*Hades*]; his body did not

rot in the grave."' 1 Peter also speaks of Jesus going to preach to the dead, 'the imprisoned spirits', presumably in the time between his crucifixion and his resurrection.

Death can be spoken of as a sleep, but 'paradise' is a word used by Jesus to describe the pleasant existence of those who die at peace with God. Paul was confident that when a Christian dies he or she is in the presence of Jesus. It is difficult to imagine an existence outside time, and the Bible writers never try to do so analytically. But the New Testament expresses confidence that Christian believers, whether dead or living, will meet with Jesus, and enter into the glory of heaven, being given new 'resurrection' bodies no longer subject to death.

Job 19:25–27; Psalms 94:17; 16:9–11; Daniel 12:2, 3; Matthew 9:24; Luke 23:43; Acts 2:31; 1 Corinthians 15:20, 35–58; 1 Thessalonians 4:13–17; 1 Peter 3:19–20; Revelation 20:11–22:5

Glory

When the word 'glory' is applied to people in the Bible, it usually refers to their wealth or position. But the 'glory of God' refers to God's unique power and greatness.

In the Old Testament God's glory is seen in history, especially perhaps in the two major events of the exodus and exile. The Israelites are shown travelling through the desert preceded by the glory of God seen in the cloud and fire which guided them on their journey. When Moses went up the mountain to receive the law of God the cloud of God's glory covered the mountain. Again, during the exile the prophet Ezekiel saw some amazing visions which showed the 'glory' of God.

The New Testament suggests that Jesus was the glory of God made visible on earth. God's glory was seen by the shepherds when they heard that Jesus was born. And those who saw Jesus recognized God's glory in him. John comments that 'We saw his glory,' while Jesus' way of life and his miracles were the vehicles that 'revealed his glory'. But in John's gospel, the glory of God was seen above all in Jesus' death on the cross, and his resurrection which followed.

Exodus 16:7, 10; 24:15–18; 40:34–38; 2 Chronicles 7:1–3; Ezekiel 1:26–28 and other passages; Mark 8:38; 13:26; Luke 2:8–14; 9:28–36; John 1:14; 2:11; 17; Romans 8:18–30; 1 Timothy 6:15–16

God

In the Bible, God is a personal, spiritual being who is beyond human understanding, revealed in creation and by continuing to be actively involved in history. God created all life, and is the one who keeps it going. In the Old Testament, God is frequently at work, helping the people of Israel. In the New Testament God is seen working especially in the life, death and resurrection of Jesus, and in a personal way in the lives of Jesus' followers.

The Bible describes by reference to actions, rather than through abstract philosophical descriptions of God's nature. Some aspects of the Bible's view of God are surprising, and quite different from the traditional views of Greek philosophers, who tended to depict God in all-powerful terms. In the New Testament, the key model of God is Jesus, through whom God suffers weakness and powerlessness – a key reason why God can also relate to the human predicament. The Bible simply takes the existence of God as a fact which needs no proof. It begins with the simple statement, 'In the beginning God created…'

People have always had many ideas about God, and they have worshipped many different gods. One of the concerns of the Old Testament is to show that Yahweh – the Israelites' personal name for God – is the only true God. God, it is stated, is the creator of all there is, the one who is 'light', who is utterly holy – and at the same time utterly loving.

In the Old Testament God was sometimes referred to as a parent (both 'father' and 'mother') of the people of Israel. Jesus laid great emphasis on this dimension of personal relationship with God, encouraging his followers to enjoy an intimate parent-child faith relationship.

The 'otherness' of God: the eternal spirit; the Creator:
Genesis 1; Deuteronomy 33:26–27; 1 Kings 8:27; Job 38ff.; Psalms 8; 100; 104; Isaiah 40:12–28; 55:9; John 4:23–24; Romans 1:19–20; Revelation 1:8
The power of God:
Genesis 17:1; Exodus 32:11; Numbers 24:4; Job 40:1–42:2; Isaiah 9:6; 45–46; Daniel 3:17; Matthew 26:53; John 19:10–11; Acts 12; Revelation 19:1–16
God's knowledge:
Genesis 4:10; Job 28:20–27; Psalm 139:1–6; Daniel 2:17–23; Matthew 6:7–8; John 2:23–25; 4:25–29; Ephesians 1:3–12
God's presence everywhere:
Genesis 28:10–17; Psalm 139:7–12; Jeremiah 23:23–24; Acts 17:26–28
The character of God; God's holiness and righteousness:
Exodus 20; Leviticus 11:44–45; Joshua 24:19–28; Psalms 7; 25:8–10; 99; Isaiah 1:12ff.; 6:1–5; John 17:25–26; Romans 1:18–3:26; Ephesians 4:17–24; Hebrews 12:7–14; 1 Peter 1:13–16; 1 John 1:5–10
God's love and mercy:
Deuteronomy 7:6–13; Psalms, such as 23; 25; 36:5–12; 103; Isaiah 40:1–2, 27–31; 41:8–20; 43; Jeremiah 31:2–4; Hosea 6; 11; 14; John 3:16–17; 10:7–18; 13:1; 14:15–31; 15:9, 12ff.; Romans 8:35–38; Galatians 2:20; Ephesians 2:4–10; 1 John 4:7–21
God as 'father' and 'mother':
Deuteronomy 32:18; Isaiah 42:14; 49:15; 66:13; 1 Chronicles 25:10; Psalms 68:5; 103:13; 131:2; Matthew 5:48; 6:1–14; 23:37; 28:19; Romans 8:14–15

Gospel

The word 'gospel' means 'good news', and is a term used to describe all that Jesus said and did in order to facilitate the restoration of good relationships between people and God.

The New Testament gospel of Mark describes itself as 'the good news of Jesus Christ', and at its simplest it states that Jesus himself *is* the good news, the 'gospel'. Paul later expressed the facts of the gospel this way: 'That Christ died for our sins, as written in the Scriptures; that he was buried, and that he was raised to life three days later, as written in the Scriptures.' Thus, people can have forgiveness and new life.

Mark 1:1, 14; Luke 2:10–11; 4:18–21; Romans 1:16–17; 1 Corinthians 1:17–23; 15:3–4; Ephesians 1:6–13

Government

The Bible does not put forward any one form of government as the right way to organize society. In fact, the Bible reflects many different forms. The Old Testament patriarchs lived in family clans. The nation of Israel had autocratic kings, like other nations of the time. And Christians in the New Testament era simply accepted the Roman system of government under which they lived.

The underlying message of the Bible is that, whether people realize it or not, all rulers are responsible to God and will be judged according to the extent to which they reflected the standards and values of God's own way of being. Consequently, God's people should pray for governments and support them insofar as they rule with justice. At the same time, the Bible contains plenty of stories describing opposition to those who flouted God's laws, not least the Old Testament prophets, some of whom (like Elisha) were actively involved in revolutionary activities to overthrow unjust rulers. At a later time, Esther, Judith and the Maccabees were unafraid to stand up and condemn those who sought to oppress them, making it clear that, in a straight choice between what the government says and what God says, God's will should always be paramount.

Judges 21:25; Isaiah 56:9–12; Jeremiah 21:11–22:19; Daniel 3; Amos and many other passages from the prophets; 1–2 Maccabees; Judith; Esther; Matthew 22:15–21; Acts 5:27–29; Romans 13:1–7; 1 Timothy 2:2; 1 Peter 2:11–25

Grace

The underlying image of God in both Old and New Testaments is of undeserved goodness and kindness towards people. This is God's 'grace'.

The Old Testament is full of reminders of God's goodness and constant love, though sometimes it was the subject of fierce debates (the books of Hosea, Jonah and Ruth all opposed another popular view, that God was predominantly fierce and warlike). For the New Testament writers, God's grace was seen most clearly in the life, death and resurrection of Jesus, and the gift of the Holy Spirit. The human race did not deserve salvation, but God freely gave it. This is what the New Testament means by 'the grace of our Lord Jesus'.

The New Testament also suggests that the Christian life, from start to finish, depends on God's grace. 'My grace', God says in answer to Paul's prayer for healing, 'is all you need, for my power is strongest when you are weak.' Paul's New Testament letters often begin or end with a celebration of God's grace.

Deuteronomy 7:6–9; Psalms 23:6; 25:6–10; 51:1; Jeremiah 31:2–3; Romans 5:8; 16:20; 3:19–24; 6:14; 2 Corinthians 12:9; Ephesians 2:8–9; 1 Timothy 1:2; 1 Peter 5:5–7; 2 Peter 3:18

Healing

In the Bible, one of the results of evil in the world is illness – not that people become sick as a consequence of their own misdeeds, but in a broader cosmic sense, as part of the suffering of alienation that afflicts all things in the cosmos. Jesus announced a new way of being in which sin, sickness and death would be no more – an age that other New Testament writers describe as beginning with Jesus' own life, but still remaining to be fully inaugurated in the future. Jesus' own healings of those who were sick in mind and body was a foretaste of this coming age.

The earliest Christians assumed they were to continue Jesus' healing work. Paul described a gift of healing given to every community of Christians. James considered it natural to call in the elders of the church to pray for a sick person, and he advised people to 'Confess your sins to one another, so that you will be healed.' In some Christian communities, such as Thessalonica, people were distressed when their friends began to die, but the New Testament makes clear that the reversal of the whole process of sickness, ageing and death will have to wait until 'all things are made new' at the end of time, a time which is depicted with great power in the visions of the book of Revelation.

Genesis 3:14–19
Some Old Testament healings:
Numbers 21:4–9; Deuteronomy 7:12–15; 28:20–23; 1 Kings 17:17–24; 2 Kings 4:18–37; 5
Some of Jesus' healings:
Matthew 8:5–13, 28–34; 9:32–33; 17:14–18; Mark 7:31–37; 10:46–52; Luke 4:18–19; 7:11–15; 8:41–42, 49–56; 17:11–19; John 9; 11

Heaven

The ancient Israelites used the word 'heaven' to refer to the sky. The phrase 'the heaven and the earth' means the same as our word 'universe'. In the Bible, heaven also refers to the place where God is. Thus, in the New Testament, Jesus taught his disciples to pray: 'Our Father in heaven…' Some passages depict God in heaven as surrounded by the angels and other celestial beings. Jesus spoke of heaven as the place where his disciples would join him after death, and this kind of teaching eventually led to the belief that 'heaven' is the experience in which all the angels and all the believers who once lived on earth join in unending worship of God.

The Bible uses many metaphors to describe heaven. It will be 'home', a place of rest but also a place to share in God's work. In 'heaven' people will be safe and happy in God's presence. In 'heaven' people will meet all those who have trusted Jesus during their lives. 'Heaven', according to the New Testament, is a 'treasure-house', where more important things than money are kept. In heaven there are no tears, pain, weakness, night or need for sleep.

Nehemiah 9:6; Matthew 6:9; Mark 13:32; Luke 6:21–23; John 14:2; Romans 8; 1 Corinthians 15; Philippians 1:21–23; 3:12–21; 1 Peter 1:3–5; Revelation 4; 21–22

Hell

Hell features mostly in the teaching of Jesus, having become an important issue in the time of the Maccabees as people tried to figure out when and where justice would be dispensed to those who seemed to do very evil things during their lifetime, without suffering any consequences. Jesus described hell as a place of punishment for those who do evil, using vivid imagery to describe it – a rubbish tip; outer darkness; a fire which never goes out; a fiery furnace where people will cry and grind their teeth; and the place where both body and soul would perish. These phrases were meant as clear warnings, emphasizing the absolute and final nature of God's judgment.

Matthew 3:12; 10:38; 13:42; 18:8–9; 25:41; Mark 9:48; Revelation 20:10–15

Holy Spirit

The Holy Spirit is, in effect, God at work in the world, and eventually the Spirit became one part of the Christian belief in the Trinity (along with God the Creator and Jesus Christ the Redeemer).

In the early Old Testament, God's Spirit empowers people for special service, and inspires and encourages the community to keep the Law. The prophets were especially regarded as Spirit-inspired people, as were kings and other community leaders. In a later period, through the figure of divine 'wisdom', the Holy Spirit's activity was traced back to the creation of the world itself.

The New Testament describes Jesus' ministry by reference to the Spirit, especially in Luke's gospel. Jesus was conceived by the power of the Holy Spirit, the Spirit descended on him in a special way at his baptism in the River Jordan, ministered to him during his temptations, and empowered him for all his work of ministry. John the Baptist spoke of Jesus baptizing people with the Holy Spirit, and the gospels depict Jesus promising his disciples that after he had left them he would send the Holy Spirit to be with them all the time, to teach and guide them as they continued his work. 'The Spirit will give me glory,' Jesus said, 'by taking what I say and telling it to you.'

On the Day of Pentecost, the disciples were baptized with the Holy Spirit, something that was obvious to everyone because of a new note of praise and boldness in their demeanour as they spoke in ecstatic tongues, and because of their powerful preaching. As Jesus' disciple Peter told his listeners on the Day of Pentecost, the prophecy of the Old Testament prophet Joel had come true: God had poured out the Holy Spirit on all believers.

The New Testament describes all Christians receiving the 'gift' of the Holy Spirit, to enable them to realize their oneness in Jesus Christ, and empowering them to live like Jesus, displaying qualities such as 'love, joy peace, patience, kindness, goodness,

faithfulness humility and self-control'. And the Holy Spirit gives Christians the power and gifts needed to serve God.
Genesis 1:2; Judges 3:10; 14:6, and many other passages; 2 Samuel 23:2–5; Psalm 139:7–12; Isaiah 11:1–3; Ezekiel 36:26–27; Joel 2:28–29; Micah 3:8; Luke 1:35; 3:22; 4:1–18; 3:16; John 14:16–17; 16:7–15; Acts 2; Romans 8; 1 Corinthians 12; Galatians 5:22–23

Hope
Hope, based on God's faithfulness, is a key theme running throughout the Bible. Even at times of apparent hopelessness – slavery in Egypt, the destruction of Jerusalem, and the exile, the time of Antiochus IV's persecution – God's people still had reason to hope for and expect a better future of prosperity, rather than disaster. In the New Testament, the resurrection of Jesus is the great foundation of the Christian's hope. 'Because of [God's] great mercy we have been given new life because Jesus rose from death,' wrote Peter. 'This fills us with a living hope.'
Jeremiah 29:11; Romans 4:18; 5:1–5; 8:24–25; 12:12; 15:4; 1 Corinthians 15:19–20; 2 Corinthians 5:1–5; Colossians 1:15; 1 Peter 1:3–6

Jesus Christ
'Jesus' was a common personal name, a form of the Hebrew 'Joshua', meaning 'Yahweh saves'. The word 'Christ' is the Greek equivalent of the Hebrew 'Messiah', God's 'anointed one' who would usher in the new age. It is a title, rather than a second name. Jesus is also given several other titles:

Jesus, the 'servant of God'. This title came from the prophecies of the Old Testament prophet Isaiah. When Jesus said that he 'came to serve and to give his life to redeem many people', he was living as the servant of God, suffering to bear the sins of humankind.
Isaiah 42:1–4; 52:13–53:12 and other passages; Matthew 12:15–21; Mark 10:45

Jesus, the 'Son of David'. The angel who announced his birth told Jesus' mother that her son would be a king, 'as his ancestor David was'. Jesus' ancestry was traced back to the Israelite king David, thereby showing Jesus as the fulfilment of the hopes of the Jewish nation. This was the title used to welcome Jesus as the Messiah in his final entry into Jerusalem, and the one placed over him on the cross.
Matthew 1:1; 21:9; Luke 1:32; John 7:42

Jesus, the 'Son of man'. This is the title most often used of Jesus in the gospels. It goes back to the prophet Daniel's vision of someone who 'looked like a human being', yet had God's authority for ever. 'His kingdom,' Daniel said, would 'never end'. The New Testament preserves this tension, as it describes Jesus as a person of both great humility and also of great glory – completely identified with humankind, yet transcending the human condition. As the 'Son of man' he came to serve all people, and to give his life to save them. 'The Son of man must suffer... He will be put to death, but three days later he will be raised to life.' As the Son of man Jesus defeated sin and death and will come again 'with great power and glory'.
Daniel 7:13–14; Mark 10:45; 9:21–22; Luke 21:25–28

Jesus, the 'Son of God'. At Jesus' baptism in the River Jordan, a voice from heaven declared, 'You are my own dear Son. I am pleased with you', a phrase taken from Psalm 2 and referring to the special relationship between God and the kings of ancient Judah. The gospel of John in particular picks up this term as its favourite way of referring to Jesus. Jesus is God's 'only Son', and his whole life and purpose is to carry out God's work: 'The Father and I are one,' Jesus said, sharing in God's cosmic work and nature.
Mark 1:11; Luke 9:35; John 1:14; 10:30; 17; Romans 1:3–4; Hebrews 1; 1 John 1:1–2:2

Jesus, the 'Lord'. In the New Testament gospels Jesus is often called 'Lord' in the everyday sense of 'master'. But 'Lord' was also the personal name of God, used in the Septuagint. When the first Christians publicly declared their faith in the words 'Jesus Christ is Lord' this was what they had in mind. Paul, in his letter to Christians at Philippi, looks forward to the time when Jesus will return as Lord, when 'all beings in heaven, on earth, and in the world below will fall on their knees, and all will openly proclaim that Jesus Christ is Lord, to the glory of God the Father'.
Luke 5:8; John 20:28; 1 Corinthians 12:3; Philippians 2:6–11

Joy
Joy in the Bible is generally described as part of a personal relationship with God: living with the presence of God in one's life is a continuous experience of joy, and can therefore be a reality even at times of difficulty or suffering. 'Rejoice in the Lord always,' wrote Paul to his readers at Philippi – even though at the time he was in prison!
Psalms 16:11; 30:5; 43:4; 51:12; 126:5–6; Ecclesiastes 2:26; Isaiah 61:7; Jeremiah 15:16; Luke 15:7; John 15:11; 16:22, Romans 14:17; 15:13, Galatians 5:22; Philippians 1:4; 1 Thessalonians 2:20; 3:9; Hebrews 12:2; James 1:2; 1 Peter 1:8; Jude 24

Judgment
The notion of judgment is always undergirded by concepts of God's sense of justice and fairness. This is the ultimate standard from which all other types of judgment take their meaning, and the basis on which human actions can be evaluated.

In the Old Testament judgment often meant 'good government'. The judges were national leaders before Israel had a king, operating under God, who could be regarded as the supreme judge, the ruler of all things. By New Testament times, Judaism had an expectation of a final, future judgment, the 'last' judgment when good would ultimately triumph over evil. This theme is elaborated in the New Testament, where Jesus is identified as the judge, and conformity to his values and standards is the ultimate test of true character. 'Whoever believes in the Son has eternal life,' wrote John, 'whoever disobeys the Son will not have life, but will remain under God's punishment.'
Genesis 18:25; Psalm 96:10; Romans 3:3–4; 1:18–2:16; 3:9–12; Matthew 10:32–33; John 3:18; 5:24–30; Acts 4:12; 10:42; 2 Corinthians 3:10–15; 5:10; 2 Thessalonians 1:5–10; Hebrews 12:22–27; Revelation 20:12–15

Justification
A complex term which represents all that a person must be in order to be accepted by God. Paul is the New Testament writer who uses this term the most, arguing that since there is nothing a person can do to make themselves right before God, being accepted and forgiven must be a free gift of God's grace, to be accepted by faith. Since such acceptance leads to a renewal of moral and spiritual life, and this flows from the death and resurrection of Jesus, and the work of the Spirit, God's acceptance of people is also rooted in Jesus' death on the cross and the new status of believers in him as children of God, new people 'in Christ'. Justification and atonement therefore belong together.
Romans 3:24; 5:1, 9; 2 Corinthians 5:21

Kingdom of God
God is often described as king in the Old Testament, and the notion of God's 'kingdom' is not so much territorial, as a way of describing how people would behave if God's values and standards were truly observed. 'God's kingdom' is therefore a way of speaking of 'God's way of doing things'. Of course, life isn't always like that, and the hope that somehow things would get better is what lies at the root of later expectations that God's rule would at some future time arrive in a final sense, as the time when God's laws would be observed, bringing human fulfilment and satisfaction.

The message of Jesus picked up this aspiration: 'The right time has come and the Kingdom of God is near! Turn away from your sins and believe the Good News.' Jesus is depicted as the one who would finally establish God's kingdom, and put an end to the evil mess into which the world had fallen, thereby making possible a fresh start, inaugurating a new age. The characteristics of how life would be when God's kingdom was fully realized were spelled out in such things as Jesus' healings and exorcisms, all of which were signs of the arrival of a new way of being, in which evil would be completely destroyed.

At the same time, the New Testament is realistic about the ongoing human struggle, and looks forward to the full revelation of the kingdom of God as a future event, when evil will be banished and all things made new. The life, death and resurrection of Jesus are presented as guarantees of the reality of God's commitment to that.
Micah 4:6–7; Matthew 5:1–20; 6:10; 13; Mark 1:15; 4; 9:45–47; Luke 7:18–23; 8; 14:16–24

Law
The law, or *torah*, was the regulations for living the good life entrusted to ancient Israel, and was the centre of Israel's devotion. It included the Ten Commandments, the heart of the moral law, together with detailed social and religious laws.

Jesus both affirmed and challenged the law, in his lifestyle, discarding some of its key teachings, notably on the sabbath and on various rituals related to food. Paul further expands on this, by arguing that the law was only relevant up to the time of Christ, whose teaching and example had now both fulfilled and displaced it. Much of Paul's writings are taken up with arguing against the notion that by keeping rules and regulations a person can earn their own salvation. Instead, he affirms the primacy of faith in Christ and the forgiveness offered freely by God's grace.
Exodus 20; 21–34; Leviticus; Numbers 2–9; 15; 18–19; 28–30; Deuteronomy; Psalms 1; 9; 119; Matthew 5:17–20; 22:36–40; Luke 10:25–28; John 7:19; Romans 2:25–29; 3:19–21; 3:31; 7:7–25; 8:3–4; Galatians 3:21–24; Hebrews 7:18–19; James 2:8–12

Life
In the Old Testament 'life' is often depicted metaphorically as the breath of God, flowing through the lungs of people and animating them. God is regarded as part of all the natural processes that keep people alive; and it is therefore God who determines when life shall end. Life is a person's most valued possession, and one of people's greatest desires is for God to bless them with a long life.

The Bible also appreciates that there is more to life than just physical existence, and throughout its pages emphasizes the social and spiritual ambition to live life on a new level – something that in the New Testament is occasionally referred to as 'eternal life', something that shares in the qualities of God's own life. 'Whoever has the Son', writes John, 'has this life.' It is given to all disciples, and is not only a new style of life, but also survives death and is therefore 'everlasting' life.
Genesis 2:7; Deuteronomy 8:3; 30:15–20; Psalm 91:16; John 10:10, 28; 11:25–26; Romans 6:4–13, 22–23; 1 John 5:12 and many other passages

Light
The Bible often uses the contrast of light and darkness to show the absolute difference between God and the forces of evil. 'God is light, and there is no darkness at all in [God].' Indeed, God can be described simply as being 'light', in contrast to the forces of evil, which are called 'dark'. Unlike the usage of similar terminology in Greek philosophy, this light/dark dualism in the Bible always has an ethical dimension, not a metaphysical one.

The gospel of John describes Jesus as 'the light of the world' and promises 'the light of life' to all who follow him. People need no longer walk in darkness, ignorant of the truth, cut off from God and blinded by evil. They can 'live in the light – just as God is in the light'. Being a Christian, is like moving out of darkness and into light, and disciples are exhorted to be 'like light for the whole world', so that others might also find the way to new life.
Matthew 5:14–16; John 1:4–9; Ephesians 6:12; 1 Timothy 6:16; 8:12; 1 John 1:5; 1:7; Revelation 21:23–24; 22:5

Love
Love is one of the key characteristics of God throughout the Bible: love for the whole world, shown first through the agency of the people of Israel and then through Jesus Christ. Israel did not always appreciate what this should mean, and frequently corrupted the notion of God's love with racist attitudes, some of which are clearly visible in the Old Testament stories. When that happened, the prophets and others both condemned the people and called them back to an appreciation of God's true character.

In the New Testament world, there were Greek words for different kinds of love: family love, sexual love, and so on. The most important term used in the Bible, however, is the word *agape*, which is used to describe self-giving love, which was portrayed above all in Jesus Christ, especially his death. This kind of self-giving love was the most useful way to describe God's love for the world, and Christians were called to practise it too: 'If you have love for one another,' Jesus said, 'then everyone will know that you are my disciples.'
Leviticus 19:18; Deuteronomy 7:7–8; 6:5; Hosea 11:1–4; 7–9; John 3:16, 35; 13:34–35; see also John 14:15, 21–24; 15:9–14; Romans 5:5, 8; 1 Corinthians 13; Galatians 5:22; 1 John 4:7–5:3

Man and woman
The Bible regards men and women as part of nature, yet uniquely 'made in God's image'. As such they are both the crowning glory of God's whole creation on earth, and co-creators with God in preserving and protecting other living things.

The faith-story of Adam and Eve emphasizes that both women and men share in this responsibility, and are to be partners together. Moreover, it affirms the sacredness of human sexuality as part of God's perfect creation. When Adam and Eve rebelled against God they lost the open fellowship with God and with one another which they had known. The results of their disobedience affected every area of their lives. Their work became burdensome, and their relationship with one another brought pain as well as pleasure.

The rest of the Bible reflects both the glory and the fallenness of men and women. They are second only to God, crowned with honour. They care for all God has made, sharing God's creativity in artistic achievement and caring for the earth's resources. But they also have the capacity – and the tendency – to spoil things, and to behave in violent and evil ways.

The New Testament announces new possibilities of redemption. Humankind, 'in Adam', is the same as ever. But those who 'one

in union with Christ Jesus' are made new and can share in the new creation as equal partners, to live life as God originally intended it.
Genesis 1:26–28; 2; 3; Deuteronomy 5; 8; Psalm 8; Romans 1–3; 5:12–19; 8:18–25; 2 Corinthians 5:17; 6:16–18; Galatians 3:28

Mediator
A 'go-between' who brings together (reconciles) two people or groups who are estranged from each other.

When Adam and Eve rebelled against God, their friendship with God was broken. This was how the Old Testament writers described the dysfunction that often seems to characterize human life: it was a broken relationship. Consequently, there was a need for a mediator to restore things between people and God. This was the purpose of the Old Testament sacrificial system, to break down the perceived barriers between people and their environment, and people and God, with the priests as the mediators.

In the New Testament book of Hebrews, Jesus emerges as the perfect mediator between God and the people, more effective than the traditional priests, who were but men themselves. And, because Jesus could be viewed as both priest and sacrifice (through his death) what he accomplished would never need to be repeated.
Exodus 32:30–32; 33:11; Leviticus 16; Numbers 12:6–8; Deuteronomy 5:4–5; Galatians 3:19–20; 1 Timothy 2:5; Hebrews 7:24–25; 8:6; 9:15; 12:24

Mercy
The Hebrew word most often translated 'mercy' (*chesed*) occurs nearly 250 times in the Old Testament. It refers to God's loving patience with the people of Israel, God's kindness and readiness to forgive. Despite Israel's tendency to disregard the covenant agreement with God, God did not disown them but was faithful and had 'mercy' on them. Some English versions translate the word 'loving kindness'.

In the New Testament, 'mercy' is a loving pity for those in need. God is 'the merciful Father, the God from whom all help

comes'. Jesus himself was often moved with pity to respond to the needs of those around him, and made clear that his disciples should show to other people the same mercy which they had received undeservedly from God.
Exodus 34:6–7; Deuteronomy 7:9; Nehemiah 9:7, 31; Psalms 23:6; 25:6; 40:11; 51:1; 103:4, 8; Daniel 9:9; Jonah 4:2; Micah 6:8; Matthew 5:7; Luke 6:36; 18:13; Romans 9:15; 12:1; 2 Corinthians 1:3; Ephesians 2:4

Messiah
'Messiah' and 'Christ' both mean the 'anointed one'. 'Messiah' is the Hebrew word and 'Christ' is the Greek equivalent.

Throughout the troubled history of the nation of Judah the hope gradually grew that God would one day send a great Messiah-king to establish God's universal and everlasting kingdom by achieving what the regular kings in Jerusalem had been unable to do. By the time of Jesus there was a widespread expectation of such a Messiah, and it was inevitable that many people would speculate as to whether Jesus might be that figure.

The first Christians certainly identified Jesus as the Messiah, encouraged in their belief by the fact that Jesus himself had behaved in thoroughly 'messianic' ways, even though he resisted claiming the title for himself, no doubt to avoid political misunderstandings.

However, the key question on which Jesus' fate eventually depended was the question asked by the high priest: 'Are you the Messiah, the Son of the Blessed God?' 'I am', answered Jesus, something that was certain to lead to a conviction for blasphemy. This did not stop the disciples continuing to believe in Jesus, though, and when the Day of Pentecost came Peter had no hesitation in declaring that 'All the people of Israel, then, are to know for sure that this Jesus, whom you crucified, is the one that God has made Lord and Messiah!'
Psalms 2; 45:6–7; 72; 110; Isaiah 9:2–7; 11; 42:1–9; 49:1–6; 52:13–53:12; 61:1–3; Jeremiah 23:5–6; 33:14–16; Ezekiel 34:22–25; Daniel 7; Zechariah 9:9–10; Matthew 1:18, 22–23; 16:16, 20; 26:68; Mark 8:27–30; 14:61–64;

Luke 2:11, 26; John 4:25–26; 7:26–27, 31, 41–42; 9:22; Acts 2:36; 3:20–21; 4:26–28; 10:38; 18:28; 26:22–23

Miracles
Miracles feature throughout the Bible story, but are mostly concentrated in the stories of Jesus' life and work. These miracles range from curing physical illnesses and performing exorcisms, to calming storms and energizing those thought to be dead.

Jesus' miracles are sometimes described as 'mighty works'. They were done through the power of God. The most important display of God's power – the greatest miracle – was the resurrection of Jesus. The miracles are also called 'wonders', for they amazed those who saw them. But Jesus resisted the image of being a mere wonder-worker, both in his temptations and throughout his ministry. He did not want people to follow him just to witness miracles. So he often told the people he cured to tell no one about it.

The gospel of John regards Jesus' miracles as 'signs' – signs that he was the Messiah, and that God's kingdom, really had come. When John the Baptist sent to find out if Jesus was the Messiah he was told of the miracles Jesus did and left to draw his own conclusions. Miracles were above all signs of the coming of God's kingdom, that God's way of doing things was breaking in and could change things.

There are also stories of Jesus' disciples carrying out healing miracles in Jesus' name, and this remained part of the practice of the early church. One of the 'gifts of the Spirit' mentioned by Paul was the working of miracles, another the gift of healing, though he was careful to insist that all healing ultimately came from God.
Matthew 4:5–7; 11:2–6, 20–21; Mark 10:27; Luke 9:1; Acts 3:6; Romans 1:4; 1 Corinthians 12:9–10 Galatians 3:5;

Jesus' healings:
Matthew 8:2–3, 5–13, 14–15; 28–34; 9:2–7, 20–22, 27–31, 32–33; 12:10–13, 22; 15:21–28; 17:14–18; 20:29–34; Mark 1:23–26; 7:31–37; 8:22–26; Luke 13:11–13; 14:1–4; 17:11–19; 22:50–51; John 4:46–54; 5:1–9; 9

Jesus' command over the forces of nature:
Matthew 8:23–27; 14:25,

15–21; 15:32–38; 17:24–27; 21:18–22; Mark 11:20–26; Luke 5:1–11; John 2:1–11; 21:1–11

Jesus restores the dead to life:
Matthew 9:18–19, 23–25; Luke 7:11–15; John 11:1–44

Some Old Testament miracles:
Exodus 14; Joshua 2; 1 Kings 17:17–24; 2 Kings 2; 4–5; Daniel 6 and many other passages

New birth
The notion of 'new birth' or 'rebirth' is a natural metaphor to use for the kind of radical change of life and attitude that God demands. In the dark days before the final collapse of the kingdom of Judah, the prophet Jeremiah spoke of the need for men and women to be completely remade from within if they were to have a meaningful relationship with God. In the New Testament, the same point comes across in Jesus' discussion with the Jewish leader Nicodemus, and Jesus' followers had no hesitation in using this imagery to describe their own experience of Jesus: 'When anyone is joined to Christ, he is a new being; the old is gone, the new has come.'
Psalm 51:10; Jeremiah 31:31–34; John 3:1–21; 2 Corinthians 5:17

Parable
A parable is a fictitious story, told for the purpose of stimulating people to reflect more deeply on their own lives, and to convey some spiritual truth. It was a characteristic of Jesus' teaching method, though there are also one or two parables in the Old Testament.
Matthew 13:45–46; 18:12–14; 20:1–16; 22:2–14; Mark 4:21–22; 6:47–49; 2:21; 4:3–8; 4:30–32; 13:28–29; Luke 15:8–10; 16:1–8; 18:10–14 and many others

Peace
The Hebrew word for 'peace' (*shalom*) has a very broad meaning, indicating 'wholeness' and fullness of life in every aspect. It can refer to bodily health, or to a long life which ends in a natural death. It also describes safety, and harmony for the individual and for the community. Peace is the most precious of all gifts, and it comes directly from God: 'The Lord is peace.'

In the New Testament Jesus is called the 'prince of peace'. He 'came and preached the good news of peace to all' – a peace

assured by his death on the cross and his ensuing resurrection. Christ's gift to every disciple is peace with God, and peace with others – a deep sense of fulfilment and acceptance, unaffected by circumstances. 'Peace,' he told his disciples on his last evening with them, 'is what I leave with you; it is my own peace that I give you. I do not give it as the world does. Do not be worried and upset; do not be afraid!'
Genesis 15:15; Judges 6:24; Psalms 4:8; 85:8–10; Isaiah 48:22; 2:2–4; 9:6; John 14:27; Romans 5:1; Ephesians 2:14–18; 2 Thessalonians 3:16

Praise
The joy that God's people have in God is expressed in 'praise'; people praise God as their creator and as their saviour. One of the Old Testament words for praise comes from a Hebrew word which means 'to make a noise'. It appears in the word 'hallelujah'. Israelite worship included joyful shouting and singing, and the sound of many musical instruments, as well as dancing and other forms of movement. The New Testament tells that the angels sang praises when Jesus was born and that heaven continually rings with praise.
Psalms 136; 135; 150; 34:3; 35:18 and many other passages; Luke 2:13–14; Philippians 4:4–8; Revelation 4:6–11

Prayer
Prayer is depicted in the Bible as a natural way of relating to God. It can be both planned and spontaneous, expressed through bodily movements as well as through words, through poetry as easily as through prose. It is a style of living, as those who trust in God share their life with God in prayer: thanking God, confessing wrongdoing and asking things of God, confident that God answers prayer.

In the Old Testament, the faithful Israelite prayed in a structured way, three times each day. Samuel was so sure of his duty to pray that he considered it a sin if he failed to pray for those in his care. The New Testament adopts a more informal approach, though prayer in its various manifestations was expected to have a central place in the life of the Christian and the church. One of the key functions of the Holy Spirit was to help Christians find appropriate ways to pray, especially non-verbal ways. As Paul wrote to the Romans: 'The Spirit personally pleads with God for us in groans that words cannot express.'

1 Samuel 12:23; Psalm 62:8; Mark 11:24; Acts 12:12; Romans 8:26; Philippians 4:6; Colossians 4:2; James 1:5–6; 1 John 1:9

Jesus' teaching on prayer:
Matthew 6:5–15; 7:7–11; 26:41; Mark 12:38–40; 13:33; 14:38; Luke 11:1–13; 18:1–14

Prayers of Jesus:
Matthew 6:9–13; 11:25–26; 26:36–44; Mark 14:32–39; Luke 10:21; 11:2–4; 22:66; 23:34, 46; John 11:41–42; 12:27–28; 17

Some other great prayers:
Exodus 15; 32; 33; Deuteronomy 32–33; Joshua 17; 10; Judges 5; 6; 1 Samuel 1; 2; 2 Samuel 7; 22; 1 Kings 3; 8; 18; 19; 2 Kings 19; Ezra 9; Nehemiah 1; 9; Job 42; Psalms; Daniel 2; 9; Jonah 2; Habakkuk 3; Luke 1:46–55, 68–79; 2:29–35; Acts 4:24–30, and many prayers in the New Testament letters

Prophecy
From an early period in Israel's history prophets played a leading part in the Bible story. It was their responsibility to reflect God's values to the community, and to chastise and challenge their people.

The Old Testament prophets typically began their message with the statement, 'The Lord says…' So it was important for people to be able to know the difference between a true prophet and an impostor. The true prophet was always called to the work by God, and someone to whom God's plans were communicated. Most prophetic messages referred directly to the situation of the prophet's own time, so it is important to read them alongside the historical accounts of the same period. They found fulfilment in the prophet's own age, though they could also point forward to future events. Some of the Old Testament prophecies are applied to Jesus by the New Testament writers.

The New Testament suggests that through the inspiration of the Holy Spirit all Christians may proclaim God's message. It also mentions a gift of 'prophecy', describing it as a special gift given by

God to people in the Christian community in order to help them build up the church.
Deuteronomy 13:1–5; 18:20–22; Amos 7:14–15; 3:7; most of the Old Testament prophecies are contained in the books of the prophets, Isaiah – Malachi; John 5:39; Acts 2:17; 11:17–28; 1 Corinthians 11:5; 12:10, 29; 14:24, 29

Reconciliation
To 'reconcile' two people is to bring them together after they have been in conflict. The story of people in the Bible begins in the Old Testament book of Genesis with the break in the relationship between the first people and God. This is followed immediately by one man's hostility to another, in the story of Cain and Abel. The Bible says that it is only when the relationship with God is restored that relations between people can be truly healed, and that this is the effect of the 'reconciliation' which God offers to all.

The New Testament links this reconciliation with the effects of the life, death and resurrection of Jesus himself. The stranglehold of sin in the world has been dealt with by Jesus, and those who follow Jesus can share in the effects of his accomplishments: they are reconciled to one another, and to God.
Genesis 3; Romans 5:10–11; 11:15; 2 Corinthians 5:18–20; Ephesians 2:11–18; Colossians 1:19–22

Redemption
To 'redeem' something is to buy it back. The Gospels describe Jesus' ministry as being to 'give his life to redeem many people', buying back those whose lives had been spoiled by forces that are opposed to God. Christians can therefore be spoken of as 'the redeemed', in much the same way as the Israelites brought out of slavery in Egypt were 'the redeemed' in the Old Testament.
Exodus 13:11–16; Mark 10:45; John 8:34; Romans 6:12–14; 8:19–23; 1 Corinthians 6:20; 1 Peter 1:18–19

Repentance
Repentance is a change of direction, a decision to abandon old ways of doing things and go a new way. Throughout the Bible, the change of heart that will be required for God's kingdom truly to come is described as 'repentance'.

In the Old Testament it was regularly accompanied by outward actions such as fasting and tearing one's clothes, though Jesus emphasized that such things were not sufficient by themselves, without a determination actually to change. His parable of the Pharisee and the tax collector shows the importance he placed on an inward change of heart.
Joel 2:12–13; Mark 1:15; Luke 18:9–14; 19:1–10 (and other examples); Acts 11:18; 17:30

Resurrection
The claim that Jesus rose from the dead is the key premise of the Christian faith: 'If Christ has not been raised, then your faith is a delusion and you are still lost in your sins,' wrote Paul.

Following his death, the followers of Jesus soon came to believe that he was alive again. They saw him on various occasions, and his tomb was empty. Paul gives a comprehensive list of the people who had seen Jesus alive, over an extended period of time. As a result, the disciples were transformed overnight, from being a weak and dispirited bunch into being a fearless group of people who preached and performed miracles in the power of the risen Christ.

Paul also taught that Jesus' own resurrection was a model for what his disciples could expect, as they looked beyond their own end. Christians would have to face physical death like everyone else, but they would be assured of a future with Jesus in a new spiritual mode of existence. Because of their belief in Jesus' resurrection, the earliest Christians did not look for the immortality of a soul, but the resurrection of the complete person in a new and more wonderful body.
Matthew 28; Mark 16; Luke 24; John 20; Acts 1:3; 4:10; Romans 1:4; 6:4–13; 1 Corinthians 15

Revelation
The Bible sees the revelation of God's nature coming in three major ways. First, God is revealed through creation and people's experience of it. Then, since people are made 'in God's image', they also have access to God's will not only through

their own conscience but through their shared experiences of life. And thirdly, God can be known in more direct ways, through psychic and mystical experiences.

The history books of the Old Testament show evidence of reflection on human experience, as people recalled the events of their national experience, and realized that God was at work there, and events like the exodus had not been mere coincidences but were part of God's intention for their nation. The prophets began their work from their own direct personal encounters with God, depending on mystical encounters with the spiritual. In the New Testament, Jesus is presented as the final and most complete revelation of God's character, demonstrating what God is like in a living form that could easily be understood.

Because the Bible itself is the source of all these various 'revelations' of God, it has often been thought of as 'revelation' in itself – its books were written by people under the direct guidance of God.
Exodus 3; 6:7; Ecclesiastes 5:2; Isaiah 1:3; 58:8–9; Amos 3:7; John 1:14; 14:26; 16:13; Hebrews 1:1–2; 1 Timothy 6:16; 2 Timothy 3:16; 2 Peter 1:21

Salvation
'Salvation' is the word used to describe the wholeness of life that is God's will.

In the Old Testament, salvation was more than just a spiritual deliverance. The major act of salvation was when God freed the Israelites from actual slavery to the Egyptians. The New Testament also teaches that God's salvation affects far more than a person's 'spiritual' life. It concerns the whole person. Nearly one-third of the references to salvation in the New Testament are concerned with being set free from specific ills such as imprisonment, disease and demon possession.
Matthew 1:21; 9:21–22; Romans 10:13; 13:11; 1 Corinthians 1:18; Ephesians 2:8–9; Philippians 2:12

Satan
'Satan' is the Hebrew name and 'devil' the Greek name for the being who personifies all that is evil and opposed

to God. Both names mean 'accuser', suggesting that Satan is the one who tempts people to do wrong so they may stand accused of transgressing God's will. The Bible does not see the battle between good and evil as an equally balanced contest for, although the powers of Satan might sometimes seem to be gaining the upper hand, God has already secured ultimate victory for the powers of good, through Jesus' death and resurrection in which he was able 'to destroy what the devil had done'. The final state of goodness, though, will only be achieved at the end of all things.

The Bible records numerous instances of Satan's opposition to the work of God. Jesus was tempted by the devil in the desert. The disciple Peter was used as a tool of Satan and had to be rebuked by Jesus. The betrayal of Jesus by Judas Iscariot was also seen as part of Satan's work.
2 Corinthians 11:14; Ephesians 6:11; John 14:30; 1 John 3:8; John 12:31; 1 Peter 5:8; Revelation 20:10; Matthew 4:1–11; 16:23; Luke 22:3; Matthew 12:22–28

Second coming of Jesus
The New Testament expects a 'second coming' of Jesus to the world. In his first coming Jesus came quietly, lived the life of the humble servant of God and died on the cross. But during his life he promised that he would return at the end of the world, this time with power and glory for all to see. This coming will be a time of accounting, when those who have resisted God's values will find themselves rejected, and those who have followed carefully will be rewarded. But Jesus told many parables to highlight that God's standards of judgment are different from human standards, and some of those who thought they should be first will discover they are last, while others who imagined they were on God's side might find themselves rejected.

No time or date was ever given in the New Testament for the return of Jesus: it will be 'at an hour when you are not expecting him'. Though some passages do speak of the gospel being preached to all nations first, and of a time when

sin will increase and people will worship someone who falsely claims to be God.
Matthew 24; 26:64; Mark 13:26; John 14; Acts 1:11; 3:19–21; Philippians 3:20; Colossians 3:4; 1 Thessalonians 1:10; 4:13–5:11; 2 Thessalonians 1:5–2:12; 2 Peter 3:8–13; Revelation 19–22

Sin
The Bible uses many words to describe sin. It can be thought of as rebellion against God (as in the Old Testament story of Adam and Eve). It is also described as 'missing the mark' or falling below the standard required by God. But the essence of all sin is that it is a rejection of God's values. As a result of sin, people find themselves cut off from God and facing God's judgment. Sin is the root cause of all that is wrong in the world.

The Bible does not concern itself with the thorny problem of where evil comes from, but simply accepts it as an obvious fact. Its influence spreads through the entire cosmos, but people are still held to be responsible for their own wrong behaviour. The goals of the entire redemptive process is often described as a time when sin and evil are banished for all time.
Genesis 3; Psalm 51; Isaiah 1:18–20; 59; Romans 1:18–2:11; 3:9–26; 5–8; Revelation 20–21

Soul
The Bible sees human beings as a unity. It does not speak of an immortal 'soul' locked up in a decaying, sinful body. This was a Greek idea, though it has been held by many Christians through the centuries.

The word 'soul' in the Old Testament means the whole of a person's being: when the psalmist said 'Praise the Lord, my soul' he was calling on himself to respond as a whole person to God. The New Testament uses the word 'soul' in a similar way, meaning 'people'. It is the word used to show that people are more than physical flesh and bone; they have a mind and will and personality. For instance, Jesus said, 'Do not be afraid of those who kill the body but cannot kill the soul; rather be afraid of God, who can destroy both body and soul in hell.'
Psalm 103:1; Matthew 10:28 and many other passages

Spiritual gifts

According to the New Testament, when Jesus left his disciples after the resurrection, he gave them spiritual 'gifts', inspired by the Holy Spirit for the edifying of the church. Ephesians lists some of the gifts which marked people out as having special work as leaders in the church, while 1 Corinthians indicates some of the gifts which would be found among church members: wisdom, knowledge, faith, healing, miracles, speaking and explaining God's message, speaking in 'tongues' and interpreting what has been said. Paul's letter to the Christians in Rome lists some other gifts: service, encouragement, sharing with others and acts of kindness. None of these lists claims to be complete.

Paul believed that in every local church each member should be free to use his or her God-given gift of ministry. Gifts of the Spirit, he wrote, are not given for private enjoyment but for the good of all, and for this reason Paul deals at some length with the question of speaking in tongues and other apparently 'supernatural' gifts. Paul himself spoke in tongues and was keen for others to have the same ability, but he insisted that there must be someone to interpret. Otherwise no one would understand it, and no one would be helped.
Romans 12; 1 Corinthians 12 and 14; Ephesians 4

Suffering

Suffering is seen in the Bible as a natural misfortune. It entered the world because of sin, and is a result of the continuing activity of Satan. The New Testament states that Jesus came into the world to free people from suffering and death. In his life on earth he showed his love and care by healing many people. And, he taught, in God's kingdom there will be no suffering.

Suffering is also a problem in the Bible, however. Because God has total control, presumably suffering also must ultimately come from God. Yet how can a God of love allow the innocent to suffer? It is easy to see that sin brings suffering – not just to the individual but to the whole family. And

it is possible to accept that God allows suffering in order that people might learn certain lessons. The Old Testament book of Job is an honest attempt to discuss all these problems, using an ancient story of the suffering of an innocent man. Job discards all the neat explanations that his friends provide, and in the end accepts his suffering, while also discovering that trusting God can and does make sense even in these difficult circumstances.

In the New Testament the life and work of Jesus highlight suffering as a way of life. Jesus, an innocent man, suffered because of the hatred of sinful people – and in order to save them from their sin. Rather than trying to provide a rational, philosophical answer to the problem of suffering, the Bible invites its readers to consider the example of Jesus, and to realize that God is not distant from human tragedy, but is actually to be found within it.
Genesis 3:15–19; Job; Psalm 39:11; Isaiah 53; Amos 3:6; Romans 8:21; 2 Corinthians 12:7; Hebrews 12:3–11; Revelation 21:4

Temptation

The word 'temptation' commonly refers in the Bible to the activity of Satan in trying to lead people into wrongdoing. Classic examples of this are the story of Adam and Eve, or the record of Jesus' temptations. Such testing gives an opportunity for people to reaffirm their commitment to God's standards, and every test that is overcome strengthens and leads them forward.

The New Testament warns Christians to be on their guard against temptation, and reminds them that God will never allow the testing to become too great to bear, but will provide the power to endure suffering.
Genesis 3; Exodus 20:20; Deuteronomy 8:1–6; Matthew 4; 6:13; 1 Corinthians 10:12–13; Ephesians 6:10–18; Hebrews 2:18; James 1:12–16; 1 Peter 1:6–9; 4:12–16

Transfiguration

The transfiguration of Jesus marks a turning point in the stories of the Gospels. The apostle Peter had just recognized Jesus as the Messiah, and Jesus went on to teach his disciples

about his coming death and resurrection. Then he went up a mountain (traditionally thought to be Mount Hermon) with Peter, James and John. There they saw Jesus transformed by a heavenly glory, and Elijah and Moses talking with him. The experience ended with a voice from heaven saying, 'This is my Son, whom I have chosen – listen to him.'

Moses and Elijah represented the two major parts of the Old Testament, the Law and the Prophets. By their presence they showed that all was fulfilled in Jesus. The transfiguration confirmed that the way Jesus had chosen was right, and it pointed to the glory that would one day be his. But before that time he had to die on the cross, and Jesus' 'exodus' was the topic of conversation with Moses and Elijah – though the disciples did not begin to understand this until after Jesus' resurrection.
Matthew 17:1–8; Mark 9:2–8; Luke 8:28–36

Trinity

The word 'trinity' is not used in the Bible. It is the name given to the statements about God made in the creeds drawn up in the early centuries of the church, to explain how God could be creator, redeemer and living presence all at one and the same time (traditionally expressed as Father, Son, and Holy Ghost or Spirit). Though the term 'trinity' is not used, these three ways of thinking of God are all clearly present in the New Testament, and were evidently used in the context of Christian baptism.

Traditional Jewish teaching was that there is only one God, and nothing was allowed to compromise that belief. Yet the New Testament writers also had the clear conviction that Jesus was, in some way, God in person, and that their own experience of Jesus' continuing presence in their lives was also therefore an experience of God. They never tried to articulate all that philosophically, preferring just to reflect on their own experience of God. But in the centuries after the New Testament period the church found it necessary to formulate

careful statements to define its beliefs more precisely, in the face of arguments about what constituted correct Christian beliefs.
Exodus 20:2–6; Deuteronomy 6:4; Isaiah 45:5; Matthew 28:19; John 5:19–29; 8:23–29, 58; 14–17; Acts 2:32–33; 2 Corinthians 13:14 and many other passages

Word

The 'word of God' is a phrase the Bible often uses when it speaks of the revelation of God to people. Just as people can only know one another well through speech, so God is revealed by words as well as actions. The 'word of the Lord' is God's spoken word, particularly in the books of the Old Testament prophets. This 'word' was not always heard audibly; sometimes it was seen, or experienced in mystical ways, or arrived at by a process of rational reflection. In John's gospel, Jesus is described as 'the word' in a different sense, originating from Greek concepts of 'the word' as the essence of all things. Here, the key thing is that 'the word became flesh', emphasizing how Christian faith is not exclusively a rational, analytical understanding of abstract beliefs, but is something that needs to be celebrated and understood in human terms, as something to be seen, touched and felt, as well as heard.
Isaiah 40:8; Jeremiah 1:4; Ezekiel 1:3–28; John 1:1–14; 2 Timothy 4:2; 1 John 1:1–3; Revelation 22:18–19

World

The Greek word *kosmos* normally means the physical created world. It is used in this way in the New Testament to describe the world God made. It is also used to speak of the 'state of the world'. In this sense, 'the world' is a way of being that is opposed to God's ways. Thus, Satan can be called the prince or ruler of 'this world', and the whole world is said to lie in his power. 'World' (represented sometimes by another Greek word, *aion*, meaning 'age' or 'spirit of the age') describes all that is in opposition to God in much the same way.

The New Testament uses the term mostly in this metaphorical sense, relating how the 'world' hated Christ and will show similar hatred to his followers. And yet

God loved the world (in both senses!). Christians do not belong to the world in a moral sense, but they live in the world in a physical sense: indeed, it is their home. These interchangeable meanings have often led Christians to imagine that God somehow disapproves of physical being, but these contrasts are always ethical ones in the Bible. Christians are warned against sharing the world's attitudes or conforming to its self-centred materialist standards. Instead, they must live in tune with God's values and standards, empowered to do so because God loves them and Jesus died for them.
John 1:10; 3:16–21; 14:30; 15:18–19; 17:16–17; Romans 12:2; 1 John 5:19

Worship

The first of the Ten Commandments in the Old Testament is: 'I am the Lord your God. Worship no god but me.' To worship is to give God honour. In the Old Testament psalms the people worship God for what God has done in creation and in redemption, and for all God's gifts and blessings to individuals.

In the New Testament, when Christians met together they expressed their gladness by 'praising God'. Filled with the Holy Spirit they spoke to 'one another with the words of psalms, hymns and sacred songs', and they sang 'hymns and psalms to the Lord' with praise in their hearts. Everyone could participate in this worship: 'When you meet for worship one person has a hymn, another a teaching, another a revelation from God, another a message in strange tongues, and still another the explanation of what is said.'

The Bible warns against the kind of worship which degenerates into only an outward show. True worship is a genuine response to God which shows itself not only in ritual actions, but especially in a style of life that pleases God. Worship centres on God, and the gospel is what fills it with content and meaning. Paul wrote in the New Testament: 'Christ's message in all its richness must live in

your hearts. Teach and instruct each other with all wisdom. Sing psalms, hymns, and sacred songs; sing to God with thanksgiving in your hearts.'

Worship is not simply a human activity on earth. The Bible also mentions that God's whole creation – humans and angels – praises and worships God in heaven.
Exodus 20:1–3; Psalms 29; 136:4–9, 10–26; 116; Acts 2:43–47; Ephesians 5:18–19; 1 Corinthians 14:26–40; John 4:21–24; Micah 6:6–8; Colossians 3:16; Revelation 4; 5; 7; 15

Index

315